INTRODUCTION TO
BUSINESS

The Economy and You

Anne Scott Daughtrey
Professor of Management
School of Business
Old Dominion University

Robert A. Ristau
Professor of Business Education
Department of Business and
 Industrial Education
Eastern Michigan University

Steven A. Eggland
Professor of Vocational Education
Teachers College
University of Nebraska

Published by

G16 SOUTH-WESTERN PUBLISHING CO.

CINCINNATI   WEST CHICAGO, IL   DALLAS   PELHAM MANOR, NY   LIVERMORE, CA

*P*reface

These are exciting times for business. Corporations and other business concerns are experiencing evolutionary and revolutionary change. Fifteen years ago computers were used mostly for accounting purposes; today they are an integral part of decision making in all facets of business. Computers have even found their way into the home. Social, economic, and technological change is evident throughout the business world.

Why is the study of business important? Everyone in our society interacts with business — through the products we buy, the advertisements we see and hear, and the money we invest in stocks, bonds, and other securities. We are all tightly woven into the fabric of our economic and business systems. Moreover, the vast majority of us, at one time or another, will work for private businesses and maybe even run them. It is critically important that we understand what the role of business is in our society and what our relationship is to business. The objectives of this book are to introduce students to the world of business and to help prepare them for a more meaningful and beneficial interaction with business.

The world of business has changed dramatically over the last decade or so. We know that change will certainly continue to be a fact of life in the years ahead. The fundamental principles of business stay the same from year to year; but recent social, economic, technological, and regulatory developments have introduced new ideas and methods into business practice and, therefore, into the study of business. We have integrated the more significant of these developments into the discussion of business principles.

A Book for Changing Times — Contemporary Topics and Format

Introduction to Business: The Economy and You is based on the twelve successful editions of its predecessor, *General Business For Economic Understanding*. It retains the best of those twelve editions, but also adds topics and concepts needed to prepare students to deal with and become part of the contemporary business world. And we have used state-of-the-art textbook production techniques to present materials in an attractive and easy-to-read format, consistent with sound educational methodology.

Text Organization

Introduction to Business: The Economy and You is divided into eleven units.

- Units 1 and 2 introduce the student to the American economic system and how it meets the wants and needs of its citizens. The first seven chapters discuss such fundamental concerns as the free enterprise system; the U.S. economy today; the basic function of business; and the impact of world trade on our economy. The decision-making process is introduced and is reinforced throughout the text.
- Unit 3, Living in the Computer Age, introduces students to the far-reaching impact of computer technology, both in the workplace and at home.
- Unit 4 encourages students to begin thinking about a career and provides some helpful tips on getting started.
- In Unit 5, students learn of their rights and responsibilities as consumers, as well as the role that careful buying plays in improving one's standard of living.
- The ever-changing world of banking and financial services is the topic of Unit 6.
- Unit 7 explores ways individuals and families can manage their finances and adjust to changing economic conditions.
- Unit 8, Using Credit Wisely, and Unit 9, Savings and Investments, introduce students to ways they can make the most of the money they earn through careful use of credit and wise savings and investment strategies.
- In Unit 10 students learn of the need for protection against economic loss through the use of insurance.
- The text concludes with a discussion of the role of government and labor in our economic system in Unit 11.

Improvements, Changes & Features

Users of *General Business For Economic Understanding* will notice significant changes in the content and organization of *Introduction to Business: The Economy and You*. For example, the text is now divided into 11 units and 42 chapters. Unit 3, Living in the Computer Age, is new. Unit 4, Your Role in Business, consolidates all of the career planning material. Five completely reorganized and rewritten chapters make up the banking unit and reflect the many changes in the financial services industry resulting from government deregulation. This unit examines the operations of banks and other financial institutions such as savings and loans, credit unions, and nonbank banks.

Material in Unit 8 has been combined into 4 chapters and completely updated. A new appendix, the Computer Glossary, has been added to help students with computer terminology.

Each unit in *Introduction to Business: The Economy and You* contains a Business Brief, highlighting a special event, person, product, or development in business. Each unit concludes with a Career Focus, a two-page career information review of jobs in a particular occupational category.

Each chapter has been rewritten using multiple-level headings to better lead students through concepts and ideas. Activities at the end of each chapter of *Introduction to Business: The Economy and You* have been carefully planned to facilitate teaching and learning.

These activities involve students in writing, investigating, interviewing, problem solving, demonstrating, computing, explaining, reporting, and learning and practicing other skills needed in today's complex economic system. These varied and challenging experiences also allow teachers to provide for a wide range of student abilities and interests.

All activities are keyed to the performance objectives provided for each unit and chapter. The end-of-chapter activities are divided into the following sections:

1. Adding to Your Business Vocabulary. This section increases word power by asking students to identify definitions of commonly used business and economic terms.
2. Understanding Your Reading. This section measures students' comprehension through oral or written responses to questions directly related to the content of each chapter.
3. Putting Your Business Knowledge to Work. Through the activities in this section, students apply what they have learned in problem situations relevant to their everyday lives.
4. Computing Business Problems. By solving the business/economic problems in this section, students strengthen and refine their basic mathematics abilities. Problems vary in level of difficulty; the first problem in each section is designed for easy and quick solution. Many chapters contain a metric activity to familiarize students with the metric system.
5. Stretching Your Business Knowledge. The activities in this section are intended mainly as optional experiences for students. The solutions require students to exercise careful thought, to investigate sources of information beyond the textbook, and in some cases to conduct studies using basic and practical research methods. Students may be expected to report their findings and to make decisions or recommendations. This section is designed particularly, but not exclusively, for the more able or resourceful students.

Finally, the workbooks that accompany *Introduction to Business: The Economy and You* have been completely revised with new activities and projects in each chapter.

In addition a short, classroom-tested, business simulation has been included in each workbook. Students should find the simulation activities instructive and fun. Teachers should find them very useful in expanding the explanation of material covered in the text chapters.

Acknowledgments

Specialists from all levels of the teaching profession have read manuscripts, offered suggestions, and otherwise contributed to the improvement of *Introduction to Business: The Economy and You*. Authorities from business and government helped significantly in updating content and illustrations relating to computer technology, banking, credit, investments, and other topics.

Many pages would be required to give proper recognition to each individual who has contributed in some way to the production of this textbook. Although it is not possible to give credit to all contributors individually, we acknowledge with deep appreciation the special assistance received from Dr. Al Brinson of Indiana Central University and Dr. Les Dlabay of Lake Forest College for their work in Units 3 and 11, and from Dr. Kenneth E. Everard of Trenton State College for preparation of workbook manuscript.

We are grateful to Dr. Brinson for his preparation of the Computer Glossary, to Dr. Dlabay for his efforts in developing the workbook simulations, and to the following individuals for their review and testing of the simulations: Mr. Craig Beacham of Lapeer West High School, Lapeer, Michigan; Ms. Connie Hilligas of Aurora High School, Aurora, Nebraska; Ms. Jean Holbrook of Roanoke County Schools, Salem, Virginia; Ms. Terry A. Hurst of Lake Park High School, Roselle, Illinois; Mrs. Linda Kruger of Maury High School, Norfolk, Virginia; Ms. Lee Palmer of Pioneer Middle School, Plymouth, Michigan; and Ms. Becky Paschal of Bellevue West High School, Bellevue, Nebraska.

A Special Acknowledgment

Although this is the first edition of *Introduction to Business: The Economy and You*, it is built upon the firm foundation of twelve successful editions of *General Business For Economic Understanding*. Several of these editions, spanning over a quarter of a century, benefited from the many contributions of Dr. S. Joseph DeBrum. We acknowledge with gratitude his dedication to business education. His enthusiastic support has made teaching and learning business an enjoyable and enriching experience for teachers and students worldwide.

Anne Scott Daughtrey
Robert A. Ristau
Steven A. Eggland

Contents

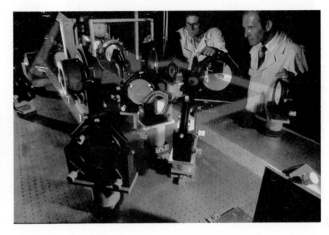

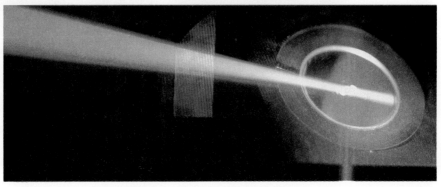

UNIT 1
YOUR ECONOMIC SYSTEM

UNIT OBJECTIVES

After studying the chapters in this unit, you will be able to:

1. Explain the basic economic problem.

2. Describe several features of the private enterprise system.

3. Give an example to show how each of your three economic roles plays a part in our economic system.

4. Discuss three ways to measure our economic progress.

BUSINESS BRIEF

Free Enterprise Is Alive and Growing

The free enterprise system has always encouraged entrepreneurs—persons willing to invest time and money to turn ideas into profits. People seeking to "make a million" or be their own boss have been venturing out on their own in growing numbers. These entrepreneurs are bringing new products and services to the marketplace and are helping to create new jobs.

Selling an innovation for profit is not a new idea. Thomas Edison is said to have been a "commercial innovator who invented the light bulb and the phonograph in the pursuit of the silver dollar." Consider a few of the things modern-day entrepreneurs have given us: the laser, optical scanner, personal computer, turbojet engine, insulin, penicillin, FM radios, zippers, ball-point pens, Velcro strips, and fast-food restaurants.

As early as her paper-route days as a teenager, Patricia Henriques dreamed of owning her own business. Today she operates her own successful business, Management Alternatives, Inc., which provides managerial consulting services to lawyers, accountants, and doctors.

The success of Steven Job and Steven Wozniak's Apple Computer, Inc., in the 70s is now a classical story in commercial innovation. When their company went public in 1980, the two young men became multimillionaires.

Teresita and Carlos Deupi fled to the U.S. from Cuba in 1961. They applied their talent, ambition, and architectural training to founding Deupi and Associates, a commercial design firm. By 1984, it was one of the country's top 100 interior design firms with annual sales of over $2 million.

John Halamka at age 17 built a computer and sold it for $4,000. Four years later, in his senior year at Stanford University, he headed his own customized tax and accounting software firm, Colossus Computers. His sales were $350,000 that year.

In 1982 Noah Flesher, at age 9, launched his business by offering handmade leather key fobs for sale through Hickory Farms of Ohio. The company ordered 250 twice at 50 cents each, and then 1,000 at 65 cents. Noah was honored in 1984 at Cornell University's Entrepreneur of the Year program.

Though history shows that 40 percent of new businesses fail within five years, those that do succeed supply us with many new products and services. A recent survey predicts that the chances for success are highest in such small businesses as computer program and software services, accounting, medical labs, and home computer stores.

One economist predicts that improving economic conditions will sweep us into the next century as a "new country" with new jobs and new opportunities. A great many entrepreneurs will help us get there.

Facts included in this Business Brief were taken from the following sources: "A Salute to Small Business." *Time* (May 7, 1984), special advertising section; Bock, Gordon M. "Capitalists Prosper on College Campuses." *U.S. News & World Report* (May 28, 1984), pp. 77-78; "11 Year Old Hits the Big Time." *The Virginian Pilot,* April 10, 1984, p. 2a; "10 Small Businesses Most Likely to Succeed." *Changing Times* (October, 1984), pp. 82-86.

CHAPTER 1

Satisfying Needs and Wants

■ CHAPTER OBJECTIVES

After studying this chapter and completing the end-of-chapter activities, you will be able to:

1. Give an example to show that human wants are unlimited.
2. Give an example to show that economic resources are limited.
3. Give an example of each of the three kinds of resources that are needed to produce goods and services.
4. Explain the importance of human resources in the production of goods and services.
5. Explain why the basic economic problem forces you to make choices.
6. State the six steps in the decision-making process.

Think about your last visit to a shopping mall. As you walked by the stores, you probably saw many things that you wanted: a radio/cassette player, a tee shirt in the newest design, a tennis racquet which was attractively displayed in a sporting goods store window, a pair of boots now on sale which you need for the winter. Or perhaps you wanted to go to a movie or to play the video games in one of the stores. No doubt you saw many things that you wanted.

Everyone Has Needs and Wants

You were not the only one wanting things. Think about all the other people walking around in the mall that day. They wanted things too. Everyone has needs and wants.

Needs Are Basic to Survival

Things that are necessary for survival are called **needs**. Food, clothing, and housing are the basic needs that most people have.

But we also desire things beyond our basic needs. It is doubtful that all of the things you saw and wanted in the mall were necessary for you to survive, but you wanted them anyway.

Wants Make Life Nicer

Things which are not necessary for survival but which add comfort and pleasure to our lives are called **wants**. The tee shirt, radio/cassette player, and tennis racquet you saw in the mall are examples of wants. You could live without them, but having them would make life easier and more fun for you. When we talk about needs and wants, we often lump them together and just call them wants.

Wants Are Unlimited

Needs and wants never end. After you ate breakfast this morning, you probably were no longer hungry. Your need for food had been satisfied. But by lunchtime you were ready to eat again. Or you may have bought that radio/cassette player you had wanted for a long time. That want was fulfilled. But then you wanted tapes to play on it and maybe a headset so that you could listen in private. (Your parents may feel that your headset is a "need" to them!) Your family may want to trade in a large car for one which uses less gas in order to save money and conserve energy. Or you may learn about a new product which has just arrived in the stores. You decide that you want the new product because it is useful or just because it is new. So, for many reasons, our wants keep changing. We can never satisfy them all. That is true for everyone—our wants are unlimited.

Illus. 1–1
Some purchases meet our basic needs; others satisfy our wants.

Satisfying Wants with Goods and Services

Some of the things you wanted as you walked through the mall were classified as goods and some as services. We satisfy most of our wants with goods and services; these are key words in the study of business and you will use them often. **Goods** are things you can see and touch. The tennis racquet, tee shirt, and radio/cassette player you wanted are goods. All the things which satisfy our material wants are goods—food, a television set, gasoline, cement, books, a bicycle, and clothes are examples. Goods are also called products.

Not all of our wants can be met with things that you can see and touch. Some wants are satisfied through the efforts of other people or by equipment. These efforts are called **services**. When you go to a movie, play a video game, make a deposit at the bank, get a haircut, take a swimming lesson, use your telephone, or ride a bus, you are using services. When you pay the hairstylist to cut your hair, you are buying a service performed by a person. When you put a coin in the video machine to play a game, or deposit coins at the car wash before you drive into the washing stall, you are buying a service performed by a piece of equipment. We need both goods and services to satisfy our wants. Supplying goods and services is what business is all about.

Goods and Services Require Economic Resources

Goods and services don't just appear as if by magic. You cannot create goods from nothing or supply a service without some effort. The means through which goods and services are produced are called **economic resources** or **factors of production.** There are three kinds of economic resources: natural, human, and capital resources. All three are needed to produce the goods and services that satisfy our wants.

Natural Resources

The raw materials supplied by nature are called **natural resources.** All the things that come from the earth, the water, or the air are natural resources. We take iron ore, gold, and oil from the earth to use in making goods. We also grow vegetables in the soil and take fish from the water for food. We use oxygen from the air in hospitals to help sick people breathe and to make such products as carbonated water for colas. All the goods we use today began with one or more natural resources.

Human Resources

Natural resources do not satisfy our wants by themselves. It takes people to turn them into goods and make the products and services available to us. **Human resources** are the people who work to produce goods and services. **Labor** is another name for this factor of production. Human resources include people who run farms and factories, manage banks, design machines to mine coal, process food, announce the news on television, check out our purchases at the supermarket, police the streets, or teach General Business. Human resources are very important in producing goods and services.

Capital Resources

The tools, equipment, and buildings which are used to produce goods and services are called **capital resources.** Office buildings, factories, tractors, carpenters' tools, computers, delivery trucks, and display cases are examples of capital resources. If you use a bicycle to deliver newspapers, your bicycle is a capital resource because it is equipment you use to provide the newspaper delivery service. Likewise, if a bank uses a computer to prepare a report of a customer's account, the computer is a capital resource. And the grill used to cook the hamburger you buy for lunch as well as the restaurant building are capital resources.

The word **capital** is often used in place of "capital resources," especially when referring to the factors of production. Capital is also thought of as money that is needed to run a business. A person may say she or he is trying to raise "$40,000 capital" to expand a business or that she or he has a "$10,000 capital investment" in a store operated by friends. Capital has a variety of meanings, but here the word is used in its economic sense to include equipment and other facilities needed to produce goods and services.

All three economic resources—natural, human, and capital—are necessary to produce goods and services to satisfy our wants. Unfortunately, we do not have an endless supply of resources.

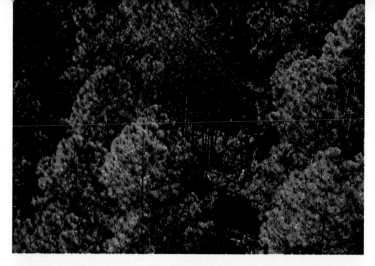

Illus. 1–2
Can you identify
the types of
resources shown
in these photos?

Resources Are Limited

If you had enough money, you could have bought all the things you wanted on your walk through the mall. But your money was limited, so you could not buy everything you wanted. That is true for people everywhere. Resources that can be turned into goods and services are limited.

Newscasters often report about shortages of certain items. In recent years oil, lumber, and sugar have been reported as scarce. There were not enough of these items for all the people who wanted them. We do not have an endless supply of economic resources. Because of pollution we do not have endless supplies of clean air, water, and land. We also have shortages in certain kinds of human resources, such as accountants, nurses, secretaries, and others with the skills and education to satisfy our unlimited wants. And since our natural and human resources are limited, our manufactured capital resources such as buildings and tools cannot be made and are therefore also limited. (See Figure 1–1.)

Scarcity Affects Everyone

Just as meeting your unlimited wants with limited resources is a problem for you, so it is for everyone—your family, your neighbors, and your school club. People all over the world are affected by scarcity. For that reason we refer to the conflict between unlimited wants and limited resources as **the basic economic problem.**

The members of your family may not be able to afford many things they want because the wages of your father or mother are

Figure 1–1
Individuals, businesses, and nations must decide how to use limited resources.

Illus. 1–3
The Alaskan Pipeline — a bold solution to resource scarcity.

needed for food, clothing, the house payment, the electric bill, or your school expenses. Your neighbors and the families of your friends face the same economic problem. Your school club might want to hire a live band to play for its annual dance, but because its money is scarce, may have to use stereo tapes instead.

Businesses and Governments Must Also Deal with Scarcity

Just as individuals face the basic economic problem, so do businesses, governments, and all agencies which supply goods and services. A business might want to enlarge its plant and parking lot to take care of its growth, but because the land it owns is limited and locating elsewhere would cost more than it can afford, it cannot do both.

All levels of government face the problem of supplying the almost unlimited wants of the citizens with limited resources. For example, your town may wish to give a large wage increase to police officers and fire fighters. However, because taxes may not provide enough money, the increase might have to be smaller in order to provide other services, such as a new school building or additional employees to collect the garbage. Cities, states, the United States, and all other nations must cope with the problem of providing the many services the citizens want from limited resources — the taxes collected to pay for the services. Someone must decide which services will be provided. How do you, other individuals, businesses, and governments decide which of the unlimited wants to supply?

You Must Make Economic Choices

Since you cannot have everything you want, you must choose which of the things you want most and can afford. Suppose you earn $10. If you spend it on movies and a pizza with your friends on Friday night, you won't have enough left to go to the amusement park on Saturday. So you must make a choice. You must decide which of your wants—the movie and pizza with friends or the trip to the amusement park—is more important to you and will satisfy you more. One of the purposes of this book is to help you learn how to make wise economic decisions.

You have already learned that businesses and governments face the problem of scarcity just as you do. They must also make choices. Every country has a shortage of economic resources in relation to the unlimited wants of its citizens. Some countries have fewer resources than others. A major problem each nation has is how best to use its limited resources to satisfy as many as possible of its people's wants. A natural resource like petroleum, for example, can be used to make gasoline for cars or nylon or polyester material for clothes and tires. Timber can be reserved for natural beauty in state and national parks or used for lumber to build houses. And people tend to want it all—gasoline, polyester and nylon products, natural forests for parks, and wood houses. Who decides how the resources will be used? You will be studying in this course how you, other individuals, businesses, and governments go about making these decisions in the United States.

Illus. 1–4

Which shoes to buy? Which plan to follow? We all must make decisions.

Learning to Make Decisions

You make decisions every day. Many are economic decisions—whether to go to a show or save your money, whether to buy new jogging shoes or make your faded ones last a little longer, whether to take a part-time job as a bagger at the supermarket or continue to deliver newspapers. You know that decisions must be made, but do you know that there is a correct way to go about making all your decisions?

The Process for Making Decisions

There is a process which you can use to make almost any kind of decision. Let us look at the way economic decisions are made. **Economic decision making** is the process of choosing which among several wants being considered at a certain time will be satisfied. Once you learn the process, your decision making will be easier.

Steps in Decision Making

You will study more about decision making later in this book when you read about choosing a career and managing your money. But let's look briefly at the steps here.

1. Define the problem. If you have only $10 and want to buy several things, the problem is how to spend the money in a way that will give you the most satisfaction. In each situation, the problem must be defined in order to make a decision that will lead to its solution.
2. Identify the choices. There may be many choices or only two or three. In the movies/amusement park decision, you had identified two wants or choices. But other choices, or alternatives, might be considered. For example, you might decide to save your money instead of going to either place. It is important to consider all the alternatives in making a decision.
3. Examine the advantages and disadvantages of each choice. If you go to the movie, you will enjoy seeing the show and being with friends; but you will have the disadvantage of missing the trip to the amusement park. You also might miss the opportunity of being with your family on a Saturday outing. If you save the money and do neither, you will have the money for other things later. But you will miss out on being with your friends

and enjoying the recreation of either the movie or the amusement park. Sometimes actually writing down your choices and listing the advantages and disadvantages of each will help with the next step.

4. Choose. This is really getting down to the "nitty gritty" of the problem. Even if you have done the first three steps as best you can, this is often a difficult step. But you must learn to select from your alternatives the one which you feel will be the best for you and your interests at this particular time.

5. Act on your choice. This is the "take-action" step. If you have chosen to go to the movie, go and enjoy it. Try not to worry about the other choices that you decided against. Some people fret so much about the choice they made that they cannot enjoy the activity they decided upon. Life is full of choices. And no doubt everyone regrets a decision from time to time. But using the decision-making process each time will help you improve your ability to make choices.

6. Review your decision. Was your decision a good one? On a scale of one to ten, what score would you give your decision for the satisfaction it provided? What was right about it? What was wrong with it? If you had it to do over, would you make the same choice? Did you miss one of the alternatives that might have been a better choice? Or did you fail to examine all the advantages and disadvantages of each choice? This step gives you the opportunity to evaluate your decision and profit by any mistakes you feel you made so that you can make a better decision in the future.

Of course there are occasions when decisions must be made quickly and you will not have time to use all the steps. For example, if your home catches on fire, you will not have time to consider many choices before you decide to get out! But for most decisions, following the process will help you make better choices.

As you progress through this course, you will have an opportunity to practice decision making and you will study how the six-step process can be used by everyone—individuals, businesses, and governments—to cope with the problem of choosing which of the unlimited wants can be satisfied with the limited resources available.

A dding to Your Business Vocabulary

The following terms should become part of your business vocabulary. For each numbered item, find the term that has the same meaning.

basic economic problem
capital resources or capital
economic decision making
economic resources or
    factors of production
goods

human resources or *labor*
natural resources
needs
services
wants·

1. The process of choosing which want among several wants being considered at a certain time will be satisfied.
2. The means through which we produce goods and services.
3. The problem—which faces individuals, businesses, and governments—of satisfying unlimited wants with limited resources.
4. Raw materials supplied by nature.
5. The tangible things you use in everyday life.
6. Tools, equipment, and buildings used in producing goods and services.
7. Those things that are necessary for survival, such as food, clothing, and shelter.
8. The people who work to produce goods and services.
9. Those things which we can live without but which add pleasure and comfort to living.
10. Those things that satisfy our wants through the efforts of other people or equipment.

Understanding Your Reading

1. Explain the difference between needs and wants.
2. Give two examples each of needs and wants.
3. Give three examples to explain why wants are unlimited.
4. Does business play a part in satisfying our needs and wants? Explain.
5. Give one example each of a service provided by a person and by a machine.
6. What role do economic resources play in satisfying our needs and wants?
7. Name the three kinds of economic resources and give two examples of each.
8. Can goods be produced with only capital and human resources?
9. Give two examples to show that economic resources are limited.
10. Explain what is meant by the basic economic problem.
11. Give one example each to show that businesses and governments must also deal with scarcity.
12. What are the six steps in the decision-making process?

Putting Your Business Knowledge to Work

1. Review the examples of limited resources given in the chapter. For each of the three economic resources, give two examples not listed in the text.
2. When you learn about a new product, you often want it. Give an example of a new good or service that you or your family learned about during the past year and wanted. Show how you learned about each item.
3. Everyone must cope with the basic economic problem. For each of the following, give one example to show how this was done and what choice was made: your family, one of your school's sports teams, your town or city, the federal government.
4. Think about the clothes you own. Name one piece of clothing that you own but no longer wear. Give two reasons why you do not wear the item and tell how this situation contributes to unlimited wants.
5. List two businesses in your community that sell goods, two that sell services, and two that sell both.
6. Without natural resources there could be no goods. Name some of the natural resources that were used in making each of the following: a digital watch, denim jeans, your classroom desk, a pizza, a wallet.

Computing Business Problems

1. The Jenkins family had a monthly take-home pay of $1,080. Each month they paid for the following needs:

House payment	$310
Electric bill	95
Water bill	15
Food	250
Clothing	50

a. What is the total monthly payment for the needs?

b. How much was left for other needs and wants?

c. What percentage of the Jenkins' take-home pay was being spent for needs?

2. Forest fires take a heavy toll on land and timber resources, as shown recently in the Wildfire Report below for protected areas (those which are under the control of state and federal agencies such as the Department of Agriculture or the Department of the Interior). Study the table and answer the questions which follow it.

Acres of
Protected Land

	Federal Acres	State & Private
Total land area	680,261,000	805,927,000
Area burned by wildfires	751,000	2,348,000
Number of fires reported	14,600	141,000

a. What is the total acreage of protected land?

b. What was the total number of fires reported in protected areas for the year?

c. How many acres were burned in the protected areas?

d. What was the average number of acres (show in rounded numbers) of federally protected land burned per fire?

e. How do these wildfires affect the problem of limited resources?

3. To protect natural resources, various levels of government recently spent the following amounts in one year for water, land, and air quality control activities.

Quality Control
Expenditures
(in millions of dollars)

Level of Government	Water	Land	Air
Federal	$4,829	$ 163	$353
State	986	188	166
Local	8,498	3,014	35

a. How much did each level of government spend during the year to protect the quality of its natural resources?

b. What was the total spent by all levels of government for water, land, and air quality control?

c. What percent of the total amount was spent by local governments?

d. On which resource was the most money spent? What amount was spent on the resource?

e. In what way might the action by all levels of government help to alleviate the problem of scarcity?

*S**tretching Your Business Knowledge***

1. What changes might occur for you and your family if any of the three factors of production — natural, human, or capital — was no longer available?

2. Most of the goods and services we want can be bought from various kinds of businesses. But many of our wants are satisfied by some level of government. On a sheet of paper write three column headings: local, state, federal. List under each heading five wants which are supplied by each level of government. How do we pay for these wants?

3. One of the economic decisions you will be making soon is whether or not you will go to college. It is economic because your decision will affect your ability to earn money (a resource) to satisfy your needs and wants. While you cannot act on your decision at this time, you can begin thinking about the decision now.

Follow this decision through the first three steps of the decision-making process. Write down your responses at each step. If you had to complete Step 4 now, what would be your choice?

4. From the local newspaper or from television or radio newscasts, make a list of items which are said to be in short supply. Classify each of the items as a good or service. Classify each as a natural, human, or capital resource, or a combination of resources.

5. The Department of Labor (DOL) issues information on human resource needs for the present and for the next few years. DOL recently stated that we will have a shortage of certain skilled workers for several years into the future. Two of these were accountants and secretaries. List as many ways as you can to ease the scarcity of these two groups of workers.

CHAPTER 2

The American Economic System —
Private Enterprise

■ CHAPTER OBJECTIVES ─────────────────────

After studying this chapter and completing the end-of-chapter activities, you will be able to:

1. State the three economic questions that must be answered by every society.
2. Describe three types of economic systems.
3. Identify five features of our private enterprise system.
4. Defend the statement that people are entitled to make profits from their business ventures.
5. Explain why competition generally results in better service and more goods at lower cost.
6. Tell who owns/controls the economic resources under capitalism, socialism, and communism.

As you have learned, resources to satisfy our many wants are limited. Every society, including America, must use whatever resources it has to provide as many of its members' wants as it can. This is a fact of life with which all societies have had to cope since time began and which will apply to all societies in the future. The limited economic resources available to each nation forces the nation to make choices on how the resources will be used. These economic resources or factors of production, you will recall, are natural, human, and capital resources. How does a nation decide how to use these resources to its best advantage?

Three Economic Questions Must Be Answered

In order to decide how to use its scarce resources, each nation must answer three economic questions: (1) What goods and services are to be produced? (2) How should the goods and services be produced? (3) For whom should the goods and services be produced? A nation's plan for answering these questions is called its **economic system** or its economy. Since these questions help us to understand different economic systems, let us think about each one.

What Goods and Services Shall Be Produced?

Nations differ in their wants just as individuals do. One country might decide to go all out to produce spaceships and to explore other planets. Another might want to use its resources to build the biggest and best military force. Some might want to use most of their resources to provide such consumer goods as cars, television sets, dishwashers, and recreational parks. Still other countries might have such limited resources that they must concentrate on providing the basic needs of food, clothing, and shelter. If a country wants to meet some or all of its people's wants, it must plan how to best use its resources. A nation which concentrates too much of its resources on military goods will not have enough left for consumer goods and services. On the other hand, a nation which uses all of its resources to supply consumer goods and services may not be able to protect its people from outside forces. Each nation must decide which kinds of goods and services it values most.

How Will the Goods and Services Be Produced?

A country which has a great many people but not much money or equipment might build roads by having many workers use picks and shovels to do the job. In another country, road building may be accomplished by using only a few people to operate heavy equipment, such as bulldozers and power earth movers. In the first case, the country is making use of its human resources to offset its lack of capital resources. In the second case, the country is doing the job with more capital resources and less labor. In either case, the road will get built. But the second method is more efficient and will enable the country to complete the road much sooner. As you can see, economic resources can be combined in different ways to produce the same goods and services. Each nation decides which combination of resources will best suit its circumstances.

For Whom Shall the Goods and Services Be Produced?

For whom should the goods and services be produced? How will the goods and services be distributed? Should the goods and services be shared equally among the people? Should people who contribute more to producing the goods and services be able to get a larger share of them? If you have the money, shouldn't you be able to buy anything you want? These are some of the questions that have to be considered.

In some economic systems you can buy whatever you want and can afford. But in others, your ability to buy may be limited by the country's answer to the question, "What shall be produced?" For example, a country might be using a large share of its resources to produce capital goods, such as tractors or industrial robots; it might, therefore, limit its production of consumer goods, such as boats and video recorders. In the United States the share of goods and services that you are able to have is largely determined by the amount of money you have to spend. And the amount of money that you receive in wages will be affected by many things, including your abilities and how you use them. Figure 2–1 illustrates a variety of responses to the three basic economic questions.

Types of Economic Systems

Another way to understand a nation's economic system is to look not only at how the three economic questions are answered, but also at who answers them. In some countries, the answers are established by custom. In a **custom-based economy** things are done the way they have always been done. Children of each generation are taught to use the same method to make the same goods their parents and grandparents produced, and a tradition develops over the years. The custom may be weaving cloth on a hand loom, making straw baskets, or planting rice by hand. Goods are typically produced by hand, by using primitive tools, and by using people or animals for energy. Change and growth occur slowly in countries whose economies follow customs and where the people are poor in material goods.

In some countries economic questions are answered by the owners of the resources. In a **directed** or **planned economy,**

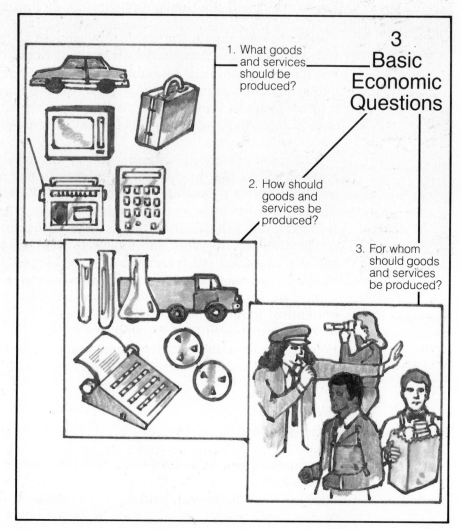

Figure 2–1
Every economic system must answer the three basic economic questions.

resources are owned and controlled by the government. The officials of the government decide what and how goods will be produced and how they will be shared. They decide how much of the nation's resources will be put to military uses and how much to producing consumer and capital goods. They decide how much grain will be grown, how many pairs of shoes will be produced, and how many people will be used to produce television sets. They plan all phases of the economy and command that the plans be carried out, using military or police force to do so if necessary. In directed economies, the average citizen has very little to say

Methods of production are slow to change in a custom-based economy.

about how the three economic questions are answered. While directed economies work for some countries, the freedom of the people is always limited.

In a third type of economy, the three questions are answered by the buying and selling activities in the marketplace. The **marketplace** is any place where buyers and sellers exchange goods, services, and some form of money. People who order goods from a mail-order catalog, go to a movie, buy food in a supermarket, lease a telephone, buy a share of stock, or have a sweater cleaned are operating in the marketplace. When an airline orders a new jet, a business launches a satellite, or the government hires computer operators, each is operating in the marketplace. No one tells the consumers what to buy and no one tells businesses what to sell. Consumers and businesses make economic decisions based on their own interests. A system in which economic decisions are freely made by buyers and sellers in the marketplace is called a **market economy.** When people in a market economy buy a product, they are helping to answer the question, "What will be produced?" Resources are combined in such a way that goods which people want and buy will be produced. This answers the question, "How will goods and services be produced?" And since people buy what they wish and can afford in a market economy, they largely answer the question, "For whom will goods and services be produced?"

Our Economic System Has Several Labels

Were you able to identify our economy as you read the three types? If you selected "market economy," you were correct. As you know, the main differences among economic systems involve who owns the economic resources and who makes the decisions about production and distribution. Our system fits the definition of a market economy—a system where economic decisions are freely made by buyers and sellers in the marketplace. But our economic system also has other labels.

Capitalism is another name used to identify the economic system in the United States. This term refers to the fact that economic resources are mostly owned by individuals rather than by government. Since most of the resources are privately owned, the individual owners are free to decide what they will produce with them. This freedom of the individual to choose what to produce provides the rationale for two other names given to our economy—a **free enterprise system** and a **private enterprise system.** All four of these terms—market system, capitalism, free enterprise system, and private enterprise system—mean about the same thing: a system in which most economic resources are privately owned and decisions about production and distribution are largely made by free exchange in the marketplace. The term "private enterprise system" will be emphasized in our discussion.

Illus. 2–2
The U.S. economic system is best described as a private enterprise system.

Features of Our Private Enterprise System

There are many things about our economic system which make it different from other systems of the world. You are aware that the words "freedom" and "individual choice" are frequently used in discussing our economy. Let us examine five major features of our private enterprise system.

Private Enterprise

A **business** is an establishment or "enterprise" that supplies us with goods and services in exchange for payment in some form. The right of the individual to choose whether to own a business, what business to enter, and what to produce with only limited government direction is referred to as **private enterprise.** Private enterprise ensures your freedom to decide how you will earn a living. In a private enterprise system, you may start or invest in any business you wish as long as you obey the law in doing so. You are free to choose to be a bricklayer, minister, karate instructor, business owner, astronaut, teacher, dancer, or anything you wish.

As a business person, you are generally free to offer goods and services at times, prices, and places of your choice. You are free to succeed or even to fail in the business of your choice. Of course there are some regulations that prevent you from doing things that would harm others. For example, you may not dispose of chemical wastes in a way that would pollute the environment. Nor can you practice surgery unless you have been granted a surgical license by the appropriate agency in the state in which you plan to practice surgery. These regulations are not designed to limit freedom but to protect people from harmful practices.

Private Property

If your family owns the home in which you live or the television set you watch, the family is enjoying the right of private property. The **private property** feature is the right to own, use, or dispose of things of value. You may dispose of things you own by selling them, giving them away, willing them to anyone you wish, or even by throwing them away. In our country you can own any item and do what you want with it, as long as you do not violate a

Illus. 2–3
Private property is the cornerstone of the private enterprise system.

law in doing so. You also have the right to own, use, and sell whatever you invent or create.

Businesses also have the right to own property. This property may be such things as land, buildings, tools, and the goods they produce. Businesses also have the right to use and dispose of their property in any lawful way, just as individuals do.

The Profit Motive

Businesses supply goods and services to the marketplace for one main reason—to earn money. Unless business owners can expect to make a profit, they would not want to put time, energy, and money into an enterprise. **Profit** is the money left from sales after subtracting the cost of operating the business. Business owners are entitled to make profits because they run the risk of losing the money they invested to start the business and because of the extra work and stress that are part of owning and running a business.

The desire to work for profit is often called the **profit motive.** This profit motive helps make our economy strong. Because of it, people are willing to invest money in business and to develop new products to satisfy consumers' wants. But the profit motive is not the only reason for putting time, money, and effort into businesses. Some people enjoy bringing out new products or improving existing ones. Others get pleasure from knowing that the goods or services they produce make other people happier. And others like the excitement of starting and running new businesses. But the profit motive is the heart of the private enterprise system.

Competition

An ad on television urges you to buy "Superior" brand instead of "DeLuxe" brand. A supermarket ad in the newspaper claims in bold letters, "Ours are the lowest prices in town." An ad in a magazine urges you to buy the designer jeans being modeled in the ad by a famous video star. The rivalry among businesses to sell their goods and services to buyers is called **competition**. This feature of our economy gives you the opportunity to make choices among countless goods and services that are available. You make these choices by comparing prices, quality, appearance, usefulness, and appeal of the things you buy. And if you are not satisfied with a purchase, you are free to buy from a competing business next time. Competition encourages business owners to improve products, offer better services, keep prices reasonable, and produce new things.

Freedom of Choice

You have learned that the private enterprise system gives you the right to enter a business or career of your choice, to own property, to make a profit, and to compete. You also have other rights that contribute to your economic freedom of choice.

You have the right to buy where and what you please, even though sales of some things that the government declares harmful to you or others may be prohibited or required to carry a warning of danger. You have the right as a worker to organize with other workers. Through organization you can strive to improve working conditions. You have the right to travel when and where you please in this country and to many other countries. And you have the right to express your opinions in newspapers, over radio and television, and in talking with others as long as you do not slander another person. The private enterprise system provides greater freedom of choice to the individual than any other economic system.

Other Economic Systems

There are many different economic systems operating in the world today. The major ones are known as the three "isms": capitalism, socialism, and communism. We have already examined capitalism, or private enterprise, as it operates in the United States.

If you examined all three systems in detail, you would find that it is very difficult to define them and explain how they work. That is true partly because none of them exists anywhere in a pure form. Two countries operating under one form may differ in a variety of ways. Economic systems are usually identified, therefore, by the major features of their organization and operation. Under pure capitalism, for example, all enterprises would be privately owned and managed. That is not true in the United States, but we call our system capitalism because most of its enterprises are privately owned and managed. Neither of the other two major economic systems exists in pure form.

Under **socialism** the government owns and operates certain basic enterprises, such as steel mills, railroads and airlines, power plants, radio and TV stations, hospital and health-care services, and banks. However, the extent of the government ownership and control is decided by the people. If they want more government control, they can vote for it. If they want less, they can vote against it. Some enterprises are also privately owned, but there is less frequency of private business ownership than in a private enterprise economy.

Under **communism** the government owns or controls most of the economic resources and has tight control over them. All economic activities are planned and directed by the state. Farms, mines, factories, stores, newspapers, railroads, telephone services—all are owned and run by the government. Officials of the government decide what goods and services are to be produced and in what quantities. They also decide how the goods are to be produced. It is true that people are free to buy whatever goods and services are offered for sale. But the prices and supplies of such products as clothing, TV sets, watches, and cars are set by the government. Wages of the workers are also set by the government. These actions by government basically answer the question of how goods and services will be distributed.

Most people living under communism today do not have the freedom to decide how far they will go in school or what job they will have. Job opportunities, like wages, are mostly fixed by government. Even the size of an apartment or house in which people are to live may be assigned by the government in directed economies.

Mixed Economic Systems

An economic system usually gets its name from the way its economic resources are owned and controlled. But most modern economic systems cannot be easily and neatly placed under such labels as capitalism, socialism, or communism. As you have read, there is no pure form of any of these systems in any country today. In general we think of most countries as having mixed economic systems. While they usually are predominantly one system, they often combine some features of others. Socialism combines government ownership and control of basic industries with some private ownership of consumer-goods businesses. In some communist countries, a limited amount of private enterprise and profit motive may be tolerated. For example, after farmers in some communist countries meet the government's quota for their crops, they may be allowed to sell the rest and keep the profit.

In our country there is some government regulation of business. There are also some government-operated enterprises, such as post offices, schools, and city water agencies. Our economic system is not pure capitalism, so it is often called modified or mixed capitalism. In Unit 11, you will learn about how government and business work together in our economic system.

A dding to Your Business Vocabulary

The following terms should become part of your business vocabulary. For each numbered item, find the term that has the same meaning.

business
capitalism, free enterprise system,
    market economy, or private enterprise
    system
communism
competition
custom-based economy
directed or planned economy

economic system
marketplace
private enterprise
private property
profit
profit motive
socialism

1. A nation's plan for making decisions on what to produce, how to produce, and how to distribute goods and services.
2. An economic system in which things are done the way they have always been done.
3. An economic system in which government owns and controls the economic resources and makes all the decisions regarding the production of goods and services.
4. Any place where buyers and sellers exchange goods and services for some form of money.
5. An economic system in which most economic resources are privately owned and decisions about production are largely made by free exchange in the marketplace.
6. The right of the individual to choose what business to enter and what to produce with only limited direction from the government.
7. The right to own, use, or dispose of things of value.
8. Money left from sales after subtracting the cost of operating the business.
9. The right to work for profit.
10. The rivalry among businesses to sell their goods and services to buyers.
11. An economic system in which government owns and operates a number of industries and provides for some degree of private property and private enterprise.
12. An economic system in which government owns most of the economic resources and has tight control over the production and distribution of goods and services.
13. An establishment or enterprise that supplies goods and services in exchange for some form of payment.

Understanding Your Reading

1. What are the three economic questions which every society must answer to set up an economic system?
2. Name the three types of economic systems and give the major feature of each.
3. Who owns and controls most economic resources in a system of capitalism?
4. In addition to capitalism, give three other names by which the American economic system is known.
5. What are the five features of our private enterprise system?
6. Why are business owners entitled to make a profit from their business ventures?
7. What does the right of private property entitle the owner to do?
8. Give three ways in which consumers benefit from competition among businesses.
9. In addition to the profit motive, give two other reasons that might encourage people to invest their time, money, and energy in operating their own businesses.
10. In addition to private property and private enterprise, what are four other rights that are included in our economic freedom of choice?
11. How does ownership of resources differ under socialism and communism?
12. Do citizens have any influence on the extent of government control under socialism?
13. Is freedom to buy goods and services

in a communist system restricted in any way?

14. What is meant by the term "mixed economy"?

15. Why is it more nearly accurate to refer to our economic system as modified or mixed capitalism rather than as pure capitalism?

*P*utting *Your Business Knowledge to Work*

1. How is the question of what goods and services will be produced chiefly determined under a custom-based system?
2. Who chiefly decides what will be produced in a directed economic system?
3. Can you think of ways in which competition among businesses might work to the disadvantage of consumers?
4. For each of the three types of economic systems, give one example of a country operating under that system in the world today. Explain your choices.
5. If we can choose any kind of work we wish under the right of free enterprise, why can't individuals open a law office, practice dentistry, or pilot a plane when they feel they are ready to do so?
6. If the United States operated as pure capitalism, what are several changes which might occur?
7. It has been said that the term, "market," in our market economy refers to an idea and not to a place. What do you think this means?
8. Explain how the decisions of buyers and sellers in the marketplace largely answer the question of what to produce in our private enterprise system.

*C*omputing *Business Problems*

1. Countries which make great use of capital goods can produce more with fewer people in a shorter time than countries where many workers perform the work by manual labor. Study the figures below for farm workers and their output; then answer the questions.

	U.S.	U.S.S.R.
Agricultural labor force	4,380,000	34,350,000
Number of persons supplied from output of each farm worker	49	7

   a. How many more people were working in agricultural jobs in the U.S.S.R. than in the U.S. in the year quoted?
   b. In which country was each farm worker more productive?
   c. In terms of persons supplied from the output of each farm worker, how much more productive was the worker cited in Item (b)?
2. Seth Gorman compared food prices in newspaper ads each week before doing his grocery shopping. One week he found these prices for Grade A eggs at three competing supermarkets: Food Mart, $1.09 per dozen; Farm-to-you, $1.17 per dozen and 20 cents off with a newspaper coupon; Kitchen Pride, special, 2 dozen for $2.09.

a. At which store would Seth pay the lowest price per dozen?
b. Will the coupon be an advantage? Explain.
c. Do you think the fact that there were three stores from which Seth could buy eggs benefited him in any way?
3. The table below shows the average number of hours a worker in the capitals of the U.S.,
   Great Britain, and Russia would have to work to earn enough money to buy the items listed
   at the left.

	Washington, D.C.	London	Moscow
Hamburger meat, 1 pound	17 min.	29 min.	56 min.
Color TV, large screen	65 hrs.	132 hrs.	701 hrs.
Toothpaste	16 min.	13 min.	27 min.
Bus fare (2 miles)	7 min.	11 min.	3 min.
Men's shoes, 1 pair	8 hrs.	7 hrs.	25 hrs.
Week's food for family of four	18.6 hrs.	24.7 hrs.	53.5 hrs.

a. How much longer than an American must a Russian employee work to earn enough to
   buy food for four for a week?
b. How much longer than an American must a British employee work to earn enough to
   buy the weekly food basket?
c. How many 8-hour days would a worker in each country have to work to earn enough to
   buy the color TV?
d. If the color TV set costs $650, what would American workers' wages per hour be?

Stretching Your Business Knowledge

1. Using library resources, such as *The Statistical Abstract of the United States,* prepare a report on the two largest directed
economies, the U.S.S.R. and The People's Republic of China. Find as much
as you can of the following information
about each of the two countries:

Population
Percent of the world's population living in
   each country
Output per person (check under the list-
   ing "GNP—per capita")
Amount of goods exported to the United
   States
Amount of goods imported from the
   United States
An example of an exported and an
   imported good. Do the exported/

imported goods give you an idea
about the advantage and the disadvantage of each country's resources? Explain.

2. Visit a mall or a shopping center in your
community and list the businesses that
sell the same or similar products. List
ways in which these businesses compete
with one another to get customers to buy.

3. Interview a person in your community
who owns and manages a business. Ask
the owner to list the advantages and disadvantages of owning a business as
opposed to working for someone else at
a salary. Find out whether the owner
would invest money and energy in the
business if he or she had the decision to
make again.

4. In our private enterprise system, you and other consumers make most of the decisions regarding what to produce by what you buy. Some products which are put on the market succeed because many people buy them. Others stay on the market only a short time because no one buys them. Consumers are saying with their purchases, "Produce this." or "Don't produce this." From discussions with your parents and other adults, identify three products which have remained on the market over a long period of time and three which were put on the market but failed in a short time.

CHAPTER 3

You and the Private Enterprise System

■ CHAPTER OBJECTIVES ──────────────────────

After studying this chapter and completing the end-of-chapter activities, you will be able to:

1. Identify three economic roles each person plays.
2. Give an example to show how dollar votes help create demand.
3. Give one example each to show how demand and supply affect prices.
4. Explain the effect that competition has on prices.
5. Explain how your worker role supports your consumer role.
6. Give one example to show the importance of productivity in your worker role.
7. Give two examples of economic citizenship.

In the early morning hours, John Bedker finished his bacon and eggs at a nearby restaurant then boarded a bus to his part-time job across town. To earn money to go back to college in the fall, John was working with the city road repair crew. When his work-day ended, he rushed for the bus which would take him to the voting precinct near his home. He was eager to vote on an issue which had been vigorously debated in the city and in which he had taken a great interest. John was preparing for a career in teaching, so he voted for the increase in taxes which was to provide an increase in teacher salaries in the city. As he headed home, John felt good about his day. He may not have been aware of it, but John had played three economic roles during the day.

Your Three Economic Roles

You play three economic roles, too, just as John did. A look at John's activities will help to identify those roles. First, John was a consumer; he purchased goods (bacon and eggs) and services (bus ride). As a worker John helped produce a service (road repair). And as a citizen he voted on an economic issue.

You and everyone you know will play many different roles in life. You may become a famous recording star, a business executive, or even president of the United States. A friend of yours may become an Olympic swimming champion, an electrician, a minister, or a computer programmer. While you and your friend may follow different career paths, some of the roles you play will be the same.

The three roles that all people share are those of consumer, worker, and citizen. It is true that some people do not work outside the home for wages, and some people may not exercise their right to vote, but we all will be affected in some way by these three economic roles. As you play these roles, you will make decisions that affect not only you, but the entire economy as well. Understanding how the private enterprise system works will help you understand the importance of your decisions — and may even help you make better ones — in each of your economic roles. In the remainder of this chapter, you will look at how the American economy works and how your roles fit into the picture.

Illus. 3–1
How will you fulfill your role as a worker?

Your Consumer Role in the Private Enterprise System

As you learned in Chapter 2, the American economic system is a market economy where buyers and sellers freely make economic decisions in the marketplace. You also learned that these decisions basically answer the question of what will be produced. The buying decisions of all consumers—individuals, businesses, and governments—provide the answer to how we will use our scarce resources. The important role you and all other consumers play in making these decisions is one of the most interesting things about our system. Individual buying decisions have a great influence on our market economy; individual consumers buy over two-thirds of all the goods and services produced in it. As you can see, consumers play a central role in a private enterprise system.

It may seem to you that the American economy is a big, unorganized system where everyone does just about as he or she pleases. You may wonder how the system can work when each business makes its own decision about what to produce and each buyer makes a decision about what and where to buy. But the system does work and it works well. Let's explore how your consumer decisions affect the system.

Your Dollar Votes Help Create Demand

As a consumer you help businesses make their decisions. You do this by buying—or not buying—certain goods and services. When you buy something, you are casting a "dollar vote" for it. You are saying to a business, "I like this product or service, and I'm willing to pay for it." When a business sees your dollar votes and those of all other consumers, it knows the demand for the product. **Demand** means the quantity of a product or service that consumers are willing and able to buy at a particular price.

Demand Helps Determine Supply

Knowing the demand tells a business what products and services to supply and how much of each. **Supply** means the quantity of a product or service that businesses are willing and able to provide at a particular price. Suppliers usually will produce a product or service as long as it can be sold for enough to cover the costs of operating the business to make and sell it, plus a reasonable profit. That is why you can buy a hamburger for about $1, but you won't find any for 10 cents. Suppliers of hamburgers could not cover their costs and make a profit at the 10-cent price.

Together, supply and demand play an important part in our market economy. Those "buyers and sellers in the marketplace" that you read about in Chapter 2 help to determine not only what will be produced but also what the price will be. Let's see how that works.

Demand and Supply Affect Prices

Have you ever wondered how a business decides what price to charge for a product or service? Why does a sweater cost $40 and a new car $10,000? Why does the price of a swimsuit drop in the fall of the year or the cost of food go up after a long summer's drought?

In addition to deciding what to produce, a business must set a price on a product or service. Generally speaking, prices are very carefully determined after a good deal of study. Supply and demand are among the most important factors to be considered.

The demand for a product affects the price. If many people want (demand) a particular product or service, its price will tend to go up, as illustrated in Figure 3–1. The price of Christmas cards is usually at its peak in November and early December when many people want to buy them. But have you noticed that the prices of the cards are often cut in half the day after Christmas? When demand is low, prices are usually low.

Supply also affects the price of a product. Remember that a supplier needs to cover the costs of operating the business and make a reasonable profit. Prices are set to do these two things. If a supplier of jogging shoes, for example, sets a price too high, people won't buy them; so the supplier will have to lower the price in order to sell the shoes. Of course, if the price is set too low, operating costs will not be covered; the supplier will lose money and soon go out of business. All this means that the supplier must produce a good product and operate in an efficient way. Prices can then be set at reasonable levels so that consumers will be willing and able to buy the products.

Of course, other things may be involved in the pricing process. The prices of some things tend to stay high, for example, because the materials from which they are made are limited by nature. Diamonds have been found in only a few countries of the

Figure 3–1
Prices are affected by the demand for and the supply of goods and services.

world and in relatively small quantities. Therefore, the price of diamonds is very high.

In recent years the people of the United States have also come to understand that the supply of oil is not unlimited as was once thought. When suppliers of oil produce less and the supply of products made from oil, such as gasoline, is reduced, the prices rise. On the other hand, when suppliers produce more oil and make it available, the prices tend to fall.

Competition Keeps Prices Reasonable

Earlier you read that suppliers set prices to cover operating costs and earn some profit. What is to prevent a seller from charging an unreasonably high price in order to earn larger profits? The answer is competition. You will remember from Chapter 2 that competition is one of the main features of the private enterprise system. If one store offers cassette tapes for $12.95 but another offers the same tapes for less, you probably would say to the merchant with the higher price, "Forget it. I can buy that same tape at a store down the street for $7.95." If the owners of the store keep the price at $12.95, they will soon go out of business because not many people will buy tapes at their price.

Competition affects prices in another way, too. When a product has a very high demand and is making money for one supplier, other business people will begin to offer the product also. With several businesses offering the product, one of the suppliers could not afford to sell at extremely high prices. Consumers would go to the competitors to buy. This also tends to cause suppliers to produce goods and services efficiently. If a supplier cannot produce the product at low cost so that it can be sold at competing prices, other suppliers who do so will get all the business and the inefficient producer will be forced out of the market. In this way, competition tends to allow only efficient producers— those who can supply good products at competitive prices — to survive in the marketplace. Competition, then, aids the consumer by helping to keep prices and profits at reasonable levels.

Your Worker Role Supports Your Consumer Role

No matter what price is set on products and services in the marketplace, you cannot enjoy the products and services unless you have the money to buy them. This is where your worker role comes into the picture.

Your Earnings Help Set Your Standard of Living

Most people earn their money by working. Of course, people work for many reasons. But probably one of the main reasons you will work is to earn money to buy things you need and want. While your parents may be supplying most of your needs now, before long you will be meeting your own needs with money you earn. How well you succeed in your chosen career will be the most important factor in setting your standard of living. We use the term **standard of living** as a measure of how well people in a country live; that usually means the quality and quantity of wants and needs which are satisfied. We use our incomes to buy the things we need to maintain and improve our standard of living. Your worker role, then, supports your consumer role.

Illus. 3–2
Your role as a
worker supports
your role as a
consumer.

Your Worker Productivity Affects the Economy

The main way we improve our standard of living is to produce more in our worker roles. When you begin your worker role, you will join over 110 million other workers in the United States. These workers produce the goods and services that consumers demand. One of the reasons this country has progressed so far in such a short time is that it has had a varied and skilled work force. We have combined with this work force better capital goods and a high level of technology to increase our productivity. That is, we have learned to work smarter. **Productivity** refers to the quantity of a good that an average worker can produce in an hour. High productivity has enabled us to achieve a standard of living which is among the highest in the world. As a worker you will want to improve your productivity so that you can increase your earnings and your standard of living. If you produce less than is expected of a worker in the job you choose, you help to lower the productivity and thus the standard of living for the nation. You will learn more about productivity and about your worker role in other chapters in this text. Now, let us consider the third role you play in the private enterprise system.

Your Role as a Citizen — Working for the Common Good

So far we have considered how you will satisfy your own wants and needs through your worker and consumer roles. But there are some needs and wants that you will not be able to satisfy for yourself. In your citizenship role, you will join other citizens in making some economic decisions for the common good.

Some Decisions Are Made Collectively

You probably will not earn enough to have your own fire department to protect your home. And you won't earn enough to build your own highways on which to drive your car. Even if you did earn enough money, it would not be very practical for each person to provide his or her own fire department or road system. Think of the confusion, to say nothing of the waste! There are many other things, such as schools, courts, and police protection, that neither individuals nor businesses can usually provide for themselves. In your role as citizen, you will join others, through different levels of government, in providing for these goods and services. Thus we collectively decide how some of our scarce resources will be used and what will be provided for our common use.

Illus. 3–3
As citizens we make economic decisions collectively through the ballot box.

Your Taxes Help Pay for Common Services

In order to pay for the goods and services which the government provides for our common use, you and other citizens will pay taxes. There are many kinds of taxes collected by local, state, and national governments. You will learn more in Unit 11 about meeting the costs of government services. In your citizenship role, you should remember that the government cannot supply all that the people want. It, too, must make choices as to which services it can afford to provide. When John Bedker voted for the teacher-salary increase through increased taxes, as discussed in the opening of this chapter, he helped his city decide which of the many goods and services would be provided. When you vote, as a part of your citizenship role, you will be helping to make some of these decisions.

Illus. 3–4
Taxes help to pay for goods and services provided by the government.

*A*dding to Your Business Vocabulary

The following terms should become part of your business vocabulary. For each numbered item, find the term that has the same meaning.

demand   *standard of living*
productivity   *supply*

1. The quantity of a good that an average worker can produce in one hour.
2. The quantity of a product or service that businesses are willing and able to provide at a particular price.
3. As a measure of how well people in a country live, this term indicates the quantity and quality of wants and needs which are satisfied.
4. The quantity of a product or service that consumers are willing and able to buy at a particular price.

*U*nderstanding Your Reading

1. What are the three economic roles that most people in the United States play?
2. Give an example of the way your dollar votes help to create demand.
3. Give one example each to show how demand and supply affect prices.
4. Suppliers usually set their prices to cover what two things?
5. If a business has overstocked a product, would it be likely to raise or lower the price of the product?
6. Would the price of a product made with scarce natural resources tend to be high or low?
7. Explain the effect that competition has on prices.
8. Give an example to show how competition tends to make businesses more efficient.
9. Explain how your worker role supports your consumer role.
10. In what way might your selection of a career affect your future standard of living?
11. Give one example to show the importance of productivity in your worker role.
12. Give two examples of activities you perform in your citizenship role.

*P*utting Your Business Knowledge to Work

1. When the demand for small cars increases, what might the suppliers of large models do to sell their cars?
2. Give two examples of products whose prices are usually high because they are made from scarce natural resources.
3. Because of the central role that consumers play in it, the private enterprise system has been called a system in which "the consumer is king." What do you think this means?
4. If workers produce fewer goods and less services than they are expected to produce, what effect will their lowered productivity have on the nation's standard of living?

5. Since Americans have the freedom to make individual choices in the market-place, why would they make some decisions collectively?
6. Explain why choosing a career is one of the most important economic decisions a person makes.

7. In your citizenship role, you will be doing a variety of things in addition to voting on economic issues. After discussing this with friends and members of your family, list several things that a good citizen does for either his or her personal satisfaction or for the common good.

Computing Business Problems

1. The Video Sports Shop purchased 24 dozen computer games, at a cost of $20 per game, to sell during the Christmas season.
   a. How many individual computer games did Video Sports Shop buy?
   b. What was the total cost of the games?
   c. In January the shop had ¼ of the games left. How many games were unsold?
   d. If demand had dropped after the holidays, would the shop be more likely to increase or decrease the price to sell the games?
2. Below is a table showing information about the voting activity of young people in two national elections. Study the data and answer the questions which follow.

Year	No. of Persons 18–20 yrs. old	% Reporting They Registered to Vote	% Reporting They Voted
1978	12,200,000	34.7	20.1
1980	12,300,000	44.7	35.7

   a. How many people 18–20 years old voted in 1978?

   b. What was the percent of increase in the number of people who voted in 1980 over 1978?
   c. How many 18–20 year olds reported they registered but did not vote in 1980?
3. Products made of gold are usually high in price because the supply of gold is limited and expensive to mine. Below is a table showing the amount of gold produced in the U.S. and the value of the gold produced at three 5-year intervals.

Year	Ounces	Production Value
1970	1,743,000	$ 63,400,000
1975	1,052,000	169,900,000
1980	951,000	582,800,000

   a. In which year was the most gold produced? Was the value of the gold produced highest in the same year that the most gold was produced?
   b. What was the decrease in ounces produced in 1975 compared to 1970? In 1980 compared to 1975?
   c. What was the value per ounce of gold produced in 1980? (Round to the nearest dollar.)

*S*tretching Your Business Knowledge

1. There are other forms of competition besides price. If all stores in your area charged the same price for an electric hair dryer, there would be no competition among the stores on the basis of price. And if all the hair dryers were exactly the same, the customer would have no reason to choose one hair dryer over another. If these conditions were true, what other forms of competition could stores use in order to get customers to buy hair dryers from them?

2. Interview the manager of a local supermarket. Ask the manager how prices are determined in the store. Find out whether there have been any items recently for which there was a surge of demand. If so, did the store have enough of the item to supply the demand? Did the price change? Ask the manager to explain also how such things as spoilage, bad checks, and theft affect prices in the store.

3. Interview five seniors in your school who are or soon will be 18 years old. Find out how they feel about voting. Suggested questions: What is your age? If you are 18, have you registered to vote? Why or why not? Do you plan to register before the next election? Do you think 18-year-olds should vote? Why or why not? Report your findings to the class.

4. Visit three gasoline stations in your area and list the price each charges for a gallon of unleaded regular gas. Find out how much of the cost represents taxes and from what levels of government the taxes are imposed. Ask the owners how they compete with other stations other than by the price of the gasoline.

5. Using your local newspaper, clip articles dealing with economic citizenship. Try to find at least one article on taxes and one dealing with voting on an economic issue. Write a brief statement of your views on each article and justify your position.

CHAPTER 4

Measuring Our Economic Progress

■ CHAPTER OBJECTIVES

After studying this chapter and completing the end-of-chapter activities, you will be able to:

1. Explain how GNP is used as a measure of economic growth.
2. Tell how per capita output is determined.
3. Give an example to explain how productivity is related to the standard of living.
4. Describe economic conditions in the four phases of the business cycle.
5. List three economic problems which our country faces.

George and Sue Ellen Lester enjoy showing their friends how much their daughter, Megan, has grown over the years. They can do this by pointing to the tape measure they attached to the wall of her room when she was a year old. On each birthday Megan stands next to the tape and her father places a mark to show her new height. From this record, the Lesters can tell many things about their daughter's growth. They can compare her height from one birthday to another. They can point to years in which she grew a lot and to others in which her growth was slower. In addition, they can figure her total growth and her average annual growth.

The Lesters could also use other methods of checking Megan's growth. They could just look at her and see that she has grown taller and stronger. But they could also measure her growth by recording her weight or the size of her clothes.

Checking the Growth of the Economy

Just as the Lesters could use different ways to measure Megan's growth, we can use different methods to check on the growth of our economy. A high rate of employment and a low rate of business failures are two indications that our economy is doing well. However, the most important ways by which we can measure how well we are doing relate to how much we produce to help satisfy the needs and wants of our people. Today more than 110 million Americans work in thousands of different jobs and produce thousands of different products and services — hamburgers, snowmobiles, amusement parks, nail polish, electronic games, fire engines, carry-out chicken dinners, garbage collection, medical services, concerts. You could name many more. The total of all the goods and services that Americans produce is the output or production of our nation. We have only about 7 percent of the world's land and about 5.4 percent of the world's population, but our output accounts for about 25 percent of all goods and services produced in the world.

Measuring the Nation's Output

One way to find out how well our economy is doing is to compare output from year to year. The federal government collects information from producers and estimates our national output. The most widely used estimate is the gross national product. The **gross national product** or **GNP** is the total value of all goods and services produced in our country during one year.

GNP includes what consumers spend for food, clothing, and housing. It includes what businesses spend for buildings, equipment, and supplies. It also includes what government agencies spend to pay employees and buy supplies. There are a few things not included, of course. For example, GNP does not include

Illus. 4–1
Millions of Americans are employed in thousands of different jobs.

Illus. 4–2
Some activities
are not included
in the GNP. Can
you name some
others?

things we do for ourselves, such as cutting our own lawn or building a picnic table for our yard. But if we buy the lawn service
or the picnic table from businesses, they would be included. GNP
includes everything that goes into the price of goods and services
that we produce in a year.

If the GNP increases from year to year, this is a good sign that
our economy is growing. Even though we have had some bad
years, our economy has enjoyed a steady climb over its history.
GNP was almost $3 trillion in a recent year. Writing that figure
down—3 followed by 12 zeros—will give you an idea of how big
our economy really is when we measure it in dollars.

There is one big difficulty in comparing a country's GNP
from year to year, however. Prices of what we produce do not stay
the same from year to year. Prices go up and down—mostly up.
So in order to make comparisons that are fair and accurate, we
need to take the current prices and adjust them each year so that
they are equal in value over a period of years. Let's look at a very
easy example.

Suppose the tiny make-believe country of Logoland produces
only colorful bumper stickers with printed messages. The output
of Logoland is shown in Figure 4–1.

Year	No. of Bumper Stickers Produced	Current Price per Sticker	GNP at Current Prices	Prices Adjusted to 1965	GNP at Constant Price
1965	1,000	$ .50	$ 500	$.50	$500
1975	1,000	$1.00	$1,000	$.50	$500
1985	1,000	$1.50	$1,500	$.50	$500

Figure 4–1
Output of Logoland. Did total output actually increase?

Note that under current prices the GNP for 1985 is reported at $1,500. On this basis you could say that the GNP (or total output) increased three times since 1965. But this would be wrong. Actually, Logoland made no progress in producing bumper stickers. In each of the years, 1,000 stickers were produced. If prices had remained the same, the dollar value would have been $500 each year.

Now let's look at a different example for Logoland. Figure 4–2 shows that in 1985 Logoland produced three times as many bumper stickers as in 1965. But if the GNPs at current prices are compared, the GNP increase in 1985 was nine times that of 1965 ($4,500 ÷ $500 = 9). However, in "constant" prices, the GNP in 1985 was three times that of 1965 — exactly the same as the actual increase in the total number of bumper stickers produced. In this example we have used 1965 as the year the price is held constant so that we can use it as a measuring device. We call 1965 the base year. **Base year** means the year chosen to compare an item, such as price, to any other year. We can choose any year as the base year, just as we chose 1965 to compare the GNP of Logoland.

Figure 4–2
A second look at Logoland GNP.

Year	No. of Bumper Stickers Produced	Current Price per Sticker	GNP at Current Prices	Prices Adjusted to 1965	GNP at Constant Price
1965	1,000	$ .50	$ 500	$.50	$ 500
1975	1,500	$1.00	$1,500	$.50	$ 750
1985	3,000	$1.50	$4,500	$.50	$1,500

Measuring Output per Person

An even better way than GNP to measure economic growth is the **per capita output** or the output per person. The per capita output is found by dividing GNP by the total population. (See Figure 4–3.) For example, suppose that there is no change in GNP this year over last year. But suppose that the population increases. You can see that the same output would have to be divided among more people. An increase in per capita output means that our economy is growing. A decrease may mean that our economy is having trouble.

Measuring Productivity

As you learned in Chapter 3, productivity is the quantity of output for the average worker in an hour. Our economic history shows a steady upward climb in productivity until recently. Over the past twenty years, productivity has had some ups and downs. While there has been an increase in productivity in many of those years, the amount of the increase has become smaller than in the past. And in a few cases, productivity actually decreased. At the same time wages were steadily climbing. (See Figure 4–4.) In one recent ten-year period, wages increased five times more than did productivity. This means, of course, that the cost of producing goods increased and prices rose accordingly. So even though workers were earning more money, they were not able to improve their standard of living very much because of rising prices. For that reason, a great deal of attention has been given in recent years

Figure 4–3

Is per capita output in the United States increasing or decreasing?

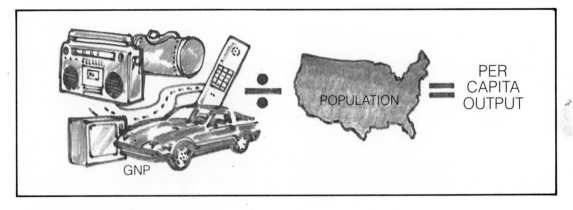

GNP ÷ POPULATION = PER CAPITA OUTPUT

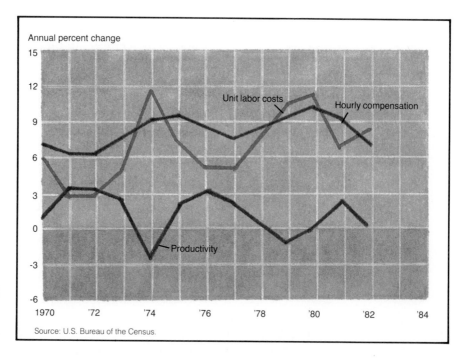

Annual percent change

Unit labor costs

Hourly compensation

Productivity

1970   '72   '74   '76   '78   '80   '82   '84

Source: U.S. Bureau of the Census.

Figure 4–4
Can you explain the importance of the relationship between wages and productivity?

to ways of motivating workers to increase productivity. By doing so the workers will be contributing to a higher standard of living in the nation as well as improving their own life-styles.

A measure of the standard of living is the number of hours one has to work in order to earn a living. Our ability to produce more and more goods and services over our history has made it possible to reduce the number of hours in a workweek. In the early 1890s, an average worker put in about 60 hours a week. Today the average workweek is a little less than 40 hours. But even though we work fewer hours and have more leisure time, we produce more and earn more than our labor force ever has before. We can produce more in less time because we use modern equipment and efficient work methods, and we have many highly skilled workers. Even though productivity in our recent past has increased nearly every year, it has been pointed out that the amount of the increase has been decreasing. When you choose your career, you will want to select one which will suit your interests and abilities and in which you can help to keep our productivity moving upward.

Coping with Economic Problems

You probably have heard adults talking about the many changes in the economy. They speak about bad times and good times, rising prices, a new business coming to town and providing new jobs, or a factory closing and causing hundreds of workers to lose their jobs. What do these changes mean? We have learned over the decades that our economy has its ups and downs. Good times and bad times seem to run in cycles.

Changing Economic Conditions—the Business Cycle

It has been said that bad times go away and good times return—if you wait long enough. If we look at the economic changes over our history, we can see that they do form a pattern: good times to bad times and back to good times. This movement of our economy from one condition to another and back again is called a **business cycle.** There are four phases of the business cycle. Let's look at the good times first.

Prosperity. At the high point of the business cycle, we enjoy **prosperity**. During prosperous times most people who want work are working, wages are good, and GNP is high. Consumers are buying and business is booming. Then, for some reason, the economy begins to cool or slow down. For example, after the successful moon landing, the U.S. government severely decreased its spending for space exploration. Jobs of engineers, technicians, and other workers in the program ended. Businesses which had contracts to supply the technology and labor for that large program had to cut production and lay people off. The nation had some serious economic adjustments to make. When people lose their jobs or hear of many others losing jobs, they begin to worry and to cut down on spending. Businesses begin to feel this through decreased sales.

Recession. When demand falls and businesses lower production, unemployment begins to rise; this phase of the business cycle is called a **recession**. It may not be too serious nor last very long. It may signal trouble only to certain groups of workers or it may spread through the entire economy. GNP slows and may even decrease. Some recessions are longer and worse than others.

Depression. If a recession deepens and spreads through the entire economy, the nation may move into the third phase, **depression**. This phase of the business cycle is marked by high

Illus. 4–3
Some businesses may not survive a recession.

unemployment and business failure. GNP is at its lowest point during a depression. Fortunately, our economy has not had a deep depression for over half a century. The last one was the Great Depression of 1930–1940. About 25 percent of the American labor force was out of work. Many people could not afford even the basic needs. Food and clothing were given out in the "bread lines" of churches and other charitable agencies. Depression was not only an appropriate name for the state of the economy, it fit the people well also. They were emotionally as well as economically depressed.

Recovery. By the end of the 1930s, things began to pick up. The sick economy began to recover. **Recovery** is the phase of the business cycle in which unemployment begins to decrease and GNP rises. People begin to find jobs and consumers regain confidence about their futures. They begin buying again. This new demand causes businesses to produce more and to employ more people to do this. Recovery may be slow or fast. As it continues, the nation moves into prosperity again.

Inflation

Another problem with which our nation has had to cope is inflation. **Inflation** is an increase in the general price level. Inflation occurs when the demand for goods and services is greater than the supply. The large supply of money, earned or borrowed, is spent for goods that are in short supply, causing further price increases. Inflation was a serious problem in the 1970s and early

1980s. Government, business, and individuals kept increasing their spending and prices continued to rise. Even though wages (the price paid for labor) tend to increase during inflation, prices of goods and services usually rise so fast that the wage earner never seems to catch up.

Controlling inflation requires reduced spending. Cuts in spending require a great deal of discipline. And reducing spending by government, business, and individuals often leads to other economic problems, such as unemployment. As you have read, this can also lead to a change in the business cycle. You will learn more about inflation in Chapter 25 when you study about the changing value of money.

Other Economic Problems

We have come a long way under our private enterprise system. We know it works well. We also know that it can be made to work even better as we find solutions to the economic problems that confront us in addition to coping with business cycles and controlling inflation.

There are still some people who do not have good food, decent housing, and proper health care. All of us may be harmed by pollution. Air and water are being polluted by gases, smoke, and waste coming from industry, from individuals, and from the products we buy and use. Government now is responding to the people's demand for action. And businesses are cooperating so that we can keep our environment healthy for future Americans. Individuals are also taking more responsibility in protecting the environment. More needs to be done.

Another challenge is that of providing proper housing for all our people, especially in large cities. Already much slum housing is being remodeled or torn down and rebuilt. Efforts are also being made to solve traffic problems in large cities, and new shopping and cultural centers are being built.

We must also find creative solutions to our unemployment problem. As our nation changes from smoke-stack industries, or factories, to greater use of technology and communications, we must find ways to retrain people whose jobs are lost in the change.

As Americans, we realize that we have some shortcomings. And as a nation we are working to eliminate economic hardship for our people. Much needs to be done to control disease and reduce human suffering. We need to find new sources of energy and to conserve all our natural resources. Much remains to be done in education, mass transportation, and human relations, and to make our government more responsive to the needs of the people.

Building the Economic Future

What lies ahead for our economy? Robots doing most of the routine work in factories? Housekeeping done entirely by machines? Farming under the ocean? Space colonies on the moon or other planets? Replacement of injured body parts with artificial ones? Working at home and communicating with employers by computer instead of going to offices? Two-way pocket telephones and three-dimensional TV? Germproof, tornadoproof, earthquakeproof, soundproof, fireproof, burglarproof houses? These are some of the things scientists have predicted for the year 2000. Some are already being developed. No one knows for sure what will happen in the future.

To provide a better quality of life for everyone, each of us has the responsibility of understanding how our economic system works, of being aware of our problems, of helping solve our problems, and of realizing the impact of our own productivity on the nation's economy and standard of living.

Illus. 4–4
What does the economic future hold in store for the United States? No one knows for sure.

A dding to Your Business Vocabulary

The following terms should become a part of your business vocabulary. For each numbered item, find the term that has the same meaning.

base year
business cycle
depression
gross national product or *GNP*
inflation

per capita output
prosperity
recession
recovery

1. The total value of all goods and services produced in a country in one year.
2. The year chosen to compare an item, such as price, to the same item in another year.
3. The figure that results from dividing the GNP of a country by the population of that country.
4. The movement of our economy from one condition to another and back again.
5. A phase of the business cycle in which employment is high, wages are good, and GNP is high.
6. A phase of the business cycle in which demand decreases, businesses reduce production, and unemployment rises.
7. A phase of the business cycle in which unemployment and business failures are high and GNP is at its lowest point.
8. A phase of the business cycle in which unemployment begins to decrease and GNP rises.
9. An increase in the general price level.

U nderstanding Your Reading

1. How does the United States compare with the rest of the world in land size, population, and output of goods and services?
2. "One way of finding out how well our economy is doing is to compare output from year to year." What does this statement mean? Do you agree with it?
3. GNP includes the spending of what three groups?
4. If prices of goods and services remain exactly the same over a long period of time, would it be fair and accurate to compare a country's GNP from year to year at current prices?
5. Explain the use of a base year in measuring output.
6. What is the difference between "current prices" and "adjusted prices" of goods and services?
7. How is per capita output determined?
8. How is per capita output used in measuring economic growth?
9. Name three things that have contributed to the high output over the history of our economy. What changes have taken place in productivity in recent years?
10. Give an example to explain how productivity is related to the standard of living.
11. Describe the general economic conditions in each of the four phases of the business cycle.
12. Is there room for improvement in our economic system? What are some of the economic problems that need solving?

*P*utting *Your Business Knowledge to Work*

1. The GNP of a small island in the Caribbean increased 10 percent in one year—from $300,000 to $330,000. Does this mean that this little economic unit had a 10 percent increase in the amount of goods and services produced?
2. Make a list of some things that you and your family have contributed to the GNP during the past few months.
3. The GNP of Country A is $400,000. The GNP of Country B is $800,000. Does this mean that the per capita output of Country B is about twice that of Country A? Explain.
4. In a recent year the GNP of the United States was almost $3 trillion in current dollars. Ten years before, it was less than $2 trillion. In the next ten years, the GNP is expected to reach the $3.5 trillion mark. What differences does it make to you and to other people in your community whether GNP is increasing or decreasing?
5. Explain how high wages and low productivity can increase the price you pay for goods and services.
6. Explain how productivity has helped to increase the U.S. worker's leisure time.
7. Suppose that many auto and steel plants close throughout a country and that thousands of workers lose their jobs in a relatively short period. If the country has been enjoying prosperous times, it may now be headed into what phase of the business cycle? Describe other conditions which might begin to occur.
8. List three things that you and your classmates could do to prevent or reduce pollution.

*C*omputing *Business Problems*

1. The 1985 production schedule of Logoland listed on page 47 shows its GNP at current prices of $4,500 and at constant 1965 prices of $1,500. If Logoland's population in 1985 was 500, what was its per capita output
   a. at current prices?
   b. at constant prices?
2. Some very simple machines such as the wheelbarrow and the hand truck have increased productivity or output per worker hour. Jorg Bensen, who works in a warehouse, can move one 60-pound box at a time by hand. Using a hand truck, he can move four 60-pound boxes at once in the same length of time.
   a. Jorg can move 15 boxes in one hour without using a hand truck. What is his productivity in boxes?
   b. If he uses a hand truck, what is Jorg's productivity?
   c. How many workers without hand trucks would it take to do the work Jorg does with a hand truck?
3. A small island in the Pacific Ocean produces shell jewelry to sell to tourists from cruise ships. The island's production record is shown below:

Year	No. of Items Produced	Current Price per Item
1975	1,000	$ .25
1980	2,000	$ .50
1985	4,000	$1.00

   a. What is the island's GNP at current prices for each year?

b. What is the amount of increase in number of items produced in 1980 over 1975?

c. What is the rate of increase in number of items produced in 1980 over 1975?

d. If the island expects to maintain the same rate of increase for 1990, how many shell items will it produce?

4. Study the graph on page 49 and answer the questions below:

a. In what year was productivity lowest?

b. What happened to the cost of producing each unit of goods in the year cited in a above?

c. What was the approximate percentage of decrease from the previous year to the year cited in a?

d. In most years an increase in GNP is shown, even though the amount of the increase was down from the previous year. In what years was there an actual decrease in GNP?

Stretching Your Business Knowledge

1. The GNP does not include the services of homemakers and other services we perform without pay for ourselves and others. Aren't these services as important as the ones we pay for? Why do you think that they are not included in the GNP?

2. Look through some recent newspapers and news magazines for items which mention any of the nine business terms in the "Adding to Your Business Vocabulary" section. Mount your clippings on sheets of paper. Below the article, write one statement that the article tells you about the term mentioned.

3. In determining our GNP, only *final* goods and services are included. This avoids having some items counted more than once. For example, a mining company sells iron ore to a company that makes steel. The steel company sells the steel to an automobile manufacturer who produces finished cars. The iron ore is not counted at each step. Its value is included only once: in the price paid for the final product, the car.

Below is a list of things produced in our economy. Tell whether you think each item should be counted as part of GNP. If you do not think it should be counted, tell why.

a. An electric toaster bought as a gift for newlyweds.

b. Telephone service installed in your home.

c. Telephone service installed in a government office.

d. Tires sold to a company to install on the motorcycles it produces.

e. Grooming services for a poodle.

f. Paper sold to the publisher of this book.

g. Flowers sold to a florist.

h. Flowers sold by a florist.

i. A computer paid for by a city government.

j. An automobile for your family's use.

k. An automobile for the state highway patrol's use.

l. Videodiscs bought by a music store for resale.

m. Peaches sold to a cannery.

4. Using the telephone directory and other sources of information, find out whether any agency in your area recycles materials. Prepare a brief report showing what

materials are recycled, how the recycling is done, and for what the recycled materials are used. Include in your report a statement of the benefits you think come from recycling.

5. The Environmental Protection Agency was established by the federal government to help in cleaning up and maintaining the environment. Write a brief report on what the EPA does to carry out this responsibility. Your school library probably has government publications and other resources to help you find the information.

CAREER CATEGORY: Economics

A career in the American free enterprise system could be anything you want it to be. If you have enough interest to acquire the training for it, you could be a corporate executive, a crossword puzzle maker, or a professional clown. The choice is yours.

Each unit in this text will help you prepare to make your choice by outlining career opportunities in the area discussed in the unit. Since this unit introduces you to the economics of our system, this career section will focus on the people who work in the economics profession; they are called economists.

Job Titles: Job titles commonly found in this career area include:

Economists	Statisticians
Financial Analysts	Actuaries
Investment Analysts	Credit Analysts
Consultants	Budget Officers

Employment Outlook: The economics profession is small. In 1982 about 30,000 economists were employed, half of them in government agencies. The remaining 15,000 taught economics in colleges and universities. Only average growth in the number of jobs is expected in the next few years, reaching about 39,000 by 1995. Competition for most jobs in economics will therefore be keen, especially in teaching where the number of jobs is expected to decline. Most of the new jobs will be in government, research, and consulting.

Future Changes: Computers have had, and will continue to have, a great impact on the economics profession. They have provided economists with more information at very rapid speeds; information is the resource with which economists work. Economists who have strong backgrounds in math

and computers and the ability to analyze numerical data will have the best job opportunities in the future.

What Is Done on the Job: Economists study the way a society uses its scarce resources—natural, human, and capital—to provide goods and services. They analyze and interpret their research to find the best ways of using resources to produce and distribute these goods and services. They also measure economic growth, which you learned about in Chapter 4. Some economists are concerned with economic theory; they study how and why economic events, such as recessions, happen as they do. Most economists, however, apply economics in specialized areas such as agriculture, housing, or banking. Some economists collect and analyze data about population changes, such as the number of people in various age groups or the movement of large numbers of people from one section of the country to another. Through their understanding of economic relationships, economists can advise businesses and government about the possible results of various actions or decisions.

Education and Training: A bachelor's degree is usually required to enter the field of economics. Top economists typically have doctoral degrees. Since beginning jobs often involve the collection and compilation of information, the entrant must understand statistics and research methods. The ability to handle details accurately and to analyze objectively are important personal skills. Courses in advanced mathematics and computers, along with advanced degrees in economics and related fields, provide the best opportunities for advancement.

Salary Levels: Salaries vary widely depending upon the educational background and experience of the worker and the place of employment. In 1982 the average beginning salary for economists with bachelor's degrees was about $13,000 a year; for those with master's degrees, about $19,700; and for those with Ph.D's, about $23,800. Average salaries for federal government economists in 1982 was about $34,900. Overall, salaries ranged from $13,000 to over $50,000.

For Additional Information: An interview with a banker in your community or an economics professor in a college or university would be helpful if you are interested in exploring a career as an economist. Such publications as *U.S. News and World Report* and *BusinessWeek* regularly feature economic data as well as economists' views on the state of the economy and the outlook for the future. Your school counselor can provide information about colleges and universities offering degrees in economics. The National Association of Business Economists may provide information on careers in business economics. The Association's address is

28349 Chagrin Blvd.
Suite 201
Cleveland, OH 44122

UNIT 2

THE ECONOMIC ROLE OF BUSINESS

UNIT OBJECTIVES

After studying the chapters in this unit, you will be able to:

1. Describe the four basic types of businesses.

2. Cite the main features of the various forms of business ownership.

3. Give examples to illustrate how the interdependence of nations makes world trade necessary.

BUSINESS BRIEF

Ray Kroc—The Hamburger King

While he did not invent either the hamburger or the "golden arches," Ray Kroc is credited with building a hamburger empire which helped to change American eating habits. In 1983 he presided over a chain of more than 7,500 outlets spread over the United States and 31 other countries, with sales of $8 billion.

Kroc was a man of ideas, energy, and innovative management abilities. He held a variety of jobs before becoming a sales manager for a paper product company where he worked for 17 years. Later, as agent for a company selling a machine that could make 6 milk shakes at a time, Kroc was amazed when a California hamburger stand owner ordered eight of them. Curious about a firm which needed to make 48 milkshakes at once, he visited the busy hamburger operation and convinced the owners, Maurice and Richard McDonald, to let him take their golden arches hamburger stand idea back to Illinois as a franchise. They agreed, and in 1955 at age 52 Kroc opened his first McDonald's in a Chicago suburb. Five years and 250 McDonald's outlets later, he bought out the McDonald brothers for $2.7 million.

Kroc insisted that managers of his franchises and of his company-owned stores be skilled in working with people. He stressed cleanliness and strict quality control for his all-beef-patty operation. He applied a streamlined team approach to food preparation. His firm became one of the country's largest employers of part-time teenage workers.

The firm has not been without problems, however. Some critics have called it the top symbol of the "asphalt and chrome culture;" the nutritional value of hamburgers was once debated in Congress; the struggle to keep prices down has been on-going; and competition from a growing field of fast-food outlets has often been fierce. Kroc always met the problems head-on and survived them. His enormous success has been credited to his genius in innovative management techniques, including fine tuning the fast-food retailing operation and convincing people worldwide to eat and enjoy his products.

Kroc had other interests along the way. He became influential in the sports world as the outspoken owner (1974-1979) of a professional baseball team, the San Diego Padres. His humanitarian efforts have benefitted many people. Most notable among them are the Ronald McDonald Houses that have been established near several children's hospitals to house parents who are visiting their sick children in the hospitals. Ray Kroc's business has made both a social and an economic impact on America.

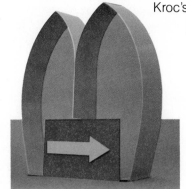

Facts included in this Business Brief were taken from the following sources: Moskowitz, Milton (ed.). *Everybody's Business, An Almanac.* New York: Harper & Row, Inc., 1980; "Ray Kroc Dies; Built McDonald's." *Virginian-Pilot/Ledger Star,* January 15, 1984, pp. 1, 3.

CHAPTER 5

What Business is All About

■ CHAPTER OBJECTIVES ────────────────────

After studying this chapter and completing the end-of-chapter activities, you will be able to:

1. Give an example of the four basic kinds of businesses.
2. Explain how marketing adds value to products.
3. Explain the difference between direct and indirect marketing channels.
4. Describe six kinds of activities that are performed by most businesses.
5. Explain the difference between gross profit and net profit.
6. Give the average percent of profit made by manufacturers.
7. Describe two benefits that come to a community as a result of new or expanded business activity.
8. Give two examples of ways through which businesses carry out social responsibility.

Burt Cayton and all his friends wear jeans. In fact, jeans are the most popular item of clothing among all the students in Burt's school. When Burt bought a new pair recently, he looked for just the right style, the right stitching, and the right fit. But neither Burt nor his friends give much thought to the chain of businesses involved in getting the jeans to the store where they buy them.

First the cotton is planted and harvested; then it is made into cloth and dyed different colors. The jeans are designed, made up in various sizes, labeled, boxed, and then stored until they are sold to the store from which Burt and his friends buy them.

Several businesses are involved in this process. These businesses are different in many ways, but all are alike in one way: they are helping put a product or service that you want on the market. That is what business is all about. There are over 16 million business firms in the United States. While there are some differences among them, they all supply or help to supply goods and services to satisfy your wants and needs. Learning about them will help you understand what business does.

Illus. 5–1
There are over 16 million businesses in the United States.

Basic Kinds of Businesses

You and your family buy from many kinds of businesses. You buy food from a supermarket, shoes from a shoe store, furnace repairs from a plumbing and heating company, financial services from a bank, a car from an auto dealer, and electricity from a utilities company. In all of these cases, you are dealing with firms that sell products and services to you and to other consumers. But have you ever wondered where they get the products and the materials for the services they sell to you? Often these products and materials have moved through several businesses before they get to the store from which you buy them. There are four basic types of these businesses: extractors, manufacturers, marketers, and service businesses.

Extractors Get Products from Nature

Businesses that grow products or take raw materials from nature are called **extractors**. The farmer who grew and sold the cotton for your jeans is an extractor. Silver and coal miners are also extractors. So are those who dig copper in Montana, fish for salmon in Alaska, pump oil in Texas, grow fruit in Florida, and run lumber camps in Washington. Sometimes the extractor's products are ready to be sold just as they come from the earth or the sea, like the clams in New England, oranges from California, or pecans from Georgia. But most food products and raw materials need some processing or change in form before the consumer can use them.

Manufacturers Make Products

The **manufacturer** takes the extractor's products or raw materials and changes them into a form that consumers can use. The manufacturer might make a product, such as a moped, or process a product, such as packaging and freezing vegetables. Some manufacturers are only a part of the total activity of producing goods from the extractor's products. Think about Burt's jeans again. The full process might be something like this: A textile mill in North Carolina takes cotton grown on an Alabama farm, spins it into yarn, and makes the yarn into cloth. A plant in New England dyes or prints the cloth. And a clothing factory in New York buys the cloth and makes it into jeans. Together, extractors and manufacturers change the form of resources from their natural states into products for consumers.

Marketers Bring the Products to Consumers

Our skilled labor force and our advanced technology enable producers to make thousands of different products at a reasonable cost. But if these products are not available where and when you and other consumers want to buy them, they are of no use.

If all the goods you use had to be bought directly from their producers, it would be very hard and very expensive for you to buy things. You might have to go to Central or South America to get a banana. What an expensive banana that would be!

The services of many businesses are often needed before goods actually reach consumers. All the activities involved in moving goods from producers to consumers are performed by marketers; the activities themselves are called **marketing** or **distribution**.

Marketing includes more than transporting and selling products. Marketers test new product ideas to see whether consumers like them and will buy them. They package goods to protect products and to present them in attractive and convenient sizes. They store goods until they are needed by other marketers or consumers. They even design store windows and arrange displays in supermarkets to attract your attention. All these marketing activities add value to products by bringing them where the consumer is, at the time they are wanted, in the assortment wanted, and at prices the consumer is willing to pay.

Bridging the gap between producers and consumers can be very complicated. Of course, you can buy certain products directly from the producer. For example, you may buy tomatoes directly from the farmer who grew them or a handmade basket from a basket weaver. But most products will be handled by several marketers before they reach the store where you buy them. The path that a product travels from producer to consumer is called the **marketing channel** or **channel of distribution**. Figure 5–1 illustrates three possible marketing channels.

Figure 5–1
Channels of distribution link producers and consumers.

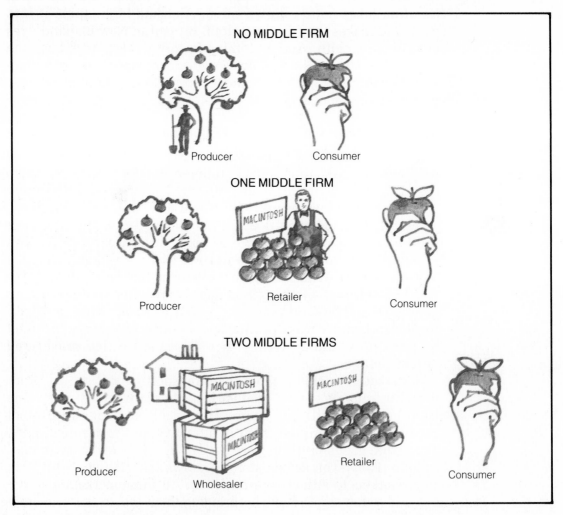

NO MIDDLE FIRM

Producer   Consumer

ONE MIDDLE FIRM

MACINTOSH

Producer   Retailer   Consumer

TWO MIDDLE FIRMS

MACINTOSH   MACINTOSH

Producer   Retailer
        Wholesaler   Consumer

When goods are bought by the consumer directly from the producer, the process is called **direct marketing.** The tomatoes and the basket purchases are examples of direct marketing. Most goods, however, will travel through at least one and sometimes several middle firms before they get to the consumer; this process is called **indirect marketing.**

The farmer may sell tomatoes to your local grocery store, a retailer, from which you buy them. A **retailer** is a middle firm which sells directly to the consumer. Or the farmer may sell the entire crop of tomatoes to a wholesaler, such as a large distribution firm. A **wholesaler** is a middle firm which sells to other wholesalers or to retailers. The wholesaler will then sell the tomatoes to the grocery store, the retailer, which in turn sells them to you. A product may travel through several middle firms in the marketing channel.

Service Businesses Do Things for Us

Firms that do things for you instead of making or marketing products are called **service businesses.** These businesses are perhaps the fastest growing part of our business world. Between 1970

Illus. 5–2
How many businesses that offer services rather than goods can you name?

and 1980 the number of people employed full time in service industries increased almost 30 percent. By 1995 it is expected that over 25 million people will be working in businesses that provide services to others.

Some service businesses serve individual consumers. Some serve other businesses. And some serve both. Today you can find a service business to move you from New Jersey to Arizona, style your hair, wash your car, figure your income tax, board your dog, give you computer lessons, clean your clothes, rent you a pair of skis, pull a tooth, take you on a tour, cook the food for your party, and almost any service you need and don't want to do for yourself.

As people have more leisure time and more money to spend, they want more and more businesses to do things for them. Also, as more women enter the labor force, they tend to pay someone to perform many services that they once did for themselves and their families. All this tends to increase the size of the service industry.

Activities Performed by Most Businesses

Businesses come in all types and sizes. A business may be as small as a newspaper stand on a street corner, or as large and complex as an oil company which has wells, refineries, and service stations in many different countries. Although individual businesses differ in the way they operate, most of them perform basically the same kinds of day-to-day activities. Let's examine some of these important activities.

Reprinted by permission of Jefferson Communications, Inc., Reston, Va.

Buying

Businesses buy goods and services both for resale and for their own use. The owner of a men's clothing store, for instance, must buy slacks, jackets, suits, coats, and other items to sell. The store owner also needs sales tickets, a cash register, display cases, and other supplies. Services offered by other businesses, such as advertising space in a newspaper or a window cleaner to wash the display windows, will be needed.

Selling

Businesses must sell goods and services if they expect to stay in operation. Some businesses — grocery, hardware, jewelry, and other stores — sell goods. Other businesses — telephone companies, airlines, hospitals, law firms, and so on — sell services.

Storing

Goods must be stored until they are sold or until the customer wants them delivered. For example, toys are produced the year round, but most of them are stored until merchants order them for Christmas. Manufacturers need storage yards and warehouses to store raw materials, supplies, and finished products.

Handling Money and Keeping Records

All businesses must handle money and keep records. Business owners need to know how much they have sold, how much of what they sold was returned by customers, and how much they owe to others. They need to know the amount they are spending for building repairs, rent, salaries, and other expenses. Their records show whether their business is making or losing money and give them information they need for government reports.

Extending Credit

Most businesses extend credit to their customers. Many businesses would not be able to operate if manufacturers and other businesses did not allow them to buy on credit. And merchants find that most customers today expect credit at stores where they shop.

Providing Services

Almost all businesses provide certain services with the goods they sell to customers. Often a customer will buy from the business that offers the most service. A store may provide parking space, lounges, a coffee shop, telephones, and delivery service.

Packaging

Many businesses package and divide goods to meet customer needs. For example, marketers design packages to protect goods and make them more attractive. Businesses that sell goods may buy them in large quantities and divide them into small quantities for resale to customers. A supermarket might buy oranges by the bushel and package them into trays of six oranges each, which is a convenient size for the customer.

Businesses Make Profits

As you learned in Section I, business owners are entitled to profits because of the risks they take in investing their money and because of the extra work and responsibilities that go with ownership and management. But most do not make the huge profits that some people think. The average profit on sales for manufacturing businesses is about 5 percent a year. As you know, competition with other businesses helps keep prices and profits down to reasonable figures. One reason for inaccurate beliefs about profits, however, is that some people don't understand the difference between gross and net profit. **Gross profit** or **margin** is the difference between the selling price and the cost price of an article. **Net profit** is what is left after all expenses have been paid. Suppose Ruby Doss, the owner of a camera shop, sells a camera for $40. She bought the camera for $24, so she has a gross profit of $16. But out of this $16, she must pay rent, supplies, advertising, taxes, and many other expenses. Her records show that all expenses related to the sale of the camera amount to $14. She has therefore made a net profit of $2 on the camera—or a net profit of 5 percent ($2 ÷ $40) on the selling price.

Businesses Help the Local Economy

Communities often spend much effort and large sums of money persuading new businesses to locate within their boundaries. Almost everyone is pleased when new businesses open in the community. And no wonder. A new business benefits the local economy in many ways.

The Multiplier Effect

Perhaps the most important benefit of a new business investment in the community is that new jobs are created. This means that the people who work directly for the business have incomes to support themselves and their families. As they spend this income for goods and services, the money multiplies as it is spent again by each person who receives it. The increase in income caused by the chain of spending by consumers of a new investment by business is called the multiplier effect. Let's see how that works.

When a new factory opens, it begins paying wages to its employees. This is money that has not been in the community before. Workers spend this money for the goods and services they want and need. The money is then spent again by the businesses from which those goods and services were bought. For example, part of each worker's income is spent for food. The food store manager pays out part of this money for stock. The manager also pays part of it to employees, who in turn spend their money somewhere else for other goods and services. If new people come to the community to work, more houses will probably be needed. This means that local builders will hire more workers and buy more materials. As each dollar is spent, each business is likely to buy more goods and hire more people to meet its customers' demands. This endless spending chain started with the original investment in wages by the new business in the community. Of course, most people and most businesses don't spend all of their income as in this simplified example. People might spend, say 90 percent of their income and save 10 percent. But the multiplier effect works the same way on whatever amount is spent in each round, and it always adds up to more than the original amount. (See Figure 5–2.) You can see, then, that when new jobs are created in a community, each dollar paid to workers is said to multiply itself. That is why most cities and towns seek new businesses.

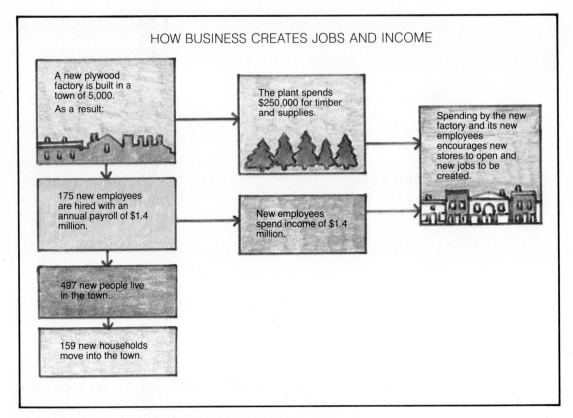

HOW BUSINESS CREATES JOBS AND INCOME

A new plywood factory is built in a town of 5,000.
As a result:

The plant spends $250,000 for timber and supplies.

Spending by the new factory and its new employees encourages new stores to open and new jobs to be created.

175 new employees are hired with an annual payroll of $1.4 million.

New employees spend income of $1.4 million.

497 new people live in the town.

159 new households move into the town.

Figure 5–2
A new business can benefit the whole community. Here is how the multiplier effect works.

Other Effects on the Local Economy

Another benefit from a new or expanded business is that it pays taxes to the community. This means that the community has more money to build new schools, repair its streets, provide better police and fire protection, and improve other services such as parks.

When a new business comes to a community, it buys such things as electricity, office furniture and supplies, equipment, and tools. Some of these things will be bought from firms in other towns, but many will be bought locally. This gives income to local businesses, and, in turn, paychecks to their employees.

Businesses also tend to attract other businesses. When one business settles in a community, other businesses often come to supply it. For example, small businesses may spring up to supply a large factory with such things as small parts, office supplies, cleaning services, and advertising services. Each of these smaller firms hires people and buys goods and services. So still more jobs and more income are created in the community.

Businesses Carry Out Social Responsibilities

Business owners and managers today must do more than just provide a worthwhile product or service at a reasonable price in order to make a profit and stay in business. They must hire workers without discrimination; they must pay competitive wages and provide other benefits, such as insurance and holidays. They must provide a safe working environment; and they must show concern for the general welfare of their workers. These are economic benefits that workers in any community expect.

In addition, businesses today assume social responsibilities in the community. Many firms participate in training programs for unskilled workers. Some firms provide advice and managerial assistance to members of minority groups in setting up and operating their own businesses. They cooperate with schools in many ways—by providing speakers, by employing students in part-time jobs, and by sponsoring such programs as Junior Achievement.

Illus. 5–3
Many firms provide scholarships for deserving students.

Many business firms contribute generously to education, to charities, and to civic and cultural projects. In fact, business leaders are often also the leaders of these projects.

The acceptance of social responsibility by businesses is also seen in the efforts of many firms to avoid polluting the air, the water, or the natural beauty of the countryside. Helping to keep a clean environment is an important part of business planning today. Before they allow a new business to locate in their area, most communities require the firm to show that its operation will not cause pollution. There are still many problems to be worked out to improve the environment and keep it clean, but progress is being made through cooperation between businesses and the communities in which they are located. Adding the economic and social benefits together, you can see why most communities welcome new businesses.

A dding to Your Business Vocabulary

The following terms should become part of your business vocabulary. For each numbered item, find the term that has the same meaning.

direct marketing
extractor
gross profit or margin
indirect marketing
manufacturer
marketing channel or
    channel of distribution

marketing or distribution
net profit
retailer
service business
wholesaler

1. The activities that are involved in moving goods from producers to consumers.
2. The path that a product travels from producer to consumer.
3. The difference between the selling price and the cost price of an article.
4. The process through which goods are bought by the consumer directly from the producer.
5. A business that takes an extractor's products or raw materials and changes them into a form that consumers can use.
6. The amount left over after expenses are deducted from the gross profit.
7. The process through which goods move through one or more middle firms between the producer and the consumer.
8. A middle firm which sells directly to the consumer.
9. A business that grows products or takes raw materials from nature.
10. A business that does things for you instead of making or marketing products.
11. A middle firm which sells goods to other firms like itself or to other retailers.

Understanding Your Reading

1. Give an example of the four basic types of businesses.
2. What is meant by the statement that some extractors' products are ready to be sold to the consumer in their natural states?
3. Name several marketing activities other than transporting and selling goods.
4. How does marketing add value to a product?
5. What is the difference between a direct and an indirect marketing channel?
6. To whom do wholesalers and retailers sell their products?
7. What similar activities are performed by most businesses? Give at least six examples.
8. What is the average percent of profit on sales made by manufacturers?
9. What is the difference between gross profit and net profit?
10. How does the multiplier effect of new businesses result in more jobs and income in the community?
11. Give two examples of ways through which businesses carry out social responsibilities in the community.

Putting Your Business Knowledge to Work

1. List three marketing activities that might be involved in getting a home computer from the manufacturer to the retail store which sells it.
2. If two firms make the same percentage of profit on sales, will they also make the same amount of dollar profit from their business operations? Explain.
3. Name two products which you might buy through a direct marketing channel.
4. Lani Kokua owns and operates the Islands Gift Shop where she sells arrangements of fresh flowers and shell jewelry. Give two examples of each of the following:
   a. goods which she would buy for resale
   b. goods she would buy for use in her store
   c. services she might offer to her customers
   d. services she might buy from other businesses
5. The Chamber of Commerce and the Economic Development Council of Metro City have persuaded the Plastics Processing Company to open a plant in the city's industrial park. The company expects to employ 250 people there. Name at least five ways in which the city would probably benefit from the new business.

Computing Business Problems

1. The Delia Telini Company is considering building a cannery in Santa Rosa. The company accountants' estimate of the monthly income and expenses for the new plant is as follows:

Income from sales	$200,000
Expenses:	
Salaries	100,000
Raw materials purchased	60,000
Rent on equipment	6,500
Miscellaneous expenses	5,000
Taxes	8,400

  a. What is the total amount of the cannery's estimated monthly expenses, including taxes?

  b. What will be the cannery's net profit if the estimates are accurate? (Calculate net profit by subtracting the total estimated expenses and taxes from estimated income.)

2. The fish catch and the value of the catch along the Atlantic coast for a recent year are shown below:

Area	No. of Workers	Catch (million pounds)	Value (million dollars)
New England states	30,500	788	$327
Mid-Atlantic states	17,700	244	$ 97
Chesapeake Bay states	25,000	718	$130
South Atlantic states	10,600	473	$148

  a. How many workers were employed in the industry on the Atlantic coast?

  b. What was the total weight of the catch for the Atlantic regions, expressed in full (including the zeros)?

  c. What was the dollar value of the catch from the area where the catch was the largest (expressed in full)?

3. Joshua Mizell has just received his first semimonthly paycheck of $1,000 from a new firm in his town, Metal Fence Manufacturing, Inc., where he works as production supervisor. His budget allows him to save 25 percent of his salary. He spends the rest at businesses in town on food, clothing, and a down payment on a car. His spending sets the multiplier effect in motion. Each time the money is spent, you can assume that the person who receives the income also saves 25 percent and spends 75 percent.

  a. Carry the income/saving through five rounds of the spending chain, beginning with Joshua's $750 spent and $250 saved. List the amount spent and the amount saved for each of the next four rounds.

  b. How much has been added to the local economy at the end of five rounds?

  c. What is the total amount saved by the five people or businesses involved?

Stretching Your Business Knowledge

1. Communities often advertise in newspapers and business magazines to encourage new businesses to locate in their towns. Find out what your community or your state is doing to attract new businesses. Consult such sources as your local newspaper, your Chamber of Commerce publications, *Businessweek, Fortune, The Wall Street Journal,* and *US News and World Report* in your library.

a. From the ads and other information you find, list the advantages cited by your city or state to encourage businesses to locate in the area.

b. Which factors among those listed do you think are the most important? Why?

c. Would some factors be more important to some kinds of businesses than others? Explain.

2. Read Question 5 of "Putting Your Business Knowledge to Work" on page 75. Some citizens prefer that businesses not locate in their communities. What are some of the arguments you think they might list opposing the locating of new businesses such as the Plastics Processing Company in their towns? Do you think that the advantages are more important than the disadvantages?

3. What social and economic changes are taking place in our country to cause more and more people to want to buy services rather than perform them for themselves? What changes will this likely cause in our business system?

4. When businesses leave a community, the multiplier effect can work in reverse. If several businesses in your community fail during the year, how might the welfare of individual consumers, workers, other businesses, and the local government be affected?

5. Interview the owner or manager of a retail store in your area. Ask him or her if most of the products in the store come through direct or indirect marketing channels. Do any products come through more than one wholesaler? If so, give an example, identifying the types of wholesalers involved. Write a brief report entitled, "The Marketing Channels for (name of store), a Local Retail Store." Share your findings with the class.

CHAPTER 6

*O*rganizing for Business

■ CHAPTER OBJECTIVES

After studying this chapter and completing the end-of-chapter activities, you will be able to:

1. Tell how ownership differs among sole proprietorships, partnerships, corporations, cooperatives, and franchises.
2. State the advantages and disadvantages of the three major types of business ownership.
3. Tell the difference between a consumers' cooperative and a producers' cooperative.
4. Explain how municipal corporations and business corporations differ.

Before the baseball team at your school starts its season, it must organize. Some players will be assigned to the bases while others will play the outfield. Players will be assigned to the positions of pitcher, catcher, and shortstop. The players are placed according to their special talents and in the way that will benefit the team most—that is, to make it easier to reach the team's goal of winning games.

In a similar way, a business also must organize to produce goods and services for the consumer. Many questions must be answered in the organizing process. Who will make the decisions? Who will buy the goods to sell? Who will keep the records on what is bought and sold? Who will get the profits? If there is a loss, who must bear it? Most of the answers to these questions are found in the way a business is owned and organized.

Three Major Types of Business Ownership

The three major types of business ownership are the sole proprietorship, the partnership, and the corporation. Later in this chapter you will learn about two other types of business ownership, the cooperative and the franchise.

A **sole proprietorship** is a business owned by one person. Most are small firms such as grocery stores, restaurants, gas stations, barber shops, and drugstores. As shown in Figure 6–1, more than three-fourths of U.S. businesses are operated as sole proprietorships.

A **partnership** is a business owned and managed by a small group, often not more than two or three people, who become "partners." By written agreement, these partners share the profits or losses and the responsibilities of their business.

A **corporation** is a business owned by a number of people and operated under written permission from the state in which it is located. The written permission is called a **certificate of incorporation.** The corporation acts as a single individual on behalf of its owners. By buying shares of stock, people become owners of corporations. They are then known as **stockholders** or **shareholders**. A corporation may have a very few owners, but most corporations have many owners. Large corporations, such as IBM, Texaco, and General Motors, may have a million or more owners. Even if you own just one share of a company, you are still one of its owners. Most mining, manufacturing, and transporting of goods is done by corporations. And many of our consumer goods are supplied by supermarkets, department stores, and other businesses organized as corporations.

Figure 6–1
Sole proprietorships, partnerships, and corporations are the major types of business ownership.

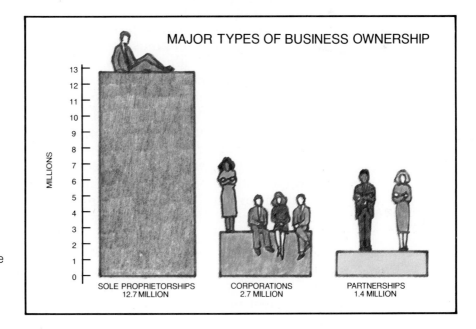

MAJOR TYPES OF BUSINESS OWNERSHIP

MILLIONS

13
12
11
10
9
8
7
6
5
4
3
2
1
0

SOLE PROPRIETORSHIPS
12.7 MILLION

CORPORATIONS
2.7 MILLION

PARTNERSHIPS
1.4 MILLION

Illus. 6–1
Over 75 percent of U.S. businesses are sole proprietorships.

The size and the nature of a business are key factors in choosing the best type of ownership and organization for it. To help you understand each type of ownership, the next few pages tell a story of how a young man started a business and worked to make it grow.

Chad Peery's Proprietorship

While in high school Chad Peery held a number of different part-time jobs after school and on Saturdays. He thought about retailing as a career and took business courses in school. He was also interested in individual sports and jogged each day before school. In his senior year he became acquainted with a jogger who was manager of a sporting goods department of a large department store. As a result of this acquaintance, he was offered a job as a part-time sales trainee in the sporting goods department. After graduation he accepted a full-time job with the store.

In the next few years, Chad worked hard and was successful as a salesperson. He prepared for advancement by taking several courses in the evening at a nearby college. Soon he was promoted to assistant manager of the sporting goods department. Chad was now married, earning a good salary, and saving money. But he wanted to own his own business. He liked the idea of earning profits for himself and of being his own boss. So in his spare time, he began planning his own business. Soon he resigned his job in the department store and was on his own.

Because of his experience and his interest in selling sporting goods, Chad decided to open a sporting goods store. He chose the name Lifetime Sports. He rented a small store in a shopping center and bought showcases and other equipment. With the help of a bank loan, he bought his stock of merchandise.

Chad had learned a lot about selling sporting goods in the department store, but he found that owning his own business required long hours and much decision making. He ordered merchandise, built window displays, and did most of the selling and the stock work. His wife helped him keep his business and tax records. A student was employed part-time. Chad owned the business by himself. So, as shown in Figure 6–2, it was a sole proprietorship. All the profits — or losses — were his.

The Partnership of Peery and Gore

Lifetime Sports was a success. Chad paid his bills on time and paid himself, his wife, and his part-time employee fair salaries. Each month he made payments on his bank loan until it was paid off. Profits were put aside in a savings account.

Soon Chad felt that it was time to expand the business, but he needed more money than he had saved. He also needed the help of someone who knew more about advertising and accounting than he did. He knew that his friend and former employer in the sporting goods department had studied advertising, accounting,

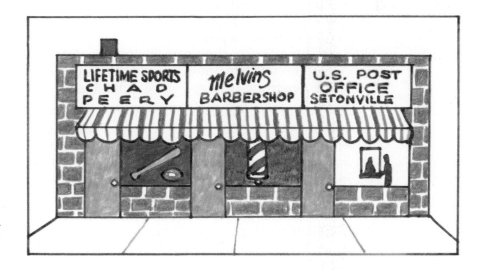

Figure 6–2
Chad Peery is the sole proprietor of Lifetime Sports.

management, and other business courses in college. His friend, Lyn Gore, also had been a salesperson for a national exercise equipment firm. He knew that this background would add a great deal to his business, so he invited Lyn to become a part owner of Lifetime Sports.

With their combined skills, experience, money, and other property, they could afford to offer a larger variety of sporting goods. They could also afford to add new lines of merchandise — camping supplies, sportswear, and exercise equipment. Offering a greater variety of items would attract more people to the store and increase sales.

They consulted an attorney, Peggy Spillios, about setting up the partnership. With her help, Chad and Lyn drew up a list of items they wished to have in their agreement. From this list, Spillios drew up a written agreement called the **articles of partnership.** Among other things, the agreement provided that:

1. The name of the firm will be Lifetime Sports.
2. Peery will invest $80,000 in cash and property. Gore will invest $40,000 in cash.
3. Each partner will draw a salary of $1,800 a month.
4. Profits and losses after salaries are paid will be shared in proportion to each partner's investment: two-thirds to Peery and one-third to Gore.
5. Peery will have main responsibility for sales, selection, and purchase of merchandise, and customer and community relations. Gore will handle financial records, payroll, store maintenance, advertising and sales promotion, and other details of operating the business.
6. In the event of the death or the necessary withdrawal of one partner, the remaining partner will have the right to purchase the departing partner's share of the business.

Before Peery and Gore signed the articles of partnership, their attorney pointed out some of the legal responsibilities of partners. For example, each partner could be held personally responsible for all the debts of the business. This would even include debts incurred by the other partner without the first partner's consent. Each partner was also bound by the agreements made for the business by the other partner. To avoid problems, the partners agreed to talk over all important business matters, such as hiring people or buying new equipment.

Under Peery and Gore's joint management, the partnership, as shown in Figure 6–3, was very successful. At the end of the first year, there was a profit of $15,000 after the business expenses and the partners' salaries had been paid. Since they had agreed to share profits in proportion to their investments in the business, Chad received two-thirds, or $10,000, and Lyn received one-third, or $5,000.

Figure 6–3
Lifetime Sports is now owned by partners Peery and Gore.

Lifetime Sports Becomes a Corporation

Lifetime Sports continued to grow under the Peery and Gore partnership, and the partners considered expanding the business even more. A new shopping center was being built on the other side of town. Should they also enlarge the present store? Should they add new sales and storage space and also a line of small boats and boating supplies? Should they open an exercise salon as part of their business? To do these things, they needed more money. They thought about adding more partners; however, they decided against this. They reasoned that they did not need partners to help them manage the business since they could hire qualified assistant managers. Also, there would be personal risks in being responsible for the actions of other partners.

Peggy Spillios advised Chad and Lyn that if they formed a corporation, they would not be personally responsible for the debts of the business. In case of a business failure, each member of the corporation could lose only the amount he or she had invested. Again with Peggy's help, Chad and Lyn dissolved the partnership and drew up a plan for a corporation, Lifetime Sports and Fitness Center, Incorporated. The corporation was to represent a total investment of $240,000. Their financial records showed that the partnership was worth $180,000, so they needed to raise another $60,000.

Chad and Lyn decided to divide the $240,000 into 24,000 shares, each with a value of $10. Based on the partnership agreement and the corporation plans, they divided the 24,000 shares this way: (1) Chad received 12,000 shares worth $120,000; (2) Lyn received 6,000 shares worth $60,000; and (3) they offered for sale 6,000 shares valued at $60,000.

The information about the division of shares of stock and other information about the corporation was put in an application submitted to the state government. The application asked permission to operate as a corporation. After approving the application, the state issued a certificate of incorporation authorizing the formation of Lifetime Sports and Fitness Center, Inc.

Chad and Lyn were no longer owners of the partnership. They had sold their partnership to the new corporation. In return they had received 18,000 shares of stock, or a part ownership in the corporation amounting to $180,000. These 18,000 shares were divided in proportion to the investment in the former partnership. The 6,000 shares offered for sale were bought by 30 people who had confidence in the new corporation, including the attorney, Peggy Spillios, who bought 1,000 shares. The corporation now had a total of 32 individual stockholders, or owners. The owners received stock certificates like the one shown in Figure 6–4 as evidence of their ownership of the corporation.

Chad and Lyn called a meeting of the stockholders to elect officers, to make plans for operating a branch store, and to transact other business. Each stockholder had one vote for each share of stock that she or he owned. Since Chad and Lyn together owned 18,000 shares, they had enough votes to control the operation of the business.

At the stockholders' meeting, seven people, including Chad and Lyn, were elected as directors of the corporation. These seven people made up the **board of directors.** The board's responsibility was to guide the corporation properly. The board's first act was to elect the executive officers of the corporation. The directors

Figure 6–4
A stock certificate shows ownership in a corporation. Peggy Spillios owns 1,000 shares of Lifetime Sports and Fitness Center, Inc.

Lifetime Sports and Fitness Center, Incorporated

This certifies that   Peggy Spillios   is the owner of
One Thousand

Dated APR 4 19--

elected Chad Peery as president, Jo Rabinski as vice president, Karen Vogan as secretary, and Lyn Gore as treasurer. As full-time employees, the officers receive regular salaries for managing the business.

At the end of a year, after all taxes were paid, the corporation had a net profit of $31,600. The board of directors voted to keep $10,000 of this in the business for expansion and to divide the other $21,600 among the stockholders. Since the corporation had issued 24,000 shares, each of the 32 stockholders received 90 cents for each share of stock that he or she owned ($21,600 ÷ 24,000 = $.90). The part of the profits that each stockholder receives is called a **dividend**. In addition to their salaries, Peery received $10,800 ($.90 × 12,000 shares) and Gore received $5,400 ($.90 × 6,000 shares). Figure 6–5 shows the prospering corporation.

Comparing Types of Ownership

You have read about Chad Peery as a sole proprietor, as a partner with Lyn Gore, and as a major stockholder in a corporation. As you have seen, Peery found some good features and some

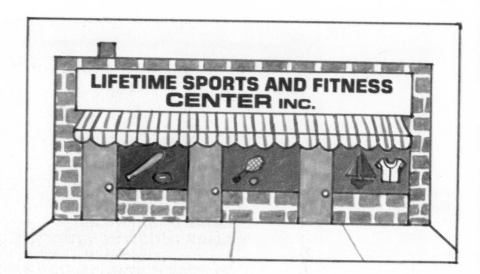

Figure 6–5
Ownership of a corporation can change without affecting the organization and life of the business.

not-so-good features about each experience. Figure 6–6 shows a summary of the main advantages and disadvantages of the three types of ownership.

Organizing Corporations for Service

When driving into towns, you probably have seen signs like "Centreville—Incorporated." An incorporated town is called a **municipal corporation.** Unlike a business corporation, it is organized to provide services for its citizens with money from their taxes rather than to make a profit. It does not issue stock representing ownership. It has its own officials, its own schools, and its own police and fire departments. It repairs its own streets; and it provides its own water supply, street lighting system, and other services for its citizens. It levies taxes and passes rules and regulations to operate effectively. It buys supplies, equipment, and services just as any business does and pays for them under the corporate name of the city. However, it is not in business to make a profit.

Other groups are also organized as nonprofit corporations. Like the municipal corporation, nonprofit organizations are those which operate to provide a service but not for profit. Among these are churches, private colleges and universities, American Red Cross, Boy Scouts of America, Future Business Leaders of

TYPE OF OWNERSHIP	ADVANTAGES	DISADVANTAGES
Sole Proprietorship	It is easy to start the business. The owner makes all the decisions and is his or her own boss. The owner receives all the profits.	Capital is limited to what the owner can supply or borrow. The owner is liable (responsible) for all debts, even to losing personal property if the business fails. Long hours and hard work are often necessary. The life of the business depends upon the owner; it ends if the owner quits or dies.
Partnership	It is fairly easy to start the business. More sources of capital are available. More business skills are available.	Each partner is liable for business debts made by all partners, even to losing personal property if the business fails. Each partner can make decisions; there is more than one boss. The partnership ends if a partner quits or dies. Each partner shares the profits.
Corporation	More sources of capital are available. Specialized managerial skills are available. The owners are liable only up to the amount of their investments. The ownership can be easily transferred through sale of stock; the business is not affected by this change of ownership.	It is difficult and expensive to start the corporation. The owners do not have control of the decisions made each day, unless they are officers of the company. The business activities of the corporation are limited to those stated in the certficate of incorporation.

Figure 6–6
There are advantages and disadvantages to each type of ownership.

America, and Distributive Education Clubs of America. Both community governments and nonprofit agencies find that the corporate form of organization provides the most effective way for them to deliver their services to the public.

Cooperatives — Businesses Owned by Members

In addition to proprietorships, partnerships, and corporations, there are other forms of organization for doing business. Sometimes people join together to operate a business known as a cooperative. A **cooperative** is owned by the members it serves and it is managed in their interest. One type is a **consumers' cooperative,** an organization of consumers who buy goods and services more cheaply together than each person could individually. For example, farmers and members of labor unions may form cooperatives to buy such products as groceries and gasoline and such services as insurance and electricity. Farmers also form cooperatives from which they buy products needed to run their farms.

Another type of cooperative is a **producers' cooperative.** It is usually a farmers' organization that markets such products as fruits, vegetables, milk, and grains. Sometimes the cooperative operates processing plants such as canneries. A producers' cooperative lets farmers band together for greater bargaining power in selling their products.

A cooperative is much like a regular corporation. Its formation must be approved by the state. It may sell one or more shares of stock to each of its members. A board of directors may be chosen by the members to guide the cooperative. But a cooperative differs from corporations in the way that it is controlled. In a regular corporation, a person usually has one vote for each share she or he owns. A cooperative may be controlled in two ways: each owner-member may have one vote; or, each member's vote may be based on the amount of service he or she has received from the cooperative.

Most consumers' cooperatives sell to nonmembers as well as members. Prices in cooperative stores are set at about the same level found in other local stores. Most of the profits a cooperative earns may be refunded directly to members at the end of the business year; part may be kept for expansion of the business.

Selling Another's Products Through a Franchise

If you have stayed in a Holiday Inn or a Howard Johnson's motel, or have eaten Kentucky Fried Chicken or a McDonald's hamburger, you have bought services and goods from a company that operates as a franchised business. A **franchise** is a written contract granting permission to sell someone else's product or service in a prescribed manner, over a certain period of time, and in a specified territory. Franchises can be operated as a proprietorship, partnership, or corporation.

In a recent year, there were 466,000 franchised businesses. Over 80 percent of these were owned by the person or group of persons who had received the franchise from a parent company to sell its products or services. This person or group is called the **franchisee**. Ownership of the remaining 20 percent was retained by the parent company granting the franchise, the **franchisor**.

The franchise agreement states the duties and rights of both parties. The franchisee agrees to run the business in a certain way. This often includes the name of the business, the products or services offered, the design and color of the building, the price of the product or service, and the uniforms of employees. This standardizing of the franchised businesses means that customers can recognize a business and know what to expect when they buy a product or service from any one of them. You know about what kind of hamburger you will get when you buy at the "golden arches" whether you are in Miami, Kansas City, or Tokyo.

Illus. 6–2

Many restaurants are part of a franchise system.

A franchise is a relatively easy business to start and the franchisor agrees to help the franchisee get started. Also the national advertising of the product or service by the parent company serves all the franchises all over the country. For its service, the franchisor collects a percentage of sales or an agreed-upon fee from the franchisee each year. Franchises usually require a large investment of capital to start and they are often very competitive. You may have seen in your town a fast-food store or other franchise fail because it was not competitive or because it was not in a good location. Nevertheless, franchises are a popular way of doing business.

A dding to Your Business Vocabulary

The following terms should become part of your business vocabulary. For each numbered item, find the term that has the same meaning.

articles of partnership
board of directors
certificate of incorporation
consumers' cooperative
cooperative
corporation
dividend
franchise

franchisee
franchisor
municipal corporation
partnership
producers' cooperative
sole proprietorship
stockholder or shareholder

1. A group of people elected by stockholders to guide a corporation.
2. An organization which farmers form to market their products.
3. A business owned by one person.
4. A written agreement made by partners in forming their business.
5. An association of two or more people operating a business as co-owners and sharing profits or losses according to a written agreement.
6. An incorporated town or city.
7. An organization of consumers who buy goods and services together.
8. A business made up of a number of owners but authorized by law to act as a single person.

9. A document, generally issued by a state government, giving permission to start a corporation.
10. The part of the profits of a corporation that each stockholder receives.
11. A person who owns stock in a corporation.
12. A business that is owned by the members it serves and is managed in their interest.
13. A written contract granting permission to sell someone else's product or service in a prescribed manner, over a certain period of time, and in a specified area.
14. The person or group of persons who have received permission from a parent company to sell its products or services.

15. The parent company which grants permission to a person or group to sell its products or services.

*U*nderstanding *Your Reading*

1. What advantages did Chad Peery find in starting his own firm?
2. What disadvantages did Peery find as the operator of a sole proprietorship?
3. What advantages over his original organization resulted when Peery entered into partnership with Lyn Gore?
4. Name six things that should be agreed upon and recorded in the articles of partnership.
5. State two advantages that a corporation has over a partnership.
6. Name two disadvantages of a corporation.
7. What evidence of ownership did Peery and Gore receive when they changed from a partnership to a corporation?
8. Who actually manages a corporation?

9. Why does a corporation's board of directors keep part of the profit before dividing the remainder among the stockholders?
10. What is the difference between a municipal corporation and a business corporation?
11. What is the purpose of a consumers' cooperative?
12. In what ways does a producers' cooperative serve its members?
13. How does a cooperative differ from a regular corporation?
14. What are the three conditions of a franchise agreement?
15. Name one advantage and one disadvantage of operating a business as a franchise.

*P*utting *Your Business Knowledge to Work*

1. Features of the five types of business organizations which you studied in this chapter are given in the following statements. Name the type of organization to which each statement applies. Some statements may apply to two types of organizations.
   a. The owner is his or her own boss.
   b. If one of the owners makes a large, unwise purchase and the business can't pay the bill, another owner might have to do so.
   c. The business can sell stock to raise more money.
   d. If a profit is made, the owner gets it all.
   e. Owners agree on how they will divide profits and share losses.
   f. Owners allow a board of directors to make decisions about the business.
   g. Owners/operators agree to operate the business in a prescribed manner set forth by the parent company.
   h. Farmers join together to transport, store, and sell their crops.
   i. Owners must get written permission from the state in which the business is located before it can operate.
   j. An owner may be added to help make business decisions.
   k. The amount of control a person has in the business may depend upon the

value of the products and services bought from the business during the year.

l. A percentage of sales or a set fee must be paid annually to a parent company.

2. Could the policies and the management of a corporation with more than 10,000 stockholders be controlled by just one stockholder? Explain your answer.

3. The community of Grandview has petitioned its state government for a certificate of incorporation so that it can become a town. When Grandview becomes a corporation, can it sell stock and issue dividends to stockholders? Explain.

4. Trish Watson and her partner, Russ Agee, fail in their business venture. The debts are about $8,000 greater than the value of the business. Ms. Watson has personal property worth more than $10,000, but her partner has nothing. How much of the debt of the business will Ms. Watson probably have to pay? Give the reason for your answer.

Computing Business Problems

1. Jake Simmons and Maury Gertz operate a small convenience store under a franchise with a national company. The franchisor requires an annual payment of 5 percent of gross sales. At the close of the current year, the accountant who keeps the records for the Simmons-Gertz store reported gross sales of $523,250. How much will Simmons and Gertz pay to the franchisor for the year?

2. As an art major at a university, Lu-yin Chang specializes in hand-tooled leather. To make extra money, Lu-yin rented a stall in the new festival marketplace in the revitalized downtown area. His income and expenses for the month of December were as follows:

Income from sales	$850
Expenses:	
Rent for stall and utilities	125
Cutting tools	45
Leather and supplies	110
Ad in the university newspaper	20

a. What was the total of Lu-yin's expenses for December?

b. How much profit did Lu-yin make in December?

c. If Lu-yin put 20 percent of his profit into savings before spending on personal needs, how much will he save in December?

3. Scott and Kristie delaGarza own stock in four corporations. Below is a record of their stock holdings and the dividend they received for each share at the end of the first quarter.

Company	No. Shares Owned	Quarterly Dividend per Share
IBM	50	$.95
Avon Products	20	.50
William Wrigley, Jr.	50	.36
Levi Strauss	100	.4625

a. How much dividend income did the delaGarzas receive from each of their stocks for the quarter?

b. What was their total dividend income for the quarter?

c. If each corporation paid the same amount per share for the remaining three quarters, how much dividend income would the delaGarzas receive from each for the year?

d. What total dividend income would the delaGarzas receive for the year?

4. After all expenses were paid, Hillsdale Consumer Cooperative had $13,000 left over. Of this amount, $3,000 was set aside for expansion of the business. According to its policy, Hillsdale would refund to each member an amount in proportion to the amount he or she bought during the year. Since total sales for the year were $500,000, the refund would be 2 percent, or 2 cents for every dollar each member had spent at the

co-op during the year. The following were among the members; their total purchases are shown in even dollars:

G. T. Frazier	$1,000
A. G. Whitbeck	650
B. R. Ricks	750
J. Fantoni	100
T. J. Reed	1,250

a. How much refund did each of these members receive?

b. What was the total amount refunded to these five members?

*S*tretching *Your Business Knowledge*

1. Be prepared to give an oral report about an interview with the owner of a local business. Plan carefully in advance for your interview. Ask the business owner questions such as these:

   a. Why did you choose to go into this particular kind of business?

   b. What risks do you take in operating your own business?

   c. What methods do you use to compete with similar businesses for customers?

   d. What training and experience should a person have before attempting to start his or her own business?

2. Visit a local shopping center. Take a pad and pencil with you and write down the names of at least 10 businesses located in the center. Beside each name, write down whether you believe the firm to be a proprietorship, a partnership, or a corporation. Be able to explain to the class what part of the firm name led you to identify it as you did. If you could not identify the type of organization by name, be able to explain why.

3. Corporations are required to issue an

annual report to their stockholders. Several ways in which you might get such a report to review are listed below:

   a. Borrow one from a member of your family or a friend who owns stock.

   b. Ask your school or community librarian if the library has corporation annual reports.

   c. Visit a corporation in your community and ask for a copy of its report.

   d. Write to a corporation and ask for a copy of its report.

   Using these suggestions, try to obtain annual reports from two corporations. Write a brief report showing the types of information contained in both reports.

4. There are several types of stock. Using a text in business principles, accounting, or business law, try to find definitions of the following types: common stock, preferred stock, cumulative preferred stock, participating preferred stock.

5. In most partnerships, the partners are general partners, but sometimes there are limited partners and silent partners. Explain the differences among these

types. (Refer to business law and business principles textbooks in your library.)

6. Franchise businesses are particularly common in the motel, restaurant, and prepared-food fields. List the names of four or five franchise businesses in your area and describe the product or services provided by each.

7. What is Junior Achievement, Inc.? Look into the nearest Junior Achievement program in your area. If possible, visit some of the Junior Achievement "companies" that are in operation. Be prepared to report orally to the class on the results of your investigation.

CHAPTER 7

World Trade and Our Economy

■ CHAPTER OBJECTIVES ─────────────────────────

After studying this chapter and completing the end-of-chapter activities, you will be able to:

1. Explain how people, communities, and nations throughout the world depend upon each other.
2. Give an example to show the difference between foreign trade and domestic trade.
3. Tell how we depend upon world trade for many goods and services.
4. Describe how tariffs, quotas, and embargoes affect world trade.
5. State an advantage and a problem associated with world trade.

If you examine the clothes you are wearing or the items you are carrying in your pocket or purse right now, you would probably find that few of the items were made in the town or city where you live. Your shoes might be from Taiwan, Korea, or Brazil; your sweater from New Zealand or Scotland; your watch from Switzerland; and your pocket calculator from Japan.

As you learned in Unit 1, our hometowns cannot supply all the things we want so we trade with other communities, states, and countries to help fulfill our needs. Likewise other communities, states, and countries buy from suppliers in our town and from others who have the things they want. This trading is an important part of our economy.

We Use Our Advantages to Specialize

Each region of our country has certain special advantages. These advantages may include climate, deposits of minerals, rich soil, a favorable location, or many workers with special skills and abilities. These kinds of advantages make it possible for a state or region to produce a certain good or service of higher quality or at a lower cost than another state or region. Thus, Florida has an advantage over Wisconsin for growing oranges. Minnesota has an advantage over Florida for producing iron ore. Georgia has an advantage over Wyoming in growing peanuts. And Michigan has an advantage over Maine in making cars. Trade among people and businesses in the same country is called **domestic trade.**

Trade allows each state or region to specialize—to devote most of its resources to producing the kinds of goods it produces best. And each state exchanges its special products for the special products of other states. What is the result for you as a consumer? You benefit by having many different kinds of products that are generally better in quality and lower in price than if each state or region tried to supply most of the things its people need.

For example, a person in Omaha, Nebraska, might buy a car that was made in Detroit from a local dealer. The heater, battery, tires, and other parts may have been produced in communities in other states and shipped to Detroit to be assembled in the car. And at least 30 raw materials used to make the car parts came from other nations.

You can see that the automobile customer in Omaha would not have been able to obtain a car if it were not for trade among communities in the United States and trade between the United States and other countries.

Other Countries Use Their Advantages, Too

Just as we specialize and trade among our states and communities, other countries also take advantage of special factors of production that they have. They produce goods according to these advantages and trade with other countries to help provide for the wants of their citizens. This trading affects your daily life more than you realize.

What did your family have for breakfast this morning? Coffee, cereal, and sliced bananas, perhaps? If it were not for trading with Brazil for the coffee and with Honduras for the bananas, you might have had only cereal. The sugar on your table may have come from the Philippines. Even your morning newspaper was printed on paper that may have come from Canada.

While our country has many natural resources, a skilled labor force, and modern machines and methods of production, we cannot provide ourselves with all of the things we want. We go beyond our borders to get many things. We carry on trade with as many as 150 foreign countries in one year. Trade among different countries is called **world trade.** It is also referred to as **foreign** or **international trade.**

Most nations of the world have special advantages. Brazil, for example, has an advantage over the United States in producing coffee. Saudi Arabia has an advantage over most other countries in crude oil. Australia has an advantage in wool. Korea and Taiwan have an advantage in the number of skilled laborers who can assemble radios and make textiles and shoes. And compared with these and many other countries, the United States has advantages in the production of airplanes, tractors, computers, office equipment, and many varieties of food and other agricultural products. Because of trade and modern means of transportation, nations everywhere can specialize in the kinds of production they can do best.

Illus. 7–1
As do most nations, the United States has advantages in the production of certain products.

Importing Goods—Buying From Other Countries

The things we buy from other countries are called **imports**. Imports account for our total supply of bananas, coffee, cocoa, spices, tea, silk, and crude rubber. About half the crude oil and fish we buy comes from other countries. Imports also account for 20 to 50 percent of our supply of carpets, sugar, leather gloves, dishes, and sewing machines. In order to produce industrial and consumer goods, we must import tin, chrome, manganese, nickel, copper, zinc, and several other metals. Figure 7–1 shows the percentage of various materials imported by the United States in a recent year.

Figure 7–1 The United States imports some of the raw materials used in the production of many products.

We depend upon imported raw materials for many of the products we use today. Also, without world trade, many of the things we buy would cost more. This is due to the fact that other countries' advantages allow them to produce goods and services

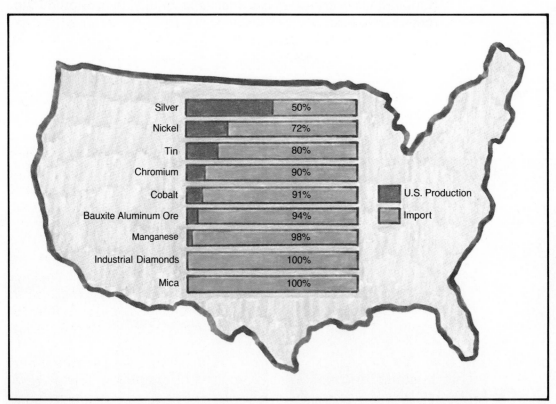

Material	Percentage
Silver	50%
Nickel	72%
Tin	80%
Chromium	90%
Cobalt	91%
Bauxite Aluminum Ore	94%
Manganese	98%
Industrial Diamonds	100%
Mica	100%

■ U.S. Production
□ Import

at lower costs. These lower production costs are largely the result of labor costs being lower in many foreign countries than they are in the United States.

Many people prefer to buy certain imported goods, even at higher prices, because of their difference or their quality. You might be willing to pay a higher price for a pair of German binoculars, a Swiss watch, or an imported cashmere sweater because you have confidence in the quality and workmanship of these products. Or, you may simply enjoy owning products made in other lands.

Exporting Products — Selling to Other Countries

The goods and services we sell to other countries are called **exports**. Just as imports benefit you, exports benefit the people of other countries. People in nations throughout the world run their factories with machinery made in the United States. They work their land and harvest their crops with American-made tools. They eat food made from many of our agricultural products. They use our chemicals, fertilizers, medicines, and plastics. They see our movies and read a good deal of our printed matter. Producing these exported goods employs many of our workers. One out of every six jobs in the United States depends upon world trade. Figure 7–2 shows some of the countries with which the United States trades.

Two segments of the American economy — machinery and agriculture — are especially dependent on selling in foreign markets. Our exports in the machinery and transport-equipment fields

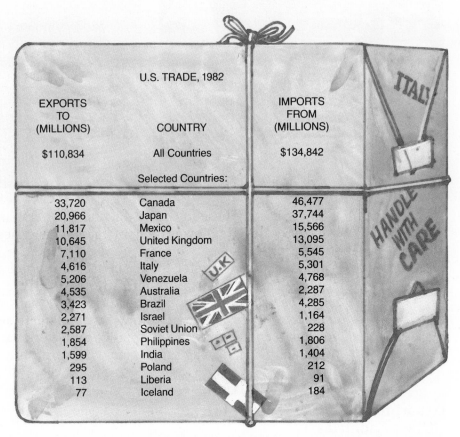

EXPORTS TO (MILLIONS)	COUNTRY	IMPORTS FROM (MILLIONS)
	U.S. TRADE, 1982	
$110,834	All Countries	$134,842
	Selected Countries:	
33,720	Canada	46,477
20,966	Japan	37,744
11,817	Mexico	15,566
10,645	United Kingdom	13,095
7,110	France	5,545
4,616	Italy	5,301
5,206	Venezuela	4,768
4,535	Australia	2,287
3,423	Brazil	4,285
2,271	Israel	1,164
2,587	Soviet Union	228
1,854	Philippines	1,806
1,599	India	1,404
295	Poland	212
113	Liberia	91
77	Iceland	184

Figure 7–2
The United States has many trading partners.

include diesel engines, buses, tractors, oil-drilling rigs, earth-moving equipment, jet planes, computers, and air-conditioning and refrigeration equipment. Large amounts of farm products are also sold abroad each year. Farmers who grow such crops as cotton, wheat, soybeans, and rice depend on selling in foreign markets.

The jobs and incomes of millions of American workers depend directly on success in exporting. And the profits of many businesses depend in part on the demands of other countries for American products and services.

Paying for Foreign Goods

Suppose that each of the 50 states had a different kind of money, each with a different value. Imagine the trouble you would have in traveling through New England if you had to change your "Massachusetts money" into "Rhode Island money" and then into "Connecticut money." If you lived in Chicago and were ordering products from Oregon, you would need to convert your "Illinois money" into "Oregon money" to make the payment. This is what we must do when we travel in or trade with other countries. It is one reason why world trade is so much more complicated than domestic trade.

Each nation has its own type of money and its own banking system. In the United States, we use dollars; Mexico uses pesos; France uses francs; Japan uses yen; and so on. When American businesses buy olive oil from Italy, for example, arrangements are made to change American dollars into lire, the Italian currency. If you were to visit Spain, you would need to have pesetas to pay for meals and other expenses. When Spanish people come to this country, they need to change their pesetas into dollars.

For experienced travelers or businesspeople, the exchange of money from one currency to another is not as difficult as it might seem. Travelers in a foreign country simply go to a local bank or other money changer and "buy" whatever amount of the local currency they want and pay for it with money from their own country. How much of the local currency they get will depend on the value of the two currencies at that time.

Because of the differences in value of the monies of the world, rates of exchange are established among countries. A **rate of exchange** is the value of the money of one country expressed in terms of the money of another country. This is the part that gets complicated. Let's take an example. If the rate of exchange for the Mexican peso is .04, this means that the peso is worth 4¢ in our money and that an American dollar could be changed into 25 pesos. A Mexican tourist in our country would need 250 pesos to exchange for $10 in American money. The approximate values of the currencies of several foreign countries on a recent date are given in Figure 7–3. Remember, though, that rates of exchange vary and sometimes change from one day to the next. In international trading, the buyer or seller must be aware of the rate of exchange for the day of the purchase.

The problem of foreign currency exchange is handled mainly by major banks around the world. The banks are willing to buy and sell the currencies of the various countries. They provide the needed and often very complex services which allow trading partners to make and receive payments.

The Government May Regulate Trade

World trade affects and is affected by the economy. But there are other factors that may be involved as well. Chief among these is our political relationship to other countries. Our government establishes a foreign policy which guides our activities, including trade, with other countries. Several devices may be used to control the importing and exporting of a product or service. Among these controls are quotas, tariffs, and embargoes.

Quotas

One of the devices used by governments to regulate foreign trade sets a limit on the quantity of a product that may be imported or exported within a given period of time. This limit is called a **quota**. Quotas may be set for many reasons. Countries that export oil may put quotas on crude oil so that the supply will remain low and maintain prices at a certain level. Quotas may also be imposed by one country on imports from another to express disapproval of the policies or behavior of that country. Quotas can also be set by one country to protect an industry from too much foreign competition. This is often done by a nation to

Figure 7–3
Exchange rates of currencies change frequently.

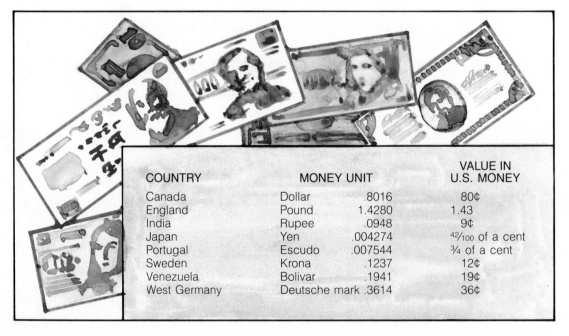

COUNTRY	MONEY UNIT		VALUE IN U.S. MONEY
Canada	Dollar	.8016	80¢
England	Pound	1.4280	1.43
India	Rupee	.0948	9¢
Japan	Yen	.004274	$^{42}/_{100}$ of a cent
Portugal	Escudo	.007544	¾ of a cent
Sweden	Krona	.1237	12¢
Venezuela	Bolivar	.1941	19¢
West Germany	Deutsche mark	.3614	36¢

shield its "infant industries" that need protection to get started. Our government in the past has imposed quotas on sugar, cattle, dairy products, and textiles.

Tariffs

Another device that governments use to regulate foreign trade is the tariff. A **tariff** is a tax which a government places on certain imported products. Suppose you want to buy an English bicycle. The English producer of the bike sets a price of $140 on it, but our government places a 20 percent tariff on the bike when it is imported. This means that you will have to pay $168 plus shipping charges for the bike. The $28 tariff goes to the government. Tariffs make up only a small part of the government's revenue. Tariffs are used not so much to produce income as they are to regulate imports. By increasing the price of an imported product, a high tariff tends to lower the demand for that product and, therefore, to lower the number imported. If a country wants to increase imports of a product, it can remove the tariff or put a very low one on it. The product can then be sold at a lower price, which encourages people to buy it and results in more being imported.

Embargoes

If a government wishes, it can stop the export or import of a product completely. This action is called an **embargo**. Governments may impose an embargo for many reasons. They may wish to protect their own industries from foreign competition to a greater degree than either the quota or tariff will accomplish. The government may wish to prevent sensitive products, particularly those important to the nation's defense, from falling into the hands of unfriendly groups or nations. As with the quota, a government may sometimes impose an embargo as a strong measure to express its disapproval of the actions or policies of another country. When it needs to do so, a government may use any of the three devices to improve its trade position. Let's take a look at the way a government measures its trade position.

Keeping Track of Trade Flows

As you learned in Unit 1, a major reason people work is to get money to buy the things they need and want; that is, they sell their labor for wages which they then spend for products and services. People usually try to keep their income and spending in balance, knowing that if they spend more than they earn, they can have some economic problems. So it is with nations regarding their trade positions.

Balance of Trade

Countries pay for their imports with the money they receive for their exports. Keeping the two in balance is often a problem, however. The difference between a country's total exports and total imports is called the **balance of trade.** If a country exports (sells) more than it imports (buys), it has a trade surplus or its trade position is said to be favorable. But if it imports (buys) more than it exports (sells), it has a trade deficit or an unfavorable balance of trade.

A country can have a trade surplus with one country and a deficit with another. Overall, however, a country tries to keep its trade in balance; if it does not, and it has no other way of making up the deficit, its money will flow out of the country to other countries. Figure 7–4 shows the three possible trade positions. After a long history of a favorable balance of trade, the United States had a trade deficit in seven years of a recent ten-year period. In 1983, the trade deficit was almost $70 billion. This has been a serious problem for our economy.

Balance of Payments

In addition to export and import flows, other forms of exchange occur between countries that affect the economy. Money flows from one country to another through investments. For example, a citizen of one country might buy stock in a firm in another country; or a business may set up a plant in a foreign country. Also, one government might give financial or military aid to another country. And banks may deposit funds in foreign banks. When tourists travel, they also contribute to the flow of money from their country to the country they are visiting. Some countries limit the amount of money their citizens can take out of the country when they travel.

The difference between the amount of money that flows into and the amount of money that flows out of a country for investments, tourism, and nontrade items is called the **balance of**

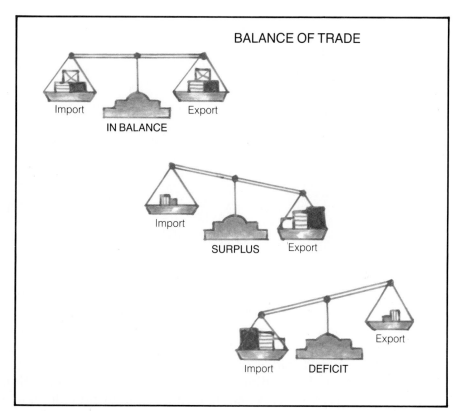

Figure 7–4
In recent years the United States has experienced a deficit in its balance of trade.

payments. A country can have a surplus in the balance of trade and a deficit in the balance of payments. A balance of trade deficit, for example, can be made up by a high level of tourism to effect a balance of payments surplus. But if a balance of payments deficit continues over a long period of time, the country could bankrupt its treasury. Countries try to review regularly their balance of trade and balance of payments positions in the interest of the health of their economies.

World Trade—Benefits and Problems

You have already learned that there are many benefits to world trade. Since countries cannot supply all of their citizens' wants and needs, trade offers a way to provide them from other countries. By increasing the abundance of products available to us, often at prices lower than we could make them, world trade enables us to increase our standard of living.

Illus. 7–3
What changes would you expect if all world trade stopped tomorrow?

Trade also creates jobs. Firms which make and market products for export may depend upon foreign trade to exist. Other firms may sell in both the domestic and foreign markets. Ships and planes which carry cargo and tourists overseas are manufactured and operated by firms that provide jobs based heavily on world trade.

International trade also increases competition among firms. As you know, competition tends to provide us with better products at lower prices.

Many people view world trade as a way to promote international understanding. Nations which are trading partners usually try to maintain friendly relations for economic reasons; this sometimes promotes better relationships and understanding between the countries.

Even though there are many benefits, world trade also creates some problems. The competition which brings in better products at lower prices can also lower demand for domestic products and cause people working in our industries to lose their jobs. In some cases it can cause domestic businesses to close when demand for their products falls in favor of imported products. The United States in recent years has experienced such problems in several of its industries, including shoes, textiles, and cars. Some people argue that when Americans buy Italian shoes, Korean sweatsuits, or Japanese cars, they are exporting American jobs to those countries. This means that their purchase of imported products creates demand for those products in the countries where they are made and therefore creates jobs in those countries. At the same time, as demand for the same domestic products decreases in favor of the import, American businesses must lay off workers and sometimes close down their plants. On the other hand, competition should, in the long run, bring about more efficient production in our country and enable American firms to recapture the market through better products at reasonable prices. Each person in our country is free to buy whatever he or she wishes.

In addition to the jobs/trade dilemma, countries also may become too dependent upon a trading partner. If one country depends heavily upon another for certain products and the exporting country decides to cut production, the importing country may have serious problems. This could be especially critical for strategic products such as energy and food.

Even though there are problems, the benefits of world trade are believed to outweigh the disadvantages. With high-speed transportation and instantaneous communication creating demand today for products from all over the world, international trade will probably increase.

*A**dding to Your Business Vocabulary*

The following terms should become part of your business vocabulary. For each numbered item, find the term that has the same meaning.

balance of payments	*imports*
balance of trade	*quota*
domestic trade	*rate of exchange*
embargo	*tariff*
exports	*world, foreign,* or *international trade*

1. Goods and services sold to another country.
2. A limit on the quantity of a product that may be imported or exported within a given period of time.
3. The buying and selling of goods and services among people and businesses within the same country.
4. The value of the money of one country expressed in terms of the money of another country.
5. Trade among different countries.
6. Goods and services bought from another country.

7. Stopping the importing or exporting of a certain product or service.
8. The difference between a country's total exports and total imports of merchandise.
9. A tax which a government places on certain imported products.
10. The difference between the total amount of money that flows into a country and the money that flows out of a country for investments, tourism, and nontrade items.

Understanding Your Reading

1. Give an example to show the difference between domestic and foreign trade.
2. Give three examples of regional advantages in production in the world and in the United States.
3. Name a food, a raw material, and a manufactured good which we would not have without world trade.
4. What percent of our supply of aluminum ore is imported?
5. State one reason why you might prefer to buy an imported product, even at a higher cost.
6. What two segments of the American economy particularly depend upon international trade?
7. Why are rates of exchange established?
8. State three reasons that are given by countries for placing tariffs on imports.
9. How does a quota limit trade?
10. What is the difference between balance of trade and balance of payments?
11. What is meant by the term "unfavorable balance of trade"?
12. State one advantage and one problem associated with world trade.

Putting Your Business Knowledge to Work

1. It is said that no community or nation today can be completely independent. Do you agree or disagree? Explain.
2. How does world trade contribute to a better standard of living for many people in various countries?
3. An American manufacturer of electric toasters wants to sell its products to the people of China. Can you think of some difficulties that this business might have in entering the Chinese market?
4. What are "infant industries"? Give a few examples of such industries, either in the United States or in other countries. Should infant industries be protected by high tariffs? If so, for how long?
5. Some people feel that the United States should place stiff controls on imports of goods that compete with our businesses to prevent the "exporting of American jobs" to other countries. Give arguments for and against such a position.

Computing Business Problems

1. The table below shows the approximate value of some imported foods for 1980 and 1981. The value is stated in millions of dollars:

Food	1980	1981
Meat and meat products	$2,300	$2,000
Fruits and nuts	1,700	2,100
Coffee	3,900	2,600
Sugar	2,000	2,100
Fish	2,600	3,000
Cocoa	400	500

   a. What is the total value in millions of dollars of the foods imported by the U.S. in 1980?
   b. What is the total value in millions of dollars of the foods imported in 1981?
   c. Was there an increase or a decrease from 1980 to 1981?
   d. What was the amount of the increase or decrease?

2. Using the information in Figure 7–3 on page 102, tell what the equal amount in U.S. dollars would be for these amounts in foreign currency:
   a. In Portugal, 100 escudos
   b. in Japan, 136 yen
   c. one Canadian dollar
   d. in India, 6 rupees

3. To make their exports suitable for use in other countries, U.S. manufacturers must produce goods that are measured in the metric system. Many of our measures do not convert exactly into a standard measure of the metric system. For example, if a manufacturer wanted to export paint, which is sold in gallon cans in this country, it would probably export the paint in 4-liter (about 1¼ gallons) cans. To what sizes would the items listed below be converted for export to countries using the metric system? (Refer to Appendix D.)
   a. a quart bottle of liquid detergent
   b. a 50-yard bolt of polyester fabric
   c. an automobile engine measured in cubic inches
   d. a 12-inch ruler
   e. a bathroom scale that measures in pounds

4. The table below shows the approximate values of the exports and imports going through the nine customs ports in a recent year:

City	Exports (million $)	Imports (million $)
Boston	$15,400	$24,400
New York	35,800	44,100
Baltimore	22,200	26,900
Miami	19,800	20,300
New Orleans	23,300	26,100
Houston	31,500	36,200
Los Angeles	19,600	24,400
San Francisco	30,600	29,700
Chicago	28,200	29,700

   a. What is the total value in millions of dollars of the exports for the year? the imports?
   b. Which port city reported the largest business in terms of value? What is the value?
   c. Which port imported and exported the least amount? What was the value for each?

*S*tretching Your Business Knowledge

1. When travelers enter a country, including their own, they are required to go through a customs check. Talk to someone who has traveled to a foreign country and ask him or her to relate this experience to you. Ask what procedure was followed at the customs check; what forms had to be filled in; how much exemption they were given on items purchased abroad before having to pay a customs levy; and what amount, if any, the traveler had to pay. Report your findings to the class.

2. Using a reference which gives governmental statistics, such as the *Statistical Abstract of the United States* or *The World Almanac,* prepare a brief table showing the U.S. balance of trade position for the past four years.

3. Look through the stock of food supplies that your family presently has on hand. Make a list of the ingredients that you think probably were imported. Indicate where some of these items may have come from.

4. Agencies are often called by a word made up of their initials. OPEC, relating to world trade, is an example of such an agency. EEC and OAS, relating to regional trade, are other examples. For each of these three terms, find the complete name, the purpose of the organization, and the nations which are involved.

CAREER CATEGORY: Management

In this unit you have learned about the types of businesses, what they do, and how they carry on trade with each other in America and throughout the world. The people who operate these businesses are called managers. It takes many managers to operate our businesses, government agencies, and other organizations. Therefore, career opportunities in management are numerous.

Job Titles: Job titles commonly found in this career area include:

Bank Managers and Officers
Public Administrators
Sales Managers
Hospital/Health Service Managers
Administrative Managers

Store Managers
Supervisors
Restaurant Managers
Personnel Human Resources Managers
Department Managers

Employment Outlook: Managers, officials, and proprietors make up one of the largest career categories. In 1982 there were over 9½ million managers, officials, and proprietors. This number is expected to increase by 28 percent to over 12 million by 1995. This means that about 207,000 new managers will be needed each year. Bank managers and health service administrators are expected to be in high demand.

Future Changes: As America moves toward becoming a service-oriented economy and high technology changes the way we produce goods, management is increasing in scope and importance. As more use is made of computers to supply data used by managers to make decisions, preparation for management careers will require an understanding of computers and superior decision-making skills. In order to direct today's more sophisticated and demanding work force, managers must also have a high level of human relations ability.

What Is Done on the Job: Managers get things done by people. They plan what has to be done, how it is to be done, by whom it is to be done, and when it is to be done. They assign tasks and see that the work is com-

pleted. Managers also evaluate the performance of workers and see that they are paid. Activities of managers fall into four categories: planning, organizing, leading, and controlling. There are many types of managers who perform specialized duties. Sales managers plan and organize sales departments. They assign sales quotas and territories to salespersons; plan ways to motivate them, such as giving bonuses for exceeding quotas; require reports from the salespeople; and evaluate them on their performances. Personnel managers handle employee-related matters including recruiting, selecting, training, and appraising the performance of employees. A manager's specialization, therefore, will dictate how he or she will plan, organize, lead, and control.

Education and Training: While it is still possible for high school graduates to become managers, it is becoming increasingly less likely. High school graduates who are experienced workers with a record of excellent performance are sometimes promoted to supervisory or lower-level management jobs. But they are usually required to get additional training through college courses or company-sponsored development programs. A bachelor's degree in business administration is a typical requirement for entering a management career. Management courses in such a program usually include management principles, human resources management and labor relations, business policy and strategy, organizational behavior,

and information management technology or computer science. People with college degrees in management usually begin their careers as management trainees. Vacancies in management are usually filled from the pool of trainees.

Salary Levels: Factors affecting salary vary widely in management; among them are the level of management in which one works, and whether one works in business, for the government or other nonprofit agency, or for oneself. In 1982 beginning salaries for management trainees with bachelor's degrees ranged between $13,200 and $21,600. During that year the top managers in several U.S. businesses earned over $1 million. As you can see, the range of salaries for managers is very broad.

For Additional Information: To learn about managers visit a local business and ask the manager to describe his or her job to you. You school counselor can advise you about colleges and universities which offer degree programs in management and business administration. Visit your library and ask for information on management careers. For example, examine the latest edition of *Defining the Manager's Job,* by Max Wortman and JoAnn Sperling (New York, NY: American Management Association, Inc., 1975). This book describes common responsibilities of all managers and gives actual job descriptions of over 125 managers of American businesses.

UNIT 3

LIVING IN THE COMPUTER AGE

BUSINESS BRIEF
Thinking Small

You can enjoy your radio, hand-held calculator, electronic game, or even a pacemaker because of the transistor. The transistor, a small electronic amplifying device made from a wafer of semiconductor material, is one of the most important inventions in the history of electronics.

In 1948 John Bardeen and Walter H. Brattain, two scientists at Bell Telephone Laboratories, invented the point-contact transistor. In 1951, William Shockley applied the ideas of Bardeen and Brattain to his invention of the junction transistor which became the model for later transistors. In 1956 the three men received the Nobel Prize for physics.

The transistor replaced the vacuum tube used in early radios and televisions, and transistor radios and miniature electronic devices quickly became common in the 1960s and 70s. Improvements in the transistor have revolutionized how the business world and private citizens use many items. In 1954 only a million transistors were produced in the United States, but by 1967 over 500 million units were produced each year. Now billions of transistors are sold annually in the United States.

Among the advantages of the transistor are its size and weight (smaller than a pinhead), its sturdiness which results in long life (speculated to be thousands of years), and its high efficiency. These advantages, aided by the development of the silicon chip—a sliver of silicon packed with hundreds of thousands of transistors, allow the transistor to be used successfully in a variety of items such as hearing aids; fire alarms; minicomputers; minicalculators; medical devices; satellites; and military data transmission, guidance, radar, and communication systems.

The first computers filled large rooms, but because of improvements made possible by the transistor and integrated circuitry, researchers have created computers that you can hold in your hand or wear on your wrist. The space required for each part of a computer, such as its memory and logic and switching circuits, keeps getting smaller. It is possible that small computers using transistors will soon be adapted to and used in many commonly used items.

Because the transistor made the computer portable, we can walk on the moon, implant artificial hearts into humans, use laser beams to dissect and examine diseased body cells too small to be seen, and grow more nutritious foods. And, yes, we can now send missiles containing computerized parts to any point in the world as a defensive measure. All types of miniature computers and electronic devices are now possible because three men thought small.

CHAPTER 8

The Computer at Work

■ CHAPTER OBJECTIVES

After studying this chapter and completing the end-of-chapter activities, you will be able to:

1. Give reasons for increased use of computers in the world of work.
2. Explain how a computer processes business information.
3. Identify and use at least 15 computer terms.
4. Tell how automated word processing is changing the office.
5. Report how computers are used in public service settings.

You have probably heard people say the world of work is changing. Or you may have seen a television report that there are fewer industrial workers each year. Perhaps you have noticed more want ads asking for workers with knowledge and skills in electronics to help in service-related jobs. Why are these changes taking place? Many changes in today's work world are due to increased use of computers. **Computers** are electronic or mechanical devices designed to store, rearrange, and report information.

The Need for Computers

The reasons for increased use of computers are simple. The amount of **data**, or facts and information, used in business is increasing. Computers enable businesses to compute numbers and arrange and store information quickly and efficiently. Because computers can make calculations so quickly, they save businesses time. Because they can store information so efficiently, they save space. Today's computers are also cheaper and smaller than the first computers. The first computers were large and expensive, but new ideas from researchers and developers have resulted in computers that can be held in your hand or placed on desks in offices. As advanced technology and competition have brought about more efficient computers at lower prices, businesses have begun to apply computers to everyday problems.

Computers enable businesses to save time. An American engineer, Herman Hollerith, designed a punched-card system for taking the 1890 census. Each punched hole represented a certain unit of information. Computers read the "holes" in the cards and stored the information they contained. As a result, the 1890 census was completed in two and one-half years, five years faster than the 1880 census was completed. In recent years the electronic computer has been developed to meet the need for a faster, more efficient method of storing the increasing volume of information and for solving problems for businesses. The list of computer time measurements in Figure 8–1 gives an idea of the speed at which a computer functions.

Computer Time Measurements
second
millisecond (one thousandth of a second)
microsecond (one millionth of a second)
nanosecond (one billionth of a second)
picosecond (one trillionth of a second)

Figure 8–1
Computers save time.

At first computers were owned only by large companies. Now most small and medium-sized companies use computers to help store the large amounts of data needed in today's business world. Businesses often have to rearrange data, however, before it can be useful. For example, a business might need the names of all its employees or clients listed in alphabetical order in a directory. This rearrangement or processing of data to make it more useful is called **data processing.**

How Computers Work

Even the most up-to-date computer needs your help to process data properly. You must always tell a computer what you want it to do. One way to give commands is to give the computer a set of instructions called a **program**. A program tells the computer what functions to complete and when to complete them. When using the program, the data you place into the computer is called **input**. When the computer rearranges the data for you by following the program, the rearranged data is known as **output**. All the input or information that a company stores to run its business, such as personnel, inventory, and accounting records, is called a **data base.** The data base is useless, however, unless the computer is told by people what to do with the data. So businesses hire people called **programmers** to write the instructions that tell the computer what to do.

The most common way to instruct your computer is by entering input on a terminal keyboard. A **terminal** consists of a keyboard and screen. The keyboard looks somewhat like a typewriter and the screen, a **visual display terminal (VDT),** looks like a television screen. The VDT shows what you and the computer are saying to each other as data is entered or revised.

When working with a computer, you must select the task to be completed from a **menu**, a list of choices of commands that appears on the VDT. For example, business employees may order their computers to recall and update information concerning invoices, customer statements, or credit memorandums. After you choose a task from the menu, you enter the input into the computer. You may then view the processed data on the VDT.

Illus. 8–1
Without an accurate set of instructions provided by the programmer, computers cannot perform properly.

Or you may tell the computer to print a copy of the processed data using the **printer**, an output device that produces written characters on paper. Figure 8–2 shows one way data can be placed into the computer to be processed into output.

Solving Problems with Computers

When you are given a problem to solve, you use facts stored in your memory to arrive at a solution. A computer can be used to solve problems in the same way. Everything the computer has stored such as facts and instructions is its **memory**, and it uses information stored in its memory to solve problems.

The amount of information a computer can store depends upon the size of the computer's memory. These amounts are measured using computer terms such as bit, nibble, byte, and kilobyte (K). Figure 8–3 shows these measures. But to give you an idea, it would take at least a 1K computer to store the information on an average page in this book. Large computers can store thousands of pages of information.

The **central processing unit (CPU)** is the control center of the computer. It follows the program you have placed in the computer's memory when processing information. The information stored in the computer's memory is used by the CPU in solving

Figure 8–2

An optical character recognition (OCR) device reads a typed page of text and transfers it to a tape or disk. The tape or disk is then processed into output.

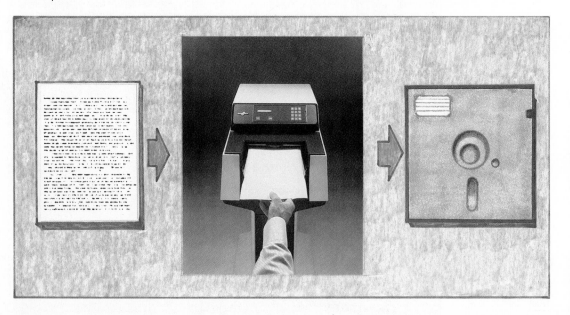

Figure 8–3
The amount of information that can be stored depends on the size of the computer's memory.

Measurements Used to Store Information
bit (smallest unit of code a computer reads)
nibble (four bits, a half-byte)
byte (eight bits)
kilobit (1024 bits)
kilobyte (1024 bytes)
megabit (a million bits)
megabyte (a million bytes)
gigabit (a billion bits)
terabit (a trillion bits)

problems. Often the processing and storing is done in a tiny wafer, or chip, no bigger than your thumbnail. **Chips** are tiny pieces of silicon, located in the CPU, which contain imprinted circuits and components. Electric pulses flow along tiny paths on the circuits which cover the chip. In a small computer, one chip may have enough circuits to do all the computer's work. A larger computer may have several chips with each chip doing a different job.

Now let's examine the problem-solving process of a computer. You may ask the computer to compare your company's profit and loss statements for the last three business years to determine

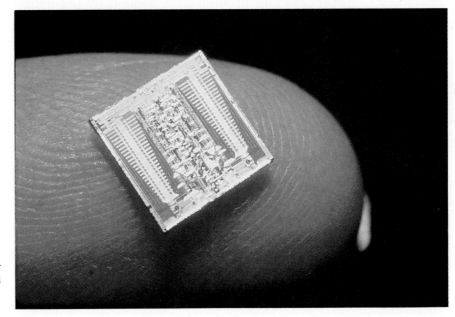

Illus. 8–2
Chips about the size of one of your fingernails make miniaturization of computers possible.

the increase or decrease of each expense. Or if you sell three different products, you might program the computer to indicate what percentage of all expenses should be assigned to each product. For the CPU to provide information necessary for a logical decision to be made in these business situations, certain steps must be followed:

1. Data concerning the profit and loss statements of the three products is recorded and placed into computer storage in a chip by using a keyboard or some other input device.
2. A program telling the computer how to use the information is also placed into computer storage inside a chip.
3. The computer operator enters any new data into storage and tells the computer to follow the program to provide the information needed.
4. When the computer begins to follow the instructions, electric pulses flow along the circuits. The pulses cause the computer to follow the program step by step using the data stored in the chip. The data is rearranged almost instantly as the computer completes the program.
5. The computer operator can request a printed copy of the rearranged data which appears on the screen.

Remember that computers do not make decisions. By following the instructions given in the program, however, computers process and provide data needed by the people who will make the decisions.

Software and Hardware

The programs and other instructional routines that direct a computer are called **software**. All other parts of the computer are called **hardware**. Examples of hardware are the keyboard, visual display terminal, chips, and the printer.

As you know, computers come in different sizes. The largest computer is called a **mainframe** computer, which can handle more instructions per second than smaller computers. A **minicomputer** is smaller and less powerful than a mainframe. The smallest computer is a microcomputer. A **microcomputer** uses a processor whose circuits are all on one integrated circuit chip. Some microcomputers will fit on the corner of a desk or in a briefcase.

Computers in Business

Information in a business office is stored on paper, on microfilm, in computers, or on magnetic disks. This stored information becomes a data base for the firm. When you request information from a business, the office worker will check the data base to answer your question.

As there is more information to store each day, many companies are putting data in the computer or on disks to save space, time, and money. To put information on disks, special equipment is needed. An example of such equipment is the disk drive. A **disk drive** is a device that stores information on a magnetic disk so the information can be recalled and used again.

A very common use of the computer in the office is the word processor. A **word processor** usually consists of a keyboard, VDT, disk drive, and printer and is designed especially for text editing. A word processor allows you to store, rearrange, and process data used in such business communications as letters, memos, reports, or standard business forms. Office workers can recall data from the disk, project it on the VDT, make changes, and print the new copy without having to retype all the data.

Illus. 8–3
Many businesses rely on computers to maintain sales and inventory records.

Increased use of word processors has resulted in changes in some offices. For example, secretaries may not have typewriters because word processing operators do most of the typing. The secretary spends more time helping with the administrative tasks such as preparing written or dictated materials to be processed, attending meetings with supervisors, or handling calls and greeting visitors. Another change is that information that must be used often by office workers can now be stored on disks to be processed on the word processor instead of in the mainframe computer. The word processor and information on the disks are easily available to the office worker, and the new storage procedure frees computer space in the larger, more expensive computer for other important information.

A Computer for Everyone

Some type of computer is now used by many people who work in offices. Managers enter a few items on a terminal keyboard, and data they need appear on a screen. Salespeople enter information about a sale electronically as the sale takes place. The computer automatically adjusts the inventory when an item is bought, sold, or returned. Although computers do the work neatly and quickly, employees still need to check the quality of the computer's work.

Salespeople can send and receive important information for you instantly although they may be a long way from their company. If you want to buy a car with special features, the salesperson can quickly tell you how many cars with those features are available and in which cities they are located. Many large businesses send memos and letters across the country in just a few seconds. Receiving this information would have taken several days just a few years ago.

Banks, grocery stores, and even gas stations rely heavily on computers for smooth operation. For example, a bank card allows you to deposit or withdraw money from your account using a computerized bank terminal. At some supermarkets, the price of a food item is recorded by a computer which reads the price and says the price aloud. Some gas stations are run by computers.

When you insert your credit card, the computer places the needed fuel into the tank, records the transaction, and then reports to the main office the amount of your purchase and the amount of gasoline on hand.

Reprinted by permission of Jefferson Communications, Inc., Reston, Va.

The Computer in Public Service

Government agencies use computers to keep the many records they need. For example, they must keep the social security records of all past and present workers in the United States and the military records of all people who have served in any branch of the military. Other service agencies are also increasing their use of computers. Medical information can be found within seconds to save lives. Police records can be sent from state to state minutes after a crime has occurred, thus aiding in solving crime. Social agencies and schools can transfer records easily when someone moves to another town.

It is important that we realize how computers are changing the business world in industry and public service. But it is more important to remember that people run computers and that people work together to keep the business world running smoothly. The computer is only a tool to help people run businesses as efficiently as possible.

*A*dding to Your Business Vocabulary

The following terms should become part of your business vocabulary. For each numbered item, find the term that has the same meaning.

central processing unit	input	printer
chips	mainframe	program
computer	memory	programmers
data	menu	software
data base	microcomputer	terminal
data processing	minicomputer	visual display terminal
disk drive	output	word processor
hardware		

1. The programs and other instructional routines that direct a computer.
2. A computer that uses a processor whose circuits are all on one integrated circuit chip.
3. A set of instructions telling the computer what to do.
4. An electronic or mechanical device designed to store, rearrange, and report information.
5. A screen that shows what you and the computer are saying to each other.
6. Facts or information.
7. Rearrangement of data in a way that makes the information more useful to you.
8. Data placed into the computer.
9. A keyboard and screen used to enter and view data.
10. The largest type of computer.
11. The decision-making part of the computer that takes the instructions from the memory and performs them.
12. Tiny pieces of silicon containing imprinted circuits and components.
13. A list of choices of commands you can perform on the computer.
14. People who write instructions for computers.
15. Everything the computer has stored.
16. A computer that is smaller and less powerful than a mainframe.
17. A term that describes the computer, terminal, disk drive units, and chips.
18. The data that exist after being processed or printed.
19. All the information a company needs to run its business.
20. An output device that produces written characters on paper.
21. A device that puts information on a magnetic disk.
22. A computer that usually consists of a keyboard, screen, disk drive, and printer designed especially for text editing.

*U*nderstanding Your Reading

1. Why do businesses need computers?
2. List two ways you can give directions to your computer.
3. Give an example of why you might use a computer during a sales transaction.
4. What is the difference between software and hardware?
5. Why might the size of a computer's

memory be important to a business?
6. Why is the central processing unit called the decision-making center of the computer?
7. How does a word processor save the office worker time?
8. Is a word processor a computer? Explain your answer.

9. Give two examples of how businesses use computers to help them save money.
10. List two types of public service work, and give an example of how the computer can be used to save either time or money for each.

*P*utting Your Business Knowledge to Work

1. In what ways do modern computers differ from early models?
2. How do you get input into the computer?
3. How does a visual display terminal help you "talk" to your computer?
4. How do you get a paper copy of data that is inside the computer?
5. Would an 8K computer be considered a computer with a large memory?
6. Which of the following items are hard-

ware and which are software?
a. visual display terminal
b. data
c. chips
d. keyboard
e. program
f. disk drive
7. What is one advantage of a computer that will fit into a briefcase?

*C*omputing Business Problems

1. Using the "measurements" chart in Figure 8–3, tell how many bytes could be stored in a 16K computer.
2. Ivan Dvorsky requested sales information from the computer about sales of Lightning pickup trucks from each of five sales districts in the United States. The computer printout is shown below. Fill in the missing blanks in the computer printout.

Region of U.S.	Trucks Allocated	Percentage Sold	Number of Trucks Sold	Current Inventory*
East	4,200	18 percent	____	____
Southern	6,425	27 percent	____	____
North Central	8,625	____	____	5,175
Southwest	____	20 percent	550	____
Northwest	100	____	____	83

*Trucks Allocated − Trucks Sold = Current Inventory

3. A minicomputer sells for $7,800. If the printer costs $2,500 and the yearly maintenance fee is $700, how much will
   a. the buyer pay for all three items if it is a cash purchase?
   b. monthly payments be if there is a 12 percent interest charge and there will be 12 payments if all items are purchased?
   c. the buyer save if there is a 2 percent discount on the computer and printer for paying cash within ten days of purchase?
4. The Second Bank of Atlanta put in a computerized walk-up window. It costs $15,000 plus $2,000 maintenance per year. If the machine replaced 2½ tellers whose salaries were $16,000 a year, how much was saved per year by installing the computer?

Stretching Your Business Knowledge

1. Businesses have different reasons for needing a computer. For example, one company uses computers to design their dolls so each doll is unique. Using recent newspaper and magazine articles, find examples of how companies use their computers to help with their businesses.
2. Part of the ad for a personal computer reads "Systems include green-phosphor monitor, 128K memory, graphic capabilities. Standard PC costs $2,595 with 320K diskette drive and $2,995 with second floppy." Explain what the following terms mean.
   a. green-phosphor monitor
   b. 128K memory
   c. graphic capabilities
   d. floppy
3. Prepare a five-person panel presentation about the evolution of the computer. The first person should be responsible for the 1890–1950 period. The last four people should each be responsible for a ten-year period which would end with the 1990s.
4. Write a brief report about computer "networking." You should find some good articles in recent magazines in your school or community library.
5. Talking to your computer is easy if you know the right language. In a five- to seven-minute oral report, share with your classmates how the BASIC language works.
6. Elizabeth Rodriguez operates a word processor at work. Sometimes she must send the same letter to over one hundred people. Sometimes she must compose letters for her employer that are for one person. She also types the company newsletter once a month. How will the word processor help her in these jobs?

CHAPTER 9

The Computer at Home

■ CHAPTER OBJECTIVES

After studying this chapter and completing the end-of-chapter activities, you will be able to:

1. Tell three ways a personal computer can help in the home.
2. Identify at least three ways to enter data into a computer.
3. List five different ways in which home software packages might help you.
4. Explain two advantages of word processors.
5. Identify five types of personal-use information available from time-sharing services.
6. Tell how the use of electronics in the home is changing American life-styles.

Kerri Adamson told her friend Julie Petroski that she had never used a computer. Actually, her home has many items with computers in them, for computers are now often used in operating other products. Most people know that home video games are operated by computers, but did you know that your digital watch and your microwave oven contain computers? Electronic calculators also store information for later use. Can you think of other examples of computers in your home?

Personal Computers

One example of a computer in the home is the personal computer. In a recent year over six million people bought personal computers to use in their homes. A **personal computer** is a small computer designed for business or home use. It usually consists of a keyboard, visual display terminal, disk drive, and printer. Some personal computers without a screen may be attached to your television screen.

Illus. 9–1
Many products
that we use
everyday have
been made
possible by
or improved
through the use
of computers.

Talking to Your Computer

A computer will do only what you tell it to do. Unfortunately, computers do not understand English. To "talk" to your computer, you should learn a simple computer language. A **computer language** is a system of letters, words, numbers, or symbols used to talk to a computer. Computer experts have devised several computer languages. Examples include FORTRAN, COBOL, BASIC, and PASCAL. A sample program, written in BASIC, and its printed output are shown on page 133. Figure 9–1 lists some of the better-known computer languages. There are, however, several ways you can communicate with your computer without knowing a computer language.

It is now possible to add extras to your home system so you can do more with your computer. For example, you may add a disk drive, which would allow you to store data on a magnetic disk so it can be read back into the computer's memory at a later time. These small, soft plastic disks are stored in protective covers and have several names such as disks, diskettes, floppies, and flexible disks. The **floppy disk,** an oxide-coated plastic disk that looks much like a phonograph record, is the most popular storage disk. Each floppy can hold a large amount of information, yet data from any part of the disk are quickly displayed on the screen when you enter the correct command.

Common Computer Languages
Ada
ALGOL (ALGOrithmic Language)
APL (A Programming Language)
ASCII (American Standard Code for Information Interchange)
BASIC (Beginner's All-purpose Symbolic Instruction Code)
COBOL (COmmon Business-Oriented Language)
FORTRAN (FORmula TRANslation)
LOGO
Pascal
PL/1 (Programming Language 1)

Figure 9–1
If you plan to do any programming, you'll need to know a computer language.

Entering Data into Your Personal Computer

There are a number of ways to enter data into a computer. Keyboarding is a commonly used method. **Keyboarding** is the entering of letters, numbers, or symbols using the terminal keyboard while keeping your eyes on the copy or the visual display terminal.

There are ways other than keyboarding to enter data into a computer. One way is to use a **mouse**, a hand-held device you point toward a certain command on the visual display terminal. For example, if you want to store a report, point the mouse toward a drawing of a filing cabinet on the screen. When the storage symbol lights up, press the "yes" command button on the mouse. The report will then move to storage in the computer. A second device, the **touch sensitive screen,** allows you to touch or point at the correct command to enter data. A third way to enter data without keyboarding is called **imaging**. Imaging occurs when a camera, or imaging system, scans a piece of paper or an object and stores an exact copy of the written data or a picture of the object in the computer system. This allows you to store entire articles, reports, or other items of personal interest without having to keyboard them. Some computers also react to voice commands.

Most personal-computer software has **graphics** capabilities which allow you to draw or display graphs or pictures on the computer screen. Many computers will plot data on a line, bar, or circle graph when you give the proper command. For example, you could compare your monthly heating expenses for two different years on two different line graphs. All you would do is

Illus. 9–2
The graphics capabilities of most software make it possible to use a computer for charting household expenses, studying a new subject, or playing a game.

enter the correct data and instructions into the computer. When the two graphs appear, you can compare the data for the two years.

One way you can use the graphics feature to produce pictures is to enter commands on the terminal to tell the computer what parts of the screen to light up. A second method is to draw on an attached graphics tablet which transfers the design to the screen. The most common method is to outline a picture on the screen with a **light pen,** an input device attached to the computer that lets you draw or write directly on the visual display terminal.

Home Software Systems

Perhaps you want to use a personal computer, but you do not know how to write programs. **Home software systems,** or special programs designed to help you use your personal computer, are available. Some can be used on only one brand of computer; some can be used on several brands of computers. Before buying software you need to know exactly what the package will do and if it is user-friendly. A **user-friendly** package will tell you when you make a mistake and how to correct it without your having to know a computer language.

If a specific task you have for the computer requires the use of software, you should buy your software packages first. Then buy a computer that can use the software you have. Many people make the mistake of buying a personal computer and then discovering there are no software packages available to perform the tasks they want to complete.

Software packages are designed to perform specific home tasks on a computer. One such task is creating and updating lists. You can keep a list of names of those people to whom you wish to mail holiday greetings, or you may wish to file your favorite recipes by food groups. The family's medical history can be kept on file, and major household purchases can be recorded by purchase date and amounts. Or you can have an inventory of your household items, insurance records, or even a complete list of books from your library.

Other software packages will help with your personal finances and will help you prepare the records we will discuss in Chapters 23 and 24. They can help you set up a budget, balance your checkbook, or prepare your taxes on your home computer. For example, a software package designed to help you complete your tax forms would guide you step-by-step through the process of filing your income taxes. The package would contain pictures of all the forms needed. As you answer each question with a "Yes," "No," or an amount of money, the programmed package would move to the next question that must be answered. It is also possible to prepare net worth statements, record investments, and keep track of stock-market activities if you have the proper software. You may wish to keep detailed automobile records that show gas and oil usage, repair costs, and mileage. Such records are easy to keep and can help you decide whether to keep, sell, or trade your car.

Some families use word processors to keep their household records or to prepare correspondence. Word processors allow people to write new copy or make lists and then make changes until they are satisfied with the copy. They can move entire paragraphs to another page, delete words or sentences, or have spelling checked for errors by pushing one or two keys. The word processor is also a useful tool for writing themes, term papers, or reports.

An important advantage that a word processor offers over a typewriter is that when the final copy is printed there will be no erasures if you have proofread carefully and made the necessary corrections. Another advantage is that you can store your copy on a diskette for later use. This allows you to recall the information and **edit**, or make changes in your copy, when you need to update it.

Home Time-sharing Services

It is possible for you to use information stored in other people's computers. Most computers can "talk" to other computers. A simple device called a **modem** allows you to connect your computer equipment to telephone lines. Your computer can then send messages to other computers and receive messages from them using the telephone.

Sometimes several people with separate terminals use the same central processing unit of a large computer. This is called **time sharing.** Time sharing allows two or more people to share information from one data bank, use each other's software, or even store information on someone else's storage devices. The user receives a monthly bill for the services from the owner of the central processing unit and the telephone company.

Certain time-sharing services allow you to sit in your home and read national headlines or want ads in another city's newspaper on your video screen. You may be able to "tap into" data banks that allow you to place an order from a special catalog at a discount or know what is happening in Congress at any time. You can even check on the times and costs of flights to another city or read the menus of restaurants in a town you plan to visit soon if the airlines or restaurants have their data available on time-sharing systems.

The Electronic Cottage

Many people see widespread use of time-sharing services as something we can have in the future. But computers are changing the way some families live now. Certain writers and sociologists see what they call the electronic cottage as changing family life-styles. An **electronic cottage** is a home in which members of the family use computers to perform personal, household, and career tasks in the home. Shopping, banking, and routine medical care handled through time-sharing services are only a few ways you and your family can use computers to make your lives more comfortable.

A growing number of people are working at home through the use of computers. Sales representatives and consultants can easily send their reports and ideas to the office by computer. This saves travel time for the worker and travel costs for the employer. It is possible that these new methods will result in less traffic and less noise and air pollution. Other ideas concerning the electronic cottage and how it might affect your life-style will be discussed in the next chapter.

This simple program in BASIC determines the average of up to three of your grades. Enter any three scores for homework, tests, or quizzes. The program will instruct the computer to compute the average and print your name and average score.

The Program

```
10 ' GRADE AVERAGE PROGRAM
20 CLS
30 INPUT "ENTER NAME OF STUDENT";N$
40 INPUT "ENTER FIRST GRADE";G1
50 INPUT "ENTER SECOND GRADE";G2
60 INPUT "ENTER THIRD GRADE";G3
70 LET A=(G1+G2+G3)/3
80 PRINT
90 PRINT
100 PRINT "NAME OF STUDENT ";N$
110 PRINT "AVERAGE GRADE ";A
120 PRINT
130 PRINT
140 INPUT "DO YOU WISH TO ENTER ANOTHER STUDENT? (Y=YES, N=NO)";Q$
150 IF Q$="Y" THEN 20
160 END
```

Sample Output

```
ENTER NAME OF STUDENT? SUSAN SMITH
ENTER FIRST GRADE? 89
ENTER SECOND GRADE? 98
ENTER THIRD GRADE? 91


NAME OF STUDENT SUSAN SMITH
AVERAGE GRADE  92.66666

DO YOU WISH TO ENTER ANOTHER STUDENT? (Y=YES, N=NO)?
```

Adding to Your Business Vocabulary

The following terms should become part of your business vocabulary. For each numbered item, find the term that has the same meaning.

computer language
edit
electronic cottage
floppy disk
graphics
home software system
imaging
keyboarding

light pen
modem
mouse
personal computer
time sharing
touch-sensitive screen
user-friendly

1. A device that lets you hook your computer equipment to telephone lines.
2. A method of entering data using a camera or device that stores a picture of written data or a picture of an object.
3. To add to, change, or delete from something you have written.
4. An input device attached to the computer that lets you draw or write directly on the computer screen.
5. A software package designed to perform home tasks on a computer.
6. A system which allows several people to use the same central processing unit.
7. Pictures or diagrams used to present data.
8. A system of letters, words, numbers, or symbols used to talk to a computer.
9. A home in which members of the family use computers to perform personal, household, or career tasks.
10. A term which describes a computer that tells you when you make a mistake and how to correct the mistake without your having to know a computer language.
11. An oxide-coated plastic storage disk.
12. A hand-held device that can be moved so it lights up a command on the visual display terminal.
13. A small computer designed for home use, although it is sometimes used in businesses.
14. A computer that allows users to point at or touch the command on the screen to give orders to the computer.
15. Entering letters, numbers, and symbols using the terminal keyboard while keeping your eyes on the copy or the visual display terminal.

Understanding Your Reading

1. What is a personal computer?
2. How can you tell if a computer is "friendly"?
3. List three types of personal record-keeping tasks a home software system package might help you do.
4. Give three examples of typing tasks you might do on a word processor that you could not do on an electric typewriter.
5. How can a mouse help you use your computer?
6. What is one major advantage of imaging?
7. How might one display his or her own

handwriting on a visual display terminal?

8. Why would you use a modem when you already have a computer?

9. How might a time-sharing service help you?

10. What are some major social problems that the electronic cottage might help solve?

*P*utting *Your Business Knowledge to Work*

1. List three tasks that a person might now complete with the help of a computer which some member of the family might have done manually in the past.

2. List three ways that you might use graphics on a computer.

3. If you were to buy a software system to help you with your budgeting, what are some questions you might ask the salesperson to assure getting a system that is best for you?

4. How could a software system help you prepare your tax forms?

5. What types of information would your family want if you had a time-sharing arrangement?

6. List as many ways as possible to talk to a computer.

7. How might a family shop by computer?

*C*omputing *Business Problems*

1. Roger Friedman bought a personal computer for $1,850. He also bought a disk-drive unit for $1,125 and a printer for $2,740. If he bought five disks at $6.00 each, how much did he pay for everything?

2. After Roger Friedman (Item 1) had his computer, disk-drive unit, and printer for a year, he decided to sell them. If he sold them for 65 percent of what he paid for them, how much did he receive for the three items?

3. Leon Fremont paid the following monthly rates for his modem service during the year.

January	$32.00	July	$32.80
February	16.50	August	19.64
March	28.38	September	27.72
April	55.13	October	29.75
May	46.05	November	76.22
June	29.60	December	45.11

a. How much was Leon's expense for the year for the modem service?

b. How much was Leon's average monthly cost for this special feature?

*S*tretching *Your Business Knowledge*

1. Using computer catalogs or computer magazines from your school library, make a list of the "extras" offered for personal computers, and identify the five most popular "extras."

2. Prepare a class bulletin board entitled "The Electronic Cottage." The visuals should consist of pictures and articles of the most recent home computer developments.

3. One of the major benefits of owning a home computer is the recreational opportunities it offers the family. Prepare a panel of five "game experts" to report to the class on the electronic games available, the goal of each game, and the method of play for each.

4. Give a three- to five-minute speech explaining features of a certain software system for a personal computer.

5. Using a copy of a typed one-page report, explain how you could use a word processor to
   a. delete copy
   b. insert copy
   c. move copy
   d. check spelling.

If there is a word processor available, you may wish to demonstrate these and other word-processing operations.

CHAPTER 10

The Challenge of Computers

■ CHAPTER OBJECTIVES ─────────────────────────

After studying this chapter and completing the end-of-chapter activities, you will be able to:

1. Explain three advantages and three disadvantages of using computers in the work force.
2. Tell how the widespread use of computers can affect your privacy.
3. Explain how the computer has made electronic mail services possible.
4. List at least three types of information that can be stored on SMART cards.
5. Explain how telecommuting will change the way some businesses operate.
6. Explain the need for computer literacy.
7. Identify future uses of the computer.

It is exciting to live in the computer age. New uses for the computer are found almost every day, and the possibilities seem endless. Medical researchers have built computerized body parts that work when the brain gives the command for action. One team of researchers expects to be able to store large amounts of information on bits of matter so small they cannot be seen with the human eye. Executives carry portable briefcase computers and work as they travel, and computers continue to get smaller. A software package has been designed that divides the computer screen into parts or windows so that you can see several computer applications at one time. Computers are even used to design unusual special effects for disaster movies and space films. It seems the computer's limits will be determined only by the human imagination.

Right now there are thousands of people planning new uses for the computer. The ideas that work will end up in toys, appliances, tools, and other items that we use every day. Perhaps you have some ideas that will expand the use of the computer.

The Challenge at Work

You may have thought that robots and other special computers existed only in science fiction stories. But **robots**, mechanical devices programmed to do routine tasks, are commonly used in many factories today. And the quality of robots is improving. An increasing number of companies are using robots for assembly line and other routine work. In 1970 there were only 200 robots in use in the United States. By 1980 that number had grown to 3,500, and it is predicted there will be at least 35,000 robots in use by 1990.

Some robots can see, hear, smell, and feel. They can even make decisions based on information they have been given. Researchers are working to expand the number of tasks a robot can perform, especially those that humans cannot do. For example, robots can work 24 hours a day without a coffee break; they can work in outer space without space suits, under water without air, and in coal mines without fear.

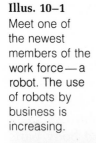

Illus. 10–1
Meet one of the newest members of the work force—a robot. The use of robots by business is increasing.

It is important to remember that a robot is a computer that depends on people to tell it what to do and to fix it when it cannot perform. While robots may replace some people on certain jobs, you should remember that the robot's existence also creates new jobs for people.

The computer is being improved to help workers in every area of business. You can find computer terminals in oil fields, warehouses, retail stores, offices, and hospitals. Such widespread

use of the computer has created a demand for more improvements, however, as the number of workers having access to the information increases.

The Ethics of Confidentiality

One of the greatest challenges facing computer users is the need to guarantee your privacy. Although it may be difficult to gain access to the information, a lot of people have learned how to break into computers' data banks. This is against the law, and some people are now in prison for stealing information from data banks of businesses or private citizens.

Existing laws are being challenged, and new laws are being written to protect your privacy. Businesses are becoming stricter about who can see and use company information. Tighter security systems are being built. Some companies change their password several times a day to protect their information. A new code of ethics is developing as a result of the growing use of the computer.

You may have seen examples of computer crimes on your favorite television show. Wide use of the computer has led to an increase in white-collar crimes, illegal acts committed by office or professional workers while they do their jobs. Some workers steal money or products from companies by changing or moving information in the computer data base. Crimes such as **piracy**, stealing and illegally copying software packages and information, are also becoming a problem. Some companies which develop software packages may lose over half their profits to information pirates who are breaking copyright laws. Laws are being updated to protect businesses from such illegal acts by workers and to handle other problems created by increased use of the computer.

Electronic Mail

Meeting the challenge of computers at work has also resulted in improvements. For example, computers are improving mail services. Let us assume Janet Roberts lives in Salem, Oregon, but is vacationing in Hawaii. John Powell, who lives in Charlotte, North Carolina, sends Janet an important letter at 10 a.m. (EST) using electronic mail services. At 11 a.m. (EST) Janet receives the message from John in her hotel room. Although John may never know that Janet is in Hawaii, she receives her message immediately.

As long as John and Janet have access to terminals and a telephone, they can use electronic mail services. When Janet left for vacation, all she had to do was command the computer to forward her incoming messages to either her hotel phone or another terminal in Hawaii. Then she simply checked at regular intervals to see if she had any incoming messages. Regular mail is sent from place to place, but **electronic mail** is sent to an electronic device to be picked up via phone or terminal at the convenience of the receiver. A paper copy of the message can be printed if it is needed.

Electronic mail services are not yet used by most businesses as they usually cost more than regular mail services. However, businesses who use the services often handle major business transactions within hours which would have taken at least five workdays by regular mail. Other businesses may have to switch to electronic mail services to remain competitive. The expected growth of electronic mail has even caused some experts to predict a paperless society.

Information Storage Cards

Perhaps we will become a society that does not carry money if some computer ideas become widely used. In France and the United States, some people use a SMART card when they shop. A **SMART card** is a plastic card with a silicon chip for storing information. The chip stores the customer's current balance with the company and credit history. Information about a new purchase can be placed on the chip at the time of purchase. SMART cards may also be used to store important medical or military information about the person carrying the card. It is also possible to have your checking and savings bank balances stored on a SMART card. If banks begin using such cards,you might never have to carry money as your money would be transferred from your bank account to the stores' accounts at the time of each purchase. The amount of the transaction would be deducted from the balance on your SMART card.

The use of the SMART card presents some challenges. The cards need to be reliable, durable, and marketable. Researchers are devoting much time and effort to make such cards workable. But an even greater challenge will result when SMART cards are improved. These cards would remove the need for much of the information in companies' mainframe computers and place the data in the wallets of the consumer. The variety of information that could be stored on SMART cards is great. This could change the manner in which many companies store their data and the number of employees needed to store and retrieve the information.

International Business

The effect of meeting such computer challenges will be felt worldwide. Imagine countries time sharing a computer. Imagine important information being passed around the world in less than a second. Satellites and computers have made the farthest point on the globe as close as the touch of a computer button. Increased world trade and dependence on other countries may result.

Imagine import and export trades taking place inside a computer with the goods being moved from the closest location, perhaps another country, to save time and money. For example, you may soon be able to order an item you want from China by using your terminal. When the Chinese marketers receive your order on their terminal, they may check their data base and discover there are five such items in Canada. They tell the Canadian importers by electronic mail to ship the item to you which you receive the next day. You pay the Chinese company, and the Chinese and Canadian companies settle their accounts later — by computer.

Computers and the Labor Force

Many people think computers are taking their jobs. What is really happening, though, is a shifting in job duties and skills needed in business and industry. For example, companies may need to retrain people who are replaced by computers to take care of the computers. **Displaced workers,** or workers who are out of

Illus. 10–2
The opportunities for exchange of information between nations are limitless through satellites such as this one.

work due to changing job demands, can be hired to perform new jobs created by the changes.

There is a good chance that the job you will have five years from now does not yet exist. The changing job market, how and where people will work, is one of the greatest challenges brought about by the widespread use of the computer. It is a challenge that government, management, and unions will have to meet.

The Challenge at Home

Such challenges and improvements are as evident in computer use at home as they are at work. Some computers now do routine household tasks. For example, a computer will adjust your home's heating and cooling system to preset temperatures. Computers can also regulate gas and oil flow in your car or remind you with a computerized voice to turn off your lights and remove the keys. The first computers to respond by voice to a human voice command exist but need to be improved before they will be in general use. Some computers not only obey your spoken command, but also answer certain questions using a limited vocabulary.

The home computer may result in the end of the nine-to-five workday. Some companies already have employees who get up from the breakfast table, go into another room, turn on their computer, and report to work. And some companies are now hiring handicapped workers who cannot leave their homes. Companies which now have **telecommuters**, or people who work from their homes by computer, have reported a large increase in the amount of work done.

The use of telecommuters results in more electronic cottages, the computer-age homes we discussed in Chapter 9. As the number of electronic cottages increases, companies may consist of a series of offices in private homes rather than in one large building in one place. It is expected that by 1990 over 18 percent of all workers will be telecommuters.

And how might the computer affect you and your education? Sociologists report the telecommuter idea also applies to students and schoolwork. There are software packages already available to tutor you in math, English, and even music. Families can use their video screen to read books located in local, state, or national libraries. It is possible that all the printed ideas in the world might soon be available to you through your computer.

The variety of applications the computer offers will result in people using the home computer more for hobbies and creative pastimes. Artists now draw and paint original art, and composers now create musical scores on computer screens. Most popular board games, word games, and action games are now available in software packages. The popularity of video games has caused researchers to try to find as many creative and fun uses of the computer as possible. Just imagine! You and three friends could play a board game while each of you sits in your own living room.

Computer Use in Specialized Fields

Illus. 10–3
Such fields as research, medicine, and space travel present special opportunities for application of computer technology.

Not only are computers having an impact at work and at home, but they also aid specialists in improving our life-styles. With computers, we can study outer space, conduct medical research, map out defense plans, solve math equations, or present traffic patterns to be used during emergencies. Genetic engineering, one of the fastest growing industries in the world which deals with experimentation with plant and animal gene characteristics, owes its rapid success to the computer. Future uses of the computer lie in our minds. And no computer begins to compare with the wonder of the human brain. Our greatest challenge is to help both reach their potentials.

Educating a Nation

As you can see from Chapters 8 and 9, computers are having and will continue to have an impact on our lives. Therefore, it is important for everyone to learn to use computers in order to have access to this vital tool. The greatest immediate challenge concerning computers is determining how to educate the people in our nation to use them properly. **Computer literacy,** or the ability to use computers to process information or solve problems, has become a major educational goal. There are computer courses taught in elementary, junior high, and senior high schools as well as in colleges and adult education programs. While you do not have to understand how a computer works to use it, you do need to know how to store, process, and retrieve information. It is becoming increasingly helpful to know a computer language. Many experts feel that computer literacy will become as important a communication skill as reading and writing.

In addition, most people will need to learn to keyboard. As we discussed in Chapter 9, keyboarding is one method of entering data into the computer. Since keyboarding is a skill you will use in your work, home, and leisure activities, it should be practiced until it is a natural skill.

A dding to Your Business Vocabulary

The following terms should become part of your business vocabulary. For each numbered item, find the term that has the same meaning.

computer literacy
displaced workers
electronic mail
piracy

robots
SMART card
telecommuters

1. A card which has a silicon chip for storing information.
2. Stealing information or copying software packages to use the information free.
3. People who are out of work because of changing job demands.
4. People who report to work from their homes by computer.
5. Messages sent to an electronic device to be picked up at the receiver's convenience.
6. The ability to use computers to process information or solve problems.
7. Mechanical devices programmed to do routine tasks.

Understanding Your Reading

1. What are some recent discoveries of ways to use computers?
2. List three advantages of robots as workers.
3. What advantage does electronic mail have over regular mail?
4. What is a paperless society?
5. What types of information might you store on a SMART card?
6. Why is piracy of software considered wrong?
7. What effect might computers have on international relations in the business world?
8. How are computers helping scientists save time?
9. How might an office building in the year 2000 differ from today's typical office?

Putting Your Business Knowledge to Work

1. Using information from the bar graph, answer the following questions:
   a. How many telecommuters are expected in 1990?
   b. How many telecommuters are expected in 2000?
   c. Which five-year period showed the greatest increase in telecommuters?

2. Give two types of work now being done by computer that used to be done by people.

3. How might a person's "right to privacy" be affected by widespread use of computers?

4. What effect might electronic mail have on the federal postal system?

5. What types of schoolwork might be completed on personal computers or word processors?

6. List three advantages you might receive from having a SMART card.

7. What effect might using a SMART card have on how businesses operate?

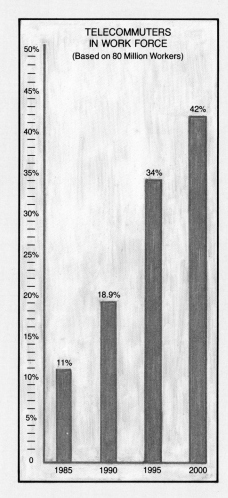

TELECOMMUTERS IN WORK FORCE
(Based on 80 Million Workers)

- 1985: 11%
- 1990: 18.9%
- 1995: 34%
- 2000: 42%

Computing Business Problems

1. Essex Corporation usually sends about 3,500 pieces of mail per month at 20¢ each. If the firm switches to electronic mail service at a cost of $1,125 per month, how much money would it save or lose?
2. Franklin Mosier can buy 500 radios from a United States business for $35 each. He can buy the same radios from a Chinese company for $27 each, but he must pay a 10 percent import tax. Which is the better buy? How much will he save by buying the cheaper radios?
3. A scientist working eight hours a day can analyze 14 specimens per hour using a computer. Before using the computer, the scientist could analyze 3 specimens per day. How many more specimens per five-day week can the scientist analyze by using the computer?
4. A robot can do as much work in eight hours as three workers earning an average of $23,000 a year. If a company buys a robot for $135,000 and uses it 24 hours a day:
   a. How many eight-hour-a-day workers will the robot replace?
   b. How much money will the company save or lose each year?
   c. How many workers can the company keep in addition to the robot without losing money?

Stretching Your Business Knowledge

1. Present an original idea to the class for which computers are not yet used. Tell the class how the product or service functions, who would use it, how you would advertise it, and how much it would cost.
2. Prepare a list of arguments for and against the use of robots on a large scale in industry. Then rank what you feel are the top three arguments in each group.
3. Discuss as a class the effects of
   a. your parents or guardians working at home with the jobs they now have.
   b. getting your education at home via computer.
   c. shopping from your home.
   d. widespread use of SMART cards.
   e. required computer literacy courses in schools.
   f. computers and robots on union membership.
4. Write a report on the changing world of work and leisure over the next ten years. Identify changes that are taking place and what they might mean before the year 2000.
5. Do you believe it is ethical to copy albums and cassette tapes onto personal tapes or to copy sheet music on copying machines to avoid buying your own copies? Explain.

CAREER CATEGORY: Computers

As you now know, computers and computer technology are influencing the lives of almost everyone, both at work and at home. No other career area offers more challenging or exciting opportunities.

Job Titles: Job titles commonly found in this career area include:

Computer Operator
Computer Programmer
Computer Systems Analyst
Computer Teacher (schools and industry)
Computer-Assisted Design (CAD) Technician
CAD Terminal Parts Cataloger
Computer-Assisted Graphics (CAG) Technician
CAG Terminal Input Artist
Computer-Assisted Manufacturing (CAM) Specialist
Computer Modeling and Simulation Technician

Computer Research and Design
Computer-Terminal Information Processor
Computerized Vocational Training (CVT) Technician
Data Processing Machine Mechanic
Editor/Proofreader
Electronic Data Processing Equipment Operator
Industrial Robot Production Technician
Sales Representative for Computer Firm
Word Processor

Employment Outlook: The United States Bureau of Labor Statistics has reported that high-technology industries will account for 17 percent of new jobs by 1995. It is predicted that at least 86 percent of workers will be service workers by the year 2000. At least half of these workers will collect, manage, and pass out information. Computer knowledge will be required in these positions.

Data processing positions are found in a wide range of industries from finance to manufacturing to electronics to transportation. Any industry with data and records to be stored, such as banks, insurance companies, or government offices must have computer departments. These organizations

need employees to enter data, code information, and manage the records. As emphasis on information storage grows, so will employment in these areas.

Future Changes: Computer use will become commonplace in most positions. Five of the 20 fastest growing occupations in the United States are in the computer field. They are data processing machine mechanics, computer programmers, computer operators, computer systems analysts, and electronic data processing equipment operators. You should know, however, that computer programmers will be needed less as input techniques are refined.

What Is Done on the Job: Workers in this area collect information, enter data, code information, and manage records; develop programs, design software, and apply different techniques, such as graphics, to software; or work as marketing representatives to sell software and/or hardware. There is great demand for teachers at all levels in the computer field, specialists to analyze existing systems and to maintain existing computers, and researchers and designers to create computers with new capabilities.

Education and Training: A recent survey concerning career opportunities stated that 56 percent of businesses were interested in hiring business majors and MBA's (people with master's degrees in business administration), and 14 percent of the companies wanted to hire liberal arts graduates. The study further indicated that most companies are not interested in hiring people who are not computer literate. A computer literate person understands how computers work,

can do basic programming, and knows how to solve problems using a computer.

Many businesses hire marketing majors and then teach them the technical information they need to use or sell software systems. Since the use of computers is expanding into many occupations, those people with training or experience in the fields of accounting, architecture, and health care will find they can make use of their background in getting jobs using computer technology. By 1990 the computer will probably be used in some way in most occupations, so any person with any specialized interest should have computer knowledge and application skills.

Salary Levels: Salaries vary widely in this career area, depending on the level of the job and training required. Most data-entry operators, for example, begin at about $10,000 a year; some people who have designed successful programs have become millionaires. Most computer salaries are in the $25,000 to $50,000 range, especially those at management levels.

For Additional Information: Additional information about this career area is available from several sources including the following:

Block, Jean Libman. *Careers for a Changing World: Communication & Media.* New York Life Insurance Company, Box 51, Madison Square Station, New York, NY 10010.

Hopke, William E. (ed.). *Encyclopedia of Careers and Vocational Guidance,* New York: Doubleday and Co., Inc., 1982.

UNIT 4
YOUR ROLE IN BUSINESS

UNIT OBJECTIVES

After studying the chapters in this unit, you will be able to:

1. *Describe our work force.*
2. *Explain how to plan for a career.*
3. *Tell how to obtain a job in the world of work.*

CHAPTER 11. You and Our Work Force

12. Planning Your Career

13. Entering the World of Work

BUSINESS BRIEF

The U.S.A.—
A Nation of Career Opportunities

You can do much to shape your own career. America continues to offer thousands of career opportunities, and new jobs emerge every year. Each individual, however, must make the most of those opportunities. For instance, a job in a fast-food restaurant could lead you into management; or it might provide the experience you need to begin your own franchise business later.

Many success stories may be drawn from actual experiences of people in our work force. The stories include men and women of all ages. As you read the following case studies, notice that each person saw an opportunity and made the most of it.

A 16-year-old student developed a system that could prevent illegal duplication of computer programs. His invention brought him earnings of over $2,000 a week. He has visions of future enterprises that may do even better.

A young assembly-line worker, through determination and careful planning, became one of the country's first black car dealership owners. He now operates his own job-training program in which he hires undereducated people at the minimum wage and gives them free job training in a variety of trades. He is a successful business person who cares for others while enjoying his own success.

One young woman had what she called a "cushy" job. After 22 years she left her job, borrowed a large sum of money, and opened the travel agency she had always dreamed about. Her agency did quite well. Soon after it opened, however, she had an automobile accident. As a result of her injuries, she has had to wear braces and use crutches to walk. In spite of her handicap, she kept her business going. In fact, she began to specialize in travel tours that would accommodate disabled persons such as herself. She offered a new and needed service. Her business now earns $2 million a year.

And here's a story about a young man whose family survived on donated food. He contracted polio early in life and grew up with severely weakened legs and arms. He and his brothers eventually were sent to a boys ranch in Texas where he was challenged to build up his body and to complete his schooling. He did both. He became interested in agriculture and rose to the executive ranks of an agriculture firm. Recently he was elected as a state senator.

This senator said this about opportunity: "One of the big advantages of living in America is freedom of choice. I tell kids, 'dream your dreams and work to make them come true.'"

CHAPTER 11

You and Our Work Force

■ CHAPTER OBJECTIVES ————————————————

After studying this chapter and completing the end-of-chapter activities, you will be able to:

1. Tell who is included in our work force.
2. Give examples of businesses in at least two of the major industry groups.
3. Give examples of jobs found in at least two worker categories.
4. Discuss several factors that are affecting the future of the work force.
5. Describe employer demand for future workers.

Jonie Williams had worked for eight years on the assembly line in an automobile plant. When the demand for new cars dropped, Jonie was laid off. After a few months of unemployment, Jonie took a job in an auto parts store. While consumers were not buying as many new cars, they were buying more parts to fix the cars they were keeping longer. Her new job does not pay as much as the plant job, but it is steady work and Jonie enjoys it.

Frank McGivern's shorthand and typewriting skills made finding an office job quite easy. It was a good-paying job in a pleasant, modern office. Two years later the company purchased some word processing equipment and reduced its need for stenographers and typists. Frank had two choices: (1) learn how to operate this new equipment and move into a new job classification, or (2) look for a job with another company where stenographers and typists still were needed. What would you have done? Frank took the special training class on the use of the word processing equipment. Today he has an important word processing job and a very good salary.

Our Work Force

There are over 110 million persons like Jonie and Frank who have jobs in our nation. There are full-time and part-time jobs, white-collar and blue-collar jobs, and goods-producing and service-producing jobs. Some jobs require a lot of education and special training while others require very little of either. Some jobs are high-paying and some are low-paying; some involve working mainly with machines and equipment while others involve working mainly with people and information.

All of the people age 16 and over who hold jobs or who are seeking jobs make up our **work force**. That work force is an important part of our economy. In spite of advancing technology and electronic innovations in business and industry, people continue to be the most important resource. Over the next decade, however, there are some sweeping changes in store for our work force.

What kinds of changes do you suppose they will be? What effect will those changes have on your career plans? What jobs are available now and what jobs will be available in the future? These are important questions. This chapter presents information that will help you answer questions such as these as you consider our work force and your role in it.

Where the Jobs Are Now

The business world is made up of thousands of companies, industries, and jobs. There are many ways to determine which jobs are or will be in demand. Our federal government's Department of Labor, through its **Bureau of Labor Statistics (BLS)**, researches thousands of different types of jobs held by persons in our work force. The BLS publishes information about the current and projected status of those jobs. Two BLS publications, *The Occupational Outlook Handbook* and the *Occupational Outlook Quarterly*, contain up-to-date information about many kinds of jobs.

Jobs by Industry Groups

One way the BLS reports its findings is by groups of industries. Figure 11–1 shows the percent of persons employed in each of nine industry groups. You will notice that three of those industries — services, manufacturing, and wholesale and retail trade — employ most of the workers. Those three industries include over 73 percent of all workers.

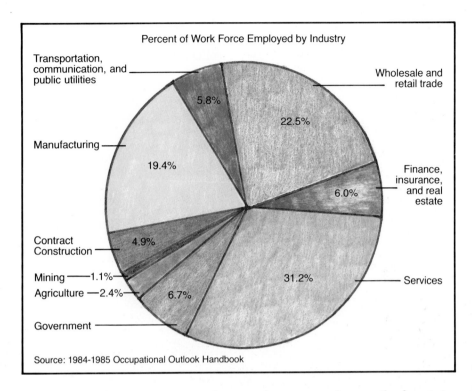

Percent of Work Force Employed by Industry

Transportation, communication, and public utilities — 5.8%

Wholesale and retail trade — 22.5%

Manufacturing — 19.4%

Finance, insurance, and real estate — 6.0%

Contract Construction — 4.9%

Mining — 1.1%

Agriculture — 2.4%

Government — 6.7%

Services — 31.2%

Source: 1984-1985 Occupational Outlook Handbook

Figure 11–1
Employment by industry group. Can you identify one company, organization, or agency in each group?

These groups are similar to those you learned about in Chapter 5. Here are some examples of the functions of businesses in each of the three largest industry groups.

Wholesale and Retail Trade: provide for the distribution and sale of goods from producers to retailers; sell goods and services to consumers.

Manufacturing: produces goods, such as automobiles, television sets, computers, clothing, food products, and medicine.

Services: operate businesses such as hotels, restaurants, ski lifts, repair shops, hospitals, barber shops, and beauty salons.

Jobs by Worker Categories

Another way of studying our work force is to look at worker categories. These categories may be the most helpful to you in looking at a possible career. Seven categories used by the BLS are shown in Figure 11–2. You will notice that the categories of "service," "marketing and sales," and "administrative support" have the largest number of workers. Jobs found in these categories include:

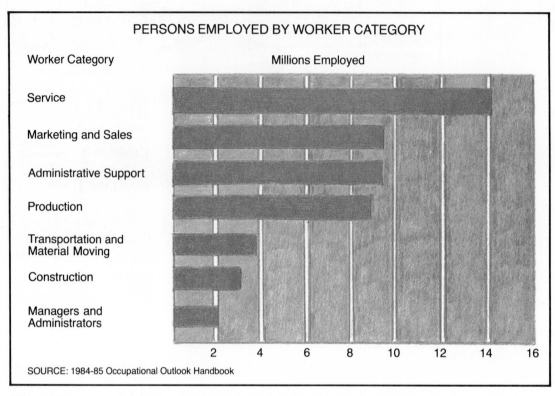

PERSONS EMPLOYED BY WORKER CATEGORY

Worker Category   Millions Employed

Service

Marketing and Sales

Administrative Support

Production

Transportation and
Material Moving

Construction

Managers and
Administrators

2   4   6   8   10   12   14   16

SOURCE: 1984-85 Occupational Outlook Handbook

Figure 11–2
You probably know people employed in each of the worker categories. Why not ask them about the work they do.

Service: social workers, hotel clerks, fire fighters, waiters and waitresses.

Marketing and Sales: retail salespersons, buyers, insurance salespersons, real estate brokers, advertising workers, graphic designers, securities brokers, and travel agents.

Administrative Support: secretaries, stenographers, typists, word processing operators, general clerks, payroll clerks, personnel clerks, credit clerks, and shipping/receiving clerks.

White-Collar and Blue-Collar Jobs

Two categories that are very broad and have been used traditionally are white-collar and blue-collar. These categories separate our work force into two large groups. **White-collar** workers are persons whose work involves a lot of contact with people and who work with or process information. Some white-collar workers are called "knowledge workers." Some are employed in offices and stores. Included are professional, managerial, and clerical workers. White-collar workers make up over half of our work force.

"**Blue-collar**" workers are persons whose work involves the operation of machinery and equipment. They are employed in factories, shops, and on construction sites. Blue-collar workers produce goods and materials.

Both white-collar and blue-collar workers are important in our work force. Both kinds of workers are needed to help meet our needs and wants. Both also are affected by factors which influence the future of the labor market.

Factors Affecting the Future of Jobs

The jobs held by persons in our work force are subject to a variety of factors that cause jobs to change. Some of these may cause jobs to be eliminated while others will cause jobs to be modified, often requiring employees to have more skills and training. New technology, economic conditions, and consumer preferences are major factors.

New Technology

New technology refers to the use of automated machinery and electronic equipment to help increase the efficiency of work being done. Computers, lasers, robots, and information processing equipment are examples of new technology. Robots and lasers are being used more and more in manufacturing plants. Computers, word and information processing, and telecommunications are being used in

Illus. 11–1
New technology will bring about exciting employment opportunities. However, workers may need to develop new skills.

offices. Retail stores are using computerized systems and services to handle sales and merchandise controls. These and other uses of new technology affect workers and their jobs.

Factory Work

The introduction of assembly lines in factories many years ago changed the nature of blue-collar work. The specialization of labor became possible with workers becoming very good at completing just one or two processes out of a larger series that developed a product. More goods were produced in less time, and higher wages could be paid. However, many of the jobs were routine and boring and employees became dissatisfied. Today, modern robots are taking over many of the unskilled jobs formerly held by assembly-line workers. Robots someday will perform more complicated job functions and other jobs will be changed or eliminated.

On the positive side of the increasing use of robots in the work place is the fact that robots have to be built and maintained. New kinds of workers are needed to develop robots and keep them working. New technology often calls for new kinds of workers, and those already employed may get new assignments.

Office Work

As you learned in Chapter 8, the use of computers in offices is growing. Computers were first used in offices over three decades ago. Today, since microcomputers and remote video display terminals are common, a dramatic change has occurred in many office jobs. Through the use of video display terminals at workers' desks, information is available almost instantly when the worker needs it. File clerks and others who used to file, locate, and deliver information are no longer needed for that purpose.

You also have learned that word processors are common in offices today. **Word processing** is an office function that involves using a word processor, or a microcomputer with a word processing software package, to produce reports, letters, memoranda, and other forms of written communication. The whole process of producing words in written form has changed. Revising written reports has been made easier, and final copies can be reproduced speedily on printers. In particular, the work of secretaries and typists has been altered. It is important for some office workers to be good at using special word processing equipment, and additional training often is required.

The use of telecommunications is another important change coming to modern offices. **Telecommunications** is a system which utilizes television, telephones, communications satellites, computers, and other electronic devices to allow both oral and visual communication to take place. With telecommunications, meetings and conferences can be held without persons having to travel to central locations. Money is saved on travel, and more time is available for decision making and other important office tasks.

Retail Sales Work

Retail salespeople are needed to assist customers in selecting a product or service. However, a good deal of the behind-the-scenes work in stores and shopping centers has been affected by new technology. Computerized cash registers automatically keep inventories of merchandise up-to-date. Analyses of sales are produced from computerized data recorded through cash registers as sales are made throughout the day. And, in some retail outlets, automated machines dispense the products to the customers. Some even "speak" a friendly message as the customer makes a selection.

While it is evident that many workers and their jobs are affected by new technology, they are not all affected in the same way. Another factor which has an important effect on workers and their jobs is the changing condition of our economy.

Economic Conditions Affect Jobs and Workers

The general condition of the economy affects both jobs and persons in our work force. Jobs are created to produce needed goods and services. As the demand for those goods and services changes, jobs are affected accordingly.

Reprinted by permission of *Jefferson Communications, Inc., Reston, Va.*

A Changing Economy

When businesses are expanding and consumers are buying more and more goods and services, new jobs are created to meet the growing demand. As workers earn more money, they spend more on goods and services which they need, and the growing demand continues.

High prices cause consumers to decrease their buying. When interest rates increase and both businesses and consumers find it difficult to borrow money or to buy on credit, demand for goods and services decreases. As a result, jobs may be eliminated or the number of workers reduced. The workers in turn have less money to spend for their needs and wants and are not sure of their future earnings. This tendency to spend less further decreases demand for goods and services.

Business Costs

The cost of running a business also affects jobs and workers. When profits begin to decrease, the business must look for ways to improve its profits. Installing new equipment or systems that allow workers to produce more goods and services in less time may be one solution. In the end, there may be a decrease in the number of workers employed.

Consumer Preferences

Another factor affecting jobs and workers is the preference that consumers have for one product or service over another. Jobs are affected by **derived demand**; that is, jobs are created or eliminated by consumer demand. Jobs disappear if the product that workers produce is no longer in demand. For instance, if most consumers decided to wear clothing made of blue denim, workers who make blue denim clothing will be needed. If consumer choice shifts away from blue denim, these workers again will be affected. The "dollar vote" which you learned about in Chapter 3 affects workers and their jobs.

Sometimes new products entering the market make those already available obsolete — at least in the mind of the consumer. Workers producing the old product may find that their jobs will disappear while new jobs will be created by the demand for the new product. These are the displaced workers we discussed in Chapter 10. Knowing what product demands will be and knowing how to respond to the changing demands are major tasks facing business managers. The job you will have in the future will be affected in some way by these and other factors.

The Future Outlook for Jobs

Given the factors which affect jobs, is it possible to look ahead and determine which jobs will be needed in the future? That is not a simple thing to do. Some of the factors which affect jobs are difficult to predict. However, there are some estimates of future job needs that are worth knowing about. The BLS, governmental agencies, and some private groups study our work force to determine what may happen to the job market in the future. They can tell us what jobs appear to be in the greatest future demand and what is needed to prepare for those jobs. There are some growth areas.

Growth Areas

It is estimated that white-collar jobs will grow faster than will blue-collar jobs. In robot manufacturing, for instance, two-thirds of the work force are white-collar workers. In most manufacturing companies, white-collar workers have been less than one-third of the work force.

As shown in Figure 11–3, the service-producing industries will grow the most in the coming years. The wholesale and retail

Figure 11–3
The service-producing industries have shown tremendous growth in the United States. That growth is likely to continue.

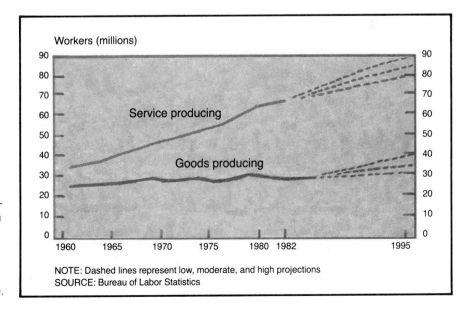

NOTE: Dashed lines represent low, moderate, and high projections
SOURCE: Bureau of Labor Statistics

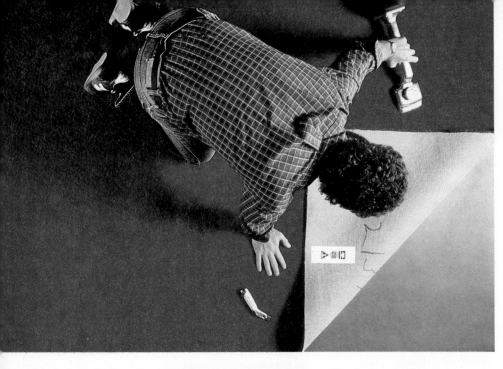

Illus. 11–2
Services may
take many forms.
How many can
you name?

trade, services, and manufacturing industry groups will continue to employ the greatest number of workers.

Workers Needed

An important part of planning, of course, is to know in which specific job areas there will be future needs. Estimates of the need for workers in any particular job category are based upon two major factors: (1) the number of new jobs to be created and (2) the number of people who will be replaced because of transfers and separations. Jobs for which future demand will very likely be above average include secretaries, general office clerks, salespeople, legal assistants, and word processing operators.

Education and Training

Another finding by the BLS and other researchers is that employers will look for persons who have a good general education and who have been trained in some specific skill area. There are many reasons for this demand by employers. New technology, competition in the market place, and the need to make a reasonable profit require that businesses employ persons who can perform their job tasks well. The increased education and training of employees are two factors that help employers use technology effectively, remain competitive, and earn a reasonable profit. And profitable businesses provide jobs.

Looking Ahead

Looking ahead to the job you will seek and the career area that is right for you is an important process. When exploring a career area, there are some important things for you to keep in mind. Chapter 12 will give you some helpful ideas on studying careers to find out which one may be best for you.

Adding to Your Business Vocabulary

The following terms should become part of your business vocabulary. For each numbered item, find the term that has the same meaning.

Bureau of Labor Statistics (BLS)
blue-collar workers
derived demand
new technology

telecommunications
word processing
white-collar workers
work force

1. The use of automated machinery and electronic equipment to help increase the efficiency of work being done.
2. All of the people aged 16 years and over who hold jobs or who are seeking jobs.
3. A system which utilizes television, telephones, communications satellites, computers and other electronic devices to allow both oral and visual communication to take place.
4. An organization which researches over 20,000 different jobs held by persons in our work force.
5. Persons whose work generally involves a lot of contact with people and who process information.
6. Causes jobs to be created or eliminated as a result of what consumers buy or do not buy.
7. Persons whose work primarily involves working with materials and using equipment and machinery.
8. An office function that involves using a word processor, or microcomputer with a word processing software package to produce written material rapidly.

Understanding Your Reading

1. How many workers are in our work force?
2. What is the most important resource in our world of work?
3. Name two publications of the BLS that deal with our work force.
4. List the three industries that employ 75 percent of the workers.
5. What are the three worker categories that have the largest number of workers?
6. What are the two major factors affecting the future of jobs?
7. Describe some of the new technologies that are causing changes in the world of work.

8. What effect are robots having on factory work?

9. How do changing economic conditions affect jobs?

10. How do consumer preferences affect jobs?

11. What are two major factors which determine the need for workers in a particular job category?

12. Why will there be a future demand for persons with good education and specific training?

Putting Your Business Knowledge to Work

1. List ways in which the *Occupational Outlook Handbook* or the *Occupational Outlook Quarterly* can help you.

2. Identify businesses in your local community that operate in each of the three industries that employ most of the workers in our nation. With which of these businesses do you have the most frequent contact?

3. What examples are there of persons in your school who work in the worker categories having the largest number of workers? List as many of their job titles as you can.

4. Give examples of new technology, in addition to those mentioned in the text, that affect jobs in our work force.

5. Can you think of one or more businesses in your community that have had to make major changes, or even close down, because of changes in consumer preferences or because of bad economic conditions? Identify as many as possible and explain what caused them to change or close down.

Computing Business Problems

1. The need for secretaries is expected to increase by .5 million workers in 10 years. If there now are 2.5 million secretaries, how many will there be in 10 years? How many secretaries will be needed if the same number of new secretaries are added in a second 10-year period?

2. Examine the two charts on page 163 and answer the following questions:
   a. How many white-collar workers and how many blue-collar workers are employed in each of the four industries?
   b. What is the total number of blue-collar and white-collar workers in these four industries?

3. One of the large stores in a shopping center employs 48 salespeople, 6 department managers, 2 credit clerks, 2 secretaries, 1 accountant, and 1 manager.
   a. How many employees, including the store manager, are there in this store?
   b. If the credit clerks, secretaries, and accountant make up the office staff, the office staff is what percent of all employees?
   c. If two-thirds of the salespeople work part time, how many part-time salespeople are there? How many salespeople are full-time workers?

4. If a community has 4,000 people employed and they are distributed in the same proportion as shown in Figure 11-1, how many people are employed in government? in services? in wholesale and retail trade? in manufacturing? What is the total number of workers employed

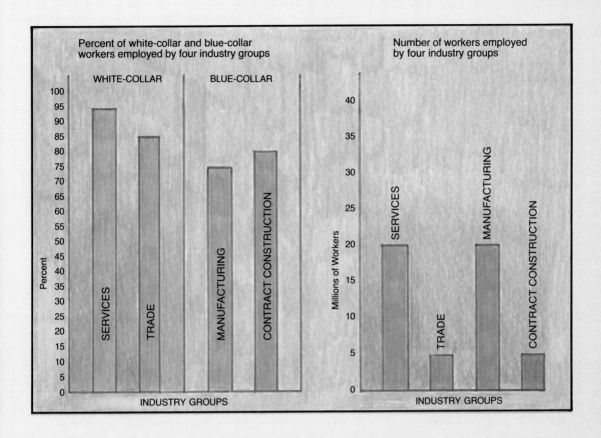

Percent of white-collar and blue-collar workers employed by four industry groups

Number of workers employed by four industry groups

in those four industries? How many people in this community are employed in the remaining five industries?

Stretching Your Business Knowledge

1. The demand for some workers depends in part on the preferences of consumers for certain goods and services. Make a list of some of the goods and services you and your friends demand that help to create jobs. Then identify the kinds of jobs that are affected. Find examples of jobs in your community that have disappeared because of changes in demand for goods and services.

2. The percentage of women entering the work force has been increasing while the percentage of men in the work force has been decreasing. What are some of the reasons for this change? What effect does this change have on employment opportunities for both men and women? Name some specific jobs or careers in which women are employed in greater numbers today than in the past.

3. Find out about the impact of new technology on businesses and industries in your community. Talk with business owners, managers, and employees about their experiences with new technology and the effect it has had on their jobs, if any.

CHAPTER 12

*P*lanning Your Career

■ CHAPTER OBJECTIVES ────────────────────────

After reading this chapter and completing the end-of-chapter activities, you will be able to:

1. Explain why career planning is important for students.
2. List at least four important sources of information about careers.
3. Identify at least two topics that should be discussed in a career information interview.
4. State three questions that can help students think through their values.
5. Suggest two ways students can learn about their talents and abilities.
6. Describe five steps to follow in making a career decision.

The mouse in Figure 12-1 has a difficult job: how to get through the maze and end up where he wants to be. He is trying to do it the easy way, but he will have to work harder to solve the problem.

The world of work sometimes appears to be a maze like the one in our cartoon. It can be a puzzle with a lot of pieces that must eventually fit together. Finding the job that is right for you among thousands of different jobs in the world of work is not an easy task. A study of careers is necessary before good career decisions can be made.

Planning your career is important, and the planning should begin while you are in school. Learning about our work force, as you did in Chapter 11, is a good beginning. The next step in getting through the maze of careers is to take the right approach in planning your career.

Career planning involves looking into possible careers. It also means looking at yourself and making decisions about what you want or do not want to do in your future career.

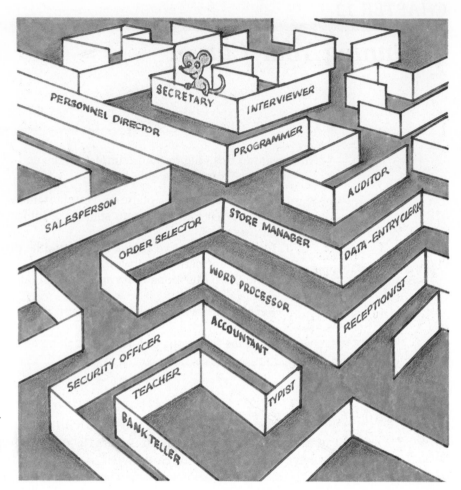

Figure 12–1
Don't cheat your-
self. Investigate
all of the careers
that might be of
interest to you.

Looking into Careers

Looking into careers means learning specific facts about jobs. It means finding out the duties performed, the education and training required, and the wages paid in different jobs. It means learning about what it takes to succeed and about the advantages and disadvantages of certain career areas. Done correctly, your job study will answer some important questions.

Career planning includes making a formal study of careers. You don't just decide to study careers for one day or one week. The study of careers is a continuous process. Because there are always new career opportunities to learn about, it even continues after you begin a career. Many people view learning about careers as a life-long activity.

There are several sources of help for you right in your school and community. Some information will cover careers in general. Other information will be more specific about careers in your town or state. You should look into both.

Sources of Information

Your own school is a good place to start looking for information about careers. Many school libraries have career resource materials. You may find the *Occupational Outlook Quarterly* or other publications of the Department of Labor and the BLS to be quite helpful. For instance, the *Occupational Outlook Handbook* gives detailed information on 250 occupations. Included are job duties, working conditions, education and training requirements, advancement possibilities, employment outlook, earnings, and a list of other occupations which require similar aptitudes, interests, or training.

Career World magazine publishes information about a variety of careers, often looking at careers of the future. The *Encyclopedia of Careers* can give you basic information about many jobs and career areas. Organizations, such as The Administrative Management Society (AMS) and the Insurance Information Institute, publish good materials dealing with their particular career areas. The AMS publication, *The Office and You,* is helpful for those interested in business careers.

Illus. 12–1
There are many publications available to help you in your search for career information. Many can be found in your school library.

Some books are written specifically to help students with career planning. *Business Careers, Secretarial and Office Careers, Accounting and Data Processing Careers,* and *Marketing Careers* are four books that give some helpful information on planning a career in business. Books that deal with other career areas are also available. Materials such as these often include activities that help with career planning.

Many schools have career resource centers. Sometimes they are located in the library, sometimes in the counseling office, and at times in departments such as Business Education. These resource centers normally have a wide variety of materials available. You may find folders, pamphlets, films, and filmstrips on careers. Or you may find video display terminals in your school hooked to centralized computer files of career and education information.

Newspaper help-wanted ads also can be of help. Reading the help-wanted ads in your local newspaper or any large metropolitan paper can give you a good idea of what jobs are in demand. You also can learn what employers are looking for in the people they hire. Sometimes ranges of beginning salaries are shown. Such information is helpful in career planning.

Another good source of information in many communities is the **government employment office**. These offices, which are tax supported, help people find jobs and provide information about careers. Employers who need workers often contact government employment offices for help. They may also contact private employment agencies for the help they need. Employment offices can help you get up-to-date information about your local job market. They also can help you look for part-time, summer, or full-time work.

Experience in the World of Work

Part-time or summer jobs are also good sources of information. You can get good information by being alert to what is going on around you on your job. You may already have had experiences with part-time or summer jobs. What did they teach you about certain jobs and the work that must be done?

Career information interviews are an excellent way to get valuable information about careers. A **career information interview** is a planned discussion with a worker to find out about the work that person does, the preparation necessary for that career, and the person's feelings about his or her career. Interviews will help you

Illus. 12–2
Have you held any part-time or summer jobs? They can provide a wealth of career information and be fun too!

gain insight into what really goes on in a career area. Most workers like to talk about their career experiences. Interviews often reveal how important it is to select and prepare for the right career.

Before you begin a career information interview, think about the questions you want to ask. Here are some questions you may want to ask:

1. How did you get your present job? Did other jobs lead you to this one? What were those jobs?
2. In what ways do you find your job to be satisfying? In what ways is it dissatisfying?
3. What are some tasks you perform in your job?
4. In what ways do you think your job is better than other jobs? In what ways is it not as good?
5. What do you believe are some of the most important qualifications for the work you do? What training and education are needed?
6. What advice would you give a young person who is considering this line of work?

You should keep notes on what you learn through career information interviews. The job experiences of others will provide important career planning information that you will continue to find valuable.

Illus. 12–3
Plan to interview several people about the career areas in which you are interested. Most people will be happy to talk with you about their jobs.

Local and Distant Careers

As you consider your future career, you may have to decide whether you want to work in the area in which you live now or whether you are willing to move to where the job you want is located. There may be reasons why you would prefer to live and work near your home. However, mobility is often necessary for persons to successfully pursue the careers of their choice.

Mobility is the willingness and ability to move where jobs are located. The lack of mobility of our work force leads to locational unemployment. **Locational unemployment** occurs when jobs are available in one place but go unfilled because those who are qualified to fill those jobs live elsewhere and are not mobile.

Your career goals and your feelings about where you live influence your mobility. You may prefer to work and live where your family and friends live. Your goals and personal qualities are important in several ways when it comes to career planning. You need to know about careers and about yourself.

Looking At Yourself

As you look into careers and learn about jobs and the work involved, you get a feel for certain jobs and career areas. You may like or dislike certain jobs and career areas without knowing why. There are personal aspects of career planning and decision making that are important. Becoming aware of these personal aspects and learning about yourself in the process are important in career planning.

Your Goals and Values

Your own **values**, the things that are important to you in life, must be considered along with facts about jobs and careers. There are a number of ways you can learn about your own value system. Your counselors or business teachers may have exercises or activities that can help you learn about your values. These exercises show how you rank items such as prestige, money, power, achievement, independence, leadership, security, or belonging. Each of these may influence you, directly or indirectly, when you select your job or career.

You can begin to check out some of your values by answering certain questions. Your answers will show which values you consider important and how you react in certain situations. Each answer should be thought through and analyzed. Here are some examples of those kinds of questions:

- Is it important to me to earn a lot of money?
- Am I mainly interested in work that provides a service for others?
- Is it important for me to have a job that others think is important even if I don't really care for it?
- Would I be willing to start in a job that pays a lower salary than another if that job were more challenging and offered better opportunities for future advancement?

There may be other questions you can think of, but these will give you a good start.

Another activity is to consider what you would do if someone gave you a large sum of money to be used in any way you desire. Would you start your own business? Or would you hire a jet and travel throughout the world? Would you develop a foundation to support athletics for underprivileged children? Or would you help build up a run-down neighborhood? Would you buy the biggest wardrobe someone your age ever had? Your answers will tell you something about your personal values.

Some jobs and careers will let you achieve your goals, use your talents and abilities, and fit your values. Those jobs bring the highest levels of satisfaction to the worker. Your talents and abilities determine to a large extent the career that you should follow.

Your Talents and Abilities

Each of us has certain talents and abilities. You may have special talents and abilities that your friends and classmates do not have. Your talents and abilities, along with your career goals and interests, are important in career planning.

There are a number of ways you can learn about your own abilities. You can begin by reviewing the courses you have taken and the grades you received in school. What kinds of courses have you taken? In which ones have you done your best work? Which courses have been easiest for you? Which have been the most difficult? Answers to questions such as these will identify your talents and abilities.

Your courses and your grades also tell you something about your likes and dislikes. You may have talent and ability but are not applying yourself. To get a good look at your talents and abilities, you should discuss this matter with your parents, counselors, teachers, and friends.

Just as there are exercises to tell you about your values, there are also tests and exercises that analyze your abilities. Your school counselors may have these tests available. Sometimes employment agencies have applicants take these special tests so that they can better match people with jobs requiring certain talents and abilities.

Abilities can be developed; that is an important point to keep in mind. If you are weak in a certain area, you may want to take courses that will improve that area. Some part-time jobs can give you important experiences in areas where you may have minor weaknesses. Weak areas should be strengthened before you go into full-time work.

Once you know your strengths and weaknesses, you can plan your courses and future activities to help you grow toward your chosen career. With this and other information gained from career planning, you can make some important career decisions.

Illus. 12–4
Some people find that their talents and abilities can benefit others and lead to a rewarding career too.

Making a Career Decision

Each person must eventually make a career decision. Too often the decision is made when full-time work begins. But that is too late, especially if certain training and education are required.

Making initial career decisions while you are in school has many advantages. One advantage is that in school you have a lot of good information readily available. But more important, early career planning will help you select the right courses. An early career decision can also encourage you to become involved with organizations such as Future Business Leaders of America, Distributive Education Clubs of America, and Junior Achievement which teach you about business and help you prepare for a career.

Your decision may be a **tentative career decision**, that is, a decision that is subject to change or modification as new information is received. A tentative decision is much better than no decision at all. Your career decision will give you a direction that is needed, and you will find a new kind of interest in what you do.

How can you be sure that you are making the best career decision possible? Well, there is no way to guarantee a perfect decision. But good decisions generally are made by those who follow the right steps. Here are some steps to follow in making your career decision:

1. Get as much information as you can.
2. Sort out and think about what you learned about careers and about yourself.
3. Think about different plans of action and what might happen if you follow each one.
4. Select what seems to be the best plan of action and follow it.
5. Evaluate your career decision from time to time.

Your search for the right career could go on for a long time. In the years ahead, some of your values and goals will change. You will develop new interests and abilities. New jobs and careers will come along for you to learn about. You should be ready to make career-decision changes when they are called for in your situation.

Chris Jones: A Dilemma

Chris Jones often thought about career planning. Still, there always were so many other things to do and to think about. In a business class, Chris prepared a career report on becoming a corporation lawyer and had learned something about that career. But Chris soon forgot about it after the career section was completed.

During the last semester of Chris's senior year, becoming a legal secretary or legal assistant became a definite career goal. But Chris had failed to plan early enough. Important business education courses, such as typewriting, shorthand, word processing, office procedures, accounting, and business law had not been taken. Too many electives had been taken haphazardly. Chris lacked skills and experience to offer an employer.

Chris had not planned on going to college. No scholarships were available, and no money had been saved for tuition and other costs of higher education. Now what should Chris do? How long will it take Chris to get ready for the desired legal office job? Career planning, with a career decision made in a timely fashion, could have saved Chris from this dilemma. Will you avoid this kind of problem?

Adding to Your Business Vocabulary

The following terms should become part of your business vocabulary. For each numbered item, find the term that has the same meaning.

career information interview
career planning
government employment office
locational unemployment

mobility
tentative career decisions
values

1. Looking into careers, looking at yourself in terms of careers, and making decisions about a future career.
2. A tax-supported office which helps people find jobs and gives out information about careers.
3. A planned discussion with a worker to find out about the work that person does, the preparation necessary for that career, and the person's feelings about that career.

4. The willingness and ability to move where jobs are located.
5. Jobs are available in one place but go unfilled because workers who are qualified live elsewhere.
6. The things that are important to you in life.
7. A career decision subject to modification or change when new information is received.

Understanding Your Reading

1. What does looking into careers involve?
2. What are several sources of information about careers?
3. Name three books that are written specifically about careers.
4. Explain how a career resource center can be helpful.
5. What help does a government employment office offer?
6. What is the purpose of a career information interview? What are some questions

that should be asked?
7. Why is mobility important in planning your career?
8. How can you learn about your value system?
9. How can courses and grades tell you something about your talents and abilities?
10. What are the five steps in making a good career decision?

Putting Your Business Knowledge to Work

1. What can be learned from working on a part-time or summer job that will help you in career planning?
2. What are materials you would expect to

find in a career resource center? State how two or three of those materials would be used in a study of careers.
3. What would you look for in want ads that

could help you learn about jobs that are in demand? What other sources of information can tell you about jobs that are in demand locally and in general?

4. Why is it important to write out questions before you interview a worker? Why is it important to be a good listener?

5. Give examples of ways you can develop your talents and abilities to help you get ready for a career.

6. Why are career decisions called tentative rather than final, once-and-for-all decisions?

7. What are some of the ways that your value system might affect your career decision?

Computing Business Problems

1. Steve Rupp got a job in a hospital as a medical secretary. He had to take extra courses at a community college for this job. These courses cost him $600. He earns $200 a week and can use one-fourth of his earnings for his college expenses.
   a. How many weeks will it take him to pay for his community college work?
   b. If he works 40 hours a week, what is his hourly rate of pay?

2. Laura Romano is trying to decide whether or not to become a legal assistant. The program she desires would require her to go to school for three more years after high school. The tuition would cost $1,800 each year. Her room and board would cost $2,100 a year. And her books and materials would be about $900 for the three-year period.
   a. What will be the total cost of the three-year course?
   b. If Laura got a part-time job to pay for her schooling and earned $6.00 per hour, how many hours would she have to work to pay for all of the above costs?

3. Dora DeTellem wants to save $1,800. Her job pays $300 per week. Taxes take 25 percent of her salary, and living expenses take another 60 percent.
   a. If she saves the balance of her salary, how many weeks will it take her to save $1,800?
   b. If her living expenses increase to 70 percent of her salary, how long will it take her to achieve her savings goal?

4. Bill Rolfsen's job as a receiving clerk involves working with figures. In just a few hours he received the following shipments:
   a. One order that came in said that the shipment was 4 meters long and 2 meters wide. Approximately how many feet long and how many feet wide was the shipment?
   b. Another sheet listed an order for 10 bottles which held 1 liter each of a new cleaning fluid. Approximately how many quarts of cleaning fluid were in that order?
   c. A box that was delivered was marked to show that it weighed 2 kilograms. That seemed very heavy to Bill. Do you think that he should be able to lift that box without much difficulty? Why or why not?

*S**tretching Your Business Knowledge***

1. Make a list of all of the career resources in your school that could be of help to someone looking into careers. Be sure to check reference shelves, the card catalog, and periodicals in the library or resource center. Your counselor's office and the Business Education Department are also places to look for materials to be included on your list.

2. Interview a worker whose occupation would be of interest to you. Develop an interview outline to help you ask the right questions. Write a report of the interview after you have completed it.

3. Write a report on a part-time job that you have now or one that you had and can still remember. Describe the job in general and then tell about some of the specific things that you had to do on the job. Write some comments about what you liked best and what you liked least about the work, the people with whom you worked, and the working conditions. End your report by writing a one-paragraph summary of how this part-time job has helped or could help you plan for your future.

4. Interview a job counselor (sometimes called a placement counselor) from a government employment agency or from your school district. Ask about jobs that are available today and those that are expected to be available in the future. You might include questions about some of the changes that have taken place in the job market in the past few years. After you have completed your interview, write a report on your findings.

5. From the list of library resources you compiled in question 1, select two or three pamphlets or books that describe a job about which you know nothing or very little. Read those materials and write a report on why you feel that career could be a good one for you or someone else (even if you decide it is not the one for you). List at least three advantages and three disadvantages of that job. Give a report to the class on your findings.

6. Locate one or more exercises that allow you to test or evaluate your own personal values. Complete the tests or exercises. Then write a short report on how what you have learned may influence you in your career decision. Be as specific as possible in relating how your values concerning such things as power, independence, security, money, and prestige would influence your decision on which career to pursue or reject.

CHAPTER 13

*E*ntering the World of Work

■ CHAPTER OBJECTIVES ————————————

After studying this chapter and completing the end-of-chapter activities, you will be able to:

1. Identify three sources of information about job leads.
2. Describe what should be included in a letter of application.
3. Explain what should be included in a personal data sheet.
4. Properly fill out a job application form.
5. List at least four questions often asked in an employment interview.
6. State at least five actions an applicant can take that will contribute to an effective interview.

Jamie Johnson walked into an employment office and was obviously nervous. Getting off to a bad start was one of Jamie's consistent traits. He looked over the application form and asked himself: "What is my social security number?" "Where have I worked before?" "What are the names and addresses of my former employers?" Jamie tried to think of the answers but could not. He was unprepared for the questions that appeared on the application. There also was a question about what job was desired and what pay was expected. Jamie decided to leave the office quietly and come back some other time.

Tracy Wilson looked over the job application form and began filling it out. It asked for printing or typing, so she printed as neatly as she could. Tracy used her personal data sheet which included the names and addresses of former employers, the dates worked, and the names and addresses of people who had given permission to be used as personal references. After filling out the application form, Tracy read it over once more to be sure she had completed every item. She handed it back to the personnel supervisor and was told to wait a few minutes for the interview. While waiting, Tracy read through several pamphlets that gave information about the company and its operation.

Who do you think is likely to get a job first? Jamie or Tracy? Jamie needs to be better prepared the next time he applies for a job. And preparation is the first step in getting started on a career.

Getting Into Your Work Career

You actually have one kind of a career under way right now: your career as a student. Doing a good job in school will be important later when you begin your full-time work career. The record you are building as a student—your attendance, the courses you take, the grades you earn, and the activities in which you participate—will someday be considered by an employer.

When and how does your work career begin? It generally begins after you graduate and get your first full-time job in the area in which you have planned your career. However, getting a part-time job in an area related to your career goal is also a beginning of that career. Whether you look for part-time or full-time work, there are a few procedures you should follow. It is a good idea to become familiar with those procedures and learn what employers expect of job applicants.

Job Leads

Finding job openings is an important part of getting that first job. No one source is necessarily better than others. You need to let as many people as possible know that you are looking for a job. Your relatives, friends, neighbors, and others will be good potential sources of job leads.

The sources you use for information about the nature of jobs are also good sources of job leads. Your school counselors and business teachers can be very helpful. If your school has a placement office, be sure to register with that office. You should also contact employment agencies. Newspaper want ads are very helpful. You also need to visit businesses and inquire about their openings. Some businesses post help-wanted signs in their windows. Getting a job means going out and looking around. Finding a job can be hard work, but it is worth the effort.

Illus. 13–1
Want ads may not be great reading, but they can provide helpful leads for job openings.

Writing a Letter of Application

If you are answering a job advertisement or following up on a friend's lead, writing a letter of application may be your first step in approaching an employer. A **letter of application** is a sales letter about yourself written for the purpose of getting a personal interview. It should be a courteous letter focusing on your interest in and qualifications for the job.

Like any good sales letter, your letter of application should gain the employer's attention and interest. It should create a desire to meet you. You should urge the reader to invite you to come for an interview. Figure 13-1 shows Jerry Miller's well prepared letter of application. The letter is neat, courteous, and to the point. A carelessly written letter may cause the employer to think you will be a careless worker. Your letter represents you, and it must compete with other letters of application for the reader's attention.

Preparing Your Personal Data Sheet

Jerry's letter mentions that a personal data sheet is enclosed with the letter. A **personal data sheet** is a summary of important job-related information about you. It tells about your education and work experience and lists the names of people who have agreed to be your personal references. The people you list as references might

```
                                520 Kenway Road
                                Iron Mountain, MI  49801-6295
                                March 20, 19--


        Ms. Elizabeth W. Chaffin
        Personnel Manager
        Tons O' Fun Amusement Park
        Iron Mountain, MI  49801-5286

        Dear Ms. Chaffin

        In yesterday's Enterprise Journal I read your advertisement
        for summer workers at Tons O' Fun Amusement Park.  I wish to
        apply for one of the positions.

        In your advertisement you mentioned that you are looking for
        cashiers at your ticket and refreshment booths.  I believe I
        could serve you well in such a position.  In addition to
        studying subjects like English and mathematics, I have taken
        typing and general business.  Therefore, I am familiar with
        businesses and how they operate.  Also, I have sold refresh-
        ments at my school's football games and served as the trea-
        surer of the youth group at my church.

        Enclosed is a personal data sheet giving my qualifications
        in more detail.  May I have an interview with you at your
        convenience?  I may be reached by telephone at 875-2129
        after 4 p.m. on any weekday.  Thank you for your considera-
        tion.

                                Sincerely yours

                                Jerry Miller

                                Jerry Miller

        Enclosure
```

Figure 13–1
Your letter of application will introduce you to your prospective employer. It should make its reader eager to meet you in person.

include teachers, religious leaders, adult friends, and others who can tell something about your character and work habits.

If you apply for a job in person, you should have a copy of your personal data sheet with you. Data sheets should outline the information in brief, readable form. Look at Jerry Miller's data sheet in Figure 13-2.

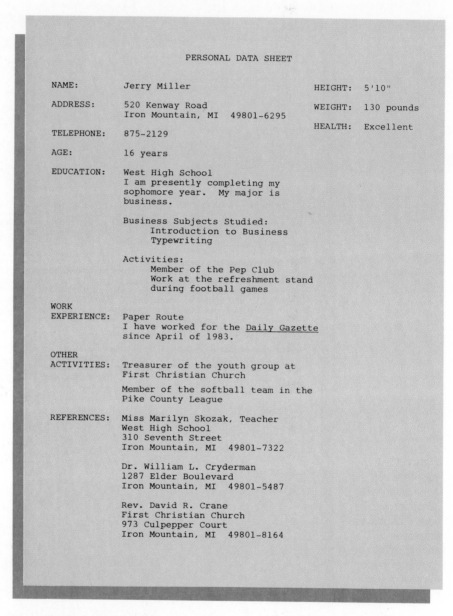

PERSONAL DATA SHEET

NAME: Jerry Miller   HEIGHT: 5'10"

ADDRESS: 520 Kenway Road   WEIGHT: 130 pounds
                Iron Mountain, MI 49801-6295
                                                HEALTH: Excellent
TELEPHONE: 875-2129

AGE: 16 years

EDUCATION: West High School
                I am presently completing my
                sophomore year. My major is
                business.

                Business Subjects Studied:
                    Introduction to Business
                    Typewriting

                Activities:
                    Member of the Pep Club
                    Work at the refreshment stand
                    during football games

WORK
EXPERIENCE: Paper Route
                I have worked for the Daily Gazette
                since April of 1983.

OTHER
ACTIVITIES: Treasurer of the youth group at
                First Christian Church

                Member of the softball team in the
                Pike County League

REFERENCES: Miss Marilyn Skozak, Teacher
                West High School
                310 Seventh Street
                Iron Mountain, MI 49801-7322

                Dr. William L. Cryderman
                1287 Elder Boulevard
                Iron Mountain, MI 49801-5487

                Rev. David R. Crane
                First Christian Church
                973 Culpepper Court
                Iron Mountain, MI 49801-8164

Figure 13–2
Jerry's personal data sheet summarizes important job-related information.

Completing An Application Form

Most companies will ask you to fill out an application form as the next step in the hiring process. An **application form** is prepared by an employer and asks for information related to employment.

Most application forms ask for your name, address, social security number, education, work experience, the job for which you are applying, references, and other qualifications.

The information on your personal data sheet will help you complete the application form. Completing the job application form should be seen as the first job task your employer asks you to perform. Supply each item requested; don't leave questions unanswered. Take this assignment seriously. A poorly prepared application form may give the wrong impression about you. Observe the application form prepared by Jerry Miller in Figure 13-3.

Having A Good Job Interview

You may be one of the persons invited to come for a personal job interview. A **job interview** is a two-way conversation in which the interviewer learns about you and you learn about the company.

Job interviews often are conducted by personnel interviewers. A **personnel interviewer** is someone who has special training in talking with job applicants and hiring new employees. The interviewer will be able to find out about your appearance, manners, use of language, and general suitability for the job. Plan for your interview as carefully as you plan your letter of application and personal data sheet. The following are some good points to keep in mind:

- Be on time for the appointment.
- Go alone to the interview. Don't take friends or relatives with you.
- Dress properly. Don't be too formal or too informal. Wear the type of clothing that is appropriate for the company and the job in which you are interested.
- Try to be calm during the interview. Avoid talking too much, but answer each question completely. Ask questions intelligently. Let the interviewer guide the discussion.
- Leave when the interviewer indicates that the interview is over. Thank the interviewer for the opportunity to discuss the job and your qualifications.
- After the interview, send a brief thank-you letter to the person with whom you interviewed.
- Be patient after the interview. It may take several weeks for the company to complete all of its interviews and make its selection.

Date _March 28, 19--_	**Tons O' Fun** AMUSEMENT PARK	**For Office Use Only** Tel. ____ ☐ ☐ ☐ ☐ Due ____ Div. ____ Sec. ____ Area ____ Rate ____ Pl. ____
An Equal Opportunity Employer		
Please Print All Information	Application For Seasonal Employment	

General — Use Full Name — No Nicknames Please

Last	First	Middle	Social Security Number
Miller	_Jerry_	_Martin_	_301-44-0262_

Number	Street	City	State	Zip Code	Home telephone number
_520_	_Kenway Rd._	_Iron Mountain_	_MI_	_49801-6295_	_875-2129_

Are you less than 18 years of age? Yes ☐ No ☑	If you are less than 18, what is your date of birth?	_March_ Mo. _16_ Day _--_ Yr.	U.S. Citizen? ☑ Yes ☐ No　If No, have you the legal right to remain permanently in the U.S.? ☐ Yes ☐ No

Have you ever been convicted of any crime(s) other than minor traffic violations? Yes ☐ No ☑	If yes, please explain when, where and disposition of the case(s) on reverse side of this form.
Have you been employed previously by Tons O' Fun? Yes ☐ No ☑	If yes, when and in what division?

The position(s) for which you are applying may require special physical abilities to safely and effectively perform the assigned duties and responsibilities of the position(s). Where there are questions in this regard, the interviewer will explain requisite abilities for specific positions. Please explain the nature of any illness, injury or disability which may restrict your ability to safely and effectively perform the duties of the position(s) for which you are applying.
If none, please check here ☑

Education

High School _West High School_	Present Grade Level (Circle)　9　(10)　11　12	List your special abilities, hobbies, awards, and honors received: _Treasurer of youth group,_
College, Business, Tech or Trade School	1　2　3　4	_softball, swimming, skiing_

Availability

Will you be able to work weekends in:	April & May? Yes ☑ No ☐ Sept. & Oct.? Yes ☑ No ☐	Date your school is out for summer _June 5_	Date your school begins in fall _Sept. 8_
Date you will be available to work daily _June 8_	Are you applying for weekend work only? Yes ☐ No ☑	Can you work an evening shift? Yes ☑ No ☐	

Employment History

DATES	EMPLOYED BY	POSITION HELD	Last Rate Of Pay	Supervisor's Name	REASON FOR LEAVING
From _4/--_ Present	Employer _Daily Gazette_	_Paper Carrier_	$_20_/_Wk._	_Joe Gaines_	_still working at it_
To	Address of Employer		Per		
From	Employer		$		
To	Address of Employer		Per		

IN WHAT POSITION(S) AT TONS O' FUN WOULD YOU PREFER TO WORK
1. _Cashier_　　2. _Ride Attendant_　　3. _____　　4. _____

Personal References　(Do not refer to relatives or former employers)

Name
Miss Marilyn Skozak, Teacher, West High School, 310 Seventh St., Iron Mountain, MI
Dr. William L. Cryderman, 1287 Elder Boulevard, Iron Mountain, MI
Rev. David R. Crane, First Christian Church, 973 Culpepper Ct., Iron Mountain, MI

Figure 13–3
Be sure that you are neat, accurate, and thorough when completing a job application.

There are many different approaches that an interviewer may take. Most interviewers will try to put you at ease when your inter-

Illus. 13–2
A job interview will be your only opportunity to make a good first visual impression. Careful planning for the interview will pay big rewards.

view begins. As the interview progresses, there are a number of questions that could be asked by the interviewer. Here are some examples:

- Why are you interested in this particular job?
- What are some of the things you like to do in your spare time?
- What courses have you taken that will help you on this job?
- What are your career goals?
- Do you plan to continue your education now or in the future?
- Do you have any friends or relatives who work here?

Succeeding on Your First Job

When you are selected for a job, remember that your employer is just as eager as you are for you to succeed. Doing well on your first job is an important first step in your career. Generally you will find the other employees willing to help you and to answer your questions. One person may be assigned to help you through the first few days. You probably will make a few mistakes in the process of learning your job. The important thing is to learn from each mistake and to avoid repeating it. You will need to be a good listener, too. Your job will test your ability to follow directions and to produce good work. It should be a challenging experience for you.

Your attitude toward your new job is important. For example, a negative attitude may result in frequent absences from work. A positive attitude, on the other hand, may mean you are willing to learn and grow in your job, and to cooperate with your fellow workers. As a bonus, you will probably find your job more satisfying too.

Adding to Your Business Vocabulary

The following terms should become part of your business vocabulary. For each numbered item, find the term that has the same meaning.

application form
job interview
letter of application

personal data sheet
personnel interviewer

1. A sales letter about yourself written for the purpose of getting a personal interview.
2. A summary of job-related information about yourself.
3. A form prepared by an employer which asks for important information related to employment.

4. A two-way conversation in which the interviewer learns about you and you learn about the job and the company.
5. Someone who has special training in talking with job applicants and hiring new employees.

Understanding Your Reading

1. How can your school record be useful to an employer?
2. List eight sources of leads on possible jobs.
3. In what ways is a letter of application a personal sales letter?
4. What kinds of information should you include on a personal data sheet?
5. Why should you be especially careful in filling out an application form?

6. What can an interviewer learn about you during an interview?
7. What can you learn about a job and a company during an interview?
8. Identify seven important points to keep in mind regarding interviews.
9. List at least five typical questions that may be asked during a job interview.
10. Why are learning and growing on the job important in a career?

Putting Your Business Knowledge to Work

1. Name at least six persons you know whom you could ask for help in finding a full-time job. Also identify several local organizations or agencies you could contact for help in finding a job.
2. If you were in charge of hiring people for jobs, what information would you want to get about applicants? How would you go about getting this information? What are some specific questions you would ask if you were to interview the applicants?

3. Your personal data sheet should list several references. Application forms also ask for references to be listed. Make a list of three or more references you could use right now. Then note the type of information each reference could give that would be of help to a potential employer.
4. Write out a personal data sheet that you could use right now if you were to apply for a part-time or full-time job. After it is completed, think about whether or not you

need to consider being more involved in school, church, or community activities. Think about whether or not your personal data sheet would impress an employer and what you could do that could be included in future personal data sheets to better present yourself.

5. You have received information about three jobs:
   a. an office job which involves assembling and stapling papers, folding leaflets, and sealing envelopes;
   b. a job in a refreshment stand at a movie theater;
   c. a part-time job in a gift shop which involves stocking shelves, checking shipments, and preparing packages for mailing.

Write a letter applying for one of these jobs. Make up the name and address of the employer. Refer to Figure 13-1 as a guide to the information you should include in your letter.

6. Draw up an application form similar to the one in Figure 13-3 and supply whatever information you think necessary to apply for one of the jobs mentioned in Problem 5 above.

Computing Business Problems

1. Jackie Lippert worked 25 hours one week and 30 hours during each of the next two weeks.
   a. What was the total number of hours she worked?
   b. If she is required to work at least 120 hours during a four-week period, how many hours will Jackie have to work in the fourth week?

2. Gregory Ellison earns $5 an hour on his part-time job. During one week he worked the following number of hours:

Monday	4 hours	Thursday	4 hours
Tuesday	3 hours	Friday	5 hours
Wednesday	4 hours	Saturday	8 hours

   a. How many hours did Gregory work during that week?
   b. What was the total amount that he earned?

3. Bill Bonkowski does volunteer work at a children's summer camp near his home. This afternoon he set up some team races for the young children. He put four runners on a team and each runner is to run 50 meters.
   a. How many meters will the winning team run?
   b. How many feet will the winning team run?

Stretching Your Business Knowledge

1. Find a copy of the classified advertising section of a Sunday newspaper from a medium- to large-size city. Examine the help wanted columns, particularly the advertisements of private employment agencies.
   a. In the listing of private agencies, what do the terms "no fee" and "fee paid" mean?
   b. Salaries for some jobs are listed as "open," "to $20,000," or "650+." What do these terms mean?

2. Check the help wanted advertisements from your local newspaper over a period of one week. Make a list of ten jobs for which you find the most ads. This list will tell you something about the kinds of work which are most readily available in your community. Make another list of those jobs for which you think you could qualify. Which of these jobs interests you the most? Why?

3. Using the list of questions often asked in job interviews on page 185 and other lists of questions, conduct mock employment interviews with other members of your class. Decide in advance the kind of job for which the interviewees have applied. Have the class observe some of the interviews and then discuss what was correct and incorrect about the interviews. An interesting result can be having the class vote on which person(s) they would hire or not hire for the job and why.

CAREER FOCUS

CAREER CATEGORY: Secretarial and Clerical

Many people find that their roles in business begin in secretarial or clerical positions. With the increased influence of the computer upon today's office, such positions can be very challenging and rewarding.

Job Titles: Job titles commonly found in this career area include:

Executive Secretary
Medical Secretary
Transcribing Machine Operator
Public Stenographer
Word Processing Operator
Correspondence Secretary

Bank Teller
Cashier
Bookkeeper
Accounting Clerk
General Office Clerk
Receptionist

Employment Outlook: There were 18.9 million workers in this career area in 1980; that number is expected to increase to over 23 million by 1990. That means that almost 500,000 new workers will be needed each year. Secretaries, general clerks, and bookkeepers and accounting clerks will be in especially high demand.

Future Changes: New developments in computers, office machines, and office systems will help secretarial and clerical workers to do more in less time. Many routine jobs will be handled through computerized systems or electronic processing. Skilled workers with appropriate training and good work habits will still be needed.

What Is Done on the Job: Workers in this career area prepare and keep records; operate office machines; arrange schedules and make reservations; collect, distribute, or account for money; deliver messages, mail, or material; type and file reports; take minutes at meetings and prepare transcripts; greet

people and answer telephones; provide a variety of important supportive work for administrators and managers.

Education and Training: High school graduates frequently find good employment opportunities in this career area. However, job applicants with specific job training beyond high school—in either two-year or four-year programs—generally find opportunities in higher level positions and are promoted more frequently. The nature of the training, however, is important as is the job performance of the employee when it comes to salary increases and promotions.

Salary Levels: Salaries vary widely in this career area, depending in part on the section of the country in which the employee is located, the level of the job, and the work record of the employee. Salaries for secretaries in 1982 ranged from an average of $10,000 in one section of the country to $20,000 in another.

For Additional Information: Additional information about this career area is available from several sources including the following:

Hopke, William E. (ed.). *Encyclopedia of Careers and Vocational Guidance,* New York: Doubleday and Co., Inc., 1982.

Can I Be an Office Worker?
Public Relations Department
General Motors
Detroit, MI 48202

Careers, Inc.
Largo, FL 33540

Administrative Management Society
Willow Grove, PA 19090

UNIT 5
YOUR ROLE AS A CONSUMER

UNIT OBJECTIVES

After studying the chapters in this unit, you will be able to:

1. Explain how you can become an informed consumer.

2. Identify nine general rules a consumer should follow in buying.

3. Describe four rights and four responsibilities that consumers have.

BUSINESS BRIEF
The Consumer Movement

Even a casual observer of business and consumption patterns in the United States would recognize the 60s, 70s, and 80s as the era of the consumer. Consumers now have several government and private agencies working to protect them. They have consumer magazines to read. They can tune in to radio and television programs designed to supply them with information about products and services. Businesses themselves even have consumer bureaus that exist to help consumers make better choices. It is now recognized by business and government that consumers do have rights that are to be protected.

It was not always this way. In fact, until the early 1900s, it was common for business owners to figure out ways to fool consumers into buying a product. The sellers of patent medicines were notorious for misrepresenting their products. Millions of bottles of various kinds of totally useless and uncontrolled medicines were sold to unsuspecting consumers who believed they would cure everything from liver cancer to the common cold. This philosophy of selling was commonly referred to by the Latin words *caveat emptor* (let the buyer beware).

The meat-packing industry in the early 1900s was another area of business where the protection of the consumer was not a high priority. Unhealthy and dangerous meat products were a very important consumer issue at this time. Journalists called "muckrakers" investigated unhealthy conditions in the meat-packing industry. The most prominent of these journalists was Upton Sinclair who, in 1906, published a book called *The Jungle*. It confirmed the American consumers' worst fears about foods. Below is part of Sinclair's description of a meat-packing plant:

These rats were nuisances, and the packers would put poisoned bread out for them and they would die, and then rats, bread and meat would go into the choppers together . . . men who worked in the tank rooms full of steam . . . fell into the vats; and when they were fished out, there was never enough of them to be worth exhibiting—sometimes they would be overlooked for days, till all but the bones of them had gone out to the world as Durham's Pure Leg of Lard![1]

Sales of meat dropped 50 percent after publication of *The Jungle* and later that year, with support from the U.S. Department of Agriculture, the American Medical Association, and the National Consumer's League, Congress passed both the Pure Food and Drug Act and a meat inspection act authorizing stricter government inspection of meat packing houses. This event probably marked the beginning of today's consumer movement. Finally *caveat emptor* has changed to *caveat venditor,* which means "let the seller beware." Businesses are now convinced that consumers are a group to be served and a force to be reckoned with in the marketplace.

[1]Upton Sinclair, *The Jungle* (New York: Doubleday & Co., Inc., 1906), p. 117.

Being an Informed Consumer

After studying this chapter and completing the end-of-chapter activities you will be able to:

1. Tell why consumers are important to businesses.
2. List seven important decisions you should make before purchasing a product or service.
3. Name at least four sources of information you can consult when planning a purchase.
4. Describe the kinds of information contained on a label.
5. Explain how advertising can help you become a well-informed consumer.
6. List the types of information provided by print and broadcast media.
7. Name the services provided by Better Business Bureaus.

Everyone is a consumer. We all consume or use products or services every day. We buy snacks, tape recorders, clothing, and bicycles. We also purchase movie tickets, telephone services, and legal advice. All of these activities make us consumers. It is the job of American businesses to provide goods and services for us to consume. And it is our job to be wise consumers.

The Consumer

What is a consumer? A **consumer** is a person, business, or government that buys and uses goods or services. A consumer may buy goods such as cosmetics, radios, toys, or oranges. Or a consumer may buy services such as dry cleaning, insurance protection, a haircut, or a car wash. You are a consumer.

The Importance of Being a Good Consumer

How you consume, to some degree, defines who you are. Your consumer habits reflect and determine your life-style. You may choose to be thrifty and buy only the products and services you need to live. On the other hand, you may buy many products and services that you could easily do without. To some extent you are known by your spending habits. Have you ever heard of a person being called "a real tightwad" or a "cheapskate"?

Most people seek the highest standard of living that their incomes will allow. You can raise your standard of living by becoming an informed consumer. In fact, your standard of living is probably determined more by how wisely you spend than by how much money you earn.

The Importance of Consumption in Our Economy

Over two-thirds of America's gross national product represents products and services sold to individual consumers. This means that as a consumer you are very important to businesses and to the economy. The buying decisions that you and other consumers make can lead to either success or failure for many businesses. Consumers are, then, obviously important to businesses. As a result, businesses expend great efforts to attract and keep customers. Without customers businesses would not make sales, earn profits, or remain in business.

Illus. 14–1
An informed consumer is a wise consumer. Take time to learn about the products and services you want and need.

Using Good Judgment in Buying

It is not realistic to expect that you will use great consumer skill in the purchase of every product or service. Sometimes there won't be time to do so. It may not be worth the effort when making a minor purchase. Or maybe it just won't be reasonable. You can, however, develop the habit of using good judgment in most of your purchases.

Whenever you plan to buy anything, you must make a number of important decisions. Your answers to the following questions will help you choose the best product or service for you:

1. Would you rather buy this item instead of another desired item that costs the same amount of money?
2. Which business or businesses should you visit?
3. What quality of goods or services do you want to buy?
4. What price are you willing to pay?
5. Should you pay cash or buy now and pay later?
6. Do you really need this item now, or can you wait awhile?
7. If you make this purchase, what other important item may you have to do without?

Judge each purchase according to whether it will meet your needs better than something else you could buy instead. Purchases must be guided by the relationship between the need or want for one article and the possible needs or wants for other articles.

Not buying one article so that you can buy another article can be viewed as a cost. It is called an opportunity cost. An **opportunity cost** is the cost of giving up something in favor of buying something else. For example, suppose you want both a new sweater and a seat for your bicycle but have only enough money for one or the other. If you choose the seat, you must give up the sweater. Part of the "cost" of the seat, then, is the opportunity to have a new sweater.

Consumer Information from Business

To make wise purchasing decisions, you must have factual information about the products and services you want to buy. There are many ways to get the information you need. But where should you begin?

Suppose, for example, you wanted to buy a stereo receiver. How would you determine which receiver was the best value for your money? Would you ask a friend? Or would you go to the store and talk with a salesperson? You could read the labels and booklets that accompany each receiver. Any of these methods may work for you. There are several very reliable ways to go about gathering product or service information.

A major source of consumer information is business itself. Businesses provide information through product labels, various forms of advertising, and customer-service departments and specialists.

Product Labels

A **label** provides written information about a product. It may tell you what the product is made of, its size, how to care for it, and when and where it was made. For example, if you want to buy a pair of running shorts, you need to know whether or not they will shrink when washed or dried. The label on the shorts should tell you what they're made of and provide laundering instructions.

A label may be printed on a carton, can, wrapper, or on a tag attached to the product. It may also be stamped or sewn onto the product. Whatever the form, a label gives useful information about a product. Study it carefully and you will be a better-informed consumer.

Advertising

Advertising is a very popular source of consumer information. Since the main purpose of an advertisement is to convince you to buy a product or service, you should use it with care as a source of consumer information. Advertising can be useful to you if you know what product or service you want and if you can overlook strong appeals to buy a particular product or service.

Useful advertisements tell you what the product is, how it is made, and what it will do. They give facts which you can use to compare the product with other products. Beware of claims made that really tell you nothing about the product. If an advertisement states, "Buy Acmes, they're better!" you should ask, "Better than what?" and "How are they better?"

Customer Service Departments

Many businesses have special departments devoted to customer service. Some firms provide customers with booklets on a variety of consumer topics. Banks and insurance companies publish booklets to help consumers manage their money. Some large

Illus. 14–2
Not all advertisements can provide a great deal of product information. Billboards, for example, can present little more than a product, service, or brand name.

retail firms provide printed materials to help consumers with their buying problems. J. C. Penney and Sears, for example, publish pamphlets to help customers improve their buying skills.

Business Specialists

Sometimes it is wise to get advice from an expert before purchasing a product. This is especially true if you have never bought such an item, if the item is very complicated, or if it is very expensive. Houses, business machines, and used cars are examples of products that should not be purchased without an expert's advice. For example, most of us could not judge whether a used car's transmission is worn or its brakes need to be replaced. But an automobile mechanic could give reliable advice about the condition of the car.

Consumer Information from Public Sources

Many agencies and organizations that serve the public provide product and service information to consumers. Among them are product testing agencies; print and broadcast media; Better Business Bureaus; and local, state, and federal government agencies. In general, these organizations are completely independent of business interests and can be trusted to be honest and objective.

Product Testing Agencies

There are a number of organizations which can help consumers become more informed about the goods and services they buy. Two such organizations are Consumers' Research, Incorporated, and Consumers Union of the United States, Incorporated. They perform independent tests on consumer goods and publish reports on the quality of the goods. Consumers' Research publishes its findings in *Consumers' Research Magazine.* Consumers Union publishes its findings in a magazine called *Consumer Reports.* Another testing organization is Underwriters Laboratories. It is a nonprofit independent testing organization that examines products for fire, casualty, and electrical safety. They do not judge products for performance or quality. Their symbol, shown in Illus. 14–3, means only that a product has been judged safe.

Print and Broadcast Media

These terms are used to describe magazines, newspapers, radio, and television. Interested consumers can find these media to be rich with information about products and services.

Magazines and newspapers often carry articles designed to help consumers. Many newspapers contain weekly columns written by home economists on best food buys. Other articles may deal with such topics as what to look for in a used car and how to cut home heating costs.

Illus. 14–3
The Underwriters Laboratories' symbol is an indication of safety to buyers of electrical products.

Some magazines also test and rate products. *Good House-keeping* and *Parent's Magazine* are examples. When a product has been tested by one of these publications and meets standards of performance or quality, the product can display the magazine's seal of approval on its label. There are also magazines devoted to information on special products, such as stereo equipment and cars.

Like magazines and newspapers, radio and television are sources of consumer information. Many stations carry regular programs which inform the public about product safety, care and use of products, and shopping tips, such as the best food buys of the week. In addition, many stations now broadcast talk-shows designed to help listeners with their immediate consumer problems.

The Better Business Bureau

Most communities have a Better Business Bureau. Better Business Bureaus are supported by dues paid by businesses. The bureaus work to maintain ethical practices in the advertising and selling of products and services and to combat consumer fraud. They are chiefly concerned with problems arising from false advertising or misrepresentation of products and services. Better Business Bureaus can provide very helpful information. For example, suppose you were planning to buy a used car from a dealer. You could call the Better Business Bureau to find out what experiences others have had with that dealer. If consumers have reported problems they have had with the firm, you can find out about these complaints. Better Business Bureaus give facts only; they do not recommend products or firms. They give you the information they have, but you are free to interpret it and to make your own decision.

Consumer Information Provided by Government

Federal, state, and local governments also provide assistance to persons wishing to become informed consumers. The federal government, for example, formed the Consumer Product Information Center to serve as a headquarters for consumer information. In addition to making government publications available, the Center publishes the results of government research and product tests. The agency has distribution centers in several major cities.

The U.S. Department of Agriculture (USDA) is another source of consumer information. USDA publications specialize in information about food—judging quality, buying wisely, improving buying practices, planning meals, improving nutrition, and other farm- and home-related topics.

The USDA also inspects and grades foods and makes that information available to consumers in the form of labels. Labels often show the grade of a product. A **grade** indicates the quality or size of a product. For example, beef may be stamped "prime," "choice," "good," or some other grade. Look at the label in Illus. 14–4. The USDA shield means that the product has been inspected and approved by that government agency.

You should not overlook sources of information made available by state and local governments. Most states and many cities and counties have some type of consumer agency from which you can get information.

Other Sources of Consumer Information

Labor unions, civic clubs, and some churches provide materials, sponsor programs and fairs, and hold meetings on topics of consumer interest. Look around you. You will be surprised to find that with just a little effort you can find sources that will help you become an informed consumer.

Illus. 14–4
Through the grading process, government agencies provide consumers with needed product information.

Adding to Your Business Vocabulary

The following terms should become part of your business vocabulary. For each numbered item, find the term that has the same meaning.

consumer   *label*
grade   *opportunity cost*

1. A person who buys and uses goods or services.
2. An indication of the quality or size of a product.

3. The cost of giving up something in favor of buying something else.
4. A statement attached to a product giving information about its nature or contents.

Understanding Your Reading

1. What are common activities of consumers?
2. Why are consumers important to businesses?
3. What are the seven important decisions you should make before purchasing a product or service?
4. Name four sources of consumer information about a bicycle.
5. What kinds of information can you find on labels?
6. How can advertising help you become a better consumer?
7. Name one form of consumer information provided by businesses.
8. How do product-testing agencies help consumers?
9. What kinds of information do print and broadcast media provide for consumers?
10. What does it mean if a product displays the *Good Housekeeping* seal?
11. List the services a Better Business Bureau can provide for you.
12. Identify some of the major government sources of consumer information.
13. What is meant by the grade of a product?
14 What does it mean if you find the USDA shield on a product?

Putting Your Business Knowledge to Work

1. Why is it important to be a well-informed consumer?
2. Why do you think a good businessperson with good products or services to sell would like to have customers who are well informed?
3. What kinds of advertisements are most valuable to consumers? Give an example.
4. If you were to purchase the following items, for which of them would you seek the advice of a specialist. Give reasons for each answer.
   a. a study desk   c. a pair of jeans
   b. a microcomputer   d. a used car
5. Do you feel a report on an item from a product-testing agency would be reliable? Explain your answer.
6. On which of the following items would you

be likely to see the UL seal?
a. electric blanket
b. laundry detergent
c. scissors
d. study lamp
e. baby's
   pajamas
f. carton of milk

7. One autumn day a woman and a man came to Dorothy Franklin's door. They said they were chimney sweeps and would like to clean Mrs. Franklin's chimney before she began using her fireplace. They said it would be inexpensive and make her home safer because it would reduce the chances of a chimney fire. Mrs. Franklin looked out her window and saw the name "Chim Chim Chimney Sweeps" on the truck they were driving. How can she find out if the firm is reliable and if their price is a fair charge for the service they wish to provide?

*C*omputing Business Problems

1. Two grocery stores advertised carrots in the newspaper. One store offered 3 lbs. for 99 cents. The other offered 2 lbs. for 68 cents.
a. Which carrots are less expensive per pound?
b. At a price of 3 lbs. for 99 cents, how much would 5 lbs. of carrots cost?

2. The advertisement below appeared in a newspaper during the month of March:

CLEARANCE SALE
SAVE   SAVE   SAVE
Buy NOW! Buy for NEXT YEAR!
A small deposit will hold your selection!
Don't miss these fine values!

	Regular Price	Sale Price
Fur-Trimmed Coats	$259.95	$174.95
Finer Winter Coats	$199.95	$149.95
Raincoats	$ 34.95	$ 26.95

a. How much were the fur-trimmed coats reduced?
b. How much were the finer winter coats reduced?
c. How much were the raincoats reduced?

3. Near the end of the summer, Wheeler's Garden Store marked down a number of items for quick sale. The regular selling price, reduced price, and cost of each item to the store are shown below. Each item was sold at the reduced price.

Item	Regular Price	Reduced Price	Cost
21-inch power mower	$194.99	$179.25	$151.50
Riding lawn mower	675.00	599.95	562.50
Electric hedge trimmer	54.00	49.32	40.50
Deluxe barbecue grill	97.45	74.52	81.75
Lawn furniture set	224.99	169.32	135.00

a. By what amount was each item marked down?
b. How much markup or markdown was realized on the sale of each item?
c. What was the total markup received from the sale of the five items?
d. By what percentage of the regular price was each item marked down?

Stretching Your Business Knowledge

1. Make a list of all the types of information contained on any package of food.
2. Think of a person whose life-style you admire. Tell how that person's consumption habits help to define his or her life-style.
3. Collect advertisements from newspapers and magazines that represent each of the following appeals:
   a. desire for comfort
   b. pride of ownership
   c. desire to be healthy
   d. desire to be famous
   e. desire for security.

   Write a short statement explaining how each advertisement makes the appeal.
4. Use a telephone book to find the address and telephone number of the nearest Better Business Bureau. List the kinds of information it has available.
5. Newspapers carry both news stories about consumer events and columns which provide consumer information. Examine one issue of your local newspaper and make a list of all articles about consumers. Indicate which articles are published as a consumer information service.
6. Look through your weekly local radio or television listing to see if you can find a program designed to provide information to consumers. Watch it or listen to it and write a paragraph about the kind of information it broadcasts.

CHAPTER 15

*S*hopping Wisely

■ CHAPTER OBJECTIVES

After studying this chapter and completing the end-of-chapter activities, you will be able to:

1. List at least six general rules for shopping.
2. Tell why time is important to shoppers.
3. Give a reason to avoid impulse buying.
4. Describe how unit pricing can benefit you.
5. Tell how a promotional sale is different from a clearance sale.
6. Describe two types of product brand names.

Once you have gathered as much information as you can about a product or service you wish to purchase, you are ready to go shopping. The term shopping can have several meanings. For our purposes **shopping** means going to businesses to find out about the products or services they have for sale. While shopping you have the opportunity to compare prices, quality, guarantees and other product or service features. Shopping allows you to compare the consumer information you possess with the actual features of the products and services as they exist in the business.

Some people view shopping as recreation. Others think of shopping as a social event. Take time to watch people shop. Many seem to lack purpose in their shopping activities. Others seem to have definite plans, shopping from a list and carefully comparing items. It is this last group of people who are usually the best shoppers and who get the most value for their money. This chapter will help you learn some general rules for shopping and buying. Figure 15–1 gives several rules for buying wisely.

General Rules for Shopping

When to Buy

- Take your time.
- Buy at the right time.
- Avoid impulse buying.

How to Buy

- Compare prices, services, and quality.
- Look for unit prices.
- Look for genuine sales.
- Examine before buying.

From Whom to Buy

- Buy from businesses you trust.
- Know brand names.

Figure 15–1
How many of
these rules do
you follow?

When to Buy

Timing is a key part of good shopping. It takes time to buy wisely. A smart shopper spends time planning a shopping trip. Once in the marketplace it is important to shop slowly and thoughtfully to find the best buys. Smart shoppers also know that there is often a right time of the day, month, or year to buy.

Take Your Time

"I just don't have the time" is the cry of many people. It is often tempting to spend only a little time shopping. This is usually not a good practice. Spending more time planning purchases and shopping usually results in savings that reward you for the time spent. Taking your time usually means slowing down, visiting more stores, and giving yourself a chance to look for the best values. If you learn to pace yourself, you will probably find that your money goes farther toward buying the things you need and want. As a good shopper, you should refuse to be hurried into buying anything. In this way, you avoid buying merchandise that you really do not want or need.

Sometimes consumers become impatient. They want to buy right now which often costs them money. Being patient might mean postponing a purchase until you have saved enough money to pay cash, until you can afford to make a larger down payment, or until you know a special sales event is coming.

Buy at the Right Time

In some businesses prices are lowest at predictable times. A good shopper will learn about those times and take advantage of them. Certain times and conditions favor goods and services being sold at reduced prices. Here are just a few examples:

1. When fresh fruit and vegetables are at their peak, they are usually lower in price.
2. Automobiles are usually less expensive at the end of a model year (September) before the new models are displayed.
3. Winter clothing is often on sale in January.
4. February "White Sales" are a good time to buy bedding and towels.
5. Airline tickets cost less when travel is at off-peak times (such as flights to Florida in the summer.)
6. Chimney sweeps often charge less in the summer.

You can probably add to the list of products and services that are less expensive on a seasonal basis. Consumer magazines and newspaper articles, as well as radio and television programs for consumers, can help you add to this list.

Avoid Impulse Buying

The opposite of spending time and thought in shopping is buying too rapidly without much thought. This type of buying is called **impulse buying** and should be avoided to keep from making costly mistakes. Impulse buying often happens when you see an item attractively displayed and suddenly decide to buy it. Sometimes impulse buying is harmless. Purchasing some small item like a bag of popcorn, a small gift for a friend, or a magazine is a pleasant part of life. The cost is small and the item is usually worth the price. But buying more expensive items like clothing, radios, or even automobiles on impulse can be costly. You may not really need the item. Or it might not be the best value for the price, as you might discover if you collect information about the item and then carefully shop for it.

One of the best ways to avoid impulse buying is to make a shopping list and stick to it. Many people use lists when shopping in grocery stores and supermarkets. Market research firms who study consumers' buying habits have found that, in supermarkets, people without shopping lists tend to buy more items (many of them luxury items) than do people with shopping lists. Since most consumers are open to suggestion, an attractive display of products can tempt them to buy something that they had not planned to buy. You can save money if you make and stick to a shopping list whether it is for groceries, hardware, or clothing.

How to Buy

You can be a better shopper; all it takes is a little skill. Once you gain that skill, you should get greater value for your money each time you shop. You can learn how to compare prices, services, and value. You can also learn about sales and how to examine what you buy. You can become more efficient in your shopping activity.

Compare Prices, Quality, and Services

A skillful consumer is a comparison shopper. **Comparison shopping** means comparing the price, quality, and services of one product to those of another product. Except for utilities, such as water and electricity, or for very specialized goods, there are few things that are not produced or sold by more than one business. Therefore, you can choose where to buy and you can compare prices, quality and services.

Smart shoppers, of course, compare the prices of products. They question advertisements that use such phrases as "normally sells for" or "sold elsewhere for." Sometimes these ads are honest. But sometimes the prices mentioned in them are not really the prices normally charged. The smart shopper compares prices to find out if what is being offered is a true bargain.

Reprinted by permission of Jefferson Communications, Inc., Reston, Va.

All shoppers want to get their money's worth. Good quality merchandise and services generally cost more, but buying lower-quality items can sometimes turn out to be even more costly. For example, if you buy a blank tape on which you plan to record music for a very low price, it may break or fail to give you the quality of sound you want. A good-quality tape may cost more but it may last twice as long as the poor-quality tape and will probably give you more pleasure.

The wise shopper also compares services offered by businesses. Most dealers try to give good services, but types of services may differ. Some businesses sell for cash only; others extend credit. Some businesses deliver goods; others do not. Some keep a very large stock from which selection may be made; others may have fewer items in stock.

Service is important, but you should not pay for more service than you actually need. As a wise shopper you should know what you want, seek out what you want, and buy what you want at the best prices. In short, develop your skills as a comparison shopper.

Look for Unit Prices

Unit price is the price per unit of measure. To compute unit price, you must divide the price of the item by the number of units of measure. For instance, suppose you need to buy a can of frozen orange juice. In the supermarket you see that a 12-ounce can of Tropical Sunshine orange juice costs $1.26. Nearby in the freezer case are 6-ounce cans of Golden Citrus orange juice for 69¢ per can. Which is the better buy? Comparing the total prices only, it isn't easy to decide. But if each can also showed the cost per ounce—the unit price—you could quickly compare prices. In this case, the 12-ounce can would show a unit price of 10.5¢ an ounce ($1.26 ÷ 12). The 6-ounce can would be 11.5¢ per ounce ($.69 ÷ 6). Unit pricing would quickly tell you that the 12-ounce can is a better buy per ounce. Larger sizes do not always mean better value, though. And you often are not aware of this if the label does not show the unit price. Also, you should not buy a larger size if it is more than you need. Buying more of a product than you can use is not smart shopping.

To help shoppers compare value among various brands and sizes of the same product, many stores show the total price and the price of one standard measure, or unit, of the product. In the case of orange juice, a standard unit would be one ounce. If the store

Illus. 15–1
Unit prices enable shoppers to compare the costs of various sizes and brands of products.

showed how much one ounce of each brand of orange juice costs, you could easily tell whether Tropical Sunshine or Golden Citrus was a better buy regardless of the size of the containers.

The good shopper, then, will look for the store that features unit pricing. Or, as an alternative, it might be a good idea to take a pocket calculator with you when you go shopping. Armed with this inexpensive tool, unit prices are easy to determine.

Look for Genuine Sales

The word "sale" may be the most over-used and least-trusted word in marketing. You have probably seen "Sale" signs a thousand times. They are used so much as gimmicks to try to sell goods that many shoppers no longer know when a real sale is going on. When an item is really on sale, it is offered at a price lower than its normal selling price. Many so-called sales are not really sales at all, and you should check them carefully. Sometimes they consist of regular goods at regular prices being heavily advertised with the word "sale."

Retailers run three main types of sales. With **promotional sales,** the merchants promote the sale of their regular merchandise by making temporary price reductions. They may do this to open a new store or to publicize the new location of an established store. Merchants may have promotional sales to build acceptance for new products by offering them at low introductory prices. The retailers hope that customers will buy the products at the reduced prices, like them, and then buy at the regular prices in the future. Retailers also use promotional sales to draw customers into their stores. They hope that customers who buy the sale merchandise will buy other products at the regular prices.

Clearance sales are used to "clear" merchandise that retailers no longer want. This may be shopworn stock; leftovers, such as odd sizes and models; or a line of merchandise that the store no longer carries. Clearance sales usually offer some bargains, but it is important to be sure that you can use a sale item before you buy it.

There are sales, however, which feature special-purchase merchandise. This is merchandise bought for a special sale rather than marked down from the regular stock. Special-purchase merchandise may include goods purchased from a manufacturer who is overstocked, goods that are no longer made, or stock from a company that is going out of business.

Illus. 15–2
New retailers often hold grand opening sales to encourage consumers to try shopping in a new store.

To be able to take advantage of sales, you have to look for sales which are genuine and which are truthfully advertised. Even then you must know the regular price of the product so that you can buy only those items which represent a real savings.

Examine Before Buying

Always try to examine a product before you buy it. Even if you are not an expert, you can often tell whether it is exactly what you want. With experience you will learn to recognize differences in quality.

As you examine the quality of a product, remember an important rule of buying: "Don't buy quality you don't need." This means that the intended use of the product determines the level of quality you need. For example, you wouldn't need to buy expensive designer jeans for working in the yard. Less expensive, strong jeans would serve just as well.

From Whom to Buy

Often it is important to know who is supplying the goods and services you wish to buy. The reputation of a business can mean a great deal to you if you should have trouble after a purchase.

Buy From Reputable Businesses

You should make every effort to judge quality for yourself. But sometimes you may have no way of knowing exactly what you are getting. One of the best guarantees you can have that the things you buy are of good quality is to buy from businesses that have good reputations. The wise business owner knows that a satisfied customer is likely to return. The salespeople know the uses and the quality of the goods being offered for sale. They are also concerned about matching the proper goods with customers' needs. If you buy from a business with a good reputation, you can usually rely on its salespeople to help you make wise selections.

Know Brand Names

A **brand name** is a special name given to a product by a manufacturer to distinguish it as being made by that particular firm. Many goods are advertised nationally and are sold in almost every community. Among these goods are clothing, shoes, tools, canned foods, toothpaste, cosmetics, furniture, and appliances. Manufacturers of such goods often place brand names on the items they make. "General Electric," for example, is the brand name of a world-famous line of electrical appliances.

Many brands are available nationally. Learning to recognize national brand names can help you in several ways. First, you can usually expect uniform quality even when brand-name goods are bought in different stores. This is especially helpful in buying goods that are difficult to inspect for quality, such as canned goods. Second, brand names make comparison shopping possible. Third, brand-name items often have better guarantees behind them. It is true, of course, that some unbranded items are comparable in quality to brand name items and are less expensive. They can be good buys if you carefully examine them and choose only quality goods.

Some stores have their own brand names. These are called **house brands** or **store brands.** For example, "Kenmore" is the house-brand name for appliances sold by Sears, Roebuck and Co. House brands are usually sold for less than national brands. Buying house brands, therefore, may often save you money and offer good quality at the same time.

Some supermarkets now carry unbranded items at reduced prices. They are called **generic products**. Generic products are less expensive because they do not require advertising and fancy packaging, thus saving the manufacturer money. These savings are passed on to consumers. The labels on generic products are usually written with large bold print identifying the contents. There are sometimes minor differences in quality and uniformity between generic and branded products. However, these differences can save a careful shopper between 15 and 25 percent over branded products.

Efficient Shopping

Skillful shoppers are efficient in their shopping activities. They save time, energy, and money by planning. You can become a skillful shopper too. There are at least three specific steps you can take. First, plan your purchases carefully and make a shopping list. As you already know, a shopper with a list makes better decisions in the store and avoids impulse buying. Next, use the telephone to help you. Using the classified ad section of the telephone book and calling businesses to find out if they have what you need is a very efficient practice. Often you can order goods and services by telephone. Finally, you can save fuel by carefully planning the route of your shopping trip. Unnecessary travel can add a lot to the total cost of a shopping trip.

You can see that with a little attention to timing, learning simple shopping skills, and gaining knowledge of sellers, you can become a much better shopper. You can then expect to make the best buy each time you shop.

A dding to Your Business Vocabulary

The following terms should become part of your business vocabulary. For each numbered item, find the term that has the same meaning.

brand name
clearance sale
comparison shopping
generic products
house brand or store brand

impulse buying
promotional sale
shopping
unit price

1. Going to a business to find out firsthand about the products or services it has for sale.
2. Buying too rapidly without much thought.
3. Comparing the price, quality and services of one product to those of another product.
4. The price per unit of measure of a product.
5. Using a price reduction to sell items that a business no longer wishes to carry in stock.
6. Selling items below regular price to increase the sales of regular merchandise or to draw customers into the business.
7. A special name given to a product by a manufacturer to distinguish it as being made by that particular firm.
8. A special name used for products sold by one store or chain of stores.
9. Unbranded products sold without advertising and fancy packaging in order to reduce prices.

U nderstanding Your Reading

1. What are the nine general rules for shopping?
2. Why are automobiles usually a good buy in September?
3. Why should you avoid impulse buying?
4. How can unit pricing help you?
5. Distinguish between a promotional sale and a clearance sale.
6. What is the difference between a house brand and a national brand?
7. What is a generic product?
8. Why might a grocer reduce the price of bananas?
9. Name two ways you can be an efficient shopper.

Putting Your Business Knowledge to Work

1. In what ways is timing important to a shopper?
2. List three examples of products or services that might be less expensive in July and August and tell why.
3. When would you consider an impulse purchase to be a harmless activity?
4. What does the phrase, "Don't buy quality you don't need" mean?
5. List the steps an efficient shopper might take in planning the purchase of a pair of hiking boots.

Computing Business Problems

1. Sandy Rasmusson wanted a new corduroy blazer. The price in August was $89.00. Sandy knew that in January the price would be reduced—probably to about $59.00.
   a. If Sandy waited until January to buy it, how much would she save?
   b. If the clothing store purchased the coat at $45.00 and sold it to Sandy for $59.00, what is the difference between the store's cost and selling price of the coat?
2. Popper's peanut butter comes in an 18-ounce jar and is priced at $1.98. Georgia Pride peanut butter comes in a 24-ounce jar and is priced at $2.52.
   a. What is the unit price of each brand?
   b. Assuming the quality of each is equal, which is the better buy?
3. Western Furniture and Appliance is moving to a new store. To avoid having to move a lot of merchandise, it is having a pre-moving clearance sale. Western has advertised that it will reduce the price of all merchandise in the store by 20 percent for one day.
   a. What would the sale price of a $979.00 sofa be?
   b. A customer paid $439.20 for a microwave oven during the sale. What was the original price of the oven?

Stretching Your Business Knowledge

1. Many supermarkets carry three types of brands—national, house, and generic. Name two food products you would feel comfortable buying under each type of brand. Tell why you made the selections you did.
2. For each article listed below, tell whether you would choose to buy a higher-quality item or whether you would choose a lower-but-acceptable-quality item. Which would, in turn, be lower in cost? Give reasons for each choice.
   a. outdoor paint for your two-story frame home
   b. tires for the car your brother drives a few miles into town to work each day
   c. shoes for school
   d. a wallet to give to your father, who is a salesperson
   e. a ball-point pen for school use
3. Are there supermarkets in your area which display unit prices? If you do not know, check the newspaper ads. If a store uses unit pricing, it will usually advertise this

fact. Visit a supermarket that uses unit pricing to see how the prices are displayed for the customers. Ask the store manager how customers reacted when the store began using unit pricing.

CHAPTER 16

A Consumer's Rights and Responsibilities

■ CHAPTER OBJECTIVES ────────────

After studying this chapter and completing the end-of-chapter activities, you will be able to:

1. List four rights and four responsibilities of consumers.
2. Give an example of an express warranty.
3. Explain how the Federal Trade Commission helps consumers.
4. Tell how the Better Business Bureau works with businesses for consumers.
5. List at least three examples of consumer dishonesty.
6. Explain why you should report a business's unethical practices.
7. Describe how trade associations help consumers.

After owning her new compact car for four months, Roselle noticed that the turn signal mechanism wasn't working properly. This was annoying and unsafe. She decided to take the car back to the dealership where she had purchased it for repair.

She explained the problem to the service manager. The service manager told Roselle if she could leave her car there for the afternoon, the turn signal would be repaired at no charge and with as little inconvenience to her as possible.

She returned in the late afternoon to find the turn signal repaired and, as promised, no bill for the work. As she climbed into the car, the service manager said, "When we sold you the car, the turn signal switch worked. You have a right to expect it to continue to work—certainly longer than four months. It was our responsibility to fix it at no charge."

That scene is being played out more and more frequently between businesses and consumers. It hasn't always been that way, however. Businesses have become more aware of the importance of good relationships with their customers. And consumers are certainly more aware of their rights and responsibilities in the marketplace.

There was a time when unfair actions by businesses were very common. To fight against those unfair practices, consumers joined together to demand fair treatment from business. This banding together became known as the consumer movement.

Your Consumer Rights

President John F. Kennedy, recognizing the growing consumer movement, declared that every consumer has the following basic rights:

1. The right to be informed — to be given the correct information needed to make an informed choice.
2. The right to safety — to be protected from goods and services that are hazardous to health or life.
3. The right to choose — to be assured of the availability of a variety of goods and services at competitive prices.
4. The right to be heard — to be assured that consumer interests will be fully considered by government when laws are being developed and enforced.

Actions by government, private groups, and individuals work together to protect these rights.

Protecting Your Rights as a Consumer

As was suggested by Kennedy, consumers have the right to expect honesty and fair treatment from businesses. These practices usually do not have to be demanded. Few businesses are ever dishonest on purpose. However, being a skillful consumer means that you know what your rights are and how to protect them.

The Right to be Informed

You have a right to expect accurate product information. Most products and services that you buy are described in advertisements, on labels, or by a salesperson. You are entitled to know what the product or service is and what it will do for you. But sometimes we buy carelessly. We may not weigh the facts given in advertising or by a salesperson, and we blame the seller for our poor purchases.

There are other times, though, when false information is given to a customer in an effort to make a sale. This type of dishonesty is

Illus. 16–1
Manufacturers provide product information in several ways. Many use the product itself or its package to carry information to buyers.

known as **fraud**. To be defrauded you must actually be deceived. Suppose you were looking for a small desk for your personal computer. If a salesperson told you she thought the desk would be sturdy enough to hold the computer—but it was not—you were not deceived, even though the salesperson may not have been accurate in judging the strength of the desk.

When a salesperson "puffs up" the product—says "It's the best." or "It's a great buy."—there is no fraud. If, however, the salesperson tells you the desk is made of oak when, in fact, it's made of pine, this is fraud.

The Right to Safety

Consumers also have a right to be safe from harm associated with using products or services. People could be endangered by taking harmful medication. Children have been hurt playing with unsafe toys.

There are several agencies that work to assure the safety of consumers. The Consumer Product Safety Commission (CPSC) is one of them. The CPSC has the authority to set safety standards, to ban hazardous products, and to recall dangerous products from the market.

The Food and Drug Administration (FDA), makes sure that food, drug, and cosmetic products are not harmful to consumers. It enforces laws and regulations which prevent distribution of unsafe or misbranded foods, drugs and cosmetics. The FDA also works to assure that product labels do not mislead consumers.

The United States Department of Agriculture (USDA) also helps insure consumer safety by setting standards for grading farm products sold from one state to another. It also controls the processing of meat, the inspection of meat, and the stamping of meat products with grades according to their quality.

The Right to Choose

The right of consumers to choose from a variety of goods and services has become a well-established principle. In fact, one of the main activities of the Federal Trade Commission (FTC) is to prevent one firm from using unfair practices to run competing firms out of business. When a business has no competitors and controls the market for a product or service, it is said to have a **monopoly**. Competing firms try to get your business by offering a variety of products and services at various prices. By driving out this competition, monopolies limit your right to choose.

Illus. 16–2
Competition is the cornerstone of our economic system. As consumers, we have the right to choose from among competitive products.

The Right to be Heard

Another of your rights that has developed during this century is the right to be heard by firms and government agencies whenever you have a valid complaint. Most firms are glad to take care of problems you have with their products or services, and many operate departments to handle customer complaints. Several federal government agencies also have the responsibility to assure the consumer's right to be heard.

The Office of Consumer Affairs (OCA) coordinates and advises other federal agencies on issues of interest to consumers. Its primary concerns are to represent the interests of consumers, to develop consumer information materials, and to assist other agencies in responding to complaints. The OCA normally refers consumer problems to other appropriate agencies and uses complaints from consumers to promote legislation.

The Federal Trade Commission (FTC) also protects your right to be heard. As a consumer, you can report directly to the FTC if you feel that any of your rights which come under its protection have been violated. The FTC regulates advertising and encourages informative and truthful advertising. It also requires textile firms to label wool and other fabrics with information telling what the material is made of and how to care for it. By responding to complaints in these and other areas, the FTC guards your right to be heard.

State governments also support public agencies that are interested in hearing consumers' concerns. Usually the Office of the Attorney General and the Department of Consumer Affairs have some responsibility for protecting the rights of consumers. They can prosecute businesses for violation of state consumer-protection laws and inspect advertising practices. They can also handle other types of consumer matters such as automobile-repair problems, credit problems and door-to-door sales practices.

Help From Private Agencies

In addition to publicly supported consumer protection agencies, there are some privately funded groups that help to make sure that you are heard. Perhaps the best known of these is the Better Business Bureau.

As discussed in Chapter 14, the Better Business Bureau is chiefly concerned with problems which arise from false advertising or misrepresented products and services. If you feel that your consumer rights have been violated by such practices, you can get help from the Better Business Bureau in your community. The bureau will usually ask you to report your problem in writing so that it can get all the details straight. It will then try to persuade the firm to correct the practice or fulfill its promises for the product or service in question. Most businesses willingly carry out the bureau's requests.

One of the bureau's most powerful tools of persuasion is publicity in local news media about unfair practices of firms that deliberately deceive customers. Also, because all bureaus have access to the information of other Better Business Bureaus, the report would follow the firm all over the country. Such bad publicity would cause the firm to lose customers, and most firms will change their practices to avoid losing customers.

There are a number of other private organizations which help protect your right to be heard. Groups of like businesses frequently form **trade associations**. These are organizations of firms engaged in one line of business. Many trade associations establish standards of quality for the products that their members manufacture. These standards of quality help assure that customers get the quality they expect when purchasing a product. Some trade associations also publish codes of ethics that members are urged to follow. Several trade associations now serve as central complaint departments to resolve consumer problems which may have been mishandled on the retail or manufacturer levels.

Recently, several newspapers and radio and television stations have added features designed to publicize consumer complaints and to help consumers solve problems. They respond to complaints by acting as mediators between consumers and businesses.

A Guarantee

While it is not a right, in the case of some purchases a consumer can expect to get a guarantee. A **guarantee** is a promise by the manufacturer or dealer, usually in writing, that a product is of a certain quality. A guarantee may apply to the entire item or only to some parts of it. It may promise that defective parts will be replaced only if a problem occurs during a specified period of time. No guarantee, however, covers damages caused by misuse.

When making a purchase, a skillful consumer asks about a guarantee. A guarantee is frequently in the form of statements like these: "The working parts on this watch are guaranteed for 1 year." "This sweater will not shrink more than 3 percent." "This light bulb is guaranteed to burn for at least 5000 hours." These kinds of guarantees are sometimes called **express warranties**. They are made orally or in writing and promise a specific quality of performance.

You should insist on seeing a copy of the guarantee when you buy an item. And you can require the business to put in writing any other guarantees that have been offered. Written guarantees are useful if you need to seek replacement of a faulty product. Guarantees are sometimes included in ads for the product. Keep a copy of the ad as evidence of the guarantee. Read the guarantee carefully to find out just what is covered and for what period of time.

Some guarantees are not written. They are often called **implied warranties**. They are imposed by law and are understood to apply even though they have not been stated either orally or in writing. In general, the law requires certain standards to be met. For example, it is implied that health aids purchased over the counter at a pharmacy will not harm you in any way.

Meeting Your Responsibilities as a Consumer

As we have seen, consumers in our country are very well protected. We have hundreds of laws and groups to protect us. Yet every day examples of consumer fraud are reported. Why? The answer probably lies in consumers themselves. They don't carefully exercise their responsibilities as consumers. What are those responsibilities?

Be Informed

The most important responsibility you have as a consumer is to be informed. Just having the right to be informed will not make you an informed consumer. You must find and use the information available to you. A producer might put a complete label on a product, but it is up to you to read and use the information on the label. To be an informed consumer, you should continually learn about the many goods and services available.

You should also keep informed about your rights as a consumer. Learn about the laws and agencies that protect your rights and how to report a violation of your rights. Being an informed consumer is hard work. But the extra effort spent in making your dollars go as far as possible will be worth it.

Illus. 16–3
Clothing manufacturers provide care labels on their garments. It is up to consumers to read and follow the instructions.

Be Honest

Most people are honest, but those who are not cause the rest of us to pay higher prices. Shoplifting losses have been estimated to be in the billions of dollars each year. Businesses usually make up losses that result from shoplifting by charging everyone higher prices.

Some people who would not think of shoplifting may be dishonest in other ways. Businesses report many dishonest acts by customers. For example, a customer might wear an outfit once for a formal occasion and then return it. Another customer might buy a stereo from a discount store but have it repaired at a retail store which has a generous repair plan on the same brand of stereos. Also, customers have been seen taking low price tags from articles and putting them on more expensive items which they buy. And there have been many complaints about customers who try to use discount coupons for merchandise they have not purchased.

As a responsible consumer, you must be as honest with a business as you want it to be with you. You should be as quick to tell the cashier that you received too much change at the checkout counter as you are to say that you received too little. Remember that dishonesty, in addition to being illegal and unethical, usually results in higher prices for all consumers.

Complain Reasonably

As a buyer you are usually responsible for what you buy if the merchant has been honest with you. If you are dissatisfied, however, and wish to complain, you should complain in a reasonable way.

You should first be sure that you have a cause for complaint. Be sure that you have followed the directions for using the product. One consumer angrily returned a record player because it would not work. The store found that the customer had failed to remove a piece of plastic placed under the turntable for safe shipping.

After you have confirmed the details of your complaint, calmly explain the problem to an employee of the firm from which you bought the item. In most cases the firm will be glad to correct the problem because it doesn't want to lose you as its customer. But if you become angry or threatening, you risk getting an angry response which will only delay the solution to your problem.

If you feel that your complaint is not handled fairly by the salesperson or the complaint department, take the matter up with

Illus. 16–4
Accepting returned items is one way retailers try to assure customer satisfaction.

the owner or an official of the firm. If that fails and the firm is a part of a national company, a letter to the customer relations department at the main office often gets results. If you do not get a response within a reasonable time, a second letter with copies sent to several consumer agencies will often bring a quick reply. If your complaint is about your charge account, the firm is required to answer your letter within 30 days. If you fail to get what you think is a fair adjustment, you may contact one of the following organizations:

1. the Better Business Bureau

2. the local or state Bureau of Consumer Affairs or the state Attorney General's office

3. your social welfare agency if you or your family are receiving financial aid from the government

4. a lawyer or the Legal Aid Society if the problem is quite serious

5. in larger cities, the Small Claims Court which is operated for filing small claims only

6. a consumer help department of a local or national newspaper or radio or television station.

Report Unethical Practices

As a responsible consumer, you should report unethical business practices to protect other consumers from becoming victims. Suppose the hand brake on your two-week-old bicycle fails to work and the shop from which you bought the bike refuses to honor its guarantee to replace all parts that break under normal use within 90 days. After several unsuccessful attempts to get the bicycle fixed, you might be tempted to give up, pay someone else to fix your bike, and mark it off as a bad experience. This might solve your problem, but it won't prevent other people from losing money as you did. Report the matter to an agency discussed in this chapter which might be able to get the shop to keep its word both to you and to future customers.

As you have seen, rights are only one aspect of the consumer movement. You also need to consider consumer responsibilities. As a consumer, you should be aware that rights and responsibilities are equally important if you are to get the best value for your money.

Adding to Your Business Vocabulary

The following terms should become part of your business vocabulary. For each numbered item, find the term which has the same meaning.

express warranty implied warranty
fraud monopoly
guarantee trade association

1. When false information is given to a customer in order to make a sale.
2. A promise that a product is of a certain quality or that defective parts will be replaced.
3. A firm that has control of the market for a product or service.

4. An organization of firms engaged in the same type of business.
5. An oral or written guarantee that promises a specific quality of performance.
6. A guarantee imposed by law which is not stated orally or in writing.

Understanding Your Reading

1. What are the four basic consumer rights as listed by John F. Kennedy?
2. What is the difference between "puffing up" a product and fraud?
3. Why should you get a good description of a product or service before you buy it?
4. Give an example of an express warranty.
5. How does the Federal Trade Commission help consumers?
6. What are the duties of the Office of Consumer Affairs?

7. How does the BBB work with businesses on consumers' behalf?
8. What are four responsibilities that every consumer has?
9. What is the most important responsibility that you have as a consumer?
10. Give at least three examples of consumer dishonesty.
11. Why should you report businesses that are following unethical practices?

Putting Your Business Knowledge to Work

1. What is the difference between an express warranty and an implied warranty?
2. Give a real or imaginary example of a business monopoly. Tell why it is a monopoly.
3. Why do you suppose the government supports agencies that protect consumers?
4. Which of the following would be considered fraud? Explain your answers.

a. A salesperson says the sound system you are looking at is the best brand made. After you buy it, you find it rated in a consumer magazine as the second best.
b. The label in a shirt says the colors will not fade. After washing it, you find that instead of a bright red shirt you now have a pale pink one.
c. The person who sells an electric pop-

corn popper says it is completely wash-able. Before using it, you put it into a sink filled with water to wash it. The first time you try to make popcorn, there is a flash and the popper's electrical unit catches fire. When you return the pop-per to the store, the salesperson tells you that she did not mean the popper could be put under water. She says you should have known that electrical appliances should not be put in water. She refuses to give you either a refund or an exchange.

5. What is one of the Better Business Bureau's most powerful tools of persua-sion?

6. Why, with all of the laws and organi-zations to protect consumers, do we con-tinue to hear of examples of consumer fraud?

7. Suppose that the first time you wash a new wool sweater it shrinks so much that it no longer fits you. You washed the sweater in hot water, but you notice that the label in the sweater says to use cold water. Would you have a fair complaint against the business that sold you the sweater? Why?

Computing Business Problems

1. The Art Mart Gallery, a shop dealing mainly in prints and drawings, guarantees satisfaction with every purchase for one month. That means a customer can re-turn a print or a drawing anytime within 30 days of purchase for a full refund. Last year's sales are given below:

Total sales $320,000
Products returned for refund $ 6,400

a. What percent of total sales was re-turned for refund?

b. What was the total amount of net sales, deducting the cost of refunds?

2. If you purchased a pair of jeans that had a waist size of 33 inches and were guar-anteed not to shrink more than 3 percent, approximately how many inches would you expect the waist size to shrink?

3. Jane Franklin is thinking about sub-scribing to a weekly consumer magazine so that she can be better informed. The magazine is offering a special trial sub-scription of 26 weeks for $19.50. The normal subscription rate for 26 weeks is $32.50.

a. What is the normal cost per issue?

b. What is the cost per issue under the special subscription rate?

c. How much would Jane save per issue by taking advantage of the special subscription rate?

Stretching Your Business Knowledge

1. Find out if there is a Better Business Bu-reau in your area. If there is, ask them to send you a brochure describing their function.

2. If you were a business person selling tools, what two express warranties would you put on your tools? Tell why you chose these two kinds.

3. Because business losses to shoplifters have been growing so rapidly, more and more businesses are prosecuting offend-ers who are caught. Through your library

and interviews with local business people, the police department, and the Chamber of Commerce, prepare a report on this problem. Consider these questions:

a. What is the extent of the problem in your area?

b. What is the estimated amount of loss by all local businesses in a year?

c. What are businesses doing to prevent shoplifting?

d. What are the penalties for those found guilty of shoplifting?

4. Gather four written guarantees and read them carefully. Make two lists from the guarantees. First, list all statements that give you specific information or instructions. Second, list all statements that are vague or general. Finally, evaluate each guarantee and rate it as either acceptable or unacceptable.

CAREER CATEGORY: Retail Selling

Much of this unit has dealt with your behavior as a consumer. Consumers, by definition, are involved in buying things from various businesses. Many of those businesses are retail businesses — businesses in which you might someday like to become employed.

Job Titles: Job titles commonly found in this career area include:

Divisional Merchandiser	Department Store Salesperson
Retail Buyer	Department Manager
Stock Room Supervisor	Cashier/Checker
Advertising Assistant	Buyer
Stock Clerk	Assistant Store Manager
Salesperson	Aisle Manager
Sales Manager	Advertising Manager
Home Furnishings Salesperson	Marketing Manager
Fashion Coordinator	Merchandise Checker
Fashion Buyer	Rackjobber

Employment Outlook: The outlook for employees in the area of retailing is very good. In a recent year retail sales workers held 3,367,000 jobs. They worked in many different kinds of stores, including drugstores, grocery stores, department stores, hardware stores, and sporting goods stores to name just a few. Through 1995 the number of retail workers employed is expected to grow about as fast as the average for all workers. However, while the volume of goods sold is expected to grow rapidly, the adoption of self-service and computerized checkout systems by more retailers will limit the need for additional sales workers. Retail sales work will nonetheless continue to provide more job openings than most other occupations through the mid 1990s.

Future Changes: Prospects for employment in retail stores are very good because of the many selling jobs available and the high turnover rate for sales jobs. There will continue to be many opportunities for part-time workers as well as for temporary workers during peak selling periods such as holiday seasons.

What Is Done on the Job: Most employees in retailing work in clean, comfortable stores. While helping customers make purchases, many retail workers must stand for long periods. Although many sales workers have a five-day, 40 hour week, in some stores the standard workweek is longer and includes weekend employment. Longer-than-normal hours may be scheduled before holidays and during other peak buying periods. Many employees in retailing regularly work one evening or more per week. Part-time workers in retailing generally work during peak business hours which are daytime rush hours, evenings, and weekends.

In addition to selling, most retail sales workers also make out sales checks, receive cash payments, and give change and receipts. They also handle returns and exchanges of merchandise and keep their work areas neat. In smaller stores they may help order merchandise, stock shelves or racks, mark price tags, take inventory, and prepare displays.

Education and Training: Many people enter retailing as a way to earn money in order to do something else such as complete a college education. Frequently students enter retailing as part-time employees while in high school.

It has often been said that retailing is a people-oriented business. It follows that retailers like people and like to work with people. Beyond human relations skills, it is important that retail employees have ambition and skills in marketing. It is useful but not always necessary to have college preparation for upper level jobs in retailing.

Salary Levels: The starting wage for most retail employment is the federal minimum wage. Weekly earnings of full-time sales workers in large stores are about $400. Sometimes employees in retail stores receive salaries plus commissions based on a percentage of sales. Some others are paid only commissions. An additional fringe benefit that many retail sales workers receive is a discount on merchandise that they purchase from the store.

For Additional Information: You may wish to speak with your marketing or distributive education teacher at the high school you attend. You may also receive information on careers in retailing by writing to the following organization:

Marketing and Distribution Career Information
The American Vocational Association
1510 H Street, N.W.
Washington, D.C. 20005

UNIT 6
USING BANKING AND FINANCIAL SERVICES

UNIT OBJECTIVES

After studying the chapters in this unit, you will be able to:

1. *List six services provided by banks.*

2. *Explain how to open and maintain a checking account.*

3. *Write an error-free check.*

4. *Reconcile a bank statement.*

5. *Name five means of payment other than cash or personal checks and tell when each should be used.*

BUSINESS BRIEF

The Evolving Financial Services Industry

From banking in formal halls of marble by business and the wealthy to electronic banking on street corners by the masses, banking has come a long way. Some highlights of the past fifty years show that it is still evolving.

The 30s and 40s. Banking meant a trip downtown. Bars separated tellers from customers, but the tellers knew most customers by name. Transactions were recorded by hand.

Consumer banking was growing. Formerly catering to the financial needs of business, banks began to welcome consumers.

A run on banks during the Great Depression brought about the birth of the Federal Deposit Insurance Corporation to protect customers' deposits. The 30s and 40s ushered in banking for the masses.

The 50s. America was becoming a mobile society. We fell in love with cars and the freedom they gave. They took us to drive-in hamburger stands and drive-in movies. Banks took the cue. Drive-up windows added convenience and come-as-you-are informality to banking.

The 60s. Americans were still on the move—from the cities to suburbia. Shopping malls followed, making "downtowns" into "ghost towns." Banks took their services to the suburbs, and branch banking was born. By the mid-60s, branch banks outnumbered main banks by three to one.

The 70s. Big things happened in the 70s. The automatic teller machines (ATMs) meant 24-hour banking and they moved to malls, airports, supermarkets—everywhere. Through electronic funds transfer (EFT), ATMs let us deposit money, withdraw cash, pay bills, or transfer money instantly.

A savings bank in Massachusetts found a legal way to allow customers to write special checks—negotiable orders of withdrawal—on savings accounts, introducing the concept of interest on checking. The NOW account idea would soon spread throughout the industry.

The 80s. Federal deregulation of banking in the early 80s erased many differences among financial institutions. Rules allowing savings and loans (S & Ls) to pay higher interest than banks were erased, putting both in competition for the same savings dollars. S & Ls and credit unions began allowing checks on savings. Financial institutions were allowed to transact business formerly assigned to specific types of firms. Now investments, real estate transactions, insurance, and other financing could be added to a financial firm's services. Department stores, brokerages, and other firms began offering certain financial services, giving birth to "nonbank" banking. Increased uses of EFT began reducing the need for checks. Home computers are viewed as tools for the increasing use of "home banking." It is likely that the public will soon find little or no difference between financial institutions in form and function.

CHAPTER 17

*T*he Business of Banking and Financial Services

■ CHAPTER OBJECTIVES ─────────────────────────

After studying this chapter and completing the end-of-chapter activities, you will be able to:

1. Give two reasons for putting your money in a bank or other financial institution.
2. Explain how banks earn most of their income.
3. Give two examples of ways the Federal Reserve System serves its member banks.
4. Name two federal government agencies that insure depositors' money.
5. Explain the difference between demand deposits and time deposits.
6. List six services provided by banks.
7. Give two examples of electronic funds transfer.

Imagine a city with no banks or other financial institutions. You would have to carry cash around with you to pay for everything you buy. You couldn't pay your bills through the mail because if the money were lost, you couldn't recover it. You would have to travel to the realty company to pay your rent, to the telephone company to pay your phone bill, and to the electric power company to pay for the electricity in your home. You would also have to find a safe place to hide the rest of your money until you needed it. And of course your idle money wouldn't be earning more money while it was hiding in the cookie jar at home. These are just a few of the many problems you and everyone else would face without banks.

Fortunately, we don't have to handle our money in this way because banks are in business to serve us. They provide services that help you and the community to carry out daily business activities. These services are available to individuals, to businesses, and to government agencies in the community. One of the major ways banking serves you is by providing a safe place to keep your money until you need it. Banks can also help your money grow by putting it to work in the community through loans. And banks offer advice on how to manage money so that it will be used in the best way. There are over 150 ways in which banks and other financial institutions serve their customers.

Banking as a Business

Have you ever thought of a bank as a business and yourself as its customer? Many people don't think of banks in this way. Yet a bank is a business just as stores and factories are businesses. As a business a bank sells services. For their services banks expect to earn a profit. Banks earn most of their income by charging for loans they make to individuals, businesses, and government and by investing part of the money customers put into the bank. Later in this chapter you will learn about other sources of income for banks.

Since banks are businesses, can anybody start one? Well, not exactly. People who wish to start a bank must meet certain qualifications set up by federal and state governments. Since the bank owners are going to handle other people's money, they are expected to be responsible citizens of high moral character. They also must have enough capital to start the business operations.

People who want to start a bank must apply for a charter from their state or from the federal government. If they apply to their state and a charter is granted, the bank will operate as a state bank. If the charter is from the federal government, the bank will operate as a national bank. Most national banks have the word "national" in their names, such as First National Bank or American National Bank. However, state bank names usually do not include the word "state."

Banks Are Regulated by the Government

A bank's operations are regulated more strictly than the operations of most businesses. If a business other than a bank fails, only a few people lose money. But if a bank fails, thousands of people are affected. Government regulation is necessary to assure the safety of customers' money. Even though Congress removed many regulations in 1983 and 1984, the government still exercises a great deal of control over the financial industry. State banks operate under the banking laws of the state in which the banks are located. National banks operate under federal laws as well as those of the state in which they are located.

The Federal Reserve System

Figure 17–1

Locate the Federal Reserve district in which you live. Is there an FRS branch bank in your town or city?

The federal government set up the **Federal Reserve System** to help banks serve the public efficiently. All national banks are required to join the Federal Reserve System (FRS or "the Fed"), and state banks may join. Banks that join the system are known as member banks. The United States is divided into 12 FRS districts, with a central FRS bank in each district, as shown in Figure 17-1.

As an individual, you cannot open a savings account in an FRS bank or borrow money from it. An FRS bank is a bank for banks. Its relationship to member banks is similar to that of your bank to you.

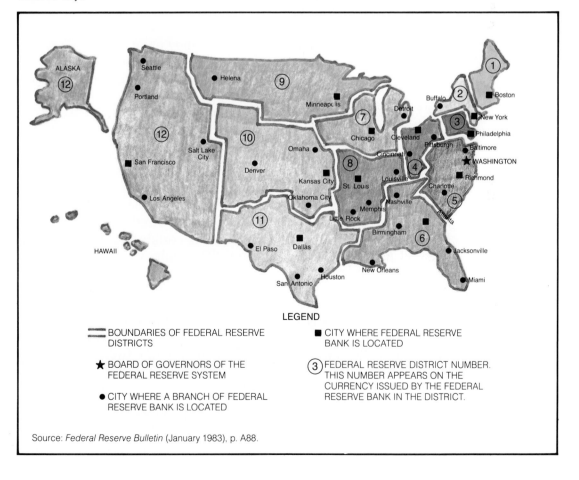

LEGEND

≡ BOUNDARIES OF FEDERAL RESERVE DISTRICTS

★ BOARD OF GOVERNORS OF THE FEDERAL RESERVE SYSTEM

● CITY WHERE A BRANCH OF FEDERAL RESERVE BANK IS LOCATED

■ CITY WHERE FEDERAL RESERVE BANK IS LOCATED

③ FEDERAL RESERVE DISTRICT NUMBER. THIS NUMBER APPEARS ON THE CURRENCY ISSUED BY THE FEDERAL RESERVE BANK IN THE DISTRICT.

Source: *Federal Reserve Bulletin* (January 1983), p. A88.

Illus. 17–1
FRS banks serve
other banks.

You may go to your bank to deposit money or get a loan. The FRS bank serves its members in the same way. It accepts their deposits, lends them money, and provides them with other banking services.

The Federal Deposit Insurance Corporation

Another federal agency that helps to regulate banks is the **Federal Deposit Insurance Corporation (FDIC).** It protects depositors' money in case a bank fails. At present, the FDIC insures each account up to $100,000. Although the FDIC is a government agency, money for its operation is provided by banks rather than by government. All member banks of the FRS are required to join the FDIC. Nonmember banks may join by meeting certain requirements. Almost 99 percent of all banks are FDIC members.

Types of Banks

Banks are usually classified by the number and kinds of services they offer. There are several types of banks and financial institutions. Let's look at the most common one first.

Commercial Banks

Most banks are organized as **commercial banks**. These are often called **full-service banks** because they offer a full range of financial services. Commercial banks handle checking accounts, make loans to individuals and to businesses, and provide a variety of other services. These services may be handled in different departments, such as a savings department, a trust department, a real estate department, or an investment department. Because commercial banks have so many different departments, they have been called "financial department stores." There are over 15,000 commercial banks in the United States.

Banks for Special Purposes

Some banks are organized for special purposes. **Savings banks**, for example, often provide a variety of services, but they are organized mainly to handle savings accounts and to make loans to home buyers. The major purpose of **trust companies** is managing people's money and property for them. **Investment banks** help large corporations get money for new buildings, machinery, and other long-term needs.

Other Financial Institutions Offering Banking Services

When you see "bank" in the name of a firm, you expect it to accept deposits and make loans; it may also offer a variety of other banking services. But there are businesses other than banks that offer banking services. Among these are **mutual savings firms** and **savings and loan associations (S&Ls)** which specialize in savings accounts and in making loans for mortgages. Savings in S&Ls are usually protected by a government agency, such as the **Federal Savings and Loan Insurance Corporation (FSLIC),** which insures accounts in S&Ls in much the same way that the FDIC insures bank accounts.

A **credit union** is a kind of a bank formed by workers in the same firm, government agency, labor union, or other agency. Credit unions serve members only. They accept members' savings deposits and make loans to them for a variety of purposes. In a recent year, there were over 20,000 credit unions in operation.

Consumer finance companies specialize in making loans for durable goods, such as cars and refrigerators, and for financial emergencies. Because they make loans, they are a part of the financial services industry; but they do not accept savings as do banks and other financial firms. You will learn more about this type of firm in Unit 8.

As a result of decreased government regulation of the banking industry, the differences among banks, S&L firms, and credit unions are not as evident as they once were. Some banks now compete with S&Ls and credit unions for savings and other services. At the same time, some S&Ls and credit unions offer special checking services on their savings accounts.

Other changes are also occurring. Firms not usually associated with banking now offer selected financial services. These "nonbank" banks include brokerage firms, credit agencies, and department stores. For example, brokerage firms that buy and sell stocks for their customers now also provide special savings accounts on which customers can write checks. Also, some large department stores, such as Sears, Roebuck & Co., after buying a brokerage firm, have established "financial service centers" in their retail stores. These centers offer, through the firm's brokerage divisions, a broad range of financial services, including savings and checking accounts and investments.

Other nonbank banks include the small out-of-state branches of large banking firms which opened after deregulation. In the past, a bank could operate only in the state in which it was originally

Illus. 17–2
Deregulation of the banking industry has resulted in significant changes. The Sears Financial Network is an example of nonbank banking.

chartered. But since these branches do not offer a full range of banking services, they are not technically defined by the government as banks and are, therefore, permitted to operate in other states. Typically these branches offer savings and checking accounts but do not make loans.

Other types of banks will probably also emerge as financial institutions adapt to deregulation. Whether or not these nonbanks continue to develop and become a permanent part of the financial-services industry is a question that will be decided by Congress and the marketplace.

Services of Banks

While some banks and financial institutions are organized for special purposes, commercial banks offer a variety of services, including some of those offered by special-purpose banks. Let's take a look at some of the most common of the many services offered by banks.

Accepting Deposits

One of the main services that banks offer is accepting money from their customers for safekeeping. Rick Schwartz, a student who works part-time and summers, is an example of a customer who uses this service. Rick gets $130 a week take-home pay from his summer job. He wants to save most of this for a down payment on a car. Rick knows that if he carries the money with him or keeps it at home, he may be tempted to spend it or it may be lost or stolen.

To protect his money, Rick puts most of his weekly pay into the bank. The money he puts in the bank is called a **deposit**. When he makes a deposit to his account, he becomes a depositor.

Demand and Time Deposits. Rick may put his money into a checking account where he can use it at any time by writing a check. A **check** is a depositor's written demand to a bank to pay out money from his or her account. Money put into a checking account is called a **demand deposit.** But since Rick does not plan to use his money until he saves a large amount, he has chosen a savings account and will make time deposits instead. A **time deposit** is one that usually will be left in the bank for a long time. Since Rick's money is in a savings account, he is saying to the bank, "I'm going to leave this money in my account for a fairly long period of time—maybe six months to a year or longer—and you can use it

Illus. 17–3
What a piggy bank! Security is, of course, a major concern for financial institutions and their customers.

until I need it." The bank can then make loans to other customers with Rick's money, along with the funds of other depositors, and Rick will be paid by the bank for the use of his money. The amount paid for the use of money is called **interest**. Let's say that Rick deposits $500 of his summer wages in a savings account and leaves it there for a year. If the bank pays 8 percent interest on savings, Rick's savings will have earned $40 interest at the end of the year and his car fund will have grown to $540.

Checking and Savings Accounts are Changing. At one time, there were two clear differences between checking and savings accounts: (1) Checking accounts did not earn interest as did savings accounts, and (2) you could not write checks on savings accounts. The differences between checking and savings accounts no longer exist to the extent that they once did. Certain types of checking accounts now earn interest. The bank may require the depositor to keep a minimum balance, such as $2,500, to earn the full interest on the account.

You can also write checks on certain types of savings accounts. A check written on a savings account is called a **negotiable order of withdrawal**. The account is known as a NOW account, getting its name from the name of the check. The number and frequency of checks allowed on certain NOW accounts may be limited. For example, a bank may limit the number of checks on certain types of NOW accounts to three a month.

Transferring Funds

Let's say that Megan Stewart has a checking account which she uses to pay bills. She can pay her bills by telling the bank to pay out, or transfer, a certain sum from her account to someone to whom she owes money. The bank provides different ways through which Megan can do this. One of the most common transfer methods is by check. When Megan writes a check to her rental agent to pay her rent, for example, the bank subtracts the amount of the check from Megan's account and, if the rental agent has an account at the same bank, the bank adds the amount to the rental agent's account. If the agent's account is at another bank, Megan's bank will transfer the funds to the agent's bank to be added to the agent's account there. The transfer of funds is simply an accounting entry in the records; no actual cash has been handled in the transaction.

More and more banking is done through electronic funds transfer. **Electronic funds transfer (EFT)** is a system through which funds are moved electronically from one account to another and from one bank to another. You can instruct your bank to transfer funds automatically, for example, from your savings to your checking account without writing a check. Or you can pay monthly bills, such as your phone bill or your rent, by instructing your bank to transfer the amount automatically each month from your account to the phone company or the rental agent.

You can go to your bank in person or write a letter instructing the bank to make electronic transfers for you. Or you can give the instructions to the bank at an automatic teller machine. An **automatic teller machine (ATM)** is a computer terminal provided by a bank to receive, dispense, or transfer funds electronically for its customers. ATMs provide automatic teller service quickly and easily and are available twenty-four hours a day. Their popularity has brought about considerable growth in the EFT system, which is changing the way people do their banking.

Lending Money

Many people, businesses, and government units need to borrow money at some time. For example, a business may want to

Illus. 17–4
Thanks to ATMs, customers can complete many banking transactions even when the bank is closed.

borrow money to expand, to build a new warehouse, or to buy merchandise for resale. Individuals may borrow to buy a car or pay college tuition. Banks are glad to lend money to those who need to borrow if it seems likely that the loans will be repaid when due. In fact, a bank needs to make loans. You will recall that it receives most of its income from the interest it charges borrowers. Even when you buy items like clothing or sports equipment and pay for them with a bank charge card (such as MasterCard or VISA), you are borrowing money from the bank.

But banks can't lend all the money they receive from their customers. The government requires banks to keep a certain amount of their customers' money on deposit with the FRS so that the banks can meet the daily needs of their customers. Therefore, a bank will lend only a certain part of its customers' deposits and keep the rest in reserve. For example, if a customer deposits $1,000 and the bank is required by the FRS at that time to hold 15 percent of all deposits in reserve, it can lend $850 ($1,000 − 15% or $150 = $850). This regulation is designed to help the banking system and the economy operate efficiently and to protect depositors' money.

Storing Valuables in Safe-Deposit Boxes

Besides offering a place to deposit money, banks offer **safe-deposit boxes** where you can store valuables. Since these boxes are in well-guarded vaults, they are the safest places to keep such things as jewelry, bonds, birth records, lists of insurance policies, and copies of wills. Not even the bank has the right to open your safe-deposit box unless it is ordered to do so by a court of law. The box can be opened only by you or by someone who has been given the right to open it for you. Safe-deposit boxes are rented by the year, and you can choose from a variety of sizes to suit your needs.

Providing Financial Advice and Investment Services

Many banks help their customers by offering financial advice and investment services. Officers of a bank can advise customers about such things as whether it is wise to buy a certain house, how to manage money better, or how to exchange United States money for foreign money.

Most banks offer advice on investments that customers can make. **Investments** are savings that are put to work to earn more money. For example, money in a savings account is an investment because the savings account earns interest. Federal government bonds are another kind of investment that can be bought through a bank. If a depositor wants to buy bonds regularly, once a month, for example, the bank can automatically deduct the cost of each bond from the depositor's account. A bank can also cash government bonds for its customers and pay them whatever interest the bond has earned. Usually depositors are not charged for these services. You will learn more about investing in government bonds in Unit 9.

Banks also buy for their customers bonds issued by businesses, by state and local governments, and by school districts. Since the deregulation of the banking industry, banks can buy and sell stock for their customers. At present, however, banks cannot advise customers as to which stocks to buy or sell, as stockbrokers can; but this may change in the future.

Managing Trusts

Many banks manage investments for their customers. When they do this, the money or other property that is turned over to the banks for investment is said to be held in trust. This service can be offered through a trust company or through trust departments in banks.

Trust departments are used by people of all ages, but they are especially useful for very young people and for elderly people. A young person who inherits money may not have the skill and experience to manage it wisely. The bank will take care of the money and will make proper investments with it. Elderly persons may have the trust department of a bank manage their money because they no longer want to do it. The bank makes investments and keeps the customers informed about what is happening to their money.

Banks Help Communities Grow

There is a great deal more to banking than that which you have read in this chapter. But from what you have learned so far, you can see that banks are important to all of us. Over a million people work in America's 59,000 banking offices. Banking services help build homes, start new businesses, plant crops, finance educations, buy goods, pave streets, build hospitals, and buy new equipment. These services are made possible because of the savings of many people.

Bank deposits do not remain idle in bank vaults. They are put to work. When you deposit money in your bank, you are making your money work for you and your community.

Adding to Your Business Vocabulary

The following terms should become part of your business vocabulary. For each numbered item, find the term that has the same meaning.

automatic teller machine	interest
check	investment bank
commercial or full-service bank	investments
consumer finance company	mutual savings firms and savings
credit union	and loan associations
demand deposit	negotiable order of withdrawal
deposit	safe-deposit box
electronic funds transfer	savings bank
Federal Deposit Insurance Corporation	time deposit
Federal Reserve System	trust company
Federal Savings and Loan	
Insurance Corporation	

1. A bank that handles the transactions of businesses that need to obtain large amounts of money.

2. A bank that mainly handles savings accounts and makes loans to home buyers.

3. A bank that handles checking accounts, makes loans to individuals and businesses, and provides other banking services.

4. Money that is placed in a bank account by a customer.

5. A nationwide banking plan set up by our federal government to assist banks in serving the public more efficiently.

6. An amount paid for the use of money.

7. An order written by a depositor directing a bank to pay out money from his or her account.

8. A bank that manages the money and property of others.

9. A financial institution, much like a bank, which specializes in savings accounts and making loans for mortgages.

10. A financial institution formed by workers in the same agency which serves only its members.

11. A financial firm which specializes in making loans for durable goods and financial

emergencies but does not accept deposits.

12. A federal regulating agency which insures depositors' money in member banks for up to $100,000.

13. A check written on a savings account.

14. A deposit that will be left in the bank for a fairly long period of time.

15. A box in a bank vault for storing valuables.

16. A system through which funds are moved electronically from one account to another or from one bank to another.

17. Savings that are put to work to earn more money.

18. A federal agency which insures depositors' money in member savings and loan institutions up to $100,000.

19. A computer terminal provided by a bank to receive, dispense, and transfer funds electronically for its customers.

20. A deposit to a checking account, making the money available at any time.

Understanding Your Reading

1. Give at least two reasons for putting money in a bank.

2. How do banks earn most of their income? Name two other ways in which banks earn income.

3. Why is government regulation of banks thought to be necessary?

4. Name two services the Federal Reserve System provides for its member banks.

5. Name two federal agencies which insure depositors' money. How do they differ?

6. How is a full-service bank different from a special-purpose bank?

7. How does a credit union differ from a savings and loan association?

8. How are banks and S&Ls becoming more alike?

9. Explain the difference between demand deposits and time deposits.

10. What is a negotiable order of withdrawal? What is the name of the account in which it is used?

11. Give an example of an electronic funds transfer.

12. Give three examples of the kinds of financial advice a customer might seek from a bank.

13. What two age groups find trust departments of banks especially helpful? Why?

14. Give three examples to show the importance of banks to the economy of the community.

*P*utting Your Business Knowledge to Work

1. Olaf Anders and Jean Myers operate a small bookstore. Each day they deposit all the cash they received except a small amount of change and a few bills which they keep in their safe. Explain why they are wise to follow this method of handling their money.
2. List the types of banking services that each group or individual below would be most likely to use. Explain your answer.
   a. a person planning to open a ski lodge
   b. a rock band
   c. a retired person
   d. a car buyer
   e. a high school ecology club
3. Agnes Sandski won $1,000 in an "original recipe bake-off" contest sponsored by the local TV station. She has decided to put all of her winnings in the bank. List several questions Agnes might want to ask before choosing whether to put the money in a demand-deposit or time-deposit account.
4. "In a private enterprise system, anybody who wants to open a bank should be allowed to do so." Do you agree with this statement? Give reasons for your answer.

*C*omputing Business Problems

1. Rick Schwartz, as you remember, is saving money for a car. He worked 12 weeks during the summer on a road construction crew. His take-home pay was $130 a week.
   a. If he deposited each paycheck in the bank, what was the total amount he deposited during the summer?
   b. If he put $50 each week in his savings account, how much did he have saved at the end of the summer?
2. On October 1 Christine Prado had a checking account balance of $120. She has her paychecks automatically deposited into her account. Her earnings for October were $920. During the month she wrote checks for $75, $125, $25, and $250. She also had $100 automatically transferred from her checking account to her savings account. In addition she used her EFT card at an automatic teller machine to withdraw $50 in cash. Find Christine's bank balance after these transactions.
3. To raise money for a class outing, a business class at Martin Luther King High School sold cans of dry-roasted nuts. The 0.05-kilogram cans sold for $1.25 each. The students deposited the total amount of their sales each week in the school's accounting office. During one month the records of the three students with the highest sales showed the following:

Date	Addie Smith	Jack Heinz	Rosa Ramirez
Oct. 5	8 cans	3 cans	5 cans
Oct. 12	6	5	5
Oct. 19	5	4	1
Oct. 26	11	7	4

a. How many cans did each student sell?
b. How much did each student deposit during October?
c. How many kilograms of nuts did each student sell?
d. Suppose a student in the class had not had any instruction in the metric system and wanted to know how many pounds of nuts were sold. Find the

number of pounds sold by each of the three students. (You will find help in the Appendix.)

4. The table which follows shows the total number of S&Ls in the United States in a recent year. It also shows the total assets (the value of all property) of S&Ls in the six states which have the highest number of S&Ls for the same year. Study the table and answer the following questions.

   a. What is the total number of S&Ls in the six states?
   b. What percent of the total number of U.S. S&Ls are located in the six states?
   c. In what state are the S&Ls with the highest total assets located?
   d. What is the total value of the assets of the S&Ls in the six states? (Write the figure in full.)

State	No. of S&Ls	Total assets ($ millions)
All states	4,591	$627,560
Ohio	384	40,587
Illinois	371	45,882
Pennsylvania	356	24,969
Texas	320	35,088
New Jersey	207	25,142
California	195	120,536

Stretching Your Business Knowledge

Many changes have taken place in banking during the last 25 years. You have read about some in this chapter. Talk with your parents and neighbors and see how many changes in banking you can list which have taken place during the last 25 years. As a start, you might list night banking hours. Compile a single list from all the changes noted by all the members of your class.

2. Find the following information about at least one bank in your community:
   a. What is the name and address of the bank?
   b. Is it a state bank or a national bank?
   c. Does it belong to the Federal Reserve System?
   d. Is it a commercial bank, or has it been organized for a special purpose?
   e. Does it provide safe-deposit facilities for its customers?
   f. Does the bank offer services other than those presented in this chapter? If so, give a brief explanation of each.

3. Five examples of items which might be kept in a safe-deposit box were given in this chapter. Talk with several adults and try to find out at least five other items which are stored in safe-deposit boxes. One bank gives its customers a list of 27 items to be stored in safe-deposit boxes. Also ask if there are items which should not be kept in safe-deposit boxes and tell why they should be kept elsewhere.

4. A bank's advertisement reads, "All major employees bonded for your protection."
   a. What does "bonded" mean?
   b. How does it protect the bank's customers?
   c. Why is bonding important to the bank?

5. Interview a manager of a credit union or savings and loan association and find out how NOW accounts work. You might include such questions as these in your interview:
   a. How is a NOW account opened?
   b. Must a certain balance be maintained?

If the balance falls below the required amount, what happens?

c. Is there a limit to the number of checks (negotiable order of withdrawals) which may be written on the account?

d. What are the advantages and disadvantages of NOW accounts?

6. Some people prefer to continue the use of checks rather than switch to EFT. Talk with several people who have bank accounts and find out their opinions about EFT. Report your findings by listing several advantages and disadvantages of the EFT system.

7. Some banks offer a service called "debit cards." Are debit cards offered by banks in your town? Explain what debit cards are and give an example of how they are used.

CHAPTER 18

Your Checking Account

After studying this chapter and completing the end-of-chapter activities, you will be able to:

1. List four advantages of having a checking account.
2. Explain the difference between the two major types of checking accounts.
3. Tell why a bank requires you to sign a signature card when you open a checking account.
4. Describe the procedure for making a deposit.
5. Show how to record your first deposit on a check stub or register.

Kim Po wrote the last of several checks to pay his monthly bills, placed them in stamped envelopes, and took them to the mailbox on the corner near his home. "How would I handle my business affairs without a checking account?" he asked himself as he dropped the envelopes into the mailbox. He would have to travel long distances to deliver each payment in cash, he thought. And with all his bills, he mused, he probably would need a wheelbarrow to carry all that cash. "Well," Kim said, "I surely don't have to put up with all that inconvenience and risk, thanks to my checking account."

A lot of people agree with Kim. In a recent year, over 112 million checking accounts were in use. A look at some of the advantages will show why checking accounts are so popular.

Advantages of Paying Through a Checking Account

When you open a checking account you will find, as Kim Po did, that it will be a convenient way to handle your business affairs. With a checking account, you can write checks at home and pay your bills by mail. Or, as you have learned, you can make payments automatically through the EFT system. Both methods will save time, energy, and money.

In addition to convenience, paying through a checking account also has many safety advantages. People who keep a lot of money on hand risk losing it by fire, theft, or carelessness. And when money is at home, there is a greater temptation to spend it needlessly. With a checking account, you will need to keep only a little cash on hand for small purchases.

Another safety feature is that you can safely send a check through the mail because it can be cashed only by the person or business to whom it is made payable. It is not safe to send cash through the mail because if it is lost, there is no way to recover it. But if a check is lost in the mail, it can be replaced at very little or no cost.

As you learned in Chapter 17, the money you deposit in the bank is safe in another way. If the bank is a member of the Federal Deposit Insurance Corporation, your account will be insured up to $100,000. You should always check to see that the bank in which you deposit your money is an FDIC bank. If you deposit your money in a savings and loan firm, you should verify that it is a member of FSLIC. The same caution applies wherever you deposit your money: first find out what kind of insurance protection your money will have.

A third advantage of paying by check is that, once cashed, a check is legal proof of payment. For example, suppose you write a check each month for $20 to pay for tennis lessons at the Indoor Tennis and Fitness Center. The Center will deposit your check at its bank; the Center's bank will then send the check to your bank where it will be subtracted from your account. Most banks return checks to depositors with "paid" stamped on the back. If the Center makes an error in its records and later tells you that a past month's fee has not been paid, your returned check will prove that you made the payment. Even if your bank does not return checks, it keeps a record of all checks paid and you can request that a copy of the check be sent to you. You can use the copy as proof of payment.

Another advantage of checking accounts is that they provide a record of your finances. With a checking account, you must record every deposit you make and every check you write. You can tell from these records how much you're spending, where it goes, and how much you have left in your account. The organized records you keep help you manage your money.

There are many advantages to paying through a checking account. Now that you know some of the main ones, your next step is to learn what kinds of checking accounts are available.

Kinds of Checking Accounts

Many things in banking have changed in recent years; the kinds of checking accounts offered by banks are among those changes. Checking accounts differ from one bank to another and from one part of the country to another. They differ in the features they offer customers. They also differ in costs, such as service charges. A **service charge** is a fee a bank charges for handling an account. When you are ready to open a checking account, you should visit several banks to find out what each offers. A bank employee will explain the advantages and disadvantages of each kind of account the bank offers. Shopping for your checking account will enable you to choose one that best suits your needs.

While there are still many types of accounts in use, recent changes have tended to put them into two basic groups: regular checking accounts and interest checking accounts.

Regular Checking Accounts

If you write a large number of checks each month, you probably should use a regular checking account. With some banks there is no service charge for a regular checking account as long as the account balance does not fall below a certain amount during a month. This balance varies, but it may be as high as $300 or more. Sometimes the charges are figured on the average balance of the account during the month. This means that the account may fall below a certain minimum on some days but must average at or above the minimum at the end of the month to avoid a service charge. Note the minimum and average balance requirements for regular checking accounts in Figure 18-1. Some banks also do not charge service fees on checking accounts to persons who keep a certain balance, usually $1,000, in a savings account in the bank. Service charges are also waived by some banks for persons 65 years old or older.

Interest Checking Accounts

If you are able to keep a rather large balance in your account, you may choose an interest checking account. Banks differ in their requirements. Some banks require a minimum balance of $500 or an

Interest rates and service charges.

	Minimum Balance		Average Monthly Balance	Interest	Monthly Service Charge
Regular Checking	$300 $0—299	or and	$600 $0—599		$0 $4
Interest Checking	$500 $0—499	or and	$1,500 $0—1,499	5¼%	$0 $5
Preferred Interest Checking			$10,000 + $5,000—9,999 $2,500—4,999 $0—2,499	premium rate money market rate money market rate 5¼%	$0 $0 $5 $8

Interest Checking and Preferred Interest Checking Accounts closed between interest payment periods will not receive interest for that monthly period.

GULFSTREAM BANK   Member FDIC

Figure 18–1
Fees charged and interest rates paid by banks may vary from bank to bank.

average daily balance of $1,000. As long as the account meets the balance requirement, the bank will pay interest on the checking account. If the account falls below the required amount, the bank usually pays no interest and may also add a service charge to the account. The charges may include a monthly charge, a fee for each check written, or both of these service charges.

The rates of interest which banks pay their customers also vary. A typical rate is 5¼ percent a year when required balances are maintained. In some cases, a bank may offer a higher rate of interest for a higher maintained balance. The interest rate may be based on the current cost of money in the marketplace. This rate is known as the **money market rate**. It is the interest rate that big users of money, such as governments and large corporations, pay when they borrow money. For example, the federal government announces each week what interest rate it has to pay to borrow money from citizens, banks, and businesses. This rate, along with other rates that make up the money market rate, may vary from day to day.

Banks offer interest checking accounts with varying rates tied to the money market rate. As this rate changes, so does the rate the banks pay depositors in certain types of accounts. To avoid changing rates daily or weekly, the bank, at the end of a month or a three-month period, determines the average of the daily money market rates for the month and pays the depositor that average rate for the period. Even higher rates than money market rates are sometimes available for very large accounts. Gulfstream Bank's interest checking account requirements are shown in Figure 18–1 as an example.

Variations of Basic Checking Accounts

In addition to the two basic kinds of checking accounts, there are several other types that you may want to examine as you shop for an account.

You may need to write only a few checks each month and may wish to keep only a small balance in your checking account. For depositors with such needs, many banks offer special checking accounts. Charges on these accounts vary, but the basic charge is about 10 cents to 20 cents for each check written and paid by the bank. There may also be a small monthly service charge for the account.

Some banks also offer a variety of banking services along with the usual checking account services in a package-plan account. With such an account, you may use a variety of bank services for a monthly fee. The fees vary from bank to bank according to the number of services included in the package. The package plan eliminates separate fees usually charged for such services as checking account maintenance, traveler's check fees, and charge card privileges.

In Chapter 17 you learned that financial institutions other than banks offer banking services. Savings and loan associations, for example, offer NOW accounts. You will recall that these accounts earn interest and allow you to write checks called negotiable orders of withdrawal. These accounts may require large balances, often $2,500 or more. Interest rates paid to depositors in S&Ls may be higher than those paid on interest checking accounts in banks. The rates often vary according to money market rates. The rate of interest earned by an account may change with the number of checks a customer is allowed to write. For example, one S&L offers an account called a SuperNOW Checking Account with these features: $2,500 minimum balance required, 8½ percent interest paid, and 4 checks allowed per month. The S&L may offer an option which allows unlimited checks but pays a lower interest rate, such as 7 percent.

Some credit unions also provide checking account privileges to members. Members in credit unions are called shareholders when they have money on deposit, and their checks are called **share-drafts**. This means a draft (withdrawal) is made on the member's shares of ownership (deposits) in the credit union. Interest rates may vary and the number of sharedrafts may be limited, as in NOW accounts.

As you also learned in Chapter 17, brokerage firms also offer NOW accounts on which checks can be written. These accounts usually earn interest at money market rates.

Now you know the most common kinds of checking accounts that are available. Which kind would you choose if you were opening a checking account?

Opening Your Checking Account

The procedure for opening a checking account is the same regardless of the kind of account you choose. Opening a checking account is easy. Just take your paycheck or cash to the new-accounts clerk in any bank and say that you want to open an account. The clerk will help you sign a signature card, make your deposit, and select your checks.

Signing the Signature Card

A bank will take money from a checking account only when authorized to do so by the depositor. Therefore, the bank must keep the depositor's signature on record to compare with the signature that appears on his or her checks. For this reason you will be asked to sign your name on a card when you open your account. This card is called a **signature card** and is the bank's official record of your signature. You must use the same signature on each check you write. Figure 18-2 shows a signature card for Kris Garza.

Sometimes two or more people have an account together. This is known as a **joint account**. Each person who will write checks on the account must sign the signature card. Any signer of the card in a joint account can write checks on the account as if he or she were the only owner. A signature card for a business would show the name of the business and the signatures of everyone authorized to sign checks for the business.

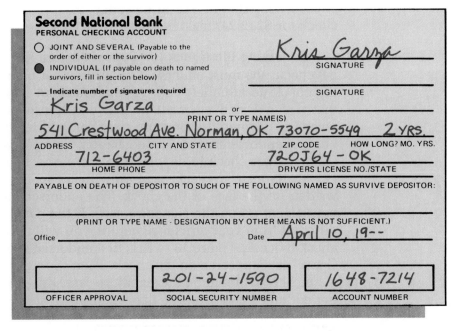

Figure 18–2
The signature on your checks must match the signature on your signature card that is on file at your bank.

Making Your First Deposit

When you deposit money in your checking account, you will fill out a **deposit slip** or a **deposit ticket**. This is a form on which you list all items you are depositing—currency, coins, or checks.

The deposit slip shows your name as depositor, your account number, the date, the items deposited, and the total amount of the deposit. Most banks print the depositor's name and account number on deposit slips and checks. Since these will not be ready when you open your new account, you will use a blank deposit slip. Figure 18–3 shows a deposit slip made out by Kris Garza. Her

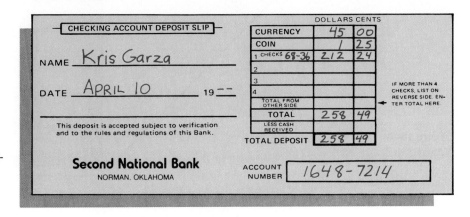

Figure 18–3
Kris Garza has completed a deposit slip for a total deposit of $258.49.

deposit consisted of $45 in currency, $1.25 in coin, and her paycheck for $212.24, making a total of $258.49.

Endorsing the Check for Deposit. Before Kris can deposit her paycheck, she must endorse it by writing her name on the back of the check near the left end. An **endorsement** is written evidence that you received payment or that you transferred your right of receiving payment to someone else. You will learn about different kinds of endorsements in a later chapter. Here you will see how Kris endorsed her check to deposit it to her new account.

To endorse a check, sign your name in ink exactly as it is written on the face of the check. The endorsement should match your signature on the signature card. If the name on the check is different from your official signature, you will need to endorse the check twice. In Figure 18–4 Kris first endorsed her paycheck "K. S. Garza" as it appeared on the check. Then she signed it "Kris Garza" as she had written it on the signature card. Kris is now ready to list her endorsed check on the deposit slip.

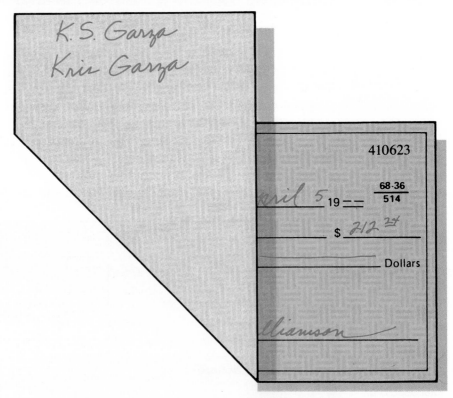

Figure 18–4
Why did Kris have to endorse this check twice?

Recording Checks on the Deposit Slip. Each check is identi-fied by the number of the bank on which it is drawn. This number is assigned to each commercial bank by the American Bankers Association. You can see the three parts of this number in Figure 18–5. The first part of the number above the line indicates the city or state in which the bank is located. The second part is the number assigned to the individual bank. The number below the line is a Federal Reserve number that banks use in sorting checks. Only the two top numbers are listed on the deposit slip, as shown in Figure 18–3.

Sometimes checks are listed on the deposit slip by the name of the person from whom the check was received or by the name of the bank on which it was drawn. You should use the method your bank prefers.

Figure 18–5
Each commercial bank in the United States is assigned a number by the American Bankers Association.

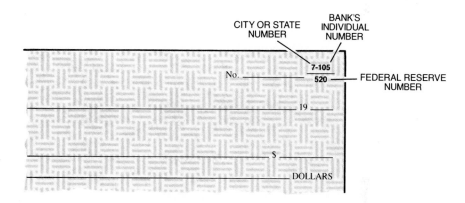

Getting a Receipt for Your Deposit. When you make a deposit to your checking account, the bank teller will give you a receipt. The receipt may be printed by a machine at the same time that it registers the deposit in the bank's records. This type of receipt is shown in Figure 18–6.

Another type of receipt has a stamped or written acknowl-edgment of the deposit on a duplicate copy of the deposit slip. Deposits may also be made at automatic teller machines located away from the bank building. Figure 18–7 shows a receipt for a deposit made at an automatic teller station.

Deposits may also be sent through the mail. The bank records your deposit and mails a receipt back to you. Remember, mail deposits should not include cash because it may be lost.

FIRST NATIONAL BANK OF DAWSON

MEMBER
FEDERAL DEPOSIT INSURANCE CORPORATION

DAWSON, ALASKA

ALL ITEMS ARE CREDITED SUBJECT TO PAYMENT
THIS IS YOUR RECEIPT
THE BANK SYMBOL, TRANSACTION NUMBER, DATE, AND AMOUNT OF YOUR DEPOSIT ARE SHOWN BELOW

FNB425 JUN 1 50.00D44

ALWAYS OBTAIN OFFICAL RECEIPT WHEN MAKING DEPOSIT

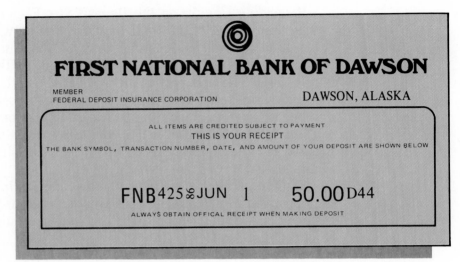

Figure 18–6
No matter how you make deposits to your account, be sure to get a receipt each time.

Selecting Your Checkbook

When you become a depositor, your bank will supply you with blank checks bound in a **checkbook**. Checkbooks may be supplied without charge on some kinds of accounts, but usually banks charge a fee when the depositor's name and address are printed on each check and deposit slip. Today, checks may be personalized in ways other than just printing the depositor's name. You may also choose from a variety of colors and designs: an example is shown in Figure 18–8.

TRANSACTION RECORD

This transaction is subject to verification and adjustment and will become final in accordance with the Bank's rules and regulations and as provided by law

CARD NUMBER: 611929001655848302
TRANSACTION: DEP 0202

AMOUNT: $150.00
DATE: 1/12/--
TIME: 3:14PM

FROM:
TO: CHK
LOCATION: WARDS CORNER

PLEASE KEEP THIS FOR YOUR RECORD.

Second National Bank

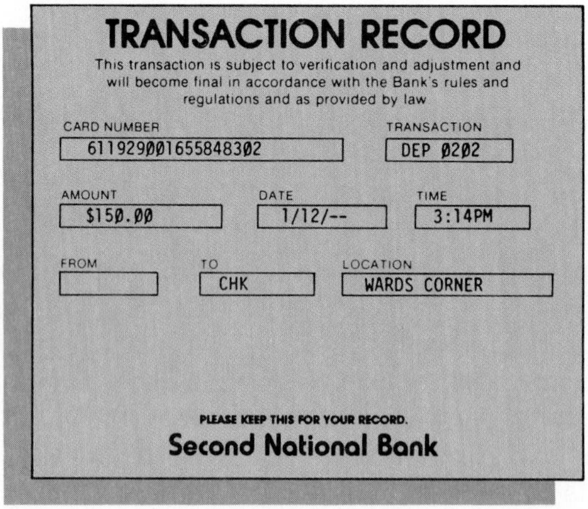

Figure 18–7
This receipt for a deposit to a checking account was issued at an automatic teller location.

Figure 18–8
Depositors may now choose from a wide variety of check designs.

Besides the checks, a checkbook also contains forms on which a depositor writes a record of deposits made and checks written. In some checkbooks, this record is kept on the **check stub**, which is attached to each check, as shown in Figure 18–9. Another type of checkbook provides a **check register**, which is a separate form for recording deposits and checks. Checkbooks also often contain deposit slips.

Figure 18–9
The check stub attached to a check provides one way to keep checking account records. The stub is completed when the check is written.

When checks are printed, the bank number and the account number are usually printed in magnetic ink. These magnetic ink numbers enable banks to sort checks quickly using machines that "read" the numbers. Figure 18–8 shows magnetic ink numbers in the lower left corner of the check. These odd-looking numbers are especially designed to be read electronically.

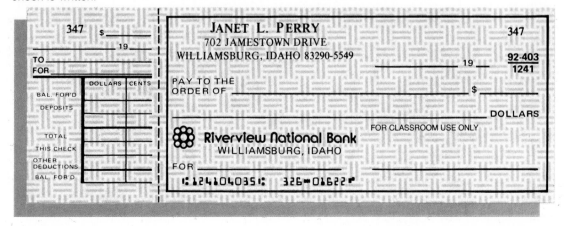

cathy®

Figure 18–10

A check register is a second way to maintain checking account records. Like the stub, the register is completed at the time each check is written or a deposit is made.

Recording Your Deposit

When you make a deposit to your checking account, you should immediately enter the amount on the check stub or in the check register. Figure 18–10 shows how Kris Garza recorded the information for her deposit in her check register. Since Kris is opening a new account, there is no balance to be entered on the "Balance Forward" line.

Kris Garza is now ready to write checks up to the amount she has deposited in her account. In the next chapter, you will learn how this is done.

PLEASE BE SURE TO DEDUCT ANY PER CHECK CHARGES OR MAINTENANCE CHARGES THAT AFFECT YOUR ACCOUNT

ITEM NO.	DATE	PAYMENT ISSUED TO OR DESCRIPTION OF DEPOSIT	AMOUNT OF PAYMENT	✓	AMOUNT OF DEPOSIT OR INTEREST	BALANCE FORWARD	
D	4/10	To *Opening deposit* For Paychk 212.24 ; Cash 46.25			258 49	Payment or Deposit	
						Balance	258 49
		To For				Payment or Deposit Balance	
		To For				Payment or Deposit Balance	
		To For				Payment or Deposit Balance	
		To For				Payment or Deposit Balance	
		To For				Payment or Deposit Balance	

*A*dding to Your Business Vocabulary

The following terms should become part of your business vocabulary. For each numbered item, find the term that has the same meaning.

checkbook

check register

check stub

deposit slip or deposit ticket

endorsement

joint account

money market rate

service charge

sharedraft

signature card

1. A form that accompanies a deposit and shows the items deposited.
2. A form attached to a check on which a depositor keeps a record of the check written and any current deposit.
3. A signature on the back of the check that transfers ownership of the check.
4. A separate form on which the depositor keeps a record of deposits and checks.
5. A card, kept by a bank, that shows the signatures of persons authorized to draw checks against an account.
6. A bank account that is used by two or more people.
7. A bound book containing blank checks and check stubs or accompanied by a check register.
8. A charge made by a bank for handling a checking account.
9. The current cost of money in the marketplace.
10. A withdrawal from a member's shares of ownership in a credit union.

*U*nderstanding Your Reading

1. What are the advantages of paying bills through a checking account?
2. Why should a person who wishes to open a checking account be interested in knowing whether or not the bank is a member of the FDIC?
3. Explain the difference between the two major kinds of checking accounts.
4. Describe several variations of the two basic kinds of checking accounts.
5. Name two kinds of fees that go into service charges.
6. What is the difference between a minimum balance and an average monthly balance?
7. Why does a bank require you to sign a signature card when you open a checking account?
8. Describe the process for making a deposit.
9. If the name on the face of a check and the depositor's official signature are not alike, how should the depositor endorse the check?
10. Explain the meaning of each of the three parts of an ABA number.
11. How may checks be listed on a deposit ticket?
12. If you have both cash and checks to deposit, should you send the deposit by mail? Why?
13. Explain the difference between check stubs and a check register.
14. Why are account numbers printed in magnetic ink on checks and deposit tickets?
15. Explain the procedure for recording the first deposit to a new account on a check stub.

*P*utting *Your Business Knowledge to Work*

1. "You should shop for the best place to open a checking account as carefully as you shop for the best buy in any product or service." Give two reasons to support this statement.
2. If you sign your full name on the signature card when you open your checking account and then sign your nickname on a check, do you think the bank should pay the check? Give a reason for your answer.
3. Alice and Steven Kranebill have a joint bank account and both have signed the signature card. Must they both sign each check? Why?
4. Greg Johannsen attends a technical school in the morning and works afternoons and weekends as a receptionist at a skating rink. He believes that if he deposits his earnings in a checking account and writes checks to pay the few monthly bills he has, he could better manage his money. What kind of a checking account would you recommend for Greg? Why?

*C*omputing *Business Problems*

1. Steve Tolson wrote a check for a deposit to his savings account and three checks to pay his monthly bills. Here are the amounts: savings, $100; rent, $325; electric bill, $92.50; gasoline bill, $72.25. This left a new checkbook balance of $290.25.
   a. What is the total amount of Steve's monthly bills?
   b. What is the total amount of Steve's four checks?
   c. What was Steve's checkbook balance before he wrote the four checks?
2. Service charges for Julie Poynter's regular checking account at Second National Bank are based on the bank's rate schedule, which follows:

Minimum Balance	Charge
0–$100	$3.00
$101–$300	1.50
$301 & over	no charge

During a recent six-month period, her balances were: April, $142.71; May, $194.20; June, $97.70; July, $302.43; August, $38.74; and September, $154.36.
   a. How much was Julie's service charge for each month?
   b. What was the total service charge for the six-month period?
3. The rate schedule at Gulfstream Bank is shown in Figure 18–1 on page 252. Wanda Settle's interest checking account at Gulfstream had an average monthly balance for June of $1,621.80.
   a. Is Ms. Settle eligible to earn interest on her account for June?
   b. If the bank paid 5 1/4% annual interest on the average monthly balance, how much interest will she earn for June?

Stretching Your Business Knowledge

1. The numbers printed in magnetic ink in the lower left corner of a check are written in a kind of computer language called Magnetic Ink Character Recognition or MICR. In Figure 18–8 you will notice two groups of MICR numbers. The first group is the bank's number and the second group is the customer's number. When the bank pays a check you have written, the check is returned to you with another number in MICR printed in the lower right corner. Ask your parents or another person who has a checking account to let you examine the returned check and find out what the added MICR number is. Report your findings to the class.

2. Some banks advertise as "24-hour banks" or "anytime banks." Do any banks in your community offer after-hours services? If so, write a brief description of how a customer would use these services. Why might after-hours services be needed?

3. Many banks today do not have a minimum age requirement for a person who wants to open a checking account. Visit a local bank or talk with a bank employee to find out if there is an age requirement at the bank. Write a brief report on the reasons given for having or not having an age requirement.

4. Interview an employee at a savings and loan association and one at a credit union. Find out what kinds of checking accounts, if any, each offers. Ask each person you interview what advantages, if any, an account in her or his firm would have over an account in a bank.

5. Find out what a "split deposit" is and prepare a deposit slip to show how such a deposit is made.

6. Below is a list of terms that relate to joint bank accounts. Write a short definition of each term. You might refer to a high school business law textbook or ask a bank employee to help you with your definitions.
   a. joint and several
   b. tenants in common
   c. joint tenants with right of survivorship
   d. tenants by entirety

CHAPTER 19

*W*riting and Receiving Checks

■ CHAPTER OBJECTIVES ───────────────────────

After studying this chapter and completing the end-of-chapter activities, you will be able to:

1. Correctly maintain checking account records on check stubs or in a check register.
2. Write error-free checks.
3. State three purposes of endorsements.
4. Identify three types of endorsements and tell when each is used.
5. Correctly endorse a check.

After you have opened your checking account, you will probably write so many checks that you will wonder how you ever got along without it. You will join over 100 million other owners of checking accounts who write over 40 billion of these "orders to pay" each year.

Checks are important pieces of paper. They travel across town and across the country to make both personal and business payments. Each check is finally either returned to the person who wrote it or filed at the bank. Most people consider their checking accounts an important part of their money management. They provide a handy record of income when checks received are deposited. And the record of checks written shows where the money goes. If you learn to write checks and record your banking activities correctly, you will find that using your checking account is easy and enjoyable.

Getting Acquainted with Your Checks

A good way to get acquainted with checks is to examine several different checks belonging to relatives or friends. You will find that the checks look alike although they are from different banks.

Compare them to the check shown in Figure 19–1. Note that all checks have basically the same kinds of information printed in the same places.

As you study the parts of the check in Figure 19–1, you will find some terms on its face, or front, that you have not learned. At the upper left and the lower right, you will see the word, "drawer." The **drawer** is the owner of the account and the person who signs the check. The **payee** is the person to whom the check is written. The payee's name always appears after the words, "Pay to the order of." The **drawee** is the bank or other financial institution in which the account is held. Three parties, as you see, are shown on each check: the drawer, the payee, and the drawee. You may want to refer to the parts of a check in Figure 19–1 as you learn to write checks in the next section.

Writing a Check

Figure 19–1
The parts of a check.

In addition to checks, your checkbook will have a form for recording the activities of your account. Two kinds of these forms are available. A check stub is a form attached to the check by a

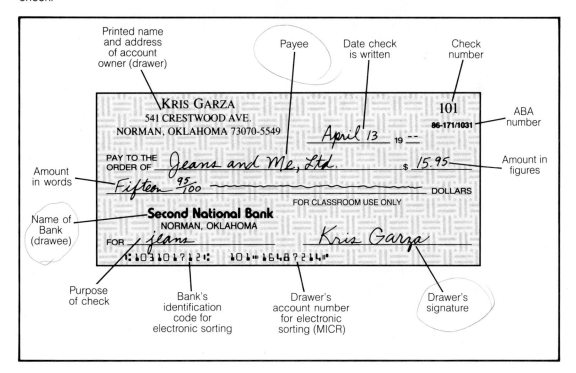

perforated line. After the check is written, it is torn off at the line and the stub remains in the checkbook. A check register is a separate book of forms, usually the same size as the checkbook. Compare the two forms shown in Figure 19–2. Note that both provide blanks to fill in the same type of information about the check.

Figure 19–2
Which form would you prefer?

ITEM NO.	DATE	PAYMENT ISSUED TO OR DESCRIPTION OF DEPOSIT	AMOUNT OF PAYMENT	✓	AMOUNT OF DEPOSIT OR INTEREST	BALANCE FORWARD	
						PLEASE BE SURE TO DEDUCT ANY PER CHECK CHARGES OR MAINTENANCE CHARGES THAT AFFECT YOUR ACCOUNT	
D	4/10	To *Opening deposit* For *Paychk 212.24; Cash 46.25*			258 49	Payment or Deposit	
						Balance	258 49
101	4/13	To *Jeans and Me, Ltd.* For *jeans*	15 95			Payment or Deposit	– 15 95
						Balance	242 54
102	4/15	To *Second National Bank* For *Cash – current expenses*	40 –			Payment or Deposit	– 40 00
						Balance	202 54
D	4/16	To *Deposit* For *Birthday-Mom & Dad*			20 50	Payment or Deposit	+ 20 50
						Balance	223 04
103	4/22	To *Spangler Gifts, Inc.* For *postage due on 4/8 order*	– 88			Payment or Deposit	– 88
						Balance	222 16
AT	4/23	To *Cash from Automatic Teller* For *Game tickets and dinner*	30 – –			Payment or Deposit	– 30 00
						Balance	192 16

	101	$ 15.95	
April 13		19 – –	
TO *Jeans and Me, Ltd*			
FOR *jeans*			
		DOLLARS	CENTS
BAL. FOR'D		–	
DEPOSITS 4/10		258	49
TOTAL		258	49
THIS CHECK		15	95
OTHER DEDUCTIONS		–	–
BAL. FOR'D		242	54

Fill Out Your Record First

The check stub or register is your record. Fill out the stub or register first. If you write the check first, you may forget to record the information. Later, when you need to refer to the information, you may not remember the amount of the check or to whom it was written.

Study Figure 19–2. It shows how Kris Garza would record her check for $15.95 to Jeans and Me, Ltd., using both a check stub and a register. Of course, she would use only one type, but you can see from Figure 19–2 that she would record the same information on either form.

Let's consider the check register here. Recall that in Chapter 18 Kris opened her new account with a deposit of $258.49. That is her first entry in the register. It is entered in the Additions column and Balance column. Since this is her first deposit, there is no "balance forward" to record.

The second entry is for the check that Kris wrote to Jeans and Me, Ltd. (Figure 19–1). Kris has entered the check number in the first column and the date of the check in the second. In the next column, she has recorded the payee and noted that the payment was for jeans. The amount of the check has been written in the Amount of Payment or Withdrawal column and subtracted from the beginning balance of $258.49. She recorded her new balance, $242.54, in the Balance column on the same line as the amount of the check.

Filling Out the Check

After you have completed the entry in the check register, you are ready to fill out the check. Remember that a check is an order to the bank to pay out your money, so fill out the check completely and carefully.

There are usually seven items which you will write on the check: the check number, the date, the payee, the amount in figures, the amount in words, the purpose of the check, and your signature. Complete the following steps in writing your checks:

Step 1. Number your checks in order. These numbers help you to compare your records with the checks that have been paid and returned to you. If the numbers are not already printed on the checks, write them in the space provided. Check numbers are usually printed both on the checks and the check stubs. Check registers have a space for you to write the check numbers.

Step 2. Write the date in the proper space on the check just as it was entered in the register.

Step 3. Write the payee's name on the line following "Pay to the Order of." The payee for Kris's first check is Jeans and Me, Ltd., as shown in Figure 19–1.

Step 4. Write the amount of the check in figures after the printed dollar sign. Write the amount close to the dollar sign so that a dishonest person cannot insert another figure between it and the amount. A check on which the amount has been dishonestly increased is called a **raised check**. Cents are usually written somewhat smaller so that the amount in dollars and the amount in cents can easily be distinguished. Write cents figures close to the dollar figures so that additional numbers cannot be inserted.

Step 5. Write the amount in words on the line below the payee's name. Spell out the amount in dollars. Write the cents in figures as a fraction of a dollar. Begin writing at the far left end of the line so that the amount cannot be changed by adding a word at the beginning of the line. Draw a line from the fraction to the printed word "Dollars" to fill all unused space. If a check must be written for less than a dollar, write the amount as shown in Figure 19-3.

If the amount written in figures does not agree with the amount written in words, the bank may pay the amount written in words. But the bank is not obligated to

Figure 19–3
Most people would rather not write a check for less than $1.00. However, sometimes it is necessary, and this is how it should be done.

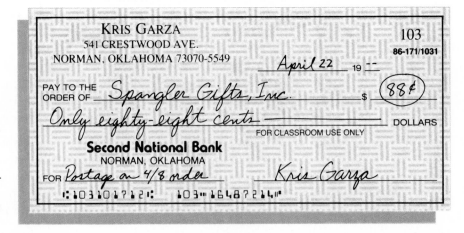

pay a check containing errors. If there is a serious difference between the two amounts, the bank may call you and ask for instructions concerning payment. The bank may also return the check to you and ask you to replace it. There is usually a charge when a check is returned for any reason. If a firm receives a check from you on which the amounts disagree, the firm will probably return it to you and ask for another check.

Step 6. Write the purpose of each check on the line labeled "For" at the bottom of the check. Writing the purpose will later help you remember why you wrote the check. Note that Kris Garza wrote "jeans" as the purpose of Check 101.

Step 7. Sign your checks with the same signature that you wrote on your signature card. A married woman should use her given name in signing checks. For example, she should sign Racquel Waterman, not Mrs. Jack Waterman. Kris Garza is the drawer of the check in Figure 19–1 and has signed her name on the proper line.

On checks issued by a business or other organization, the firm's name may appear as a printed signature and is often followed by the word, "By." The person who signs the check writes his or her name after "By." This shows that the firm is the drawer and that the check should not be charged to the person who has signed the check. An example of a business signature is shown in Figure 19–4.

The bank may subtract from the depositor's account only the amounts of checks and electronic funds transfer (EFT) transactions that the depositor has authorized. Your signature as drawer on a check tells the bank to pay the amount from your account. EFT payments require special arrangements with the bank. By using your private code

Figure 19–4
Who is the drawer of a business check? Should Sarah Adams' account be charged for this check?

number at an automatic teller machine (ATM) to give instructions for EFT payments, you authorize the bank to subtract money from your account.

If a bank cashes a check signed by someone who had no right to use the depositor's signature, the bank may be held responsible. Writing another person's signature on a check without his or her authority is a crime called **forgery**. A check with such a signature is a forged check.

Tips for Good Check Writing

Figure 19–5
Here are eight tips for good check writing.

Anyone who writes checks has a great deal of responsibility. But if you remember the tips shown in Figure 19–5, there is little chance of your losing money because of poorly written checks.

1. Write checks only on the forms provided by your bank. It is possible to write checks on just about anything—even a paper bag. But sorting and exchanging the millions of checks that are written every day is a tremendous job for banks. This job is done at a reasonable cost due to the use of machines that sort the checks according to the MICR numbers printed on the check. (See Figure 19–1). If the check does not have these numbers, the sorting will be interrupted, the check may be delayed, and a charge for handling the check may be made.

2. Tear up all checks on which you make errors. Don't try to erase or retrace your writing. No one who handles your check can be sure whether the changes were made by you or by someone who had no right to make them. Before destroying the check, record its number and write the word, "void" on the register to show that the check was not used.

3. Avoid making checks payable to "cash" or to "bearer." If such a check is lost, it can be cashed by anyone. For this reason, you should never make a check payable to "cash" unless you are going to cash it at the time it is written—at the teller's window in the bank. Even then, it is usually preferable to make the check out with the bank as payee.

4. Always fill in the amount. If you leave it blank, you may be held responsible for amounts filled in by others.

5. Write a check only if you have enough money in your account to cover it. A bank is not expected to cash checks for more than the amount that is in your account. Writing a check for more than you have in your account is called **overdrawing**. When an account is overdrawn, the bank may not pay the check. In addition, most banks charge the depositor a fee for checks they have to return marked "insufficient funds." Special arrangements can be made with the bank to give you an automatic loan if you overdraw your account. Intentionally overdrawing without an arrangement with the bank, however, is against the law.

continued

6. Use the current date. A **postdated check** is one which is dated later than the day on which it is written. For example, a check written on October 1 but dated October 5 is postdated. You might postdate a check because you do not have enough money on deposit on October 1 to cover the check but plan to deposit money on October 3. This is a bad business practice because you may not be able to make the deposit or may forget to make it as planned. Also, you must be sure that your deposit is actually entered into your account by the bank before you write checks using the money. This usually takes one or two days after the deposit reaches the bank, but it may take longer. Writing checks before your deposit is put into your account will result in an overdraft unless you have funds to cover the check amount in your account before your deposit is made. Before you open an account, get information on when the bank enters deposits into customers' accounts.

7. Record every payment from your checking account, whether the payment is by check or EFT. Some people carry a few blank checks in their wallets instead of carrying their checkbooks. When one of these checks is used, the drawer should make a note of it and record it in the register as soon as possible. It is also important to record promptly all transactions made at an ATM. Since no check is written, it is easy to forget to record withdrawals. But a receipt is given for each transaction. Note the last entry in the register in Figure 19-2.

8. Write all checks in ink. This prevents someone from raising the amount of the check. Some businesses use small machines called check protectors or check writers to guard against possible changes in the amount of a check. These machines stamp the amount on the proper line of the check so that the amount cannot be changed. Many businesses, especially large ones, use computers to print their checks; this also helps to prevent raising of checks.

Following the eight guidelines in Figure 19-5 will help prevent losses on checks that you write.

Stopping Payment on a Check

In certain situations you may want to tell your bank not to pay a check that you have written. Suppose Kris Garza's check for $45.67 to Joseph Fields was lost. Before she writes a new check, Kris should ask the bank not to pay the first one. This is called **stopping payment**. The bank will ask Kris to fill out a stop-payment form such as the one shown in Figure 19–6. This form is a written notice from the drawer telling the bank not to pay a certain check. Note the items included on the stop-payment form: date, check number, amount, payee, and the drawer's signature. Most banks charge a fee for stopping payment on a check.

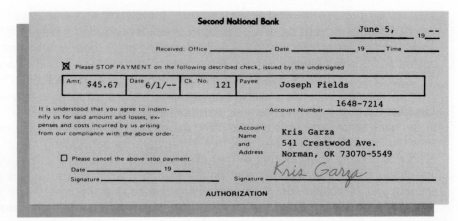

Figure 19–6
A stop-payment form tells your bank not to pay a check that you have written.

Payment of a check should be stopped only for good reasons. You may learn, for example, that a check you have written to pay a bill was lost in the mail. Before you write a new check, you should stop payment on the one which was lost. Or, a check you have written may be stolen. To prevent the wrong person from cashing the check, you can instruct the bank to stop payment. Remember, however, that once you have issued a check, it may be passed from one person to another. You can be held responsible for damages that stopping payment on a check may cause to rightful holders of the check.

Now you have learned how to write your own checks correctly and to stop payment on a check if a problem arises which demands this action. But what about checks written by others which you receive? How do you handle those?

Handling Checks You Receive

You will no doubt receive many checks in your lifetime. You should learn to handle them as carefully as you do cash. As the payee, you can do one of three things with a check: you can cash it, deposit it to your bank account, or transfer it to another person or business as a payment. To do any of these things, you must first endorse the checks you receive.

As you remember from Chapter 18, Kris Garza had to endorse her paycheck before she deposited it to her account. In doing so, she was following one of the basic purposes of endorsements.

Endorsements Serve Several Purposes

When you endorse a check, your responsibilities are almost as great as if you had written the check yourself. As an endorser, you are actually making this promise: "If this check is not paid by the bank, I will pay it." To enable you to handle properly the checks you receive, you should understand the purposes of endorsements. Here are the three basic purposes:

1. Endorsements allow the payee of the check to carry out his or her plans for the check, either to cash it, deposit it, or transfer it to someone else.
2. Endorsements serve as legal evidence that the payee had the check and that he or she cashed it or transferred it to someone else.
3. Endorsements mean that the endorser will pay the check in case the next owner of the check cannot collect the money.

Studying the kinds of endorsements will help you to understand these purposes.

Kinds of Endorsements

Different endorsements serve different purposes. Learn the kinds of endorsements, what each one means, and when to use each kind. As you handle the checks you receive, you will probably use each of the four types of endorsements discussed below. Let's start with the endorsement that Kris Garza used for her paycheck in Figure 18–4.

Blank Endorsement. An endorsement that consists of only the endorser's name is called a **blank endorsement**. Kris Garza signed her name exactly as it was written on the face of the check. She then signed her name as she had written it on the signature card.

A blank endorsement makes a check payable to anyone who has the check. This endorsement may be used whenever a check is to be transferred, but sometimes another type is better.

Special Endorsement. Suppose Nancy R. Brooks receives a check made payable to her. She then wants to make that check payable to Alan C. Friedman, who operates a service station where she buys gas. The check is a payment on the bill she owes Mr. Friedman. If she uses a blank endorsement and sends the check to

Mr. Friedman, he can cash it when he receives it. But if the check is lost before it reaches him, anyone who finds it can cash it.

To make sure that no one except Mr. Friedman will be able to cash the check, Miss Brooks may use a **special** or **full endorsement**. With this endorsement, she places the words "Pay to the order of Alan C. Friedman" before her signature as shown in Figure 19–7. Mr. Friedman must sign the check before it can be cashed.

Restrictive Endorsement. A **restrictive endorsement** limits the use of the check to the purpose given in the endorsement. For example, you may have several checks that you want to mail to the bank. If you write "For deposit only" above your signature, as in Figure 19–8, you have restricted the use of the check so that it can only be deposited to your account. If a check with such an endorsement is lost, it cannot be cashed by the finder.

Businesses often use rubber stamps to imprint restrictive endorsements that require checks to be deposited to their accounts. A business thus has no risk of loss if an unauthorized person uses the stamp to endorse a check..

Multiple Endorsements. After endorsing a check, the payee usually cashes it or deposits it in a bank. But the payee may transfer the check to another person, who in turn may transfer it to someone else, and so on. Each person who transfers a check should be required to endorse it, for each endorsement is another promise that

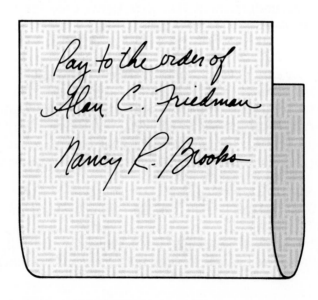

Figure 19–7
A special or full endorsement.

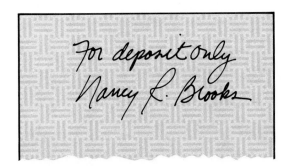

Figure 19–8
A restrictive endorsement. If this check is lost, it cannot be cashed by the finder.

the check will be paid. In actual use, checks with more than one, or multiple, endorsements are rare.

An endorsement serves as a promise only to those who receive the check after the endorsement is written. It does not apply to persons who held the check before the endorsement. Suppose that Jean Whitfield signs a check and gives it to Sam Corbett and that Corbett endorses it and gives it to Earl Foster. Suppose also that Foster endorses the check and gives it to Harry Paulsen. As shown in Figure 19–9, Paulsen sends the check to his bank for deposit. If the bank refuses to pay the check for any reason, Paulsen may collect the amount from the drawer (Whitfield) or from either of the two endorsers (Corbett or Foster). If he collects from Foster, Foster has a claim against the drawer (Whitfield) and against the first endorser (Corbett). But if Paulsen collects from either of them, neither has a claim against Foster. As you can see, the collection process can become quite involved; for this reason, many people will not accept checks with multiple endorsements.

Tips for Accepting and Cashing Checks

It is important that you understand your responsibility as a signer and as an endorser of checks. According to law, a check is payable on demand, that is, at the time the holder of the check presents it for payment at the bank on which it is drawn. But a bank may refuse to accept a check if it is presented for payment long after the date on which it was written. Some checks carry a printed notation, "Please cash within 60 days." So you should present a check for payment within a reasonable time after you receive it.

A check is valuable only when it is drawn on a bank in which the drawer has money on deposit. For this reason you should accept

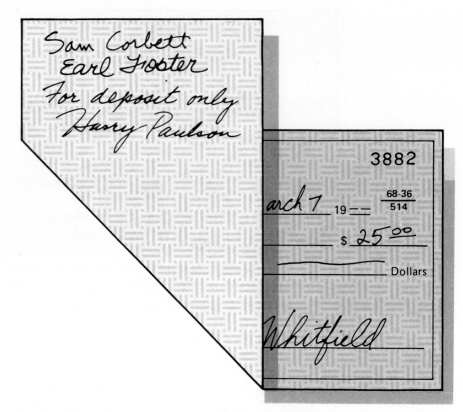

Figure 19–9
A check
with multiple
endorsements.

checks only when they are written or endorsed by people whom you know and trust or those who can provide clear identification. A check received from a stranger who cannot provide acceptable identification may turn out to be worthless, and it may be impossible for you to find the person to collect the money.

Just as you should be cautious in accepting checks, you should not expect strangers to cash checks for you. If you must ask a business or a person who does not know you to cash your check, you will probably have to prove your identity. You may do this by showing your driver's license or some other form of identification. Some businesses require a second identification, such as a credit card, before accepting a personal check. Some banks furnish identification cards which can be used on a terminal in a business to verify electronically that a customer presenting a check has funds on deposit to cover the amount of the check.

Checks are used so commonly instead of cash that you will usually have no trouble cashing them where you are known. However, legally, no one has to accept your checks.

Illus. 19–1
Check acceptance policies may vary from store to store. Remember that no one is legally bound to accept checks.

Adding to Your Business Vocabulary

The following terms should become part of your business vocabulary. For each numbered item, find the term that has the same meaning.

blank endorsement
drawee
drawer
forgery
overdrawing
payee

postdated check
raised check
restrictive endorsement
special or full endorsement
stopping payment

1. The person who signs a check.
2. The crime of signing another person's name on the check form without authority to do so.
3. A check dated later than the date on which it is written.
4. The person to whom a check is made payable.
5. The bank or other financial institution in which the account is held.
6. Instructing a bank not to pay a certain check.
7. Writing a check for more money than is in one's account.
8. A check on which the amount was increased by a dishonest person.
9. An endorsement including the name of the person to whom the check has been transferred.
10. An endorsement that limits the use of a check to a specific purpose.
11. An endorsement consisting of a name only.

Understanding Your Reading

1. Name the three parties involved with a check and tell where their names are shown on the face of a check.
2. What two numbers are included in the MICR figures printed on the lower left edge of the check?
3. Why should the check stub or register be filled in before the check is written?
4. Explain the difference between the way check numbers are recorded on a check stub and on a register.
5. Name the seven steps in writing a check and tell how each part of the check should be written.
6. How does the signature section of a business check usually differ from that of a personal check?
7. What is a forged check?
8. What risk is involved in making a check payable to "Cash" or "Bearer"? What can you do to avoid the risk?
9. Is it always illegal to overdraw intentionally? Explain.
10. Under what conditions might you stop payment on a check? How would you stop payment?
11. What are the three purposes of endorsements?
12. If you wish to transfer ownership of a check from yourself to another person, would you use a blank, a special, or a restrictive endorsement? Explain.
13. Which endorsement would you use to limit the use of your payroll check to being deposited in your bank account?
14. What is meant by multiple endorsement?

Putting Your Business Knowledge to Work

1. Olivia Moreno likes the convenience of the automatic teller for her banking. She often makes deposits at the automatic teller station which she passes on her way to work. But she frequently forgets to record these banking activities in her check register and never seems to know how much money she has in the bank. Also she has overdrawn her account twice and has had to pay a fee each time. Can you suggest a plan for Olivia to follow which would allow her to use the automatic teller services and still be sure of having an accurate record?
2. Tina Hobbs feels that it is a waste of time to record information on check stubs. "The bank sends me a statement each month; that's all I need," she says. How could you convince Tina that she should keep records?

3. On October 28 Henry Santee selected a $59.95 sunshield helmet to wear when he commutes to work on his motorbike. The merchant agreed to take his personal check, using Henry's driver's license and his company ID card for identification. However, when the merchant saw that Santee had dated his check November 1, he refused to accept it. Santee explained that he would deposit his paycheck on October 30, and that by the time the merchant sent the check through the bank, it would be covered. The merchant still refused to take the check. Do you agree with the merchant? Why?
4. The NaturFresh Supermarket requires its checkers to follow four rules in the following order when accepting checks: (1) Get two forms of identification (ID) from the customer. (2) Hand the check and the IDs

to the manager for approval. (3) Stamp the check with the store's rubber endorsement stamp. (4) Place the check under the cash tray in the register drawer.

a. Why do you think the store requires two IDs?

b. Why do you think the check must be approved by the manager?

c. What kind of endorsement would most likely be on the rubber stamp?

d. What are the advantages of stamping the check immediately after accepting it?

e. Why do you think checks are placed under the cash tray instead of with the cash?

5. For each of the following situations, (a) name the endorsement which should be used, (b) write the endorsement, and (c) explain each of your responses.

a. John C. Houchens is in the bank and wants to cash his payroll check.

b. Megan T. Pickthorne wants to deposit her payroll check by mail.

c. Lloyd B. Kilgore uses a check received from Howard W. Sloan to pay for groceries at TruValu Supermarket.

d. Martha S. Markowski gives two checks to a friend, Caron Ann Talbot, who is to deposit them to Martha's account.

e. C. R. Smythe deposits a check on which his name has been misspelled as C. R. Smith.

*C*omputing Business Problems

1. Kathy Whiteside opened a checking account on June 1 and deposited $122.47, the amount of her first paycheck from her summer job as a day-camp counselor. During the month she deposited three more paychecks of the same amount.
   a. What was the total of Kathy's deposits?
   b. During June Kathy wrote four checks for the following amounts: $37.50, $25.00, $7.35, and $4.20. What was the total amount paid out in checks?
   c. What was Kathy's balance at the end of June?

2. As treasurer of the Glendale High School Student Council, you are to fill out check stubs and write checks for the following transactions of the council. If forms are not available, draw forms similar to that shown in Figure 19-2. The beginning balance is $277.60. Use the current date. Number the stubs and checks beginning with 26.
   a. Pay $9.25 to the Iowa Bookstore for the book, *Parliamentary Procedure*.
   b. Pay 82 cents to Sandy Graham for a record book (79 cents plus tax).
   c. Pay $27.50 to Latimer's Sporting Goods for a basketball trophy.
   d. Pay $43.04 to Don Smedke for his traveling expenses to the state convention of student councils.

3. On September 1 Tomas Gibran had a balance of $678.25 in his checking account. By arrangement with his bank, his electric bill is automatically paid each month through EFT — the amount of his electric bill is deducted from his account and added to the account of the utility company. He also has his payroll check automatically deposited to his account by his employer. His checks and deposits for the month are shown on page 280. Record the beginning balance, the checks, the deposits, and his EFT transactions in a check register similar to the one in Figure 19-2.

September	Check No.	To	For	Amount
1	AD	Automatic deposit	8/15-31 check	$575.24
3	AT	Danville Public Uti.	August electric	98.65
4	134	Century Realty Co.	September rent	395.00
9	135	J. F. Todd, M.D.	Chip's sprained ankle	52.50
13	136	Jerome's Fashions	Balance on suit	64.22
16	137	Morrisette Hardware	Paint, wallpaper	72.20
16	AD	Automatic deposit	9/1-15 paycheck	575.24
20	138	Sun Fuel Co.	Oil contract	88.20
24	139	Food Emporium	Groceries	97.91
25	AT	Automatic withdrawal	Cash for expenses	50.00
28	140	United Fund Drive	Contribution	35.00
30	141	Frazier's Drugstore	Chip's medicine	18.11

4. Paul D. Redford stopped at an automatic teller station to deposit three checks he had received. The amounts were $142.75, $64.50, and $13.80.
  a. What was Paul's total deposit?
  b. Write the correct endorsement that Paul would use. His name was spelled out on two of the checks; on the other it was P. D. Redford.
  c. In order to prepare a deposit slip, what other information would Paul need?

Stretching Your Business Knowledge

1. Listed below are some errors that were made in filling out checks. Explain which errors would probably not affect the use of the checks and which would probably cause the checks to be void.
  a. The check number is omitted.
  b. The check stub was not filled out.
  c. The drawer forgot to sign the check.
  d. The check was dated 1984 instead of the current year.
  e. The drawer forgot to fill in the name of the payee.
  f. The payee's name was misspelled.
  g. The amount of the check was $54.50. It should have been $45.50.
  h. The drawer omitted the amount of the check since that information was not available, and in a letter instructed the payee to fill in the correct amount.

2. "The float" is a term often used in banking and finance. Some states have laws regulating the float period.
  a. What is meant by "the float"?
  b. Survey two or three banks in your community and find out the float for each.
  c. Interview a banker or a lawyer and find out what laws, if any, your state has passed regarding the float.

3. Harvey Graham owed Leonard Saunders $58. He wrote a check to Mr. Saunders and mailed it to him. Later, Mr. Graham decided that he did not want to pay all of the debt at once. He therefore asked his bank to stop payment on the check. Do you think it was wise for Mr. Graham to make this request? Why?

4. Some large supermarkets have rules posted about cashing checks. Some of

these rules include the following: only checks in the amount of the purchase will be accepted; no checks will be accepted unless ID cards are on file in the store; anyone paying by check will be photographed; each person paying by check must record her or his thumbprint on the back of the check. Find out whether these or other rules are posted in a supermarket near you. Ask the manager whether the amount of bad-check loss has gone down since the store began using these methods. Report your findings to the class.

5. Some banks offer special ID cards to their customers. These cards allow the customer to have checks approved electronically in firms that have credit-check terminals connected to the computers in the customer's bank. Visit a large supermarket, drugstore, or department store and find out if the store has a credit-check terminal. Ask for a demonstration. Write a brief description of the procedure and report to the class.

CHAPTER 20

Your Returned Checks and Your Bank Statement

■ CHAPTER OBJECTIVES

After studying this chapter and completing the end-of-chapter activities, you will be able to:

1. Explain how a check is cleared.
2. Tell why a canceled check is valuable to the drawer.
3. Explain how a depositor whose bank does not return paid checks can prove that a certain payment was made.
4. Reconcile a bank statement.

In the last chapter you learned how to write checks and how to handle the checks you receive. You also learned that the checks you write will be handled with billions of other checks written each year by people everywhere. Before the checks you write are returned to you, their course is long and lively as they travel to pay your bills.

Checks travel around the country in wallets, handbags, envelopes, mail pouches, planes, trucks and on trains. They crisscross the nation's cities and towns and travel to farms, to ships at sea, and to foreign countries. They go in and out of houses, businesses, government offices, and banks of all shapes and sizes. They are written on, typed on, stamped on, and imprinted with oddly shaped characters in magnetic ink. They are shuffled by hand, stored temporarily under money trays of cash registers, and stacked and bound with rubber bands. They are sped through machines which read and sort them by the thousands a minute. Finally, they find their way, still in good shape, back to the bank of the drawer. The bank will either return them to the drawer — as most banks do — or file them with the depositor's account. In either case, the checks will be available to the depositor as proof of payment. For many

Illus. 20–1
Checks must
be sorted
and delivered.

checks, the journey from drawer and back is a long one. You may wonder how all the checks ever find their way back to the right person. Let's see how that happens.

How Your Checks Get Back to You

Though getting checks back to their original drawers may seem an impossible task, it happens through a carefully planned system. You have learned how checks are passed from one person to another by an endorsement. So the check you write or receive may be owned by several persons before it gets back to you as the drawer. But eventually it is returned to the drawer's bank to be paid and charged to his or her checking account. This process is called **clearing a check**. Clearing may be done locally on the books of one bank, through a specially designated place for clearing, or through the Federal Reserve System.

Clearing Checks Locally

Check clearing may involve one, two, or several banks and drawers within the same city. Let's see how these differ.

The Same Bank. If both the drawer and the payee have accounts in the same bank, clearing is simple. The bank subtracts the amount from the drawer's account and adds it to the payee's account. It is simply an accounting transaction.

Two Banks.   When two different banks are involved, clearing is somewhat different, although it is still fairly simple if the two banks are in the same small town.

Suppose Jon Gable's neighborhood rock group feels its new song will make it big if the group can get more practice time and get the song recorded. Jon persuades his father to rent a garage on the outskirts of town (the Gable's neighbors' suggested the location!) for rehearsals. The rent for one month is $50. Mr. Gable sends the rental check, written on his account with the North River National Bank, to Arlene-Bayne Realty. Look at Figure 20-1 and follow the check

Figure 20–1
Follow Mr. Gable's check through the clearing process.

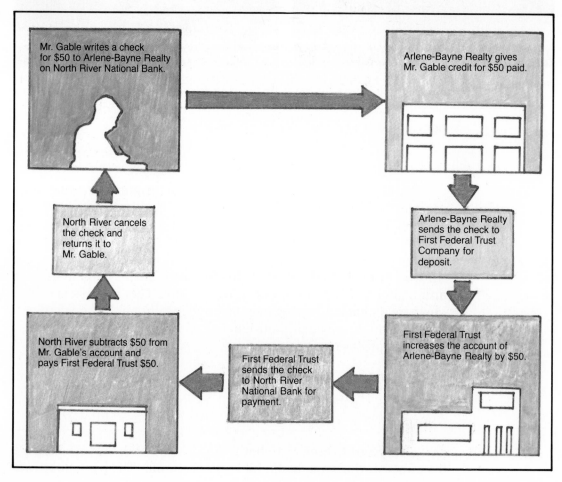

Mr. Gable writes a check for $50 to Arlene-Bayne Realty on North River National Bank.

Arlene-Bayne Realty gives Mr. Gable credit for $50 paid.

North River cancels the check and returns it to Mr. Gable.

Arlene-Bayne Realty sends the check to First Federal Trust Company for deposit.

North River subtracts $50 from Mr. Gable's account and pays First Federal Trust $50.

First Federal Trust sends the check to North River National Bank for payment.

First Federal Trust increases the account of Arlene-Bayne Realty by $50.

on its trip to the two banks in the town where the Gables live and back to Mr. Gable.

Arlene-Bayne Realty endorses the check and deposits it in its account in the First Federal Trust Company. When First Federal receives the check, it adds $50 to the account of Arlene-Bayne Realty, endorses the check, and sends it to North River National for payment. After North River National receives the check, it pays First Federal $50 and subtracts that amount from Mr. Gable's account. The check is then marked paid by North River National and returned to Mr. Gable as his record of payment.

Several Banks.   When there are several banks in the same town, the banks usually agree on a certain time each day to clear checks. Each bank makes up one package of its paid checks which were drawn on the other banks—one package for each bank. A messenger may be sent to each bank to exchange packages of checks and pay or collect any difference that might be due. Or, each bank may send a representative to a central place which the banks have selected as an exchange office; here they exchange checks and settle the accounts with each other.

Suppose that when the bank representatives meet, it is found that the First Federal Trust Company has checks totaling $4,000 drawn on the North River National Bank. Also, the North River National Bank has checks totaling $4,250 drawn on the First Federal Trust Company. First Federal thus owes North River National $250. It may pay this amount in cash, but usually a method is worked out that makes the handling of cash unnecessary. For example, both banks may maintain accounts with the same bank in a neighboring city. In this case, the bank in the other city may be notified to transfer $250 from the account of First Federal to the account of North River National.

Clearing Checks Through a Clearinghouse

In large cities where there are many banks, it would not be practical for each bank to send checks for payment to all banks on which the checks were written. Usually city banks are members of an association which operates a place for members to clear their checks every day. This place is called a **clearinghouse**.

The method of clearing checks through a clearinghouse is similar to the method followed between banks in a small town, except that thousands of checks are handled for many banks. Entries may be made in accounts that the banks maintain with the clearing association or with a Federal Reserve bank.

Clearing Checks through the Federal Reserve System

One of the services of the Federal Reserve System, which you learned about in Chapter 17, is clearing checks between banks in different cities. This process is more complex than clearing through a clearinghouse because of the volume of checks that must be cleared.

The Federal Reserve System handles millions of checks every day. In a recent year, for example, the Federal Reserve Bank of New York handled almost six million checks every business day. Because of the services of the Federal Reserve System, checks can be used to make payments in any part of the country as easily as they can be used locally. Even so, you can see that the actual handling of the checks to get them back to the drawer is expensive. Banks use EFT wherever they can to speed up the process. EFT, as you have learned, eliminates the use of checks. You can understand why EFT will probably become more widely used in the future. In the meantime, a great number of checks still must be cleared.

After your bank subtracts all your cleared checks from your balance, the checks will either be filed at the bank or sent back to you with a report of your account. Reviewing this report will be the last step in the process of maintaining your checking account.

Reviewing Your Bank Statement

As a depositor you will need to review the record of your account which the bank keeps. At regular intervals, usually monthly, the bank will send you a report on your account known as a **bank statement**. Statement forms vary, but most of them show these things:

1. the balance at the beginning of the month
2. the deposits made during the month
3. the checks paid by the bank during the month
4. any electronic or automatic teller transactions made during the month
5. any special payment the bank has made at your request, such as a transfer of funds from your checking to your savings account, or the automatic payment of a monthly bill such as a car payment
6. service charges for the account for the month, including charges

for special services, such as stopping payment on a check

7. the balance at the end of the month.

See if you can locate an example of each of these items on the bank statement shown in Figure 20-2.

Second National Bank

Checking Account Statement

ACCT. 1648-7214
DATE 5/1/--
PAGE 1

Kris Garza
541 Crestwood Ave.
Norman, OK 73070-5549

Please examine at once. If no errors are reported within 10 days, account will be considered correct.

BALANCE FORWARD	NO. OF WITH-DRAWALS	TOTAL AMOUNT	NO. OF DEP.	TOTAL DEPOSIT AMOUNT	SERVICE CHARGE	BALANCE THIS STATEMENT
0.00	15	350.10	4	651.23	1.25	299.88

CHECKS AND OTHER DEBITS		DEPOSITS AND OTHER CREDITS	DATE	BALANCE
		258.49	4/10	258.49
101	15.95		4/13	242.54
102	40.00		4/15	202.54
		20.50	4/16	223.04
103	.88		4/23	222.16
	30.00 ATW		4/23	192.16
		160.00	4/23	352.16
104	16.30		4/24	335.86
105	6.22		4/24	329.64
106	25.78		4/26	303.86
107	18.95		4/26	284.91
109	65.33		4/26	219.58
110	33.46		4/27	186.12
111	24.33		4/27	161.79
112	5.80		4/27	155.99
113	12.85		4/27	143.14
		212.24 ATD	4/29	355.38
114	4.25		4/30	351.13
	50.00 AP-Valley Power Co.		4/30	301.13
	1.25 SC		4/30	299.88

KEY TO SYMBOLS

AD -	AUTOMATIC DEPOSIT	PC -	PAID OVERDRAFT CHARGE
AP -	AUTOMATIC PAYMENT	PR -	PAYROLL DEPOSIT
ATD -	AUTOMATIC TELLER DEPOSIT	RC -	RETURN CHECK CHARGE
ATW -	AUTOMATIC TELLER WITHDRAWAL	RT -	RETURN ITEM
CC -	CERTIFIED CHECK	SC -	SERVICE CHARGE
EC -	ERROR CORRECTED	ST -	SAVINGS TRANSFER
OD -	OVERDRAFT	TC -	TRANSFER CHARGE

Figure 20–2
Kris Garza's bank statement showing transactions completed during April.

Examining Your Returned Checks

If your bank returns checks, it will return all of the checks that it has paid during the month with your statement. Before the bank sends you your checks, it cancels each one, usually using a machine that stamps or punches holes in the check. The paid checks are called **canceled checks**. Be sure to save them. They are valuable records. Your check stub or register is your own record, but the canceled check is evidence that payment was actually received. Since the payee must endorse a check before it can be cashed, the endorsement proves that the payee received the check.

But suppose your bank does not return checks to depositors and you need a certain check to prove that a payment was made. Banks which do not return checks often send a more detailed statement than banks which return checks. In most cases, information on the statement will be sufficient to prove payment. But if the check showing the endorsement is needed, a copy of it can be obtained by giving the bank enough of the details of the check to allow a clerk to identify it. Banks keep a photographic record of all checks paid. Your check will be located in this record and a copy sent to you. There may be a small charge for this service.

You receive computer-printed receipts for all transactions made at an automatic teller station. Some banks send another receipt of the transaction with your statement; other banks do not. In either case, your statement will show a record of each transaction. You should have kept your own record of each EFT transaction in your register.

Now you have your returned checks and your bank statement. Your next step is to compare your record of your account with the bank's record.

Reconciling Your Bank Statement

You have learned about keeping a record of your account on check stubs or in a register. The bank statement gives you a copy of the bank's record of your account. The balances on the two may differ. Bringing the balances into agreement is known as reconciling the bank balance. The statement showing how the two balances were brought into agreement is called the **bank reconciliation**. Forms for reconciling are often printed on the back of the bank statement.

There are several reasons why the balances shown by your records and the bank statement may be different. Here are the most common reasons:

1. Some of the checks that you wrote and subtracted from your balance may not have been presented to the bank for payment before the bank statement was made. These checks, therefore, have not been deducted from the bank-statement balance. Such checks are known as **outstanding checks**.
2. You may have forgotten to record a transaction in your register. This is especially true if you use an automatic teller or have other EFT transactions. Failure to record these is a frequent cause of errors.
3. A service charge which you have not recorded may be shown on the bank statement.
4. You may have mailed a deposit to the bank that had not been received and recorded when the statement was made.
5. If yours is an interest-bearing account, you may not have added to your balance the interest shown on your statement.
6. You may have recorded the amount of the check incorrectly in your check register or on the check stub.

Illus. 20–2

Reconciling your bank statement is easier if your records are accurate. Record all transactions, including those at ATMs, as they are completed.

7. A computation error may have been made by you or your bank. Mistakes made by the depositor are the most frequent causes of differences.

Let's see how a bank reconciliation is made. On May 4, Kris Garza received the bank statement shown in Figure 20-2. The statement balance is $299.88. Kris's checkbook balance is $302.63. She examined her canceled checks which were returned with the statement and found that her checks numbered 108, 115, and 116 were outstanding. She listed these on the reconciliation form with the amounts for each and recorded the total. Her bank reconciliation is shown in Figure 20-3.

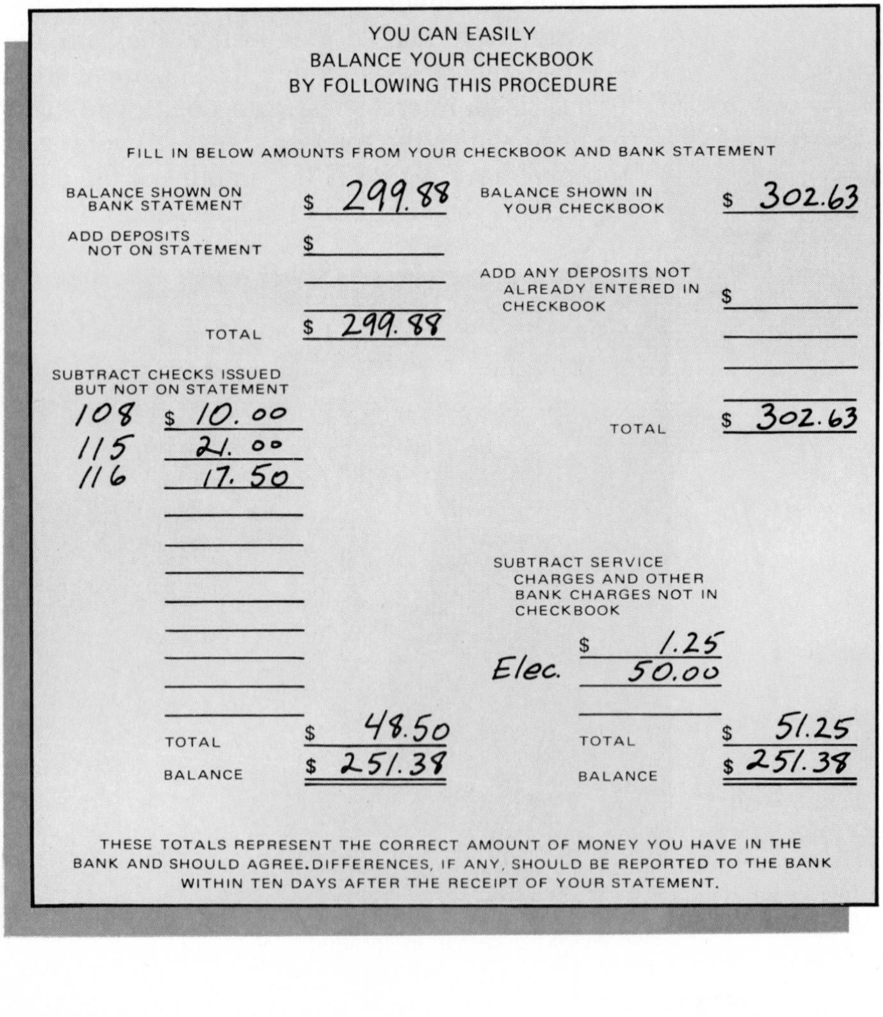

Figure 20–3

A bank reconciliation helps you bring your records and the bank's records of your account into agreement.

YOU CAN EASILY
BALANCE YOUR CHECKBOOK
BY FOLLOWING THIS PROCEDURE

FILL IN BELOW AMOUNTS FROM YOUR CHECKBOOK AND BANK STATEMENT

BALANCE SHOWN ON BANK STATEMENT $ 299.88

BALANCE SHOWN IN YOUR CHECKBOOK $ 302.63

ADD DEPOSITS NOT ON STATEMENT $ _____

TOTAL $ 299.88

ADD ANY DEPOSITS NOT ALREADY ENTERED IN CHECKBOOK $ _____

SUBTRACT CHECKS ISSUED BUT NOT ON STATEMENT
108     $ 10.00
115   21.00
116   17.50

TOTAL $ 302.63

SUBTRACT SERVICE CHARGES AND OTHER BANK CHARGES NOT IN CHECKBOOK
          $ 1.25
Elec.   50.00

TOTAL $ 48.50
BALANCE $ 251.38

TOTAL $ 51.25
BALANCE $ 251.38

THESE TOTALS REPRESENT THE CORRECT AMOUNT OF MONEY YOU HAVE IN THE BANK AND SHOULD AGREE. DIFFERENCES, IF ANY, SHOULD BE REPORTED TO THE BANK WITHIN TEN DAYS AFTER THE RECEIPT OF YOUR STATEMENT.

By using the reconciliation form, Kris proved the accuracy of the bank statement and her record by (1) subtracting the total of the outstanding checks she had listed on the form from the bank statement balance, and (2) subtracting the service charge and the automatic payment of her electric bill from her checkbook balance.

In some cases, other additions or subtractions might have to be made in the reconciliation. For example, a charge made for stopping payment on a check should be subtracted from the checkbook balance. Also, a deposit made so late in the month that it did not appear on the bank statement should be added to the balance on the bank statement.

If the balances do not agree, either you or your bank has made a mistake. In that case, you should compare your canceled checks with those listed on the bank statement and with those recorded in your check register. Be sure that you have recorded all EFT transactions. Then carefully go over the calculations on your register. If you do not find an error in your calculations, take the matter up with the bank right away.

After you have reconciled your bank statement, correct any errors that you made on your register. Note how Kris has entered her reconciliation in her check register in Figure 20-4. Some people like to note the reconciliation entry in a different color so that next month they will know where to start with the new bank statement. On Kris's reconciliation entry, she has subtracted the service charge and the electric bill payment. The new balance now agrees with the bank statement. With her account now in order, she can feel free to write checks on her new balance.

Figure 20–4
Kris finds it helpful to make reconciliation entries in her check register in a different color.

CHECK NO	DATE	CHECK ISSUED TO	BAL. BR'T. F'R'D.	√	341	13
115	4/30	TO Madsen's Fashions	AMOUNT OF CHECK OR DEPOSIT		21	00
		FOR Skirt	BALANCE		320	13
116	4/30	TO Nelson's Garage	AMOUNT OF CHECK OR DEPOSIT		17	50
		FOR Auto Repairs	BALANCE		302	63
Recon	4/30	TO Service Charge	AMOUNT OF CHECK OR DEPOSIT		1	25
		FOR April	BALANCE		301	38
AP	4/30	TO Valley Power Co.	AMOUNT OF CHECK OR DEPOSIT		50	00
		FOR Automatic Payment—electric	BALANCE		251	38
		TO	AMOUNT OF CHECK OR DEPOSIT			
		FOR	BALANCE			
		TO	AMOUNT OF CHECK OR DEPOSIT			
		FOR	BALANCE			

PLEASE BE SURE TO DEDUCT ANY PER CHECK CHARGES OR MAINTENANCE CHARGES THAT AFFECT YOUR ACCOUNT

Adding to Your Business Vocabulary

The following terms should become part of your business vocabulary. For each numbered item, find the term that has the same meaning.

bank reconciliation
bank statement
canceled check

clearing a check
clearinghouse
outstanding check

1. A place where banks exchange checks to clear them.
2. Returning a check to a drawer's bank to be paid and charged to his or her account.
3. A report given by a bank to a depositor showing the condition of his or her account.

4. A check that has been paid by a bank.
5. A check given to the payee but not yet returned to the bank for payment.
6. A statement showing how the checkbook balance and the bank statement were brought into agreement.

Understanding Your Reading

1. How are checks cleared
   a. in the same bank?
   b. between different banks in a small town?
2. In large cities where there are many banks, how are checks cleared?
3. Explain the role of the Federal Reserve System in clearing checks.
4. What seven items of information are included on a bank statement?
5. How does a depositor know that his or her checks have been paid?
6. Explain how you can prove that a certain payment was made if your bank files your checks instead of returning them to you.
7. Why should you save canceled checks?
8. For what five reasons might your bank statement and your checkbook balance differ?
9. When EFT transactions are involved in a bank statement error, what is the usual cause?
10. How do you reconcile a bank statement? State the steps briefly.
11. How would you record a service charge on your check stub or in your register?

Putting Your Business Knowledge to Work

1. Sandra and Tom Wyatt are talking about whether or not to save their canceled checks from their joint account. Tom says, "Throw them out; I hate a cluttered house." Sandra reminds him, "Remember what happened last year when you tried to use your check register to prove you paid the furniture bill? I think we should save the canceled checks." Do you agree with Tom or Sandra? Why?

2. Edo Chan has received his bank statement for the month of May. The bank statement shows a balance of $401.19, but his check register shows a balance of only $364.52.
   a. What is the most likely reason that the bank balance is larger than Mr. Chan's?
   b. What steps should Mr. Chan take to bring the balances into agreement?
3. The Second National Bank of Valleydale offers free checking account services to three groups: persons over 60 years of age, disabled veterans, and churches. Why do you think the bank does not charge these groups while it records charges on the statements of other customers?
4. Look at Kris Garza's bank statement in Figure 20-2 and answer these questions:
   a. What is her account number?
   b. How many deposits did she make?

c. How many checks were paid?
d. Is there a service charge? If so, how much is it?
e. Does the statement show any outstanding checks? If not, how would Kris find out if there are any?
f. How many EFT transactions were made during the month?
5. Burt Engles maintains a checking account at the Fulton Trust Company. He drew a check on his account for $97.31 and gave it to the Edison Electric Company. The Edison Electric Company deposited the check in the Fifth National Bank, which in turn sent the check to the Fulton Trust Company for payment. Assuming that all parties concerned were located in the same city, draw a chart similar to the one in Figure 20-1 showing the movement of the check from the time it was issued by Mr. Engles until it was returned to him.

*C*omputing Business Problems

1. When Cindy Olander began to reconcile her bank statement, she found that four checks she had written had not been paid by the bank. The amounts of the checks were: $14.50, $9.25, $10.00, and $26.50.
   a. What is the total amount of unpaid checks?
   b. In order to reconcile the statement, should Cindy subtract this total from the bank statement balance or from her checking account balance?
2. When the four banks in the town of Butler prepared to clear checks one day, they found that they had paid checks drawn on the other banks as shown in the following table:

Checks Held By	Drawn on			
	First National	Farmers' Trust	Merchants' Mutual	Butler Bank
First National	······	$938.57	$644.63	$1,158.64
Farmers' Trust	$443.74	······	$711.44	$ 208.45
Merchants' Mutual	$304.36	$522.82	······	$ 639.28
Butler Bank	$988.95	$326.31	$783.30	······

Assuming that each bank makes an individual settlement with every other bank, calculate the amount that each bank will either pay or receive from every other bank.

3. In October Leo Kishman received a bank statement that showed a balance of $378.65. The service charge was $2.25. Mr. Kishman found that the following checks were outstanding: No. 31, $7.16; No. 34, $15.10; and No. 35, $9.95. His checkbook balance at the end of October was $348.69. Reconcile the bank balance.

4. Some service charges are paid at the time the service is performed. Others are charged to the customer's account and reported on the monthly statement. In a recent five-year period, most service charges have increased, as shown in the following table which gives the average charges among U.S. banks. Using the data in the table, complete the following activities:
   a. Find the percent of increase over the five-year period for each charge.
   b. Identify the service charges which would probably be included on the customer's monthly statement.

Service Provided by Bank	Year 1	Year 5
Bounced Check	$5.07	$9.46
Overdraft Paid by Bank	$4.72	$9.01
Safe-deposit Box Annual Rental Fee	$6.96	$11.37
Checking Account Monthly Fee	$1.17	$2.51
Check Cashing for Non-Customers	$ .40	$1.87
Inquiry about Balance	$1.20	$1.28

Stretching Your Business Knowledge

1. Among the EFT programs offered by some banks are "debit cards" and "smart cards." By interviewing a banker or using library sources, answer the following questions:
   a. What is the basic use of debit cards?
   b. What are several uses of the smart card?
   c. Is there a difference between debit cards and smart cards? If so, what?
   d. Are these cards offered by banks in your community?

2. Statements of interest-bearing checking accounts show interest earned each month. The statement will be the first record of the interest earned that the customer sees. The statement will therefore be out of balance with the customer's

records. Using the form in Figure 20-3, show how this interest on checking will be handled in reconciling the account.

3. Below is a list of items for which many banks charge a fee:
   a. overdraft
   b. insufficient funds
   c. stop-payment order
   d. photocopy of a paid check
   e. extra statement
   f. dormant account
   g. postdated check
   h. returned deposit item
   i. counter check used on restricted account.

State briefly the meaning of each item. Find out if a local bank charges for these services and, if so, what amount?

4. Visit a bank in your community that has automatic teller service. Write a brief report describing how a customer would use the automatic teller for the following transactions:
   a. obtain $50 in cash
   b. pay a utility bill of $87.92
   c. transfer $200 from a savings to a checking account.

CHAPTER 21

*O*ther Ways of Making Payments

After studying this chapter and completing the end-of-chapter activities, you will be able to:

1. State three points to consider in choosing the best method of making a payment or transferring money.
2. Name four basic methods of payment other than cash or personal checks.
3. Explain how four kinds of money orders are purchased and used.
4. Explain why traveler's checks are considered to be a good way for travelers to make payments.
5. Explain how payments are made through electronic funds transfer.
6. Tell where you could go for advice on the best method of making a payment.

As safe and convenient as checks are, there are times when personal checks are not the best way to transfer money. There are even situations in which personal checks may not be accepted. Persons traveling far from home may have difficulty in cashing a check because they are not known. People making large purchases may find that the seller questions whether or not there is enough money in the purchaser's account to cover the check offered in payment. For a variety of reasons, other means of making payments are needed. Fortunately, other means are available. These include money orders, traveler's checks, certified checks, bank-guaranteed checks, and electronic funds transfers. In choosing the best method, you will need to consider where and to whom the money is going, how fast it must get there, and how much you are sending.

Money Orders

A person who does not have a checking account and who wants to send a small payment through the mail may purchase a money order. A **money order** is a form of payment which orders the issuing agency to pay the amount printed on the form to another party. When you buy a money order, you pay the issuing agency the amount of the payment you want to make and a service fee.

Money orders are convenient because they can be purchased in many places. They are sold by banks, post offices, express companies, and telegraph offices. Many retail stores, such as supermarkets and drugstores, also sell them.

Let's look at an example of how money orders work. Jack Trippett wants to order a metric tool kit from the Jarris Company. The company does not take personal checks on first orders and it would take several weeks for Jack to establish credit with the company. He needs the tools right away to work on his car. How should he pay for it? There are several kinds of money orders that he could buy.

Illus. 21–1
Money orders are sold in many locations. Service fees may vary.

Bank Money Orders

One way Jack Trippett could pay for his metric tool kit is to buy a money order from his bank. A bank money order is a form sold by a bank stating that money is to be paid to the person named on the form.

In the bank money order shown in Figure 21–1, Jack Trippett is sending $22.50 to the Jarris Company. He pays the bank $22.50 plus a service charge, which may be about $2.

When this money order has been paid, it will not be returned to Jack as a canceled check would be. It will be returned to the bank that issued it. However, the money order can be obtained if Jack wants to prove that payment was made. Since bank practices in issuing money orders vary, check with your bank to find out what its practice is before you buy a money order.

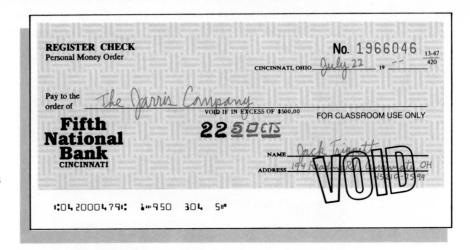

Figure 21–1
After payment is made, a bank money order is returned to the issuing bank.

Postal Money Orders

Jack Trippett may also purchase a money order from the post office. When you buy a postal money order, the postal clerk registers by machine the amount in figures and words. You then complete the form by filling in the payee's name, your name and address, and the purpose of the money order. Figure 21–2 shows a sample postal money order.

You can send a postal money order safely through the mail because it can be cashed only after it is signed by the payee. If a money order is lost or stolen, the receipt copy that you receive may

Figure 21–2
A postal money order can be cashed only after it is signed by the payee.

be used in making a claim with the post office. The payee may cash the postal money order at a post office or a bank or may transfer it to another person by filling in the information requested on the back of the money order.

Postal money orders are issued only in amounts up to $500. If you want to send a larger amount, you may buy more money orders. Fees for postal money orders vary with the amounts that are purchased, but the charge is small.

Express Money Orders

Jack Trippett could have used an express money order to pay for his tool kit. Express money orders are sold by offices of the American Express Company, Federal Express Services Corporation, some travel agencies, and many retail stores. Figure 21–3 shows an American Express money order.

An American Express money order can be written only for amounts up to $200, but you may buy as many as you want. Charges are about the same as the charges for postal money orders. If you buy an express money order, you should keep the receipt as proof that you bought the money order.

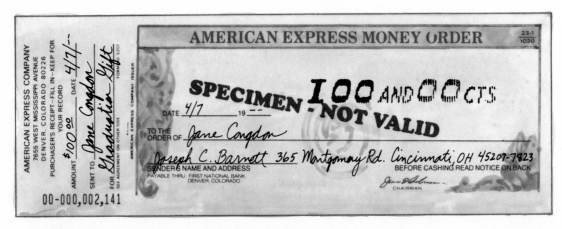

Figure 21–3
An express
money order.

Telegraphic Money Orders

When buying a telegraphic money order, you buy a message directing a telegraph office to pay a sum of money to a certain person. Although his situation was not urgent, Jack Trippett could have used one. A telegraphic money order is used mainly in an emergency—when money must be delivered quickly. Suppose that while Agnes Wilcox is on a school band trip to Pasadena, California—2,000 miles from home—she loses her wallet with all her money. Agnes may phone her parents requesting $75 spending money for the rest of the trip. A telegraphic money order will probably be the best way to get the money to her fast. Her father will pay the $75 plus a handling fee to his telegraph office in Dundee, Illinois. A telegram like the one shown in Figure 21–4 will be sent ordering the Pasadena telegraph office to pay Agnes $75. If the message is sent promptly, Agnes should have the money soon after her call is made or the telegram is sent.

To be sure that the right person gets the money, a test question may be sent free. The sender may choose to ask a personal question, such as "When is your father's birthday?" Agnes's father would tell the clerk the answer to the question. In order to get the money, Agnes would have to give the Pasadena clerk the correct answer. Mr. Wilcox could request a report that the money was paid to Agnes. For this service, he would pay an additional fee.

A charge is made for any other message sent with the telegraphic money order. Sending money in this way is somewhat expensive when one considers the cost of telegrams both ways and the cost of the money order. However, this form of payment is very useful in an emergency.

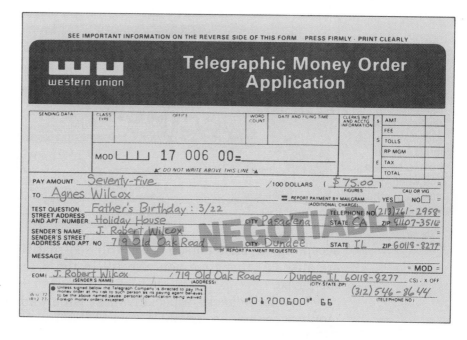

SEE IMPORTANT INFORMATION ON THE REVERSE SIDE OF THIS FORM   PRESS FIRMLY · PRINT CLEARLY

western union

Telegraphic Money Order Application

SENDING DATA	CLASS TYPE	OFFICE	WORD COUNT	DATE AND FILING TIME	CLERKS INIT AND ACCTG INFORMATION	S	AMT
							FEE
						S	TOLLS
MOD └┴┴┘ 17 006 00=							RP MGM
						E	TAX
✈ DO NOT WRITE ABOVE THIS LINE ✈							TOTAL

PAY AMOUNT _Seventy-five_ /100 DOLLARS (_$75.00_) =
FIGURES

TO _Agnes Wilcox_   ☰ REPORT PAYMENT BY MAILGRAM YES ☐ NO ☐   CAU OR VIG =
                                                    (ADDITIONAL CHARGE)

TEST QUESTION _Father's Birthday : 3/22_   TELEPHONE NO _(213)761-2958_

STREET ADDRESS AND APT. NUMBER _Holiday House_   CITY _Pasadena_ STATE _CA_ ZIP _91107-3516_

SENDER'S NAME _J. Robert Wilcox_

SENDER'S STREET ADDRESS AND APT NO _719 Old Oak Road_ CITY _Dundee_ STATE _IL_ ZIP _60118-8277_
                                          (IF REPORT PAYMENT REQUESTED)

MESSAGE

= MOD =

EOM(_J. Robert Wilcox_   / _719 Old Oak Road_   / _Dundee IL 60118-8277_ CS) · X OFF
         (SENDER'S NAME)   (ADDRESS)   (CITY STATE ZIP)

Unless signed below the Telegraph Company is directed to pay this money order at my risk to such person as its paying agent believes to be the above named payee personal identification being waived. Foreign money orders excepted

W12 72
(R12 77)

‖°0 6700600‖° 66   _(312) 546-8644_
                              (TELEPHONE NO)

Figure 21–4
Telegraphic money orders are usually used in emergencies — when money is needed quickly.

Traveler's Checks

It is risky to carry a large sum of money when you travel, since it can be lost or stolen easily. It is also difficult to pay traveling expenses with personal checks. You will be dealing mostly with strangers and, as you have learned, strangers may not accept personal checks. Even money orders may not work out for traveling, as you may not have the identification that is necessary for cashing them.

Special forms designed for the traveler to use in making payments are called **traveler's checks**. You can buy them at banks, express companies, credit unions, and travel bureaus. They are sold in several denominations, such as $10, $20, $50, and $100. In addition to the value of the checks, there is usually a charge of 1 percent of the value with a minimum charge of 50 cents. This means that $100 worth of traveler's checks will cost $101. However, some banks and credit unions do not charge for traveler's checks if customers have certain types of accounts.

As shown in Figure 21–5, traveler's checks have two places for your signature. When you buy the checks, you sign each one in the presence of the selling agent. When you cash a check or pay for a purchase with it, you sign it again in the presence of the person

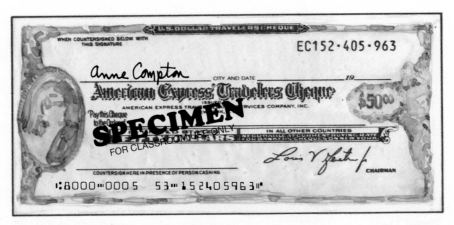

Figure 21–5

You must sign traveler's checks twice, once when you purchase them, a second time when you make a purchase with them.

accepting it. That person checks to see that the two signatures are alike. At that time you also fill in the date and the name of the payee.

Traveler's checks, especially those widely advertised, are commonly accepted throughout the world. Almost any business is willing to accept a traveler's check since there is little chance of its not being signed by the right person.

When you buy traveler's checks, you should immediately record the serial number of each check on a form that is generally given to you by the issuing agency. Then, on the same form, record the place and date you cash each check. Keep this record separate from your checks so that you can refer to it if your checks are lost or stolen. If they are lost or stolen, report it at once to the nearest bank or office where such checks are sold. The company that issued them will replace them.

Bank-Guaranteed Checks

There are many times when a personal check will not be the best means of paying for a product or service. But there is a way to have a bank guarantee that the check will be good, and this makes the check acceptable when it otherwise would not be. Banks provide several kinds of checks which they guarantee. Learning about these will give you several options to choose from when deciding the best way to make a payment. Let's look at three bank-guaranteed checks.

Certified Checks

A **certified check** is a personal check on which the bank has written its guarantee that the check will be paid. Suppose Hazel Carter wants to make a payment to someone who does not know her and who does not want to accept her personal check. She could use several forms of payment, as you have learned, but she may want to have the transaction recorded in her checking account. Ms. Carter could have her bank certify her check, as shown in Figure 21–6. She will pay a fee of as much as $4 for this service.

When the bank certifies Ms. Carter's check, the amount of the check is immediately subtracted from her account. This makes it impossible for her to withdraw the money or to use it for other checks. If the check is not used, it may be returned to the bank and credited to her account.

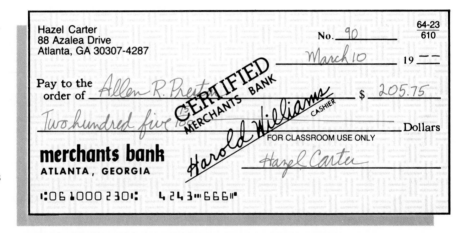

Figure 21–6
The Merchants
Bank guarantees
that this certified
check will
be paid.

Bank Drafts

For certain large payments, a bank's own check may be purchased. Banks usually deposit part of their funds in other banks. An officer of a bank may draw checks on these deposits in the same way that you may draw on funds that you have deposited in your bank. A check that a bank official draws on the bank's deposits in another bank is known as a **bank draft**. Anyone can buy a bank draft simply by going to a bank and requesting one for a certain amount. Let's see how that works.

Suppose Sam Welton, a builder in Middleton, Oregon, wanted to make a large payment to the M & G Lumber Company in Eugene,

Oregon. M & G does not accept personal checks from new customers. Mr. Welton could pay the $1,247.55 with a bank draft. In this case, the draft would be a check which Mr. Welton's Middleton bank wrote on funds it has on deposit in another bank. The other bank may be a commercial bank in Eugene or a western district Federal Reserve Bank. Mr. Welton would pay his bank $1,247.55 plus a small fee for issuing the draft. The service charge is usually based on a small percentage of the amount of the draft, with a set minimum fee. Mr. Welton's bank draft is shown in Figure 21–7.

Figure 21–7
A bank draft may be used when a personal check is not acceptable.

Cashier's Checks

Banks also keep funds within their own banks on which they can write checks. A **cashier's check** is a check that a bank draws on its own in-house funds. It was so named because such checks were originally written by a bank employee known as a cashier. Some banks refer to checks drawn on their own funds as officer's checks, treasurer's checks, or manager's checks, depending upon who is authorized to sign them. A cashier's check is shown in Figure 21–8.

As with bank drafts, a cashier's check costs the amount of the check plus a service fee. Both are often used to make rather large payments. These banker's checks are more acceptable than the personal checks of an individual whom the payee may not know.

Bank checks, as well as money orders, can also be used for sending payments to other countries. Information about the methods of making payments to businesses or persons in foreign countries may be obtained from the bank or from the place where the money order is purchased. Any time you do not know the best means of making a payment, ask your bank for advice.

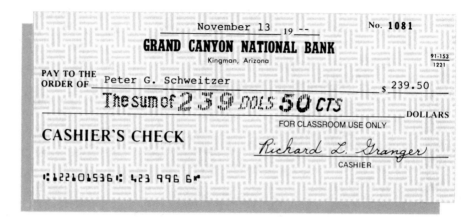

Figure 21–8
A cashier's
check is drawn
on a bank's own
in-house funds.

Electronic Funds Transfer

As you learned in Chapter 17, electronic funds transfer (EFT) is the moving of funds from one account to another and from one bank to another by computer. This means that payments can be made without a written form such as a check. Electronic funds transfer gives faster and less costly service than has been possible in the past. Let's discuss some of the EFT services that are now becoming commonplace.

Individuals can direct their banks to pay automatically such monthly bills as utility and telephone charges. Each month the utility company, for example, sends to the bank the bills for everyone who has instructed them to do so. The bank subtracts the amounts due from the accounts of the customers who have instructed the bank to make monthly utility payments automatically for them. The amounts from the customers' accounts are added to the utility company's account.

Many businesses hesitate to accept a personal check as payment without proof that the customer's account contains at least the amount of the check. With EFT, however, customers can often have their checks approved at a terminal located in the store where they are shopping. The information from the terminal tells the merchant that the amount of the check is covered by the current balance in the customer's account. This verifies the check at the point of sale and the merchant then is willing to accept the personal check for payment.

Another development in the EFT system is the debit card. A **debit card** is a programmed card which provides evidence of funds on deposit and allows access to the depositor's account through a special computer terminal. Using a debit card permits the transfer of money from a customer's checking account to the account of the firm from which a purchase is being made. Using a debit card is like paying cash, but no cash is handled. As with cash, the business receives payment at the time of the sale. The amount of the purchase is subtracted from the customer's account and added to the business's account.

As you have learned, automatic teller machines are increasing in popularity. ATMs — actually computer terminals — allow customers to make payments or transfer money for a variety of reasons at any hour of the day or night. Bank customers can also make deposits and withdrawals, transfer money from savings to checking accounts, make a loan payment, or even get a loan at these electronic terminals. Automatic tellers are placed in convenient locations outside the bank, such as in shopping malls, airports, and on street corners.

Your employer can also pay your salary through EFT. Some businesses have practically eliminated payroll checks by directing their bank to pay their employees through EFT. The bank subtracts the total amount of the payroll from the firm's account and adds the amount earned to each employee's account, even if the employees' accounts are in several different banks. The computer is programmed to transfer electronically the amount of the salary to the appropriate bank for each employee.

Other EFT services are available and more are being developed all the time. As more people buy their own personal computers, more payments will be made electronically. The customer's computer will be able to communicate with the bank's computer, permitting the customer to do a great deal of banking electronically. EFT has helped banks reduce paperwork and it has sped up the transfer of funds. But EFT is not expected to eliminate checks or traditional banking methods completely.

*A*dding to Your Business Vocabulary

The following terms should become part of your business vocabulary. For each numbered item, find the term that has the same meaning.

bank draft	debit card
cashier's check	money order
certified check	traveler's check

1. A personal check that is guaranteed by a bank.
2. A check that a bank draws on its deposits in another bank.
3. A form sold by a bank, express company, or other agency to take care of the financial needs of travelers.
4. A form sold by banks, post offices, express companies, and telegraph offices to be used for making payments.
5. A check that a bank employee draws on the bank's own in-house funds.
6. A programmed device which provides evidence of funds on deposit and allows access to the depositor's account on a special computer terminal.

Understanding Your Reading

1. Why are personal checks not always the best way to make payments?
2. In choosing the best method of making a payment, what three things should you consider?
3. Name five methods of payment other than cash or personal checks.
4. What happens to a bank money order after it has been paid?
5. Why is it considered safe to send a postal money order through the mail?
6. In what ways is an express money order different from a bank money order and a postal money order?
7. What is the procedure for sending money by telegraphic money order?
8. Why are traveler's checks better for the traveler to carry than personal checks or cash?
9. What are the steps taken by the bank to certify a personal check?
10. What is the major difference between a bank draft and a cashier's check?
11. Explain how payments are made through EFT. Give an example of an EFT payment.
12. If you do not know which type of special money payment to use in a certain situation, where can you find out?

Putting Your Business Knowledge to Work

1. While on a vacation trip, the Macon family found an old jukebox made in the 1930s and in good working order in an antique shop. The family decided that it would be a good addition to the family recreation room. The jukebox cost $500 and the dealer would not accept a personal check or credit cards. What method could be used to pay for the jukebox?
2. Suppose you want to send $24 to Classic Car Parts, Inc., in another city for parts needed to repair an old car. You have no checking account. Would you make the payment with a certified check, money order, or a bank draft? Explain.

3. Billie Jo and Tom Reid are moving to a distant city where Billie Jo has been transferred by her employer. The moving company has instructed them to have a cashier's check ready to pay the driver when their furniture is delivered. What reasons can you give for the request for this type of payment?

4. Listed below are some of the money payments that the Graham family made during a six-month period. In each case, tell what method of making payment you would recommend.

   a. Mrs. Graham paid the phone bill at the local office.
   b. Mr. Graham made the monthly payment on their house at the local bank.
   c. The Grahams paid their federal income tax.
   d. Mr. Graham bought his automobile license plates.
   e. The Grahams paid $125 for goods they ordered from a Chicago mail-order house. They wanted the goods shipped at once, but they had never bought goods from that firm before.
   f. Mr. Graham had an automobile accident 300 miles from home. Mrs. Graham sent him $250 by the fastest method.
   g. Mr. Graham paid $14.75 for repairs at a local garage.
   h. Mrs. Graham paid $125 each month on a loan from her bank.

Computing Business Problems

1. Margaret Clay bought traveler's checks from her credit union to pay for her family's vacation. She must pay a fee of 1 percent of the value of the checks. The denominations she chose were $400 in $50 checks and $200 in $20 checks.
   a. How many $50 checks did she receive? How many $20 checks?
   b. How much was the bank's charge for the checks?
   c. What was the total cost of Mrs. Clay's checks?

2. Jim Foley ordered a country-western tape to add to his collection. It was advertised on TV as available only through the station address. Customers could pay by check or money order for $7.95 or C.O.D. (collect on delivery) for an additional fee for postage and handling. Since Jim did not have a checking account, he used a postal money order for the tape. The cost of the order was 75 cents.
   a. What was the total cost of the tape?
   b. If postage and handling charges for delivery to Jim's home were $2.64, how much would the tape cost if it came C.O.D.?
   c. How much did Jim save by sending payment with his order?

3. Guido Alba's ability to repair bicycles has developed into an after-school business. He can get parts cheaper by ordering from wholesale houses in several cities. He pays by postal money order. During the last three months, he made the following payments:

   National Cycle Co. $7.42, $18.12, $31.04
   Wheels, Inc. $41.74, $3.19, $67.18, $10.00

The post office fee schedule is as follows:

Amount of order	Fee
$ 0.01 to $ 25	$ .75
$25.01 to $ 50	$1.10
$50.01 to $500	$1.55

a. What was the cost of each postal money order? List the payments in a column and write the fee beside each.
b. What was the total cost of Guido's postal money orders for the three months?
c. What was the total cost of the bicycle parts Guido ordered, including the cost of the money orders?

On September 11, Albert Hutton of Tacoma suddenly remembered that it was the sixteenth birthday of his favorite nephews, Ronnie and Reggie, of Cheyenne. He had forgotten to send his usual gift of $1 per year of age to each nephew. To get his gift to them on time, he decided to send a telegraphic money order for the total amount, addressed to both young men, and have it delivered to their home. He included this message: "Happy Birthday, Ronnie and Reggie. Our love and a dollar per year." The fee schedule was as follows:

Base fee for office delivery		Additional for	
Amount	Fee	home delivery	Message
.00-$ 50.00	$10.95	$8.95	$2 minimum, 10 words
$50.00-$100.00	$11.95		20 cents per word over minimum

a. How much money was sent by money order as a combined gift?
b. What was the fee for the delivered money order, not including the message?
c. What was the charge for the message?
d. What was the total cost of Mr. Hutton's gift to Ronnie and Reggie?

Stretching Your Business Knowledge

1. A memo from an employer gave employees the option of receiving their paychecks as usual or having their wages deposited automatically to their accounts at their individual banks. List some advantages and disadvantages of the automatic deposit plan that you would consider if you were one of the employees. Which method would you choose? Why?

2. List the name of at least one place in your community where each type of money order can be bought. What is the cost of each kind of money order for $10? For $50?

3. Certified checks are often required in real estate closings. Why might a personal check not be acceptable? A real estate agent, lawyer, or banker might help you with your answer.

4. Some banks include in their certifying stamp on certified checks the words, "Do not destroy." To whom is this addressed? Why are the words included? If the words were not included, is it all right to destroy the check?

5. There are several types of traveler's checks. Figure 21–5 shows the American Express traveler's check. Find out what other types are sold in your community. Is there a difference in the cost?

6. Certified checks sometimes are imprinted with the words, "collectible at par." Find out what this means and whether a bank in your community issues certified checks including these words.

CAREER CATEGORY: Banking and Finance

The financial industry offers a variety of career opportunities. More than 2.5 million people are employed in over 59,000 banks and almost 28,000 other financial institutions. Most of these workers are employed in commercial banks. Others work in specialized banks and in savings and loans, credit unions, and finance companies.

About two-thirds of all bank employees are clerical workers. Bank officers and managers make up about 30 percent of the total. A small percentage are professional workers, such as economists, attorneys, investment analysts, and specialists in computer technology, marketing, personnel, and public relations. The remaining employees include guards, maintenance workers, and other service personnel.

Job Titles: Job titles commonly found in this career area include:

Trust Officer	Loan Officer
Branch Manager	Commercial Teller
New Accounts Clerk	Systems Analyst
Word Processing Specialist	

Employment Outlook: The Department of Labor (DOL) estimates that there will be almost 200,000 new jobs for bank officers and managers in 1995, an increase of over 45 percent over the early 1980s. The DOL also estimates a need for over 150,000 additional bank tellers, up 29 percent over the same period. Computer programmers, systems analysts, and computer service technicians are predicted to be the jobs in which there will be the greatest growth over the next decade. During this same period, the number of computer operator jobs is expected to increase 27 percent.

Future Changes: As the financial industry continues to expand the use of electronic technology, a large number of these specialized workers will be needed. Also, as dereg-

ulation allows banks to expand their services into other fields, such as investment counseling and real estate, there will be a need for employees for these special fields.

What Is Done on the Job: The types of jobs in financial firms are about the same across the industry. However, all of the jobs are not found in all institutions.

Tellers spend most of their time working directly with customers, receiving and paying out money. At the end of the day, tellers must count the money, balance their cash drawers, and reconcile their daily computer-terminal printouts with their cash transactions. They may then help to sort and file checks, notes, and other papers. In a large bank, tellers' duties are often specialized. A loan teller, for example, receives only loan payments; a payroll teller handles payroll accounts for firms that are the bank's customers.

Most clerical workers perform their jobs behind the scenes, handling routine paperwork and record keeping. They may operate computer terminals, word processors, and sorting machines. They may write computer programs, record transactions in customers' accounts, or sort and file checks and other papers. Some clerks handle specialized duties. An interest clerk, for example, is responsible for keeping the records of notes on which the bank must collect or pay interest.

The bank may have many officers and managers. A loan officer is responsible for making loans to businesses and individuals. The operations officer is responsible for seeing that the daily operations of the bank flow smoothly and efficiently. This officer usually directs the work of tellers, clerks, data processors, and word processing specialists.

Education and Training: Most beginning jobs in banking require at least a high school education. Many beginners also have had additional business preparation in community or technical colleges. Officers, professional personnel, and executives usually have college degrees.

Bank workers who meet the public must be able to communicate well. They must be tactful and have a businesslike appearance. Most bank workers must be able to handle details and to work well under stress. They must also be able to work at routine tasks for long periods.

Salary Levels: In 1982 the salary range of officer trainees with bachelor's degrees was $1,100 to $1,800 per month; for those with a master's degree in business administration, the range was $1,800 to $2,900. The average salary for bank officers in 1982 was $24,500 a year; the top 10 percent earned over $46,800. For tellers, the average salary was $10,300; the top 10 percent earned over $16,800. Banking salaries are influenced by the type of position and the size and location of the bank.

For Additional Information: One of the best ways to learn about banking careers is to talk to a banker. Many banks have brochures which describe opportunities in banking. The *Occupational Outlook Handbook* usually lists with its banking sections several organizations relating to banking and careers within the financial industry. Consult a current edition of this publication for addresses of these organizations.

UNIT 7
MANAGING YOUR MONEY

UNIT OBJECTIVES

After studying the chapters in this unit, you will be able to:

1. *Explain why it is important for individuals and families to develop money management goals.*

2. *List the steps that should be followed in preparing an individual's or family's budget.*

3. *Keep records of income and expenditures for an individual or a family.*

4. *Explain why it is difficult to compare prices of goods and services from one year to the next.*

BUSINESS BRIEF

The Money Manager—New Popularity

Can you imagine a time when you will need someone to help you manage your money—to help you decide how to save, invest, and plan for your retirement years? Believe it or not, many people are doing just that. They are hiring specialists in money management to advise them on how to make the most of the money they earn now and will earn in the future.

It is possible that in a few short years you will earn enough money that it will pay you to hire someone to assist you in managing and investing it. The world of finance—even personal finance—is becoming more and more complex and sometimes it is appropriate to hire an expert to assist you. You employ experts to assist you in other areas of your life such as law, medicine, or construction. Why not hire an expert in financial management?

Just how would a money manager help you? While services vary among managers, most assist their clients in four ways: they help clients set short- and long-term financial goals; they analyze clients' current financial condition; they suggest ways clients can meet their goals; and they help reevaluate their clients' financial plans as their goals or economic conditions change.

Some money managers also serve as investment advisers, and even make investments for their clients in accordance with their clients' goals and tolerances for risk. In addition, these managers give general advice regarding taxes and other significant financial matters. They are normally paid a small percentage of the amount of money in a client's account.

Until recently, the ablest professional money managers were very expensive and kept their account minimums high. Unless you had over $100,000 to invest, you weren't welcome as a client. Now, however, some money managers with impressive records and credentials accept customers who have as little as $10,000 to work with.

In selecting a money manager, pay close attention to the financial success they have achieved with other clients and to your ability to get along with them. They must share your financial objectives and philosophy.

While it may seem remote to you now that you would ever need a professional money manager, you may find that in a few short years a money manager may be just what you need. Professional money managers are definitely part of the contemporary business scene.

CHAPTER 22

Sensible Money Management

■ CHAPTER OBJECTIVES ─────────────────────

After studying this chapter and completing the end-of-chapter activities, you will be able to:

1. Name the two main parts of a good financial plan.
2. List four factors that affect a person's goals.
3. Tell what three decisions are associated with money management.
4. Discuss how proper use of your possessions is related to good money management.
5. List the five items on which most families spend the largest part of their incomes.

Stories describing someone's rise from rags to riches are common in popular literature. It is an important part of the American ideal that a person can start with nothing and, through hard work, can achieve financial success. Sometimes financial success comes through luck or a generous inheritance. But more often it results from a combination of hard work and careful financial planning.

Financial Planning

It has been said that if you don't know where you are going, you will never get anywhere. This is especially true with personal finances. Everyone should have a carefully developed financial plan. **Financial planning** includes evaluating one's financial position, setting financial goals, and guiding activities and resources toward reaching those goals. The plan should be developed thoughtfully and should be evaluated and updated frequently. There are two main parts of a good financial plan. The first is a realistic evaluation of your current economic situation. The second is the setting of attainable goals.

Current Evaluation

In order to prepare a good financial plan, you must have a realistic view of your present financial situation. You must honestly and carefully evaluate your financial position to determine what you can and cannot do financially. This includes realistic estimates of your earning power, life-style, wants, and needs.

Developing Goals

Once you have an idea of what is possible, you can begin setting financial goals. **Goals** are those things you want to achieve. Goals may be short-term or long-term. A short-term financial goal, for example, might be to pay off debts, go on a trip, or buy new carpeting. As a student, your short-term goal might be to buy an electronic calculator. Long-range goals often involve large amounts of money. A family's long-range goal might be to buy a new car or provide college educations for the children. Your long-range goal might be to open your own business.

Goals are personal. They are not the same for all people, or even for everyone within a given age group. Goals are affected by such things as a person's age, environment, interests, and values.

Goals also change from time to time. A family's goals change as its needs change. For example, an apartment or a small house might best suit the needs of a newly married couple. As their family grows, however, they might set the goal of buying a larger house. Think about how your goals have changed in the last few years and what your goals may be at age 20 or 30.

No matter how often goals change, they are the basis of good financial planning. Working to achieve a certain goal probably gives an individual or a family the best reason for practicing good financial planning and money management.

Money Management

As a high school graduate, you will probably earn over $500,000 in your lifetime. That is a lot of money, but there will be many demands on it. You will have to pay for food, shelter, clothing, transportation, and the other goods and services you need. When you begin a career you will face the same problem you face now — you have a limited amount of money to pay for all the goods and services you need and want. We discussed this basic economic problem in Chapter 1. One solution to the problem is learning to manage your money carefully and wisely within the limits of your financial plan.

Money management, then, is acting, on a day-to-day basis, on the goals set in your financial plan. It involves refining or "fine tuning" your financial plan. Money management also means getting the most for your money. It means careful planning, saving, and spending. Many people have the wrong idea about money management. They think it means pinching pennies, doing without things, and not having any fun. They are wrong. If you learn to manage your money well, you may be able to buy the things you really want that you have not been able to buy before. Planning ahead and deciding what is really important will help you to have money to spend on the things you enjoy.

Making Choices

Money management can be seen as a process of making economic choices. Money, of course, is limited and individuals and families must decide how to use the money that is available to them. They must determine the amount of their income that can be used for meeting basic needs, saving for future expenses, and spending on special wants.

Illus. 22–1
Stretching your dollars can be fun. This couple will save money by making a parka rather than buying one ready-made, and will enjoy working on it too.

The Basic Needs. The first step in money management is to decide how much money you will spend to meet basic needs. Basic needs are things you must have to live. But everyone's needs are not the same. Needs depend on where you live and what life-style you follow. If you live in a southern city, for example, you have different transportation and clothing needs from those who live on a large ranch in a northwestern state. For some people, an apartment is ideal; others may need a house. In any case, after you have met basic needs, you must decide how to use the money that remains.

Saving for Future Expenses. After providing for your basic needs, you should decide how to prepare for large expenses in the future. You do this by developing a savings program.

Everyone has special reasons for saving. Maybe you want to buy a car or save for college. Perhaps you want to be a beautician or an auto mechanic and will need equipment. Unless you manage your money wisely and plan your savings, you may not be able to do or buy the things you want. You will learn about saving in Chapter 30.

Spending Discretionary Income. The third choice you must make in managing your money is to decide how to spend any money you have available after you have taken care of your basic needs and future expenses. This is called your **discretionary income**. It is the money you spend to buy things you want for pleasure, satisfaction, and comfort rather than for the things you need. It is, for example, money spent for entertainment, travel, tapes or records, or hobby supplies. Spending discretionary income is usually more fun and can be seen as your reward for good money management.

Buying Wisely

Most of us have so many needs and wants that we could never manage to meet all of them. We must stretch our limited incomes as far as possible. Wise buying is an important way to stretch an income.

To buy wisely, you must gather information carefully before making your purchases. You must plan your purchases so that you buy the right item or service at the right time and at the right price. Unplanned buying often leads to disappointment and wasted money. Planned buying leads to better use of money and greater satisfaction from the things you buy.

Illus. 22–2
How we manage our money in meeting basic needs and saving for the future determines the amount we have left to spend on things we want and enjoy.

Using Possessions Properly

After careful planning and buying, you should use your possessions properly. Use your possessions carelessly, and you lose money. A radio in an unlocked locker can be stolen. Clothing must be cleaned and repaired or it will soon be unwearable. Cars and motorcycles need regular tune-ups and oil changes. Things you own will give you greater satisfaction and last longer with proper care. Taking care of your possessions is an important part of money management.

Living Within an Income

Do you ever run out of money before the end of the week? A lot of people have that problem. They have not learned to live within their incomes. Living on the amount of money that you have available to you is a central idea in money management.

It isn't always easy to live within your income. But if you don't, you will probably have to borrow money. Borrowing money isn't bad, but it is expensive. It costs money to borrow money. If you avoid the costs of borrowing you will have more money to satisfy other needs and wants. We will talk more about borrowing in Unit 8.

Illus. 22–3
Many people enjoy saving money by buying items they want or need at yard sales.

Household Spending Patterns

You may have wondered what kinds of spending patterns are typical among U.S. households. While no two households are alike in their spending, the U.S. Department of Labor has compiled some averages to help you compare your spending patterns with those of other people.

Figure 22–1 shows the average spending of a city family of four in the United States. As you can see, basic needs take a large share of a family's income. The biggest expense for the average family is food. The second largest expense is housing. Clothing and transportation are important basic expenses too. Almost 80 percent of a typical family's income is spent for the first five items listed in Figure 22–1.

SPENDING FOR A TYPICAL CITY FAMILY OF FOUR

Expense Category	Amount	Approximate Percent of Total
Food	$ 5,586	25
Housing	4,916	22
Income taxes	3,352	15
Clothing and personal care	2,011	8.5
Transportation	1,788	8
Social security and disability taxes	1,341	6
Medical care	1,341	6
Other (savings, gifts, contributions, recreation)	2,123	9.5
TOTAL SPENDING	$22,458	100%

Source: U.S. Department of Labor

Figure 22–1
Food and housing are the major expenses for most families.

A dding to Your Business Vocabulary

The following terms should become part of your business vocabulary. For each numbered item, find the term that has the same meaning.

financial planning   *discretionary income*
goals   *money management*

1. Requires evaluating one's present financial position, determining financial goals, and guiding activities and resources toward attaining those goals.
2. The day-to-day activities associated with carrying out a financial plan.
3. Income available to spend after money has been set aside for basic needs and future expenses.
4. The things you want to achieve.

Understanding Your Reading

1. What are the two main parts of a good financial plan?
2. List four factors that affect a person's goals.
3. What three choices are associated with money management?
4. List five items you think might be purchased with discretionary income.
5. How is proper use of your possessions part of good money management?
6. What are the five items on which the typical household spends the largest part of its income?

Putting Your Business Knowledge to Work

1. Describe the difference between short-term and long-term goals. Give two examples each of short- and long-term goals that could be a part of a financial plan.
2. What is the most common problem people face in relation to their income and expenses?
3. The income of the Cortey household is well above the national average. Therefore, the Corteys feel it is not necessary to plan the use of their income. They find, though, that they are having difficulty making ends meet. Suggest some reasons why the Cortey household may be having financial difficulty.
4. How would you save for the future expense of buying and operating an automobile, using your knowledge of financial planning and money management?

Computing Business Problems

1. One of Mike's long-range goals is to buy an automobile. His mother is willing to give him the down payment. But after that, he would need to pay $95 per month to repay the loan balance. Mike's monthly income is $1,135. What percentage of his income would be consumed by auto loan payments?
2. Dorothy Christensen decided to change the oil and filter in her car. She bought five quarts of 10W40 multi-weight oil for $1.35 per quart and an oil filter for $4.29.
   a. How much was the total bill (including 4 percent sales tax) for the oil and filter?
   b. How much did she save if a service garage would have charged her $18 including tax?
3. Figure 22–1 shows the spending for a typical family of four in dollars and percentages. Sometimes this kind of information has more meaning when presented as a chart. Use the percentages given on the figure to construct and label a pie chart showing how this typical family spends its income.

Stretching Your Business Knowledge

1. With a small amount of research in your school library, you should be able to find at least one piece of fiction by Horatio Alger. Read the story and then tell how good financial planning and money management contribute to the success of a modern-day Horatio Alger character.

2. What conclusions would you draw from the following statements?
   a. A popular cliché in the business world is, "Never take business advice from someone who has something to sell."
   b. Many businesses, including brokerage firms, banks, and insurance companies offer services called "financial planning."

3. Find out approximately how much your household spends for some of the categories of spending shown in Figure 22-1. What are some of the reasons why differences exist between the figures in the illustration and your household's spending?

4. Ask your grandparents or someone their age what kinds of money management problems they had when they were your age. What differences exist between now and then?

5. "The more your earn, the more you spend." Do you agree or disagree with this statement? Why? How does a person's lifestyle relate to this statement?

CHAPTER 23

*M*anaging *Your Personal Finances*

■ CHAPTER OBJECTIVES ────────────────────

After studying this chapter and completing the end-of-chapter activities, you will be able to:

1. Name the first step in preparing a good budget.
2. List three ways a budget can aid you financially.
3. Describe the relationship between a budget and a financial plan.
4. Prepare an Income and Expenditures Record.
5. Prepare a Comparison of Savings and Expenditures with a Budget Allowances Record.
6. Explain why budgets must be changed from time to time.

Fourteen-year-old Erin Angland always seemed to have what she called "money problems." She always seemed to be a little short of cash. (And long on ways to spend it.) Her wants and needs were usually greater than her income. Erin's situation is not uncommon.

Her income for a typical week included $25 for delivering papers, $10 for one baby-sitting job, and a $10 allowance from her parents. For some this would seem like an adequate amount of money, but not for Erin. If she bought everything she wanted during the week, she wouldn't have any money for her savings account.

She thought of several possible solutions to her problem, including delivering more papers, seeking more baby-sitting jobs, and asking her parents for a raise in her allowance. After a discussion with her business teacher, she decided that the best solution was for her to learn to manage her money more wisely. She decided to set up a plan for spending and saving money. Such a plan is called a **budget**.

What is a Budget?

A budget is one means of carrying out a good financial plan. It enables you to save the money you need to meet your goals and encourages you to spend wisely. It may be just a simple record of how much money you make, how much you plan to spend and how much you want to save. Or it may be more detailed and include specific amounts to be spent in categories such as food, clothing, and transportation. A good budget should take very little of your time, and it can aid you in several ways. It is a basic step toward better money management. Also, a budget will help you set goals for yourself. Further, putting your plans in writing will help you follow them.

Planning Your Budgetary Goals

A good budget begins by establishing goals. These goals are shorter term than the financial plan but consistent with it. Do you want to save money for a special occasion? Do you want to buy a record album or a new sweater? You must decide which of the things you want are most important. Then you can budget your money to meet your goals.

Illus. 23–1
Living within a budget means planning ahead for purchases. You may want to save money for those purchases you think are important.

Erin's goal is to save enough money to buy a horse. She has decided to save $15 a week. To do this she needs to plan very carefully how she will use her available money. This means Erin must plan her **expenditures**—amounts actually spent for goods and services. By remembering what she usually spends, Erin has developed the budget shown in Figure 23–1.

Keeping the Accounts

It is usually easier to prepare a budget than it is to follow it. Regularly updating your records, however, can help you stick to your budget. This is called "keeping the accounts." Updating records can be done using expense record sheets that are available in stationery and office-supplies departments of several stores. The information recorded on these record sheets includes such figures as budgeted amounts, cash on hand, income and expenditures, totals of each category, and ending balances.

Erin tried to follow her budget but she kept no records to show how she actually spent her money. At the end of a few weeks, she found that she hadn't saved anything, but she couldn't remember where her money had gone. Erin then decided that she needed not only a budget, but also records to show exactly how her money was spent.

Recording Income and Expenditures

A part of every budget is a plan for how money should be spent. Accounts of records show how money has actually been received and spent. Both are necessary, but records can become burdensome if they are too detailed. They should be as simple as possible

Figure 23–1
Erin has prepared her weekly budget. Have you prepared yours?

Erin Angland Weekly Budget					
Estimated Income			Estimated Expenditures		
Allowance	10	00	Savings	15	00
Delivering Papers	25	00	Entertainment & Recreation	12	50
Baby-sitting	10	00	School Supplies	7	50
			Clothes & Personal Items	10	00
Total Income	45	00	Total Savings and Expenditures	45	00

and yet show the information that is needed. Erin decided to keep her record of income and expenditures on the form shown in Figure 23–2. Study this form carefully, and follow the steps Erin completed in filling out this record.

1. Erin recorded the total amount budgeted, $45. She also recorded the amount budgeted for each item. These amounts were to remind her of how much she had allowed for each item. She then drew a line across the whole page so that she would not confuse the budget amounts with the amounts she received and spent.

2. On January 3, the day she started the record, Erin had $7.50 in cash. To distinguish between the beginning balance and the amounts to be received during the week, she wrote the word "Balance" in the Explanation column. Notice how the year, month, and day are entered in the Date column.

3. Also on January 3, Erin received $25 for delivering papers and spent $2.50 for a ticket to a school dance. She also put aside the $15 she wanted to save. She saved the $15 early in the week because she knew how easy it was for money to slip through her fingers if she didn't deposit it in her savings account. Notice how these three entries have been made.

4. A similar entry has been made for each day of the week. When amounts were spent for two or more purposes, the total was entered in the Payments column and the individual amounts were entered in their own columns. Look at the entries for January 5, for example.

5. Erin proved, or balanced, her record at the end of each week to be sure that she had kept it accurately. After her last entry for the week, she drew a single line across all the money columns to indicate addition.

6. Next she found the totals of the Receipts and Payments columns. She wrote these totals directly under the last line on which she had recorded an entry. At any time, the difference between the total of the Receipts column and the total of the Payments column should be the same as her cash on hand. The difference between Total Receipts and Total Payments was $7.50. Erin counted her money and found that she had exactly $7.50 in cash. So she knew that her record was correct.

7. Erin found the totals of each of the special columns. She then added these totals and compared the sum with the total of

Figure 23–2

An accurate record of income
and expenses is important.

Erin Angland
Income and Expenditures Record

Date		Explanation	Totals Receipts	Totals Payments	Savings	Entertainment and Recreation	Clothes and Personal Items	School Supplies
(1)		Budget $45			15 00	12 50	10 00	7 50
(2) 19-- Jan.	3	Balance	7 50					
(3)	3		25 00	17 50	15 00	2 50		
	4			2 50			2 50	
	5			8 25		4 00		4 25
	6			4 00			4 00	
(4)	7		10 00	2 00		2 00		
	8		10 00	2 00				2 00
(5)	9			8 75		4 00	4 75	
(6)	9	Totals	52 50	45 00	15 00	12 50	11 25	6 25
(7)	9	Balance		7 50				
(8)			52 50	52 50				
(9) Jan.	10	Balance	7 50					
	10		25 00	15 00	15 00			
	11			5 75		4 50		1 25
	12			6 00			6 00	
	13			3 50			3 50	
	14		10 00	9 50		3 75		5 75
(10)	15		10 00					
	16			4 00		4 00		
	16	Totals	52 50	43 75	15 00	12 25	9 50	7 00
	16	Cash short		1 00				
	16	Balance		7 75				
			52 50	52 50				
Jan.	17	Balance	7 75					

the Payments column. The two amounts were the same. This gave her further proof that she had recorded everything she had spent.

8. She added the cash balance of $7.50 to the payments total and then brought the totals of the Receipts and Payments columns to the next line. This showed that the Receipts equaled the sum of the Payments and the Balance.

9. Erin then drew a double line across the Date column and all the money columns to show that her record book had been balanced. To show the amount of money on hand at the beginning of the second week, she recorded the balance of $7.50 in the Receipts column.

10. Erin recorded receipts and payments during the second week as she had during the first week. When she totaled the Receipts and Payments columns at the end of the second week, she found her cash balance to be $8.75. But when Erin counted her money, she found that she had only $7.75. She probably had lost a dollar or had forgotten to record a payment. So she entered $1 in the Payments column. She usually did not write an explanation of an entry, but in this case she wrote "Cash Short" in the Explanation column. She wanted to know how much her cash was short from week to week. After making an entry for the cash shortage, Erin balanced her record as she had done at the end of the first week.

Comparing Savings and Expenditures With Your Budget

As a reminder of how much she had decided to save and spend, on the first line of the record Erin had written her budget **allowances** — amounts of money budgeted for savings and for each expenditure. But at the end of each week she wanted to know exactly how her savings and spending compared with her budget allowances. To get this information she used the form shown in Figure 23–3. Study it to see how Erin prepared this record.

1. Erin entered her budget allowances for the week of January 3 to 9.

2. She entered the amounts that she had actually saved and spent during the first week, getting this information from the Income and Expenditures Record.

3. The differences between her budget allowances and the amounts she actually saved and spent told her how well she had kept

within her budget. For example, she saved exactly $15 as she had planned. She had allowed $7.50 for school supplies but spent $6.25, thus having $1.25 to carry over to the next week. She recorded the difference between her budget allowances and her expenditures on the next line and wrote "Carried Forward" in the explanation column.

4. Erin again entered the amounts that she had budgeted for the week.

5. She added the amounts carried forward and the budget allowances to find the amounts available for the second week. For example, the amount available for school supplies was $8.75, and the amount available for clothes and personal items was $8.75. During the first week she had spent $1.25 more for clothes and personal items than she had planned. To show that she had spent more than her budget allowance for these items, she circled the $1.25.

cathy®

Adjusting the Budget

The estimates of how much money you expect to receive and spend may be wrong and need adjusting. The first estimates may not have been very accurate. Then, too, everyone's spending requirements change from time to time. At the end of the second week, Erin decided that she should make some changes in her budget allowances. For one thing, another of her neighbors wanted her to baby-sit a few hours a week, so this meant she could earn an extra $8 a week. Also, Erin knew that several school activities were coming up and that she would probably be spending more for recreation, clothes, and personal expenses. And she wanted to put aside another $4 a week in savings.

After considering her new income and plans, Erin revised her budget estimates as follows:

Savings	$19.00
Entertainment and recreation	14.50
Clothes and personal items	12.00
School supplies	7.50
Total estimated savings and expenditures	$53.00

Erin recorded these new budget allowances in her comparison form (Figure 23–3) and added them to the amounts carried forward to show the budget amounts available for the third week.

If your budget is carefully planned, estimates will not need to be changed very often. Spending more than the amount allowed for a particular budget item is usually the result of one of the following situations: (1) an unexpected expense may have occurred; (2) the cost of the item may have increased; or (3) you may have been careless in spending. Remember that increasing an allowance for one item requires a decrease in the allowance for one or several other items unless your income has also increased.

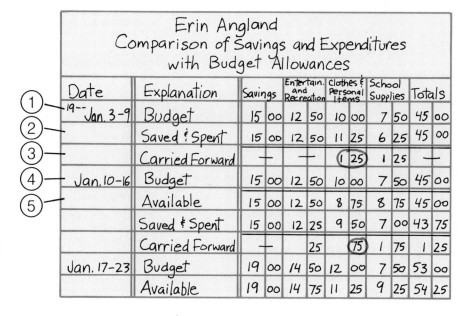

Figure 23–3
Has Erin stayed within her budget? A comparison form like this one shows Erin how well she's doing.

Erin Angland
Comparison of Savings and Expenditures with Budget Allowances

	Date	Explanation	Savings	Entertain. and Recreation	Clothes & Personal Items	School Supplies	Totals
①	19-- Jan. 3-9	Budget	15 00	12 50	10 00	7 50	45 00
②		Saved & Spent	15 00	12 50	11 25	6 25	45 00
③		Carried Forward	—	—	(1 25)	1 25	—
④	Jan. 10-16	Budget	15 00	12 50	10 00	7 50	45 00
⑤		Available	15 00	12 50	8 75	8 75	45 00
		Saved & Spent	15 00	12 25	9 50	7 00	43 75
		Carried Forward	—	25	(75)	1 75	1 25
	Jan. 17-23	Budget	19 00	14 50	12 00	7 50	53 00
		Available	19 00	14 75	11 25	9 25	54 25

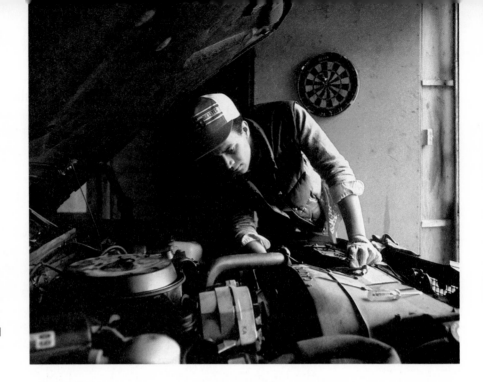

Illus. 23–2
Unexpected expenses may mean you need to adjust your budget.

*A*dding *to Your Business Vocabulary*

The following terms should become part of your business vocabulary. For each numbered item, find the term that has the same meaning.

allowances   *expenditure*
budget

1. The amounts of money budgeted for savings or expenditures.
2. A plan for saving and spending income.

3. An amount actually spent for food, clothing, or other items.

*U*nderstanding *Your Reading*

1. What is the first step in developing a good budget?
2. In what three ways can a budget aid you financially?
3. What relationship does a budget have to a financial plan?
4. Why did Erin Angland decide the amount of savings as her first step in preparing her budget?

5. Why did Erin's first try at budgeting her money fail?
6. Why did Erin write the budgeted amounts in her income and expenditures record before she recorded any transactions?
7. What information did Erin write in the Payments column of her income and expenditures record?

8. Why did Erin total the individual expenditures columns at the end of each week?

9. Why might you have a cash shortage at the end of the budget week?

10. State three reasons for changing budgets from time to time.

*P*utting Your Business Knowledge to Work

1. After her second week with her budget, Erin found she could earn an extra $8.00 per week from another baby-sitting job. How did she budget this extra money? How would you have budgeted the additional money?

2. Some people claim that living by a budget is too structured and restrictive. That is, they don't like to live such a planned and strict economic life. What would you say to those who have that point of view to convince them that budgets can work, even for them?

3. Every week Chris Thorson puts any amount he has not spent during the week into savings. If he needs more money than he has budgeted, he withdraws it from his savings to meet expenses. Is Chris following a good money management plan? Explain.

4. A goal of many teenagers is to own a car. If you became the owner of a car, what major changes would you make in a budget like Erin Angland's.

*C*omputing Business Problems

1. On January 17, Erin Angland revised her budget estimates as shown on page 331. Her new total of estimated savings and expenditures increased to $53 a week. In this problem you will keep Erin's record for January 17 to 23. Draw a form like the one shown in Figure 23–2.

   a. On the first line write Erin's revised budget allowances. Then draw a line across the entire page.

   b. On the second line write the balance of cash on hand as of January 17. Obtain this information from Figure 23–2.

   c. Enter the following financial activities that Erin completed:

   Jan. 17 Received $25 pay for newspaper route; placed $19 in savings.

   18 Expenditures: Container of shoe polish, $1.90; movie ticket, $4.75.

   19 Received $18 for baby-sitting; expenditure: notebook paper, $2.95.

   20 Expenditures: School biology lab fee, $5.

   21 Expenditures: Hairbrush, $4.75.

   22 Received $10 for weekly allowance; expenditures: stereo tape, $8; ball-point pens, $1.85.

   23 Expenditures: ticket to basketball game, $2; socks, $4.95.

   d. Rule and balance the record in the same way Erin did at the end of the first and second weeks. Refer to Figure 23–2. Erin's cash on hand at the end of the third week was $5.60.

   e. Draw a form similar to Figure 23–3 and

prepare a comparison form for the week of January 17 to 23.

f. On the first line of the comparison form, record the amounts available for the week of January 17 to 23. Obtain this information from Figure 23–3.

g. On the second line of the form, enter the amounts saved and spent. Then determine the amounts carried forward and enter them on the third line.

2. Complete the instructions given below for Erin Angland's budget for the week of January 24 to 30.

a. On the next line of the comparison form, enter the budget allowances. Calculate the amounts available for the week of January 24 to 30 and record them on the following line.

b. Prepare a second page for the income and expenditures record. On the first line, write Erin's budget allowances and draw a line across the entire form. On the second line, write the balance of the cash on hand of $5.60.

c. Record the following transactions that Erin completed during the week:
Jan. 24 Received $25 pay for news-

paper route; placed $19 in savings.

25 Expenditures: magazine for English class, $1.50; ticket to dance, $3.

26 Received $8 for helping neighbor.

27 Received $10 for baby-sitting; expenditure: gloves, $6.50.

28 Received $10 for weekly allowance; expenditure: school newspaper, 75 cents (charge to entertainment).

29 Expenditure: watchband, $8.50.

30 Expenditures: ticket to basketball game, $2.00; protective goggles for biology lab, $6.

d. Rule and balance the record. Erin's cash on hand is $11.35.

e. Complete the comparison for the week.

3. Erin's parents have promised her that her allowance will be increased each year by the amount of inflation during the year plus five dollars. If inflation is 6.5 percent in the coming year, what will her allowance be one year from now?

Stretching Your Business Knowledge

1. It has been said many times and in many ways that if one doesn't have goals or objectives, one will never get anywhere. While this statement may be a bit harsh and not always correct, it certainly contains a grain of truth. Develop a paragraph encouraging the use of a budget using this philosophy.

2. Besides the money they spend themselves, teenagers have another important effect on the American economy. This effect results from what they have to say about how their family's money is spent.

In what ways does having a teenager in the family influence a family's spending?

3. Do you have a budget? Whether you have a job or not, you probably receive and spend some money each week. Using the budget set up by Erin Angland in this chapter as a model, prepare an estimate of your weekly income and expenditures. Then make an income and expenditures record for yourself similar to the one shown in Figure 23–2. Keep an exact record for one week. How does your record compare with your estimate?

CHAPTER 24

*M*anaging Household Finances

CHAPTER OBJECTIVES ─────────────────────────

After studying this chapter and completing the end-of-chapter activities, you will be able to:

1. Tell why it is usually recommended that savings be considered the first item in a household budget.
2. Give three examples of fixed expenses.
3. Name the eight types of items a family usually includes in a budget.
4. Describe how a filing system can help to remind you of the date bills are due.
5. Explain why a statement of net worth should be prepared every year.
6. Tell how long income tax records should be kept.

You will remember from the last chapter that Erin Angland had a few small money problems that she was able to solve by planning her spending and saving. This plan, called a budget, had been suggested by her business teacher. Budgets are an important part of any sound financial plan.

A budget is especially important for a household consisting of several members. When more than one person is earning and spending money, it is quite easy to lose track of finances. The members of a household with a good money management plan will usually live better than they could without a plan.

Preparing a Household Budget

Just as in a personal budget, savings should be considered first in a household budget. If savings are not considered first, the allowances for other expenditures may use up all the income and leave nothing to save. After savings, two other types of expenses must be considered, fixed expenses and variable expenses. **Fixed expenses** are bills that occur regularly and are for the same amount each time such as house payments and insurance payments. **Variable expenses** are expenses that occur less frequently, are for widely differing amounts, and are usually more difficult to estimate. For example, medical and dental expenses may not occur very often, but they may be large when they do occur. Such expenses should be provided for somewhere in the budget. If allowances are not made for them, variable expenses may use up a large part of savings.

The Anglands' Budget

As did Erin, the Anglands decided that a budget would improve their financial situation. They had no particular financial difficulties but felt that a lot of money "slipped through their fingers" each month. They were correct in thinking a budget would remedy that feeling by providing them with an accurate record of all of their income and expenditures.

Marie Angland is a computer sales representative. Although it varies slightly from month to month, her average monthly net income, or take-home pay, is about $1,250.00. **Net income** or **take-home pay** is the amount a person receives after taxes and other deductions have been taken from his or her earnings. Hans Angland is an electrician and earns slightly less than Marie; however, because his company pays for more of his insurance and retirement program, he takes home slightly more ($1,325.00) in net income each month.

To gather more information on budgeting, the Anglands read several booklets on income planning. They learned that savings and expense items are often classified under eight main divisions:

1. Savings. Savings accounts, government bonds, and stocks.
2. Food. Food eaten at home and meals eaten away from home.
3. Clothing. Clothing, dry cleaning, sewing appliances, and shoe repairs.
4. Household. Rent, mortgage payments, taxes, insurance, gas and electricity, coal or fuel oil, telephone, water, household furnishings, household supplies, and painting and repairs.
5. Transportation. Automobile payments, automobile upkeep and operation, fares for public transportation, and auto and drivers' licenses.
6. Health and personal care. Medical and dental expenses, drugs, eyeglasses, hospital and nursing expenses, accident and health insurance, barber and beauty shop, and children's allowances.
7. Recreation and education. Books, magazines, newspapers, theaters,

movies, concerts, vacations, school expenses, hobbies, radio and TV, musical instruments, and club dues.

8. Gifts and contributions. Gifts to church, charitable organizations, and personal gifts.

Illus. 24–1
The Angland household budget shows allowances for clothing, recreation, food, and several other expense categories.

The Anglands first decided they wanted to save $235 a month. They made an estimate of their past expenditures based mainly on their checkbook record. They then prepared the budget shown in Figure 24–1.

Figure 24–1
The Angland Family's monthly budget

The Angland Household
Monthly Budget
January, 19--

Estimated Income			Estimated Expenditures		
Hans' net income	1,325	00	Savings	235	00
Marie's net income	1,250	00	Food	400	00
			Clothing	325	00
			Household	540	00
			Transportation	475	00
			Health & Personal Care	150	00
			Recreation & Education	325	00
			Gifts & Contributions	125	00
Total Income	2,575	00	Total Savings & Expenditures	2575	00

Income and Expenditures Records

After planning their budget, the Anglands set up an Income and Expenditures Record to show them whether or not their plan was working. This record is shown in Figure 24–2. Notice that this record is similar to the one kept by Erin in Chapter 23. The Anglands' first entry at the beginning of the month was for money put in their savings account. By setting aside that amount first, they could be sure of saving part of their income. Entries for expenditures were recorded each Saturday and at the end of the month, except for especially large payments which were recorded immediately. Incomes were entered on the days they were received. The Anglands ruled and balanced their records at the end of the month as Erin did at the end of each week.

Comparing Records with the Budget

At the end of each month, totals of the columns in the income and expenditures record were entered on the comparison form

The Angland Household
Income and Expenditures Record

Date	Explanation	Totals		Distribution of Savings and Expenditures							
		Receipts	Pay-ments	Savings	Food	Clothing	House-hold	Trans-portation	Health & Personal Care	Rec. & Educ.	Gifts & Contrib.
	Budget $2,575			235 00	400 00	325 00	540 00	475 00	150 00	325 00	125 00
19-- Jan. 1	Balance	300 00									
2			235 00	235 00							
7			345 00		95 00	50 00	30 00	30 00	75 00	20 00	45 00
14	Hans' Salary	662 50	199 00		80 00	29 00	5 00	20 00	10 00	45 00	10 00
15	Marie's Salary	625 00									
16	Mortgage Payment		450 00				450 00				
17	Car Payment		325 00					325 00			
21			350 00		95 00	140 00	60 00	20 00		25 00	10 00
28	Hans' Salary	662 50	281 00		90 00	87 00	3 00	30 00	6 00	60 00	5 00
29	Marie's Salary	625 00									
31	Totals	2,875 00	2,185 00	235 00	360 00	306 00	548 00	425 00	91 00	150 00	70 00
31	Balance		690 00								
		2,875 00	2,875 00								
Feb. 1	Balance	690 00									

Figure 24–2

The Anglands recorded their income and expenses for January.

shown in Figure 24–3. The Anglands spent $8 more on household expenses than they had budgeted. To show that they overspent the budget in this category, they circled the $8.

When the Anglands set up their budget, they had $300 in cash on hand and in their checking account. They decided to keep this amount in reserve to meet any unusual expenses. So this amount was not budgeted for current expenses. That is why the $300 is shown in the Income and Expenditures Record but not in the comparison form.

As far as the Anglands could tell from their records, they were following their budget satisfactorily. At the end of January, the

Month 19--	Explanation	Savings	Food	Clothing	Household	Transportation	Health & Personal Care	Recreation & Education	Gifts & Contrib.	Totals
Jan.	Budget	235 00	400 00	325 00	540 00	475 00	150 00	325 00	125 00	2575 00
	Saved & Spent	235 00	360 00	306 00	548 00	425 00	91 00	150 00	70 00	2185 00
	Carried Forward	—	40 00	19 00	8 00	50 00	59 00	175 00	55 00	390 00
Feb.	Budget	235 00	400 00	325 00	540 00	475 00	150 00	325 00	125 00	2575 00
	Available	235 00	440 00	344 00	532 00	525 00	209 00	500 00	180 00	2965 00

The Angland Household
Comparison of Savings and Expenditures with Budget allowances

Figure 24-3

As this comparison form shows, the Anglands are generally staying within their budget.

Recreation and Education category had a fairly large balance. However, the Anglands planned to go on a weekend skiing trip in late February, so this would reduce the Recreation and Education balance considerably by the end of February. Some of the other categories had large balances at the end of January, but these balances will be used to take care of large expenditures in future months. For example, auto insurance will be paid from the Transportation account, and medical and dental bills will be paid from the Health and Personal Care category.

Keeping a File

In order to assure that a budget works well, it is a good idea to have all of one's financial papers in one location and filed in an orderly fashion. In addition to eliminating the frustration associated with lost records, a good filing system is simply a wise business practice. Stationery and office supply stores sell a wide variety of filing equipment suitable for home use.

Unpaid Bills

The Anglands receive monthly bills for utilities and also make a monthly payment on their house. Since these payments are made regularly each month, there is little chance that the Anglands will forget about them. But other bills are paid less often. For example, life insurance premiums are due twice a year, in March and September. Property taxes must be paid in June and December. If there is no record to remind the Anglands when such bills are due, they may fail to budget for them.

The Anglands bought a file box similar to the one shown in Illus. 24–2. The box contains a folder for each month of the year. As bills are received, they are placed in the folder for the month in which they are to be paid. When preparing the monthly budget, the Anglands check the proper folder and make provisions to pay any debts that appear in the folder. There is also an extra folder marked "Next Year" in which the Anglands keep all bills, and papers, and reminders about such things as property taxes and insurance premiums to be paid in the following year.

Business Papers

Current bills, receipts, income and property tax records, wills, insurance policies, and deeds to property are important in a family's business affairs. Records such as these must be kept in an orderly manner so that they can be located easily when needed.

Some business and personal papers should be filed for long periods of time. An insurance policy, for example, should be kept until the contract has been fulfilled or canceled. Records involving the transfer of property should be held for as long as the property is owned. Receipts for payment of bills, especially those involving large sums of money, should be kept until there is no possibility that payment will be demanded a second time.

Illus. 24–2
Finding needed information quickly is made easier when your financial papers are organized.

Records for Taxes

It is very important to have accurate and complete records when preparing income tax returns. Many kinds of expenditures can be subtracted from your income to lower the amount of taxes you must pay. However, you must have records of these expenses if you are ever asked to verify them. As a general rule income tax records and returns should be kept for at least three years from the deadline date for filing the returns. If the government audits or checks the accuracy of your tax returns, you can be required, by law, to produce tax records for the three preceding years.

Determining Net Worth

Sometimes families or individuals want to know what they are worth financially. This can be done by listing everything of value that is owned (**assets**) and all debts that are owed (**liabilities**). The value of some assets is determined by estimating their present resale value. Information that may be helpful in preparing a statement of financial worth is available from the expenditure records of previous years.

The Angland's statement of **net worth** is shown in Figure 24–4. As you can see, net worth is determined by subtracting liabilities

The Anglands' Statement of Net Worth December 31, 19--					
Assets			**Liabilities & Net Worth**		
Cash (checking acct.)	300	00	First National Bank	620	00
Cash (savings acct.)	5,000	00	G. Wilcox & Co.	700	00
U.S. Saving Bonds	6,200	00	Mutual Savings & Loan	35,420	00
Clothing	5,000	00	Total Liabilities	36,740	00
House and Lot	87,300	00	Family Net Worth	87,620	00
Household Furnishings	5,560	00			
Automobile	15,000	00			
Total Assets	124,360	00	Total Liabilities & Net Worth	124,360	00

Figure 24–4
The Angland family's statement of net worth.

from assets (Total Assets $124,360 − Total Liabilities $36,740 = Family Net Worth $87,620). By preparing such a statement every year, families or individuals can obtain a fairly good idea of how well they are doing with their money management. A net worth that increases from year to year usually indicates that a household or individual is making financial progress and is practicing good money management.

A dding to Your Business Vocabulary

The following terms should become part of your business vocabulary. For each numbered item, find the term that has the same meaning.

assets   net income or take-home pay
fixed expenses   net worth
liabilities   variable expenses

1. Everything of value that a person, household, or business owns.
2. Expenses which occur infrequently, are for widely differing amounts, and are sometimes difficult to estimate.
3. The difference between the assets and the liabilities of a person, household, or business.
4. Expenses, such as house payments and insurance payments, that occur regularly and are for the same amount each time.
5. The amount a person receives after taxes and other deductions are withheld from his or her earnings.
6. Debts that a person, household, or business owes.

U nderstanding Your Reading

1. Why is it usually recommended that savings be considered first when preparing a budget?
2. What is a fixed expense? List three examples of fixed expenses.
3. Into what eight divisions are family savings and expense items usually classified?
4. Why did the Anglands not include the $300 they had in reserve as part of their budget?
5. Why did some categories of the Angland's budget have large balances at the end of January?
6. Why did the Anglands need a file box?
7. How can a filing system be used to keep track of when bills are due?
8. How long should records for taxes be kept?
9. Is the furniture that a family owns an asset or a liability?
10. Why should a statement of net worth be prepared every year?

*P*utting Your Business Knowledge to Work

1. You have probably heard someone say "I just don't know where all our money goes." What they are really saying is "we seem to have an adequate income but we don't keep very good track of how it is spent." After reading this chapter, what advice would you have for them?
2. Consider a family of four people: the mother, a supermarket manager; the father, a department store salesperson; and two children, ages 14 and 11.
   a. List four fixed expenses that this family will be likely to meet weekly or monthly.
   b. What are some variable expenses that they might have to meet?
3. Look at the Angland's comparison record on page 340 and answer these questions:
   a. At the end of January, for which item had the Anglands spent more money than the budget allowed?
   b. At the end of January, for which items had they spent less money than the budget allowed?
   c. Why do you think that the amount of money spent rarely equals the budgeted amount?
4. Some people keep their business papers in drawers in their desks. Each time a bill or receipt is received, they place it in the drawer. What drawbacks can you see in that system of storing records?
5. Do you agree or disagree with these statements? Why?
   a. A large income is necessary to have security and happiness.
   b. Budgets take the fun out of spending.
   c. Every member of the family should have a part in deciding how the family income should be used.

*C*omputing Business Problems

1. In this problem you will continue the Angland's household record of income and expenditures for February. Draw a form similar to Figure 24–2.
   a. On the first line of the record write the Angland's budget allowances for February, obtaining the information from Figure 24–2. Draw a line under this information across the entire form.
   b. On the second line write the balance of cash on hand as of February 1, $690.
   c. Enter the following activities that the Anglands completed during February. Use Figure 24–2 as a guide.
      Feb. 2 Payments: food, $87; clothes, $25; gasoline and oil, $25; cosmetics and medicine, $21; household supplies, $12; church contribution, $20; deposited in savings, $235.
      13 Income: Hans, $662.50. Payments: food, $68; clothes, $185; car maintenance and two new tires, $210; dental bill, $63; movie tickets, $16; church contribution, $25.
      15 Income: Marie, $625. Car payment: $325.
      16 Mortgage payment: $450.
      18 Payments: food, $79; electric and telephone bills, $80; gasoline, $12; church contribution, $20.
      22 Payments: stereo record, $8; doctor bill, $37; prescription medicine, $8; children's allow-

ances, $14; shoes, $46; church contribution, $20.

28 Income: Hans, $662.50; Marie, $625. Payments: food, $65; gasoline, $15; school supplies, $10; sports equipment, $19; birthday present for grandmother, $18.

d. Rule and balance the Angland family's record for February. Cash on hand was $1,047.

e. Now prepare a comparison form similar to the one on page 340. Draw a form similar to the one shown in Figure 24–3.

f. On the first line of the comparison form, record the amounts available for February, obtaining this information from Figure 24–3.

g. On the second line enter the amounts saved and spent as shown in the income and expenditures record.

h. Calculate and record the amounts carried forward at the end of the month.

2. What percentage of the Angland's total income of $2,575 per month is budgeted for their home mortgage payment? their food expenses?

3. By what percentage did the Anglands overspend their transportation budget in February?

*S*tretching Your Business Knowledge

1. Most discussions of budgeting strongly suggest that an amount for savings always be considered first. Try to describe a situation for an individual or a household when it would be appropriate not to follow this guideline.

2. Every family has the problem of arranging records in an orderly way. Suggest a plan for filing and organizing each of the following materials so that a particular item can be located quickly when it is needed.
   a. children's health records
   b. Christmas card list
   c. family members' birth certificates
   d. manufacturer's instructions for care and use of appliances
   e. telephone numbers
   f. product guarantees

3. From newspapers, libraries and other sources, try to find out how much money was budgeted for the following items by your town, county, or district.
   a. school needs
   b. street or highway maintenance
   c. police department
   d. fire department
   e. public welfare
   f. mayor's office
   g. public library
   h. parks

CHAPTER 25

T*he Changing Value of Money*

After studying this chapter and completing the end-of-chapter activities, you will be able to:

1. Tell how the value of a dollar is measured.
2. List several causes of inflation.
3. Discuss the changes in the value of a dollar over the years.
4. Explain what happens to prices during periods of inflation and deflation.
5. Explain the three actions that government can take to control inflation or deflation.
6. Describe the consumer price index.

Some measures in our society are constant and almost never change. A yard is always 36 inches. A gallon is always four quarts. A liter is 2.1 pints and a kilometer is .6 of a mile. However, as you learned in Unit 1, prices are not constant. They change—sometimes often. The price of a dozen eggs in your supermarket may change every week. The price of a new automobile changes every year. Prices change even though the quality of the goods or services we buy stays the same.

These price changes for the same or similar products indicate that the value of money changes. Unfortunately, a dollar is not a fixed measure like a quart or a kilometer. The value of a dollar, as measured by what it can buy, changes from year to year.

The Value of a Dollar Changes

The constant change in the value of the dollar has been a source of confusion and frustration to consumers for many years. Generally, the prices of goods and services tend to rise over the years. This makes a dollar worth less from one year to the next. In fact, the

Illus. 25–1
The changing value of the dollar usually means that the prices of goods and services increase.

prices of goods and services have risen so rapidly that a dollar buys a great deal less now than it did just a few years ago. Suppose that a school lunch cost 80 cents a few years ago and that it now costs $1.12. That is an increase of 40 percent. If the average price of all goods and services has risen 40 percent, the consumer will need $1.40 to buy what $1.00 used to buy. At times prices for some items have doubled or even tripled in just a few months. Such price increases make it difficult for many consumers to live within their budgets.

Inflation

As you will recall from Chapter 4, a general increase in prices is called inflation. Inflation occurs whenever the demand for goods and services tends to be greater than the supply. In a period of prosperity when almost everyone has a job, many people spend their earnings freely. As a result, the demand for goods and services of all kinds tends to increase rapidly. This causes prices to rise and may result in inflation.

Less Buying Power With Inflation

As prices rise, wages and salaries also tend to rise. But each wage and salary dollar has less buying power because prices are now higher. If productivity increases along with wages and salaries, there is no effect on prices. But if increases in wages and salaries are greater than increases in productivity, there are more dollars to be spent for a limited amount of goods. That gives prices another push upward. To meet the demand or the expected demand for more goods and services, businesses expand. They build new stores and factories and spend large amounts for equipment. All this spending in turn increases demand and adds to the upward movement of prices.

Local and federal governments may also contribute to inflation. Governments spend enormous amounts of money for defense, education, welfare, roads, and many other goods and services. If governments collect enough in taxes to match all their payments, their expenditures do not increase demand. For each dollar they spend, the public has one dollar less to spend. But if governments borrow large amounts from banks and then spend those amounts, they increase demand. Governments spend their borrowed funds, but the amount that the public has to spend is not decreased because taxes have not been raised.

Reprinted by permission of Jefferson Communications, Inc., Reston, Va.

Combating Inflation

In general it is thought that inflation—especially excessive inflation—is bad. But, as individuals, we cannot do very much to affect inflation. When prices seem to be too high, we may postpone making some purchases. If many consumers do this, the demand for goods may drop, and prices may decrease as a result. But most of us are not able or willing to postpone many of our purchases. We must spend regularly for food, clothing, and shelter. And if we need or want something like a new car or a refrigerator, we probably want it now and not three or four years from now when prices *may* be lower. We, of course, have no way of knowing that prices will be lower in the future. In fact, history shows that they are more likely to be higher.

Government, acting for all of us, can help to fight inflation. Among other things, it can:

1. Increase taxes. An increase in taxes takes money away from consumers and thus reduces their demand for goods and services.
2. Reduce government spending. A reduction in spending, especially when accompanied by higher taxes, decreases demand and thus decreases prices.
3. Encourage higher interest rates. Higher interest rates make it cost more to borrow money to buy such things as a car or a house. Higher interest rates also increase what a business must pay if it wants to borrow to expand its facilities. Some buying may therefore be postponed or avoided entirely. Decreases in purchases may result in a decrease in the demand for goods. A smaller demand for goods may help bring down prices.

Deflation

The opposite of inflation is deflation. Deflation is a decrease in the general level of prices. With deflation there is an increase in the purchasing power of a dollar. Deflation tends to occur when the supply of goods and services is greater than the demand. When prices increase during inflation, consumers may cut down on their purchases. Consumers may stop buying either because they think that prices are too high or because they have already bought to the limit of their money and credit.

Deflation Through Decreased Buying

Because of the decreased buying by consumers, there is less demand for goods and services. Businesses may lay off employees or have employees work fewer hours. The employees then have less money to spend and decrease their buying. The decreased buying by employees further decreases demand and makes deflation even more serious. As business becomes less active, stores and factories may delay expansion. This again decreases demand and helps push prices down.

Illus. 25–2
Decreased buying by consumers may mean increased unemployment.

Deflation Through Increased Taxes

Deflation also occurs when government increases taxes more than it increases spending. When this occurs, government takes money from consumers that they might otherwise spend, but does not increase its spending. This decreases the total demand for goods and services and tends to cause prices to decrease. Although prices are lower, unemployment is higher. While the dollar's buying power is increased, consumers have less money to spend.

The Government Can Act Against Deflation

To combat deflation, government can follow policies just the opposite of those used to combat inflation. Among other things, it can:

1. Decrease taxes. A decrease in taxes leaves more money in the hands of consumers. Consumers then can increase their purchases of goods and services.
2. Increase government spending. An increase in spending that is not offset by an increase in taxes increases demand and, thus, prices.
3. Encourage lower interest rates. Lower interest rates tend to encourage individuals and businesses to borrow in order to buy.

With increased borrowing, consumers have more money to spend. This helps to increase the demand for goods and eventually will encourage higher prices.

Why More Is Done About Deflation Than Inflation

When deflation threatens, quick action is usually taken. Everyone notices the slowing down of business and the loss of jobs that deflation brings. Public officials do whatever they can to avoid the hardships that deflation causes. Furthermore, the actions taken to combat deflation are usually welcomed. Almost everyone likes to have taxes reduced. Few object to increased spending by government for public works or services that benefit them. Also, few object to lower interest rates, especially if they want to borrow to buy a home or some other major item.

When inflation threatens, however, such prompt action is not likely to be taken. The strong demand for goods and services that usually occurs during inflation makes businesses prosperous and jobs plentiful. Wages and salaries increase. Prices also increase but the increases are not as noticeable at first. So before inflation becomes really serious, most people do not want anything done that will affect what seems to be a good condition. Often nothing is done to control inflation until it has gone so far that it can no longer be reduced easily. Then it can only be slowed down or kept from increasing.

Usually the means of fighting inflation are unpopular. Few people like to pay higher taxes or higher interest rates. The idea of reduced government spending is approved by many people, but few favor reductions in the public works or services that affect them and their jobs.

The Consumer Price Index

In order to make information about inflation and deflation available and understandable to everyone, the federal government publishes price indexes. A **price index** is a series of numbers showing how prices have changed over a number of years. The **consumer price index (CPI)** shows the changes in the average prices of goods and services bought by consumers over a succession of months and years.

Figure 25–1 gives the consumer price index for the period of 1967 to 1983. In compiling the chart, the average prices of 300 goods and services in 1967 were taken to represent 100 percent. The year 1967 is then known as the **base year.** The figure given for each year is a percentage of the base year average. For example, the amount 160 for year 1975 means that an item that cost $1.00 in 1967 had increased in cost to $1.60 by 1975. Changes in prices may not seem important from day to day. But over a number of years the changes may be very important.

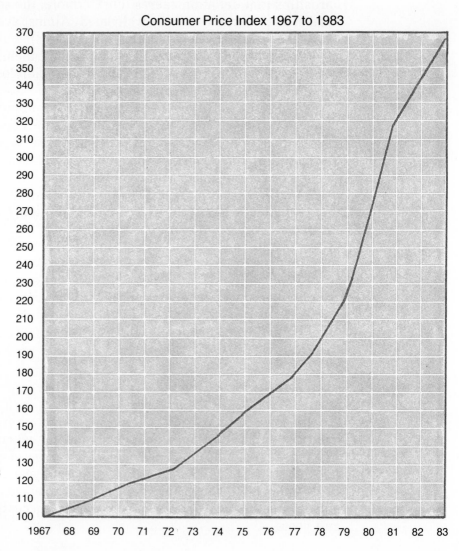

Consumer Price Index 1967 to 1983

Figure 25–1

As the consumer price index shows, the prices of goods and services have risen significantly since 1967.

Because 1967 was chosen as the base year, the consumer price index is shown as 100 in 1967 in Figure 25–1; by 1983 the CPI had climbed to 363. That means that the prices of goods and services increased by 263 percent in 16 years (363 − 100 = 263). A person with a take-home pay of $500 a month in 1967 would have needed a take-home pay of about $1,820 in 1983 to be equally well off.

What Can a Consumer Do?

Trying to predict the trend of inflation or deflation is very difficult. Further, there is little one consumer alone can do to affect the trends. But that does not suggest inactivity. A consumer can:

1. Avoid the temptation to carelessly spend money during a period of inflation just because it is available.
2. Elect responsible government officials who will try to stem inflation and/or deflation through sound economic policies.
3. Try to have money invested during inflationary times in assets that will increase in value, such as a home or securities.
4. Have a savings account that can tide you over if deflationary times result in unemployment.

Adding to Your Business Vocabulary

The following terms should become part of your business vocabulary. For each numbered item, find the term that has the same meaning.

> base year
> consumer price index
>
> deflation
> price index

1. A series of figures showing how prices have changed over a period of years.
2. A decrease in the general price level.
3. A price index that shows the changes in the average prices of goods and services over time.
4. The year in which average prices for a price index were taken to represent 100 percent.

Understanding Your Reading

1. Name two units of measure used in our society that are constant.
2. How is the value of a dollar measured?
3. What has happened to the general price level of goods and services over the past years?

4. List causes of inflation.
5. What usually happens to prices when the demand for goods increases rapidly?
6. List causes of deflation.
7. Name three things that the government can do to act against inflation and three things it can do to act against deflation.
8. What are some effects on businesses of decreased demand for goods?
9. Why is quick action usually taken against deflation but not against inflation?
10. What is the consumer price index?
11. How much did the consumer price index increase from 1967 to 1983?
12. According to Figure 25–1, what was the consumer price index for 1977? for 1981?

*P*utting Your Business Knowledge to Work

1. How is the value of a dollar measured?
2. If Andrea Lewis puts $1,000 away in a safe place in her house, can she expect that at the end of five years the money will buy more than, the same as, or less than it would have when she put it away? Explain your answer.
3. What are some of the ways in which credit purchases affect inflation and deflation?
4. Which is more likely to increase inflation: (a) an increase in government spending with no increase in taxes; (b) an increase in government spending with an equal increase in taxes; (c) a decrease in government spending with an increase in taxes?
5. The average family spends from 18 to 25 percent of its take-home pay for food. If prices for food increase very rapidly, what effects would such increases have on a family's life-style?

*C*omputing Business Problems

1. Jim Crain is 42 years old. When he was a tenth grader, his school lunches cost 50 cents. His daughter Amy is 16 and a tenth grader now. If the cost of lunches has increased by 90 percent, how much do her lunches cost?
2. In a recent year the consumer price index rose by 6.8 percent. Franklin R. Jones' employer promised him that his $21,000 per year salary would be increased by an amount equal to the CPI change that year. What was his salary?
3. The Franklin family buys and consumes 16 liters of milk per month. Using information found in the metric conversion chart in Appendix D, determine how many gallons of milk the Franklin family consumes each month.

Stretching Your Business Knowledge

1. It has been said that the purchase of a home is a very good way for one to counteract inflationary damage to one's personal financial situation. Why do you think this may be so?
2. Explain how the federal government can use its authority to tax to affect inflation or deflation.
3. Possible trends toward inflation and deflation in our economy are important to consumers. Look through last month's newspapers and magazines and clip any stories that you find which deal with economic problems. Do they indicate that the country is in good or bad economic shape? Are we in a period of inflation, deflation, or neither? Report to your class.
4. Several price indexes are used as indicators of business activity in the United States. Besides the consumer price index, which you learned about in this chapter, indexes are prepared for wholesale prices and industrial goods, industrial production, and retail store sales. You can find information about these indexes in the *Statistical Abstract of the United States, The Wall Street Journal,* or in almanacs. What effects do you think a drastic change in one of these indexes would have on our economy?
5. Two problems which our economy has had to face at some time are recession and depression. (You may want to read again about recessions and depressions in Chapter 4.) Perhaps you have read about the depression that the United States experienced during the 1930s. Do some library research about depressions. What usually causes them? What brought the U.S. out of the 1930s depression?

CAREER CATEGORY: Bookkeeping and Accounting

You are now aware of the importance of keeping accurate and up-to-date financial records. If you find that the record keeping activities associated with managing your money are easy and somewhat enjoyable, you might consider a career as a bookkeeper or accountant.

Job Titles: Job titles commonly found in this career area include:

Accountant	Auditor
Bookkeeper	Data Entry Clerk
Bookkeeping Machine Operator	Tax Accountant
Cost Accountant	Bank Clerk
Public Accountant	

Employment Outlook: The number of bookkeepers and accountants is expected to grow through the 1990s, but that growth will be slower than the average growth of all occupations. There will be good job prospects, however, because of the number of replacement workers needed to fill the jobs of those leaving employment in these occupations. Since the number of people who are bookkeepers and accountants is extremely large, the replacement needs produce numerous openings.

Future Changes: Everyone expects the volume of business transactions to increase in the future. As a result, more energy will be spent in the accounting functions of business. However, the need for workers in this area will probably be somewhat limited because of the use of advanced data processing equipment to keep track of these transactions.

What Is Done on the Job: Bookkeepers and accountants provide systematic and up-to-date information to business managers about the financial situation of the business and the business transactions that take place in the business. This information is maintained in journals, ledgers, and computer memory.

Bookkeepers and accountants analyze and record all financial transactions such as orders and sales. They check money taken in against money paid out to be certain accounts balance. They also keep payroll records and prepare employees' paychecks.

Bookkeepers and accountants must be good at working with numbers and concentrating on details. They need to be very accurate and orderly in their work.

Education and Training: The minimum requirement for a bookkeeping job is a high school education that includes courses in business math, bookkeeping, and principles of accounting. An accounting preparation program from a community or junior college would be appealing to some employers.

Some bookkeepers who enroll in college accounting programs may advance to jobs as accountants. As a general rule, an accountant is a bookkeeper with advanced training and increased responsibilities.

Salary Levels: Starting salaries for accounting clerks are about $15,000 per year. This can increase to about $25,000 for top-level employees. Persons with the job title of "bookkeeper" earn somewhat less. Sometimes accountants and bookkeepers are in business for themselves and can earn more.

For Additional Information: Many associations, government agencies, and other organizations provide useful information on bookkeeping and accounting careers. Specific information about careers in accounting is available from:

American Institute of Certified Public Accountants
1211 Avenue of the Americas
New York, NY 10036

State employment service offices.

UNIT 8
USING CREDIT WISELY

UNIT OBJECTIVES

After studying the chapters in this unit, you will be able to:

1. *Explain what credit is and why it is important in our economy.*

2. *Discuss the use of charge accounts, credit cards, and installment loans and compare their use as forms of credit.*

3. *Explain why credit costs and give several examples of the costs of credit.*

4. *Tell why credit records are important and how they are used.*

5. *Give examples of ways in which consumers can build and protect a good credit record.*

BUSINESS BRIEF

Using Credit To Build a Business

Kemmons Wilson is a millionaire who is well known for his Holiday Inn motels and other business ventures. He also is known as a dedicated worker who continued to put in 80- to 100-hour workweeks even after accumulating his fortune. He worked hard at meeting needs that he saw.

Kemmons Wilson once was quoted as saying, "I never wanted to own a million dollars; I just wanted to *owe* a million." He learned early that the ability to borrow money was important to business success.

His first credit transaction was at the age of 17 when he borrowed $50 to begin a popcorn business. Wilson bought a popcorn machine, rented space in a local theater, and was in business. He was so successful that the theater manager bought Wilson's popcorn machine and took over the business operation himself.

Wilson next borrowed $6,500 using a house he owned as security. He used the money to expand a wholesale business. His business experiences continued to yield good results.

Wilson also worked as a traveling salesperson and had spent many nights in hotels and motels. He often was dissatisfied with his accommodations, frequently finding hotel policies that bothered him. For example, he objected to the practice of charging an extra amount for children because it made it difficult for families to enjoy traveling. He set out to do something about the problems he saw. As usual, raising money was the first step.

Facts included in this Business Brief were taken from the following sources: Armour, Lawrence A. *The Young Millionaires.* New York: Playboy Press, 1973; Ingham, John. Biographical Dictionary of American Business Leaders. Westport: Greenwood Press, 1983.

His reputation as a successful businessperson allowed him to secure a loan for $350,000. With that loan he had a 120-room motel built—the first Holiday Inn. It was a bright, pleasantly decorated motel unit and there was no charge added to the bill if children were in a room.

The motel was another business success. People liked the treatment they received. His motel did not have a "No Vacancy" sign. If someone needed a room and all rooms were taken, Mr. Wilson or one of his employees would help them find motel accommodations elsewhere.

Wilson decided to expand to other cities. To get money to help build the new units, he turned to local people who would lend him money to build something that would benefit their own communities. To help develop local interest, he hired local contractors to build the units. He also set up franchise operations so that local people could operate the motels. Before long, he had over 1,100 motels in over 750 cities in the United States.

Success for Wilson was built on a foundation of hard work, the wise use of credit, and good business sense. He was alert to needs that existed and took action to meet them. The land of opportunity is real to Kemmons Wilson, and today "Holiday Inn" signs can be seen throughout the world.

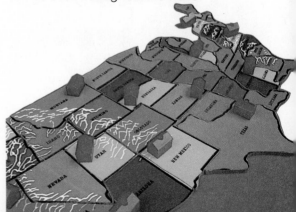

CHAPTER 26

*W*hat is Credit?

■ CHAPTER OBJECTIVES

After studying this chapter and completing the end-of-chapter activities, you will be able to:

1. Explain what credit is.
2. Give examples of how credit is used by consumers, businesses, and governments.
3. State the difference between loan credit and sales credit.
4. Discuss at least two sources of loans.
5. Tell how businesses use the three C's of credit.
6. Explain four benefits of credit.
7. Give at least three examples of ways in which credit can be a disadvantage to a consumer.
8. State four questions to be answered before using credit.

Have you ever charged a purchase or received a loan? If you have, you are among the more than 85 million American consumers who use credit. Consumers in our country buy goods and services involving billions of dollars of consumer credit each year. The use of credit is common for businesses and governments as well as consumers. Credit in various forms is an important element in doing business. Here are some examples of the uses of credit:

Alex buys gas for his car and uses his oil company credit card.

Betty buys a blouse and charges the purchase to her revolving charge account.

Charlie applies for and receives a government loan to help with his college expenses.

Diana borrows $1,000 from her credit union to take a summer cruise.

Edward takes his family out for dinner and pays the bill using his bank charge card.

Faye's family pays its telephone and electricity bills the

month after those services have been used.

Ginger and her husband apply for and receive a mortgage so that they can build a new house.

The city of Howardsville borrows $250,000 to make needed road repairs.

J. J. Nees and Company receives a $2 million loan to build a new tire store in the downtown area.

Karie asks a friend for a $10 loan until payday.

Using Money You Don't Have

Credit is the privilege of using someone else's money for a period of time. That privilege is based on the belief that the person receiving credit will honor his or her promise to repay the amount at a future date. The credit transaction creates a debtor and creditor. Anyone who buys on credit or receives a loan is known as a **debtor**. The one who sells on credit or makes a loan is called the **creditor**.

Although the credit system uses forms and legal documents, it also depends on trust between the debtor and creditor. **Trust** means that the creditor believes that the debtor will honor the promise to pay later for goods and services that have been received and used. Without that trust, our credit system could not operate.

When you borrow a large amount of money or buy on credit from a business, you usually will be asked to sign a written agreement. The agreement states that you will pay your debt within a certain period of time. For example, when Diana borrowed $1,000, she signed a paper which said that she would make a payment on the first day of each month for 24 months. Charlie had to agree to pay his tuition loan in full within two years after graduation. When Alex used his credit card to buy gas and signed the receipt form, he agreed to pay for his purchase when the bill came at the end of the month or pay interest charges. A credit agreement means that the debtor promises to pay and the creditor trusts that the debtor will pay the amount that is owed.

Loan and Sales Credit

If you borrow money to be used later for some special purpose, you are using **loan credit.** Loans are available from several kinds of financial institutions. Banks, credit unions, savings and loan associations, and consumer finance companies are the primary businesses that make consumer loans. As you learned in

Chapter 17, they lend money to earn a profit through interest and other loan charges.

Loan credit usually involves a written contract. The debtor often agrees to repay the loan in specified amounts, called installments, over a period of time. You will learn more about installment and other loans in Chapter 27.

If you charge a purchase at the time you buy the good or service, you are using **sales credit.** Sales credit is offered by most retail and wholesale businesses. Sales credit involves the use of charge accounts and credit cards. The different types of charge accounts and credit cards are discussed in Chapter 27. Both loan and sales credit are important forms of credit and are used often in our economy.

Who Uses Credit?

If you are a typical American consumer, you will use credit for many purposes. You may buy fairly expensive products that will last for quite a while, such as a car, furniture, or major appliances. Or you may use credit for convenience in making smaller purchases, such as meals and stereo tapes. Paying for medical care, vacations, taxes, and even paying off other debts are other common uses of credit.

Illus. 26–1
Businesses may use credit to finance their own operations, or to buy materials used in the products they sell.

Businesses also rely on credit. Business firms may secure loans to buy land and equipment and to construct buildings. They also use short-term credit, usually from 30 to 90 days, to meet temporary

needs for cash. For example, merchants buy goods on credit, and manufacturers buy raw materials and supplies on credit. Businesses borrow on a short-term basis to get the cash they need while waiting for goods to be sold or for customers to pay for their purchases.

Local, state, and federal governments often use credit in providing for the public welfare. Governments may use credit to buy such items as cars, aircraft, and police uniforms. They may also borrow money needed to build hospitals, highways, parks, and airports.

Basis For Granting Credit

You already have read that trust between the debtor and the creditor is essential if credit is to be granted. To become a debtor, you must be able to show that you are dependable. Not everyone who desires credit will get it.

The business which is considering you as a credit risk will generally ask you about your financial situation and for credit references. **Credit references** are firms or individuals from whom you have received credit in the past and/or who can help verify your credit record. Answers to the questions and information received from credit references will help the firm decide whether or not loan or sales credit should be granted to you.

You should be willing to give all required information readily and honestly. You may be asked questions such as these: How much do you earn? How long have you worked? What property do you own? Do you have any other debts? Recent laws, such as the Consumer Credit Protection Act, regulate the kinds of information that can be used in evaluating credit applicants. The questions listed above can be legally asked. Credit decisions cannot be made without reliable information.

The Three C's of Credit

In deciding whether or not to grant you credit, businesses consider three factors, known as the three C's: character, capacity, and capital.

Character refers to your honesty and willingness to pay. If you have a reputation for paying bills on time, you probably will receive credit. How you will pay your bills in the future usually can be judged by how you have paid them in the past.

Capacity refers to your ability to pay. The lender or seller must consider whether your income is large enough to permit you to pay your bills. If your income is too small or unsteady, granting you additional credit may not be wise even though you have had a good credit record in the past. On the other hand, your income may be very high, but if you already have many debts you may not be able to handle another one.

Capital is the value of your possessions. (It includes the "capital resources" you learned about in Chapter 1.) The money you possess and property you own may be your capital. Or you may have a car that is paid for and a house on which a large amount has been paid. You also may have a checking account and some savings which add to your capital. Or you may have nothing except your present income. The value of your capital helps give the lender some assurance that you will be able to meet your credit obligations.

Benefits of Credit

Both businesses and consumers benefit from the use of credit. Most businesses would find it difficult to compete if they did not extend credit to their customers. Sellers believe they can increase sales and profits by using credit to attract customers.

Credit benefits the consumer, too. Here are some ways in which consumers benefit from credit:

1. Convenience. Credit can make it convenient for you to buy. You can shop without carrying much cash with you. There may be times when you do not have enough cash and have a real need for something. If your car needs emergency repairs, you may have to wait until payday unless you can have the work done on credit.

2. Immediate possession. Credit allows you to have immediate possession of the item that you want. A family can buy a dishwasher on credit and begin using it immediately rather than waiting until enough money has been saved to pay cash for it.

3. Savings. Credit allows you to buy an item when it goes on sale, possibly at a large saving. Some stores, especially department and furniture stores, often send notices of special sales to their credit customers several days before sales are advertised to the general public. Credit customers thus have first choice of the merchandise and may obtain real bargains.

4. Credit rating. If you buy on credit and pay your bills when they

Illus. 26–2
Using credit may allow you to take advantage of special sales.

are due, you gain a reputation for being dependable. In that way you establish a favorable **credit rating,** your reputation for paying bills. This credit rating is valuable during an emergency when you must borrow money or when you desire to make a major purchase. It is also valuable in obtaining credit if you move to another community.

Is Credit Always Good for You?

Buying on credit is convenient and is usually beneficial. But there are some disadvantages if you are not careful in your use of credit. Some problems you can encounter with unwise use of credit include the following:

- Overbuying is one of the most common hazards of using credit. There are several ways in which this can happen. One way is to purchase something that is more expensive than you can afford. It is easy to say, "All right, charge it," for a suit that costs $190 when you would purchase one for less if you had to pay cash. Attractive store displays and advertisements attract us and invite us to make purchases. As a credit customer, you may be tempted to buy items that you do not really need.

● Careless buying may result if you become lazy in your shopping. You may stop checking advertisements carefully. You may fail to make comparisons, causing you to buy at the wrong time or the wrong place. Smart shoppers know that at certain times of the year, prices of some goods go down. Credit can tempt you not to wait for a better price on an item you want.

● Higher prices may be paid. Stores that sell only for cash are able to sell at lower prices than stores which offer credit. Granting credit is expensive. It requires good accounting to keep accurate records of each charge sale and each payment. When customers do not pay as agreed, there are collection expenses. Increased costs are passed on to customers in the form of higher prices. The cost of credit will be discussed in greater detail in Chapter 28.

Before making the final decision on whether or not to buy on credit, here are several questions you should answer:

1. Is this the best buy I can make? Is someone else selling the same product, with better service, at the same price?
2. What will be the total cost of my purchase? How much are the interest and finance charges? What would I save by paying cash?
3. If I need an installment contract, could I possibly make a bigger down payment? If so, how much will it reduce the finance charges and the cost of my purchase?
4. What percentage of my monthly income will the payments take? In case of an emergency, will I have enough money to make other required monthly payments?

Illus. 26–3
Be careful! Buying on credit may lead to overbuying.

*A*dding to Your Business Vocabulary

The following terms should become part of your business vocabulary. For each numbered item, find the term that has the same meaning.

capacity   credit reference
capital   debtor
character   loan credit
credit   sales credit
creditor   trust
credit rating

1. The factor in credit that refers to a customer's honesty and willingness to pay.
2. Credit that is offered at the time of sale.
3. The factor in credit that refers to a customer's ability to pay.
4. A person's reputation for paying debts on time.
5. One who buys or borrows and promises to pay later.
6. Borrowing money to be used later for special purposes.
7. The privilege of using someone else's money for a period of time.
8. Firms or individuals who have given credit to someone in the past and can give information on an individual's credit record.
9. The factor in credit that has to do with the property and money that the debtor owns.
10. A creditor's belief that debtors will keep their promises to pay for goods and services that they have already received and used.
11. One who sells or lends on another's promise to pay in the future.

*U*nderstanding Your Reading

1. Our credit system is based in part on trust. Who does the trusting, the debtor or the creditor? What does this person trust?
2. As a debtor, what are you promising to do?
3. Name several sources of loans. How do these sources differ from one another?
4. What are some typical uses of credit by consumers?
5. List some goods and services which a business might buy on credit.
6. Give examples of things which local, state, and federal governments might buy on credit.
7. What kinds of information do creditors need before granting credit?
8. What are the three C's of credit? Why is each one important?
9. Why would a business want to offer credit rather than selling for cash only? What advantages would a business have if it sold for cash only?
10. What are four advantages of buying on credit?
11. Name three problems that can be caused by the unwise use of credit.
12. List the four questions you should answer before using credit.

*P*utting Your Business Knowledge to Work

1. Why is trust important in a credit trans-action? Why is it necessary to have written agreements to repay a loan?
2. Some people think it is a good idea to buy a few things on credit, even when you could pay cash. Why might this be a good idea?
3. Sam Shonard buys all he possibly can on credit. If he doesn't have enough money to cover his monthly payments when they are due, he borrows money to make them. His sister, Debbie, likes to buy things only after she has saved enough money to pay cash for them.
   a. Whose plan do you think is better? Why?
   b. What suggestions about the use of credit might you make to Sam and Debbie?
4. Rosie Cooper owns and operates a flower shop. She is considering expanding her shop to include home decorator items. At present, Ms. Cooper sells for cash only. How might granting credit help or hurt this business?
5. Here are some statements that people have made about credit. Read each state-ment and tell whether you agree or dis-agree and why.
   a. "I should buy as many things as I can on credit because credit increases sales and helps business."
   b. "If things were sold for cash only, in the long run, prices would be lower and everyone would be better off."
   c. "Buy on credit at least occasionally; make your payments on time; and keep a good credit rating which will be valuable in an emergency."
   d. "Credit should be used only in making expensive purchases, such as houses and cars, and never for everyday pur-chases, such as food and clothing."

*C*omputing Business Problems

1. The following amounts of consumer credit in the United States were reported for the three years shown below:

Year	Consumer Credit in Billions of Dollars
1970	$148
1976	250
1982	430

   a. What was the increase in consumer credit, in billions of dollars, from 1970 to 1976? from 1976 to 1982? from 1970 to 1982?
   b. What was the average increase per year, in billions of dollars, for the six-year period from 1976 to 1982?
   c. If consumer credit continues to in-crease by the 1976–1982 annual rate of increase, what will be the total of consumer credit (in billions of dollars) in 1987? in 1990?
2. Last year O'Leary's Cycle Shop sold 2,200 ten-speed bicycles. The average sale price was $145, including tax. Seven out of every ten customers bought their bikes using O'Leary's credit plan.
   a. What was the amount of the total sales of ten-speed bicycles?
   b. What was the amount of total credit sales of ten-speeds?
3. The Capital Area Transit System borrowed $1,800,000 to buy six new buses to

expand its service to the suburbs. It is estimated that each bus will earn about $6,500 per month. It will cost approximately $1,500 per month for fuel, operating costs, and repairs on each bus. How many months will it take to pay for the six buses?

4. Amy Markson would like to be an airline pilot someday. Right now, she wants to learn to fly and get a private license. Her parents have agreed to pay half the cost of the lessons if Amy pays the other half. Amy checked with the Superior Air Service and was told that the cost would include the following:

fees and materials for $480
    ground instruction

24 hours of in-flight $ 50 per hour
    instruction
20 hours of solo flight $ 32 per hour
    time
third-class student's $ 80
    license

a. How much will it cost Amy to learn to fly and to get her license?
b. If Amy borrows her share of the cost, how much will she borrow?
c. If Amy repays her loan in 50 equal weekly payments, how much will each weekly payment be? If she repays $75 each month, how many months will it take to repay the amount she borrowed?

Stretching Your Business Knowledge

1. In addition to the three C's of credit, some add a fourth called collateral. Find the meaning of *collateral* as it is used in connection with credit and explain how it is used.
2. A family with a relatively low income and little property might have a better credit rating than a family with a large income and considerable property. Likewise, a small business might have a better credit rating than a much larger business owning millions of dollars worth of property. Explain the circumstances under which each of these conditions might exist.
3. Suppose that you and your parents decide to open a snack shop near your school to sell light lunches and snacks. Most of the customers will be junior and senior high school students. Since many students will forget to bring money or will want to treat friends when they haven't enough money, they will sometimes ask you to charge their purchases. Make up a set of rules that you would use to make it sound business to extend credit to teenage customers.
4. Suppose everybody decided to stop granting credit to customers. What do you think would be the effects on each of the following:
   a. a recently married couple who have to buy furniture for their apartment
   b. a small retail store which is trying to build its sales
   c. a large manufacturer which wants to expand its line of machines
   d. a local school district similar to the one your school is in.
5. Get copies of one or more installment sales or installment loan contracts. Read them over carefully. What questions do you have as you read them? Are there provisions that you do not like or understand? What additions, if any, would you like to make to the contracts?

CHAPTER 27

*W*ays of Using Credit

■ CHAPTER OBJECTIVES

After studying this chapter and completing the end-of-chapter activities, you will be able to:

1. Compare four kinds of charge accounts.
2. Explain how bank charge card transactions are handled.
3. Contrast bank charge cards and travel and entertainment credit cards with oil company credit cards.
4. Tell how installment credit sales differ from charge account or credit card sales.
5. Discuss three kinds of loans available to consumers.
6. List seven questions that should be answered before signing an installment sales contract.

Laura was shopping in her favorite department store. After selecting her purchase, Laura was asked by the sales clerk, "Will this be cash or charge?" "Charge," replied Laura; "I will use my bank charge card." Laura also had a revolving charge account at that store which she could have used.

Max purchased a color television with remote control and advanced electronic tuning. He agreed to make equal monthly payments—which included a finance charge—and signed an installment sales contract.

Jessica talked with the loan officer at the Savings and Loan Company. She needed a loan to pay off her charge accounts and to make some home improvements. Jessica signed a promissory note to get a loan.

Michael needed an addition to his print shop. He applied for a loan. His banker said that Michael could get either a personal loan or a secured loan. The secured loan sounded like a better deal. Several pieces of Michael's printing equipment were used as collateral to secure his loan.

From the above situations, you can see that there are a number of ways to obtain and use credit. In deciding what kind of credit to use, you should understand the different kinds of credit that may be available. Let's consider charge accounts first.

Types of Charge Accounts

If you are able to get credit, you may open an account at a retail store, a public utility, or a supplier (if you are in business). When you make a purchase from the business that granted you credit, the amount you owe is added to your account with that business. Three types of charge accounts are available for your use. You may have an open, budget, or revolving account.

Open Charge Accounts

An **open charge account** is one in which the seller expects payment in full at the end of a specified period. A common open period is one month. The seller may set a limit on the total amount that may be charged during a period. Open accounts generally are used for everyday needs and small purchases. With an open charge account you very likely will be given a **credit identification card** which has your name, account number, and signature on it. It identifies you as a customer who has a charge account.

At times a cashier may call the credit office when you present your card for a charge sale. This call is to verify that your account is in good standing. It also may be to check the credit limit if a limit has been set for your account.

Budget Charge Accounts

Some merchants and public utilities offer budget charge accounts. **Budget charge accounts** require that payments of a certain amount be made over several months. This arrangement helps consumers with their budgets. One budget plan offered by merchants is the 90-day, 3-payment plan. Under this plan, you pay for your purchase in 90 days, usually in 3 equal monthly payments. There is generally no finance charge if payments are made on time.

In a budget plan offered by many utility companies, an estimate is made of how much you will buy during a certain period of time, such as a year. You then agree to pay a certain amount each month to cover those purchases. For example, you may be permitted to pay a certain amount of money each month to cover the cost of energy used for heating. This plan avoids payments of large amounts during winter months. However, you pay the same amount during warm months when heating is not required.

Many customers like budget plans because they spread the cost of large or expensive purchases over several months. Such plans also allow customers to make accurate allowances in their budgets.

Revolving Charge Accounts

The revolving charge account is a popular form of credit. With a **revolving charge account** purchases can be charged at any time but at least part of the debt must be paid each month. It is similar to an open account but has some added features. There is usually a limit on the total amount that can be owed at one time. A payment is required once a month, but the total amount owed need not be paid at one time. An interest charge is added, however, if the total amount is not paid.

Revolving charge accounts are convenient, but they can tempt you to overspend. The interest charged on unpaid balances is usually quite high, often 1 1/2 percent per month or higher. Since they are commonly used for low-priced, frequently purchased items,

Illus. 27–1
Revolving charge accounts are convenient, but they may be very expensive.

revolving accounts can be expensive unless you watch charges and payments carefully. Many customers do not pay the full amount when it is due and thus remain in debt for long periods of time.

Teenage Charge Accounts

There is a special charge account that is sometimes made available to responsible teenagers. These accounts usually have a limit on the amount which can be charged. Generally a parent must agree to pay if the teenager does not. Sometimes the parent must also have an account with the firm granting the credit. The teenager receives a credit identification card and can charge purchases without permission from parents.

Teenage charge accounts may be open or revolving. They give teenagers the freedom in buying that they otherwise would not have. This privilege must be used wisely since it is often a first experience with credit.

Credit Card Accounts

Most consumers today have one or more credit card charge accounts. In fact, over 208 million charge cards were in use in a recent year. Accounts for these cards are set up by banks and oil companies, or by business firms which specialize in granting credit for special purposes such as travel and entertainment. These accounts are similar to revolving charge accounts. A special credit card is issued to allow individuals to charge purchases to the account.

Bank Charge Cards

You read about bank charge cards in Chapter 17. These charge cards have become very popular. MasterCard and VISA are two of the best-known. Most of the banks in the United States are part of a world-wide bank charge-card system. There usually is an annual fee that must be paid for the privilege of using the card.

Bank charge cards are issued to people whose credit ratings meet banks' standards. A bank charge card, in effect, indicates that the credit rating of the cardholder is good. Agreements are made between banks and various merchants to accept the charge cards.

When you use your bank charge card, a credit sales ticket that requires your signature is made out. The merchant collects all credit sales tickets prepared during the day and sends them to the bank.

Illus. 27–2
This merchant is validating the buyer's bank charge account. If the account is overdue, the bank will not approve the charge.

The bank charges your account for your charge purchases and bills you once a month for all the purchases you made. You usually do not pay a finance charge if you pay your bill in full. However, if you pay only part of your bill, there is a substantial finance charge on the unpaid balance.

The bank totals all the sales tickets received from each business. The firms are paid for the amount of the sales minus a service fee. This fee is usually about 4 to 6 percent. At the 4 percent rate, a merchant would receive $960 from sales tickets totaling $1,000 ($1,000 minus 4 percent or $40.) This fee covers the bank's expenses of processing the sales tickets and collecting amounts owed from customers. The bank is doing the work that the firm's own credit department would have to do otherwise.

Business owners like bank charge cards for several reasons. For one thing, the bank decides if a customer is a good credit risk. The bank also assumes most of the trouble and expense of granting credit. Merchants get their money, minus the service fee, right away.

Customers like bank charge cards because they are accepted by so many businesses throughout the United States and in many foreign countries. Bank charge-card users also like the fact that they receive only one monthly bill rather than many from the various businesses where they charge purchases.

Travel and Entertainment Credit Cards

Travel and entertainment (T&E) cards are similar to bank charge cards. However, an independent firm performs the functions for T&E accounts that a bank performs with bank charge-card accounts. The T&E cards are used mainly to buy services such as lodging in hotels and motels, meals, and tickets for entertainment. Purchases are billed like bank charge-card purchases, and T&E card users also pay annual fees for the privilege of having the card. Examples of nationally known T&E cards are Diners' Club, Carte Blanche, and American Express.

Travelers especially like T&E credit cards because they do not have to carry much cash with them. The cards are good at many different businesses in all parts of the world. Firms which accept T&E credit cards often find that their sales increase because more customers are attracted if T&E cards can be used. Customers also often buy more than they might buy if they had to pay cash.

Illus. 27–3
Many travelers enjoy the convenience of using T&E credit cards.

Oil Company Credit Cards

Oil companies, such as Texaco, Standard Oil, and Shell, issue their own credit cards. As with banks, accounts are opened for customers who apply for credit and have their applications approved. Oil company credit cards can generally be used only for purchases from gasoline stations selling that company's brand of gasoline. It may also be possible to charge car maintenance service and merchandise sold by that station.

Some consumers find it advantageous to have credit cards with oil companies from whom they frequently purchase gasoline. The oil companies like to extend credit to encourage consumers to buy their products.

Installment Sales Credit

Another way of making a charge purchase is to use installment sales credit. **Installment sales credit** requires that payments be made at specified times. Such plans are normally used for items that are expensive and will last for long periods of time such as furniture and large appliances.

The requirements of installment credit differ from those of a charge account or credit card. Under an installment credit plan, you will:

1. sign a written agreement (a sales contract) which shows the terms of the purchase, such as payment periods and finance charges.
2. receive and own the goods at the time of purchase. However, the seller has the right to repossess them (take them back) if payments are not made according to the agreement.
3. make a **down payment** which is a payment of part of the purchase price; it is usually made at the time of the purchase.
4. pay a finance charge on the amount owed, because this amount is actually loaned to you by the seller.
5. make regular payments at stated times, usually weekly or monthly. For example, if a total of $120 is to be repaid in 12 monthly installments, $10 is paid in each month. In some cases, a penalty is charged if a payment is received after the due date. In others, all remaining payments may become due at once if only one payment is missed.

Getting a Loan

A loan is an alternative to charge-account buying or installment sales credit. There are several kinds of loans available. The terms of the loan and the requirements for securing the loans differ.

One type of loan is called an installment loan. An **installment loan** is one in which you agree to make monthly payments in specific amounts over a period of time. The payments are called installments. The total amount you repay includes the amount you borrowed plus the interest on your loan.

Another kind of loan is called a single-payment loan. With a **single-payment loan** you do not pay anything until the end of the loan period, possibly 60 or 90 days. At that time you repay the full amount you borrowed plus the interest.

A lender needs some assurance that each loan will be repaid. If you are a fine credit risk, you may be able to get a promissory note. A **promissory note** is a written promise to repay based on the debtor's excellent credit rating. The amount borrowed, usually with some interest, is due on a certain date. The names given to the different parts of a promissory note are shown in Figure 27–1.

Illus. 27–4
For a major purchase such as an auto-mobile, you will receive a coupon payment book. One coupon is returned with each monthly payment.

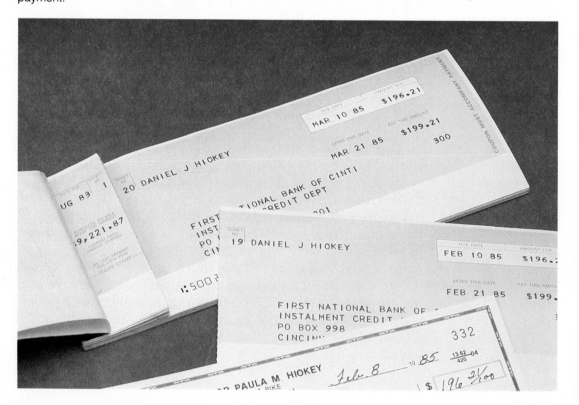

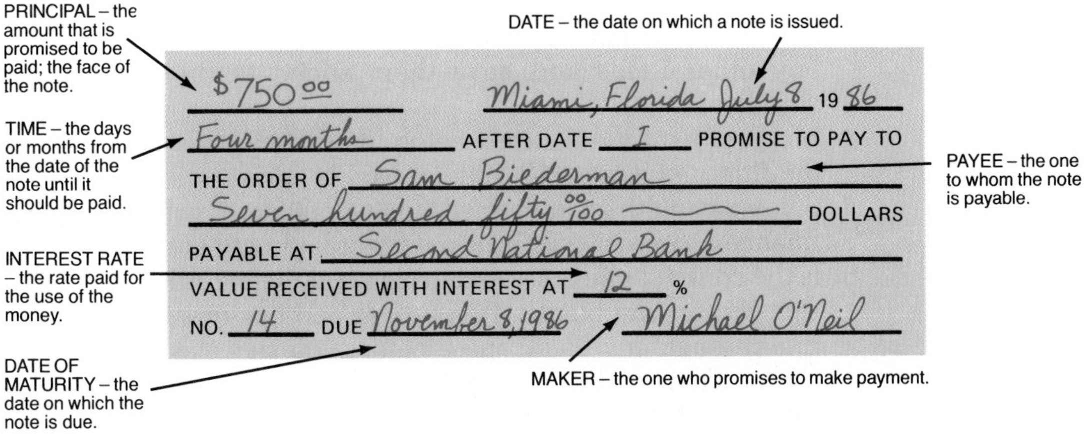

PRINCIPAL – the amount that is promised to be paid; the face of the note.

DATE – the date on which a note is issued.

TIME – the days or months from the date of the note until it should be paid.

INTEREST RATE – the rate paid for the use of the money.

DATE OF MATURITY – the date on which the note is due.

PAYEE – the one to whom the note is payable.

MAKER – the one who promises to make payment.

$750⁰⁰ Miami, Florida July 8 19 86
Four months AFTER DATE I PROMISE TO PAY TO
THE ORDER OF Sam Biederman
Seven hundred fifty ⁰⁰⁄₁₀₀ DOLLARS
PAYABLE AT Second National Bank
VALUE RECEIVED WITH INTEREST AT 12 %
NO. 14 DUE November 8, 1986 Michael O'Neil

Figure 27–1
A promissory note.

In some cases, you may be asked to offer some kind of property you own, such as a car, a house, or jewelry, as security. This means that you give the lender the right to sell this property to get back the amount of the loan in case you do not repay it. This is called a **secured loan.**

If you do not have a credit rating established or property to offer as security, you may be able to get a relative or friend who has property or a good credit rating to cosign your note. The **cosigner** of a note is responsible for payment of the note if you do not pay as promised.

The Legal Contract

Credit is important in many ways. It is a privilege which millions of consumers and businesses enjoy. No matter what kind of credit is involved, legal responsibilities are created for both parties.

"KWYS" are four letters to keep in mind when signing any legal form; the letters stand for "know what you're signing." This applies to all credit forms and contracts.

The installment sales contract is one of the most important forms you may sign. Before signing one, answer the following questions:

1. How much are the interest and finance charges? The total financing cost must be clearly shown in your contract.
2. Does the contract include the cost of services you may need, such as repairs to a TV or a washing machine? If there is a separate

repair contract, is its cost included in your sales contract? Will you be billed for anything separately?

3. Does the contract have an add-on feature so that you can later buy other items and have them added to the balance that you owe?

4. If you pay off the contract before its ending date, how much of the finance charge will you get back?

5. If you pay off the contract within 60 or 90 days, will there be any finance charge or will it be as if you had paid cash?

6. Is the contract you are asked to sign completely filled in? (Do not sign if there are blanks. It is proper and businesslike to draw a line through any blank space before you sign the contract.)

7. Under what conditions can the seller repossess the merchandise if you do not pay on time?

*A*dding to Your Business Vocabulary

The following terms should become part of your business vocabulary. For each numbered item, find the term that has the same meaning.

budget charge account	open charge account
cosigner	promissory note
credit identification card	revolving charge account
down payment	secured loan
installment loan	single-payment loan
installment sales credit	

1. Credit that is normally used for expensive items with payments to be made at specified times.

2. A type of loan in which a debt is repaid fully at one time.

3. A loan for which some kind of property you own is used to help guarantee payments.

4. A card which has your name, account number, and signature on it and identifies you as a customer who has a charge account.

5. A credit plan in which the seller expects payment in full at the end of a specified period, usually a month.

6. A credit plan which allows purchases to be charged at any time but requires that at least part of the debt be paid each month.

7. A type of loan in which you agree to make monthly payments in specific amounts over a period of time.

8. A credit plan similar to an open charge account but which requires that regular

9. Someone who becomes responsible for your loan if you do not pay as promised.
10. A payment of part of the purchase price that is made as part of a credit agreement.
11. A written promise to repay based on the debtor's excellent credit rating.

Understanding Your Reading

1. What is an open charge account?
2. Why do consumers and business people like budget charge accounts?
3. In what ways are revolving charge accounts different from open charge accounts?
4. What is the advantage of having a teenage charge account?
5. List two dangers of using revolving charge accounts or credit card charge accounts.
6. Describe briefly how bank charge-card plans work.
7. What information do installment sales credit contracts normally contain?
8. How do installment loans and single-payment loans differ?
9. What kind of persons can get loans through promissory notes?
10. How does the pledge of security and the use of cosigners help some people get a loan?
11. List five questions that you should answer before signing an installment sales contract.

Putting Your Business Knowledge to Work

1. Various attitudes toward the use of credit are found in the following statements. Tell whether you agree or disagree with each statement and why.
   a. "A bank card is nice to have. If I'm out of cash, I can still buy what I want."
   b. "I don't believe in using credit for most purchases. I pay cash for everyday items and use credit only for big items like a new refrigerator, carpeting, or a new car."
   c. "If I can't pay cash, I know that I can't afford it. I won't buy anything unless I can pay cash."
   d. "I often don't pay the full amount of my charge account when it is due; the interest charges are quite reasonable."
2. Many merchants would rather take credit cards than accept personal checks. Why do you think merchants feel this way?
3. Jerry Ripley owns a sporting goods store and is considering joining a bank charge-card plan. Answer the following questions for him.
   a. What advantages would there be for his business if he did join?
   b. What will it cost him for the services the bank will provide?
   c. In what ways are the services the bank provides important?
4. Answer the following questions concerning teenagers having charge accounts.
   a. Why might a teenager want such an account?
   b. Why might parents agree that their son or daughter should have a charge account?

c. Why might parents oppose teenage credit?

5. Which of the following items might be wisely purchased on the installment sales credit plan? Which items do you feel should not be bought on the installment plan? Give reasons for your answers.
   a. vacation trip
   b. used car
   c. suit of clothes
   d. personal computer
   e. tropical fish aquarium
   f. encyclopedia set
   g. refrigerator
   h. video games

6. The following provision was contained in an installment sales contract: "Failure to make any payment on the due date specified shall cause the balance in full, plus accumulated interest, to be payable immediately upon the demand of the contract holder. Failure to pay the full amount due when demanded shall be declared a forfeiture, and any and all merchandise included in this contract shall be subject to repossession."
   a. Is the above provision legal? Is it fair?
   b. Why is such a provision common in installment sales contracts?

Computing Business Problems

1. Alexis Ramirez bought three gallons of paint on credit. The paint cost $8.40 a gallon. A finance charge of $.25 was added to the purchase price of the paint. What was the total cost of Alexis' purchase?

2. Charlene Presley owns a pet store and hobby shop. She thinks she should join a bank charge-card plan so that she can better compete with some large department stores. Her credit sales each month on a bank-card plan will be about $10,000.
   a. If the bank plan she joins charges Ms. Presley 3 percent of her billings, how much would she pay for the bank's services in one month?
   b. How much would the bank owe her for that month?
   c. If her annual credit sales amount to $120,000 what would she pay for the bank's services for the year?

3. Flora Ruiz can buy a TV set for $260 in cash. She has, however, only $60 to spend.
   a. Flora could buy the TV on credit by paying $60 down and a total of $225 over 10 months. How much would the TV cost her under this plan?
   b. Flora could also borrow the $200 that she needs in addition to her $60 to make the total cash payment. If she did this, she would have to repay a total of $244 on her loan. How much would she pay for the TV in this case?

4. Sue Perkowski has a charge account with a department store. Her account is billed to her on the 20th of each month, and she is expected to pay in full by the last day of the month. If she does not, the store charges her a 1½ percent finance charge on the balance of the account. This past month Sue made the following purchases: two skirts at $15.55 each; one pair of children's shoes at $16.95; costume jewelry at $11.15; and a lamp at $22.10.
   a. What is the total amount for which Sue will be billed on the 20th of the month?
   b. If she pays only $20 on her account this month, what will be the amount of the finance charge when her bill comes next month?

Stretching Your Business Knowledge

1. Businesses often give special names to their credit plans in order to attract customers. For example, a revolving charge account may be called a Basic Charge Account plan. Find two businesses in your community which offer at least two kinds of charge accounts. What names do these businesses give to their charge account plans? How do the plans differ?

2. Before revolving charge accounts became common, layaway plans were often used.
   a. What is a layaway plan?
   b. Is the layaway plan still used by businesses in your community?

3. Get an application form that is used by a bank when a person wants to apply for a bank charge card. Notice the information that is requested and compare it with information that is requested when someone applies for a loan. Do you think that bank charge cards are easier to get than are loans? Why or why not?

4. In most states, the age of majority has been lowered from 21 to 18 or 19 years. This change means that those who reach age 18 or 19 have the legal rights and duties of adults. How does this change affect a 19-year-old's ability to get credit? Is a person of this age able to make wise credit decisions? Give reasons for your opinion from the point of view of both the seller and the 19-year-old.

CHAPTER 28

The Cost of Credit

■ CHAPTER OBJECTIVES

After reading this chapter and completing the end-of-chapter activities, you will be able to:

1. State the formula for calculating simple interest.
2. Determine the amount of interest due when given the principal and a stated percentage rate for a period of days or months.
3. Explain what a discounted note or loan is.
4. Determine the maturity date for a loan, given the date on which it was made and the terms of the loan.
5. Tell what charges are included in the finance charge for a loan or a credit account.
6. State what should be considered before taking out a loan or using an installment sales contract.
7. Give examples of the costs of credit.

Over the past few years Quenton charged a lot of purchases, large and small. During that time he also received one personal loan. He now finds that the total amount of his payments require more of his monthly income than he can afford. Through careless use of credit, he has spent too much of his future income. Now he is unable to buy some of the things he feels he really needs. He will have to delay some purchases until he gets some of his present debts paid. Quenton is experiencing one of the "costs" of credit.

Rosalynne purchased a professional computer system on sale. She believed that she had made a good buy. However, after reading her installment sales contract carefully, she discovered that her interest payments and other charges made the total cost quite high. It was not the bargain she thought it was. However, it was still a little less expensive than the regular price of the computer system. Rosalynne is satisfied with her purchase, but the cost of credit added more to the price than she had expected. She did not realize that there are several costs of credit.

Interest as a Cost of Credit

Money has earning power. It can be invested where it will earn interest or dividends, or it can be used for business purposes where it can earn a profit. One who lends money or gives credit gives up the right to use that money to earn interest, dividends, or profit in the marketplace. Interest paid by debtors makes up for the earning power lost through granting credit. The financial institutions which are in the business of lending money charge interest as a source of income to offset their costs of doing business and to earn a profit.

How Interest Is Calculated

The amount of interest that you must pay on a loan or on a charge account should be clearly understood. Sometimes the stated rate of interest is misleading. To determine the amount you have to pay, it is necessary to know three things: (1) the rate of interest (expressed as a percentage), (2) the amount to which the percentage is applied or the **principal** which is the amount you have borrowed, and (3) the length of the period for which the interest will be charged. Let's look at how interest is calculated on loans.

Calculating Simple Interest

Interest is often expressed in terms of simple interest. **Simple interest** is interest based on one year. The formula for computing simple interest is:

$$I \text{ (interest)} = P \text{ (principal)} \times R \text{ (rate)} \times T \text{ (time)}$$

If $1000 (P) is borrowed at 9 percent (R), for one year (T), the amount of interest would be calculated as follows:

$$I = \$1,000 \times 9/100 \times 1 = \$90$$

In calculating interest, there are three basic things to remember: (1) the rate of interest must be expressed in the form of a fraction or decimal; (2) interest is charged for each dollar or part of a dollar borrowed; and (3) the interest rate is based upon one year of time. Here is how it works:

1. Interest is expressed as a part of a dollar. This part of a dollar, or percent, is called the rate of interest. Before using a percent rate in a problem, you must change it to either a common fraction or a decimal. For example, a rate of interest of 12 percent would be changed to a common fraction of 12/100 or a decimal of .12.

2. When a rate of interest is expressed as 12 percent per year, you must pay 12 cents for each dollar you borrow for a year. At this rate, if you borrow $1, you pay 12 cents in interest. If you borrow $2, you pay 24 cents. If you borrow $10, you pay $1.20, and so on. The amount of interest charged is found by multiplying the principal by the rate of interest and then multiplying that product by the time period. Suppose that you borrow $100 for one year at 12 percent per year. Here is how the amount of interest is figured:

$$I = P \times R \times T$$
$$I = \$100 \times 12/100 \times 1 = \$12$$

3. If you borrow $100 at 12 percent for 1 year, you must repay the $100 plus $12 interest, as you have just seen. If you borrow the same amount of money at the same rate of interest for 2 years, you pay twice as much interest, or $24. If the money is borrowed for 3 years, you pay $36, and so on. The amount of interest on $100 borrowed at 12 percent for 2 years is calculated as follows:

$$I = P \times R \times T$$
$$I = \$100 \times 12/100 \times 2 = \$24$$

How is interest found if you borrow money for less than a year? The amount of interest is calculated on the fractional part of the year. The fraction may be expressed either in months or in days. A month is considered to be one twelfth of a year, regardless of the number of days in the particular month. If you were to borrow $100 at 12 percent for 1 month, the interest would be:

$$I = P \times R \times T$$
$$I = \$100 \times 12/100 \times 1/12 = \$1$$

When a loan is made for a certain number of days, such as 30, 60, or 90 days, the interest is determined by days. To make the calculation easy, a year is usually considered 360 days. The interest on a loan for $100 at 12 percent for 60 days would be $2.

$$I = P \times R \times T$$
$$I = \$100 \times 12/100 \times 60/360 = \$2$$

Discounting Notes

A **note** is a written promise to repay an amount that is borrowed. Sometimes interest is subtracted from the amount borrowed at the time the note is written. Paying interest in advance in this manner is called **discounting**. When a note is discounted, you receive the principal minus the interest that must be paid. The amount you actually receive is called the **proceeds**.

Suppose that on July 9 James Peterson borrows $1,000 to be repaid in 60 days. Suppose also that the bank deducts interest at the rate of 12 percent. The discount will be $20 ($1,000 × 12/100 × 60/360 = $20). So the proceeds—the amount that James will receive on July 9—will be $980 ($1,000 − 20 = $980). At the end of the loan period the full $1,000 must be paid.

When interest is charged in advance, the agreement does not call for the payment of additional interest when the loan is due. But if you do not pay in full when payment is due, interest is charged from that date.

Finding Maturity Dates

The date on which a loan must be repaid is known as the **maturity date.** How is the maturity date found? When the time of the loan is stated in months, the date of maturity is the same day of the month as the date on which the loan was made. If a loan is made on January 15 and is to run 1 month, it will be due February 15. If it is to run 2 months, it will be due March 15, and so on.

When the time of a loan is given in days, the exact number of days must be counted to find the date of maturity. This can be done by (1) finding the number of days remaining in the month when the loan was made and then (2) adding days in the following months until the total equals the required number of days. Suppose you wanted to find the date of maturity of a 90-day loan made on March 3. Here is how it would be done:

$$
\begin{array}{ll}
\text{March} - 28 \text{ days } (31\text{–}3) \\
\text{April} - 30 \text{ days} \\
\text{May} - 31 \text{ days} \\
\underline{\text{June} - 1 \text{ day}} \\
\phantom{\text{June} - } 90 \text{ days} \\
\text{Due Date} - \text{June 1}
\end{array}
$$

Calculating Installment Interest

Simple interest, as you have just learned, is calculated on the basis of one year of time. Installment credit, however, involves a monthly charge for interest on unpaid balances. An interest charge of 1 percent a month is the same as 12 percent for a year. If you borrowed $100 at 2 percent for one year at simple interest, you would repay $102 ($100 principal + $2 interest) at the end of one year. And if you borrowed $100 at a monthly rate of 2 percent, you would repay $102 at the end of one month. Your interest charge, then, would be at a rate of 24 percent a year (2 percent × 12 months) since you had the use of the money for only one month. The annual rate of interest must be stated on installment contracts.

On installment loans, interest is calculated on the amount that is unpaid at the end of each month. Suppose that Armando Rivera borrowed $120 and agreed to repay the loan at $20 a month plus 1½ percent interest each month on the unpaid balance. Figure 28–1 shows Armando's schedule of payments. The interest rate on the loan was 18 percent a year (1½ percent per month × 12 months).

Figure 28–1
On an installment loan, interest is charged on the monthly unpaid balance.

Months	Unpaid Balance	Interest Paid	Loan Repayment	Total Payment
1	$120	$1.80	$ 20	$ 21.80
2	100	1.50	20	21.50
3	80	1.20	20	21.20
4	60	.90	20	20.90
5	40	.60	20	20.60
6	20	.30	20	20.30
Totals	—	$6.30	$120	$126.30

With some loans, the amount of the interest is added to the amount you borrow, and you sign a note for the total amount. The note may then be repaid in equal monthly installments. Sylvia Messinger borrowed $100, signed a note for $108, and agreed to repay the loan in 12 monthly installments of $9.

If Sylvia had borrowed $100 for one year and paid $8 interest, the interest rate would have been 8 percent ($8 ÷ $100 = .08, or 8%). But Sylvia repaid the loan in monthly installments. She had the use of the entire $100 for only one month and a smaller amount each succeeding month as she repaid the loan.

Other Costs of Credit

When you use credit, you are not only using someone else's money, you are also spending your own future income. Interest paid on the amount charged or borrowed adds to the cost of what is

Illus. 28–1
When you use credit, you are spending your future income.

purchased and to what must be repaid. While credit allows us to buy an item now rather than wait until later, the interest that we pay may prevent us from buying another item later. The money we use to repay debts, including interest and other charges, cannot be used for other purchases. This is what happened to Quenton and is an example of an opportunity cost. As you recall from Chapter 14, an opportunity cost is what you must give up when you buy one thing rather than another. For instance, Rosalynne also wanted to buy a high-quality stereo system. Because she bought her computer system, she was not able to buy the stereo system. The stereo system is the opportunity cost of the computer system.

Other costs of credit include charges such as service fees or special financing charges. These fees are added to the principal and interest and increase the amount that you owe. Lenders also commonly require the borrower to purchase a form of credit insurance.

cathy®

Credit insurance is special insurance that repays the balance of the loan if the borrower dies or becomes disabled prior to the full settlement of the loan. These fees, charges, and insurance premiums add to the cost of credit and must be considered when determining credit costs.

Knowing the Total Finance Charge

Before you borrow money or charge purchases, you should have some idea of how much using credit is going to cost you. In addition to interest, consider the other charges that may be made. The interest you pay may not cover all of the creditor's costs. Creditor's costs include the time and money it takes to investigate your credit history, process your loan or charge account, and keep records of your payments and balances. As the debtor, you pay for such costs.

To make you aware of the total cost of credit, a federal law requires that you be told the total finance charge. The **finance charge** is the total cost of your loan including interest and all other charges. This finance charge must be stated in writing in your contract or on your charge account statement. Figure 28–2 on page 392 shows how the annual interest rate and the finance charges are shown on a credit card account bill and on an installment loan contract.

Making the Final Decision

Illus. 28–2
Would these people buy on credit if they knew the cost?

If you have to borrow money or make a purchase on credit, consider not only the total cost but also the available alternatives. Check with several lenders and compare their total finance charges.

If you must purchase on credit, consider whether an open charge account or a credit card charge account will involve the least amount of interest. If an installment sales contract is required, consider whether or not a personal loan from your credit union or another financial institution may be cheaper for you.

Comparing interest rates is not always easy since there are different ways to state them. To help you make comparisons, lenders must give you the annual percentage rate. The **annual percentage rate (APR)** is the percentage cost of credit on a yearly basis. If interest is stated at 1¼ percent per month, the APR lets you know that it is equal to 15 percent per year (1¼% × 12 months = 15%).

When borrowing money, shop around just as carefully as you would for a new stereo, car, personal computer, or any other major purchase. Borrowing money is costly, so make sure that you get the full value for your dollar. Some of the things you should check include the annual percentage rate, the length of the loan period, the amount of the monthly payments, and the total finance charges. As an example, suppose you want to borrow $4,000 to buy a car. After checking three lenders, you find the following information:

	APR	Loan Length	Monthly Payment	Total Finance Charges	Total Cost
Lender A	11%	3 yrs.	$131	$ 716	$4,716
Lender B	11%	4 yrs.	$103	$ 962	$4,962
Lender C	12%	4 yrs.	$105	$1,056	$5,056

Which of the loans would be best for you? The answer depends on whether you want the lowest monthly payments or the lowest

DESCRIPTION		AMOUNT
PREVIOUS BALANCE		182.57
NEW PURCHASES	+	275.70
NEW CASH ADVANCES	+	.00
NEW MICHIGAN BANKARD PLUS™ PURCHASES	+	.00
CREDITS	−	.00
PAYMENTS	−	30.00
FINANCE CHARGE	+	4.70
NEW BALANCE	=	432.97
PAYMENT DUE DATE*		9/23/--

20989 7 28792

ACCOUNT INFORMATION

DESCRIPTION	AMOUNT
MICHIGAN BANKARD PLUS BALANCE	.00
AVERAGE DAILY BALANCE	312.81

ANNUAL PERCENTAGE RATE 18%

*DATE NEW BALANCE MUST BE PAID IN FULL TO AVOID FINANCE CHARGE ON TRANSACTIONS BEING BILLED FOR THE FIRST TIME ON THIS STATEMENT (EXCEPT CASH ADVANCES AND MICHIGAN BANKARD PLUS PURCHASES).

NOTICE—SEE REVERSE SIDE FOR IMPORTANT INFORMATION

INSTALLMENT CONTRACT AND SECURITY AGREEMENT

S) Sergio Sound Systems, Inc.
The South Mall ● Amarillo, TX 79199

I (we) the undersigned buyer(s) buy from, and grant a security interest, to SERGIO SOUND SYSTEMS, INC. in this property:

Buyer's Name _Maria Benitez_
Buyer's Address _805 Elberon Ave_
City _Amarillo_ State _TX_ Zip _79199_

Quantity	Description	Amount	
1	Model XV-466 Turntable	400	00

Description of Trade-in:

	Sales Tax	16	00
	Total	416	00

Insurance Agreement

Credit life insurance is available at a cost of $_3.00_ for the term of the credit. The purchase of insurance is voluntary and not required for credit.

I want insurance.
Signed:_____ Date: _____

I do not want insurance.
Signed:_Maria Benitez_ Date: _1/15/--_
Signed:_____ Date: _____

1 Cash Price	$ 400.00
2 Less: Down Payment $ 40.00	
3 Trade-in $	
4 Total Down	$ 40.00
5 Unpaid Balance of Cash Price	$ 360.00
6 Other charges: Sales Tax	$ 16.00
7 AMOUNT FINANCED	$ 376.00
8 FINANCE CHARGE	$ 37.68
9 Total of Payments	$ 413.68
10 Deferred Payment Price (1 + 6 + 8)	$ 453.68
11 ANNUAL PERCENTAGE RATE	18.5 %

The Buyer(s) agrees to pay to SERGIO SOUND SYSTEMS, INC. at their store the "Total of Payments" shown above in _12_ monthly installments of _34.47_ and a final installment of _34.51_. The first installment is due _February 15, 19-_ and all other payments are due on the same day of the month until paid in full. The finance charge applies from _1/15/--_.
Signed:_Maria Benitez_ Date: _1/15/--_

Notice to Buyer: You should get a copy of this contract when you sign. You can pay in advance the unpaid balance of this contract and get a partial refund of the finance charge based on the "Actuarial Method."

Figure 28–2
You must be informed of interest rates and finance charges associated with credit purchases.

total finance charges. Lender C would not be considered because it has the highest APR and the highest total finance charges. Lender B offers the lowest monthly payments, but Lender A has the lowest total finance charges. If you can afford the monthly payments, you will borrow from Lender A. If the monthly payments with Lender A are too high for your budget, you will borrow from Lender B.

The cost of loan or sales credit is not generally unreasonable considering the creditor's expenses and what you get for your money. Giving careful thought to the use of credit will help you get the most for your money.

*A*dding to Your Business Vocabulary

The following terms should become part of your business vocabulary. For each numbered item, find the term that has the same meaning.

APR	note
credit insurance	principal
discounting	proceeds
finance charge	simple interest
maturity date	

1. An expression of interest based on one year of time.
2. Deducting interest from the total amount borrowed in advance.
3. The amount of money you borrow.
4. The net amount of money a borrower receives after the discount has been subtracted from the principal.
5. The date on which a loan must be repaid.

6. The total cost of a loan including interest and other charges.
7. Special insurance that repays the balance of the loan if the borrower dies or is disabled before the loan is repaid.
8. A written promise to repay an amount that is borrowed.
9. The percentage rate of credit on a yearly basis.

*U*nderstanding Your Reading

1. Why must lenders and creditors charge interest for money that is used for loans or credit?
2. What are some of the costs of credit other than interest?
3. What three things must you know to be able to calculate interest?
4. In calculating interest, how many days are normally considered to be in one year?
5. How is the maturity date of a loan determined?
6. What is the formula for simple interest?
7. What makes up the finance charge?
8. List some things you need to consider when making a decision on getting a loan or using an installment sales contract.

Putting Your Business Knowledge to Work

1. Steve Beyer has charge accounts at three different stores. He also has a bank charge card and an oil company credit card which he uses quite frequently. Last month he took out a personal loan which requires him to pay $60 a month for the next 18 months. The total of the payments he makes on his three charge accounts is $142 per month. His credit card accounts require him to pay $80 per month. His monthly income, after taxes and other deductions, is $750. His normal expenses for an apartment, car, food, clothing and other necessities amount to over $500 per month. Should Steve continue to make more credit purchases? What problems does Steve face at this time? What cost of credit is he experiencing?

2. Find the date of maturity for each of the following notes:

Date of Note	Time to Run
March 15	4 months
May 26	3 months
July 31	5 months
April 30	30 days
October 5	45 days

3. Donna Mahoney needs $3,000 to purchase a new desk top copier. Rather than using an installment sales contract to purchase it, she prefers to get a loan. Her banker offers her a $3,000 discounted note with 15 percent interest for one year. What problem will Donna have in paying for her copier if she takes this discounted note?

4. Ulysses McCray checked into several loan possibilities. One company offered him a one-year loan at 12 percent interest, which would result in interest of $120. In addition, the company has a $20 handling and processing fee and requires the purchase of credit insurance which adds another $4. Another company offered Ulysses a similar loan at 14 percent but it does not add any additional charges to the loan. Why does one company add finance charges while the other does not? Which loan would you select?

Computing Business Problems

1. Using the formula for simple interest, find the interest charge for each of the following amounts for one year.
   a. $100 at 10 percent interest rate
   b. $500 at 12 percent interest rate
   c. $1,000 at 18 percent interest rate
   d. $25,000 at 10 percent interest rate

2. Calculate the interest charge and the proceeds for each of the following discounted notes:

	Face of Note	Interest Rate	Time to Run
a.	$ 500	6%	1 year
b.	900	8	2 years
c.	1,000	12	3 months
d.	2,000	15	5 months
e.	750	9	60 days
f.	520	7	90 days

3. Jennifer Ward owns a large ranch and has a chance to buy additional land next to her ranch. She would need to put in a road so that she could move equipment onto the new land. The gravel road would be 3.3 kilometers long and would cost $800 per kilometer.
   a. How much would the road cost?
   b. If Ms. Ward had to pay 14 percent interest on a two-year loan to pay for the road, how much interest would she pay over that period?
4. Before borrowing $200, Laura Demetry visited a small loan company and the loan department of a bank. At the loan company, she found that she could borrow the $200 if she signed a note agreeing to repay the balance in six equal monthly installments of $36.50. At the bank she could borrow the money by signing a note for $215 and repaying the balance in six equal monthly payments.
   a. What would be the cost of the loan at the small loan company?
   b. What annual rate of interest would Ms. Demetry be paying if she borrowed at the small loan company?
   c. What would be the cost of the loan at the bank?
   d. What annual rate of interest would she pay if she borrowed at the bank?

S*tretching Your Business Knowledge*

1. Look for magazine articles which tell about experiences of people who are deep in debt or talk with someone involved with credit counseling and find out why people have these problems. Record the reasons given and report them to your class.
2. Many lenders use a "Rule of 78's" in determining how much interest should be returned to the borrower when discounted loans are paid before the maturity date. Check with financial institutions and loan companies in your area to find out how they use the "Rule of 78's." Report your findings to your class.
3. People borrow money for many different reasons. Some people borrow money to consolidate their debts.
   a. Find out what is meant by "consolidating debts."
   b. Is there any advantage in consolidating debts and making a single monthly payment on a single loan?
   c. How might consolidating debts reduce the amount of each payment? Does this mean that the borrower would be saving money?
4. Recent credit laws, designed to protect consumers, have imposed requirements on lenders to provide certain kinds of information. Some of these are called "disclosure laws." Find out from one of the businesses which lends money in your community if the business finds these disclosure laws to be a help in dealing with persons who want to borrow money. Ask for copies of forms that have been changed to comply with the new laws and note the changes that are on them. Find out what the APR and total finance charge would be for a personal unsecured loan of $1,000 for one year. Compare what you discover with information gathered by other students.

CHAPTER 29

Credit Records and Regulations

■ CHAPTER OBJECTIVES

After studying this chapter and completing the end-of-chapter activities, you will be able to:

1. Identify three specific factors that make a person creditworthy.
2. Describe what a retail credit bureau does.
3. Identify information shown on a statement of account.
4. Tell why receipts, credit memorandums, and canceled checks are important.
5. Explain what should be done when errors are found in credit statements.
6. Tell how provisions of several credit laws help consumers.
7. Explain how a good credit record can be established.

Wayne Oldtun applied for credit to buy a chord organ. The manager read Wayne's application, called the local credit bureau, and approved the amount of credit requested.

Van Aswell wanted a loan to buy a used car. After reading Van's application for credit, the manager called the credit bureau. Following a brief phone conversation, the manager explained to Van that it would not be possible to honor his request.

Angela Morgan received a statement showing how much she owed on her charge account. She did not recall making one of the purchases shown on her statement and she had no record of it in her file. She was sure that the statement was wrong so she called the department store to report the error.

Van was not satisfied about not getting his loan. When it was revealed that Van's record at the local credit bureau was unsatisfactory, he went to the credit bureau to find out why. Van discovered some information he felt was misleading, so he wrote out a short statement to correct his record. Angela found that her records and the store's records did not agree. She made an appointment to see the store manager to discuss the problem further. Both Van and Angela took legal and proper action.

Records about credit are very important. Let's look at the kinds of records kept and the rights and responsibilities connected with them.

What Creditors Need to Know

Federal and state laws and regulations help consumers receive fair treatment when applying for credit. However, becoming credit-worthy and staying that way is largely up to each individual. To be **creditworthy** means that you have established a record that shows you are a good credit risk. What do creditors need to know about you when you seek credit? How is such information made available?

Credit managers must consider several things when deciding whether to grant or deny credit. They may want to know about your finances: how much you earn, what kinds of savings and investments you have, and whether you have any other sources of income. They may want to know about your reliability: your occupation, how long you have been employed, how long you have lived at the same address, whether you own or rent your home, and what your school records reveal about you. They may also examine your credit record. Your **credit record** shows the debts you owe, how often you use credit, and whether you pay your credit obligations on time.

In general, credit managers want to be assured of two things: your ability to repay a debt and your willingness to do so. If you rate high on those two points, and if your credit record supports your reliability, you very likely will be given the credit you desire.

Credit Application Forms

One way for a credit manager to get information about those who desire credit is to have them complete an application. Figure 29–1 shows a credit application. You will note as you read through the application that credit references are requested. Your signature on the application gives the credit manager permission to make such inquiries as are necessary and assures that the information you have provided is accurate. The credit application form is important in getting credit or a loan. Being honest and accurate in completing this form is an important first step in the credit or loan transaction.

Bankard™ Application

THIS APPLICATION IS FOR VISA® AND MASTERCARD® (UNLESS OTHERWISE INDICATED) VISA ONLY □.   MASTERCARD ONLY □.
IF YOU ALREADY HAVE A BANKARD ACCOUNT
PLEASE PROVIDE ACCOUNT NUMBER.

VISA: 4460-
M/C: 541169-

ABOUT YOU, THE APPLICANT   PLEASE PRINT YOUR NAME EXACTLY AS YOU WISH IT TO APPEAR ON YOUR CREDIT CARDS.

LAST NAME	FIRST NAME	INITIAL	DATE OF BIRTH	SOCIAL SECURITY NUMBER

STREET ADDRESS	CITY	STATE	ZIP CODE	NO. DEPENDENTS	AREA CODE/PHONE NO.

LENGTH AT PRESENT ADDRESS (YRS.) (MOS.)	PLEASE CHECK BUYING OR OWN □ LIVE WITH □ RENT □ RELATIVE □	MONTHLY PAYMENT	NAME AND ADDRESS OF LANDLORD OR MORTGAGE HOLDER

PREVIOUS ADDRESS	CITY/STATE	YEARS	MONTHS

PRESENTLY EMPLOYED BY	STREET ADDRESS	CITY/STATE	YEARS	MONTHS

POSITION/EMPLOYEE NO	MONTHLY INCOME $	BUS. PHONE NO	AMOUNT AND SOURCE OF OTHER MONTHLY INCOME Except Alimony, Child Support, or Maintenance (See ADDITIONAL INFORMATION Below) $

PREVIOUSLY EMPLOYED BY (OR UNIVERSITY IF RECENT GRADUATE)	CITY/STATE	POSITION (OR DEGREE)	HOW LONG (OR YR. GRAD.)

NAME AND STREET ADDRESS OF NEAREST RELATIVE NOT LIVING WITH YOU	CITY/STATE	RELATIONSHIP

NAME AND LOCATION OF YOUR BANK	SAVINGS ACCT. NO.	CHECKING ACCT. NO.

ABOUT JOINT APPLICANT (IF ANY)   RELATIONSHIP TO APPLICANT _____

LAST NAME	FIRST NAME	INITIAL	DATE OF BIRTH	SOCIAL SECURITY NUMBER

STREET ADDRESS	CITY	STATE	ZIP CODE	AREA CODE/PHONE NO.

PRESENTLY EMPLOYED BY	STREET ADDRESS	CITY/STATE	YEARS	MONTHS

POSITION/EMPLOYEE NO	MONTHLY INCOME $	BUS. PHONE NO.	AMOUNT AND SOURCE OF OTHER MONTHLY INCOME Except Alimony, Child Support, or Maintenance (See ADDITIONAL INFORMATION Below) $

NAME AND LOCATION OF YOUR BANK	SAVINGS ACCT. NO.	CHECKING ACCT. NO.

CREDIT REFERENCES (OPEN AND/OR CLOSED)

PLEASE LIST ALL DEBTS PRESENTLY OWING INCLUDING ALIMONY, CHILD SUPPORT OR MAINTENANCE PAYMENTS WHICH YOU ARE OBLIGATED TO MAKE. ATTACH ADDITIONAL SHEETS IF NECESSARY, AND INDICATE ANY OF YOUR ACCOUNTS LISTED UNDER ANOTHER NAME

NAME OF CREDITOR OR INDIVIDUAL	CITY/STATE	ACCOUNT NO	MO. PAYMENT	BALANCE
AUTO FINANCED BY				

ADDITIONAL INFORMATION

YOU ARE NOT REQUIRED TO DISCLOSE INCOME FROM ALIMONY, CHILD SUPPORT, OR MAINTENANCE PAYMENTS. HOWEVER, IF YOU ARE RELYING ON INCOME FROM ALIMONY, CHILD SUPPORT, OR MAINTENANCE PAYMENTS AS A BASIS FOR REPAYMENT OF THIS OBLIGATION, PLEASE COMPLETE BELOW

ALIMONY/MO. $	CHILD SUPPORT/MO. $	MAINTENANCE/MO. $

SIGNATURES
WHEN I RECEIVE MY CREDIT CARD(S), I AGREE AND UNDERSTAND THAT I AM CONTRACTUALLY LIABLE ACCORDING TO THE APPLICABLE BANKARD TERMS AND CONDITIONS, AND IF THIS IS A JOINT APPLICATION WE AGREE SUCH LIABILITY IS JOINT AND SEVERAL. YOU HAVE THE RIGHT TO TAKE ANY ACTION(S) YOU FEEL NECESSARY TO DETERMINE THE CREDIT WORTHINESS OF ANY PARTY SIGNING BELOW AND BY SIGNING BELOW I (WE) CONFIRM THAT THE INFORMATION GIVEN TO YOU ON THIS APPLICATION IS TRUE.

APPLICANT'S SIGNATURE X	DATE	DRIVERS LICENSE NO
JOINT APPLICANT'S SIGNATURE X	DATE	DRIVERS LICENSE NO

OTHER PERSONS PERMITTED TO USE ACCOUNT(S)

SIGNATURE(S)	RELATIONSHIP(S)

BANK USE ONLY

									BANK NAME AND OR NUMBER

	TC	08	09	13	17	27	31	33
□ VISA	#							
□ M/C								
□ BOTH	APPROVED BY			DATE APPROVED				

Figure 29–1
A credit
application

Retail Credit Bureaus

In addition to checking with your employer, your landlord (if you rent a house or an apartment), and your credit references, the credit manager also will check your records with a retail credit bureau.

Retail credit bureaus are organizations that keep records on people in their area who have obtained and used credit. Each credit bureau is usually linked with similar organizations in other communities. If you are new to the area in which you are applying for credit, the local credit bureau can call the bureau in the community in which you formerly lived and check your record.

Your credit record with a bureau is used to grade you as a credit risk. Credit bureaus do not make value judgments about any individual; they simply gather facts as reported to them. Their record may describe what you owe now and how your payment record has been in the past. Your credit record is confidential. That is, it can be given out only to those who have a legitimate reason for seeing it.

Illus. 29–1
Credit bureaus maintain confidential records of buyers who have used credit. A good credit record can be very important when it's time to borrow again.

There are times when seemingly minor actions can affect your credit rating. For example, you might be on vacation and fail to make an installment payment when it is due. Or, you may have delayed depositing money in your checking account and caused a check to be returned because of insufficient funds. These actions on your part may become part of your credit record. One small blot on your record may not hurt you, but many blots suggest an unfavorable pattern of behavior.

Other Sources of Information

Verifying information about your credit record is an important matter for credit managers. The business with whom you are dealing wants to grant you credit if at all possible. Nevertheless, granting credit to poor credit risks is a costly matter. A business cannot afford to grant credit to customers who fail to pay their debts.

Employers and former employers can verify the dates of employment and salary figures which are included on credit applications. Banks and other financial institutions can report whether or not the applicants have the accounts listed on the applications. Landlords can indicate the length of time tenants have been renting and whether or not they pay their rent on time. Other creditors can report on how credit applicants make payments to their accounts and how they repay their loans.

If you list a personal reference because you do not have sufficient credit references, the person you list can indicate how he or she feels you conduct your personal business affairs. School personnel can indicate how reliable and trustworthy you were in school. In each case, the reference checked merely helps the credit manager to get a better picture of you as a credit risk so that an accurate appraisal of your creditworthiness can be made.

Checking Your Credit Statement

You can help keep your credit record clean by keeping accurate records of your purchases and payments. When a merchant sells goods on credit, a record of the sale is made on a sales ticket. Usually two or more copies of the sales ticket are made. One copy is given to the customer as a receipt. The other copy or copies are kept by the merchant for billing purposes.

At regular intervals, usually monthly, a business sends each credit customer a record of the transactions that the customer has completed with the business during the billing period. This record is known as a **statement of account** or, simply, a **statement.** For credit card accounts, the statement lists all of your purchases from various businesses. Names of the businesses involved are identified. Most statements show:

1. the balance that was due when the last statement was mailed
2. the amounts charged during the month for the merchandise or services you bought
3. the amounts credited to your account for payments made during the month or for merchandise returned
4. the current balance, which is the balance from the last statement, plus interest charges and the amounts of any new purchases, less the amounts credited to you (old balance + interest + purchases − payments = current balance)
5. the minimum amount of your next payment and when it is due.

Most statements are prepared by special accounting machines or by computers. Some statements list separately each item that was purchased. Some list only the totals purchased, paid, and owed. In any case, a statement serves two purposes: (1) it shows you how much you owe, and (2) it gives you a record of your business transactions. A statement is shown in Figure 29–2.

You should check the accuracy of the statement by comparing it with your copies of sales tickets and with your record of payments and credit memorandums. A **credit memorandum** is a written record the seller gives you of the amount subtracted from your account when you return merchandise. If you discover an error on a statement, you should notify the seller at once.

Credit card account statements need to be checked very carefully for errors. Credit card fraud is a major problem in our business community. One system used by consumers is to keep a file of sales slips when a credit card is used — each form normally has "sales draft, cardholder copy" printed on it. It is yours; keep it. When the statement arrives, check the items on the statement against the sales slips on file. If something shows on the statement for which you do not have a sales draft, check that item out and report any error to the bank or credit card company immediately. Staple to the statement the sales slips for the items listed on the statement and file them for future reference. Also compare payments and previous balances with your records.

Figure 29–2
Check your
monthly
statements
carefully.

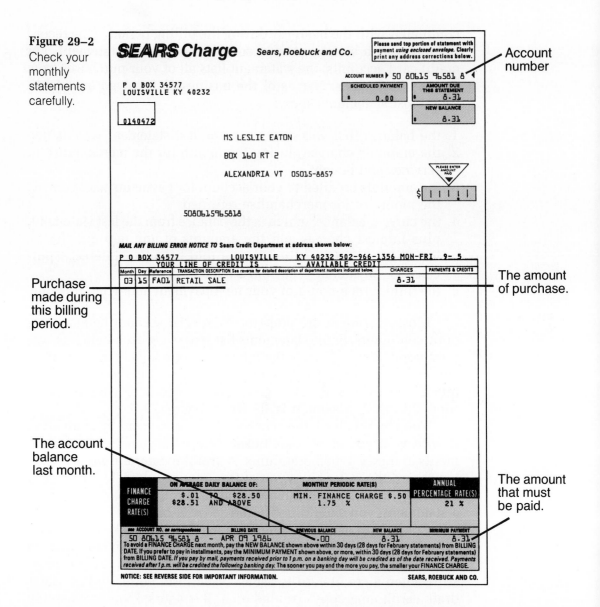

Account
number

Purchase
made during
this billing
period.

The amount
of purchase.

The account
balance
last month.

The amount
that must
be paid.

Keeping Accurate Records

Many errors are simply honest mistakes, and businesses are as
eager to correct them as you are. Your credit worthiness may be at
stake, and the business's reputation may be hurt by bad publicity if
errors are not corrected. When you receive a sales ticket, a credit
memorandum, or a monthly statement, you should examine it to

make sure that it is correct. A business may mistakenly charge you for goods you did not buy. Or it may fail to give you credit for a payment or for goods that you returned.

Unless you maintain accurate records, it will be difficult for you to check your credit statements. When making a payment by check, write the date and the check number on the statement. Keep your statements and sales tickets. They will be valuable in the future if any questions arise as to whether or not they have been paid. It is not enough for you to know that you have paid a bill. You should be able to prove that payment was made. Otherwise, you may be required to pay a second time. In Chapter 18 you learned that a canceled check is valuable as evidence that payment has been made because it has the endorsement of the payee on the back.

When you do not pay by check, however, you need some other method of showing that you have made payment. A written form that acknowledges that payment was made is called a **receipt.** Receipts are usually given to people who pay their bills by cash and should be kept as proof of payment. Receipts are sometimes bound in books, along with stubs that are similar to check stubs. The receipt form has spaces for entering the number of the receipt, the date, the name of the person making payment, the amount of the payment in words, the reason for the payment, the amount in figures, and the signature of the person receiving the payment. The stub is filled out to show the same information. Figure 29–3 shows a receipt properly filled out.

The information recorded on a receipt stub may later be needed by the one who writes the receipt to tell the amount a customer paid and when. Each stub and receipt is numbered so the customer's receipt can be compared with the stub if a dispute arises.

Sometimes a receipt is not given. Instead, the word "paid" is written or stamped on the bill or statement. The date and the initials

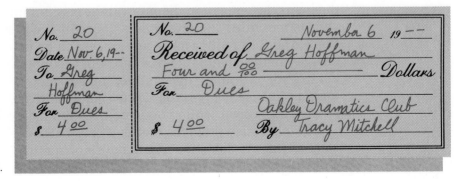

Figure 29–3
Tracy has given Greg a receipt for his $4.00 payment of dues.

or signature of the one who received your money should be included. If you pay in cash, keep the cash register receipt or the sales ticket as evidence of payment. You will need one or both of these documents if you have to return your purchase.

Credit Legislation

Many credit laws have been passed by federal and state legislatures since the early 1970's. These laws are intended to protect consumers in credit transactions. They also help assure that all individuals who seek credit are given fair treatment. The Truth in Lending Act of 1968 started a series of bills that dealt with various aspects of credit and lending practices. It was followed in 1980 by the Truth in Lending Simplification Act.

The Truth in Lending Act of 1968 requires that you be told the cost of a credit purchase before you sign any credit agreement. It requires that the annual percentage rate, the amount of interest, and the total finance charge be stated clearly in writing.

The Equal Credit Opportunity Act prohibits creditors from denying credit because of age, race, sex, or marital status. Young people who may have just entered the labor market cannot be denied credit based only on their ages. Older, possibly retired, persons also have special protection under this act. Married women who previously found it difficult to establish credit in their own names now have a legal right to do so. Under this law a woman has a right to her own credit if she proves to be creditworthy.

The Fair Credit Billing Act requires prompt correction of billing mistakes when they are brought to the attention of the business. The procedure for getting a correction in a credit billing involves four steps: (1) notify the creditor in writing within 60 days after your bill was mailed; (2) while you are waiting for an answer, you are not required to pay the amount in question; but you must pay the items that are not in dispute; (3) the creditor must acknowledge your letter within 30 days unless your bill is corrected before that time; (4) if the creditor made a mistake, you do not pay any finance charges on the amount in error and your account must be corrected. If no error is found, the creditor must bill you again and may include finance charges that accumulated and any minimum payments you missed while you were questioning the bill.

The law also provides that you may withhold payment of any balance due on defective merchandise or services purchased with a credit card. This is true, however, only if you have made a good faith effort to return the goods or resolve the problem with the business from which you made your purchase. There is a limitation to this provision that you must keep in mind: If the business did not issue your card, then (1) the purchase must have exceeded $50 and (2) the sale must have taken place in your state or within 100 miles of your current address.

The Fair Credit Reporting Act is another law which helps assure fair credit treatment. It requires that credit bureau reports identify both husband and wife if both are liable for the debt involved. This allows a credit history to be developed for each spouse. You also are guaranteed access to your own credit bureau record if you request it. Credit bureaus are entitled to charge you a reasonable fee for doing so. You may correct any errors found in your credit record by writing a statement of not more than 100 words explaining your side of the story. Your statement must be made part of your permanent record.

Building Your Credit Record

Building a credit record which establishes your creditworthiness is an important matter. To some extent you can begin that while you are still in school. Since trust and reliability are important when it comes to matters of credit, you can help to establish yourself by having a good record of grades and school attendance. Both employers and creditors know that behavior patterns developed in school tend to carry on after graduation.

In addition, it is good to have both a checking and a savings account. If you have a balance in each account and do not overdraw your checking account, a lender can see that you can handle money. Making regular deposits to your savings account also suggests that you will be a good credit risk.

Some people establish credit records by making small purchases. For instance, if you buy a sweater on credit and make the payments according to the agreement, you have taken an important step toward proving you are a good credit risk. Or you may want to pay off your account within 30 days and avoid an interest charge. Either way you will be building your credit record.

Having a good part-time or full-time employment record also helps to establish a good credit record. Changing jobs often does not

Illus. 29–2

Careful handling of your checking and savings accounts is the first step to establishing your creditworthiness.

look good to a creditor. Being on a job for two or more years is a positive part of a good credit record.

If you find that you just cannot pay your bills when they are due, you should follow these four steps: First, contact your creditors and explain your situation. Second, make a realistic proposal for when and what you can pay; don't just say "I can't pay." Third, keep any promises you make. Fourth, make a written copy of your agreement to avoid disagreements later.

Some of the options you can consider are partial payments, refinancing, and extensions of due dates. But you have little bargaining power as such, even though your creditor may be willing to work things out with you. Legally you are indebted and could be sued for nonpayment, so be open minded if a creditor has other ideas for you to consider.

Your credit rating is an important matter. You can build it and maintain it if you are careful in your business dealings.

Adding to Your Business Vocabulary

The following terms should become part of your business vocabulary. For each numbered item, find the term that has the same meaning.

credit memorandum   receipt
credit record   retail credit bureau
creditworthy   statement of account or statement

1. An organization that keeps records on people who have obtained and used credit.
2. A written acknowledgment that payment was made.
3. A record of the transactions that a customer has completed with a business during a billing period.
4. A written record of the amount to be subtracted from your account that the seller gives you when you return merchandise.
5. Having an established record that indicates being a good credit risk.
6. Shows the debts you owe, how often you use credit, and whether you pay your credit obligations on time.

Understanding Your Reading

1. What do credit managers look for when making decisions on credit?
2. Where might a credit manager get information on your history of paying bills?
3. In what ways is a credit application form important to credit managers? To you?
4. What is the purpose of a credit bureau?
5. Why is more than one copy made of sales tickets? Of what value is a sales ticket to you and to a business?
6. What important information is usually shown on the statement of account?
7. What should you do with the receipts and memorandums that you receive?
8. How can you prove the accuracy of statements you receive?
9. What evidence can a person give to prove that a bill has been paid if the payment was by check? by cash?
10. What action should you take if you find errors in a credit statement?
11. How does the Truth in Lending Act help consumers?
12. List four things you can do to establish a good credit record.

Putting Your Business Knowledge to Work

1. Keith Packard operates a book store. One day Bill Cross, a total stranger, asked if he could buy a set of manuals on credit. Mr. Cross explained that he had just moved into town two weeks ago. The moving expenses took most of his cash, but he has a good job and will be able to pay $30 a month beginning next month.
   a. What should Keith do?
   b. If he decides to extend credit to Bill Cross, what precautions should he take?

2. Ms. Oakwood wants to open an account in the Hewitt Road Department Store. She objects, however, to giving the credit manager information about such things as where she has other charge accounts, whether she owns real estate, where she works, and in which bank she maintains an account. Does the credit manager have a right to ask for this information? Explain your answer.

3. Donna Stratford has been working on her first job for seven months. Her checking account has a balance of $159. She has also put aside $50 in cash for an emergency. She wants to buy a clock radio which sells for $69.95 at a store that offers credit. Donna has never used credit and would like to establish a credit rating. What can she do to get a credit record started? What advice would you give her if she decided to buy this clock radio on credit?

4. Mrs. Summit never saves the sales tickets listing merchandise that she buys for cash. Mrs. Emmet saves her sales tickets for at least a month. Who is following the better business practice?

5. Below is a list of some common business transactions. Assuming that you are paying cash in each case, for which payments would you wish to have receipts and for which payments are receipts unimportant? Explain your answers.
   a. bought 10 gallons of gasoline
   b. paid for shoe repairs
   c. paid to have the car repaired
   d. bought a ticket to a football game
   e. paid the telephone bill
   f. paid tuition for a course at a college

Computing Business Problems

1. Shana's Boutique grants open credit to people who have been steady customers. Today the boutique received checks in the mail from several customers as shown below.
   a. What was the balance in each account?
   b. What was the total amount received from charge customers?

Name	Amount Owed	Amount Paid
Jose Navarro	$ 44.22	44.22
Lynne Goldberg	10.00	5.00
Eloise Little	102.67	50.00
Sam Nader	54.89	25.00
Ruth Smith	19.35	19.35

2. Linda Nees made the following credit purchases: gloves, $18; purse, $18; necklace, $55; shoes, $42. Later she returned the gloves and the purse and received a credit memorandum.
   a. What was the total of Linda's purchases before she returned the gloves and the purse?
   b. What was the amount of the credit memorandum?
   c. How much did she owe after she received the credit memorandum?

3. Wholesalers usually offer cash discounts to retailers to encourage them to pay their bills promptly. The following discount terms appeared on a bill received by Lisa's Lumber Yard: 5/10, 2/20, n/30. The term 5/10 means that a 5 percent discount will be allowed if the bill is paid within 10 days. The term 2/20 means that a 2 percent discount will be allowed if the bill is paid within 20 days. The term n/30

means that it is expected that the full amount of the bill will be paid no later than 30 days after the date on the bill.

a. The amount of the bill was $526.70. If Lisa's Lumber Yard paid the bill within 5 days, what was the amount of the payment?

b. What was the amount of the payment if the bill was paid on the 15th day? on the 30th day?

4. Bobby Jeffrey uses his bank charge card at several stores. During this past month, the following purchases were charged to his bank charge card account: Andy's Clothing Store, 2 shirts, $28; Julie's Hard-ware Store, 2 gallons of paint, $21.50; Charlie's Family Restaurant, $24.75. A credit sales slip for $10.75 from Julie's Hardware Store was also received this month. Bobby's statement showed a balance from the previous month of $152.00 and a finance charge of $2.28 was added by the bank this month.

a. If Bobby decides to pay his account in full, how much will he pay?

b. If he decides to make a minimum payment of $30, how much will he still owe?

c. If the finance charge is 1 1/2 percent per month, what will the next month's finance charge be if he pays only $30?

Stretching Your Business Knowledge

1. When businesses have difficulty in collecting amounts that customers owe them, they sometimes hire collection agencies. Prepare a report on collection agencies. Tell what they do, what methods they use, and what their services cost. You should be able to find most of the information you need in the library. However, you might call or visit a local collection agency to get additional information. Collection agencies are listed in the Yellow Pages of your telephone book.

2. States set a limit on the rate of interest that can be charged for different kinds of credit. Find out what the maximum allowable rates of interest are in your state. Write a report on what you discover.

3. Assume that you checked your credit bureau record and discovered an error: an account with a local department store reportedly was overdue twice during the past year. Actually you had paid the correct amount on time in each instance but your payment had been credited to someone else's account. After checking with the store's credit manager, you were able to have the situation corrected with the store, but apparently the correction was not reported to the credit bureau. Write a statement of not more than 100 words to correct the information in your credit bureau record.

4. The Equal Credit Opportunity Act permits lenders and creditors to use a credit scoring system. The credit scoring system assigns points to various factors which relate to whether or not a person is a good credit risk. Find out more about credit scoring systems by visiting your library and looking up articles dealing with this system. Visit a retail store, a bank, or some other lending institution and find out what you can about the experience that businesses have had with credit scoring. If you can, bring an example of a credit scoring system to class for discussion.

5. Bankruptcy is an alternative for consumers who are hopelessly in debt. Bankruptcy laws have been changed recently to make it easier for consumers to declare bankruptcy. Find out about bankruptcy cases in your community. Do many consumers declare bankruptcy? Is bankruptcy a good solution for some consumers? What are some advantages and disadvantages of bankruptcy? Report your findings to your class.

CAREER CATEGORY: Credit

In Unit 8 you learned of the important role credit plays in our economy. Most individuals and businesses find it necessary to use credit for some purchases. As a result, many workers are involved in the processing of credit transactions.

Job Titles: Job titles commonly found in this career area include:

Credit Clerk	Credit Department Manager
Credit Authorizer	Credit Union Manager
Credit Reporter	Credit Bureau Clerk
Loan Clerk	Credit Bureau Manager
Loan Officer	Credit Counselor

Employment Outlook: The demand for workers in credit-related occupations is expected to be above average through the next decade. An increasing use of credit by both consumers and businesses will cause the demand for credit services to continue although automation will tend to soften that demand. Professional employment in credit counseling very likely will increase steadily as individuals and families seek help with credit management problems.

Future Changes: New developments in computer applications and systems for handling credit transactions will affect the need for credit workers who normally handle paperwork and routine activities.

What Is Done on the Job: Clerical workers in this area perform functions similar to clerical workers in other areas of work. They must keep accurate records of amounts borrowed, paid, and owed by customers. They must be efficient in working with figures and must be able to handle confidential information in a responsible way.

Managers and other professional workers must decide whether or not to grant credit or extend a loan. They must analyze information and provide explanations for their actions.

Credit counselors meet with people who have credit problems and who seek help. The counselor must analyze credit problems and help clients move toward solutions.

Education and Training: High school graduates with good clerical skills will find employment in this career area. Job applicants who have continued their education beyond high school with courses in credit, finance, and counseling will be able to obtain higher-level positions. In addition to a knowledge of credit laws, financial operations, and management procedures, professional credit workers must have good public relations and communication skills.

Salary Levels: Salaries vary widely but are competitive with salaries paid to similar workers in other career areas. The average annual salaries for credit clerks and credit authorizers range from $10,000 to $15,000; managerial and loan officer positions pay in the $20,000 to $60,000 range, depending upon the experience of the worker and the size of the business.

For Additional Information: Interviewing a credit worker from a local credit bureau, visiting the loan department of a bank or credit union, or observing the credit department of a retail store are good ways to get additional information on this career area. A speaker from a credit counseling service can provide up-to-date information on credit counseling work. Special sources of information include the following:

Consumer Credit Career Information Kit
International Consumer Credit
    Association
243 N. Lindbergh Blvd.
St. Louis, MO 63141

Careers in Collections
American Collectors Association
PO Box 35106
Minneapolis, MN 55435

Opportunities in Credit Management
National Association of Credit
    Management
475 Park Avenue
New York, NY 10016

UNIT 9
SAVINGS AND INVESTMENTS

UNIT OBJECTIVES

After studying the chapters in this unit, you will be able to:

1. Explain how investors can use savings plans to their advantage.

2. Describe several kinds of savings accounts which should be considered when investing money.

3. Give examples of how stocks and bonds fit into a consumer's investment plan.

4. List several advantages and disadvantages of real estate as an investment.

BUSINESS BRIEF
From Football To Finance

When Larry Brown was a boy growing up in Clairton, Pennsylvania, few of his friends would have guessed that someday he would write and publish his autobiography. They also would have doubted that his biography citation would appear in the distinguished publication, *Who's Who In Corporate Black America.* But it did happen.

Larry Brown liked sports and worked hard at them. His capacity to be a winner was evident early in his life. Football, in particular, was important to him.

An impressive high school football record helped lead Brown into a collegiate program at Dodge City Junior College and Kansas State University. His performance on the gridiron was significant and caught the attention of the professional football scouts. After graduating from Kansas State University, Brown began a professional football career. He joined the Washington Redskins of the National Football League.

Brown's career in professional football was a distinguished one. He was elected a co-captain of his team and, in 1972, he received honors as the "Player of the Year." From 1969 to 1977 he "gave his all" to his football career.

Career changes are a way of life for most Americans, and so it was with Larry Brown. Leaving his career in professional football behind, he turned to the world of finance for which he had prepared during his professional football years. He joined the investment firm of E. F. Hutton & Company as a financial management advisor. Brown again displayed a talent for achievement. He drew upon his professional football experience and developed a National Football League investment program.

Larry Brown's drive and dedication to his professional pursuits are accompanied by a desire to improve the quality of life for those around him. He is alert to human needs and helps meet those needs whenever he can. His autobiography, *I'll Always Get Up,* reflects his dedication to excellence and achievement in all aspects of his life.

Larry Brown's civic involvement and contributions to the betterment of society are evident. He was named "Washingtonian of the Year" and has served on several boards of directors, including the following: Children's Hospital Speech and Hearing Center, Charles Edison Memorial Fund, Deafness Research Foundation, National Capital YMCA, Reading Is Fundamental Program, and the Washington Correctional Foundation. His community service also includes advisory committees for the Better Hearing Institute and the United Negro College Fund. Larry Brown is now employed by the Xerox Corporation as Business and Community Relations Manager for the Mid-Atlantic Region.

Facts included in this Business Brief were taken from the following sources: Matney, William C. (ed.). *Who's Who Among Black Americans*, 3d ed. Lake Forest: Who's Who Among Black Americans, Inc., 1981. Reed, William (ed.). *Who's Who in Black Corporate America, 1982.*

CHAPTER 30

*B*uilding Your Savings

■ CHAPTER OBJECTIVES ─────────────────────────

After studying this chapter and completing the end-of-chapter activities, you will be able to:

1. Give at least two reasons for saving money.
2. Describe four different ways you can save money.
3. Explain how interest makes your savings grow.
4. Tell how the safety of an investment affects the rate of return.
5. Describe a liquid investment.
6. Give an illustration of how investments help our economy.

American consumers are very good at using credit and, as you know, they use a lot of it. American consumers, however, do not save much of what they earn. In fact, among the people of modern nations, American consumers save the lowest percentage of their incomes.

Developing a savings habit should be a part of each person's financial plan. Savings are needed to buy the things we need and want and to prepare for future expenses and emergencies. Savings can also be used to help keep our economy healthy.

Having a Savings Plan

People save money for different reasons and in different ways. Loretta Sherman's father and mother use their savings to buy land. In addition to making payments on their home, the Shermans make payments on ten acres of land they bought in a newly developed lake area. Mr. and Mrs. Sherman also feel it is important to have money in the bank that can be used for emergencies. Every week they deposit 10 percent of their income into their savings account.

Loretta's older brother buys stocks and bonds with part of his wages. He is planning for his retirement years. Loretta takes a certain amount of the money she earns baby-sitting and puts it in an envelope which she keeps in a drawer in her room. As soon as she saves enough, she plans to buy her own stereo.

There is one common trait in Loretta's family: all family members save. But each member has a different savings plan. All except Loretta invest their savings. **Investing** means using your savings to earn more money for you. Loretta is saving but not investing. She has a savings plan, but it offers no opportunity to earn money. How will you save and invest your money?

How Savings Grow

Saving a regular amount of money, even a few dollars at a time, is a good idea. Any amount of savings can be put to work to earn an income. Interest which is paid on your savings is one of the ways in which your money can earn more money. Savings put to work to earn interest is one form of investment.

Earning Interest

When savings are invested and the income from them is also invested, the increase over a number of years is larger than many people realize. For instance, David Skinner is able to save $50 a month. In a year, his savings will amount to $600. In 10 years, he will have saved $6,000. If he deposits his money in a savings account, he can earn 6 percent interest. If that interest is paid every three months and added to his account, his savings will increase rapidly. At the end of 10 years, he will have over $8,200 in his account rather than $6,000. His savings will have grown more than $2,200.

As an investor, David realizes the importance of this increase in his savings. He looks at a chart (Figure 30–1) to see how much his savings will grow if he saves for a longer period. At 6 percent, his $50-a-month savings will grow to $14,500 in 15 years. Since interest rates change, David's account may grow even more. At the 6 percent rate, the interest he receives by the 15th year is more than $50 a month. He could then take out $50 each month without decreasing the amount he has on deposit. He would have a permanent income of $50 a month. Often people fail to do that kind of planning for the future. Figure 30–1 shows how interest can cause savings to grow over a period of years.

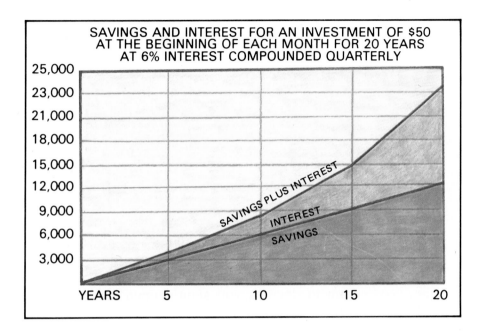

SAVINGS AND INTEREST FOR AN INVESTMENT OF $50
AT THE BEGINNING OF EACH MONTH FOR 20 YEARS
AT 6% INTEREST COMPOUNDED QUARTERLY

Figure 30–1
Interest helps savings grow.

Earning Compound Interest

In David's case, the interest he earns is compounded. That means the amount of interest paid is added to the amount saved. Then interest is computed on the amount saved plus the interest previously earned; this is called **compound interest.** David is paid interest on interest. For instance, annual interest of 10 percent on $1,000 is $100. If the interest is compounded, then the interest computed at the end of the next year will be based on $1,100 ($1,000 + $100 interest). The 10 percent interest earned would amount to $110. Interest the following year would be figured on $1,210 ($1,100 + $110) and would amount to $121. When interest is compounded, the amount of interest paid increases each time it is figured. If the interest were not compounded, the interest paid would be $100 each year.

Interest can be compounded daily, monthly, quarterly (every three months), semiannually (twice a year), or annually. The use of computers to calculate interest makes compounding relatively easy. The more frequent the compounding, the greater the growth in your savings. Figure 30–2 shows how rapidly monthly savings of different amounts increase when interest is compounded quarterly at 6 percent.

Monthly Savings	End of First Year	End of Second Year	End of Third Year	End of Fourth Year	End of Fifth Year	End of Tenth Year
$ 5.00	$ 61.98	$ 127.76	$ 197.76	$ 271.68	$ 350.32	$ 822.16
10.00	123.95	255.52	395.15	543.35	700.47	1,644.32
25.00	309.89	638.79	987.87	1,358.38	1,751.62	4,110.79
30.00	371.86	766.55	1,185.45	1,630.05	2,101.94	4,932.95
35.00	433.84	894.30	1,383.02	1,901.73	2,452.26	5,755.11
50.00	619.77	1,277.58	1,975.74	2,716.75	3,503.24	8,221.59

Figure 30–2
Even small amounts grow when interest is compounded.

Investing Promptly

You may not have a large amount of money to invest at one time. In fact, you may have to build up your savings with just a dollar or two at a time. Instead of waiting until you have a large sum to deposit, you should open a savings account as soon as you can.

Financial institutions often allow you to invest money in small amounts as you save it. Deposits are accepted whenever you want to make them, and interest is paid at regular periods. Banks, credit unions, and savings and loan associations usually welcome small as well as large savings.

Investing Carefully

The savings that you invest will grow if invested wisely. The American humorist Will Rogers is quoted as saying, "It's not the return *on* my money I am concerned about, it is the return *of* my money." Today, financial institutions — as you learned in Chapter 17 — have their savings accounts insured up to very large sums. It assures you that your money will be returned to you when you need it.

But suppose you lend $100 to a friend who promises to pay it back with 15 percent interest at the end of one year. That is a higher interest rate than banks pay. If the loan is paid back, you will receive $115 ($100 + $15 interest). But if the borrower has no money at the end of the year, you may get nothing back. You may lose both the $100 you lent and the $15 interest you should have earned. Investments are satisfactory when the safety of the amount invested and the interest to be paid can be depended upon. **Safety** is assurance that the money you have invested will be returned to you.

Not all investors need the same degree of safety. Someone may have enough money to make 20 different investments. If one of them is lost, the investor still has the other 19. On the other hand, suppose that a person has only a small amount of money and makes only one investment. One loss would be serious. If you have limited funds you should be careful to make investments that are as safe as possible.

Choosing the Right Plan

When deciding how to invest your savings, there are several things to consider. In addition to considering the safety of your savings, you should consider the plan's yield. You should also determine how quickly you can get your money out of your investment if you need it.

Yield Makes a Difference

A good savings plan should earn a reasonable amount of interest. That is, it should have a satisfactory yield. The **yield** is the percentage of interest which will be added to your savings over a period of time. Figure 30–3 shows the value of an original investment of $100 in 20 years at several different yields.

Usually the higher the yield, the greater the risk of loss. Loans to the federal government are the safest. When money is loaned to

Illus. 30–1
Interest rates paid on accounts will vary among financial institutions.

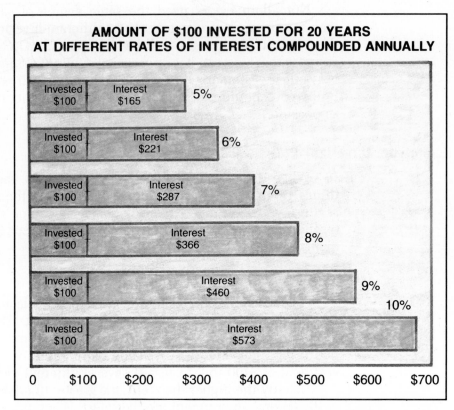

Figure 30–3
While a higher yield means greater growth, it may also mean greater risk.

individuals or businesses, because there is less safety, it usually earns higher interest rates than those paid by the government. For example, when the government is paying 6 percent interest, one business may pay 8 percent and a more risky business may have to pay 12 percent.

The offer of a low rate of interest, however, does not guarantee safety. Similarly, high rates of interest do not mean that a loss will surely occur. The higher yields mean that investors generally believe that the situation involves a higher risk.

Money Available When Needed

When an investment can be turned into money quickly, it is said to be a **liquid investment.** This feature of an investment is important if you should need money to take care of emergencies. Suppose, for example, that you have $5,000 on deposit in a bank. If you need money right away, you can go to your bank and withdraw it. On the other hand, suppose you own a piece of land which

Illus. 30–2
Not all investments are liquid. Selling a home quickly may be difficult.

you bought for $5,000. The land may be a safe investment and yield a satisfactory return; but if you need money at once, you may find it difficult to sell the piece of land right away. You might even have to sell it for less than you paid for it if you cannot wait for a buyer who is willing to pay your price.

When you make a number of investments, you do not need to have all of them in a liquid form. How much you need in liquid investments will depend on your situation. Your investment plan should meet your short- and long-term needs.

Investments and the Economy

No matter how you invest, those investments serve a very useful economic purpose. Invested money is used to operate businesses, governments, and other organizations. A business, for example, sells bonds or stocks to investors to raise money to operate and/or expand the business. We, as individuals, borrow money from banks and other organizations to buy what businesses produce. The money we borrow often is someone's invested funds. Without sources for borrowing and investing, our economic system would be greatly hurt. Your investments contribute to keeping our economic system healthy.

Adding to Your Business Vocabulary

The following terms should become part of your business vocabulary. For each numbered item, find the term that has the same meaning.

compound interest   safety
investing   yield
liquid investment

1. Interest computed on the amount saved plus the interest previously earned.
2. The percentage of interest which is added to your savings over a period of time.
3. An investment which can be turned into money quickly.
4. Using your savings to earn more money for you.
5. Assurance that the money you have invested will be returned to you.

Understanding Your Reading

1. What are four different ways of saving?
2. When does money saved become an investment?
3. Why is interest that is compounded better than interest that is not compounded?
4. What will be the total savings if $10 is deposited monthly at 6 percent interest compounded quarterly for a period of 10 years? (Use Figure 30–2.)
5. Suppose you save $20 a month. If your savings plan compounds interest monthly, should you wait six months and invest $120 at that time, or should you make deposits each month? Why?
6. Cindy Redmond has $500 in a savings account that is paying her 6 percent interest. A friend, Rosalind Tate, knows of a local business project where the $500 could be invested at a 10 percent rate of return. What might be the advantages and disadvantages for Cindy of taking her money out of savings and putting it into this other investment?
7. Which of the following investments are liquid?:
   a. land
   b. a bank savings account
   c. a loan made to a friend.
8. What are some advantages of a savings plan for you as an individual? for the economy?

Putting Your Business Knowledge To Work

1. Yolanda Miller has a pizza business. She works out of her home and makes a nice profit. She keeps all of her business cash in a small fireproof safe in her basement. She has accumulated over $2,000 — more than she needs to buy supplies and meet unexpected business expenses. She wants to be sure that her money is safe and that she can get it when she needs it. What advice can you give Yolanda so that she can make better use of her money?

2. Donald Gorski has been saving money for the past year since he started working part time. He keeps the money in a metal box in his bedroom. Donald's mother gives him $10 for every $100 saved to help him pay for a new car when he graduates from high school in two years. Donald has saved almost $1,000. Someone told him about a new business firm that pays 20 percent on money it borrows. Should Donald consider lending his money to this business? Why or why not?

3. Frank Brokaw, a wealthy businessperson, invests $5,000 in a newly organized manufacturing company. Ella Chapman owns a small house and has $5,000 in a savings account. She knows of Mr. Brokaw's investment. Because Mr. Brokaw has a reputation for being a good investor, Ella decides to invest in that company, too. Does the fact that the investment may be a good one for Mr. Brokaw mean that it is also a good investment for Ella? Explain your answer.

4. Jill Young worked hard all summer and saved $2,000. She wants to go to college in three years, so she has decided to put $500 of her savings in a bank savings account. With the balance, she is thinking of buying a piece of land outside of the city that her father said is a pretty good investment that should increase in value over the next five to ten years. What advice would you give to Jill?

5. Gary Reibling wanted to borrow $1,000 from Cliff Mathis. Gary offered to pay 10 percent interest although the usual loan rate at that time was 6 percent. Suggest why Gary may be willing to pay the higher rate of interest.

*C*omputing Business Problems

1. There are several different savings plans, but in each case saving on a regular basis is important. Even small amounts build up to large sums in a short time. How much would each person below have saved in one year (365 days) if he or she saved the following amounts without interest being added?
   a. Charles Jason — 10 cents a day
   b. Carla Spivak — 75 cents a week
   c. Alice Farney — $5 every two weeks
   d. Nolan Robinson — $10 a month

2. Ramon Valdez wants a savings plan that will permit him to buy a stereo that costs $270.
   a. How much will he have to save each month to be able to make his purchase at the end of 6 months? at the end of 12 months? If he saves at the 12-month rate, how much longer would he have to save to buy a stereo that costs $450?
   b. Ramon learned that interest can double the amount of money you deposit if you leave it on deposit long enough. To find the number of years required to double the amount deposited, divide the interest rate into 72. If Ramon deposited $180, how long would it take for his deposit to double if this account paid 6 percent interest? 8 percent interest? 12 percent interest?

3. Cindy Hamon deposited $50 in a bank each month for 15 years.
   a. What is the total amount that she has invested?
   b. How much money is in her account if her deposits earn 6 percent interest compounded quarterly? (See Figure 30–1.)

4. Barbara Maxwell finds that she can save $25 a month.
   a. If she receives no interest on her savings, how much will her savings amount to in one year? in ten years?
   b. If she deposits her money in a savings account and receives an income of 6 percent compounded quarterly (the rate used in Figure 30–2), how much will she have at the end of one year? At the end of ten years?
   c. At the end of ten years, how much of the value of the savings as found in (b) will be made up of interest?

Stretching Your Business Knowledge

1. If you deposit money in a savings account at a bank, savings and loan, or credit union, the financial institution will protect it and will return it to you when you ask for it. In the meantime, you will be paid interest on the amount deposited.
   a. Why do financial institutions do that? Are you providing a service for which you should be paid?
   b. Where do financial institutions get money to lend if funds from depositors are not sufficient?
2. Steve Bella has decided to save $30 monthly and to invest the money in a bank that pays 6 percent interest compounded quarterly. While he does not know how many years he will be saving and investing this money, he would like some idea as to the total amount he will have each year for up to five years. Using the table in Figure 30–2, prepare a rough chart for Steve much like that shown in Figure 30–1.
3. If everyone began saving money and did not buy such things as cars, furniture, household equipment, and new houses, problems would result. If no one buys, merchants will not make sales, factories will not need to produce goods, and, as a result, many people will lose their jobs. Ideally, what part of a person's income should be saved? Are there general rules for spending and saving for individuals? for families?
4. Lending institutions now compute interest for many differing time periods. Visit some lending institutions in your area and find out how much interest you could receive if you were to deposit $500 for one year. Find out what rates of interest would be paid and at what time period they would be compounded. Report your findings to your class; compare answers with other members of your class.
5. Find out from your local banks or savings and loan associations what kinds of investments they have made in your community with the money that has been placed in savings accounts in their institutions. Analyze how they have helped your community.

CHAPTER 31

Using a Savings Account

CHAPTER OBJECTIVES

After studying this chapter and completing the end-of-chapter activities, you will be able to:

1. Explain how to open and use a regular savings account.
2. Describe a certificate of deposit and explain its advantages.
3. Compare a NOW account with a money market account.
4. Explain several features of an IRA.
5. Name four things you should consider when deciding where to invest.

As you have learned, saving is simply postponing spending. It is taking some of what you have today and putting it aside so that you will have more to spend later. When you save, you are working toward the fulfillment of your goals.

A common way to put your savings to work for you is to use a savings account. You may be saving so you can provide for unexpected expenses or you may be saving for a trip or a special purchase. Savings accounts can be very valuable to you; but selecting an account from the many different savings account plans available today is not an easy matter.

Regular Savings Accounts

A savings account may be opened in a commercial bank, a savings bank, a savings and loan association, or a credit union. Opening a regular savings account in any of these institutions is similar to the procedure for opening a checking account. You fill out a signature card, make a deposit to your account, and receive a savings account passbook or a savings account register. A passbook, as shown in Figure 31–1, shows your deposits, withdrawals, interest earned, and the balance of your account. If a register is used, you

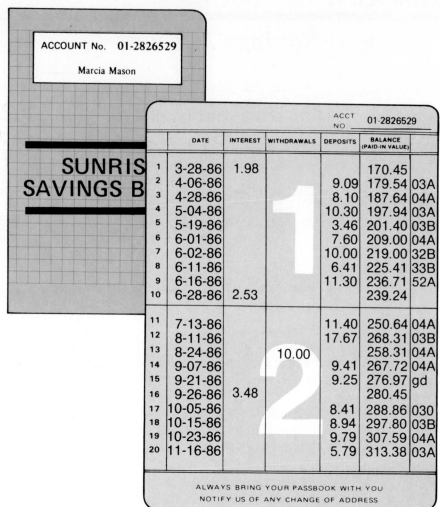

Figure 31–1
A savings account passbook provides a handy and complete record of account transactions. The teller records each transaction in your passbook.

ACCOUNT No.   01-2826529

Marcia Mason

SUNRIS
SAVINGS B

	DATE	INTEREST	WITHDRAWALS	DEPOSITS	BALANCE (PAID-IN VALUE)	
1	3-28-86	1.98			170.45	
2	4-06-86			9.09	179.54	03A
3	4-28-86			8.10	187.64	04A
4	5-04-86			10.30	197.94	03A
5	5-19-86			3.46	201.40	03B
6	6-01-86			7.60	209.00	04A
7	6-02-86			10.00	219.00	32B
8	6-11-86			6.41	225.41	33B
9	6-16-86			11.30	236.71	52A
10	6-28-86	2.53			239.24	
11	7-13-86			11.40	250.64	04A
12	8-11-86			17.67	268.31	03B
13	8-24-86		10.00		258.31	04A
14	9-07-86			9.41	267.72	04A
15	9-21-86			9.25	276.97	gd
16	9-26-86	3.48			280.45	
17	10-05-86			8.41	288.86	030
18	10-15-86			8.94	297.80	03B
19	10-23-86			9.79	307.59	04A
20	11-16-86			5.79	313.38	03A

ACCT NO ____ 01-2826529

ALWAYS BRING YOUR PASSBOOK WITH YOU
NOTIFY US OF ANY CHANGE OF ADDRESS

must record each deposit or withdrawal when it is made. The bank then sends a statement to you at the end of each month or quarter. This statement shows deposits and withdrawals, the addition of interest (if any), and the balance of the account.

When making a deposit, you fill out a deposit slip much like the ones used in making a checking account deposit. You present this slip, your passbook, and the money or checks you are depositing to the bank teller. The teller then enters the deposit in your passbook. If your bank uses savings account registers or electronic funds transfer (EFT), you will be given a receipt for your deposit. You must then enter the deposit on your register. You may also mail in your deposits.

Normally, checks cannot be written against a savings account. If you need money that is on deposit in your savings account, you must fill out a withdrawal slip. A withdrawal slip is a written request to take money out of your account. You give the withdrawal slip and your passbook to the bank clerk. Your withdrawal is then recorded in your passbook and your new balance is shown. Usually money cannot be withdrawn from a passbook savings account unless the passbook is presented.

If savings account registers are used, the teller checks the bank's records to make sure your balance is large enough to cover the withdrawal. After the withdrawal is recorded on the bank's records, you receive your money and a duplicate copy of the withdrawal slip for your records. You should record the withdrawal on your register to keep your balance current. Figure 31–2 shows entries that have been recorded in a register.

To discourage customers from using a regular savings account as a checking account, banks sometimes restrict the number of withdrawals that can be made. They may also charge a service fee for withdrawals. NOW accounts, as discussed in Chapter 17, should be used if you can maintain the minimum balance required. Although the number of checks you can write may be limited, you have the advantage of earning interest on your deposits.

Figure 31–2
If a savings account register is used, it's up to you to record each account transaction in the register.

DATE	MEMO	(-) AMOUNT OF WITHDRAWAL	(+) AMOUNT OF DEPOSIT	(+) INTEREST CREDITED	BALANCE *0*	00
July 2	opened account		15 00		+15	00
					15	00
July 25	part of summer earnings		50 00		+50	00
					65	00
aug. 5	birthday gift from parents		25 00		+25	00
					90	00
aug. 28	supplies for school	12 00			-12	00
					78	00
Sept. 1	interest received			75	+	75
					78	75

Special Savings Accounts

Savings institutions earn money by using your deposits to make other kinds of investments. The amount they can earn depends in part on how much money they have available to invest and how long they can invest it. So, if you make large deposits and leave that money in your account for specified periods of time (for example, some special accounts require a minimum deposit of $5,000 and you agree to leave that amount on deposit for 3 months), the savings institution can earn higher yields on its investments. They can then pay higher interest rates on your special account.

Special savings accounts are given different names by different institutions. The amount of interest earned also varies quite a bit. To earn a higher rate of interest, there usually are three special conditions which you need to keep in mind:

1. A minimum deposit ($100, $250, $500, $1000, or more) may be required.
2. Your money must be left on deposit for a certain period of time. This period varies from a few days to several years.
3. If your money is withdrawn before the stated time, much of your interest may be lost or penalties may be assessed.

Figure 31–3 lists a variety of special savings accounts. Note the minimum deposits required, the length of time the deposits must stay in the financial institution, and the yield that is possible from each of the savings plans. Figure 31–4 shows how one bank advertises its savings plans. Note the variation in compounding of interest, accessibility of funds, and special fees to be paid.

NOW Accounts

A NOW account is a combination of a savings account and a checking account. Interest is paid on the amount left on deposit. Generally you must maintain a minimum balance in your NOW account to earn interest. The rate of interest paid is usually higher than that paid for regular savings accounts. The account can be used in the same way that ordinary checking accounts are used, but the number of checks written on a NOW account may be limited.

Certificates of Deposit

Long-term time deposits which have certain restrictions and pay higher interest than regular savings accounts are commonly referred to as **certificates of deposits,** or "**CDs.**" When you purchase

	Minimum Deposit	Maturity	Yield
Passbook savings	None	None	5.5%
NOW accounts	Varies	None	5.25%
Super NOW accounts	$2,500*	None	Yields vary, average 7.20%
7-to-31-day time deposits	$2,500*	7-31 days	Yields vary
Money-market deposit accounts	$2,500*	None	Yields vary, average 8.47%
Short-term certificates	Varies	3 months	Yields vary, average 8.86%
	Varies	6 months	Yields vary, average 9.21%
	Varies	12 months	Yields vary, average 9.61%
Long-term certificates	Varies	2½ years	Yields vary, average 10.17%
	Varies	48 months	Yields vary, average 10.58%
	Varies	60 months	Yields vary, average 10.76%
IRA certificates	Varies	Varies	Yields vary

Figure 31–3
Not all savings accounts are the same. You need to know the conditions of the account you select.

a CD, you receive a certificate (see Figure 31–5 on page 431) instead of a passbook or a register. The certificate is numbered and is an important document. It indicates how much you deposited, what the interest rate will be, and when you may withdraw your deposit plus interest. The certificate lists the rules and regulations which must be followed for the certificate to be honored and the higher interest rate to be paid. It also states the penalties for withdrawing your deposit before the maturity date. To cash your CD, you must present and endorse it at the financial institution.

Money Market Accounts

Most savings accounts pay a specified rate of interest. In the business world, it is possible to earn various rates of interest depending upon the type of investment involved. The **money market,** a name given to reports of national credit and investment dealings, usually has relatively high rates of return compared with either

Savings Plans	Minimum Deposit	Term of Interest Rate	Interest Compounding	Accessibility	Fees Assessed
Statement Savings	$50	Fixed at 5½%	Quarterly	Anytime	When the balance falls below $100 at anytime during a calendar quarter, no interest will be paid for that quarter and a fee of $3.00 will be assessed.
The Money Market Account	$2,500	Varies weekly	Monthly*	Anytime	When the balance falls below $100 at anytime during a monthly statement cycle, no interest will be paid for that month and a fee of $3.00 will be assessed.
7-31 Day Certificate	$2,500	Fixed for 7-31 days	Simple	At maturity	None
91 Day Certificate	$2,500	Fixed for 91 days	Simple	At maturity	None
26 Week Money Market Certificate	$2,500	Fixed for 26 weeks	Simple*	At maturity	None
18 Month Small Saver Certificate	$500	Fixed for 18 months	Quarterly*	At maturity	None
30 Month Certificate	$500	Fixed for 30 months	Quarterly*	At maturity	None
Individual Retirement Account (Fixed Rate)	$50	Fixed for 18 months	Quarterly	At maturity	None
Individual Retirement Account (Variable Rate)	$50	Varies monthly	Quarterly	At maturity	None

*Interest payment options are available.

Figure 31–4
Financial institutions must inform their customers about the services they offer. This advertisement provides information about savings plans.

regular savings or NOW accounts. But, as mentioned in Chapter 18, money market dealings usually involve large sums of money.

Recent changes in regulations allow financial institutions to offer consumers special money market accounts. A **money market account** is one which pays a variable interest rate based on rates reported in the money markets. These accounts do not require long-term deposits. With these plans, the interest paid will vary daily or weekly. It is important to know the current rate when opening a money market account. Normally the yield from money market accounts will be much higher than regular savings but somewhat less than long-term CDs.

Individual Retirement Accounts

One of the recent changes in our tax laws permits you to plan ahead for your retirement in a unique way. You can set up a personal retirement plan called an Individual Retirement Account or IRA. An **IRA** is a special account which gives you an incentive to save for your future. You determine how much money to deposit (up to a certain limit per year) as well as how the money is to be invested. Most financial institutions offer one or more IRA plans. To qualify for an IRA you must have your own earned income and be under 70½ years of age. Currently, you may contribute up to $2,000 each year to your IRA. CDs and money market funds, in addition to a variety of other forms of investments, may be used in the IRA.

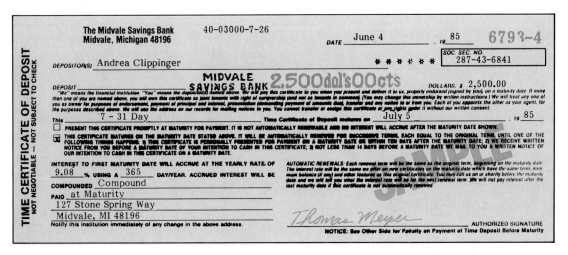

Figure 31–5
Many people find CDs an attractive way to save.

Because an IRA is considered a retirement plan, penalties are usually assessed if withdrawals are made prior to your reaching age 59½. One exception is if you incur a permanent disability. Young people must take the long time period into account in deciding whether or not to open an IRA. Money placed into an IRA should be considered unavailable for many years.

The IRA has another advantage that is important to many consumers: it is tax sheltered. That is, the amounts placed into an IRA are deducted from the individual's taxable income for that year. In addition to the fact that deposits are not taxed, earnings on IRAs also are not taxable until the time that they are withdrawn.

Illus. 31–1
IRAs help you save for the future and shelter your income today.

Reprinted by permission of Jefferson Communications, Inc., Reston, Va.

Where to Save

Today many types of financial institutions offer savings plans to consumers. Commercial banks, savings banks, savings and loan associations, and credit unions provide savings accounts for their customers. Some nonbank business firms, such as Sears, Roebuck and Co., also offer financial services. The institution you choose depends upon your individual situation.

In choosing a financial institution for your savings, your personal needs are very important. Your answers to the following questions can help you choose an institution that meets your needs: How much interest do you want to earn? What important services does the financial institution offer? How can the financial institution help you select the best savings plan for you from the available plans? What are the institution's business hours? Can you conveniently reach the financial institution, either in person or by telephone? How safe is your money in that institution?

The safety of your investment is an important consideration. As you learned in Chapter 17, special insurance corporations have been set up to protect the amounts on deposit in certain financial institutions. They include, the Federal Deposit Insurance Corporation (FDIC) and the Federal Savings and Loan Insurance Corporation (FSLIC). Deposits in credit unions are usually insured by an agency of either a federal or state government.

Illus. 31–2
There are many places where you can invest your savings. You must select the one that best meets your needs.

There are a number of things to consider when deciding where to invest your savings. For those who feel they can take greater risks, investing in stocks and bonds is still another investment alternative.

Adding to Your Business Vocabulary

The following terms should become part of your business vocabulary. For each numbered item, find the term that has the same meaning.

certificate of deposit (CD)   money market
IRA   money market account

1. Name given to reports of national credit and investment dealings.
2. A long-term time deposit which has certain restrictions and pays higher interest than regular savings.
3. A special account which pays a variable interest rate based on interest being paid in the money markets.
4. A special account which gives you incentive to save for your future.

Understanding Your Reading

1. What types of businesses offer savings accounts?
2. What steps would you follow in opening a savings account?
3. How does a depositor withdraw money from a savings account?
4. Why do financial institutions pay higher interest on special savings accounts?
5. Name three conditions that a depositor must accept to earn a higher rate of interest on a special savings account.
6. Why is the certificate you receive when you purchase a CD important?
7. Name two restrictions that are placed on IRAs?
8. Identify a special advantage of opening an IRA.
9. What should you consider in choosing a place to invest?

Putting Your Business Knowledge to Work

1. What characteristics of savings accounts make them especially good for students?
2. Financial institutions commonly pay a higher interest rate on special savings accounts than they do on regular accounts. Explain how they can afford to pay a higher interest rate on special accounts.
3. Give the name of a commercial bank, a savings and loan association, and a credit union in your community. What rate of interest does each pay on regular savings accounts?
4. What are some procedures that you should follow if you receive a savings account register rather than a passbook for your savings account? When should withdrawals and deposits be recorded in your register? How should the monthly or quarterly statements be used?

5. What is wrong with each of the following statements made by students who were discussing investing their savings:
   a. You can invest in a savings and loan association only if you plan to buy a house.
   b. Credit unions are run by labor unions.
   c. All young people should have IRAs.
   d. A bank is the only safe place for your money because a bank's accounts are insured by the government.
6. Melody Krider has $6 to invest; her older brother, Harmon, has received a gift of $2,000 which he wants to invest. Why should Melody consider a regular savings account rather than a special account? Why should Harmon consider a special savings account rather than a regular one?

Computing Business Problems

1. Joanne Olson plans to deposit $8 a month in a savings account.
   a. How much will she deposit in the first 6 months?
   b. If she then increases her monthly deposit to $11, how much will have been deposited in 12 months?
   c. How much will she have deposited in the first 18 months of her savings plan?
2. Three people had the following amounts deposited in regular savings accounts at different places: Dan Schweizer, $10,000 in a commercial bank; Margaret Zimmerman, $20,000 in a savings bank; and Stephanie Nudo, $45,000 in a savings and loan association. Each financial institution has insurance on account balances up to $100,000.
   a. What was the total amount of money invested by all three depositors?
   b. How much money would be lost (if any) by each depositor if all of these savings institutions went bankrupt?
3. Bernard Hamilton can earn 5 percent on a regular savings account, 8 percent on a CD, and 11 percent on a money market account. If he invests $5,000, how much interest will he earn in one year (compute simple interest) in each of these plans?

How much more will he earn on the money market account than he would with the regular savings account? If he decided to invest $2,000 in each plan, how much total interest (compute simple interest) would he earn in one year? In five years?
4. The table below shows the amount of money in savings deposits in four types of organizations for two recent years.

	Savings Deposits (in billions of dollars)	
	Year 1	Year 2
Commercial banks	$576.4	$1,023.8
Savings banks	158.2	163.1
Savings and loan associations	431.0	566.2
Credit unions	53.1	90.0

   a. What were the total deposits in all four types of organizations in each year?
   b. Which two organizations had the largest deposits in Year 2?
   c. In which type of organization did deposits increase the most in dollars from Year 1 to Year 2?
   d. What was the percent of increase between Year 1 and Year 2 in deposits received by credit unions?

Stretching Your Business Knowledge

1. Most savings institutions have a rule that permits them to delay the withdrawal of money from savings accounts if necessary. One bank has the following provision: "While it is extremely unlikely, the bank reserves the right to require depositors to give 30 days written notice of intent to withdraw funds." Why would institutions have such rules if they are seldom used?

2. The government does not guarantee that all investments will be successful. For example, it does not provide insurance for investments in land, stocks and bonds, or small businesses. Since it does not provide insurance against losses in other investments, why should it set up the Federal Deposit Insurance Corporation and the Federal Savings and Loan Insurance Corporation to insure deposits in banks and savings and loan associations?

3. A savings bank advertises its services under these headings: Business Services, Special Services, Savings Plans, Checking Accounts, and Loan Services. Under savings plans it lists: Golden Passbook, Certificates of Deposit, Regular Passbook, Individual Retirement Account, and Statement Savings Account. Each of these savings plans has special features and earns a different rate of interest. Visit one of your community's banks, or get some descriptive literature from them, and make a report to your class on the different kinds of savings plans which they offer. Find out what rules affect each of the plans and what the interest rates are for each plan.

CHAPTER 32

Stocks and Bonds for Investors

■ CHAPTER OBJECTIVES

After studying this chapter and completing the end-of-chapter activities, you will be able to:

1. Give three reasons why organizations sell bonds.
2. Explain how investing in bonds is different from investing in stocks.
3. Describe investment services offered by brokers.
4. Tell how an investment club operates.
5. List questions that should be answered when deciding whether or not to invest in stocks.

Depositing money in a savings account is an easy way to invest money. The variety of savings accounts available has made them popular with many consumers. But there are other ways to invest, too, such as buying stocks and bonds. Some people do not consider investing in stocks and bonds because they are unsure about the safety of such investments. Let's consider Alexis Ramirez, for example.

Alexis earns $45,000 a year as a data processing manager for an insurance company. He and his wife, Terress, have $22,000 in a savings account and own their home. They also have a good insurance program. One of his friends suggested that Alexis invest some of his savings in **securities**—a general term for stocks and bonds which are sold by corporations and governments to raise large sums of money. Alexis has heard about people who lost money by investing in stocks and bonds and wonders if stocks and bonds would be a good investment for his family.

Alexis is right to be concerned about the safety of investments. If you have only a small amount of savings, they should be invested where they are safe. They should also be liquid. But Alexis can increase the earnings on his savings and still have safe investments.

After they learn more about stocks and bonds, Alexis and Terress will be in a better position to decide whether or not to invest in securities and what kinds to consider.

Investing in Bonds

Bonds are sold by the federal government, by local and state governments, and by many corporations. Because there are so many types of bonds, it is helpful to know the answers to two questions: What is a bond? Why are bonds sold?

A **bond** is a printed promise to pay a definite amount of money, with interest, at a specified time. Bonds are similar to the promissory notes discussed in Chapter 27. When you buy a bond, you are lending money to the organization selling the bond. You become its creditor. Interest is typically paid twice a year on most bonds. Each bond has its face value printed on the front of the certificate. The **face value** is the amount being borrowed by the seller of the bond. Interest is paid to the investor on that amount. The face value is paid on the bond's maturity date.

Corporate and Municipal Bonds

Bonds are sold to raise large sums of money for a specific purpose. A corporation may want to build a new office building. A city may want to build a new park. Bonds issued by corporations are called **corporate bonds.** Bonds issued by city and state governments are called **municipal bonds.** Municipal bonds have an advantage over corporate bonds since federal or state income tax may not have to be paid on the interest earned on municipal bonds. That encourages people to buy municipal bonds even though the interest rate may not be as high as that offered on corporate bonds.

Corporate and municipal bonds are normally sold in $1,000 amounts. Municipal bonds often are sold in smaller amounts and pay a lower rate of interest than corporate bonds. Municipal bonds, however, are usually considered to be the safer investment.

Federal Savings Bonds

The safest investments in securities, especially for small investors, are federal government savings bonds. There are several types of these bonds but the series EE savings bonds are the most popular. Series EE bonds can be purchased for as little as $25 or as much as $5,000. See Figure 32-1.

Illus. 32–1
School districts often issue bonds to raise cash needed for operation or expansion.

Savings bonds are bought at a lower price than their face value. For example, Series EE bonds are bought at half their face value. A $50 Series EE bond costs $25. When the bond is cashed in (redeemed) at the end of the stated period, the government pays the face value. The difference between the cost of $25 and the face value of $50 is interest earned. A lower amount of interest is earned if these bonds are cashed before the end of the stated time period.

Figure 32–1
A series EE savings bond with a face value of $100.

The stated time period for Series EE bonds is 10 years. A Series EE bond held beyond 10 years continues to accumulate interest.

In addition to being a safe investment, federal savings bonds are easy to purchase. Alexis can purchase Series EE bonds at his local bank. Or he may wish to have an amount deducted from his paychecks to go toward the purchase of savings bonds. For example, Alexis could have $10 deducted from each week's paycheck. At the end of 5 weeks his employer would use the $50 to buy a $100 bond for him. This is a convenient way to invest in federal savings bonds.

Investing in Stocks

Investing in stocks is quite different from investing in bonds. When you invest in bonds, you lend money. When you invest in stock, you become a part owner of a firm. As you learned in Chapter 6, you become a stockholder when you buy one or more shares in a corporation. Ownership is shown by a printed form known as a stock certificate. If a business is profitable, part of the profits may be paid to the stockholders in the form of dividends.

The chance to earn a high rate of return attracts many people to invest in stocks. But the risk of losing your investment is usually greater with stocks than with bonds. A company must pay bondholders the rate of interest promised before it can pay any dividends to stockholders. If there is not enough money left to pay dividends or if the company decides to use the money earned for business expansion, stockholders receive no dividends. If a company goes out of business, a stockholder may get little or nothing back from the investment. Bondholders, on the other hand, are more certain of getting back the amount invested plus interest.

On the other hand, the market value of the stock may increase. The **market value** is the price at which a share of stock can be bought or sold. The market value of the stock of a business which is doing well usually goes up. Market value drops when the record of a business is poor or the economy is weak.

Preferred Stock

Preferred stock is one of two main classes of stock issued by corporations. **Preferred stock** has priority over common stock in the payment of dividends. A preferred stockholder, for example, is paid first if profits are used to pay any stock dividends.

The dividends paid to preferred stockholders are usually limited to a certain rate, such as 6 percent. The stock certificate shows the rate to be paid. Preferred stock may also have priority on the return of the amount invested if the firm goes out of business. Preferred stock is less risky than common stock.

Common Stock

Common stock provides ownership in a company and shared profits, but it has no stated dividend rate. Common stockholders receive dividends only after preferred stockholders are paid their share of any dividends. Yet, if the profits of a company are large, the common stockholders may receive more in dividends than preferred stockholders. For example, suppose that a company has issued $100,000 worth of common stock and $100,000 worth of preferred stock with a stated dividend rate of 6 percent. If the company earns a profit of $20,000 and pays dividends, preferred stockholders would be paid $6,000 in dividends ($100,000 × .06 = 6,000). The remainder, or $14,000 ($20,000 − $6,000), would be available to pay dividends to the common stockholders. If all of the profits are paid out in dividends, the common stockholders would be paid $14,000, a return of 14 percent.

Illus. 32–2
Wall Street in New York City is the financial heart of the United States, and home of the New York Stock Exchange.

Another incentive to buy common stock is the chance that its value will increase. The market price of a share of common stock can change rapidly — either up or down. Common stockholders expect the value of their shares to increase.

Buying Stocks and Bonds

If Terress and Alexis Ramirez decide to buy some stocks or bonds, they will probably contact someone to help them. They may go to a broker or a banker.

Help In Buying and Selling

Illus. 32–3
Exchanges specialize in buying and selling stocks and bonds.

A **broker** is a specialist who helps investors buy and sell stocks and bonds. For their services, brokers charge a fee called a **commission.** Brokers work through **exchanges**, which are business organizations that specialize in the buying and selling of securities. While there are many exchanges in the U.S., the best known are the New York Stock Exchange, the American Stock Exchange and the Midwest Stock Exchange. Brokers throughout the nation deal directly with these exchanges by telephone and by computer.

Some banks also buy and sell stocks for their customers. Buying stocks at a bank where you regularly conduct business may be the first stock investment step for you. Commissions charged by banks often are lower than those charged by brokerage houses. But banks may not offer the advice and research services that are offered by brokers.

The prices at which stocks and bonds are bought and sold change constantly. Through brokers, stockholders state prices at which they are willing to sell their shares. Interested buyers tell brokers what they would be willing to pay for those shares. The brokers then work out a price that is acceptable to both. The highest, lowest, and closing prices at which stocks sell are listed in the newspaper for every business day, as shown in Figure 32–2.

Questions To Be Answered

In selecting a stock or bond to purchase, you should learn about the business record of the firm. Has the company been profitable? Does its management seem to make good decisions? Is the company likely to grow in the coming years? Brokers spend much of their time studying stocks and price trends. They are able to provide helpful information and recommend stocks to their customers.

There also are personal questions to be considered. For instance, ask yourself which of these factors are most important to your personal investment plan: safety, liquidity, or rate of return?

Figure 32–2
Most newspapers provide a stock market summary every business day.

The current dividend rate in dollars per year.

The hundreds of shares sold during the day.

The highest price in dollars at which a sale was made during the day.

The lowest price at which a sale was made during the day.

The last price at which a sale was made during the day.

The net change between the closing price and the closing price of the preceding day.

Div.	Sales in 100's	Hi	Lo	Clo.	Net Chg.		Div.	Sales in 100's	Hi	Lo	Clo.	Net Chg.
MesaR 1.72e	6	30¼	30	30¼	+ ½	Pacif pf4.07		23	32½	32⅛	32⅜	+1⅛
Mesab .78e	355	7⅜	7	7⅛	+ ⅛	PainWb .60		3172	42½	40½	42	+1½
Mestek	6	3½	3½	3½	- ⅛	PainW pf2.25		787	33¾	32¼	33½	+1¼
MtE pfG7.68	z100	u53¼	53¼	53¼	+1¼	PalmBc 1.20		133	37⅞	37⅞	37⅞	......
MtE pf8.32	z10	56½	56½	56½	......	PanABk .70		108	26⅞	26¼	26⅞	+ ⅝
MexFd .17e	252	2¾	2½	2¾	......	PanAm		1266	4⅜	4¼	4⅜	......
MhCn pf2.05	4	19¼	19¼	19¼	- ¾	PanA wt		388	2	2	2½	......
MhCn pf3.19	45	u26¼	26	26	......	Pandck n.20		545	u20½	19½	20¼	+ ½
MchER 1.38	18	15¾	15⅜	15¾	- ⅛	PanhEC 2.30		777	37⅞	37¼	37¾	+ ½
Micklb s.06	11	6¼	6¼	6¼	......	PantPr		843	4½	4⅜	4⅜	- ⅛
Midcon 2.36	779	44¾	43¾	44½	+ ½	Paprcft .80		98	16	15¾	15⅞	- ⅛
MidSUt 1.78	7127	014¾	14⅛	14⅜	+ ⅛	Pardyn		1064	16¾	16¼	16½	+ ¼
MidRos 1	144	19¾	19	19¼	......	ParkE s		175	17	16	16⅞	+ ⅞
MWE 2.68	64	27	26⅝	26⅞	+ ⅛	ParkDrl .16		911	7½	6⅞	7½	+ ⅜
MiltnR .40	9	14⅞	14⅞	14⅞	+ ⅛	ParkH 1.12		275	39⅜	38¾	39⅜	+ ⅛
MMM 3.50	3722	85½	84½	84¾	+ ⅜	ParkPn .52		103	16½	15⅞	16½	+ ⅜
MinPL 2.76	123	30⅜	30⅜	30½	+ ⅛	PatPtrl	,1001	2⅜	2¼	2¼	- ⅛
Misnins	458	8⅛	7¾	7⅞	- ¼	PayINW .34		10	26⅞	26⅞	26⅞	- ⅛
MoPSv 1.32b	21	20¾	20¾	20¾	+ ⅛	PayNP .60		400	14	13⅜	14	+ ⅛
MoPS pr2.61	2	21¾	21¾	21¾	- ¼	PayCsh .16		3527	19⅞	19½	19⅞	+ ⅜
MoPS pf4.13	7	32⅞	32⅞	32½	+ ½	Peabdy .20		323	9	8¾	9	+ ¼
Mitel	1254	7¾	7⅜	7¾	+ ⅛	Pengo		676	1⅛	⅞	1⅛	+3-16
Mobil 2.20	11014	29⅛	28¼	29	+ ⅜	PenCen		656	53⅜	52¾	53½	+ ¾

From your answer, an investment plan can be determined. As shown in Figure 32–3, no single investment can give you the highest possible return and still be very liquid and safe.

Also consider your savings. If you have little put aside as savings, you will want safe and liquid investments. Low-risk bonds could be included in your investment plan. If your savings are more than adequate for your basic needs, however, investing in stocks to gain a higher rate of return may be advisable. Your investment goals should be determined carefully.

Figure 32–3
Your investment goals will determine which investments are best for you.

Which Investment?	How Safe?	How Liquid?	How Is Rate of Return?
Savings accounts	Excellent	Excellent	Fair to Good
Savings bonds	Excellent	Very good	Good
Other bonds	Very good	Good	Good
Preferred stocks	Fair to good	Good	Very good
Common stocks	Fair	Good	Poor to excellent

Investing in Stocks with a Group

Some investors like to join with others in making investments. There are several advantages in doing so. Investment clubs and mutual funds are two common ways you can pool your investments.

Investment Clubs

An **investment club** is a small group of people who organize to invest their money. An agreement is usually drawn up which states how often the club will meet and how much the members will invest each month. At the meetings, members report on stocks they have studied. The group makes decisions on what stocks or bonds to buy. The club's earnings are shared in proportion to the members' investments. Brokers often help groups form investment clubs.

One advantage of an investment club is that membership encourages regular saving. Another advantage is that you learn a great deal about how to judge a stock. Members of the club spread their risk because the combined funds of all members are used to buy stocks in a number of corporations. If the club loses money on one investment, the loss may be offset by other investments that do quite well.

Mutual Funds

Investment clubs are not for everyone. You may not want to take the time needed to study stocks and bonds and make decisions. A good understanding of securities is needed to purchase wisely. A mutual fund is an alternative, and it takes some of the worry and problems out of investing.

Mutual funds are funds managed by a company which receives money from many investors and buys and sells a wide variety of stock or bonds. Investors receive shares of the mutual fund. Part of the interest and dividends received from investments are used to pay operating expenses. The amount that is left may be distributed to the mutual fund shareholders or reinvested.

An investor may choose a mutual fund because of the kinds of securities that are included in the fund. Some mutual fund companies invest in bonds, preferred stocks, and common stock (balanced funds). Some buy only common stock of young, fast-growing companies (growth funds). Some companies invest only in securities that pay good dividends and interest (income funds). A few investment companies invest only in municipal bonds which pay high interest rates. There are hundreds of funds available. It should not be difficult for Alexis and Terress to find a fund that will meet their needs.

Deciding Whether or not to Buy Stocks

The decision to buy stocks should be made carefully. It would be possible for Alexis and Terress to increase their savings quite a bit if the right stock purchases were made. But they could also lose all or most of what they invest. That is a risk they must be willing and able to take.

One important guide in the decision to buy stocks is whether you can afford to lose part or all of your investment. If you have to sell your stock quickly, it might sell for much less than the amount you paid for it. Before investing in stocks you should have adequate savings in a safe place, such as in a savings account or in bonds. You also should have sufficient insurance coverage. The money invested in stocks should not be needed to meet basic living expenses.

*A*dding to Your Business Vocabulary

The following terms should become part of your business vocabulary. For each numbered item, find the term that has the same meaning.

bond
broker
commission
common stock
corporate bonds
exchange
face value

investment club
market value
municipal bonds
mutual fund
preferred stock
securities

1. A specialist who helps investors buy and sell stocks and bonds.
2. Bonds issued by city and state governments.
3. Another name for stocks and bonds.
4. A printed promise to pay a definite amount of money, with interest, at a specified time.
5. Stock that has priority in payment of dividends and in return of the investment.
6. A fee charged by brokers for their services.
7. A fund managed by a company which receives money from many investors and buys and sells a wide variety of stocks or bonds.
8. The price at which a share of stock can be bought and sold.
9. Stock which provides ownership and shared profits but that has no stated dividend rate.
10. A small group of people who organize to study stocks and invest members' money.
11. A special place of business where stocks and bonds are bought and sold.
12. The amount borrowed by the seller of a bond.
13. Bonds issued by corporations.

*U*nderstanding Your Reading

1. Why do businesses and other organizations sell bonds?
2. How much does a $50 Series EE bond cost? What is the difference between the purchase price and the face value called?
3. What are two ways in which you might buy Series EE bonds?
4. In what ways is investing in bonds different from investing in stocks?
5. When might common stock pay more dividends than preferred stock?
6. What are some of the services that a broker offers persons who are interested in buying stocks?
7. Who selects the stocks that are purchased through an investment club?
8. What are the advantages of a mutual fund?
9. What are some important points to consider when deciding whether or not to purchase stocks?

*P*utting Your Business Knowledge to Work

1. Compare bonds and promissory notes.
2. Why does the government pay a higher rate of interest on Series EE bonds held for their full time than if cashed in earlier?
3. Why do municipal bonds usually pay a lower rate of interest than corporate bonds?
4. Company A wants to borrow $1,000. Company B wants to borrow $10,000. Company C wants to borrow $1,000,000. Which business is most likely to issue bonds? Why?
5. Give several reasons why people buy stocks even though they are not as safe as other investments.
6. Why would a broker be interested in helping a group of people form an investment club?
7. One mutual fund is advertised as a growth fund. Another is advertised as an income fund. What would you expect to be the difference in the investment practices of the two funds?
8. Susan Haugen bought $5,000 worth of gold mining stocks a few years ago. Last week she received a letter saying that the company went out of business. It could not operate profitably so it closed down. How much of her investment might Miss Haugen lose?
9. Robert Holihan wants to invest in stocks that will be very safe, highly liquid, and earn an excellent income. What is wrong with his investment goals?
10. On January 1 Carl Nees purchased one share of stock for $100 plus a broker's commission of $7. At the end of the year the stock's market value was $114. Has Carl earned an income on his investment, at least on paper?

*C*omputing Problems in Business

1. Shana Lindsay bought the following Series EE bonds: three $50 bonds, and one $5,000 bond.
   a. How much did she pay for the bonds?
   b. How much will the bonds be worth when the stated time period is reached?
   c. How much interest will she have earned when the stated time period is reached.
2. Jerome Aili owns five Morgan Enterprises bonds, each with a face value of $5,000. Morgan Enterprises pays 8 percent interest on the bonds it has issued.
   a. How much interest does Jerome receive each year on each bond?
   b. What is the total amount of interest Jerome receives each year?
   c. If the interest payments are made semiannually to each bondholder, how much total interest does Jerome receive every 6 months?
3. At the stock exchange, the last sale on Tuesday for the Dandy Auto Corporation was $9.50. The next day it closed at $11.
   a. How much was the net change from Tuesday to Wednesday?
   b. By what percent did the stock increase in value between the close of the first and the close of the second day?
   c. How much would 100 shares have cost on Tuesday at the closing price?
4. The table on page 448 shows the price paid and the annual dividend on six different stocks. What is the rate of return on each of these stocks?

	Price Paid	Annual Dividend
Consolidated Engineering	$48	$2.40
Electro-Jet Company	50	3.00
Federated Industries	30	1.60
Instrumentation, Inc.	30	1.30
Magus Corporation	38	1.90
Seaboard Steel	65	2.60

Stretching Your Business Knowledge

1. U.S. savings bonds pay competitive rates of interest today. For many years they paid relatively low rates of interest. Give several reasons why the rate has been increased.

2. Within a few weeks the market price of a stock decreased from $32¾ per share to $26½. Find out several possible causes for such a decrease.

3. Check the library to find what each of the following pairs of terms about stocks and bonds means:
   a. registered bond and coupon bond
   b. callable bond and convertible bond
   c. par value stock and no-par value stock
   d. cumulative preferred stock and non-cumulative preferred stock
   e. load fund and no-load fund.

4. The National Association of Investment Clubs (NAIC) can be of great assistance to persons who want to form an investment club. Through research in your library, by writing to the NAIC, or by contacting a stock broker, make a report on the specific aids available for persons interested in organizing an investment club. Why might it be a good idea for someone unfamiliar with stocks to join an investment club?

5. The financial or business section of many daily newspapers includes a list of mutual funds. Study such a list; then answer these questions:
   a. Which fund has the highest price per share? The lowest?
   b. What is the difference in meanings between the headings "bid" and "asked"? (Check the library for your answer.)

CHAPTER 33

Real Estate as an Investment

You have already learned about a variety of savings plans and investment opportunities. Investment opportunities exist in still other areas and should also be considered. Investors may deal in coins; stamps; antiques; commodities; precious metals, such as gold and silver; and real estate. To invest wisely in such items, investors must know what they are buying and the potential for gaining or losing from their investments. This is especially true of real estate, an investment that concerns almost everyone at some time. **Real estate** is land and anything that is attached to it.

Nearly two out of three families own real estate. It is very likely that you, too, will own some kind of real estate. Because real estate is an important investment that you will probably make, it will be helpful for you to learn about real estate ownership. Let's begin where thoughts about owning real estate often begin, the need for housing.

When Andy and Carrie Redfield were first married, one of their problems was meeting their housing needs. Buying a house was one of their goals, but was not immediately possible. They decided to rent an apartment as their first real estate transaction.

Renting a Place to Live

Paying rent to live in a house or an apartment is not a real estate investment. However, it is an alternative to consider in meeting your housing needs. Andy and Carrie were aware of the advantages of renting when they decided to rent an apartment. One advantage of renting is that it is easier to move if you do not have a house to sell. You may, however, have to agree to rent for a certain period of time. Renters are free from much of the work and expense of keeping property in good condition. They are expected to take good care of the property, but most repairs are the responsibility of the owners. Renting makes it easier to keep money available for immediate use. With too much of your savings invested in a house, for instance, you may not have money available to pay emergency bills. Those who purchase houses need some savings in addition to the amount paid for the house.

Owning a Mobile Home

Purchasing a mobile home can be a step toward owning a house. During their first few years of married life, Andy worked as a mechanic and Carrie worked as a computer operator. They saved as much of their income as possible. Because they changed jobs and locations several times, renting was ideal for them. When Carrie and Andy began working for large corporations, however, they were ready to settle down. But they still could not afford a house. After careful consideration, they decided to withdraw part of their savings, borrow a small sum of money, and buy a mobile home.

To Carrie and Andy Redfield, the biggest advantage of the mobile home was owning a place of their own. Buying a mobile home also was less expensive than buying a house. And since their monthly payments were smaller, they could still save part of their incomes. The Redfields planned to use their savings, plus the money they would get later from selling the mobile home, to buy a house someday.

Owning a House

Andy and Carrie built up their savings over a number of years. Their family now includes two children, and they are ready to buy a house.

Advantages

The advantages of owning a house are similar to those of owning a mobile home. Homeowners experience the pride of ownership. They can remodel or improve their house as they wish. There is also a feeling of security. People who own the houses they live in tend to move less frequently and to become stable members of their communities.

There are also important advantages in home ownership from an investment standpoint. Homeowners receive tax benefits, such as being able to deduct the cost of interest payments and real estate taxes when calculating income taxes. **Equity**, the difference between what your house and property are worth and what you owe on it, builds up over the years. After Andy and Carrie had lived in their house for five years, they owed $35,000. Their house had cost them $60,000. Now, because of **appreciation**, the amount of increase in the value of property, their house is worth $65,000. Their

Illus. 33–1
To buy or to lease? Consider the options carefully. Each has advantages and disadvantages.

equity is $30,000 ($65,000 − $35,000). Appreciation and equity are two important factors to keep in mind when considering a house as an investment.

Costs

While equity and appreciation are important investment considerations, there also are costs which must be considered. Important costs which occur yearly include taxes, insurance, upkeep, and interest.

1. Taxes. Local property taxes are one of the certain costs of home ownership. Taxes are not the same in all communities, but they tend to increase from year to year. On the average, they are about 3 percent of the market value of the property.

   The tax rate is based on the **assessed value** of the home. This is the amount which the property is determined by the government to be worth for tax purposes. The assessed value is often quite a bit less than the actual market value of the property. For example, a house which can be sold for $80,000 may be assessed at only $40,000.

   The property tax rate is stated as dollars per $1,000 of assessed value. If the tax rate is $60 per $1,000 of assessed value, the annual taxes on the property assessed at $40,000 would be $2,400. This is 6 percent of the assessed value but only 3 percent of the market value of the property.

   Before you buy a house, you should know the assessed value of your property. You should also learn about the tax rate to determine how much you must allow in your budget to cover the costs of taxes.

2. Insurance. The cost of insurance is usually much less than the cost of taxes, but it is an important expense of home ownership. The cost of insurance is affected by the value of the house, the material from which it is made, how near it is to other buildings, and the availability of fire protection. The annual cost of insurance is about ½ of 1 percent of the market value of the house, or $5 for each $1,000 of value.

3. Upkeep. **Upkeep** refers to the cost of keeping your property in good condition. It is a cost that must be kept in mind. Annual upkeep costs average about two percent of a house's value. The costs do not necessarily occur every year. But, if repairs are delayed too long, the house will fall into poor condition and the cost of repairing it will increase.

Illus. 33–2
Many hidden
expenses and
responsibilities
accompany
home ownership.

4. Interest. Most people must borrow money to buy a house. The amount borrowed often is large, and the house is used as security for the loan. The lender receives a mortgage. A **mortgage** is a legal document giving the lender a claim against the house if the principal, the interest, or both are not paid as agreed. The borrower usually agrees to make a payment every month over the life of the mortgage. The amount of the monthly payment varies according to the amount of the loan, the interest rate, and the number of payments to be made. The monthly payment includes repayment of part of the principal plus interest. Some mortgage payments also include an amount to cover taxes and insurance on the house.

When the Redfields bought their house at a cost of $60,000, they paid $20,000 down and borrowed $40,000 for 20 years at an interest rate of 12 percent. The monthly payment to the bank was $440.44. (See Figure 33–1). Payment tables often are used by lenders to determine the monthly rate needed to repay the principal and interest on mortgage loans.

MONTHLY HOUSE PAYMENTS AT 12% INTEREST				
Amount Borrowed	5 Years	10 Years	20 Years	25 Years
$ 5,000	$ 111.23	$ 71.74	$ 55.06	$ 52.57
10,000	222.45	143.48	110.11	105.33
20,000	444.90	286.95	220.22	210.65
30,000	667.34	443.42	330.33	315.97
40,000	889.78	573.89	440.44	421.29
50,000	1,112.23	717.36	550.55	526.62

Figure 33–1
The monthly house payment is usually the largest item in a family's budget.

Interest rates on mortgages are traditionally set for long periods of time and do not change during the life of the mortgage. These are called **fixed rate mortgages.** But market interest rates generally increase or decrease quite a bit during the life of a mortgage depending upon economic conditions. Therefore, it is now common for lenders to offer an **adjustable rate mortgage (ARM).** The interest rate of an ARM is changed up or down periodically depending upon the current interest rate being charged by lenders. Monthly payments for ARMs often are lower, especially in the early years of the mortgage, compared with fixed rate mortgages. As with all loans, it is wise for consumers to shop around for mortgages to get the one that best fits their needs and circumstances.

Condominium Living

When the life-style of a person or family changes, the need for housing also changes. Carrie and Andy Redfield, for instance, outgrew their need for a house. Their children moved away and the house became too large for them. It became difficult to handle the upkeep work.

The Redfields sold their house. Since they received more than they had paid for it, the house proved to be a good investment for them. But what would they do now? They considered renting, but they still liked the idea of owning their home. They decided to look into condominiums. A **condominium** is an individually owned unit of an apartment-like building or complex.

Condominiums give people the advantages of home ownership without some of the difficulties. Upkeep of the lawn and shrubbery is usually done by others for a service fee. And condominiums are sometimes less costly than houses. This makes them attractive to young couples, singles, and retirees as well.

Other Real Estate Investments

There are many types of real estate investments. Buying a home to live in is only one type. Some people buy two-family houses and live in one half while renting the other. The rented half helps to pay for the property. The homeowner, of course, is responsible for the upkeep of the property. Real estate investors may also buy an apartment building and hire someone to manage it. Still other investors buy land and then hope to sell it when the market value goes up.

Shared-time property purchase plans are popular in many areas of the country. The property involved in these plans is usually resort or recreational property. There are several owners, and a schedule is made up to determine who will occupy and enjoy the property at certain times of the year. This property generally is quite expensive and is used by owners for short periods of time. The shared-time plan allows persons to invest in property which they could not otherwise afford to buy.

Illus. 33–3
In many cities, older buildings are being renovated and sold as condominiums.

There are also people who form groups to purchase real estate as an investment only. They combine their money to purchase apartment buildings, shopping centers, or other commercial buildings. The money received from rents and the increases in the value of the properties make this kind of investment attractive to some investors.

Getting Help with Real Estate Transactions

Buying and selling real estate is complicated. Most consumers are not likely to be knowledgeable about such matters. Therefore, it is important to hire specialists to help you avoid problems in real estate transactions.

Realtors are experts in buying and selling real estate. They receive special training and are licensed by states to do business. Land, houses, apartments, condominiums, and other properties are listed for sale with realtors. Realtors can help you think about what you want in real estate and then compare the different real estate investment opportunities that are available. The realtor helps work out a purchase price that is acceptable to both the buyer and the seller. The realtor may also help a buyer get a mortgage.

Before signing any papers and before deciding on how much to pay for a house, you should get an appraiser's report. An **appraiser** is an expert who estimates the value of property. The appraiser also reports on the quality of construction and identifies repairs that may be needed.

To prevent legal problems, it is important for you to hire a lawyer. A lawyer is needed during several stages of buying and selling. For instance, when you are buying real estate you should be certain that you are obtaining a good title to the property. You need a lawyer's opinion that you are obtaining complete and clear ownership of the property. There may be claims against the property for which the new owner will be responsible. If there are unpaid taxes on the property, these taxes are a claim against the property itself. If they are not paid, the property may be taken and sold so that the government may collect the taxes. A lawyer can help you avoid these and other legal problems.

Adding to Your Business Vocabulary

The following terms should become part of your business vocabulary. For each numbered item, find the term that has the same meaning.

adjustable rate mortgage (ARM)   fixed rate mortgage
appraiser   mortgage
appreciation   real estate
assessed value   realtor
condominium   upkeep
equity

1. Land and anything attached to it.
2. An expert in buying and selling real estate.
3. An individually owned unit of an apartment-like building or complex.
4. The amount of increase in the value of property.
5. The cost of keeping property in good condition.
6. An expert in estimating the value of property.
7. The difference between what your house is worth and what you owe on your mortgage.

8. A traditional mortgage with an interest rate that does not change during the life of the mortgage.
9. The amount which property is determined to be worth for tax purposes.
10. A mortgage where the interest rate changes up or down periodically depending upon the current interest rates.
11. A legal document giving the lender a claim against the property if the principal, interest, or both are not paid as agreed.

Understanding Your Reading

1. Name two advantages of owning a house and two advantages of renting an apartment.
2. Why is owning a mobile home a good way for some people to get started in home ownership?
3. What items, in addition to the original cost, are included in the cost of owning a house?
4. On the average, the annual cost of taxes is what percent of the market value of the property?
5. What should you find out about taxes on property you want to buy?

6. What factors help determine the amount charged for insurance on a house?
7. What percent of the market value of a house do the annual costs for upkeep average?
8. What factors help to determine the amount you have to pay each month on your mortgage?
9. Name some ways of investing in real estate other than buying property in which you will live.
10. In what ways can realtors, appraisers, and lawyers help in real estate transactions?

Putting Your Business Knowledge to Work

1. Blair West owns a house which has a value of $80,000. For the past three years the upkeep has averaged less than $500 a year. Can Mr. West assume that his expenses will be only $500 in future years?
2. Why is a condominium often desirable to retired people? to others?
3. What can you do to help assure the increase in value of a home you purchase?
4. Under what circumstances is an adjustable-rate mortgage better for a buyer than a fixed-rate mortgage?
5. Robin Greer has decided to purchase a house. She has also decided to take care of all the details herself and avoid paying a realtor, an appraiser, or a lawyer. Why might Robin find that her decision is not a good one?

Computing Business Problems

1. The Brocks own a house valued at $65,000 and they have a balance on their mortgage of $40,000. Last year they had the following expenses:

Interest on mortgage	$4,000
Upkeep	900
Insurance	250
Taxes	1,500

   a What was the total of their expenses for last year?
   b. What is the amount of equity the Brocks have in their house?
2. Don Smith invests $10,000 with a group that buys apartment buildings as investments. At the end of the first year, he received earnings of 10 percent of his investment.
   a. What amount did he receive the first year?
   b. If he receives the same amount for the next 6 years, what is the total he will receive?
3. Bill Fields has been renting an apartment for three years and pays $250 per month for rent. He has an opportunity to buy a house which will require him to pay $320 per month as a mortgage payment.

   a. In one year, how much more will he have to pay for house payments than he now pays for rent?
   b. During the first year, 90 percent of each payment will be for interest and 10 percent will be for principal repayment. What will be the amount he pays for interest for the year? for principal repayment for the year?
4. Gold is considered to be a good investment in addition to real estate, stocks, and bonds. Yet the price of gold has changed drastically over the past few years. Gold is priced on the basis of troy ounces. The chart on page 459 shows the price per troy ounce of gold over a three-year period. Use the chart to answer the following questions:
   a. What was the highest price paid for gold in the first year? the second year? the third year?
   b. How much did the price of gold increase from the beginning of the first year to the end of the second year? What was the percent of increase?
   c. How much did gold decrease in price during the third year? What was the percent of decrease?

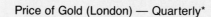

Price of Gold (London) — Quarterly*

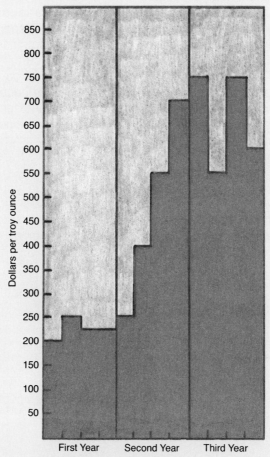

(*At end of each quarter; rounded to the nearest $25.)
Source: First National Monetary Corporation.

Stretching Your Business Knowledge

1. Investigate the changes in rents charged for apartments in your community over the past five years. What factors have caused rents to increase or decrease? Report your findings to your class.

2. Visit a local realtor's office or invite a realtor to speak to your class. Find out what you can about the changing values of real estate in your community. Also find out about some of the problems that people are having today with the purchase of houses and other real estate.

3. Call or visit a bank or savings and loan association. Ask for information about getting a mortgage on a home costing $50,000. Get answers to the following questions and make a report to your class:
   a. What is the minimum down payment needed?
   b. What is the average interest rate for a fixed-rate mortgage?
   c. What is the current rate on an adjustable-rate mortgage?
   d. What is the monthly payment on a 25-year loan at the current interest rate if the minimum down payment is made?
   e. If you decide to repay the loan early, will there be a financial penalty?
4. Investing in precious metals is an investment alternative that is attractive to many people. Precious metals commonly purchased by investors today include gold, silver, platinum, and copper. Check several newspapers and magazines or talk with precious metal dealers to determine the current price of each of these metals. Find out what trends there have been in the price of each precious metal. Do you consider investing in one or more of these precious metals to be a good idea? Why or why not?
5. Cooperatives are places to live that are somewhat like condominiums. Through research in your library, find out what cooperatives are and how they are like and unlike condominiums. Make a report of your findings.

CAREER CATEGORY: Investments

There are many ways in which people can save and invest their money. Some people turn to savings and investment workers for guidance and assistance in choosing just the right plan. This results in employment opportunities for those interested in helping others plan their financial futures.

Job Titles: Job titles commonly found in this career area include:

Securities Clerk	Securities Analyst
Real Estate Clerk	Stock Broker
Order Clerk	Stock Specialist
Comparison Clerk	Investment Advisor
Figuration Clerk	Investment Counselor
Transfer Clerk	Real Estate Agent
Margin Clerk	Real Estate Broker
Receive and Deliver Clerk	Real Estate Appraiser

Employment Outlook: The job demand in this career area is expected to be better than average with securities salespersons and real estate agents being in highest demand. Clerical workers are used in a variety of areas with securities and real estate firms; the need for clerical workers in this career area will parallel the general trend.

Future Changes: It is anticipated that more and more individuals will find it possible and desirable to become involved in securities investments; this will tend to increase the demand for securities sales workers. However, as the use of automation increases and as banks and discount brokers expand their securities sales operations, the need will be somewhat lessened. Real estate workers will be needed to respond to what is anticipated to be a growing demand for housing and other properties.

What Is Done on the Job: Clerical workers in this area perform a variety of functions related to the purchase and sale of stocks and real estate. Familiarity with legal terminology as well as the technical terms used is desirable.

Securities analysts work with market, economic, and company data to determine the desirability of investing in certain stocks. Sales workers generally serve as brokers; they meet with those who wish to sell or buy securities or real estate and work out a price acceptable to both parties. The sales worker handles legal forms and documents and may specialize in certain kinds of securities or real estate.

Education and Training: Clerical workers must possess good clerical skills and be especially reliable since huge amounts of money are involved in daily transactions.

Sales workers must obtain a state license to sell securities and/or real estate. A college education with courses in finance, real estate, marketing, and economics is desirable. College degrees are commonly required.

Salary Levels: Salaries vary widely with levels of work, experience, and geographic area. Brokers and sales agents generally work on a commission basis. For instance, beginning securities salespersons average about $1,300 per month; with experience, they eventually will earn in the $40,000 to $70,000 annual salary range.

Additional Information: A visit with workers who are involved with real estate and stock market dealings will give you some additional insight into this career area. Reading periodicals about careers will also add to your information about this career area.

UNIT 10

PROTECTING YOURSELF WITH INSURANCE

UNIT OBJECTIVES

After studying the chapters in this unit, you will be able to:

1. Explain how insurance works to protect you against economic losses.

2. Describe the various kinds of insurance available for vehicles and tell how each kind can be useful.

3. List the main types of life insurance.

4. Give examples that show how health insurance provides needed protection.

5. Describe the kinds of property insurance you can buy to protect your possessions.

6. Explain why you need to insure your future income and how you can do so.

BUSINESS BRIEF

Your Insurance Company—Friend or Foe?

For many years, people usually viewed their relationships with their insurance companies as unfriendly relationships that they had to tolerate. Even though they were insured, most people dreaded confrontations with their agents after calamities as much as they dreaded the calamities themselves.

Stories abound that described unhappy experiences with insurance company representatives after disasters. Insured people claimed their agents have lied to them about coverage, disagreed unreasonably about the monetary amount of the loss, or hid behind long contracts full of fine print that tended to disallow their specific losses.

Whether these stories are true or not, the insurance industry, following the lead of financial institutions, has adopted a new posture designed to respond more positively to the claims of policyholders. One move in this direction by the insurance industry for example, is the simplification of the language in policies. Most policies are now much easier to read and understand than in the past. And policyholders can more easily determine what claims will be covered by their policies.

Insurance companies realize that their reputations are based largely on their willingness to pay in the event of a loss. The following quote by an insurance company claims manager illustrates this point very well.

"Regardless of the type of loss, be it in commercial or personal lines, an insured judges the agent and the carrier by the manner in which they handle the loss. Whatever the company's underwriting and marketing approach and whatever type of coverage selected and premium paid by the insured, satisfaction with the insurance program is determined by the quality of service after a loss . . . The insured decides whether to continue with the present carrier and agency or to select new ones based on (the) loss service received."[1]

In addition to providing fair and equitable economic treatment to policyholders suffering losses, insurance companies are also concerned about responding to the human side of various tragedies. They try to help make the insured feel as good as possible in the face of a loss. Another claims manager says, "When an insured calls in an accident or serious loss, I feel they are in need of some consolation . . . I believe in the Golden Rule, 'Do unto others, as you would have others do unto you.' I try to be as kind and helpful as I would want to be treated, if I were the customer."[2]

[1]Thomas H. Arnold, "Satisfaction After a Loss," *Rough Notes* (October, 1984), pp. 31, 47-49.

[2]Vera Bleke, "Claims Service Builds Business," *Rough Notes* (September, 1984), p. 44.

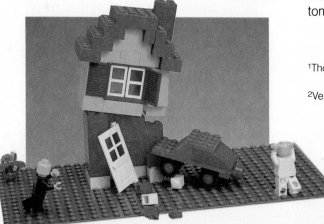

CHAPTER 34

*H*ow Insurance Works

■ CHAPTER OBJECTIVES ─────────────────────────

After studying this chapter and completing the end-of-chapter activities, you will be able to:

1. Name several economic losses that people commonly risk.
2. Tell how insurance protects against financial losses.
3. Name at least four kinds of insurance protection that are important to most people.
4. Describe how everyone benefits from fewer insurance claims.
5. Tell how insurance provides economic security.
6. List the two main factors that determine the level of insurance premiums.

A casual glance at almost any daily newspaper will reveal many tragedies, large and small. Stolen property, wrecked automobiles, tornado damage, broken bones, and burned buildings are only a few of the problems reported on a daily basis. You can probably think of a problem such as an accident, an illness requiring hospitalization, property damage, or some other loss that has affected you or someone you know within the past year.

Unfortunately, events like these are common. Hopefully they won't happen to you very often, but you will probably experience at least one of them in your lifetime. While you may not be able to avoid such disasters, you can protect yourself against the economic losses that they may cause.

Dealing with Economic Losses

Almost all losses can, in part, be seen as **economic losses.** That is, they usually cost money in one way or another. For example, the loss of an heirloom ring would certainly be a family tragedy. Family members would be unhappy about the loss of an irreplaceable part of the family heritage. That portion of the loss is noneconomic. The

Illus. 34–1
Drought can
bring tremen-
dous economic
loss to farmers.

ring, however, also has some economic value, perhaps thousands of dollars. Therefore, losing it could be seen as an economic loss.

The chance of losing property or earning power is called **economic risk.** That is, if there is a loss of property or earning power, money will be spent to repair the damage or solve the problem.

Using Insurance to Share Economic Losses

No matter how careful you are, you cannot completely remove the risks that may cause financial loss. You can, however, avoid a large financial loss all at once by sharing the loss with other people. Suppose you and 49 other people form an organization called the Broken Arm Insurance Club. The purpose of the club is not to protect its members against broken arms but to protect them against having to pay medical bills resulting from broken arms. To provide that protection, each member agrees to share the medical expense of a broken arm. So, if you break your arm and your medical bills total $500, each member, including you, contributes $10 to pay the bill.

If you are not a club member, you must pay the whole $500 medical bill. As a member your broken arm costs you only $10. When a member of the Broken Arm Insurance Club plan breaks an arm, each member suffers only a small economic loss. In that way the members help one another by sharing the risk of economic loss.

It would not be practical to share all losses as the Broken Arm Insurance Club does. There are too many kinds of risks and too many people to be protected. Loss protection must be carefully planned. **Insurance** is the name for planned protection provided by sharing economic losses. **Insurance companies** are the businesses that provide this protection against economic loss.

An insurance company, like the Broken Arm Insurance Club, agrees to take on a certain economic risk for you and to pay you if a loss occurs. The person for whom the risk is assumed is known as

Figure 34–1
Economic losses to individuals are reduced through insurance.

the **insured** or the **policyholder**. To show that risk has been assumed, the company issues a policy. A **policy** is a contract stating the conditions to which the insurance company and the policyholder have agreed. For example, a policyholder may agree not to keep gasoline in the house, not to allow an unlicensed person to drive an insured car, or not to go skydiving. If the policyholder experiences a loss that is covered by insurance, she or he must file a claim with the insurance company. A **claim** is a policyholder's request for payment for a loss that is covered by the insurance policy.

In return for taking on a risk, the insurance company requires that the policyholder pay a certain amount of money. The amount the policyholder must pay is called a **premium**. The insured usually makes payments once a month, once every six months, or once a year. The premiums from all the policyholders make up the funds from which the company pays for losses.

Insurance companies invest the premiums that they collect. The earnings from these investments make it possible to provide insurance at lower cost. Premium rates charged by insurance companies are reviewed by a state **insurance commission.** This is a state agency which makes sure that insurance premium rates and practices are fair.

Self-insurance

Another way to protect against economic losses is through self-insurance. Self-insurance means that a family assumes the total risk of economic loss. For instance, a family might regularly place money in a savings account to cover possible financial losses. But most families would find it almost impossible to self-insure against economic catastrophes such as the cost of an extended illness or the cost of replacing a house that burned.

Sometimes large businesses are able to insure themselves against certain kinds of losses. A company might, for example, determine that the average cost for damages to its fleet of company cars is $12,000 per year. It then establishes a special self-insurance fund for this purpose each year. In this way the business can insure itself against the economic losses associated with automobile damage.

Kinds of Insurance

Consumers and businesses are able to buy insurance to cover almost any kind of economic loss. Violinists can insure their fingers, professional athletes can insure against injuries, and writers may insure their manuscripts. Businesses are able to insure against the loss of rent from property damaged by fire, injury to consumers caused by a faulty product, or theft by employees. The kinds of insurance protection that will be important to most people, however, are insurance for automobiles and homes, life insurance, health insurance, and insurance for income security.

Policyholders should know exactly what protection is provided by the kinds of insurance they have. Some people have failed to tell their insurance companies about losses they have suffered because they did not know that their policies covered those losses. Other people have assumed that losses they suffered were covered by their insurance, only to find out by reading their policies that the losses were not covered.

Illus. 34–2
There is insurance to cover almost any kind of economic loss. Athletes can insure against injuries that might end their earnings.

The Cost of Insurance

Insurance companies use the premiums they collect to pay claims, to pay operating expenses, and to make a profit. The premium for each policy is determined partly by the experience of insurance companies in paying for losses of the kind covered by each policy. For example, a 20-year-old driver is more likely to have an auto accident than a 40-year-old driver. Therefore, car insurance premiums for 20-year-old drivers are higher than they are for older drivers. In general, the greater the risk insured and the more claims the company has to pay, the higher the premiums.

Insured people also play an important part in determining the cost of insurance. They can reduce property losses by being careful. Locking doors and driving defensively, for example, will help to reduce losses associated with thefts and automobile accidents. Practicing good health habits will reduce life and health insurance claims. On the other hand, if losses paid by insurance companies increase because of policyholders' carelessness or poor health habits, premiums will usually increase.

Illus. 34–3
A lifetime of good health habits can reduce insurance claims as well as premiums.

Everyone benefits if the losses covered by insurance decrease. Assume, for example, that there is a decline in losses caused by fire and that fire insurance premiums are reduced as a result. If your family owns a house and has fire insurance on it, you gain directly because you pay lower premiums. If a business owner pays lower premiums, expenses will be less and prices on goods may be less. Anything that you can do to reduce losses covered by insurance helps you and the entire community.

Buying Insurance

Individuals can buy some kinds of insurance through their employers, but most people buy insurance through an **insurance agent.** The insurance agent works for an insurance company or for an independent agency which sells many kinds of policies from a number of different companies. You can learn a lot about insurance by reading about it, but it is hard for anyone to know about all the types that are available. The best thing to do is to choose an agent who can explain the various policies to you.

Paying for Insurance

When you agree to buy insurance, you normally pay the premiums on a regular time schedule. The two main factors that determine the premium you pay are the cost of replacing the object you are insuring and the probability that there will be a loss. For example, if you owned two similar brick houses in a given area worth $95,000 each and wanted to insure them for fire damage, the premiums for the houses would be about the same. But if one house was on high ground and the other near a river, and you wanted to purchase flood insurance, the premiums for the latter would be greater.

Insurance for Economic Security

Insurance is important to everyone because it provides economic security. If you had no insurance, you could probably take care of small losses such as those resulting from minor accidents. However, a large loss from a fire or serious illness could be a real financial hardship. Protection against such major events gives everyone a feeling of security.

Insurance is also important because it helps our economy. Insurance makes it possible for many people and businesses to do things they otherwise could not do. Suppose that someday you want to buy an $80,000 home but can make only a $10,000 down payment. You will need to borrow $70,000. It is very doubtful that anyone would lend you that amount at a reasonable rate if the house were not insured. Money to buy a new car can't be borrowed at a reasonable rate unless the car is insured against risks such as theft and collision.

You have learned that part of the money collected in premiums is invested. Many insurance companies, mainly life insurance companies, also use premiums to make loans. The loans are used to build government and private business projects which help our economy grow.

Insurance companies also perform educational services by conducting campaigns on safety, health, and accident prevention. They conduct these activities to help reduce both losses and premiums.

A dding to Your Business Vocabulary

The following terms should become part of your business vocabulary. For each numbered item, find the term that has the same meaning.

claim
economic loss
economic risk
insurance
insurance agent
insurance commission

insurance companies
insured or policyholder
policy
premium
self-insurance

1. When something that has some financial value is lost or destroyed.
2. Insuring oneself against economic losses.
3. The chance of losing the financial value of something.
4. The planned protection provided by sharing economic losses.
5. Businesses that provide economic protection to others by sharing economic losses.
6. The person for whom risk is assumed by an insurance company.
7. A contract between one who buys insurance and the company which provides it.
8. The amount that a policyholder must pay.
9. A state agency which makes sure that insurance premium rates and practices are fair.
10. A person who sells insurance.
11. A request for payment due to a loss covered by an insurance policy.

Understanding Your Reading

1. Name some possible economic losses that people face.
2. Why aren't most people able to use a self-insurance plan?
3. How does insurance protect against financial losses?
4. What are some unusual kinds of economic losses against which people may be insured?
5. Name at least four kinds of insurance protection that are important to most people.
6. How do insurance companies use the premiums they collect?
7. What does a state insurance commission do for consumers?
8. Give three examples of how people benefit from fewer insurance claims.
9. How can policyholders play a part in determining the cost of insurance?
10. What are the two main factors that determine the amount of insurance premiums?
11. How does insurance provide economic security?

Putting Your Business Knowledge to Work

1. Think of three items that have both economic and noneconomic value. To what extent would you insure each of these items? Have you ever heard of an attempt to place a price on a noneconomic value? Describe it.
2. Some people feel most comfortable when they are insured for almost every loss — large or small. Others feel that most people can handle small losses and favor insuring against only major or catastrophic losses. In which group would you place yourself? Why?
3. The residents of a subdivision of 100 homes decide that they can save money by providing their own fire insurance. Since the houses in the area are of equal value, each owner agrees to contribute $500. The money is to be placed in a savings account in a bank. When a homeowner suffers a fire loss, the loss would be paid out of this account. Do you think this is a wise plan? Why or why not?
4. Why do you think insurance companies are willing to spend large amounts of money on health and safety education?

Computing Business Problems

1. John O'Hanlon is a single college student living in an apartment. He pays the following insurance premiums every year: life insurance $225, renter's insurance $165, automobile insurance $295, and health insurance $650.
   a. What is the total annual cost of John's insurance premiums?
   b. If he paid his insurance costs in equal monthly payments, how much would his total monthly insurance cost be?
2. Joan Nakoma's auto insurance company believes it can reduce its premiums by an average of 10 percent. This reduction is

possible because of lowered speed limits with fewer and less costly accident settlements. Miss Nakoma's last annual premium was $380.

a. How much will she save if the proposed premium reduction is put into effect?

b. What will be the amount of her new premium?

3. The residents of a small town hold the following numbers of the given insurance policies:

Life insurance	1,240
Health insurance	1,280
Automobile insurance	1,434
Property insurance	1,358
Other	188

a. What is the total number of policies in effect?

b. What percent of the total number of policies are automobile policies?

Stretching Your Business Knowledge

1. Make a list of problems you think you might encounter if you tried to start a Broken Arm Insurance Club in your school. Are all students equal risks?

2. It has been said that some people are "insurance poor." That means that they are insured against so many possible economic losses that paying all of the premiums is a financial hardship for them. How do you think the condition of being "insurance poor" might develop? What is the danger of not having enough insurance?

3. Some states carry no insurance on state-owned buildings. Why do you think they do this? What would they do in case of a loss?

4. Examine two or three issues of your local newspaper. Look for the news items reporting injuries to people or property damage. Think about the types of mishaps reported and the cost involved. Which of the situations may have been covered by insurance? Prepare a short report on your findings.

5. Contact a representative of the insurance commission of your state. Report on its purpose and the types of activities in which it is involved. Find out whether it investigates complaints from policyholders.

CHAPTER 35

*I*nsuring Vehicles

■ CHAPTER OBJECTIVES

After studying this chapter and completing the end-of-chapter activities, you will be able to:

1. Name the six basic types of automobile insurance coverage.
2. Tell what type of property is covered by property damage liability coverage.
3. List the factors that determine the cost of automobile insurance coverage.
4. Explain what no-fault insurance is.
5. Identify who is covered by bodily injury liability coverage.

Most people in their mid-to-late teen years become interested in learning to drive an automobile. Along with the rite of maturing goes a freedom of movement. But along with the word "freedom" goes another word—a word used by almost every adult who ever talked to young people about driving. That word is "responsibility."

Driving and owning a car usually bring pleasure, but they also bring a great deal of risk. Every year there are over 25 million auto accidents with tens of thousands of people killed and millions injured. Financial losses due to these accidents amount to over $50 billion each year. The costs of treating injured people and repairing damaged property could easily bring financial ruin to the people who must pay. Court action is costly, and awards to injured people and to owners of damaged property have increased tremendously. Vehicle insurance is designed to provide protection from the financial risks involved in owning and driving a car or other vehicle.

Protect Yourself with Automobile Insurance

Protection against the economic risks associated with driving a car is available through an automobile insurance policy. You can

Illus. 35–1
Owning a car can bring great pleasure; it can also mean financial loss. Carefully planned insurance protection can reduce the amount of loss.

buy insurance to protect yourself from the financial loss caused by almost anything that could happen to your car.

More importantly, however, you can buy insurance to protect yourself against financial loss if you injure someone else or damage someone else's property in an automobile accident. This protection is referred to as **liability insurance.**

Sometimes an accident is unavoidable; that is, no one can be directly blamed for it. In most cases, however, someone is at fault. The person who is found to be at fault is responsible for damages which result from the accident. Although you may think you are completely faultless, you can be sued. If you are insured, your insurance company will provide legal defense for the suit. If the court decides that you are legally liable for injuries and damage to property, your insurance company will pay the costs up to the limits stated in your insurance policy.

Several kinds of protection are available through companies that provide automobile insurance. This coverage is available in different combinations and for different amounts. Although some of the coverage can be bought separately, many car owners prefer a package policy which includes most or all of the coverage. Let's look at the more common kinds of coverage.

Types of Automobile Insurance

As shown in Figure 35-1, automobile insurance coverage can be classified into six types. Three of them deal with bodily injury. They are (1) bodily injury liability, (2) medical payments, and (3) protection against uninsured motorists. The other three are called property damage insurance. They are (1) property damage liability, (2) collision, and (3) comprehensive physical damage.

Bodily Injury Liability Coverage

Bodily injury liability insurance protects you from claims resulting from injuries or deaths for which you are found to be at fault. This kind of insurance covers people in other cars, guests riding with you, and pedestrians. It does not cover you or, in most cases, your immediate family.

Dollar amounts of bodily injury coverage are generally expressed as two numbers divided by a slash, such as 25/50, 50/100, or 100/300. The first number refers to the limit, in thousands of dollars, that the insurance company will pay for injuries to any one person in an accident. For example, if you had bodily injury coverage of 25/50 and had an accident for which you were found to be at fault, the insurance company would pay up to $25,000 if just one person were injured. The second number, in this case 50, refers to the limit, in thousands of dollars, that the insurance company would pay if more than one person were injured.

Some states' financial responsibility laws require as little coverage as 10/20, but car owners should consider carrying much

Figure 35-1
The six types of automobile insurance coverage.

A Summary Chart of Automobile Insurance Coverages		
Types of Coverage	**Coverage on**	
Bodily Injury Coverages	Policyholder	Others
Bodily Injury Liability	NO	YES
Medical Payments	YES	YES
Protection Against Uninsured Motorists . . .	YES	YES
	Policyholder's Automobile	Property of Others
Property Damage Coverages		
Property Damage Liability	NO	YES
Collision	YES	NO
Comprehensive Physical Damage	YES	NO
Source: Insurance Information Institute		

larger amounts. It is not unusual for juries to award an injured person $100,000 or more. If this happened to you and you only had 10/20 coverage, your insurance company would pay the $10,000 limit and you would have to pay the rest. Additional coverage is not very expensive.

Medical Payments Insurance

Through **medical payments insurance,** policyholders and their family members are covered if they are injured when riding in their car or in someone else's car. It also covers them if they are walking and are hit by a car. Guests riding in the insured car are also protected.

Medical payments insurance also covers the costs of medical, dental, ambulance, hospital, nursing, and funeral services. Payment, up to the limit stated in the policy, is made regardless of who is at fault in the accident. Normally car owners purchase medical payments insurance along with their bodily injury liability coverage.

Uninsured Motorists Protection

Sometimes injuries are caused by hit-and-run drivers or by drivers who have no insurance and no money to pay claims. Therefore, insurance companies make available a coverage called **uninsured motorists protection.** This coverage is available only to those people who carry bodily injury liability insurance. In addition to covering the policyholder and family members, it also covers guests riding in the policyholder's car.

The dollar amount of coverage provided by uninsured motorists protection is limited to the liability that state financial responsibility laws require. Unlike medical payments coverage, which pays regardless of who is at fault in the accident, uninsured motorists protection covers the insured person only if the uninsured motorist is at fault.

Property Damage Liability

Everyone who drives a car is responsible for any damage he or she causes to another's property. **Property damage liability insurance** protects you if your car damages someone else's property and you are at fault. The damaged property is often another car, but it may also be property such as telephone poles, fire hydrants, and buildings. Property damage liability insurance does not cover damage to the insured person's car.

Collision Insurance

Collision insurance protects a car owner against financial loss associated with damage resulting from a collision with another car or object or from the car turning over. It does not cover injuries to people or damage to the property of others. Most collision coverage is written with a deductible clause. A **deductible clause** indicates the amount car owners are willing to pay themselves for damage to their autos in the event of an accident. This means that the car owner may agree to pay the first $100 or $200 of damage to the car in any one collision and the insurance company agrees to pay the rest. Larger deductible amounts are available and reduce the premium paid by the policyholder.

Collision coverage does not provide for payment of damages greater than the car's value. Suppose your car receives $2,500 in damages in a collision with another vehicle. If your car has a value of only $2,100, the collision coverage would pay $2,100, not $2,500.

Illus. 35–2
Most owners save on the cost of collision insurance through the use of a deductible clause.

Collision coverage should not be carried on cars that are of little value. This is because the cost of repairing some cars may be more than the car is worth. The car's worth is normally set by a book that reports the value of similar cars that have been sold recently.

Comprehensive Physical Damage Insurance

Even if you do not have an accident with another vehicle, your car can still be damaged or destroyed. The car could be stolen, or it could be damaged by fire, tornado, windstorm, vandalism, or falling objects. **Comprehensive physical damage insurance** protects you against almost all losses except those caused by a collision or turning over.

If your car is totally destroyed or stolen, the amount paid to you is not necessarily equal to the amount you paid for the car. Rather, it is equal to the car's estimated value at the time of the loss. Suppose your car costing $7,000 is stolen soon after you buy it. The insurance company will probably pay you almost as much as the car cost, perhaps $6,600. However, if the car is stolen two years after you buy it, the insurance company may pay you only $4,500. The car has grown older and its value has decreased.

Buying Auto Insurance

There are several factors that an insurance company uses to determine the cost of automobile insurance. Some of those factors include the following:

1. your age and other characteristics, such as accident record, marital status, or academic standing
2. the purpose for which you use your car
3. the value and type of car
4. the community in which you live
5. types of coverage and deductibles.

Since some drivers are more likely to have accidents than others, they must pay higher premiums. To determine premium rates, drivers are classified according to age, marital status, driving record, and scholastic achievement. The lowest rates are reserved for the best risks, those least likely to have an accident. The cost of insurance is usually higher when one of the drivers in the insured's family is under 30 than it is if all family drivers are over 30.

The purpose for which a car is driven and the number of miles it is driven in a year are also important in determining insurance

Illus. 35–3
How might the insurance coverage on these vehicles differ?

rates. Cars used for business purposes are generally driven more miles in a year than are cars driven for pleasure and so are more likely to be involved in an accident.

The value of your car naturally has an important effect on the cost of insurance. Premiums for collision coverage and comprehensive physical damage coverage must be higher for a car worth $8,500 than for a car worth only $4,000. The insurance company runs the risk of paying out much more to the insured if the $8,500 car is destroyed or stolen. The type of car also affects the rate. If you have a high-performance car or an expensive sports car, you may have to pay higher rates.

Basic rates for automobile insurance are not the same throughout the country. Rates vary from state to state, and even from city to city within a state. Auto insurance rates are also affected by the population in a particular area and the number of accidents that occur over a certain period of time in the area. Insurance companies gather statistics on the dollar amount of claims paid for an area and base their insurance rates on this information.

The cost of your auto insurance will also vary according to the types of coverage you have and the amounts of the deductibles you choose. Naturally, the more coverage you carry, the higher will be the cost.

Reducing the Cost

If you plan your auto insurance purchase carefully, you can save a great deal of money. For example, the extra amount charged for young drivers may be decreased if they have completed approved driver education courses. Also, companies in most states offer young people who have good scholastic records a good-student discount. The discount may amount to as much as 25 percent of the premium. Figure 35–2 provides you with several additional suggestions for reducing the cost of automobile insurance.

Selecting the Company

Just as auto insurance premiums vary with the conditions associated with your car and your driving, they also vary from company to company. It pays to shop around and compare rates.

While it is very difficult to find out all of the possible rates from all companies, you should compare a few companies. The cost of the insurance will depend greatly on your choices.

Insurance for Motorcycles and Other Vehicles

Insurance on motorcycles, recreational vehicles, boats, and snowmobiles is similar in some respects to automobile insurance. For example, bodily injury liability, property damage, collision, and comprehensive physical damage insurance are the most important coverages on these vehicles. The engine size and value

SUGGESTIONS FOR BUYING AUTOMOBILE INSURANCE

1. Decide on the types and amounts of coverage you need.
2. Check with several reputable insurers, keeping in mind that the least expensive coverage is not necessarily the best for you. Consider also such things as the company's reliability and its reputation for service including claims handling. If you're in doubt about a company, check with your state insurance department and your local Better Business Bureau.
3. Consider the savings in premiums available through the purchase of a higher deductible—you may find it pays in the long run to take care of small losses yourself.
4. Check with your agent regarding your eligibility for premium discounts for:
   ● safe driving
   ● graduates of recognized driver education courses
   ● good students
   ● students attending school over 100 miles from where the family car is garaged
   ● drivers over 65
   ● low annual mileage
   ● farmers
   ● multi-car families with all cars insured on the same policy
   ● car pools
5. Consider special coverages or higher policy limits if you frequently drive other commuters to work or groups of children to school or special events.
6. Consider dropping collision coverage as cars get older.

Adapted from the Insurance Information Institute

Figure 35–2
There are ways to reduce the cost of insuring your car. Here are several money-saving suggestions.

of the vehicle are the important factors in determining the cost of insurance. Generally, the larger the vehicle, the higher the insurance cost.

Legal Aspects of Auto Insurance

There are several legal principles associated with auto insurance. To be a good consumer, you should at least know about financial responsibility laws, compulsory insurance laws, assigned risk, and no-fault insurance.

Financial Responsibility Laws

Every state has some kind of financial responsibility law. **Financial responsibility laws** provide that if you cause an accident and cannot pay for the damages either through insurance, your savings, or by selling property you own, your driver's license will be suspended or taken away. Most of these laws do not state that you must have insurance, but they do make you legally liable (responsible) for any damage you cause to people or their property.

Compulsory Insurance Laws

Several states have adopted **compulsory insurance laws,** laws requiring you to carry certain types of automobile insurance before your car can be licensed. In those states, you may not register a car or obtain a license to drive without presenting proof of having the minimum amounts of insurance coverage required.

Assigned-Risk Plan

Usually because of bad accident records, some drivers are unable to buy auto insurance in the normal fashion. Because of this, every state also has an **assigned-risk plan.** This is how it works. Every auto insurance company in the state that sells liability insurance is assigned a certain number of high-risk drivers. That number is based on the amount of insurance each company sells. Using this plan, each company has to insure a fair proportion of high-risk drivers. Drivers in high-risk categories must, of course, pay much higher premiums than those who are not high risks.

No-Fault Insurance

A major reason that court cases involving accidents are long and costly is the difficulty of proving who is at fault; that is, who is legally to blame for the accident. The average settlement time in a serious injury case is about 16 months. Some cases, however, take as long as 5 years. Meanwhile, injured persons may have very large medical expenses and less income for paying expenses because of time off the job.

In an attempt to speed up the payment of claims and reduce the hardship of long delays, **no-fault insurance** is being adopted by a growing number of states. Under this plan, people injured in auto accidents can collect for their financial losses — such as their medical bills, loss of wages, and other related expenses — from their own insurance companies no matter who is at fault.

Let's look at an example. Robert Wilson, who is insured with Auto-surance Company, and Dolores Spagnola, who is insured with All-Nation Insurance Company, are injured in a serious two-car accident. Under a no-fault policy, Wilson would collect from Auto-surance, and Spagnola's claims would be paid by All-Nation. It would not be necessary to decide whether Wilson or Spagnola caused the accident.

No-fault laws vary in some ways from state to state. Ordinarily the right to sue is kept for the more serious injury cases and for death. In such cases, it is necessary to decide who was at fault in the accident.

Auto insurance is very complex, but it is the best way to share the risk of financial loss resulting from auto accidents. You should learn all you can about the subject before buying auto insurance.

*A*dding to Your Business Vocabulary

The following terms should become part of your business vocabulary. For each numbered item, find the term that has the same meaning.

assigned-risk plan	*financial responsibility laws*
bodily injury liability insurance	*liability insurance*
collision insurance	*medical payments insurance*
comprehensive physical damage insurance	*no-fault insurance*
compulsory insurance laws	*property damage liability insurance*
deductible clause	*uninsured motorists protection*

1. Insurance coverage which provides medical-expense protection for the policyholder, immediate family members, and guests while in the insured person's car.
2. Auto insurance which provides coverage to high-risk drivers who are unable to purchase insurance through regular methods.
3. Insurance coverage which pays for damages to your car caused by events other than a collision or by turning over.
4. A plan in which people injured in auto accidents can collect for their financial losses from their own insurance companies no matter who is at fault.
5. Insurance that protects you from claims resulting from injuries or deaths for which you are found to be at fault.
6. A clause in an insurance contract that says how much car owners are willing to pay for damage to their autos in the event of an accident.
7. Laws whereby your driver's license will be suspended or taken away if you cause an accident and cannot pay for the damages through insurance, your savings, or the sale of property.
8. The general term used to describe insurance you buy to protect yourself against financial loss if you injure someone else or damage someone else's property in an automobile accident.
9. Laws that say you may not register a car or obtain a license to drive without presenting proof of having the minimum amount of insurance coverage.

10. Insurance coverage which pays for damages to the insured's car caused by collision or by turning over.
11. Insurance coverage which protects the policyholder against losses resulting from injuries caused by a hit-and-run driver or by a driver who has no insurance and no money to pay claims.
12. Insurance coverage which provides protection against claims if your car damages someone else's property and you are at fault.

Understanding Your Reading

1. What are the six basic types of automobile insurance coverage? Into what two classifications can they be grouped?
2. What type of auto insurance protects you against damage caused by a hit-and-run driver?
3. Collision coverage will pay for damages to a car up to what amount?
4. Do financial responsibility laws make automobile insurance compulsory? What can happen to an uninsured motorist who is found to be at fault in an accident, but does not have enough money to pay for the damages?
5. If a driver carries medical payments coverage, in which of the following situations will benefits be paid?
   a. A passenger in the driver's car is injured.
   b. The driver is injured in an accident.
   c. The insured person is crossing the street and is struck and injured by a passing car.
6. What does 100/300 mean in terms of bodily injury liability coverage?
7. Who is covered by bodily injury liability insurance?
8. What type of property is covered by property damage liability coverage?
9. What is a main reason for a person wanting insurance to be forced to accept the assigned-risk plan for purchasing auto insurance?
10. What is no-fault insurance?
11. Some automobile insurance companies give premium discounts to certain drivers. List two types of drivers likely to receive discounts.
12. What factors determine the cost of insurance coverage?

Putting Your Business Knowledge to Work

1. If you lost control of your car on an interstate highway and drove across the median and hit an on-coming car, what types of insurance would pay the other driver's accident expenses?
2. Why do you think it is less important to carry collision insurance on a six-year-old car than a two-year-old car?
3. If there was a four-car pileup in foggy conditions on the interstate highway, how would claims be settled in a state with a no-fault insurance law? What would happen in a state without such a law?
4. Which type of automobile insurance coverage would Tamra Hoffman need in order to be covered in the following situations?
   a. Tamra, in an attempt to avoid hitting a dog in the street, ran into a parked car.
   b. Tamra's daughter, who was riding in the back seat, was injured when Tamra

ran into the parked car.

c. During a storm, a heavy tree branch damaged Tamra's car, breaking the windshield and denting the hood.

d. Tamra was found to be at fault in an accident in which a pedestrian was injured.

5. Frank Hartley was the driver at fault in an accident in which his three passengers were badly hurt. The court awarded two of the injured people $30,000 and it awarded the third person $45,000. Hartley had bodily injury liability coverage in the amount of 50/100. Was this enough insurance to protect him from financial loss? Why or why not?

6. Joe Dubinsky is a traveling salesperson and usually drives his $9,000 car over 500 miles per week. His twin sister, Annie, drives a $5,500 economy car and seldom goes farther than the local shopping center. Who probably pays higher insurance rates? Why?

7. Jimmy Franklin has had several speeding tickets and three auto accidents in the past 18 months. His auto insurance company does not want to renew his policy. What would he do if he lived in a state that had a compulsory insurance regulation?

Computing Business Problems

1. Janice Spivah carried a $200 deductible collision insurance policy on her automobile. She had an accident that was determined to be her fault. The cost of repairing her car was $750. How much of the repair bill would her insurance company pay?

2. When Julia England drove 53 kilometers round trip to work each day, her auto insurance premium was $300 a year. Julia changed jobs and now drives 24 kilometers round trip. Her insurance company gives a 10 percent premium discount to policyholders who drive less than 25 kilometers to and from work each day.
a. How much will she save per year?
b. How much is Julia's present premium?

3. In a recent month, an insurance company reported receiving the following numbers of claims for losses:
    75 bodily injury liability
    50 medical payments
    18 uninsured motorists protection
    87 property damage liability
    130 collision
    90 comprehensive physical damage
a. What was the total number of claims made to this company?
b. If the total amount the company paid out to satisfy the claims was $270,000, what was the average settlement per claim?

Stretching Your Business Knowledge

1. Owning and driving an automobile are great responsibilities. A part of the responsibility is making certain you and your car are appropriately insured. Why is this so?

2. Ralph and Marvin had an accident in which one person was slightly injured. Although there appeared to be great damage to the two cars, Ralph suggested that they give each other their license numbers and driver's license information,

and then leave. Marvin felt that they should call the police and wait for an officer to come. With whose position do you agree? Check with your local police and report to the class on what to do at the scene of an accident. Check with an insurance agent to learn the procedure for reporting an accident to your insurance company.

3. Ask an automobile insurance agent to explain to you how he or she feels about the appropriateness of the assigned-risk plan for auto insurance. Record his or her response and share it with others.

CHAPTER 36

L *ife Insurance*

■ CHAPTER OBJECTIVES

After studying this chapter and completing the end-of-chapter activities, you will be able to:

1. Identify the most important reason for buying life insurance.
2. Describe the procedure for buying life insurance.
3. List four basic types of life insurance.
4. Name the two factors that determine the cost of life insurance.
5. Explain how term insurance and whole life insurance are different.

Rosa Gomez is the single parent of two teenagers. She has insurance on her car in case she has an accident. She also has a comprehensive insurance policy on her house that covers losses resulting from fire, wind, vandalism, and other tragedies. But she has no insurance against a risk that would be even greater than the loss of her car or her house. She has no insurance on her earning power.

Rosa is a salesperson employed by a medical supply firm. Her salary is a comfortable $3,000 per month. But if she died, how would her children survive financially? In the absence of friends or relatives to take care of them, what would the children do about housing, food, clothing, and other living expenses?

It is clear that Rosa needs a plan for the financial welfare of her children in the event of her death. Developing a life insurance program should be a part of that planning process. She needs to answer several questions such as: What kind of life insurance should she buy? How much life insurance does she need? Where should she buy life insurance?

What Is Life Insurance?

Life insurance is protection against the financial loss associated with dying. Specifically, it is designed to replace a loss of income for those who are financially dependent upon another person. Life insurance can also be considered a means of saving or investing, but its primary purpose is always protection against financial loss.

Who Needs Life Insurance?

Anyone with dependents needs life insurance. A dependent is a person who must rely on another for financial support. You will one day need to ask the question, "What would happen to the people who are financially dependent on me if I died tomorrow?" If they could not live financially in the manner in which they lived before your death, you probably need life insurance.

Another common, though far less important reason for buying life insurance is to assure that there is enough money to cover "final expenses." Many people believe that everyone should have enough life insurance to cover funeral and burial or cremation expenses.

Illus. 36–1
People with dependents need adequate life insurance to insure against financial loss.

Benefiting from Life Insurance

When you buy life insurance, you will be asked to name a beneficiary. A **beneficiary** is the person named in the policy to receive the insurance benefits.

You may insure not only your own life, but also the life of any other person in whom you have an insurable interest. To have an **insurable interest** in the life of another person, you must receive some kind of financial benefit from that person's continued life. You have, for example, an insurable interest in the lives of your parents. You do not have an insurable interest in a stranger's life. A partner in a business has an insurable interest in the life of his or her partner. The insurable interest must exist at the time the policy is started, but generally it need not exist at the time of loss.

Kinds of Life Insurance Policies

It is probably obvious that people have many different life insurance needs. A recent high school graduate would not have the same life insurance needs as someone who is ready to retire. A young single person has insurance needs that are different from those of a married person with small children. To provide for the different types of protection that are needed, insurance companies offer a variety of policies. The four basic types of life insurance are term, whole life, endowment life, and universal life. Two other types of life insurance arrangements will also be discussed in this section. They are group plans and combination policies.

Term Life Insurance

Term insurance provides financial protection from losses resulting from loss of life for a definite period of time, or term. It is the least expensive form of life insurance. Policies may run for a period of from one to twenty years or more. If the insured dies during the period for which the insurance was purchased, the amount of the policy is paid to the beneficiary. If the insured does not die during the period for which the policy was purchased, the insurance company is not required to pay anything. Protection ends when the term of years expires.

By paying a slightly higher premium, a person can buy term insurance that is renewable, convertible, or both. A **renewable policy** allows the policyholder to continue her or his term insurance for one or more terms without taking a physical examination to determine whether she or he is still a good risk physically. A **convertible policy** allows the insured to have his or her term insurance changed into some kind of permanent insurance without taking a physical examination.

Term insurance policies may be level term or decreasing term. With **level term insurance,** the amount of protection and the premiums remain the same while the insurance is in effect. With **decreasing term insurance,** the amount of protection gradually becomes smaller but premiums remain the same during the term.

An example of decreasing term insurance is **mortgage insurance.** It protects homeowners from losing their homes in case the insured person dies before the mortgage is paid off. Suppose the Carter family bought an $80,000 house on which they paid down $10,000 and took a 30-year mortgage for the remaining $70,000. The Carters want to be sure that the mortgage will be paid off if one of them should die, so they buy a $70,000 mortgage insurance policy. The amount of coverage decreases as the Carters repay what they have borrowed; so the amount of coverage is about the same as the decreasing balance of the debt.

Whole Life Insurance

Whole life insurance is permanent insurance that extends over the lifetime of the insured. One type of whole life insurance is called **straight life insurance.** Premiums for straight life insurance remain the same as long as the policyholder lives. Some whole life insurance policies are intended to be paid up in a certain number of years and are called **limited-payment policies.** They may also be designated by the number of years the insured agrees to pay on them, such as 20-payment life policies. They are like straight life policies except that premiums are paid for a limited number of years — 20 or 30, for example — or until a person reaches a certain age, such as 60 or 65. Limited-payment policies free the insured from paying premiums during retirement when his or her income may be lower.

Endowment Life Insurance

Endowment life insurance is really a savings plan which also gives insurance protection. An endowment policy may provide a fund of money for the insured at the end of a certain period, such as 10 or 20 years, or at a certain age, such as 60 or 65. If the insured

Illus. 36–2
Endowment life insurance is a combined savings/protection plan. Some people use endowment policies to provide money for retirement years.

dies before the end of the endowment period, the face value of the policy is paid to the beneficiary.

Assume that Joe Kaipo wants to make sure that money will be available to send each of his children to college. When each child is born, he takes out a $20,000 endowment policy on his own life. Each policy is to mature in 17 years and will be payable to Joe if he is living at the end of the 17-year period. If he dies before that time, it will become an educational fund for the child. In either case, the face value of the policy—$20,000—will be available for each child's education.

Universal Life Insurance

Universal life insurance also provides both insurance protection and a savings plan. The premium that you pay for universal life insurance is divided three ways. One portion of it pays for insurance protection. A second portion is taken by the insurance company for its expenses and profits. The third portion is placed in interest-earning investments for the policyholder. The most important feature of universal life insurance is that the savings portion of the policy earns a variable (and usually higher) interest rate than is paid on other permanent insurance. Universal life insurance is gaining popularity among buyers and sellers of life insurance. Figure 36–1 compares the features of the different types of life insurance.

Comparisons of Alternative Life Insurance Programs

| | Term Insurance | Whole Life | | Endowment Life | Universal Life |
		Straight Life	Limited Life		
Premium	Lowest available	Higher than term insurance	Higher than straight life insurance	Highest available	Higher than term; may vary from one payment period to another
Payment Period	Specified number of years — normally 5, 10, or 15 years	Life of the insured	Specified number of years — normally 20 or 30 years	Specified number of years — normally 20 or 30 years	Specified period
Cash Value	None	Some cash value	More cash value than straight life but less than endowment insurance	Largest cash value — equals the value of the policy	Varies with amount "invested" by the insured
Collection Time	Upon the death of the insured	Upon the death of the insured	Upon the death of the insured	Upon the death of the insured or at the time the policy is fully paid for	Upon the death of the insured
Purposes	Protection for a specified period of time; to cover specific and temporary risks	Protection for life; some cash value for insured	Protection for life; some cash value for insured	To create a guaranteed estate; to provide insurance and help finance retirement	Life insurance plus high rate of return

Figure 36–1
Alternative life insurance programs.

Combination Policies to Meet Special Needs

The life insurance policies you have just read about can be combined or modified to meet special needs. A combination plan that is popular with many people with young children is the family income policy. A **family income policy** combines straight life insurance with decreasing term insurance. The family income plan pays a monthly income to the policyholder's family if he or she dies within the period of time specified in the policy. The monthly income payments are provided through the decreasing term insurance part of the policy. In addition, the family receives the full amount of the straight life part of the policy.

Joan and Charles Roosevelt have two small children. The Roosevelts have purchased a family income policy with a face amount of $20,000. The policy also provides that in the event of death, the beneficiaries will receive a monthly income of $400 for 15 years from the date the insurance coverage began. If Mr. Roosevelt were to die five years after buying the policy, Mrs. Roosevelt and the children would receive $400 a month for the next 10 years. They would also receive $20,000 from the straight life part of the policy.

Group Life Insurance

An insurance policy that covers a group of people is called a **group life insurance** policy. The group acts as a single unit in buying the insurance. The cost of group life insurance is less than the cost of a similar amount of protection bought individually because insurance covering many people can be handled economically in one policy. Most group life insurance contracts are issued through employers. Some policies, though, are available through unions, professional associations, and other similar organizations.

Group life insurance is most often issued on a term basis, but whole life policies may be purchased. When employees leave the group in which they are insured, they usually do not have to drop their insurance. They can convert the group insurance to some kind of individual policy if they do so within a given period of time, such as 30 days. No physical examination is required, but the premium is often higher and is based on the age of the person when the conversion takes place.

The amount of protection available to an individual under a group insurance plan is generally limited. Many people, therefore, supplement their group insurance with policies of their own.

The Economics of Life Insurance

Next to a home, a life insurance plan may be the largest lifetime expenditure for many people. It is important, therefore, that you understand how to buy and benefit from life insurance.

Purchasing a Life Insurance Policy

To buy life insurance, you usually apply for a policy through an insurance agent. Normally you will be required to take a physical examination so that your state of health can be determined. Assuming that you have no serious health problems, you then pay a premium to get your life insurance policy. If you are in poor health or work in a dangerous occupation, you may be considered a poor risk. For example, if you drive racing cars to earn a living, you are in a dangerous occupation. Even if you are in poor health or work in a dangerous job, you may be able to obtain insurance. However, you will likely pay higher premiums than people who are in good health and are employed in less dangerous occupations.

The Cost of Life Insurance

In addition to the health and occupation of the insured, the cost of a life insurance policy depends on the type of life insurance being purchased and the age of the person being insured.

Illus. 36-3
Life insurance is available for almost everyone. Some people, however, may have to pay higher premiums.

Premiums for straight life insurance are higher than those for term insurance, but the annual premium stays the same throughout the insured's life. The premiums on limited-payment life insurance are higher than those for straight life insurance, but they are payable for only a limited number of years. Although the premiums on a 20-payment life policy are payable for only 20 years, the policy remains in force for the lifetime of the insured.

The premiums on endowment policies are higher than the premiums for limited-payment life, straight life, or term insurance policies. Endowment policies are payable upon the death of the insured and are also payable to the insured at the end of the policy period. Therefore, the insurance company must collect enough in premiums to: (1) give the insured protection in case he or she dies before the end of the policy period, and (2) pay to the insured the amount of the policy if she or he is living at the end of the period.

Cash Value of Life Insurance

As long as they are kept in force, whole life policies and endowment policies accumulate a cash surrender or loan value or, simply, cash value. The **cash value** of an insurance policy is the amount your insurance company will pay you if you give up your policy. The longer you keep your policy, the higher its cash value will be. If you give up or surrender your policy, you are paid the amount of the cash value. If you need money but do not wish to cancel your policy, you can borrow from the insurance company an amount up to the cash value. If you should die before the loan can be repaid, the unpaid amount will be deducted from the face value of the policy.

Insurance as a Form of Saving

With the exception of term insurance, life insurance can be seen as a part of a savings plan as well as financial protection for beneficiaries. This savings feature is the main advantage of cash-value life insurance. The return on the money you invest in cash-value life insurance is often not as large as other investments. However, insurance premium-payment plans have the advantage of a built-in incentive to save for people who lack discipline.

*A*dding to Your Business Vocabulary

The following terms should become part of your business vocabulary. For each numbered item, find the term that has the same meaning.

beneficiary
cash value
convertible policy
decreasing term insurance
endowment life insurance
family income policy
group life insurance
insurable interest
level term insurance

life insurance
limited-payment policies
mortgage insurance
renewable policy
straight life insurance
term insurance
universal life insurance
whole life insurance

1. Life insurance that covers a group of people who are usually employed by the same firm or are members of the same organization.
2. Permanent life insurance on which premiums are paid for a stated number of years.
3. The person named in an insurance policy to receive the insurance benefits.
4. A policy that combines standard whole life insurance with decreasing term insurance.
5. A life insurance policy that protects beneficiaries from losing their home if the insured dies.
6. The amount that an insurance company will pay to the insured if a policy is given up.
7. A life insurance policy that protects against risk only for a specified period of time.
8. A term life insurance policy that may be changed into another type of insurance.
9. A life insurance policy payable to the beneficiary if the insured should die, or payable to the insured if he or she lives beyond the number of years in which premiums are paid.
10. Life insurance in which a portion of the premium is placed in interest-earning investments that grow at a variable rate for the policyholder.
11. Permanent life insurance on which the insured pays equal premiums throughout his or her life.
12. A term life insurance policy that the policyholder can continue for more than one term without taking a physical exam.
13. Insurance designed to protect against the financial risk associated with dying.
14. A financial interest in or benefit from the continued life of a person.
15. Term life insurance on which the amount of protection and the premiums remain the same during the term.
16. Permanent insurance that extends over the lifetime of the insured.
17. Term life insurance on which the amount of protection gradually decreases but the premiums remain the same during the term.

Understanding Your Reading

1. What is the most important reason for buying life insurance?
2. What question should you ask yourself to determine whether or not you need life insurance?
3. What must you do to buy life insurance?
4. What determines whether you have an insurable interest in someone else's life?
5. List the four basic types of life insurance.
6. How do term insurance and whole life insurance differ?
7. What does it mean if a term life insurance policy is convertible and renewable?
8. In what way is a limited-payment policy different from a straight life policy?
9. Explain why a family income policy is referred to as a combination plan.
10. Why is the cost of group life insurance less than the cost of insurance that is bought individually?
11. What two factors determine the cost of life insurance?
12. What advantage does cash-value life insurance have to a person who is not regarded as a good saver?

Putting Your Business Knowledge to Work

1. Tell why the loss of income to a family is of greater concern than the loss of property.
2. Does a company president have an insurable interest in a lawyer who has represented the company for 14 years? Why or why not?
3. What happens to the insurance protection of a whole life policy if the insured borrows the cash value of the policy?
4. What purpose does a physical examination serve during the process of purchasing a life insurance policy?
5. What kind of life insurance policy would you recommend for each of these people?
   a. Doris Brown, age 27, wants to buy a policy on which the premiums will be as low as possible for the next ten years.
   b. Maria Flores, who works as a mechanic, wishes to have maximum protection for her invalid and widowed mother in case anything should happen to Maria.
   c. John Olson, age 45, wants to buy a policy that will not require payment of any premiums after he retires.
6. Why should a term policy that is renewable or convertible cost more than one which is not?
7. Endowment insurance is sometimes called an insured savings plan. Can you explain why it is given this title?
8. When a person buys life insurance as a member of a large group, no physical examination is ordinarily required. Why do you think this is so?

Computing Business Problems

1. Persons who have permanent life insurance with cash value can borrow up to the cash value of the policy from the insurance company. Gary Hardesty had a $50,000 life insurance policy with a current cash value of $7,000. He decided to borrow $5,000 from that amount to make a down payment on a small house he wanted to buy.
   a. If he died before repaying the loan, how much insurance would his beneficiary receive?
   b. If Gary repays the loan in one year at 8 percent annual interest, what is the total amount he will pay back?
2. John Larson needed $2,400 for one year's tuition at a technical school. He decided to borrow the money from a bank for 4 years and pay $600 on the principal each year, plus interest of 12 percent a year on the unpaid balance. To be sure that his debt would be paid if he should die, he took out a $2,400, four-year decreasing term insurance policy with an annual premium of $22.00.
   a. How much did John pay in premiums and interest each year?
   b. What was the total cost of premiums and interest for the four years?
3. When Kim Sakamoto took out a life insurance policy she was told that she could pay the premiums quarterly, semiannually, or annually. Quarterly premiums were $53; semiannual premiums were $105; and annual premiums were $205.
   a. How much would Kim save by paying the premiums annually instead of semiannually?
   b. How much would she save by paying the premiums annually instead of quarterly?

Stretching Your Business Knowledge

1. Term life insurance premiums are higher per thousand dollars of coverage for persons who are older. This is, of course, because an older person is more likely to die sooner. Make a list of other reasons why life insurance premiums might be higher for others.
2. There is a great deal of debate in the insurance industry and among consumers regarding the merits of term and cash-value life insurance. Research the subject and prepare a list of the positive and negative aspects of each type of life insurance. That research should include reading articles in consumer and insurance magazines and talking with consumers and insurance representatives.
3. Alice and Joel Sorenson have two young children. For an annual premium of $350 they can obtain a five-year, $30,000 term life insurance policy covering either Alice or Joel. For the same premium, they can obtain a $16,000 whole life policy. What factors would you take into account in advising the Sorensons about the two policies?
4. Airports often have machines or booths where life insurance can be purchased for the length of a trip. Why would someone be interested in travel insurance? How would such insurance differ from whole life insurance? If possible, obtain a travel-insurance policy to show the class. Why do you think airline pilots are against the sale of such insurance?

CHAPTER 37

Health Insurance

■ CHAPTER OBJECTIVES ────────────────────

After studying this chapter and completing the end-of-chapter activities, you will be able to:

1. Tell what kind of health insurance is purchased most often.
2. Discuss the seven types of coverage available in health insurance policies.
3. Tell the purpose of a deductible clause in a health insurance policy.
4. List the three coverages that are included in basic health coverage.
5. Name three health insurance programs operated by government agencies.

You will recall from Chapter 25 that the federal government uses the consumer price index (CPI) to measure the prices consumers pay for various goods and services. The goods and services are divided into categories such as food, housing, energy, etc. Health care is one of the categories included in the CPI. For several years the annual increase in health care costs has been well above the overall increase in the CPI. These costs have risen so high that most people do not have the financial reserves to pay for even a short hospital stay or a minor operation. Figure 37–1 shows the predicted increase in health care costs through 1997. Almost everyone needs some form of health insurance.

Health care needs vary widely. One person may suffer from an illness or injury that requires surgery or physical therapy. Another may be injured in an auto accident and become permanently or temporarily disabled. And almost everyone requires some dental care. Health insurance provides protection against the economic hardships associated with paying for medical care and the loss of income that results when an injury or illness prevents you from working.

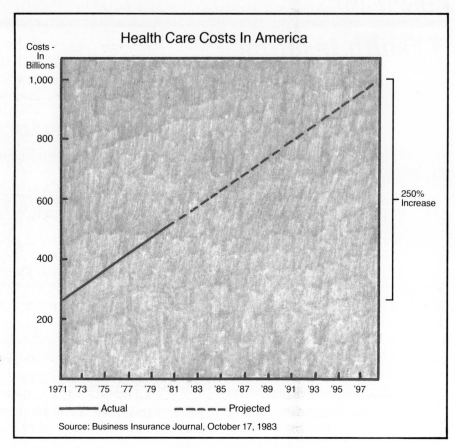

Figure 37–1
Health care costs in America are expected to continue to rise throughout this century.

Medical Insurance

Several kinds of health insurance can be purchased and each kind provides a different type of coverage. Five of the categories of health insurance can be classified as medical insurance. They include: (1) hospital expense, (2) surgical expense, (3) regular medical expense, (4) major medical expense, and (5) comprehensive medical expense.

Hospital Expense Insurance

When an illness or injury requires you to be hospitalized, **hospital expense insurance** usually pays most or all of the charges for your room, food, and such items as use of an operating room, anesthesia, X rays, laboratory tests, and medicines. Because of the high cost of hospitalization, more people purchase hospital expense insurance than any other kind of health insurance.

Hospital expense insurance can be purchased from insurance companies or from nonprofit corporations. The most well-known nonprofit organization that offers hospital insurance is Blue Cross. Blue Cross plans usually pay hospitals directly for care provided to their policyholders. If expenses go beyond the amount covered by the Blue Cross contract, the patient must pay the difference.

Surgical Expense Insurance

Surgery is one of the major reasons for hospitalization and is normally very expensive. **Surgical expense insurance** covers all or part of the surgeon's normal fees for an operation. The typical surgical policy lists the types of operations that it covers and the amount allowed for each. Some policies allow larger amounts for operations than others. This, of course, requires that a higher premium be paid. Surgical expense insurance is frequently bought in combination with hospital expense insurance.

Surgical expense insurance can be purchased from insurance companies or from nonprofit organizations such as Blue Shield. Unlike Blue Cross, Blue Shield plans cover mainly medical and surgical treatment rather than hospital care. Most Blue Shield plans list the maximum amounts that will be paid for different types of surgery. They also cover the doctor's charges for care in the hospital and some plans pay doctor's charges for office or home care.

Regular Medical Expense Insurance

Physicians charge for services in addition to surgery. **Regular medical expense insurance** pays part or all of the fees for non-surgical care given in the doctor's office, the patient's home, or a hospital. The policy states the amount payable for each call and the maximum number of calls covered. Some plans also provide payments for X-ray and laboratory expenses. This type of insurance is usually bought along with hospital and surgical insurance. The protection provided by these three coverages is referred to as **basic health coverage**.

Major Medical Insurance

Long illnesses and serious injuries can be very expensive. Medical bills of $50,000 to $100,000 and even more are possible. Most people cannot afford to pay such amounts out of their earnings and savings. **Major medical expense insurance** provides protection against the high costs of serious illnesses or injuries. It complements the other forms of medical insurance. Major medical expense insurance helps pay for most kinds of health care prescribed by a doctor. It covers the cost of treatment in and out of the hospital, special nursing care, X rays, psychiatric care, medicine, and many other health care needs. Maximum benefits range up to $250,000 and higher.

All major medical policies have a deductible clause similar to the one found in automobile collision insurance as described in Chapter 35. In this clause, the insured agrees to pay the first part — perhaps $100 or $500 — of the expense resulting from sickness or injury. Major medical policies also usually contain a coinsurance clause. A **coinsurance clause** means that the policyholder will be expected to pay a certain percentage — generally 20 or 25 percent — of the costs over and above the deductible amount.

The deductible clause discourages the filing of minor claims. The coinsurance clause encourages the insured to keep medical expenses as reasonable as possible. Thus, both clauses help to make lower premiums possible because they help to lower payments of insurance claims.

Illus. 37–1
Most families and individuals cannot afford the costs of long illnesses or serious injuries. Major medical expense insurance provides protection against such financial disasters.

Comprehensive Medical Insurance

Comprehensive medical insurance is usually purchased as a group plan and combines hospital, surgical, and medical and major medical insurance in one policy. Comprehensive medical insurance retains the features of each of the combined plans such as deductibles, amounts payable, limits, etc. It is usually less expensive than the total of the separate plans because of the advantage provided by purchasing it as a group plan.

Dental Expense Insurance

Dental expense insurance helps pay for normal dental care, often including examinations, X rays, cleaning, fillings, and more complicated types of dental work. It also covers dental injuries resulting from accidents. Some dental plans contain deductible and coinsurance provisions, while others pay for all claims. Dental expense insurance is offered mainly through groups and is growing in popularity.

Disability Income Insurance

Disability income insurance is designed to protect you against the loss of income because of an extended illness or an accident. It provides you with weekly or monthly payments until you are able to return to work. Disability income policies frequently include a waiting period provision which requires that the insured wait a specified length of time after the disability occurs before payment begins. The purpose of the waiting period is to keep people from making frequent claims for small losses, thus reducing premium costs.

Sources of Health Insurance

Health insurance is available from several sources and in many different forms. You can buy health insurance as an individual or as a member of a group. Private companies and government agencies provide many kinds of health insurance.

Individual Health Insurance

Individual health insurance is health insurance that is available to individuals and is adaptable to individuals' health insurance needs. Individual health insurance policies are usually rather expensive and require a physical examination and a waiting period before the policy is in force. Individual health insurance policies are most commonly purchased by people who are not eligible for a group insurance plan.

Group Health Insurance

Most Americans are protected under group health insurance. Like group life insurance, such policies are made available by employers to their employees and by unions and other organizations to their members. The company, union, or other organization receives a master policy or contract. Those insured under the plan are given certificates to indicate their participation in the plan. Companies that sponsor group policies often pay part or all of the premium costs for their employees. The cost of group health insurance is lower than the cost of a comparable individual policy. This is possible because insurance companies can administer group plans more economically, thus lowering costs for each person in the group.

Health Maintenance Organizations

Developed recently as an alternative to health insurance, **health maintenance organizations (HMOs)** normally consist of a staffed medical clinic organized to serve its members. You may join an HMO for a fixed monthly fee. As a member you are entitled to a wide range of health care services. HMOs emphasize preventive care. Early detection and treatment of illnesses help to keep people out of hospitals and costs down.

Help from State Governments

Our local, state, and federal governments are involved in activities that improve the health of the entire nation. An especially important health insurance program established by state governments is workers' compensation. **Workers' compensation** is an insurance plan that provides medical and survivor benefits for persons injured, disabled, or killed on the job. Accidents may occur on almost any job. Employees may suffer injuries or develop some illness as a result of their working conditions. To deal with this problem, all states have passed legislation known as workers' compensation laws. These laws provide medical benefits to employees who are injured on the job or become ill as a direct result

Illus. 37–2
Injuries or illnesses resulting from one's employment are covered by worker's compensation.

of their working conditions. Under these laws, most employers are required to provide and pay for insurance for their employees.

The benefits provided through workers' compensation vary from state to state. In some states, all necessary expenses for medical treatment are paid. In others, there is a stated payment limit. Usually there is a waiting period of a few days before a worker is eligible for loss-of-income benefits. If unable to return to the job after this waiting period, the worker is paid a certain proportion of wages as benefits. This often amounts to about two thirds of the worker's normal wages. Payments are also made to dependents if the worker is killed in an accident while on the job. Benefits for injury to or death of a worker are usually paid without regard to whether the employee or the employer was at fault.

State governments also provide a form of medical aid to low-income families known as **Medicaid**. The federal government shares with states the cost of providing health benefits to medically needy families. A medically needy family is one whose income provides for basic necessities but who could not afford adequate medical care or pay large medical bills.

The services covered by Medicaid include hospital care, doctors' services, X rays, lab tests, nursing home care, diagnosis and treatment of children's illnesses, home health care services, and family planning. States may provide additional services if they wish.

Help from the Federal Government

The nation's social security laws provide a national program of health insurance known as **Medicare**. It is designed to help people age 65 and over and some disabled people to pay the high cost of health care. Medicare has two basic parts: hospital insurance and medical insurance.

The hospital insurance plan includes coverage for hospital care, care in an approved nursing home, and home health care up to a certain number of visits. No premium payments are required for the hospital insurance, and almost everyone 65 years old and older may qualify.

The medical insurance portion of Medicare is often called supplementary or voluntary insurance. The services covered under this plan include doctors' services, medical services and supplies, and home health services. The medical insurance requires a small monthly premium. The federal government pays an equal amount to help cover the cost of the medical insurance. Some features of the Medicare plan are similar to the deductible and coinsurance provisions in other health policies.

The Cost of Health Insurance

No matter who pays the premium, the cost of health insurance, like the cost of health care, is very high. The cost is usually determined by at least four factors: the extent of the coverage, the number of claims filed by policyholders, the age of the policyholder, and the number of dependents. You will have little control over your age and the number of people dependent on you. But you can make sure

Reprinted by permission of Jefferson Communications, Inc., Reston, Va.

you buy only the kind and amount of insurance you need. You can also be careful not to abuse your benefits by using medical services when they are unnecessary. By doing so you will be doing your part to keep health insurance costs down.

*A*dding to Your Business Vocabulary

The following terms should become part of your business vocabulary. For each numbered item, find the term that has the same meaning.

basic health coverage
coinsurance clause
comprehensive medical insurance
dental expense insurance
disability income insurance
health maintenance organization
hospital expense insurance

major medical expense insurance
Medicaid
Medicare
regular medical expense insurance
surgical expense insurance
workers' compensation

1. Insurance that combines hospital, surgical, and medical insurance into one policy.
2. Insurance that provides a worker with weekly or monthly payments when he or she is unable to work as a result of an illness or injury covered by the policy.
3. Insurance that pays part or all of a doctor's fees for nonsurgical care given in the doctor's office, the patient's home, or a hospital.
4. An organization which provides complete health care to its members for a fixed regular payment.
5. A combination of hospital, surgical, and regular medical expense insurance.
6. Insurance that pays for normal care of and accidental damage to teeth.
7. Insurance that provides payments to employees or their survivors for injuries, loss of income, or death caused by acci-

dents on the job.
8. Insurance that provides benefits to cover part or all of a surgeon's fee for an operation.
9. Medical expense assistance provided by state governments to medically needy families.
10. Insurance that pays part or all of the charges for room, food, and other hospital expenses that the insured person incurs.
11. Insurance that provides protection against the high costs of serious illnesses or injuries.
12. Health insurance provided by the federal government for aged and disabled people.
13. A provision in which the insured agrees with the insurance company to pay a certain percentage of his or her medical expenses.

Understanding Your Reading

1. What kind of health insurance is purchased most often?
2. What are the two types of losses for which health insurance provides protection?
3. If hospital expenses are greater than the amount covered by a hospital expense policy, who pays the difference?
4. What are the seven basic types of coverage provided by health insurance? Explain the kinds of expenses each covers.
5. The combination of which three health insurance coverages is referred to as basic health coverage?
6. What is the purpose of a deductible clause in a health insurance policy?
7. What types of dental care are covered by a dental expense policy?
8. Why is being insured under an individual health insurance policy more expensive than under a group policy?
9. What three health insurance programs are operated by government agencies?
10. Explain what Medicaid is.
11. What are the two basic parts of the Medicare plan?
12. What kind of health insurance covers you if you are injured on the job?

Putting Your Business Knowledge to Work

1. Crystal Smith is studying to be a commercial artist and has a part-time job to help pay her college expenses. She does not have health insurance because she feels she cannot afford it. She also feels that she does not really need health insurance.
   a. Give several reasons why Crystal should protect herself with some type of health insurance.
   b. Where might she find a policy at a reasonable premium?
   c. What can she do to keep the policy premium at a reasonable level?
2. Many major medical policies contain a coinsurance clause. These policies are usually less expensive than a policy without such a clause. What advice would you have for a person or group considering purchasing a major medical expense insurance policy containing a coinsurance clause?
3. Robert Campbell found that he could buy major medical expense insurance with a maximum coverage of $10,000 for about the same cost as regular medical expense insurance with a maximum coverage of about $2,000. Why do you think the cost of the two types of insurance is about the same when the maximum coverage is so different?
4. The Lopez family is trying to determine which kinds of health insurance coverage would best fit their needs. On one hand, they feel that a Blue Cross hospital expense plan and a Blue Shield surgical expense plan would be sufficient. On the other hand, a major medical plan might better serve their needs. Mr. and Mrs. Lopez are both 48 years old and are employed by the same company. They have two children. There is a history of heart disease in Mr. Lopez's family. Mrs. Lopez smokes cigarettes. They have about $20,000 in a savings account. What advice would you offer this family relative to their health insurance needs?

Computing Business Problems

1. Chris Abboud is considering job offers from two different companies. The jobs seem equally desirable to him. The Marxel Company provides health insurance benefits to their employees that total $97 per month. The Hardity Company provides no health insurance for its workers. How much money would the Marxel health insurance benefit be worth to Chris each year?

2. Jolene Franklin had a serious illness requiring hospitalization and a lengthy recovery period. When they were all recorded, her medical bills totaled $12,700. Her major medical insurance policy had a $500 deductible clause and a 20 percent coinsurance clause. How much of the bill will Jolene be required to pay?

3. The following shows the health insurance carried by Sang Fen and the monthly cost for each kind of coverage:

Blue Cross	$75.00
Blue Shield	$16.25
Major Medical	$17.90

   a. What is the total cost of his health care coverage each month?

   b. How much does each policy cost him annually?

   c. What is his total annual insurance cost?

4. Jonathon Rozier was hospitalized as a result of an auto accident. His medical expenses were as follows:

6 days in hospital	$200 per day
Lab tests and X rays	$385
Surgeon's fees	$975

   Jonathon is covered by hospital expense insurance which pays the cost of his hospital room for up to 120 days for any one illness. Coverage for lab tests, X rays, and other hospital extras is limited to $300. His surgical expense insurance plan limits benefits to $600 for the type of surgery involved.

   a. What was the total cost of Jonathon's medical services?

   b. How much of this total cost was paid by his insurance?

   c. How much of the medical cost did Jonathon have to pay?

Stretching Your Business Knowledge

1. Employees often are injured on the job. States have passed laws that provide medical benefits to people who suffer this fate. Why do you think a state government has a specific concern for people injured on the job?

2. One of the stated goals of health maintenance organizations is to work to keep people healthy. Are there any health maintenance organizations in your community? If there are, see what their brochures have to say about preventative care and health maintenance. Report your findings to your class.

3. Schools often arrange with an insurance company to provide students with coverage that protects the students in case of accidents on the way to and from school and on school grounds. They also provide coverage for members of school athletic teams. Does your school provide such coverage? If so, how much does it cost? What coverage is provided?

4. New forms of protection that are beginning to receive attention are eye-care insurance, home care services insurance, and prescription drug insurance. What kinds of expenses would likely be covered under such policies? Do you think there is a need for these types of protection?

CHAPTER 38

*P*roperty Insurance

■ CHAPTER OBJECTIVES

After studying this chapter and completing the end-of-chapter activities, you will be able to:

1. Identify three types of economic losses against which property insurance protects.
2. Tell what kind of protection is provided by personal liability coverage.
3. Explain the difference between real property and personal property.
4. Name six examples of perils against which a basic homeowners policy provides protection.
5. State the advantage a homeowners policy has over policies that cover separate perils.
6. Explain why a person who rents an apartment needs property insurance.

Almost everyone owns some property. Sometimes that property is as inexpensive as a pencil, a record album, or a tee shirt. If one of these items were lost or stolen, you might be upset but probably not devastated financially. Other property, however, has a great deal of economic value. Furniture, jewelry, and, of course, houses are in this latter group.

Furniture can be damaged. Diamond rings are frequently stolen. And houses can be destroyed by fire or wind. In each of these cases, the owner of the property would suffer considerable financial loss without the protection of property insurance. Fire, theft, vandalism, floods, windstorms, and other hazards cause severe personal and financial hardships. Property owners also run the risk of being sued by people who are injured on their property. Because the risks of loss in such situations are high, property owners should carry property insurance.

Illus. 38–1
Though the sentimental value of some items makes them irreplaceable, everyone has possessions that should be insured against loss.

Protecting Your Property With Insurance

Home and property insurance protects you against three kinds of economic losses: (1) damage to your home or property, (2) the additional expenses you must pay to live someplace else if your home is badly damaged, and (3) liability losses.

Damage to Home or Property

If your home and its contents are damaged by fire, lightning, vandalism, earthquake, or some other disaster, home and property insurance will pay for repairs or replacement. These kinds of losses are very common and everyone should be insured against them. On the average, a residential fire breaks out somewhere in the United States every 35 to 40 seconds. The resulting property damage totals several billion dollars each year. Several more billions of dollars worth of property is stolen each year.

Additional Living Expenses

When you suffer a major property loss, you may have to pay additional living expenses because you can no longer use that property. These losses are also covered by home and property insurance.

For example, if your home were badly damaged by fire, your insurance would pay for the higher-than-normal living expenses that would result from living in a hotel and eating in restaurants while your home was being repaired. These expenses could be very high.

Liability

The third kind of loss, liability loss, is protected by personal liability coverage. **Personal liability coverage** protects you from claims arising from injuries to other people or damage to other people's property caused by you, your family, or your pets. If a neighbor trips on your sidewalk and you are shown to be at fault, personal liability coverage will pay for any medical and legal costs involved up to a stated limit. If a child damages a car in an adjacent driveway with her tricycle, claims will be paid through the provisions in the policy of the child's family that covers liability for physical damage to the property of others.

Property Insurance Policies

When considering the purchase of property insurance, you must first decide what should be insured and against what perils it should be insured. **Perils** are the causes of loss, such as fire, wind, or theft. Property attached to land, such as a house or a garage, is known as **real property.** Property not attached to the land, such as furniture or clothing, is known as **personal property.** Real and personal property may be protected by separate policies or by a combination homeowners policy. If you are a renter, there are also special policies that will cover your property.

Separate Policies

A property owner can buy separate policies which insure against certain perils. For example, a **standard fire policy** insures against losses caused by fire or lightning. **Extended coverage** can be included in a standard fire policy. This expands the coverage to include damage caused by perils such as wind, hail, smoke, and falling aircraft, among other things.

Illus. 38–2
What happens if the owner of this house has no insurance? The cost of a policy is small compared to the total loss of a house and possessions.

Homeowners Policies

Today most people buy a combination package policy known as a **homeowners policy.** The number of perils covered by a homeowners policy depends on whether the insured chooses the basic form, the broad form, or the comprehensive form.

The basic form of a homeowners policy insures property against the first 11 perils listed in Figure 38–1. The broad form, which is very widely purchased, covers 18 different risks. The comprehensive form covers all perils shown in Figure 38–1 and many more. It is sometimes referred to as an all-risk policy. Actually, such a policy insures against all perils except those excluded by the policy. Personal liability coverage is included with all forms of the homeowners policy.

With a homeowners policy you are as protected as you would be if you bought several different policies. Yet the cost of a homeowners policy is usually 20 to 30 percent less than if the same amount of coverage were obtained by buying separate policies. Also, there is the convenience of having only one policy to handle and one premium to pay. However, some people still buy separate policies because they can be better suited to individual requirements.

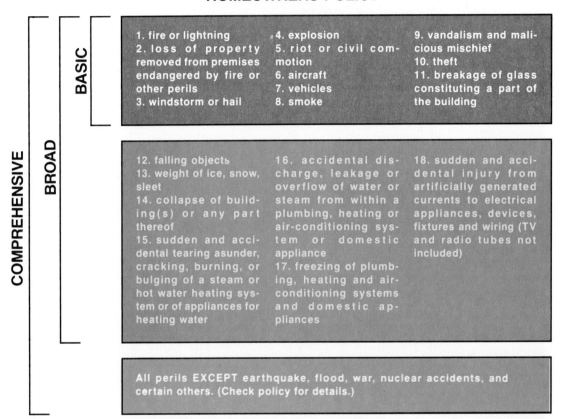

PERILS AGAINST WHICH PROPERTIES ARE INSURED
HOMEOWNERS POLICY

COMPREHENSIVE
BROAD
BASIC

1. fire or lightning
2. loss of property removed from premises endangered by fire or other perils
3. windstorm or hail
4. explosion
5. riot or civil commotion
6. aircraft
7. vehicles
8. smoke
9. vandalism and malicious mischief
10. theft
11. breakage of glass constituting a part of the building

12. falling objects
13. weight of ice, snow, sleet
14. collapse of building(s) or any part thereof
15. sudden and accidental tearing asunder, cracking, burning, or bulging of a steam or hot water heating system or of appliances for heating water
16. accidental discharge, leakage or overflow of water or steam from within a plumbing, heating or air-conditioning system or domestic appliance
17. freezing of plumbing, heating and air-conditioning systems and domestic appliances
18. sudden and accidental injury from artificially generated currents to electrical appliances, devices, fixtures and wiring (TV and radio tubes not included)

All perils EXCEPT earthquake, flood, war, nuclear accidents, and certain others. (Check policy for details.)

Figure 38–1
Perils covered by homeowners policies.

Tenants Policies

If you live in a rented home or apartment, you can also get a package policy. It is called a **tenants policy.** It covers household goods and personal belongings and provides protection against the same kinds of perils covered by homeowners policies, including personal liability coverage.

Buying Property Insurance

As when making other large insurance purchases, a wise consumer will work to find the most appropriate property protection at the lowest cost. That involves making certain that the property is insured for the correct amount and that the factors affecting property insurance costs have all been carefully considered.

Insuring for the Correct Value

Suppose that Frank Stenerud built his house in 1983 for $90,000 and that he insured it for that amount. It might cost $105,000 to build a similar house today, so the house has a current replacement value of $105,000. Yet, if Mr. Stenerud's house is completely destroyed by fire, the insurance company may pay him only $90,000. Some insurance companies provide for automatic increases in property coverage as the price level increases. Others will pay the current replacement value if the property is insured for at least 80 percent of that replacement value.

Building costs and property values have increased greatly in recent years. Property owners should review the value of their property and insurance coverage every few years. They should determine the cost of replacing their property and make sure that their insurance policies give enough protection.

Illus. 38–3

It is important to insure your home and personal property at to-day's value. Coverage amounts should be reviewed and updated periodically.

Special care should be taken to estimate accurately the value of personal property. Since personal property includes many different items, some may be overlooked if a careless estimate of value is made. Most homeowners policies provide personal property coverage at 50 percent of policy value. For example, if your home is insured for $80,000, your personal property is insured for 50 percent of $80,000 or $40,000. The value of personal property that you collect over the years is often surprisingly high. In many cases a homeowner's personal property is worth considerably more

than 50 percent of the coverage on the home. Additional coverage is available for a slightly higher premium.

Factors Affecting the Cost of Homeowners Insurance

The price that homeowners pay for insurance on homes and furnishings is based on a number of factors. One of the most important is the estimated danger of loss based on the insurance company's past experiences. In addition to the loss experiences, an insurance company considers the following factors in determining homeowners insurance premiums:

1. the value of the property insured
2. the construction of the building; that is, whether it is made of brick, wood, or concrete, and the construction of the roof
3. the type of policy (basic, broad, or comprehensive)
4. the number of perils covered
5. the distance to the nearest fire department and water supply
6. the amount of deductibles (the higher the deductibles, the lower the premium).

Proving a Loss

In order to show proof of a loss, you should keep a list of personal property that you have insured. The list, called an **inventory,** should include: (1) the original cost of each article, (2) when the article was purchased, and (3) how long the article is expected to last. The age of an insured article of personal property is quite important. As most property becomes older, it gradually wears out and decreases in value. This decrease in value, called **depreciation,** affects the amount the insurance company will pay if the property is destroyed. For example, a sofa costing $500 that is expected to last 10 years would depreciate $50 each year. Its value after five years would be $250.

As soon as possible after you discover a loss, you should file a claim with your insurance company. However, before the company will pay, you must provide proof of your loss. This is not a problem with real property. A representative of the insurance company can look at the damaged property, determine the extent of loss, and pay you according to the terms of the policy. The destroyed contents of a house, however, would pose a problem. In order to prove the amount of personal property loss, you must know the approximate value of each article damaged or destroyed.

In addition to maintaining an up-to-date personal property inventory, some insurance companies suggest taking photographs of furniture and other property. These photos can be used to support claims. Insurance companies can provide you with inventory forms and information about how to make claims for losses.

*A*dding to Your Business Vocabulary

The following terms should become part of your business vocabulary. For each numbered item, find the term that has the same meaning.

> *depreciation*
> *extended coverage*
> *homeowners policy*
> *inventory*
> *perils*

> *personal liability coverage*
> *personal property*
> *real property*
> *standard fire policy*
> *tenants policy*

1. Property that is attached to land.
2. Additional protection of property against losses from such causes as windstorms, hail, and smoke.
3. Insurance to protect against claims arising from injuries to other people or damages to other people's property which are caused by you, your family, or your pets.
4. A basic type of property insurance that protects against losses resulting from fire or lightning damage to a home.
5. Property that is not attached to land.
6. A package policy covering a wide range of risks for homeowners.
7. The decrease in the value of property as it becomes older and wears out.
8. Insurance on household goods and personal belongings for those who rent.
9. A list of goods showing the cost of each item, when it was purchased, and how long it is expected to last.
10. The causes of loss, such as fire, wind, or theft.

*U*nderstanding Your Reading

1. List the three kinds of economic losses for which home and property insurance provides protection.
2. What kind of loss would you have to suffer in order to take advantage of additional living-expense coverage in your insurance policy?
3. What kind of protection is provided by personal liability coverage?
4. Describe the difference between real property and personal property.
5. Name six examples of perils against which a basic homeowners policy will insure you.
6. How does extended coverage affect the standard fire policy?

7. What advantage does a homeowners policy have over a policy that covers separate perils?
8. Which homeowners policy covers more perils, the comprehensive or the broad policy?
9. Why would a person who rents an apartment purchase property insurance? What kind of policy should a renter purchase?
10. How is the cost of property insurance determined?
11. Name two good methods of keeping an inventory of your personal property.

*P*utting Your Business Knowledge to Work

1. It snowed in Esterville one night in January. John Gardner didn't take the time to shovel the snow from his front steps. Two days later a salesperson slipped on John's unshoveled steps and broke an arm. The salesperson has asked John to pay the medical expenses associated with the broken arm. Will John's homeowners policy cover the expenses?
2. In a recent year several homes in a Colorado canyon were destroyed when a heavy rain in the Rocky Mountains caused the river flowing through the canyon to rise to several feet above its normal level. Do you think those canyon residents who had homeowners policies suffered any financial losses? Why or why not?
3. Jane Elliot's property is covered by the basic form of homeowners insurance. Against which of the following losses is she insured? Which of the losses would be covered if she had the broad form?
   a. A smouldering fire breaks out in a bedroom closet and her clothing is damaged by smoke.
   b. Her home is broken into and vandalized, but nothing is stolen.
   c. A storm knocks out the electricity for two days in midwinter and the pipes burst, causing flooding.
4. Carlos Jimney and Joe Torres were playing golf together. Carlos hit a ball which accidentally struck and injured Joe. On the way to the hospital, Carlos told Joe that he would pay Joe's medical expenses. Joe answered that he would pay his own expenses since Carlos hit him accidentally. Then Carlos remembered that he was covered by personal liability insurance. Will this insurance cover Joe's medical expenses?

*C*omputing Business Problems

1. If Michelle Smith owned a home worth $92,000 and wanted to be certain it was insured for at least 80 percent of its value, for how much should it be insured?
2. A thief broke the lock on Knute Peterson's garage and stole the following items:

   15 liters of oak stain, valued at $4.25 a liter
   6 liters of motor oil, valued at $1.45 a liter
   3 kilograms of 2.5 cm finishing nails, valued at 85 cents a kilogram
   68 meters of 2.5 cm × 30.5 cm pine shelving, valued at $4.50 a meter

Since Peterson had recently bought these items and had not yet used any of the material, for what amount should he make his claim under his homeowners policy?

3. Cloris Lang lives in an apartment. Her furniture and other personal property are covered under a tenants policy. Miss Lang's apartment was broken into and the following items were stolen:

A stereo, bought 3 years ago for $350 and estimated to last 10 years.

A camera, bought 4 years ago for $160 and estimated to last 10 years.

A suede jacket, bought 2 years ago for $80 and estimated to last 5 years.

If the insurance company pays Miss Lang the estimated present worth of the lost articles, what amount will she receive?

Stretching Your Business Knowledge

1. Most people tend to undervalue the total amount of their personal property. First make an estimate of the value of all the personal property you own (clothes, records, radio, etc.). Then list and actually add up the value of your personal property. Are you surprised at the difference?

2. Property insurance policies usually set certain limits on the amount of protection allowed for such personal property as stamp and coin collections, jewelry, furs, and rare paintings. Why are such limitations established? If a person wants to be covered for the full value of such property, what can he or she do?

3. You have learned about group insurance plans associated with life insurance and health insurance. Why do you suppose you have not seen any discussion of group homeowners insurance plans?

CHAPTER 39

Insuring Your Income

■ CHAPTER OBJECTIVES

After studying this chapter and completing the end-of-chapter activities, you will be able to:

1. Name the two most common causes of income loss.
2. Explain the difference between an annuity and an insurance policy.
3. Identify the purpose of state unemployment insurance.
4. Name the three groups of people who receive monthly incomes from social security.
5. Discuss how social security provides protection for future income.

In order to survive economically everyone needs a regular source of money. In your youth, that source of money is usually a parent or guardian who supplies you with food, clothes, housing, etc. As you grow to adulthood you become self-reliant financially, normally by working and earning a salary. Once you retire, your income is usually in the form of a retirement plan that provides payments for your living expenses. In each case, you would have problems if your income were interrupted or discontinued. There are ways, however, of insuring your income.

Insuring Against Loss of Current Income

There is little you can do to insure the regularity of your parents' or guardians' incomes. But once you are employed, there are ways to assure that you can maintain an income. Insurance is available that will provide an income to those who face the two most common causes of loss of income: disability and unemployment.

Disability Insurance

Disability income insurance helps replace income that is lost when you cannot work because of an illness or accident. Many different individual and group disability income policies are available. The amount of each payment, the length of the waiting period before benefits are paid, and the length of time that payments are made should be chosen on the basis of the needs of each family. Most companies from which you can buy disability income insurance will pay from 40 to 60 percent of your salary while you are disabled. However, before the benefits begin, there is usually a waiting period of from one week to 90 days after you are disabled. As with other kinds of insurance, the more benefits provided, the higher premiums will be.

Unemployment Insurance

Unfortunately people do sometimes lose their jobs. In this case, their incomes would be cut off entirely. Unemployment may be caused by business failures, strikes, changes in methods and in equipment, and the temporary or seasonal nature of certain jobs.

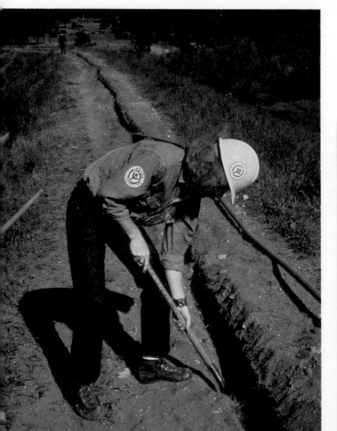

Illus. 39–1
Unemployment may be the result of new technology, strikes, boycotts, or the seasonal nature of some jobs.

To reduce the financial hardship of unemployment, most states have an unemployment insurance program which they operate in cooperation with the federal government. **Unemployment insurance** provides cash payments for a limited time to people who are out of a job for a reason other than illness. Unemployment office staff will provide guidance to help you find a new job. But if no suitable job is found, you may receive payments to replace part of your lost wages. The number of payments varies, but most states will provide benefits for as long as 26 weeks after a one-week waiting period. Ordinarily, the amount you receive when you are unemployed is based on your previous earnings. It is usually low enough to encourage you to search for another job.

Planning for Future Income

Once people retire, their salaries, of course, stop. But they continue to need money on which to live. There are several ways for workers, sometimes with the help of their employers and the government, to insure that they will have an adequate income during their retirement years.

Pension Plans

A **pension** is a series of regular payments made to a retired worker under a privately organized plan. Most employers offer plans that provide monthly payments, or pensions, to retired workers. Similar plans are often established by professional and trade associations or unions.

To qualify for a pension under most private plans, you must work for the same company or belong to the same organization for a minimum number of years. Pensions are commonly paid not only to retired workers of industries but also to retired workers of institutions such as schools, hospitals, and government agencies. It is possible for some workers to retire on pensions which together with their social security benefits give them an income of slightly over half of their earnings during employment.

The Employee Retirement Income Security Act of 1974 (ERISA) defines the rules for company pension plans. The act assures that people under pension plans will receive their pensions even if the companies they work for go bankrupt. Also, most workers who change jobs will keep some of their pension rights instead of losing them as many workers have in the past. This law also makes it possible for self-employed business and professional people and for employees not covered by a pension plan to set aside tax-sheltered income to provide for their retirement.

Individual Retirement Accounts

It is also possible for people to develop their own retirement income plans. The most popular of these plans is the individual retirement account (IRA). As described in Chapter 31, this is an account in which people can invest money each year during their working years for retirement. The money and the interest are tax free until the time of withdrawal at age 59½ or later.

Annuities

An amount of money that the insurance company will pay at definite intervals to a person who has previously deposited money with the company is called an **annuity**. An annuity is an investment plan for retirement income that is usually purchased from an insurance company. You pay the insurance company a certain amount of money either in a lump sum or in a series of payments. In return,

Illus. 39–2
Some people plan annuities as a supplement to other retirement income.

the company agrees to pay you a regular income beginning at a certain age and continuing for life or for a specified number of years.

Because annuity contracts are often sold by life insurance companies, they are sometimes thought to be a form of life insurance. However, they are really quite different. You buy life insurance mainly to protect your dependents; you buy an annuity to protect yourself against not having an adequate income in retirement years. It has been said that life insurance insures against dying too soon and an annuity insures against living too long.

The Social Security System

One of the most important forms of future income protection comes through the federal government's social security system. The Medicare program which you learned about in Chapter 37 is one part of the social security system. The other important part is **Retirement, Survivors, and Disability Insurance.** This part of the insurance system provides pensions to retired workers and their families, death benefits to dependents of workers who die, and benefits to disabled workers and their families.

Illus. 39–3
Social security is not just for retirement—it also pays survivors benefits to dependents.

The basic idea of social security is not difficult. During working years, employed people pay social security taxes. The taxes are deducted from the employees' paychecks. Employers match the amounts paid by their employees. Self-employed people, such as farmers, retail merchants, and professional people, pay the entire tax themselves. But the amount they pay is less than the total amount paid by both the employer and the employee on the same income. Self-employed people pay their social security tax when they file their income tax returns.

The taxes collected are put into a special trust fund. When a worker retires, becomes disabled, or dies, monthly payments from the trust fund are made to replace part of the income the family has lost.

Getting a Social Security Number. If you work in a job covered by social security, you must have a **social security number.** This number is used to identify your record of earnings. The social security benefits that you and your dependents may someday receive will be determined by this record of earnings.

A social security number is also needed by anyone who fills out a federal income tax return. The Internal Revenue Service uses this number as a taxpayer identification number for processing tax returns. People who receive interest or dividends also need a social security number.

To get a social security number, you must fill out an application form. You may get a form from your employer, from a social security office, or from a post office. The federal government then issues a **social security card,** such as the one shown in Figure 39–1, which shows your number. You use the same social security number during your entire life. If you lose your card, you can get a duplicate from a social security office. If your name changes, you should obtain a new card showing the account in your new name.

Applying for Social Security Benefits. Social security benefits are not automatically paid when you become entitled to them. To receive any benefits, you must apply at a social security office. The amount of benefits you receive depends to a great extent on how much you earned during your working years. Social security monthly benefits usually increase as the cost of living rises. The cost of living increase is based in part on the consumer price index discussed in Chapter 25.

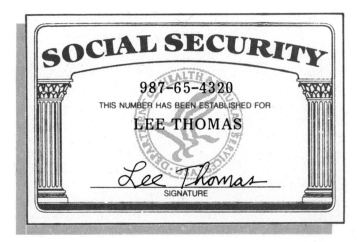

Figure 39–1
You will receive a social security card when you apply for a social security number.

Those who are covered by social security can receive the full amount of the monthly payments to which they are entitled when they reach age 65. But if they choose, they can retire as early as age 62 by accepting lower payments. Workers may be entitled to full benefits if they become disabled at any age before 65. If an insured worker dies, a lump-sum payment is made to the surviving spouse even though monthly benefits are also payable to a surviving spouse and/or dependent children.

*A*dding to Your Business Vocabulary

The following terms should become part of your business vocabulary. For each numbered item, find the term that has the same meaning.

annuity
disability income insurance
pension
retirement, survivors, and
   disability insurance

social security card
social security number
unemployment insurance

1. Insurance that helps replace income when you are unable to work because of an illness or accident.
2. An amount of money that an insurance company will pay at definite intervals to a person who has previously deposited money with the company.
3. The number used to identify one's record of earnings under social security laws.
4. Payments made to a retired worker under a privately organized plan.
5. Insurance that provides cash payments

for a limited time to people who are out of a job for a reason other than illness.

6. Government insurance that provides, among other things, for benefits to be

paid to retired workers and their families.

7. A document showing one's social security number.

*U*nderstanding Your Reading

1. What are the two most common causes of income loss?
2. What is the purpose of state unemployment insurance?
3. Why are unemployment insurance benefits lower than the unemployed person's former salary?
4. What is a pension?
5. What are some of the ways the Employee Retirement Income Security Act of 1974 helps workers?
6. What is the difference between an annuity and an insurance policy?
7. Explain how the social security system works.
8. What three groups of people receive monthly incomes from social security?
9. What does the federal government do with social security taxes after it collects them?
10. Even if you do not have a job, what is one reason you might need a social security number?
11. How can you get a social security card?

*P*utting Your Business Knowledge to Work

1. Benefits from unemployment insurance begin after a waiting period and usually end after about 26 weeks. Why do you think this is so?
2. Name the type(s) of insurance for future income that the following people would be most likely to receive:
   a. The restaurant in which Richard Saulsovich is a maître d' declares itself bankrupt and goes out of business, costing Richard his job.
   b. Alice Wait retires, at age 65, from a career as a warehouse manager.
   c. Helen Jones retires and receives

monthly checks from an insurance company under a plan bought with a lump-sum payment.

3. With unemployment insurance available in every state, why would anyone want to buy loss-of-income insurance from a private insurance company? Does loss-of-income insurance provide any benefits that unemployment insurance does not?
4. If Franklin Eldridge felt his social security retirement benefits were going to be too small, what could he do to assure greater retirement benefits?

Computing Business Problems

1. The federal government has made an attempt to keep social security benefits rising as consumer prices rise. If Charlene Thompson's social security benefits were $355 per month and consumer prices went up by 5 percent, by how much would her benefits have to increase to equal the consumer price increase?

2. James Burrow, who has worked for 24 years in occupations covered under social security, became disabled as a result of an accident. His average monthly earnings covered by social security amount to $650. The social security office used the following percentages to decide the amount of the monthly check to which Mr. Burrow is entitled:

114% of the first $110 of average monthly wage

42% of the next $290
38% of the next $150
25% of the next $100

How much will Mr. Burrow's monthly disability check be?

3. June Parder is about to retire. She will collect social security and a pension from the gas and electric company where she has been employed in a city in New York. She has always planned to retire to Florida, but she is worried about missing her children and grandchildren who live in New York. She plans to return to New York twice a year by car for a visit. If the distance from the New York city she lives in now to her new home in Florida is 2,050 kilometers, how many kilometers will she travel the first year, counting the first trip to Florida? How many miles is this?

Stretching Your Business Knowledge

1. Do you think social security was designed to be a retired person's sole source of income during retirement years? Do library research to help you answer this question.

2. There are some types of workers who are not covered under social security. Find out from your local social security office who these workers are. What types of protection for income security are available to them?

3. The most frequent retirement age is 65. Some people, however, choose to retire earlier. When they do, the social security benefits they are paid become lower. Why is this so?

4. Some insurance companies offer variable annuities as a protection against inflation. What is a variable annuity? Which type of annuity do you think is better, fixed or variable?

CAREER CATEGORY: Insurance

Just as there are many types of insurance, there are also many jobs within the insurance industry. Most of those jobs provide workers the opportunity to meet people and to plan strategies for avoiding financial loss.

Job Titles: Job titles commonly found in this career area include:

Sales Agent   Insurance Broker
Insurance Clerk   Insurance Investigator
Claims Adjuster   Actuary
Underwriter   Policywriter
Claims Examiner   Accountant
Data Processing Manager

Employment Outlook: Insurance employment is usually not seriously affected by changes in economic conditions since most individuals and businesses consider insurance to be a necessity. The volume of insurance sales is expected to grow through the 1990s, indicating an increasing demand for workers in the insurance industry. That growth plus a rather high turnover of insurance agents and brokers will cause this field to continue to be a popular employment area.

Future Changes: The demand for insurance workers will probably always be dependent on the volume of future sales. This volume will probably increase rapidly over the next decade as many more workers enter the 25–54 age group — an age period when insurance is especially important. Employment in insurance may not keep pace with increased insurance sales, however, because it is expected that more policies will be sold to groups and by mail than in the past.

What Is Done on the Job: Most positions in insurance involve frequent contact with the public, either policy owners or potential customers. Claims adjusters and claims examiners, for instance, must meet policy owners when they investigate a claim and decide how much, if anything, should be paid. They must treat policy owners fairly and courteously. Sales agents, those workers who find customers and sell them the kinds of insurance needed, also may deliver claim checks to those who have had a loss. Sales agents must be able to get along well with people. All workers who have contacts with the public should have pleasant manners and should be able to talk easily with a great variety of people. An honest desire to help people is also important for workers in this career area.

Some insurance specialists must be very good in math and statistics. Actuaries, for example, are responsible for determining the risks taken on by insurance companies when they sell policies. Accountants and data processing managers also are important in seeing to it that appropriate records are maintained and analyzed. Actuaries, accountants, and data processing managers work together as an important management team.

Education and Training: Most insurance companies prefer employees with college training but usually are willing to hire high school graduates, especially people who are ambitious and show it. Many community colleges and other colleges and universities offer training in insurance to help prepare workers for this industry.

In addition, all states require people who market insurance to be licensed by the state.

The license is issued only after the applicant has passed a test.

Salary Levels: Salaries in the insurance field vary widely, but are competitive. The largest single group of employees is sales agents and insurance brokers. As beginners they are guaranteed a moderate salary and later begin earning good commissions as a percentage of their insurance sales.

A typical salary for a new agent is about $1,800 per month. Life insurance sales agents with five years experience will earn about $40,000 per year with many eventually earning over $100,000 per year.

For Additional Information: Many insurance companies provide information free of charge to people interested in their business. Information on state licensing requirements can be obtained from the department of insurance at any state capital. Information about careers in insurance is also available from the following organizations:

American Council of Life Insurance
1850 K Street, N.W.
Washington, D.C. 20006

The National Association of Life
    Underwriters
1922 F Street, N.W.
Washington, D.C. 20006

Insurance Information Institute
110 William Street
New York, NY 10038

Alliance of American Insurers
20 N. Wacker Drive
Chicago, IL 60606

UNIT 11

GOVERNMENT AND LABOR IN OUR ECONOMY

UNIT OBJECTIVES

After studying the chapters in this unit, you will be able to:

1. Describe how government serves you as a citizen, consumer, and worker.

2. Explain how we pay for government services.

3. Describe the role of labor in our economy.

BUSINESS BRIEF
Employee-Owned Companies

Workers are taking over many American businesses. But this is not being done with the use of strikes or violence. Employees are using personal funds to purchase a controlling interest of the organization for which they work.

While most businesses are owned by investors, some are owned by the workers. In recent years, several companies were purchased by their employees. As a result, the organizations continued to operate and provide jobs. Workers and the community were able to avoid the difficult economic situation brought about by the loss of jobs and income. Outright purchase of a company by workers is one type of employee-owned business.

Another method in which workers can obtain partial ownership of their company is with employee stock ownership plans (ESOPs). An ESOP may be an employee fringe benefit similar to a pension or profit-sharing plan. An ESOP may also be used when a company cannot afford to give workers an increase in wages. Instead of higher wages, employees receive shares of ownership in their company. Many well-known businesses, such as Sears and Quaker Oats, are partially owned by employees. Nearly ten million workers are involved in employee stock ownership plans.

Studies indicate that workers often put forth a better effort on the job when they are part-owners of the company. Employee-owned companies are often more productive and have better morale than other organizations. Strong cooperation is usually present since workers are not just paid employees, they are also part owners of the business.

However, employee-owned companies are not without problems. For example, members of one organization argued between sharing profits with the worker-owners and using the funds to expand the business. This disagreement resulted in lowered productivity and lost company sales. Another problem for every company, regardless of ownership, is poor economic conditions. Employee-owned businesses must compete with all other profit-making organizations.

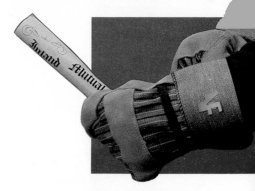

Government plays a role in employee-owned companies in two ways. First, since ESOPs are a type of employee benefit, government regulates how workers will be taxed on company stock received. Second, as a result of a high level of productivity, company profits are high which results in increased tax revenue from the business. This allows government to reduce other taxes or to have additional money available to provide public services.

Saved jobs, improved productivity, and worker participation are some of the advantages of employee-owned companies. These organizations are excellent examples of successful cooperation among business, labor, and government in our economic system.

CHAPTER 40

Government Serves Us All

■ CHAPTER OBJECTIVES ─────────────────────

After studying this chapter and completing the end-of-chapter activities, you will be able to:

1. List five services provided by government.
2. Describe how government protects you as a citizen, consumer, and worker.
3. List at least three ways government influences our economy.
4. Describe government's role as a purchaser of goods and services.
5. Tell how government activities are changing.

Each day you are free to make many decisions as a consumer, worker, and citizen. You are usually allowed to buy the goods and services you desire. But sometimes restrictions are placed on consumers buying such products as alcoholic beverages, cigarettes, and medications. Government tries to protect consumers from purchasing potentially dangerous items.

In a similar manner, you have the freedom to select a career. But for some jobs, such as a doctor, lawyer, or teacher, you must meet certain requirements. These requirements are designed to protect consumers. You certainly do not want an untrained doctor treating you when you are ill.

Government also requires business owners to follow certain safety and labor laws. Government attempts to balance and serve the interests of everyone in our economy.

Government as a Provider of Services

Government is organized into three levels — federal, state, and local — as shown in Figure 40-1. The main goal of the federal government is to oversee the activities which involve two or more

Figure 40–1
Different levels of
government have
different duties,
concerns, and
responsibilities.

Levels of Government		
Local	**State**	**Federal**
Government units include county city park district library district school district	concerned with the regulation of intrastate commerce	concerned with interstate commerce and trade between the United States and other countries

states or other countries. Business transactions involving companies in more than one state are called **interstate commerce.** Therefore, a trucking company which ships products to several states would be regulated by the federal government.

State governments regulate business activities within their own boundaries. **Intrastate commerce** refers to business transactions involving companies which do business only in one state.

Local governments include county boards and city or town councils. These local government units provide many of the day-to-day necessities for an orderly society, such as police and fire protection.

Government officials are elected or appointed to serve you. Their job is to serve all citizens based on the choices made by voters. As a citizen, one of your responsibilities includes participation through the ballot box in our society's decision-making process.

Group Decision Making

Choices about who will govern result from voting. In an election citizens decide who will represent them. Our elected officials then have the task of making choices which will affect everyone. For example, state legislators may decide to spend more money for schools and provide less funds for building new highways.

While many believe political power to be in the hands of a few, decisions are really made by many in our form of government. By voting, citizens influence the choices which will be made by our public officials. As discussed in Chapter 3, a vote to increase or decrease taxes will affect the government services available.

Meeting the Needs of the People

We enjoy freedom and safety because of the services furnished by government. The efforts of government which benefit citizens are called **public services.** Examples include fighting fires, maintaining roads, and teaching young people. Protecting our basic rights and providing economic stability are also fundamental government activities.

Government as a Protector

One of the most important government services is protection. Safety of our personal well-being, property, and national security is vital. Government also protects our rights as consumers, business owners, and workers.

Protecting Society

Providing local police and fire-fighting services is a basic duty of government. The protection of property is necessary for our survival. On a larger scale, the armed forces provide for our national defense. The security of our country is a major concern of the federal government.

Government also protects us from an unsafe environment. Several laws exist to prevent air, water, noise, and chemical pollution. If people could do as they pleased, we might not have clean air

Illus. 40–1
Through laws, government protects the environment.

or water for future use. Federal, state, and local government agencies enforce laws which prevent the dumping of chemicals and waste in rivers and lakes. Other regulations forbid the burning of substances which make our air unsafe to breathe. Protection of our communities from pollution is an important government service for everyone.

Protecting Consumers and Businesses

Every business transaction involves an agreement to exchange goods or services for something of value, usually money. This agreement is called a **contract**. A contract may be written or unwritten. The enforcement of contracts is necessary for an orderly economic system. If you agree to have repairs made on your car for $45, the work must be paid for when completed. If you fail to make payment, legal action can be taken to force you to pay. Both consumers and businesses benefit from contract enforcement. Without it, dishonest consumers or business owners could refuse to honor their agreements, and our daily business activities would be very confusing.

We are also protected by special property rights. When individuals or companies create new products or ideas, they may obtain a patent. A **patent** gives the inventor the exclusive right to make, use, or sell the item for 17 years. For example, a company which creates a new method to record programs from television would obtain a patent for this process to prevent other companies from making or selling recorders using this process.

In a similar manner, a **copyright** protects the work of authors, composers, or artists. This protection continues for 50 years after the person's death. Examples of copyright statements can be found on the front pages of most books. Patent and copyright laws were passed to reward and protect creative efforts.

Another form of protection given to a business by government is a trademark. **Trademarks** are words, letters, or symbols which are associated with a specific company or product. Company names, team emblems, and label designs may be registered with the government. A trademark can be very valuable since many are famous throughout the world. What are some trademarks you see frequently?

Illus. 40–2
The government also protects creative works through patents, copyrights, and trademarks.

Protecting Workers

Employees are also protected by government. As a worker you have a basic right to safe working conditions. For example, safety standards for buildings, machines, and chemicals are set by government agencies. Government inspection of work areas helps to reduce the number of job-related accidents. For example, when machine operators wear safety glasses, the number of eye injuries can be lowered.

Additional government regulations stem from the need to protect the basic human rights of workers. For example, government does not allow people to be denied work because of their race, religion, sex, or age. Selection for a job must be based on training and experience. In addition, government does not permit wages below a set amount for certain jobs.

Other government efforts to protect basic human rights of workers include the following:

1. Government training programs assist workers in obtaining necessary employment skills.
2. Job placement services help workers find employment.
3. Unemployment benefits provide financial assistance to workers who have lost their jobs due to poor economic conditions.

Government as an Economic Manager

Our economic system is based on free choice for individuals. Buying items, selecting a career, or starting a business are usually done with limited government influence. But sometimes actions are needed to preserve economic stability. The regulation of utilities and prevention of unfair business activities help to provide a stable business environment.

Regulating Utilities

Most goods and services you use are obtained from private businesses which are relatively free of government regulation. But a **public utility** is an organization which supplies a service or product vital to all people. These include companies which provide local telephone service, water, and electricity. Most public utilities do not compete with other companies. One is selected to serve the whole community. If your city had six different electric companies, each with its own utility poles, lines, and expensive equipment, the service you would get would be more expensive and less efficient. Also, the extra poles and wires would create an unsightly environment.

While many utility companies are privately owned, they are closely regulated by government. Therefore, public utilities cannot set prices as they wish. This would be unfair since there is no competition to keep prices reasonable. The rates charged for items such as electricity, water, or natural gas must be approved by a government agency.

Promoting Competition

Most businesspeople are fair and honest, but a few may try to take advantage of their customers or competitors. Government attempts to prevent this. If a company charges different prices to different people for the same product, it is treating its customers unfairly. Likewise, if one business gets lower rates for the same quality and quantity of supplies than others, it has an advantage. Such action results in unfair competition.

As mentioned in Chapter 16, a monopoly exists when a business has control of the market for a product or service. While a public utility monopoly may be beneficial by making sure people receive a needed service at a fair price, other monopolies may not be good for the economy. For example, if all food stores in your city were owned by the same company, consumers might not be treated fairly. This business could charge high prices and provide poor-quality products. Competition exists to give customers the best items at a fair price.

One government action designed to promote competition and fairness and to prevent monopolies was the passage of **antitrust laws**. Antitrust laws also prevent other unfair business practices such as false advertising, deceptive pricing, and misleading labeling. Each of these unfair practices hurts competition and reduces consumer choice.

Providing Business Assistance

Government also aids business by collecting and reporting valuable information. Data collected by the government can assist in planning for the future. Information about incomes, prices, worker availability, and business failures can help a businessperson make wiser decisions. For example, census information can help a business decide where the most potential customers live. The Bureau of Labor Statistics, the Department of Agriculture, and the Department of Commerce are a few of the government agencies that provide information.

Financial assistance is another government effort to aid business. Loans can be obtained to help new businesses get started. Also, farmers and others may receive financial help in times of extreme hardship such as drought, flooding, or other disasters. Destruction of home and property by a tornado may qualify a person for a low-interest government loan. These programs are designed to promote the economic well-being of our society.

Government as a Purchaser of Goods and Services

All levels of government buy and use a wide range of items. They are also consumers of human services. More than 12 million people in our country work full time for federal, state, and local governments.

Buying Goods and Services

The federal government spends a great deal of money each day to buy a variety of goods and services. Buying everything from file cabinets to jet planes, government is a major customer and an important economic force. Many businesses depend on government contracts and spending for their survival. Companies in your state most likely do business with the federal government, supplying such things as computers, processed foods, and automobiles.

Hiring Public Employees

Government is the single largest employer in our economy. About one of every nine workers is a public employee. Most people think only of police officers, fire fighters, and sanitation workers as government workers, but government employs the same types of workers employed by private industries. Secretaries, lawyers, and computer programmers, for example, are employed by government. In recent years, although the number of federal employees has not grown, career opportunities in many state and local governments have increased as citizens have demanded additional public services.

The Changing Role of Government

The services provided by government units are constantly changing. Government today is involved in many more activities than ever before. In addition, areas of government activity have changed. For example, because government has removed certain regulations, the airline and banking industries have been allowed to

Illus. 40–3
Government is our economy's largest employer.

compete more freely than in the past. Many people believe government should have less involvement in business and economic activities. Others believe that government involvement in such matters as the health and safety aspects of products must increase.

Government will continue to play a major role in our economic system. The specific areas of involvement will depend on your future decisions as a citizen and voter.

*A*dding to Your Business Vocabulary

The following terms should become part of your business vocabulary. For each numbered item, find the term that has the same meaning.

antitrust laws	patent
contract	public utility
copyright	public services
interstate commerce	trademark
intrastate commerce	

1. A business that supplies a service or product vital to all people and whose prices are determined by government regulation rather than competition.
2. Business activities within the boundaries of one state.
3. Efforts of government, such as fire and police protection, which benefit citizens.
4. Laws designed to promote competition and prevent monopolies.
5. Protection of the work of authors, composers, or artists.
6. An agreement to exchange goods or services for something of value.
7. The exclusive right given a person to make, use, or sell an invention for a period of 17 years.
8. Business transactions involving companies in more than one state.
9. A word, letter, or symbol associated with a specific product or company.

*U*nderstanding Your Reading

1. What are the three levels of government?
2. How do interstate and intrastate commerce differ?
3. In what ways do individuals influence the decisions of public officials?
4. How does government protect society?
5. Explain how the enforcement of contracts aids consumers and businesses.
6. Why does the government grant special copyright and patent rights?
7. List four ways in which government protects and assists workers.

8. Why can one public utility serve a city better than several similar public utilities?
9. When is a monopoly not in the best public interest?
10. Name two ways in which government aids private businesses.
11. What types of products and services do governments buy?

Putting Your Business Knowledge to Work

1. Below is a list of some of the public services provided by government. For each service, tell whether the federal, state, or local government would most likely have the major responsibility for the service.
   a. fire protection
   b. education
   c. parks and recreation
   d. water supply
   e. highways between cities
   f. aid to low income families
   g. sewage and trash disposal
   h. public buses
   i. police protection
   j. public libraries
   k. city streets
   l. national defense
2. In protecting human rights, the government places certain restrictions, such as minimum wages, on private businesses. Do you think that in protecting human rights the government is unfairly restricting the rights of business? Explain your answer.
3. Make a list of public utilities that serve your community.
   a. What services do they provide?

   b. Do you think it would be better for these services to be offered by several competing businesses? Explain your answer.
4. Each day people enter into many contracts both written and unwritten.
   a. Give examples of contracts between a consumer and a business, between two businesses, and between a worker and a business.
   b. What services are provided by government to enforce contracts?
5. Two students are discussing the topic "Government is Our Biggest Business." Cindy believes that some government activities are in direct competition with private businesses and that this is unfair. She believes that government should limit its activities to those activities that private businesses cannot or will not undertake. Chuck thinks that government should undertake any business activities that it can perform better or less expensively than private business. What do you think? Give some examples of business activities undertaken by both private businesses and by government.

Computing Business Problems

1. A city government spends $186,000 a month on public services. Of that amount, 46 percent is used for fire and police protection.

   a. How much is spent each month for fire and police protection?
   b. How much is spent each month for other services?

c. How much is spent by the city in a year for fire and police protection?

2. In a city in which there are 90,000 employed workers, 18,000 are public employees. Of this number, 6,000 are employed by the federal government, 8,000 by the state, and 4,000 by the city.
   a. What percent of all workers are public employees?
   b. What percent of the public employees are employed by the federal government?
   c. What percent of all employees are employees of the state government?

3. The town of Clarksville wants to expand the main street from two to four lanes. To do so, 150 feet of land is needed. How many meters of land will be used for the road-widening project?

4. Listed below is the cash income and expenditures record of the Randolph Public Library for one year:

Income:

Cash on hand, beginning of year	$ 1,250
Town and state appropriations	52,000
Income from investments	1,795
Gifts	1,645
Fines on overdue books	550
Miscellaneous income	325

Expenditures:

Salaries	23,500
Books and periodicals	6,775
Utilities	1,525
Insurance	780
Equipment and supplies	1,455
Cleaning and repairs	420
Community service programs	1,800
Library binding	675
General administrative expenses	715

a. What was the total of the cash on hand and cash received during the year?
b. How much was paid out during the year?
c. What percent of the total cash received was accounted for by town and state appropriations? (Round your answer to the nearest whole percent.)
d. What percent of total expenditures was accounted for by salaries? (Round your answer to the nearest whole percent.)

Stretching Your Business Knowledge

1. Make a list of businesses in your community involved in interstate and intrastate commerce. Information can be obtained from newspaper advertisements, customers, and employees of local companies.

2. You have seen many trademarks on products as well as in advertisements on television, on billboards, and in newspapers and magazines. Make a display of 10 trademarks you recognize to show to your class. See if your classmates can tell the name of the company represented by each trademark.

3. The salaries paid to government employees are matters of public record; that is, the public can know what these people are paid. Do you think it is fair to these employees for you to know how much money they make? Why or why not?

4. Using a business-law book or information gained through library research, list the main parts of every contract. How are minors protected when it comes to contracts?

5. Government control of monopolies in the U.S. has an interesting history. Many important laws were passed to control monopolies. Through library research find out what the major provisions were and some of the results of these laws:
   a. Sherman Antitrust Act
   b. Clayton Act
   c. Federal Trade Commission Act.

CHAPTER 41

Paying for Government Services

■ CHAPTER OBJECTIVES ─────────────────────

After studying this chapter and completing the end-of-chapter activities, you will be able to:

1. Give at least two reasons for the increasing costs of government services.
2. Identify three sources of government revenue.
3. List four items which are taxed.
4. Name three factors considered when creating a tax.
5. Explain how government can meet its expenses if taxes do not provide enough revenue.

On most mornings, the Wanston family's breakfast includes food products which the government has inspected for safety. Mrs. Wanston later drives her daughter and son to school on roads built and repaired by government workers. The car Mrs. Wanston drives was built to meet federal pollution standards. The school the children attend is a service provided with local, state, and federal government funds. After school, Beth and Kenneth Wanston often go swimming in the community-supported pool of the park district.

These are just a few of the services provided by various levels of government. But how are these services financed? Government must raise money to cover the costs of public services. Since we all benefit from government services, we should also share in paying government expenses.

The High Cost of Government

Most goods and services you buy come from private businesses. But other items are provided through government efforts. Over the years government has become more involved in serving the public. People now demand more from government than in the past. We have come to expect good highways, up-to-date libraries, and other public services. This demand for more public services results in higher government costs.

Another reason for increased government spending is the complexity of our economy. A growing population and an expanding business structure require a high degree of government effort. Providing services for 230 million people is no small task.

We have all had to cope with higher costs because of inflation, and government is no different. As prices increase, it costs more to provide public services and the rising cost of government is likely to continue. As costs continue to rise, finding new ways to pay government expenses may be necessary.

Sources of Government Income

As with businesses and individuals, income is necessary for government to operate. Government income is often called **revenue**. Most revenue comes from taxes. Taxes are the payments that citizens are required to make which are used to finance the cost of government.

Illus. 41–1
The complexity of our society and a growing population require a higher degree of government effort.

There are other sources of revenue in addition to taxes. Fines for traffic violations and other violations of the law provide income for government. Fees and licenses are also a source of revenue. Certain types of enterprises require a business license. For example, insurance and real estate agents pay a fee for the privilege of conducting business. Other examples of government fees are charges for drivers' licenses and fishing licenses.

Taxes to Raise Revenue

Taxes are the main source of government income. To pay for the services it provides, government levies taxes based on (1) earnings, (2) property, (3) estates, and (4) goods and services.

Taxes Based on Earnings

Your earnings as an individual are subject to an income tax. **Income taxes** are taxes on the income of individuals and businesses. This is the largest source of revenue of the federal government as shown in Figure 41-1. Federal income tax deductions are also the largest wage deductions for most workers. Employers are required to withhold a portion of their employees' taxes from each

Illus. 41–2
Government revenue includes fees charged for various types of licenses.

Sources of Federal Government Revenue

45.2¢ — Individual Income Tax

32.6¢ — Social Security/Retirement

10.3¢ — Corporate Income Tax

5.9¢ — Excise Tax

3.6¢ — Unemployment Tax

1.0¢ — Estate and Gift Taxes

1.4¢ — Other Taxes (tariffs, fines, misc.)

Figure 41–1 Government revenue comes from several sources. The largest source is the individual income tax.

paycheck. Employers then send this money to the government. Self-employed people are usually required to make quarterly tax payments to the federal government.

By April 15 of each year, taxpayers must file their federal income tax returns. An income tax return is a form used to determine the amount of tax owed for the year. Taxpayers may have to make an additional payment to the government or may receive a refund for any overpayment.

Most states and many large cities also tax the income of individuals. This revenue helps to cover the costs of services provided by state and local government units.

Corporate income taxes also provide government revenue. These are based on business profits. As you learned in Chapter 6, the corporate form of business ownership has several advantages. But there is the disadvantage of "double taxation." First the corporation pays a tax on its profits. Then dividends paid to shareholders by corporations must be reported as income on the shareholders' individual tax returns.

The Wanston family owns stock in a corporation. The company pays corporate income tax on its profits, and pays dividends to the Wanstons. Mr. and Mrs. Wanston must then report the dividends as income on their personal income tax form.

The social security program, discussed in Chapter 39, is supported by a tax on earnings. A percentage is deducted from your pay, up to a set limit. Your employer then contributes a similar amount based on your earnings to social security. These funds provide retirement and disability benefits for workers.

Taxes Based on Property

A major source of revenue for local governments is the real estate property tax. This tax is based on the value of land and buildings attached to the land. Most property tax revenue is used to pay for schools and other local government services such as police protection and community parks. Businesses also pay a property tax. This amount, like salaries and advertising costs, is an operating expense of the company and is included in the prices charged for goods and services.

Some state and local governments also tax personal property. This tax is based on the value of items such as automobiles, boats, furniture, and farm equipment.

Taxes on Estates

In addition to taxes on property, the government also collects revenue based on the total worth of a person. Such a tax may take one of two forms. An **estate tax** is an assessment or tax based on the value of a person's property when he or she dies. The person's property may include money, investments, a house, and land.

When the property is transferred to someone else, it may be subject to an inheritance tax. An **inheritance tax** is a tax based on the value of property or the amount of money received from a person who has died. Both estate and inheritance taxes are sources of revenue for federal and state governments.

To avoid estate and inheritance taxes, some people give away their property before they die. You are, at present, allowed to give a person a tax-free amount of $10,000 each year to as many people as you wish. When amounts greater than $10,000 are given to an individual, the value of the property is subject to a **gift tax.** In many states large amounts of money and property with a high value will be taxed even if the item changes hands before the death of the original owner.

Taxes on Goods and Services

The cost of buying things can be increased by a sales tax. A **sales tax** is a tax on goods and services which is collected by the seller. Sales taxes currently range from 2 percent to 8 percent of a purchase. If you buy a can of paint for $15.00 and the state sales tax is 6 percent, the seller collects $15.90 from you. The seller then will pay 90 cents to the state, but you were the one who provided the money for the tax.

Illus. 41–3
Sales taxes add to the cost of goods and services consumers buy. Most states now charge a sales tax.

Some states do not tax the cost of food and medicine. This is to assist low-income people who spend a large portion of their income on these necessities. In recent years, all but five states had a general sales tax.

Another type of tax that consumers pay on the purchase of certain goods and services is known as an **excise tax.** This tax is imposed on such goods and services as gasoline, cigarettes, air travel, and telephone service, and is usually included in the price of the item. The excise tax is a revenue source for federal and state governments.

As you learned in Chapter 7, taxes on imports are called tariffs. Only the federal government can impose an import tax. States cannot put a tariff on goods that are imported from foreign countries or shipped from other states.

Finding a Fair Tax

To some people, the only fair tax is the one someone else pays. Like the Wanston family, we all benefit from government services. As a result, most people are willing to share in the cost of government operations. Throughout history attempts have been made to create taxes which are fair for everyone. Several factors are usually considered when selecting a method of taxation. These are burden of payment, ability to pay, and benefits received.

Burden of Payment

Taxes are paid by two groups, individuals and businesses. A tax which cannot be passed on to someone else is called a **direct tax.** Sales taxes and personal income taxes are examples of direct taxes. These are paid directly by individuals.

An **indirect tax** is one which can be passed on to someone else. For example, corporate income taxes are paid by the business. But these taxes are paid from money received from customers. The price of products you purchase includes an amount which will be used to pay the corporate income tax.

People who rent an apartment or house also pay real estate property tax indirectly. While the tax is paid to government by the property owner, the funds come from the amount paid in rent. Every tax, both direct and indirect, is eventually paid for by individuals.

Ability to Pay

At one time property taxes were based on the number of farm animals owned or the number of windows in a person's house. Today, most taxes are related to some monetary value. This amount may be earnings, purchase price, or property value. A **progressive tax** is a tax whose rate becomes higher as the amount taxed becomes larger. For example, our federal income tax system requires a person making $60,000 to pay a larger portion for taxes than a person making $25,000. This is based on the belief that the person with the higher income is better able to pay.

Another common tax formula is the proportional method. A **proportional tax** is a tax where everyone pays the same rate; it is commonly called a **flat tax.** Most sales, social security, and some state income taxes are examples of proportional taxes.

Proportional taxes may seem fair. Unfortunately, low-income people frequently pay a larger share of their income as a result of a proportional tax. This is true because of their lower ability to pay. For example, in a state which has a 5 percent sales tax on all products, including food, the following can occur:

	Family A	Family B
Family income	$50,000	$20,000
Food budget	$ 7,000	$ 4,000
Sales tax on food (5%)	$ 350	$ 200
Portion of income spent on food sales tax	0.7%	1.0%

While Family A pays more than Family B in sales tax, B is paying a larger percentage of its income. While the tax is said to be proportional, the lower-income family pays a larger portion of its budget in taxes. This example suggests why many states do not tax the sale of food.

Benefits Received

Some people believe that taxes should be paid by those who benefit directly from the revenue. For example, these people would argue that only people with school-age children should be taxed for the cost of public schools because these parents receive the value. Others would say this is not completely true, since all citizens benefit from an educated population. There is less unemployment, better production output, and more technological discoveries with a well-educated population.

The benefits-received idea may be appropriate for a toll road. But for services like police protection, for example, it would be a difficult rule to follow.

Governments frequently change tax laws in an effort to create a fair system. Quite often, however, all that occurs is a shifting of the tax burden from one group of people to another. Recently as federal income taxes were reduced, other federal taxes as well as state and local taxes increased in many areas of our country.

The establishment of a completely fair tax system is quite difficult. People usually believe that they should pay less and benefit more. A basic understanding of the factors involved in taxation is vital as you make choices as a citizen, consumer, and worker.

Government Use of Credit

Government income from taxes and other sources may not always be enough to cover the costs of services. In a recent year, $618 billion in tax revenue was collected by the federal government. During that year, however, expenses were over $700 billion. When government spends more than it collects, a **deficit** results. This requires borrowing and increases the **public debt** which is the amount owed by government.

Governments borrow from individuals, banks, insurance companies, and other financial institutions. Those who purchase U.S. Treasury bills, notes, and bonds are actually lending money to the federal government.

In addition to paying the debt, the government must pay interest on the debt. Tax money is used to pay the interest on government loans. At the federal level, about twelve cents of each dollar spent goes for interest on the public debt.

Borrowing by government is affected by business conditions. In good economic times with high employment and strong consumer buying, income and sales taxes provide high levels of income for government. When government revenues are higher than expenses, a **surplus** exists.

We all want and expect certain services from government. But remember that we must pay for the increased services we demand. Asking for too much can result in financial problems for government. Wise money management is as important for government as it is for an individual or a family.

Influencing Government's Use of Your Money

One responsibility of every citizen is to help decide how to use tax money. The people who are elected to government positions should represent your desires. You can be involved in public decision making by:

Illus. 41–4

You do have a voice in how your tax dollars are spent.

1. Being informed about government activities.
2. Electing capable, honest people to government positions.
3. Studying and then voting intelligently on the issues presented.
4. Expressing your views to elected officials.

The wise use of your tax dollars will only come from citizen participation. Your actions must demand well-managed government at all levels.

*A*dding *to Your Business Vocabulary*

The following terms should become part of your business vocabulary. For each numbered item, find the term that has the same meaning.

deficit
direct tax
estate tax
excise tax
gift tax
income tax
indirect tax

inheritance tax
progressive tax
proportional tax or flat tax
public debt
revenue
sales tax
surplus

1. The amount owed by governments.
2. A tax which cannot be passed on to someone else.
3. Income that government receives from taxes and other sources.
4. A tax imposed on a large amount of money or property which is given away.
5. A tax on the earnings of individuals and corporations.
6. A tax on certain goods and services, generally included in the price quoted to purchasers.
7. A tax on goods and services which is collected by the seller.

8. A tax whose rate increases as the amount taxed increases.
9. A situation that exists when government has more income than expenses.
10. A tax based on the value of a person's property when he or she dies.
11. A tax which is passed on to someone else for payment.
12. A situation that exists when government spends more than it collects.
13. A tax based on the property or money received from a person who has died.
14. A tax method in which everyone pays the same rate.

*U*nderstanding *Your Reading*

1. How has inflation affected government spending?
2. List three sources of income for the federal government? For state governments? For local governments?
3. List four items on which taxes are levied.

4. How is corporate income tax a form of double taxation?
5. How are social security taxes paid?
6. Which level of government collects the most property taxes? How is this money usually spent?

7. What is the purpose of the gift tax?
8. What is the difference between a sales tax and an excise tax?
9. Who may impose tariffs on foreign imports?
10. Give an example of an indirect tax.
11. Why is it that some states do not have a sales tax on food?
12. How can the federal government pay its expenses if taxes do not provide enough revenue?
13. In what ways does government income depend on business conditions?
14. How can you help make sure that good business management is practiced in government?

*P*utting Your Business Knowledge to Work

1. As the size of a country's economy grows, the cost of government usually increases. Name some services which may not be necessary in a small country.
2. Income taxes are withheld from your paycheck throughout the year. Why do you think the government collects the taxes in this way rather than just once a year, such as when you file your income tax return?
3. In this chapter, you learned that only the federal government can impose tariffs. What do you think would happen if states were permitted to place import taxes on goods brought in for sale from other states?
4. Taxes can be classified as either direct or indirect. Tell whether consumers pay the following taxes directly or indirectly.
   a. sales tax
   b. tariff
   c. corporate income tax
   d. excise tax
   e. property tax for renters
   f. property tax for homeowners
   g. personal income tax
5. How is money received by government through the sale of bonds different from money received through taxes?

*C*omputing Business Problems

1. When Amelia Degado received her first paycheck, she was quite upset. She had been hired at a rate of $350 a week. However, her check was for an amount much less than that. The stub of her check showed that the following deductions were made from her pay:

Federal income tax	$52.50
Social security tax	$27.75
State income tax	$10.50

   a. What was the total amount of deductions from Amelia's check?
   b. What was the amount of her paycheck?

2. A state government received $3.7 million in tax revenue during a year. The costs of services for that same year were $4.1 million.
   a. What was the amount of deficit for the state for the year?
   b. If the interest rate is 11 percent, how much will the state have to pay in interest?
3. The state in which Thomas Sheehan lives has a 4 percent sales tax on all consumer purchases except food. At the supermarket one day Mr. Sheehan bought the following items:

1 box of sandwich bags, 72¢
2 liters of milk, 60¢ per liter
1 can tomato juice, 76¢
2 rolls of paper towels, 65¢ per roll
1 box of detergent, $2.43
1 package of frozen fish, $1.78

What was the total of Mr. Sheehan's bill, including sales tax?

4. The Mount Sherman School District is located in a city of 20,000. The student enrollment is 4,000. The property tax rate is $42.00 per $1,000 of assessed valuation. Of this tax rate, $20.16 is for educational needs. The total assessed valuation of all property in the city is $126 million.
   a. How much revenue should the city receive this year from the property tax?
   b. What percent of the property tax is budgeted for education?
   c. How much of the total annual revenue is budgeted for educational needs?
   d. What is the average amount of revenue received by the school district per student enrolled?

Stretching Your Business Knowledge

1. Make a list of local government services which have increased in cost over the past few years. Obtain information from articles in local newspapers or by contacting government officials.
2. The federal income tax is levied against taxable income. When you file an income tax return, taxable income is determined by subtracting certain exemptions and deductions from your total income. Through library research, find out what some allowable exemptions and deductions are. Why do you think the government allows these exemptions and deductions?
3. Tom Lee earns a salary of $18,500 a year and rents an apartment.
   a. Which of the taxes discussed in this chapter does Tom probably pay?
   b. Which of the taxes discussed are paid by others but are passed on to him as part of the cost of items he buys?
4. Besides using them as a source of revenue, government can also use taxes as a means of control. If a product is scarce and the government wants to discourage consumers from buying that product, the government can place an additional tax on that item. Is this a good way of controlling shortages? Explain your answer.
5. The federal government borrows money by selling U.S. Treasury bills, notes, and bonds. Using the financial pages of the newspaper, find the current rates people can earn by lending money to the government. Why are the interest rates for U.S. Treasury bills, notes, and bonds different from each other?

CHAPTER 42

*L*abor and Business

■ CHAPTER OBJECTIVES ─────────────────────────

After studying this chapter and completing the end-of-chapter activities, you will be able to:

1. Tell why labor is a vital economic resource.
2. Explain the difference between a closed shop and a union shop.
3. Name three economic and social concerns of workers.
4. Describe the collective bargaining process of organized labor.
5. List the actions used by workers and management to solve labor disputes.

Someday you will probably have one of the 20,000 job titles in our country. You may be a computer operator, a police officer, a store clerk, or a factory worker. Regardless of your job, you will contribute a basic economic resource—labor. As a worker you will be concerned about such things as salary level and opportunities for career advancement. The goals of labor are achieved through the combined efforts of workers and business.

Workers Provide Productive Services

The contributions of workers in our society are vital to economic growth. As presented in Chapter 1, labor includes all men and women involved in obtaining products from nature, converting raw materials into useful products, selling products, providing services, or supervising and managing others. Every human effort involved in the production of goods and services is labor.

Labor in Our Economy

Three types of economic resources are needed for production. These are natural resources, capital resources, and human resources. While labor is only one of the needed resources, many people believe it is the most important resource. Without labor, tools, machinery, and buildings could not be created. And without labor, equipment could not be used to produce goods and services for consumers.

As defined in Chapter 11, the work force includes everyone 16 years old and older who holds a job or who is seeking a job. Every business day over 110 million individuals in our country report to work. Most workers are employed either full-time or part-time in business, industry, or government. But the work force also includes professional people, such as doctors, lawyers, and teachers, and self-employed people, such as farmers and small business owners.

The Growth of Unions

Before the 1800s our economy was mainly agricultural. Most businesses were small and owners hired only a few workers. Problems of salary and working conditions were usually settled between the owner and each worker. As the use of machines increased and mass production grew, business firms became too large for owners and managers to know each employee personally.

Increased business size found many workers laboring in conditions that we would consider unbearable today. Workdays of 12 or 14 hours were common. Working conditions were often unsanitary and unsafe. Pay was frequently so low that workers could buy only basic necessities. And if employees banded together to express their discontent, they might be prosecuted in court. In some cases conflicts between employers and employees ended in violence.

Despite opposition, groups of employees continued to organize unions in order to improve their working conditions. In 1935 the legal status of unions in the United States was firmly established. In that year the National Labor Relations Act, sometimes called the Wagner Act, was passed. This law assures the right of employees to join unions and to hold fair elections to decide which union they want. It also states that workers have the right to choose representatives from their unions to make agreements with employers about working conditions.

In the beginning involvement in labor organizations was usually limited to blue-collar workers. Factories, shops, and construction sites were the main sources of union members. This is changing as more white-collar and professional workers have united to express their concerns.

Organized Labor

Many people in the work force — over 22 million workers — express themselves through labor unions. Almost 17 million of these workers belong to unions that are affiliated with one very large labor organization. This is the American Federation of Labor — Congress of Industrial Organizations, commonly known as the AFL–CIO. There are also strong independent unions, such as the International Brotherhood of Teamsters, the United Mine Workers, and the United Auto Workers.

As unions increased in size, they also became a powerful influence in the operation of businesses. Laws were created to maintain the balance of power between labor and business. For example, federal law makes the closed shop illegal. A **closed shop** exists when an employer agrees to hire only union members. At the same time, a union shop is permitted. A **union shop** exists when an employer may hire nonunion workers who must join the union within a set time period.

Illus. 42–1

Workers often band together to make their views and wishes known.

Some states have enacted **right-to-work laws** which state that no one can be required to join a union in order to get or keep a job. In the states that have right-to-work laws, unions are sometimes more difficult to organize. But workers are still allowed the choice of whether or not to join a union.

Workers often organize, though not as a union, to promote the interests of those working in their field. Examples include the American Farm Bureau, the American Medical Association, and the National Education Association. There are also special societies for sales managers, actors, and secretaries, to name just a few.

Concerns of Labor

All workers are concerned about such basic issues as job safety and a fair pay rate. Many are also interested in other benefits such as paid vacations, health insurance, and company training programs. The agreements reached between union leaders and management regarding these issues are usually written as a legally binding contract. A labor contract is designed to protect both employees and management.

Economic Issues

The main concern of most workers is their wage rate or salary. As they obtain additional skills and experience, employees desire pay increases. Workers frequently receive a raise when living costs increase. This can cause further inflation. But when a salary increase is a reward for higher productivity, improved economic stability rather than inflation results. As a company increases output and sales, higher wages and other benefits are possible.

The benefits provided by employers in addition to pay have a monetary cost. The value of benefits must be considered by both workers and management. For example, consider the benefits offered by two similar jobs:

	Job A	Job B
Salary	$28,000	$24,600
Paid vacation days (per year)	10	12
Life insurance	none	$25,000
Health insurance	$200 deductible	full coverage

While Job A pays more than Job B, the value of the additional benefits of Job B may make it a more attractive situation.

In recent years some companies have allowed individual workers to decide which benefits they will receive. Within a set limit, an employee may choose the benefits desired. A working person with several dependents may wish additional health or life insurance coverage. A single employee may want extra vacation days. These flexible benefit programs allow workers freedom to choose a plan that meets their needs.

Social Issues

A basic right of employees is safe working conditions. Unfortunately, certain methods of production can create dangers. Manufacturing equipment, factory chemicals, and building materials can be hazardous. Many labor contracts require that workers be protected from dangerous items and conditions.

As discussed in Unit 3, technology can also create problems for employees. As new equipment replaces workers, different jobs are in demand. Employers require skills related to the development, programming, and use of computerized systems. In recent years, unions have been concerned about retraining programs. As the skills of workers become outdated, labor and management can both benefit from retraining current employees.

Illus. 42–2
Worker safety is a major concern in some industries.

Grievances

Differences of opinion about a labor contract can and do occur. For example, an employee may believe extra pay is due for certain duties; the supervisor may disagree. Most union contracts outline a process for solving these disputes. This process is called a **grievance procedure.** Grievance procedures usually contain steps that allow each side to present its view of the situation.

The Collective Bargaining Process

A union contract is the result of many hours of meeting between representatives of workers and the employer. The negotiation that takes place between an organized body of workers and an employer dealing with wages and working conditions is called **collective bargaining.** This process usually involves several steps before agreement between the two sides is reached.

Starting the Process

Collective bargaining starts with a meeting where representatives of labor and management present what they believe should be in the contract. Attempts then follow to settle differences about wages, working hours, employee benefits, and other issues affecting workers. Ideally, an agreement will be reached and a contract signed. If, however, neither side will compromise on an item, other action may be necessary. In many cases others are asked to help resolve points of disagreement.

Third-Party Assistance

Sometimes negotiations between labor and management can go no further than the discussion stage. When this happens, a mediator may be used to settle the differences. A **mediator** is a neutral person, neither a member of management nor of labor, who attempts to resolve the dispute. A mediator can only recommend solutions, not enforce them.

If a disagreement cannot be settled by mediation, an arbitrator may be called in to decide the issue. An **arbitrator** is a person who makes a legally binding decision to resolve labor-management differences. Both sides present their views after which the arbitrator makes a ruling to which all are bound. Before an arbitrator can be called in, however, both sides must agree to the use of an arbitrator.

Mediation and arbitration are frequently used to settle differences as part of the grievance procedure. The people who serve as mediators and arbitrators are selected from approved lists of individuals who are acceptable to both labor and management.

Problems arising from contract disputes are also decided by the National Labor Relations Board (NLRB). This federal government agency investigates unfair practices of unions or management. The NLRB can, for example, stop union members from pressuring nonunion members to join. Or, employers can be forced to stop giving special treatment to nonunion employees.

Worker and Management Efforts to Settle Differences

The collective bargaining process may not always be successful. When neither party is willing to compromise, other actions can result. Procedures are available to both workers and management which can be used to encourage the settlement of differences.

Organized Labor's Actions

Workers who are dissatisfied with management's contract offer may vote to strike. A **strike** is a refusal to work until demands are met. A strike affects many people. Workers are not paid; the business may not have items to sell; and consumers might have to do without needed goods and services. During a recent transit strike, buses, trains, and subways did not operate. People had to find other ways of getting where they needed to go. Since many suffer during a strike, it is usually used only as a last resort.

During most strikes union members carry signs at the work site to publicize their complaints. This is called **picketing**. Picketing can encourage support from others. Customers and members of other unions often refuse to do business with a company that is being picketed.

Another action of labor is a boycott. A **boycott** is the refusal by workers to handle or buy products of a company involved in a labor disagreement. A boycott may also be a type of consumer action. If consumers believe a business is unfair to its workers, they might refuse to buy the company's products.

Management's Actions

When workers go on strike, the company may take certain actions. First, the business may try to operate as usual by hiring new employees. These people are referred to as strikebreakers. Using strikebreakers, however, may not be possible since some jobs require special training and experience.

Second, management may close all of its facilities in an attempt to put pressure on the striking union. Such action is called a **lockout**. If one union strikes, management may decide to close all offices and factories, thus involving employees not in the striking union. With many others out of work, pressure may be put on the strikers to compromise.

A third effort to stop a strike is legal action. An **injunction** is a court order directing employees to go back to work. Some strikes affect many people, such as a postal workers' strike or a truck drivers' strike. In some cases the president of the United States may obtain an injunction to get goods and services flowing again.

Illus. 42–3
Compromise is often the only road to agreement. Working together, differences can be resolved.

The Changing Role of Labor

As new types of jobs develop, the role of workers and labor organizations will change. In *recent years*, the number of employees in manufacturing industries, such as automobiles and steel, has decreased. This is the result of two main factors. First, competition from other countries has increased. While the United States was once the major producer of the world, economic development around the world has increased. Second, technology has changed the work skills that are required. Robots and computers have replaced people in various jobs.

Many new job opportunities are related to information and technology. Many employees in these industries will be white-collar workers. If unions are to grow, they will have to meet the needs of these workers. The needs and expectations of white-collar workers may differ from those of blue-collar workers. Unions will have to be aware of those differences. Organizing efforts will include clerical, professional, service, and government workers.

Illus. 42–4
New challenges
— new
opportunities!

While various factors in our economy will be different, one thing will not change. A cooperative effort among workers, business, and government will be necessary for economic success.

A dding to Your Business Vocabulary

The following terms should become part of your business vocabulary. For each numbered statement, find the term that has the same meaning.

arbitrator	lockout
boycott	mediator
closed shop	picketing
collective bargaining	right-to-work laws
grievance procedure	strike
injunction	union shop

1. An agreement requiring workers to join a union within a specified time after employment.
2. A neutral person who recommends solutions to disputes between labor and management.
3. A situation in which employees refuse to work until their demands are met.
4. A business where only union members may be hired by a company.
5. A refusal by workers to handle or buy the products of a company involved in a labor dispute.
6. Negotiations between an organized body of workers and an employer dealing with wages and working conditions.
7. A court order directing striking employees to report back to work.
8. A process in a labor contract for solving differences between workers and management.
9. A person who makes a legally binding decision to resolve a labor-management difference.
10. A situation in which a company closes all of its stores or plants in an attempt to put pressure on striking employees.
11. Laws which forbid making union membership a requirement for employment.
12. A situation in which union members carry signs to publicize their complaints.

Understanding Your Reading

1. Why is labor an important economic resource?
2. Who is included in the U.S. work force?
3. What conditions in the past contributed to the rise and growth of unions?
4. Why is the Wagner Act of special importance to workers?
5. What is the name of the largest labor organization in the United States?
6. Explain the main difference between a closed shop and a union shop.
7. What are right-to-work laws?
8. Name three examples of employee benefits.
9. How has technology affected the demands of workers?
10. What is the purpose of a grievance procedure?
11. How does the collective bargaining process work?
12. Describe the difference between a mediator and an arbitrator.
13. What is the National Labor Relations Board?
14. What techniques do unions use to persuade management to accept their demands?
15. In what ways can management reduce the effectiveness of a strike?

Putting Your Business Knowledge to Work

1. Some people are considered part of our total work force and others are not. Tell whether or not each person included in the following list is part of the work force.
   a. an airline flight attendant
   b. a bank president
   c. a homemaker
   d. a writer of mystery stories
   e. an 18-year-old high school graduate interviewing for a job
   f. a retired accountant
   g. a dentist
   h. your teacher
   i. a radio announcer
   j. a farmer
2. Certain products, such as clothing, have a label on them which indicates the manufacturer is a unionized company. Members of unions are encouraged not to buy products that do not have union labels on them. Do you think this is fair? Give reasons for your answer.
3. The demands of workers and business owners are frequently negotiated through collective bargaining. Decide if each item listed would most likely be a demand of labor or of management (or both).
   a. a day off for an employee's birthday
   b. every employee works one Saturday a month
   c. no overtime pay for cleaning machines after working hours
   d. promotions from within the company
   e. life insurance coverage for employees
4. The workers at the Browning Food Processing Company are on strike. What groups, other than the workers and the owners of the company, are affected by

the strike? In what ways?

5. Many people believe that government workers who perform vital services, such as police officers and fire fighters, should not be allowed to strike. What do you think? Why?

Computing Business Problems

1. In one city, there are 10,000 people in the work force. Of those, 21 percent are members of labor unions.
   a. How many people in the work force were members of labor unions?
   b. How many people in the work force were not members of labor unions?
2. To join a certain union, you must pay an initiation fee of $75 and monthly dues of $25.
   a. How much will it cost to be a union member in the first year?
   b. How much will it cost the second year?
3. Members of the work force are not always paid by the hour. Sometimes they are paid by the amount of work they do. Consider the following two choices that were offered to a truck driver going from Washington, D.C., to Buffalo, New York, a distance of about 560 kilometers: (1) receive 16 cents per kilometer for the entire trip; or (2) receive $14 per hour for the trip, driving at an average speed of 80 kilometers per hour.
   a. How much would the truck driver earn working by the kilometer?
   b. How much would the truck driver earn working by the hour?
4. Listed below are the hourly wages for six workers:

J. Adams	$8.65
L. Blake	8.27
K. Lomton	7.43
R. Morton	7.61
D. Roundtree	7.23
T. Washington	8.51

   a. What is the average hourly rate for these six workers?
   b. If Blake works 40 hours a week for one year, what will be his yearly earnings?

Stretching Your Business Knowledge

1. Through library research, obtain information about the growth and development of organized labor in the United States. What is the difference between a craft (or trade) union and an industrial union? What laws protect and restrict the rights of unions?
2. Discuss the questions below with relatives and friends who are members of labor unions. Summarize in writing the information you receive from your discussion and be prepared to give an oral report to the class.
   a. What social and welfare advantages do unions provide for their members?
   b. What does it cost to maintain membership in a union?
   c. What voice does the membership have in the operation of the local union? In the national union?

3. Talk to friends, relatives, and others you know who work. Obtain information about the types of employee benefits they receive. Prepare a list of the most common benefits.
4. Collect news articles about various labor and management actions. Examples could include strikes, contract agreements, or other labor issues. Prepare a display of this news for your class.
5. Unions have helped their members obtain important benefits. Have workers who are not members of unions shared in such benefits? Explain.

CAREER CATEGORY: Government

As you read Unit 11, did you find yourself wondering what it would be like to be involved in government directly—as an employee? Perhaps no other career category offers more variety in employment opportunities than does working for a government.

Job Titles: Job titles commonly found in this career area include:

Police Officer
City Manager
Postal Worker
Highway Maintenance Worker
Urban Planner
Armed Services

Health and Safety Inspector
Fire Fighter
Government Accountant
Public Librarian
Customs Agent
Social Worker

Employment Outlook: There are over 15 million people employed by local, state, and federal governments. Job opportunities include teachers, postal workers, accountants, computer programmers, custodians, and clerical employees. The variety of government careers is almost as wide as that in private business. More than one million new government jobs will be created over the next 10 years.

Future Changes: The number of federal government employees will remain fairly constant. At the same time, more local and state government agency workers will be needed as our population grows and people want more public services. Government careers especially in demand will be office workers, maintenance employees, and those with technical skills in areas such as engineering, computers, and law.

What Is Done on the Job: Because there are so many types of government jobs, we cannot describe them all here. Let's look at

two that you might find interesting, the city manager and the health inspector. Local government officials responsible for the coordination of the day-to-day operations of a city are called city managers or public administrators. A city manager usually works closely with the mayor or the city council.

A major duty of the city manager is handling finances. Tax money has to be collected and bills have to be paid. In addition, city managers work with various departments which provide police and fire protection, education, traffic control, and other government services.

City managers are also responsible for preparation of budgets and creation of future plans. Writing and reading reports are another major part of the job. A career as a local government administrator usually requires long hours and many meetings with department heads and community groups.

Health and safety inspectors are the people responsible for the safety of food products, places of employment, and our environment. Thousands of people are employed by federal, state, and local governments to protect citizens from potential dangers.

A health inspector can be involved in checking processed foods, medicines, or restaurants. Inspections are designed to insure the safety of consumer products and services. When necessary, legal action may be taken to force a business to comply with government regulations. Government inspectors are also employed in the areas of air safety, construction, customs, labor laws, mines, and occupational safety. The work in this career can be interesting and exciting as inspectors frequently encounter unusual situations.

Education and Training: Requirements for government positions vary greatly. Certain jobs are available to high school graduates. Other careers require specialized training. The college subjects most frequently recommended for government work are courses in business, office skills, communication, law, economics, and political science. Many federal government jobs require that the applicant take a civil service test. This exam is designed to measure a person's ability and potential for advancement.

Salary Levels: Just as there are many different jobs in government work, salaries also vary widely. Income can range from $11,300 for starting office clerks to over $70,000 for business administrators of large cities.

For Additional Information: Additional information about this career area is available from numerous sources, including the following:

Office of Personnel Management
1900 E Street, N.W.
Washington, DC 20415

American Federation of State, County, and Municipal Employees
1625 L Street, N.W.
Washington, DC 20036

National Association of Government Employees
2139 Wisconsin Avenue, N.W.
Washington, DC 20007

American Federation of Government Employees
1325 Massachusetts Avenue, N.W.
Washington, DC 20005

Using Information Sources

In this age of technological advancement and increased knowledge, it is impossible for you to know everything about our complex economic system. You should, however, know where to seek the information you need when you need it. By knowing what type of information is available and where to find it, you will be able to locate the desired facts and figures quickly.

Libraries

Public libraries and school libraries are among the most common and frequently consulted sources for business information. You are free to visit public libraries to read books, newspapers, and magazines. Some libraries keep files of clippings on important topics. In some of the larger libraries, films and recordings can be borrowed. Public, school, and college libraries contain those reference books most likely to help you when you need to find specific information on almost any subject, including business. Helpful librarians will assist you.

In some parts of the country, traveling libraries called bookmobiles circulate through rural and suburban areas. Special libraries are maintained by many large business firms, trade associations, and clubs. Microfilms of documents or technical and scientific reports may sometimes be obtained from government and university libraries. Also, many libraries now have back issues of major newspapers on microfilm. In the future you can expect libraries to make certain information accessible through telephone and computer hookups.

General Reference Sources

Many books are designed as sources of information. When you want information of any kind, consider first the possibility of finding it in a general reference book. If one of the popular reference sources does not contain the information needed, consult a librarian or the card index in the library.

Dictionaries

The dictionary is probably the most widely used reference book. Its chief purpose is to give the spelling, pronunciation, and meaning of words; but most dictionaries provide other useful information. Some of the more commonly used types of dictionaries are listed below.

1. *Unabridged dictionary.* This is a complete dictionary giving more information about words and their meanings than smaller editions do. Unabridged dictionaries, often containing more than 2,800 pages, provide additional information such as the following:

   Guide to pronunciation   Drawings and illustrations
   Abbreviations   Tables of measures and weights,
   Punctuation and grammar   kinds of money used through-
   Rules for spelling, forming plurals,   out the world, and common
     and capitalizing   foreign language phrases

2. *Abridged dictionary.* This is a condensed or shorter version of a larger dictionary. It is a handy reference on the spellings and meanings of words. An abridged dictionary may contain some of the special features of the unabridged dictionary.
3. *Thesaurus.* This is a book of synonyms (words similar in meaning) and antonyms (words opposite in meaning).
4. *Special dictionaries.* Special kinds of dictionaries are published for use in such fields as medicine, law, and business. Dictionaries of special interest to business people and students would include the *University Dictionary of Business and Finance* by Clark and Gottfried, the *Dictionary of Advertising Terms* by Urdang, and the *Dictionary of Business and Economics* by Ammer.

Encyclopedias

The most complete source of general information is the encyclopedia, which contains information taken from all fields of knowledge. Encyclopedias, like dictionaries, are published in brief as well as in comprehensive editions. Both one-volume editions and complete sets are available. Junior editions are also published for school-age children.

Encyclopedias are also published for special fields of interest such as business, education, engineering, sports, and religion. Munn's *Encyclopedia of Banking and Finance* is an example of one in the business area.

Almanacs

An almanac is a publication with facts and figures about government, population, industries, religions, museums, education, cost of living, national defense, trade, transportation, and many other subjects. The *World Almanac* and the *Information Please Almanac* are two books of facts that are published annually. They are among our most popular up-to-date references. Paperbound editions of these almanacs can be purchased at many bookstores.

Atlases

An atlas is a book containing maps of regions and countries of the world. It includes information on population, products, climate, history, and commerce. An atlas is very helpful in learning the location or the size of a city or a country or the agricultural and commercial products of an area.

Directories

A directory is a book listing names of people living in a certain place or engaged in a particular business, trade, or profession.

1. *Telephone.* The telephone directory gives the names, addresses, and telephone numbers of people and businesses who have telephones. Some telephone directories contain a civic section that provides a highway map of the city, information about the business and industry of the city, a list of parks and playgrounds, and a summary of traffic rules. Most telephone directories have a classified section—the Yellow Pages. This is a listing of the names, addresses, and telephone numbers of suppliers of goods and services. The names are arranged in alphabetical order under headings that describe the types of businesses and services.

2. *City.* A city directory lists the names, occupations, and addresses of persons 18 years old or older who reside in the city for which the directory is compiled. Other information usually given includes the names of business firms, streets, clubs, churches, museums, and other institutions in the city. It is among the most useful directories to persons interested in business.

3. *Government.* The *Congressional Directory* contains information about the federal government and gives the names of members of Congress. The *Book of the States* and the *Municipal Yearbook* provide similar information about state and local governments. Another important source, published annually by the federal government, is the *United States Government Manual.* This is a valuable reference book for students, teachers, business people, lawyers, and others who need information about the functions, publications, and services of U.S. government agencies.

4. *Special types.* Special types of directories include those of national businesses, public schools, school teachers and administrators, clubs, associations, and newspapers and periodicals. These can usually be found in libraries.

Books of Statistical Information

Statistics are facts that can be stated in the form of numbers. There are several excellent sources of statistical information. In addition to the almanacs previously mentioned, there are the *Statistical Abstract of the United States*, the *Statesman's Yearbook*, the *Census Reports*, and many others.

Guides to Reading

Magazines or periodicals contain many current articles on various business concerns and other subjects not found in books. Because there are so many magazines, it is impossible for anyone to find all the desired information without some aid. This aid is supplied by guides — sometimes referred to as indexes. Perhaps the most commonly used guide is the *Readers' Guide to Periodical Literature*. This guide provides an index to articles appearing in almost 200 current magazines. It is published twice a month, except for one issue in February, July, and August. Once a year, one large volume is published that combines all the listings from the indexes issued during the preceding 12 months.

The *Education Index* and the *Business Education Index* cite articles that appear in journals of particular interest to educators. The *Public Affairs Information Service Bulletin* and the *Business Periodicals Index* will also assist you in locating articles and other literature on public affairs and business topics.

Some of the larger newspapers publish their own guides that assist readers in locating articles of interest in their newspapers. Examples of these are the *New York Times Index* and the *Wall Street Journal Index*. The *Newspaper Index* indexes news items and other articles in the *Chicago Tribune*, the *Washington Post*, the *New Orleans Times Picayune*, and the *Los Angeles Times*.

Newspapers

Almost everyone refers to daily newspapers for information on radio and television programs and for announcements of movies showing at the theaters. If you are planning a trip, you may check on weather forecasts and road condition reports. Newspapers also inform us of scheduled lectures, exhibits, concerts, school affairs, sports events, and other activities. Major newspapers print information about economic conditions, prices of commodities, cost of living, prices of stocks and bonds, and other information of interest to business people and consumers.

Specialized Reference Sources

There is a wealth of information in almost any special field. You may be familiar with such special references as the *Official Baseball Guide* for baseball fans and the *Radio Amateur's Handbook* for ham radio operators. Directories, yearbooks, handbooks, and other references are available to hobbyists, artists, musicians, entertainers, workers in technical professions, ethnic groups, and many others. A few of the more widely used special reference sources are described in the following paragraphs.

Information for Travelers

Two commonly used sources of information for travelers are:

1. *Road maps.* In addition to highway routes, many road maps show places of interest, camping sites, parks, lakes, street layouts of larger cities, and other details.
2. *Guides and directories.* The *Hotel and Motel Red Book* gives information about the location and size of hotels and motels, room rates, and hotel services for thousands of hotels and motels in the U.S. and in many foreign countries.

   The *Official Airline Guide* contains airline schedules, fares, and information such as airmail rates, car rental services, and conversion of dollars to foreign currencies. The *Rand McNally Campground and Trailer Park Guide,* revised annually, contains a list of thousands of campgrounds and trailer parks in the U.S. and Canada.

Information for Consumers

Three popular monthly magazines, *Money, Consumer Reports,* and *Consumers' Research Magazine,* contain facts and advice about products and services used most by consumers. Organized consumer groups and the federal government publish newsletters and other literature of particular interest to consumers.

Many useful government bulletins, some free and others available at little cost, can be ordered from the Superintendent of Documents, U.S. Government Printing Office, Washington, DC 20402. Many libraries have the *Monthly Catalog of U.S. Government Publications,* which lists by subject all federal government publications issued during the preceding month. Bulletins of value to consumers are often available from Better Business Bureaus, labor unions, colleges, government agencies, and other public and private organizations.

Information for Business

The U.S. Department of Commerce issues many reports and studies of value to large and small business firms. It publishes *Survey of Current Business,* a monthly periodical with articles and statistics on business activity and economic conditions. The U.S. Department of Labor issues the *Monthly Labor Review* which gives information on prices, wages, and employment. National, state, and local chambers of commerce also provide many kinds of useful reports.

The *Economic Almanac* is prepared by the Conference Board. It is a standard source of facts on current business and economic developments.

Much information about business activity can be found in the financial pages of daily newspapers. Other publications such as *Fortune* and *Business Week* are devoted primarily to business and its activities. A business can subscribe to special newsletter services, such as *The Kiplinger Washington Letter,* for information not usually published in newspapers and magazines.

Many handbooks describing principles, practices, and methods for certain specialized fields of business are available. Among the handbooks of special interest to business people are:

1. *Accountants' Handbook* — a general reference book in accounting, containing answers to accounting problems and presenting the principles of accounting.
2. *Financial Handbook* — a guide to solving financial problems such as financing the growth and operation of a business and raising new capital for expansion.
3. *Office Administration Handbook* — a comprehensive volume focusing attention on the human relationships involved in the management of offices. It includes chapters on testing, hiring, supervising, training, and promoting office workers; and on office systems, policies, work procedures, correspondence, layouts, equipment, and data processing developments.
4. *Marketing Handbook* — a reference book that discusses all phases of the marketing process such as advertising, sales promotion, and marketing research.

Almost every field of business has its special trade directory. For example, special directories are published for people in such businesses as advertising, retailing, insurance, real estate, banking, plastics manufacturing, air transportation, and frozen food processing.

Information about People

Encyclopedias tell about great people of history. Other reference books give information about men and women now living. The best-known books of this type are *Who's Who* and *Who's Who in America*. *Who's Who* gives a summary of the lives and the achievements of outstanding people living throughout the world. *Who's Who in America* lists mainly those leaders living in the United States. Books similar to these are also published for special groups, such as *Who's Who in Finance and Industry, Who's Who of American Women,* and *American Men and Women of Science*. Another popular reference about people is

Current Biography, which includes sketches about individuals, many of various nationalities, who have become prominent because of their recent accomplishments.

Information about Occupations

Two important government publications giving information on occupations are the *Dictionary of Occupational Titles* and the *Occupational Outlook Handbook.* Another very worthwhile reference for junior and senior high school students is the *Encyclopedia of Careers and Vocational Guidance.* This extensive compilation is published in two volumes. Volume I contains practical guidance material and broad articles on opportunities in some 70 major industries or areas of work. Volume II contains more than 200 articles on specific occupations, such as bank teller, stenographer, travel agent, hotel manager, buyer, economist, accountant, automobile mechanic, glazier, and watch repairer. These articles give detailed information about the nature of the work, requirements, methods of entry, earnings, and sources of additional information.

Because of the recent emphasis on career education, school libraries in particular have acquired more information on different occupations. This information is presented not only in book form, but also through films, microfilm, and games.

APPENDIX B

Reviewing Arithmetic

This arithmetic review will be especially helpful to you in solving many of the end-of-chapter problems in this text and the common arithmetic problems you will encounter in business. These suggestions deal with a few of the kinds of calculations that are the most troublesome.

Multiplying Numbers Ending with Zero

When multiplying two numbers, if one or both of the numbers have zeros at the extreme right, place the zeros to the right of an imaginary line, multiply the numbers to the left of the line, and bring down the total number of zeros to the right of the line.

Examples:

$$
\begin{array}{r|l}
36 & \\
\times 25 & 00 \\
\hline
180 & \\
72 & \\
\hline
900 & 00
\end{array}
\qquad
\begin{array}{r|l}
36 & 00 \\
\times 25 & \\
\hline
180 & \\
72 & \\
\hline
900 & 00
\end{array}
\qquad
\begin{array}{r|l}
36 & 0 \\
\times 25 & 00 \\
\hline
180 & \\
72 & \\
\hline
900 & 000
\end{array}
$$

Dividing by Numbers Ending with Zero

When the divisor is 10, 100, 1,000, etc., move the decimal point in the dividend one place to the left for each zero. Moving the decimal point one place to the left divides a number by 10; two places to the left, by 100; three places to the left, by 1,000; etc.

Examples:

$$16.8 \div 10 = 1.68 \qquad 5{,}732 \div 1{,}000 = 5.732$$
$$246.9 \div 100 = 2.469$$

$$
\begin{array}{l}
930.9 \div 30 = \\
3\overline{)93.09} \\
\hline
31.03
\end{array}
$$

When the divisor is 20, 400, 3,000, etc., drop the zeros in the divisor, move the decimal point in the dividend one place to the left for each zero, and divide by the remaining number 2, 4, 3, etc.

Other examples:

$$65.8 \div 200 =$$

$$2\overline{).658}$$

$$.329$$

$$8,428 \div 4,000$$

$$4\overline{)8.428}$$

$$2.107$$

Using Decimals

Many people find the use of decimals difficult. Knowing and following a few simple rules will help improve your calculations using decimals.

1. Adding numbers with decimals — keep all decimal points in line.

Examples:

Add:
```
     33.65          26.5
     72.85            .4
      2.10          385
     30.00          400.329
    ------             .07
    138.60          -------
                    812.299
```

2. Subtracting numbers with decimals — keep decimal points in line.

Example:

```
   392.6    ← fill out spaces to the right with 0's →   392.600
 −  8.794                                             −   8.794
 --------                                             ---------
                                                       383.806
```

Subtract 12.678 from 36
```
     36.000
    −12.678
    -------
     23.322
```

3. Multiplying numbers with decimals.

Example: Multiply 7.46 by 3.2
```
    7.46        a. Keep right margin even.
    3.2         b. Keep figures in line.
   -----        c. To position the decimal point in the product, count
    1492           all digits to the right of the decimal points in the two
    2230           original figures — in this case three — count off that
  -------          number of places from the right in the product, and
   23.872          set the decimal point.
```

4. Always multiply by the simpler number.

Example: Multiply 3.7 by 327.4. This is the same as multiplying 327.4 by 3.7, which is simpler.

```
     327.4
   ×   3.7
   -------
    22918
    9822
   -------
   1,211.38
```

5. Dividing numbers with decimals.

First example: (Dividend) 129.54 ÷ .34 (Divisor) =

$$.34\overline{)129.\overset{\smile}{5}4}$$

To the right of the decimal point in the dividend count as many places as are to the right of the decimal point in the divisor. Set the decimal point in the quotient at this point. Keep figures in line.

```
      381.(Quotient)
.34 )129.54
     102
     275
     272
      34
      34
```

Second example: 420 ÷ 75 =

```
       5.6
75 )420.0
   375
   450
   450
```

The decimal point is always at the extreme right of whole numbers although it is not shown. When dividing, a decimal point may be placed at the right of the dividend and 0's added as needed.

Multiplying by Price Figures

Dealers frequently price items for sale at such figures as 49¢, $5.98, $99.95, etc. This is done because a price of $99.95, for example, seems less to the prospective buyer than an even $100.

Let us assume that 27 items are purchased at $.99 each.

The usual method of multiplication:

```
    $.99
     27
    693
    198
  26.73
```

A simpler method:

```
       27
  ×$ 1.00
    27.00
     - 27
   $26.73
```

(1) Multiply by the next higher number containing zeros—in this case $1.00.
(2) If the price figure ends in 99¢, subtract 1¢ for each item purchased—in this case 27¢.

Other examples:

If the price figure ends in 98¢, subtract 2¢ for each item purchased—in this case 64¢.

($.02 × 32 = $.64).

32 items at $4.98

```
        32
   ×$ 5.00
   $160.00
   -    .64
   $159.36
```

If the price figure ends in 97¢, subtract 3¢ for each item purchased—in this case $2.13.

($.03 × 71 = $2.13).

71 items at $9.97

```
        71
  ×$ 10.00
   $710.00
   -   2.13
   $707.87
```

In some cases the use of a hand-held calculator may make the simpler method of multiplying by price figures unnecessary.

Using Fractional Parts of $1.00 in Multiplying

While goods and services may be priced at any figure, prices are frequently expressed in fractional parts of $1.00, $10.00, $100.00, etc., that can be calculated easily and quickly. For example, 50 cents is ½ of $1.00; 25 cents is ¼ of $1.00; 33⅓ cents is ⅓ of $1.00. Thus:

24 items selling for $1.00 each would cost	$24.00
24 items at 50¢ each would cost ½ of $24 or	$12.00
24 items at 25¢ each would cost ¼ of $24 or	$ 6.00
24 items at 33⅓¢ each would cost ⅓ of $24 or	$ 8.00

With a little practice, many similar calculations can be made mentally. While there are many fractional parts of $1.00, the ones shown below will be very helpful to you from time to time in making your arithmetic calculations. This skill will be especially useful to you when comparing the prices of goods and services.

Fractional Part of $1.00	Halves	Thirds	Fourths	Sixths	Eighths
⅛					$.12½
⅙				$.16⅔	
¼			$.25		
⅓		$.33⅓			
⅜					$.37½
½	$.50				
⅝					$.62½
⅔		$.66⅔			
¾			$.75		
⅚				$.83⅓	
⅞					$.87½

You already know several of the above fractional parts of $1.00, and with practice you will be able to use those and others quickly and accurately. Four different types of calculations are involved. Master as many of them as you are able.

First type:

1. Numerator of fractional part is, "1," that is ⅛, ⅙, ¼, etc.
2. There *is no remainder*; that is, the calculations come to even dollars.

Example:

How to calculate:

12 items at $1.00 each would cost $12.00
50¢ is ½ of $1.00; hence, at 50¢, 12 items will cost ½ of
$12 or .... $ 6.00

Other examples:

$$32 \times \$.12\tfrac{1}{2} \ (32 \times \tfrac{1}{8}) = \$ \ 4.00$$
$$36 \times \$.16\tfrac{2}{3} \ (36 \times \tfrac{1}{6}) = \$ \ 6.00$$
$$48 \times \$.25 \quad (48 \times \tfrac{1}{4}) = \$12.00$$
$$39 \times \$.33\tfrac{1}{3} \ (39 \times \tfrac{1}{3}) = \$13.00$$
$$48 \times \$.50 \quad (48 \times \tfrac{1}{2}) = \$24.00$$

Second type:

1. Numerator of fractional part is "1."
2. There *is a remainder*; that is, the calculations will result in dollars and cents.

Example:

$$33 \times \$.25 = \$8.25$$

How to calculate:

33 items at $1.00 each would cost $33.00
25¢ is ¼ of $1.00; hence at 25¢ 33 items will cost ¼ of
$33 or $8¼; ¼ of $1.00 is 25¢, thus...................... $ 8.25

(Note: The fraction of a dollar obtained will always be one of the fractions illustrated on 587 so that once these fractional parts are mastered there is nothing new to be learned.)

Other examples:

$$39 \times \$.16\tfrac{2}{3} = \$ \ 6\tfrac{3}{6} = \$ \ 6.50 \ (\tfrac{3}{6} = \tfrac{1}{2} = .50)$$
$$37 \times \$.25 \quad = \$ \ 9\tfrac{1}{4} = \$ \ 9.25$$
$$28 \times \$.33\tfrac{1}{3} = \$ \ 9\tfrac{1}{3} = \$ \ 9.33^*$$
$$25 \times \$.50 \quad = \$12\tfrac{1}{2} = \$12.50$$

(*Since 1¢ is our smallest coin, if the final fraction is ½ or more, the last figure is raised 1 penny; if less than ½, the fraction is dropped. Note: Some retailers convert every fraction to 1¢, even if the fraction is less than ½.)

Third type:

1. Numerator is other than "1."
2. There *is no remainder.*

Example:

$$48 \times \$.75 = \$36.00$$

How to calculate:

Think of $.75 as ¾ of $1.00 and solve by cancellation.

$$48 \times \$.75 \left(\overset{12}{\cancel{48}} \times \frac{3}{\cancel{4}} \right) = \$36.00$$

Other examples:

$$24 \times \$.37\tfrac{1}{2} \left(\overset{3}{\cancel{24}} \times \frac{3}{8} \right) = \$ \ 9.00$$

$$32 \times \$.62\frac{1}{2} \left(\overset{4}{\cancel{32}} \times \frac{5}{\cancel{8}} \right) = \$20.00$$

$$36 \times \$.66\frac{2}{3} \left(\overset{12}{\cancel{36}} \times \frac{2}{\cancel{3}} \right) = \$24.00$$

Fourth type:

1. Numerator is other than "1."
2. There *is a remainder.*

Example:

$$34 \times \$.62\frac{1}{2} = \$21.25$$

How to calculate:

Think of $\$.62\frac{1}{2}$ as ⅝ of $1.00; but since 8 does not divide evenly into 34, first multiply by 5 and then divide by 8.

$$\$34 \times 5 = \$170$$
$$\$170 \div 8 = \$21\frac{2}{8}$$
$$\$21\frac{2}{8} = \$21.25$$

$$34 \times \$.62\frac{1}{2} \left(34 \times \frac{5}{8} = \frac{170}{8} \right) = \$21.25$$

Other examples:

$$61 \times \$.37\frac{1}{2} \left(61 \times \frac{3}{8} = \frac{183}{8} \right) = \$22.88$$

$$43 \times \$.66\frac{2}{3} \left(43 \times \frac{2}{3} = \frac{86}{3} \right) = \$28.67$$

$$21 \times \$.75 \left(21 \times \frac{3}{4} = \frac{63}{4} \right) = \$15.75$$

$$23 \times \$.87\frac{1}{2} \left(23 \times \frac{7}{8} = \frac{161}{8} \right) = \$20.13$$

Note: You will discover that after the number is multiplied by the numerator, the remaining calculation is exactly like that in the *second* type above.

Fractional parts of other amounts:

To the student who is interested in developing greater skill in calculating fractional parts of other amounts, a few additional examples will demonstrate the large number of applications possible.

First example:

.05 is ½ of	.10		24 ×	.05 =	1.20
.50 is ½ of	1.00		24 ×	.50 =	12.00
5.00 is ½ of	10.00	Thus:	24 ×	5.00 =	120.00
50.00 is ½ of	100.00		24 ×	50.00 =	1,200.00
500.00 is ½ of	1,000.00		24 ×	500.00 =	12,000.00

Second example:

.02½ is ¼ of	.10		430 ×	.02½ =	10.75
.25 is ¼ of	1.00		430 ×	.25 =	107.50
2.50 is ¼ of	10.00	Thus:	430 ×	2.50 =	1,075.00
25.00 is ¼ of	100.00		430 ×	25.00 =	10,750.00
250.00 is ¼ of	1,000.00		430 ×	250.00 =	107,500.00

APPENDIX C

Finding Percentages and Interest

What does **percent** mean?

Some students get confused when the term "percent" is mentioned. Actually the "percent" concept is very simple. Percent is derived from two Latin words, "per centum," meaning "by the hundred." This is why percent is easy — you are using a fraction whose denominator is always 100. The percent sign is %. Every percent figure can then be expressed as either a common fraction or a decimal fraction.

Examples:

Percent		Common Fraction		Decimal Fraction
3%	=	3/100	=	.03
5%	=	5/100	=	.05
7%	=	7/100	=	.07

In fact, you never use the percent figure in calculating percent. You always change the percent figure to either a common fraction or a decimal fraction.

To find:

4% of $300: multiply $300 $\times \dfrac{4}{100}$ = $12.00; or $300 $\times$ .04 = $12.00

6% of $250: multiply $250 $\times \dfrac{6}{100}$ = $15.00; or $250 $\times$ .06 = $15.00

Calculating Interest

Interest is expressed as a percent; but in calculating interest, both the percent and the length of time are considered.

Examples:

8% interest on $400 for 1 year = $400 $\times$ .08 $\times$ 1 = $32.00
5% interest on $550 for 3 years = $550 $\times$ .05 $\times$ 3 = $82.50

One method of calculating interest for less than one year is explained in Chapter 28 of this textbook; another method of calculating interest for less than a year is explained on p. 591.

The 60-Day, 6% Method of Finding Interest

There is a simple method of finding interest, known as the 60-day, 6% method. As this name indicates, the method is based on a period of time of 60 days and a rate of 6%. This method of finding interest will be explained through the use of several problems.

Problem 1: Find the interest on $100 for 60 days at 6%.

Step 1: Find the interest for one year.
$$\$100 \times .06 = \$6$$

Step 2: Find the interest for 60 days.

In interest problems a year is considered to be 360 days.

Therefore $\dfrac{60 \text{ days}}{360 \text{ days}} = \frac{1}{6}$ of a year

$6 \times \frac{1}{6} = \$1$, the interest on $100 for 60 days at 6%

Since the interest on $100 for 60 days at 6% is $1, the interest on any amount for 60 days at 6% can be found simply by *moving the decimal point two places to the left.*

Examples: Interest on $100.00 for 60 days at 6% = $1.00
Interest on $550.00 for 60 days at 6% = $5.50
Interest on $275.50 for 60 days at 6% = $2.755, or $2.76

The 60-day, 6% method may be used when the time is not 60 days.

Problem 2: Find the interest on $1,000 for 30 days at 6%.

Solve for 60 days:

The interest on $1,000 for 60 days at 6% = $10

30 days is ½ of 60 days; therefore:

$10 × ½ = $5, the interest on $1,000 for 30 days at 6%

Problem 3: Find the interest on $500 for 90 days at 6%.

Break down the 90 days into 60 days and 30 days, as follows:

The interest on $500 at 6% for 60 days = $5.00
The interest on $500 at 6% for 30 days = <u> 2.50</u>
The interest on $500 at 6% for 90 days = $7.50

To find the interest for any number of days, break down the 60 days into periods of time that are simple fractions of 60 days.

Examples: 30 days = ½ of 60 days
20 days = ⅓ of 60 days
15 days = ¼ of 60 days
10 days = ⅙ of 60 days

Problem 4: Find the interest on $420 for 105 days at 6%.

The interest on $420 at 6% for   60 days = $4.20
The interest on $420 at 6% for   30 days =   2.10
The interest on $420 at 6% for   15 days =   1.05
The interest on $420 at 6% for 105 days = $7.35

To find the interest for 1 day or for a few days, first find the interest for 6 days. Six days are 1/10 of 60 days.

Examples: The interest on $720 for 60 days at 6% = $7.20
The interest on $720 for   6 days at 6% = $ .72 (1/10 of $7.20)
The interest on $720 for   1 day at 6% = $ .12 (1/6 of .72)

(Notice that the interest on any amount for 6 days at 6% can be found by *moving the decimal point three places to the left*.)

The interest on $480 for 6 days at 6% = $.48
The interest on $480 for 1 day at 6% = $.08
The interest on $ 42 for 6 days at 6% = $.042
The interest on $ 42 for 1 day at 6% = $.007 = $.01

Problem 5: Find the interest on $412.50 for 97 days at 6%.

The interest on $412.50 at 6% for 60 days = $4.125
The interest on $412.50 at 6% for 30 days =   2.0625
    (carry to 4 decimal places)
The interest on $412.50 at 6% for   6 days =   .4125
The interest on $412.50 at 6% for   1 day =   .0688 (1/6 of $.4125)
The interest on $412.50 at 6% for 97 days = $6.6688 = $6.67

The 60-day, 6% method may be used when the rate is other than 6%.

You can find the interest on any amount at any rate of interest by adapting this method. First solve for 6%, divide by 6 to obtain the interest at 1%, and then multiply by the desired rate.

Problem 6: Find the interest on $360 for 75 days at 10%.

First, solve for 6%:

The interest on $360 at 6% for 60 days = $3.60
The interest on $360 at 6% for 15 days =   .90
The interest on $360 at 6% for 75 days = $4.50

Next, find the interest at 1%:

$4.50 ÷ 6 = $.75, the interest at 1%

Then, multiply by the desired rate of interest:

$.75 × 10 = $7.50, the interest on $360 for 75 days at 10%

Calculation of Interest on Installment Loans

The method of calculating the rate of interest on installment loans presented in Chapter 28 is sufficiently accurate for most purposes. For a more exact calculation of interest, the following method is presented.

Problem:

Martin B. Allen borrowed $120 from the small loan department of his bank and signed a note for $126. He agreed to pay back the balance in 8 equal monthly installments of $15.75. What annual rate of interest did he pay for the use of the $120 that he actually received? Assume that an interest rate of 12% a year, or 1% a month, was charged for the loan.

Solution:

The cost of the loan was $126 − $120 = $6. On this basis the interest would have been:

$120.00 borrowed for 1 month @ 1% would cost $1.20
− 15.75 1st payment

104.25 borrowed for 1 month @ 1% would cost 1.04
− 15.75 2d payment

88.50 borrowed for 1 month @ 1% would cost .... .89
− 15.75 3d payment

72.75 borrowed for 1 month @ 1% would cost .... .73
− 15.75 4th payment

57.00 borrowed for 1 month @ 1% would cost .... .57
− 15.75 5th payment

41.25 borrowed for 1 month @ 1% would cost .... .41
− 15.75 6th payment

25.50 borrowed for 1 month @ 1% would cost .... .26
− 15.75 7th payment

9.75 borrowed for 1 month @ 1% would cost .... .10
− 15.75 8th payment

Interest cost if the money had been borrowed at 1% ____
a month, or 12% a year $5.20

Notice that the interest was figured on the total $120 for the first month only, because the borrower had the use of the entire amount only during that month. During the second month the interest was figured on $104.25, as $15.75 was repaid at the end of the first month. The amount on which the interest was figured was decreased in a like manner for each month during the time of the loan.

At 1% a month, or 12% a year, the interest would have been $5.20. The actual cost of the loan was $6. How many times greater was this actual cost than $5.20? This may be found by dividing $6 by $5.20:

$$\$6 \div \$5.20 = 1.1538$$

The amount actually paid was, then, 1.1538 times greater than the amount would be if the rate had been 1% a month, or 12% a year. Since interest rates are given on a yearly basis, the actual rate was:

$$12\% \times 1.1538 = 13.85\%$$

Calculation of Interest on Installment Purchases

The method of calculating the rate of interest on installment purchases is similar to the method of calculating the rate of interest on installment loans.

Problem:

Larry Simms bought a radio on the installment plan from Ace Radio Shop for $102. A down payment of $12 was made at the time of the purchase, and $9 was paid at the end of each of the following 10 months. The radio could have been purchased for $92 in cash. What rate of interest was paid for the privilege of buying on installments?

Solution:

The amount that Larry paid for the privilege of buying on installments is found by subtracting the cash price of the radio from the installment price of the radio.

$102 the installment price of the radio
− 92 the cash price of the radio

$ 10 the amount paid for the privilege of buying on installments

The radio could have been purchased for $92 in cash. A down payment of $12 was made. The cash price was therefore $80 more than the down payment. Larry could have bought the radio for cash if he had borrowed $80 from some other source. He was, then, in reality borrowing $80 from the Ace Radio Shop. This may be shown as:

$ 92 the price that would have been paid if the purchase had been for cash
−12 the down payment at the time of the purchase

$ 80 the amount borrowed from the dealer

If Larry had borrowed $80 from some other source at a rate of 1% a month, or 12% a year, the interest would have been found as follows:

$ 80 borrowed for 1 month @ 1% would cost . . . . $ .80
− 9 1st payment

71 borrowed for 1 month @ 1% would cost 71
− 9 2d payment

62 borrowed for 1 month @ 1% would cost 62
− 9 3d payment

53 borrowed for 1 month @ 1% would cost............. .53
− 9 4th payment

44 borrowed for 1 month @ 1% would cost............. .44
− 9 5th payment

35 borrowed for 1 month @ 1% would cost............. .35
− 9 6th payment

26 borrowed for 1 month @ 1% would cost............. .26
− 9 7th payment

17 borrowed for 1 month @ 1% would cost............. .17
− 9 8th payment

8 borrowed for 1 month @ 1% would cost............. .08
− 9 9th payment

Interest cost if the money had been borrowed at 1% a   _____
   month, or 12% a year $3.96

Observe that the interest was figured on $80 for the first month only, since Larry had the use of this amount during that month only. During the second month the interest was figured on $71 because $9 was repaid at the end of the first month. The amount on which the interest was figured was decreased in a like manner for each installment paid.

At 1% a month, or 12% a year, the interest was $3.96. The actual cost for the loan was $10 ($102 − $92 = $10). How many times greater was this actual cost than $3.96? This may be found by dividing $10 by $3.96:

$$\$10 \div \$3.96 = 2.5252$$

The amount actually paid, then, was 2.5252 times greater than the amount would have been if the rate had been 1% a month, or 12% a year. The actual rate, then, was:

$$12\% \times 2.5252 = 30.30\%$$

APPENDIX D

Learning How to Use the Metric Measurement System

The metric system of measurement is used by most nations in the world. Because of our great amount of trade with other countries, the United States has taken some steps toward conversion to the metric system. The change to metric will be made gradually over a number of years. Some U.S. industries have already made the change, and you should become familiar with the metric system.

There are some things about the metric system that may already be familiar to you. For example, if you have been to a track or swimming meet or seen one on TV, you know that the distances are sometimes measured in meters, not in feet, yards, or miles. Food is often labeled to show amounts in grams as well as pounds or ounces. Meters, kilometers, and grams are examples of metric units of measurement.

Basic Metric Units

To use the metric system, you will measure weight (or mass), distance, volume, and temperature differently from the way you are used to measuring them. Once you become familiar with it, the metric system is actually simpler to use than the U.S. system. Metric has very few base units, while the U.S. system uses many base units. The following paragraphs tell you the metric base units that you need to know now.

The kilogram is the metric base unit of weight. A kilogram is equal to a little over two pounds. The kilogram and units based on the kilogram are used instead of ounces and pounds.

The meter is the metric base unit of distance. A meter is a little longer than a yard. The meter and a few other units based on the meter are used to measure things we now measure in inches, feet, and miles.

The cubic meter is really the metric base unit of volume. However, for most measurements of volume, you will use the liter. A liter is equal to a little more than a quart. You will use the liter in place of the fluid ounce, the pint, the quart, and the gallon.

The degree Celsius (named after the Swedish astronomer Anders Celsius), once called the centigrade degree, is used instead of the Fahrenheit degree to measure temperature.

Figure D-1 gives you some idea of how these metric units of measure compare with U.S. units.

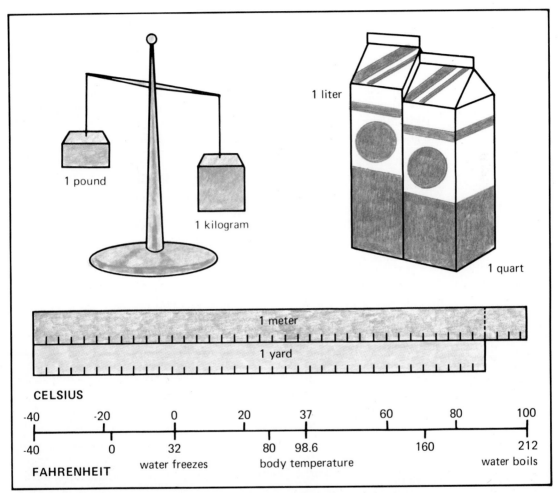

Figure D-1   Some common units of measure in the U.S. and metric systems.

Metric Prefixes

Any measure can be expressed in the base units of the metric system. But this can be awkward if very large or very small numbers are involved. By using prefixes with the units of the metric system, you can express measurements in a more convenient way. Since the metric system is a decimal system (that is, it is based on the number 10), the prefixes all mean to multiply or divide the unit by 10, 100, or 1000. There are quite a few metric prefixes, but the ones which you use in this book and in most everyday measurements are:

milli = one one-thousandth or 1/1000 or 0.001
centi = one one-hundredth or 1/100 or 0.01
kilo = one thousand or 1000

Prefixes are added to or taken away from the names of the base units to produce larger or smaller metric units. For example:

1 millimeter = 0.001 meter (about the diameter of a paper clip wire)
1 centimeter = 0.01 meter (about the width of a paper clip)
1 kilometer = 1000 meters (a little over half a mile)
1 gram = 0.001 kilogram (about the weight of a paper clip)

You may wonder why the kilogram, a base unit, has a prefix. Because the gram is extremely small, there was no way to measure it precisely when the standards for metric measurement were being set up. Therefore the kilogram is considered the base unit.

The metric base units and prefixes are shown with their abbreviations in Figure D-2. Study this illustration until you are familiar with the units, the prefixes, and their abbreviations.

The abbreviations are combined in the same way that metric prefixes and units are combined. For example, millimeter is abbreviated mm; centimeter, cm; kilogram, kg; and kiloliter, kL. The prefixes are never used with degrees Celsius. The degree is the only unit of temperature.

Figure D-2
These units and prefixes are the most commonly used ones in the metric system.

Unit	Abbreviation	Use
kilogram	kg	weight
meter	m	distance
liter	L	volume
degree Celsius	°C	temperature

Prefix	Abbreviation	Meaning
milli	m	1/1000
centi	c	1/100
kilo	k	1000

Using Units and Prefixes Correctly

It would not mean much to say that a pill weighs 0.0001 kilogram or that the distance between two towns is 77 058 meters. That would be like telling someone that the distance to the next service station is 10,560 feet instead of 2 miles. (As you see here, in the metric system a space is used instead of a comma to show thousands when grouping five or more digits.)

You would not say that your bicycle weighs 12 000 grams, but that it weighs 12 kilograms. The kilogram is ordinarily used wherever we are used to using pounds. The milligram, a very small measure, is used a great deal in the medical and scientific fields. Pills prescribed by doctors are often measured in milligrams.

Meters are used where we are accustomed to using feet or yards, and millimeters usually replace inches for short measurements. Centimeters are used for some measurements such as the dimensions of household objects, for example towels and sheets, and personal measurements, for example your height.

The liter replaces the fluid ounce, the pint, the quart, and the gallon for small quantities. Gasoline in a car's tank would be measured in liters. But the amount of gasoline in a large storage tank would be measured in kiloliters. The milliliter is used to measure very small quantities such as medicine dosages or amounts of liquid ingredients in recipes.

Changing from One System to the Other

To use the metric system well, you must learn to think in terms of metric units. However, until you get used to doing this, it is easier to convert the metric units into units you know. Figure D-3 tells you how to convert some commonly used metric units to their U.S. equivalents and some U.S. units to their metric equivalents. The numbers that you are to multiply by have been rounded off to make them easier for you to use and remember.

Take a look at Figure D-3; then study these examples.

If you buy a 6-ounce bag of candy, what is its weight in grams?

$$6 \text{ ounces} \times 28 = 168 \text{ grams}$$

If you have 9 meters of masking tape, how many yards of tape do you have?

$$9 \text{ meters} \times 1.1 = 9.9 \text{ yards}$$

What is the volume in liters of 5 quarts of oil?

$$5 \text{ quarts} \times 0.95 = 4.75 \text{ liters}$$

If the temperature is 77 °F, what is the temperature in degrees Celsius?

$$77 - 32 = 45$$
$$5/9 \times 45 = 25 \text{ °C}$$

APPROXIMATE CONVERSIONS FROM U.S. TO METRIC AND METRIC TO U.S.

	When You Know:	You Can Find:	If You Multiply By:
Distance	inches	millimeters (mm)	25.4
	inches	centimeters (cm)	2.5
	feet	meters (m)	0.3
	yards	meters (m)	0.91
	miles	kilometers (km)	1.61
	millimeters (mm)	inches	0.04
	centimeters (cm)	inches	0.4
	meters (m)	inches	39.4
	meters (m)	feet	3.3
	meters (m)	yards	1.1
	kilometers (km)	miles	0.6
Weight (Mass)	ounces	grams (g)	28
	pounds	kilograms (kg)	0.45
	grams (g)	ounces	0.035
	kilograms (kg)	pounds	2.2
Volume	pints	liters (L)	0.47
	quarts	liters (L)	0.95
	gallons	liters (L)	3.8
	liters (L)	pints	2.1
	liters (L)	quarts	1.06
	liters (L)	gallons	0.26
Temperature	degrees Fahrenheit	degrees Celsius (°C)	5/9 (after subtracting 32)
	degrees Celsius (°C)	degrees Fahrenheit	9/5 (then add 32)

Figure D–3
Table of approximate metric-to-U.S. and U.S.-to-metric conversions.

*G*lossary of Computer Terms

Auxiliary Storage A place to store data that the computer does not need at the present time.

Batch Processing Accumulating and processing data as a group so computer time can be used wisely.

Binary Digit A single bit.

Bug An error in a program.

Cathode Ray Tube Terminal (CRT) A computer screen for displaying data usually accompanied by a typewriter-like keyboard.

Central Processing Unit (CPU) The part of the computer that takes the instructions from the memory and performs them by moving data, completing instructions, and controlling the input/output operations.

Character A pattern of electric pulses forming a letter, symbol, or number which always has the same meaning for computer operators.

Chips Tiny pieces of silicon containing imprinted circuits and components.

Circuit Tiny paths on which electric pulses flow.

Coding The process of writing instructions to be used by the computer.

Command Any order the computer carries out.

Computer Electronic or mechanical device designed to store, rearrange, and report information.

Computer-Aided Instruction (CAI) The use of computers to help people learn or improve skills at their own pace.

Computer Language A system of letters, words, numbers, or symbols used to talk to a computer.

Computer Literacy The ability to use computers to process information or solve problems.

Cursor A light on the visual display terminal that shows where your next letter, number, or symbol will appear.

Data Facts or information.

Data Base The data necessary to carry on a business.

Data Processing Rearrangement of data in a way that makes the information more useful to you.

Debugging Getting rid of errors in a program.

Direct Access Having access to any bit of information immediately.

Disk Drive A device that stores information on a magnetic disk.

Down Time The time when a computer is being repaired or is not capable of being used.

Dump An unformatted listing of the contents of a file or memory.

Edit To add to, change, or take away from something you have written.

Electronic Cottage A home in which

members of the family use computers to perform personal, household, or career tasks.

Electronic Mail   Messages sent to an electronic device to be picked up at the receiver's convenience.

Floppy Disk   An oxide-coated plastic storage disk.

Flowchart   An outline of steps to be used in solving a problem or writing a program.

Garbage   Information in the computer that has not been used for a long time, or data that does not make sense.

Graphics   Pictures or diagrams used in presenting data.

Graphics Plotter   An attachment to the computer such as a plotter and pen that allows the computer to draw graphs, charts, and pictures directly on paper.

Graphics Tablet   An attachment to the computer which allows you to draw pictures on the surface of a tablet with a special pen. The drawing is transferred from the tablet to the computer screen and into the computer's memory.

Hard Copy   Information printed on paper.

Hardware   Physical equipment or devices included in computer systems.

Home Software System   A software package designed to perform home tasks on a computer.

Imaging   A method of entering data using a camera or device that stores a copy of written data or a picture of an object.

Input   Data placed into the computer.

Input Device   Any aid such as a light pen or mouse that allows you to place input into the computer.

Keyboarding   The ability to enter letters, numbers, and symbols using the terminal keyboard.

Laser Printers   High-speed printers which print thousands of lines per minute.

Light Pen   An input device that lets you draw or write directly on the computer screen.

Log Off   To stop communication between your terminal and the central computer.

Log On   To tell the central computer you are ready to begin communication from your terminal.

Mainframe   A large-sized computer.

Memory   Storage area of the computer that is addressable by the processor.

Menu   A list of choices of tasks you can perform on the computer.

Merge   Combining two or more bits of information to be used together.

Microcomputer   A computer that uses a processor whose circuits are all on one integrated circuit chip.

Microfilm   Film which stores photographs of data in reduced size.

Minicomputer   A computer that is smaller and less powerful than a mainframe.

Modem   A device used to connect computer equipment to telephone lines.

Mouse   A device that can be moved so it lights up a command on the visual display unit.

Network   A system consisting of at least one central computer and several terminals.

Off-line   A terminal or printer not currently controlled by the central computer.

On-line   A terminal or printer currently controlled by the central computer.

Optical Character Recognition (OCR) One method computers use to read input. The computer scans the new copy and matches the data with alphabetic letters or patterns stored in its memory; upon recognition, it stores the new input into its memory.

Output Data that exists after it is processed or printed.

Personal Computer A small computer designed for home use although it is sometimes used in businesses.

Piracy Stealing information or copying software packages to use the information free.

Printer An output device that produces written characters on paper.

Program A set of instructions telling the computer what to do.

Programmers People who write instructions for computers.

Real-Time System A computer system that can answer your question or give results as soon as needed information is supplied. A real-time system can handle information from several terminals at the same time.

Robots Mechanical devices programmed to do routine tasks.

Scanner A device that "reads" data in printed or written form.

Smart Card A card which has a silicon chip for storing information.

Soft Copy The information seen on a computer screen.

Software The instructions and data stored in a computer or on disks and tapes.

Supercomputer A mainframe computer that handles more instructions per second than other computers. The number of instructions per second keeps increasing, but some computers can now handle over 150 million instructions a second.

Telecommuters People who report to work from their homes by computer.

Terminal A keyboard and screen used to access a computer.

Time-sharing A system in which several input devices (usually terminals) are attached to one processor.

Touch Sensitive Screen A computer that allows users to point at or touch a command on the screen to give instructions.

Transistor The part of the computer chip that controls the flow of electric pulses.

Universal Product Code A code or pattern of stripes placed on products, that can be read by a scanner, to facilitate checkout at retail stores. The pattern of stripes contains information about the product such as the price, name of the item, and the department in which it is located.

User Friendly A term describing a computer that tells you when you make a mistake and how to correct it without your having to know a computer language.

Visual Display Terminal (VDT) An input/output device that shows what you and the computer are saying to each other.

Word Processor A computer that usually consists of a keyboard, screen, disk drive, and printer designed especially for text editing.

Glossary

A

adjustable rate mortgage (ARM). A mortgage where the interest rate changes up or down periodically depending upon the current interest rates.

allowances. The amounts of money budgeted for savings or expenditures.

antitrust laws. Laws designed to promote competition and prevent monopolies.

annuity. An amount of money that an insurance company will pay at definite intervals to a person who has previously deposited money with the company.

application form. A form prepared by an employer which asks for important information related to employment.

appraiser. An expert in estimating the value of property.

appreciation. The amount of increase in the value of property.

APR. The percentage rate of credit on a yearly basis.

arbitrator. A person who makes a legally binding decision to resolve a labor-management difference.

articles of partnership. A written agreement made by partners in forming their business.

assessed value. The amount which property is determined to be worth for tax purposes.

assets. Everything of value that a person, household, or business owns.

assigned-risk plan. Auto insurance which provides coverage to high-risk drivers who are unable to purchase insurance through regular methods.

automatic teller machine. A computer terminal provided by a bank to receive, dispense, and transfer funds electronically for its customers.

B

balance of payments. The difference between the total amount of money that flows into a country and the money that flows out of a country for investments, tourism, and nontrade items.

balance of trade. The difference between a country's total exports and total imports of merchandise.

bank draft. A check that a bank draws on its deposits in another bank.

bank reconciliation. A statement showing how the checkbook balance and the bank statement were brought into agreement.

bank statement. A report given by a bank to a depositor showing the condition of his or her account.

base year. The year in which average prices for a price index were taken to represent 100 percent. The year chosen to compare an item, such as price, to the same item in another year.

basic economic problem. The problem—which faces individuals, businesses, and governments—of satisfying unlimited wants with limited resources.

basic health coverage. A combination of hospital, surgical, and regular medical expense insurance.

beneficiary. The person named in an insurance policy to receive the insurance benefits.

blank endorsement. An endorsement consisting of a name only.

blue-collar workers. Persons whose work primarily involves working with materials and using equipment and machinery.

board of directors. A group of people elected by stockholders to guide a corporation.

bodily injury liability insurance. Insurance that protects you from claims resulting from injuries or deaths for which you are found to be at fault.

bond. A printed promise to pay a definite amount of money, with interest, at a specified time.

boycott. A refusal by workers to handle or buy the products of a company involved in a labor dispute.

brand name. A special name given to a product by a manufacturer to distinguish it as being made by that particular firm.

broker. A specialist who helps investors buy and sell stocks and bonds.

budget. A plan for saving and spending income.

budget charge account. A credit plan similar to an open charge account but which requires that regular payments be made over several months.

Bureau of Labor Statistics (BLS). An organization which researches over 20,000 different jobs held by persons in our work force.

business. An establishment or enterprise that supplies goods and services in exchange for some form of payment.

business cycle. The movement of our economy from one condition to another and back again.

C

canceled check. A check that has been paid by a bank.

capacity. The factor in credit that refers to a customer's ability to pay.

capital. 1: Tools, equipment, and buildings used in producing goods and services. (*Same as* capital resources.) 2: The factor in credit that has to do with the property and money that the debtor owns.

capitalism. An economic system in which most economic resources are privately owned and decisions about production are largely made by free exchange in the marketplace. (*Same as* free enterprise system, market economy, or private enterprise system.)

capital resources. Tools, equipment, and buildings used in producing goods and services. (*Same as* capital.)

career information interview. A planned discussion with a worker to find out about the work that person does, the preparation necessary for that career, and the person's feelings about that career.

career planning. Looking into careers, looking at yourself in terms of careers, and making decisions about a future career.

cashier's check. A check that a bank employee draws on the bank's own in-house funds.

cash value. The amount that an insurance company will pay to the insured if a policy is given up.

central processing unit. The part of the computer that takes the instructions from its memory and performs them.

certificate of deposit (CD). A long-term time deposit which has certain restrictions and pays higher interest than regular savings.

certificate of incorporation. A document, generally issued by a state government, giving permission to start a corporation.

certified check. A personal check that is guaranteed by a bank.

channel of distribution. The path that a product travels from producer to consumer. (*Same as* marketing channel.)

character. The factor in credit that refers to a customer's honesty and willingness to pay.

check. An order written by a depositor directing a bank to pay out money from his or her account.

checkbook. A bound book containing blank checks and check stubs or accompanied by a check register.

check register. A separate form on which the depositor keeps a record of deposits and checks.

check stub. A form attached to a check on which a depositor keeps a record of the check written and any current deposit.

chips. Tiny pieces of silicon containing imprinted circuits and components.

claim. A request for payment due to a loss covered by an insurance policy.

clearance sale. Using a price reduction to sell items that a business no longer wishes to carry in stock.

clearing a check. Returning a check to a drawer's bank to be paid and charged to his or her account.

clearinghouse. A place where banks exchange checks to clear them.

closed shop. A business where only union members may be hired by a company.

coinsurance clause. A provision in which the insured agrees with the insurance company to pay a certain percentage of his or her medical expenses.

collective bargaining. Negotiations between an organized body of workers and an employer dealing with wages and working conditions.

collision insurance. Insurance coverage which pays for damages to the insured's car caused by collision or by turning over.

commercial bank. A bank that handles checking accounts, makes loans to individuals and businesses, and provides other banking services. (*Same as* full-service bank.)

commission. A fee charged by brokers for their services.

common stock. Stock which provides ownership and shared profits but that has no stated dividend rate.

communism. An economic system in which government owns most of the economic resources and has tight control over the production and distribution of goods and services.

comparison shopping. Comparing the price, quality and services of one product to those of another product.

competition. The rivalry among businesses to sell their goods and services to buyers.

compound interest. Interest computed on the amount saved plus the interest previously earned.

comprehensive medical insurance. Insurance that combines hospital, surgical, and medical insurance into one policy.

comprehensive physical damage insurance. Insurance coverage which pays for damages to your car caused by events other than a collision or overturning.

compulsory insurance laws. Laws that say you may not register a car or obtain a license to drive without presenting proof of having the minimum amount of insurance coverage.

computer. An electronic or mechanical device designed to store, rearrange, and report information.

computer language. A system of letters, words, numbers, or symbols used to talk to a computer.

computer literacy. The ability to use computers to process information or solve problems.

condominium. An individually owned unit of an apartment-like building or complex.

consumer. A person who buys and uses goods or services.

consumer finance company. A financial firm which specializes in making loans for durable goods and financial emergencies but does not accept deposits.

consumer price index. A price index that shows the changes in the average prices of goods and services over time.

consumers' cooperative. An organization of consumers who buy goods and services together.

contract. An agreement to exchange goods or services for something of value.

convertible policy. A term life insurance policy that may be changed into another type of insurance.

cooperative. A business that is owned by the members it serves and is managed in their interest.

copyright. Protection of the work of authors, composers, or artists.

corporate bonds. Bonds issued by corporations.

corporation. A business made up of a number of owners but authorized by law to act as a single person.

co-signer. Someone who becomes responsible for your loan if you do not pay as promised.

credit. The privilege of using someone else's money for a period of time.

credit identification card. A card which has your name, account number, and signature on it and identifies you as a customer who has a charge account.

credit insurance. Special insurance that repays the balance of the loan if the borrower dies or is disabled before the loan is repaid.

credit memorandum. A written record of the amount to be subtracted from your account. The seller gives you a credit memorandum when you return merchandise.

creditor. One who sells or lends on another's promise to pay in the future.

credit rating. A person's reputation for paying debts on time.

credit record. Shows the debts you owe, how often you use credit, and whether you pay your credit obligations on time.

credit references. Firms or individuals who have given credit to someone in the past and can give information on that individual's credit record.

credit union. A financial institution formed by workers in the same agency which serves only its members.

creditworthy. Having an established record that indicates being a good credit risk.

custom-based economy. An economic system in which things are done according to tradition.

D

data. Facts or information.

data base. All the information a company needs to run its business.

data processing. Rearrangement of data in a way that makes the information more useful to you.

debit card. A programmed device which provides evidence of funds on deposit and allows access to the depositor's account on a special computer terminal.

debtor. One who buys or borrows and promises to pay later.

decreasing term insurance. Term life insurance on which the amount of protection gradually decreases but the premiums remain the same during the term.

deductible clause. A clause in an insurance contract that says how much car owners are willing to pay for damage to their autos in the event of an accident.

deficit. A situation that exists when government spends more than it collects.

deflation. A decrease in the general price level.

demand. The quantity of a product or service that consumers are willing and able to buy at a particular price.

demand deposit. A deposit to a checking account, making the money available at any time.

dental expense insurance. Insurance that pays for normal care of and accidental damage to teeth.

deposit. Money that is placed in a bank account by a customer.

deposit slip. A form that accompanies a deposit and shows the items deposited. (*Same as* deposit ticket.)

deposit ticket. A form that accompanies a deposit and shows the items deposited. (*Same as* deposit slip.)

depreciation. The decrease in the value of property as it becomes older and wears out.

depression. A phase of the business cycle in which unemployment and business failures are high and GNP is at its lowest point.

derived demand. Causes jobs to be created or eliminated as a result of what consumers buy or do not buy.

directed economy. An economic system in which government owns and controls the economic resources and makes all the decisions regarding the production of goods and services. (*Same as* planned economy.)

direct marketing. The process through which goods are bought by the consumer directly from the producer.

direct tax. A tax which cannot be passed on to someone else.

disability income insurance. Insurance that provides a worker with weekly or monthly payments when he or she is unable to work as a result of an illness or injury covered by the policy.

discounting. Deducting interest from the total amount borrowed in advance.

discretionary income. Income available to spend after money has been set aside for basic needs and future expenses.

disk drive. A device that puts information on a magnetic disk.

displaced workers. People who are out of work because of changing job demands.

distribution. The activities that are involved in moving goods from producers to consumers. (*Same as* marketing.)

dividend. The part of the profits of a corporation that each stockholder receives.

domestic trade. The buying and selling of goods and services among people and businesses within the same country.

downpayment. A payment of part of the purchase price that is made as part of a credit agreement.

drawee. The bank or other financial institution in which the account is held.

drawer. The person who signs a check.

E

economic decision making. The process of choosing which want among several wants being considered at a certain time will be satisfied.

economic loss. When something that has some financial value is lost or destroyed.

economic resources. The means through which we produce goods and services. (*Same as* factors of production.)

economic risk. The chance of losing the financial value of something.

economic system. A nation's plan for making decisions on what to produce, how to produce, and how to distribute goods and services.

edit. To add to, change, or delete from something you have written.

electronic cottage. A home in which members of the family use computers to perform personal, household, or career tasks.

electronic funds transfer. A system through which funds are moved electronically from one account to another or from one bank to another.

electronic mail. Messages sent to an electronic device to be picked up at the receiver's convenience.

embargo. Stopping the importing or exporting of a certain product or service.

endorsement. A signature on the back of the check that transfers ownership of the check.

endowment life insurance. A life insurance policy payable to the beneficiary if the insured should die, or payable to the insured if he or she lives beyond the number of years in which premiums are paid.

equity. The difference between what your house is worth and what you owe on your mortgage.

estate tax. A tax based on the value of a person's property when he or she dies.

exchange. A special place of business where stocks and bonds are bought and sold.

excise tax. A tax on certain goods and services, generally included in the price quoted to purchasers.

expenditure. An amount actually spent for food, clothing, or other items.

exports. Goods and services sold to another country.

express warranty. An oral or written guarantee that promises a specific quality of performance.

extended coverage. Additional protection of property against losses from such causes as windstorms, hail, and smoke.

extractor. A business that grows products or takes raw materials from nature.

F

face value. The amount borrowed by the seller of a bond.

factors of production. The means through which we produce goods and services. (*Same as* economic resources.)

family income policy. A policy that combines standard whole life insurance with decreasing term insurance.

Federal Deposit Insurance Corporation. A federal regulating agency which insures depositors' money in member banks for up to $100,000.

Federal Reserve System. A nationwide banking plan set up by our federal government to assist banks in serving the public more efficiently.

Federal Savings and Loan Insurance Corporation. A federal agency which insures depositors' money in member savings and loan institutions up to $100,000.

finance charge. The total cost of a loan including interest and other charges.

financial planning. Requires evaluating one's present financial position, determining financial goals, and guiding activities and resources toward attaining those goals.

financial responsibility laws. Laws whereby your driver's license will be suspended or taken away if you cause an accident and cannot pay for the damages through insurance, your savings, or the sale of property.

fixed expenses. Expenses, such as house payments and insurance payments, that occur regularly and are for the same amount each time.

fixed rate mortgage. A traditional mortgage with an interest rate that does not change during the life of the mortgage.

floppy disk. An oxide-coated plastic storage disk.

foreign trade. Trade among different countries. (*Same as* international trade or world trade.)

forgery. The crime of signing another person's name on the check form without authority to do so.

franchise. A written contract granting permission to sell someone else's product or service in a prescribed manner, over a certain period of time, and in a specified area.

franchisee. The person or group of persons who have received permission from a parent company to sell its products or services.

franchisor. The parent company which grants permission to a person or group to sell its products or services.

fraud. When false information is given to a customer in order to make a sale.

free enterprise system. An economic system in which most economic resources are privately owned and decisions about production are largely made by free exchange in the marketplace. (*Same as* market economy, private enterprise system, or capitalism.)

full endorsement. An endorsement including the name of the person to whom the check has been transferred. (*Same as* special endorsement.)

full-service bank. A bank that handles checking accounts, makes loans to individuals and businesses, and provides other banking services. (*Same as* commercial bank.)

G

generic products. Unbranded products sold without advertising and fancy packaging in order to reduce prices.

gift tax. A tax imposed on a large amount of money or property which is given away.

GNP. The total value of all goods and services produced in a country in one year. (*Same as* gross national product.)

goals. The things you want to achieve.

goods. The tangible things you use in everyday life.

government employment office. A tax-supported office which helps people find jobs and gives out information about careers.

grade. An indication of the quality or size of a product.

graphics. Pictures or diagrams used to present data.

grievance procedure. A process in a labor contract for solving differences between workers and management.

gross national product. The total value of all goods and services produced in a country in one year. (*Same as* GNP.)

gross profit. The difference between the selling price and the cost price of an article. (*Same as* margin.)

group life insurance. Life insurance that covers a group of people who are usually employed by the same firm or are members of the same organization.

guarantee. A promise that a product is of a certain quality or that defective parts will be replaced.

H

hardware. A term that describes the computer, terminal, disk drive units, and chips.

homeowners policy. A package policy covering a wide range of risks for homeowners.

health maintenance organization. An organization which provides complete health care to its members for a fixed regular payment.

home software system. A software package designed to perform home tasks on a computer.

hospital expense insurance. Insurance that pays part or all of the charges for room, food, and other hospital expenses that the insured person incurs.

house brand. A special name used for products sold by one store or chain of stores. (*Same as* store brand.)

human resources. The people who work to produce goods and services. (*Same as* labor.)

I

imaging. A method of entering data using a camera or device that stores a picture of written data or a picture of an object.

implied warranty. A guarantee imposed by law which is not stated orally or in writing.

imports. Goods and services bought from another country.

impulse buying. Buying too rapidly without much thought.

income tax. A tax on the earnings of individuals and corporations.

indirect marketing. The process through which goods move through one or more middle firms between the producer and the consumer.

indirect tax. A tax which is passed on to someone else for payment.

inflation. An increase in the general price level.

inheritance tax. A tax based on the property or money received from a person who has died.

injunction. A court order directing striking employees to report back to work.

input. Data entered into a computer.

installment loan. A type of loan in which you agree to make monthly payments in specific amounts over a period of time.

installment sales credit. Credit that is normally used for expensive items with payments to be made at specified times.

insurable interest. A financial interest in or benefit from the continued life of a person.

insurance. The planned protection provided by sharing economic losses.

insurance agent. A person who sells insurance.

insurance commission. A state agency which makes sure that insurance premium rates and practices are fair.

insurance companies. Businesses that provide economic protection to others by sharing economic losses.

insured. The person for whom risk is assumed by an insurance company. (*Same as* policyholder.)

interest. An amount paid for the use of money.

international trade. Trade among different countries. (*Same as* world trade or foreign trade.)

interstate commerce. Business transactions involving companies in more than one state.

intrastate commerce. Business activities within the boundaries of one state.

inventory. A list of goods showing the cost of each item, when it was purchased, and how long it is expected to last.

investing. Using your savings to earn more money for you.

investment bank. A bank that handles the transactions of businesses that need to obtain large amounts of money.

investment club. A small group of people who organize to study stocks and invest members' money.

investments. Savings that are put to work to earn more money.

IRA. A special account which gives you incentive to save for your future.

J

job interview. A two-way conversation in which the interviewer learns about you and you learn about the job and the company.

joint account. A bank account that is used by two or more people.

K

keyboarding. Entering letters, numbers, and symbols using the terminal keyboard while keeping your eyes on the copy or the visual display terminal.

L

label. A statement attached to a product giving information about its nature or contents.

labor. The people who work to produce goods and services. (*Same as* human resources.)

letter of application. A sales letter about yourself written for the purpose of getting a personal interview.

level term insurance. Term life insurance on which the amount of protection and the premiums remain the same during the term.

liabilities. Debts that a person, household, or business owes.

liability insurance. The general term used to describe insurance you buy to protect yourself against financial loss if you injure someone else or damage someone else's property in an automobile accident.

life insurance. Insurance designed to protect against the financial risk associated with dying.

light pen. An input device attached to the computer that lets you draw or write directly on the computer screen.

limited-payment policies. Permanent life insurance on which premiums are paid for a stated number of years.

liquid investment. An investment which can be turned into money quickly.

loan credit. Borrowing money to be used later for special purposes.

locational unemployment. Jobs are available in one place but go unfilled because workers who are qualified live elsewhere.

lockout. A situation in which a company closes all of its stores or plants in an attempt to put pressure on striking employees.

M

mainframe. The largest type of computer.

major medical expense insurance. Insurance that provides protection against the high costs of serious illnesses or injuries.

manufacturer. A business that takes an extractor's products or raw materials and changes them into a form that consumers can use.

margin. The difference between the selling price and the cost price of an article. (*Same as* gross profit.)

market economy. An economic system in which most economic resources are privately owned and decisions about production are largely made by free exchange in the marketplace. (*Same as* private enterprise system, capitalism, or free enterprise system.)

marketing. The activities that are involved in moving goods from producers to consumers. (*Same as* distribution.)

marketing channel. The path that a product travels from producer to consumer. (*Same as* channel of distribution.)

marketplace. Any place where buyers and sellers exchange goods and services for some form of money.

market value. The price at which a share of stock can be bought and sold.

maturity date. The data on which a loan must be repaid.

mediator. A neutral person who recommends solutions to disputes between labor and management.

Medicaid. Medical expense assistance provided by state governments to medically needy families.

medical payments insurance. Insurance coverage which provides medical-expense protection for the policyholder, immediate family members, and guests while in the insured person's car.

Medicare. Health insurance provided by the federal government for aged and disabled people.

memory. Everything the computer has stored, including programs and data.

menu. A list of choices of commands you can perform on the computer.

microcomputer. A computer that uses a processor whose circuits are all on one integrated circuit chip.

minicomputer. A computer that is smaller and less powerful than a mainframe.

mobility. The willingness and ability to move where jobs are located.

modem. A device that lets you hook your computer equipment to telephone lines.

money management. The day-to-day activities associated with carrying out a financial plan.

money market. Name given to reports of national credit and investment dealings.

money market account. A special account which pays a variable interest rate based on interest being paid in the money markets.

money market rate. The current cost of money in the marketplace.

money order. A form sold by banks, post offices, express companies, and telegraph offices to be used for making payments.

monopoly. A firm that has control of the market for a product or service.

mortgage. A legal document giving the lender a claim against the property if the principal, interest, or both are not paid as agreed.

mortgage insurance. A life insurance policy that protects beneficiaries from losing their home if the insured dies.

mouse. A hand-held device that can be moved so it lights up a command on the visual display terminal.

municipal bonds. Bonds issued by city and state governments.

municipal corporation. An incorporated town or city.

mutual fund. A fund managed by a company which receives money from many investors and buys and sells a wide variety of stocks and bonds.

mutual savings firms. A financial institution, much like a bank, which specializes in savings accounts and making loans for mortgages. (*Same as* savings and loan associations.)

N

natural resources. Raw materials supplied by nature.

needs. Those things that are necessary for survival, such as food, clothing, and shelter.

negotiable order of withdrawal. A check written on a savings account.

net income. The amount a person receives after taxes and other deductions are withheld from his or her earnings. (*Same as* take-home pay.)

net profit. The amount left over after expenses are deducted from the gross profit.

net worth. The difference between the assets and the liabilities of a person, household, or business.

new technology. The use of automated machinery and electronic equipment to help increase the efficiency of work being done.

no-fault insurance. A plan in which people injured in auto accidents can collect for their financial losses from their own insurance companies no matter who is at fault.

note. A written promise to repay an amount that is borrowed.

O

open charge account. A credit plan in which the seller expects payment in full at the end of a specified period, usually a month.

opportunity cost. The cost of giving up something in favor of buying something else.

output. Data and information generated by a computer system.

outstanding check. A check given to the payee but not yet returned to the bank for payment.

overdrawing. Writing a check for more money than is in one's account.

P

partnership. An association of two or more people operating a business as co-owners and sharing profits or losses according to a written agreement.

patent. The exclusive right given a person to make, use, or sell an invention for a period of 17 years.

payee. The person to whom a check is made payable.

pension. Payments made to a retired worker under a privately organized plan.

per capita output. The figure that results from dividing the GNP of a country by the population of that country.

perils. The causes of loss, such as fire, wind, or theft.

personal computer. A small computer designed for home use, although it is sometimes used in businesses.

personal data sheet. A summary of job-related information about yourself.

personal liability coverage. Insurance to protect against claims arising from injuries to other people or damages to other people's property which are caused by you, your family, or your pets.

personal property. Property that is not attached to land.

personnel interviewer. Someone who has special training in talking with job applicants and hiring new employees.

picketing. A situation in which union members carry signs to publicize their complaints.

piracy. Stealing information or copying software packages to use the information free.

planned economy. An economic system in which government owns and controls the economic resources and makes all the decisions regarding the production of goods and services. (*Same as* directed economy.)

policy. A contract between one who buys insurance and the company which provides it.

policyholder. The person for whom risk is assumed by an insurance company. (*Same as* insured.)

postdated check. A check dated later than the date on which it is written.

preferred stock. Stock that has priority in payment of dividends and in return of the investment.

premium. The amount that a policyholder must pay.

price index. A series of figures showing how prices have changed over a period of years.

principal. The amount of money you borrow.

printer. An output device that produces written characters on paper.

private enterprise. The right of the individual to choose what business to enter and what to produce with only limited direction from the government.

private enterprise system. An economic system in which most economic resources are privately owned and decisions about production are largely made by free exchange in the marketplace. (*Same as* capitalism, free enterprise system, or private enterprise system.)

private property. The right to own, use, or dispose of things of value.

proceeds. The net amount of money a borrower receives after the discount has been subtracted from the principal.

producers' cooperative. An organization which farmers form to market their products.

productivity. The quantity of a good that an average worker can produce in one hour.

profit. Money left from sales after subtracting the cost of operating the business.

profit motive. The right to work for profit.

program. A set of instructions telling the computer what to do.

programmers. People who write instructions for computers.

progressive tax. A tax whose rate increases as the amount taxed increases.

promissory note. A written promise to repay based on the debtor's excellent credit rating.

promotional sale. Selling items below regular price to increase the sales of regular merchandise or to draw customers into the business.

proportional tax. A tax method in which everyone pays the same rate.

property damage liability insurance. Insurance coverage which provides protection against claims if your car damages someone else's property and you are at fault.

prosperity. A phase of the business cycle in which employment is high, wages are good, and GNP is high.

public debt. The amount owed by governments.

public services. Efforts of government, such as fire and police protection, which benefit citizens.

public utility. A business that supplies a service or product vital to all people and whose prices are determined by government regulation rather than competition.

Q

quota. A limit on the quantity of a product that may be imported or exported within a given period of time.

R

raised check. A check on which the amount was increased by a dishonest person.

rate of exchange. The value of the money of one country expressed in terms of the money of another country.

real estate. Land and anything attached to it.

real property. Property that is attached to land.

realtor. An expert in buying and selling real estate.

receipt. A written acknowledgement that payment was made.

recession. A phase of the business cycle in which demand decreases, businesses reduce production, and unemployment rises.

recovery. A phase of the business cycle in which unemployment begins to decrease and GNP rises.

regular medical expense insurance. Insurance that pays part or all of a doctor's fees for nonsurgical care given in the doctor's office, the patient's home, or a hospital.

renewable policy. A term life insurance policy that the policyholder can continue for more than one term without taking a physical exam.

restrictive endorsement. An endorsement that limits the use of a check to a specific purpose.

retail credit bureau. An organization that keeps records on people who have obtained and used credit.

retailer. A middle firm which sells directly to the consumer.

retirement, survivors, and disability insurance. Government insurance that provides, among other things, for benefits to be paid to retired workers and their families.

revenue. Income that government receives from taxes and other sources.

revolving charge account. A credit plan which allows purchases to be charged at any time but requires that at least part of the debt be paid each month.

right-to-work laws. Laws which forbid making union membership a requirement for employment.

robots. Mechanical devices programmed to do routine tasks.

S

safe-deposit box. A box in a bank vault for storing valuables.

safety. Assurance that the money you have invested will be returned to you.

sales credit. Credit that is offered at the time of sale.

sales tax. A tax on goods and services which is collected by the seller.

savings and loan associations. A financial institution, much like a bank, which specializes in savings accounts and making loans for mortgages. (*Same as* mutual savings firms.)

savings bank. A bank that mainly handles savings accounts and makes loans to home buyers.

secured loan. A loan for which some kind of property you own is used to help guarantee payments.

securities. Another name for stocks and bonds.

self-insurance. Insuring oneself against economic losses.

service business. A business that does things for you instead of making or marketing products.

service charge. A charge made by a bank for handling a checking account.

services. Those things that satisfy our wants through the efforts of other people or equipment.

sharedraft. A withdrawal from a member's shares of ownership in a credit union.

shareholder. A person who owns stock in a corporation. (*Same as* stockholder.)

shopping. Going to a business to find out firsthand about the products or services it has for sale.

signature card. A card, kept by a bank, that shows the signatures of persons authorized to draw checks against an account.

simple interest. An expression of interest based on one year of time.

single-payment loan. A type of loan in which a debt is repaid fully at one time.

SMART card. A card which has a silicon chip for storing information.

socialism. An economic system in which government owns and operates a number of industries and provides for some degree of private property and private enterprise.

social security card. A document showing one's social security number.

social security number. The number used to identify one's record of earnings under social security laws.

software. The programs and other instructional routines that direct a computer.

sole proprietorship. A business owned by one person.

special endorsement. An endorsement including the name of the person to whom the check has been transferred. (*Same as* full endorsement.)

standard fire policy. A basic type of property insurance that protects against losses resulting from fire or lightning damage to a home.

standard of living. As a measure of how well people in a country live, this term indicates the quantity and quality of wants and needs which are satisfied.

statement. A record of the transactions that

a customer has completed with a business during a billing period. (*Same as* statement of account.)

statement of account. A record of the transactions that a customer has completed with a business during a billing period. (*Same as* statement.)

stockholder. A person who owns stock in a corporation. (*Same as* shareholder.)

stopping payment. Instructing a bank not to pay a certain check.

store brand. A special name used for products sold by one store or chain of stores. (*Same as* house brand.)

straight life insurance. Permanent life insurance on which the insured pays equal premiums throughout his or her life.

strike. A situation in which employees refuse to work until their demands are met.

supply. The quantity of a product or service that businesses are willing and able to provide at a particular price.

surgical expense insurance. Insurance that provides benefits to cover part or all of a surgeon's fee for an operation.

surplus. A situation that exists when government has more income than expenses.

T

take-home pay. The amount a person receives after taxes and other deductions are withheld from his or her earnings. (*Same as* net income.)

tariff. A tax which a government places on certain imported products.

telecommunications. A system which utilizes television, telephones, communications satellites, computers and other electronic devices to allow both oral and visual communication to take place.

telecommuters. People who report to work from their homes by computer.

tenants policy. Insurance on household goods and personal belongings for those who rent.

tentative career decisions. A career decision subject to modification or change when new information is received.

terminal. A keyboard and screen used to enter and view data.

term insurance. A life insurance policy that protects against risk only for a specified period of time.

time deposit. A deposit that will be left in the bank for a fairly long period of time.

time sharing. A system which allows several people to use the same central processing unit.

touch-sensitive screen. A computer that allows users to point at or touch the command on the screen to give orders to the computer.

trade association. An organization of firms engaged in the same type of business.

trademark. A word, letter, or symbol associated with a specific product or company.

traveler's check. A form sold by a bank, express company, or other agency to take care of the financial needs of travelers.

trust. A creditor's belief that debtors will keep their promises to pay for goods and services that they have already received and used.

trust company. A bank that manages the money and property of others.

U

unemployment insurance. Insurance that provides cash payments for a limited time to people who are out of a job for a reason other than illness.

uninsured motorists protection. Insurance coverage which protects the policyholder against losses resulting from injuries caused by a hit-and-run driver or by a driver who has no insurance and no money to pay claims.

union shop. An agreement requiring workers to join a union within a specified time after employment.

unit price. The price per unit of measure of a product.

universal life insurance. Life insurance in which a portion of the premium is placed in interest-earning investments that grow at a variable rate for the policyholder.

upkeep. The cost of keeping property in good condition.

user-friendly. A term which describes a computer that tells you when you make a mistake and how to correct the mistake without your having to know a computer language.

V

values. Things that are important to you in life.

variable expenses. Expenses which occur infrequently, are for widely differing amounts, and are sometimes difficult to estimate.

visual display terminal. A screen that shows what you and the computer are saying to each other.

W

wants. Those things which we can live without but which add pleasure and comfort to living.

white-collar workers. Persons whose work generally involves a lot of contact with people and who process information.

whole life insurance. Permanent insurance that extends over the lifetime of the insured.

wholesaler. A middle firm which sells goods to other firms like itself or to other retailers.

word processing. An office function that involves using a word processor, or microcomputer with a word processing software package to produce written material rapidly.

word processor. A computer that usually consists of a keyboard, screen, disk drive, and printer designed especially for text editing.

workers' compensation. Insurance that provides payments to employees or their survivors for injuries, loss of income, or death caused by accidents on the job.

work force. All of the people aged 16 years and over who hold jobs or who are seeking jobs.

world trade. Trade among different countries. (*Same as* foreign trade or international trade.)

Y

yield. The percentage of interest which is added to your savings over a period of time.

*I*ndex

A cknowledgments

For permission to reproduce the photographs on the pages indicated, acknowledgment is made to the following:

COVER PHOTO: Stephan Wilkes 1983

Contents   p. vii: (left) Arizona Office of Tourism, (center) New York State Department of Commerce, (right) TRW, Inc.; p. viii: (left) General Motors Proving Ground, (right) HUD Photo; p. ix: (left) USDA Photo, (right) Storage Technology Corp © 1984; p. x: (center) Arizona Office of Tourism, (right) Aluminum Company of America

Chapter 1   p. 4: © Randy Green for BEST Products; p. 7: (top left) Southwest Forest Industries, (bottom left and top right) Aluminum Company of America; p. 9: Alyeska Pipeline Service Company.

Chapter 2   p. 21: BLUMEBILD/H. ARMSTRONG ROBERTS.

Chapter 3   p. 33: Aluminum Company of America; p. 38: © Cheryl Rossum 1982; p. 39: David Falconer/West Stock.

Chapter 4   p. 45: Glenn Sharron for FLORIDA DEPARTMENT OF COMMERCE, DIVISION OF TOURISM; p. 46: © Four by Five, Inc.; p. 53: NASA; p. 58: Gregg Mancuso/Stock, Boston.

Chapter 5   p. 64: © Les Moore/UNIPHOTO 1983; p. 67: (right) © William Rivelli; p. 73: © Four by Five, Inc.

Chapter 7   p. 97: (right) Sperry New Holland; p. 99: (left) WORLD BANK PHOTO by Josef Hadar; p. 106: Ogden Corporation; p. 111: McDonald's Corporation.

Chapter 8   p. 118: Courtesy of CompuScan; p. 119: Courtesy of IBM Corporation; p. 121: Courtesy: Sperry Univac Division of Sperry Corp.

Chapter 9   p. 130 Reproduced with permission of AT&T Corporate Archives.

Chapter 10   p. 138: Photo courtesy of Cincinnati Milacron; p. 141: CONTINENTAL TELECOM INC.; p. 143: (left) Lockheed Corporation, (center) Photo courtesy of ITT Corporation, (right) BARNES GROUP, INC.

Chapter 11   p. 155: STORAGE TECHNOLOGY CORPORATION © 1984.

Chapter 12   p. 169: FLORIDA DEPARTMENT OF COMMERCE, DIVISION OF TOURISM; p. 173: Photo courtesy ITT Corporation.

Chapter 13   p. 189: Radio Shack, a division of Tandy Corporation.

Chapter 17   p. 236: Federal Reserve Bank—Cleveland Branch; p. 238: Courtesy Sears, Roebuck and Co.; p. 240: Federal Reserve Bank—Cleveland Branch.

Chapter 20   p. 283: (left) Federal Reserve Bank—Cleveland Branch, (right) U.S. Postal Service.

Chapter 21	p. 311: Tom Carroll.
Chapter 22	p. 319: (left) Tourism British Columbia; p. 320: © Brent Jones.
Chapter 24	p. 337: (bottom left) FLORIDA DEPARTMENT OF COMMERCE, DIVISION OF TOURISM.
Chapter 25	p. 347: © Andrew Rakoczy/Photo Researchers, Inc.; p. 350: © Charles Gupton/Stock, Boston; p. 357: © Richard Hutchings/Photo Researchers, Inc.
Chapter 26	p. 363: (right) Queen City Metro, Cincinnati, Ohio; p. 366: © Jan Halaska/Photo Researchers, Inc.
Chapter 27	p. 376: Aruba Tourist Bureau Photo.
Chapter 28	p. 389: INDIANA UNIVERSITY-PURDUE UNIVERSITY AT INDIANAPOLIS; p. 390: (left) © Janice Fullman/Picture Cube, (right) © Richard Hutchings/Photo Researchers, Inc.
Chapter 30	p. 421: © Hugh Rogers/Monkmeyer Press.
Chapter 32	p. 439: Crocker National Bank; p. 441: New York State Commerce Department; p. 442: New York City Convention and Visitors Bureau.
Chapter 33	p. 451: © 1980 J. Howard/Stock, Boston; p. 455: HUD Photo; p. 461: © Catherine Ursillo/Photo Researchers, Inc.
Chapter 34	p. 466: USDA Photo; p. 469: Queen City Metro, Cincinnati, Ohio; p. 470 (left) FLORIDA DEPARTMENT OF COMMERCE, DIVISION OF TOURISM, (right) UNRWA.
Chapter 35	p. 476: © 1984 Peter Menzel/Stock, Boston; p. 479 © Freda Leinwand/Monkmeyer Press Photo; p. 481 (bottom right) Indiana Department of Commerce, (top right) Grumman Corporation.
Chapter 36	p. 490: USDA Photo; p. 493: Virginia State Travel Photo; p. 496: Circus World.
Chapter 37	p. 504: Chesebrough Pond's Inc.
Chapter 38	p. 516: © A.B. Joyce/Photo Researchers, Inc.; p. 518: American Petroleum Institute.
Chapter 39	p. 524: (left) © Eric A. Roth/The Picture Cube, (right) The U.S. Forest Service; p. 526: FLORIDA DEPARTMENT OF COMMERCE, DIVISION OF TOURISM; p. 527: USDA Photo.
Chapter 40	p. 539: U.S. Fish and Wildlife Service Photo by Rodney Krey; p. 541: USDA Photo; p. 544: © William Mares/Monkmeyer Press Photo.
Chapter 41	p. 550: TRW, Inc.; p. 551: FLORIDA DEPARTMENT OF COMMERCE, DIVISION OF TOURISM; p. 558: United States Department of the Interior.
Chapter 42	p. 564: © Barbara Alper/Stock, Boston; p. 566: AISI; p. 570: Storage Technology Corporation; p. 575: Bohdan Hrynewych, Southern Light.

Unit Openers and Internal Art: Pete Harritos